A Co‍ı

Vocabulary Study Guide

Spanish to Portuguese to English to Chinese

MW01613557

Una Guía de Estudios Comparativa del Vocabulario Español, Portugués, Inglés y Chino

Highlighting over 5,000 selected Spanish words that have either the same spelling and meaning as their English and Portuguese language counterparts or contain easily recognizable English and Portuguese meanings, followed by their Chinese language equivalents.

Destacando más de 5,000 palabras seleccionadas en Español que tienen, ya sea la misma ortografía y significado que su contraparte en Inglés y Portugués fácilmente reconocibles, seguido por sus equivalentes en idioma Chino.

Destacando mais de 5.000 palavras selecionadas em Espanhol que tem a mesma ortografia e significado como a sua contraparte em Inglês e Português facilmente reconhecível, seguido por seus equivalentes da língua Chinesa.

精选5000个西班牙语词汇，这些词或者有与英语和葡萄要语对应的相同的拼写和意思，或者包含了容易识别的英语和葡萄牙语的含义，均附有中文的解释。

Robert D. O'Brian

Melbourne, Florida

2013

The contents of this work including, but not limited to, the accuracy of events, people, and places depicted; opinions expressed; permission to use previously published materials included; and any advice given or actions advocated are solely the responsibility of the author, who assumes all liability for said work and indemnifies the publisher against any claims stemming from publication of the work.

To Dennis M. O'Brian, Ph.D., M.B.A., M.A., M.S.

With special thanks to Maria Cristina Campos, Jin Ji (计瑾) and Mechel Pavlishin

FIRST EDITION

ISBN: 978-1-939748-38-6

Library of Congress Control Number: 2013955713

Published by
NewBookPublishing.com, a division of Reliance Media, Inc.
515 Cooper Commerce Drive, #140, Apopka, FL 32703
NewBookPublishing.com

Printed in the United States of America

Reliance
Media

Introduction

This is a four language vocabulary guide highlighting over 5,000 selected Spanish words that have either the same spelling and meaning as their English and Portuguese language counterparts or contain easily recognizable English and Portuguese meanings with a comparison to their Chinese language equivalents.

Spanish is the language base for this guide. Each Spanish listing is capitalized and followed by its Portuguese and English language equivalents. The Chinese language equivalents appear beneath. The Portuguese appears in uncapitalized bold lettering while the English is uncapitalized. For example:

ADMONICIÓN; admonição; *warning, reprimand*;
jǐng gào (n) (v): 警告, *warning; to warn*;
yù zhào (n): 预兆, *omen, sign, harbinger, warning*

All Spanish words are given the general or specific meanings of Spanish currently spoken in Argentina; the Portuguese to coastal Brazil. Spanish is the language to which the English definitions and the equivalent Portuguese are compared. The Chinese is matched to English definitions.

This guide is alphabetical, A through Z, with each letter comprising a separate listing, further divided into three sections: words that are interchangeable; nouns, adjectives and adverbs that contain easily recognizable and equivalent meanings; and verbs with easily recognizable and equivalent meanings. Not all possible words that fit this guide's purpose are listed. Only the most obvious and useful words were selected.

The English language equivalents are listed in a range of meanings with the closest in meaning listed first. The Chinese language equivalents are also listed by all relevant meanings. The Chinese is shown in both pinyin and Chinese characters. Because of the geographical diversity over which Standard Chinese is spoken there had to be a choice between forms of words. The choices of form are those which are more acceptable or those which are more widely used. This is especially true when more than one tonal form (or neutral tone) is acceptable for a word. The author gave preference to those forms which are more widely used, with some allowance for certain forms that are more acceptable.

Following are pronunciation guides for Spanish, English, Portuguese and Chinese.

Spanish Pronunciation Guide for English speakers

The vowels *a*, *e*, and *o* are "strong" vowels, *i* and *u* are "weak". When two vowels fall together the following applies: if the word has an accent mark, then that syllable is stressed (*cóncavo, enfermería*); a weak + strong combination belongs to one syllable with the stress falling on the strong vowel (*cauto, caliente*); a weak + weak combination belongs to one syllable with the stress falling on the second vowel (*construir, cuidado*); and, a strong + strong combination is divided into two syllables. *(aca-rre-ar, co-rre-a)*

A: as the **a** in *father*

B,v: when found at the beginning of a word or following a consonant, these are pronounced as a **b**. Otherwise, they have a sound which falls somewhere between the English **b** and **v** sounds.

C: before a consonant or **a**, **o**, or **u**, as the **c** in *cat*; before **e** or **i** as an **s**

CH: as the **ch** in *church*

D: as the English **d** except between vowels and following **l** or **n** where it is pronounced as the **th** in *this*

E: for a syllable ending in a vowel, as the **e** in *they*; for a syllable ending in a consonant, as the **e** in *get*

F: as the **f** in *for*

G: before **e** or **i**, as the Spanish **j**; otherwise as the **g** in *get*

H: silent

I: as **i** in *machine*

J: as an **h** but stronger; silent when at the end of a word

K: as the **k** in *kilo*

L: as an **l** in *lee*

LL: as the **y** in *you*. However, in Argentina it is pronounced as **sh** in *shoe*

M: as an **m** in *mother*

N: as an **n**; except where it appears before a **v**, as an **m**

Ñ: as the **n** in *onion*

O: for a syllable ending in a vowel, as the **o** in *vote*; for a syllable ending in a consonant, as the **o** in *pot*

P: as a **p** in *pot*

Q: as a **k**; always followed by a silent **u**

R: pronounced with a strong trill at the beginning of a word and following an **l**, **n**, or **s**; very little trill when at the end of a word; and medium trill in other positions

RR: strongly trilled

S: before consonants **b**, **d**, **g**, **l**, **m**, **n**, as a **z**; otherwise as an **s**

T: as a **t**

U: as the **u** in *rule*; silent after **q** and in the groups **gue** and **gui**

V: see **b**, **v**

W: usually pronounced as a **v**

X: when between vowels, as the **x** in *box*; before a consonant, as an **s**

Y: when used as a vowel, such as in the words **y** and **voy**, it is pronounced as the Spanish **i**. As a consonant it is pronounced as in **Y** in *yes*

Z: as an **s**

Spanish Pronunciation Guide for Spanish speakers

Algunas letras en Inglés tienen varias formas de pronunciación. Los sonidos proporcionados en Español son sólo una aproximación.

Letra en Inglés	Sonido aproximado	Ejemplo
A	a como en *arco*	car
	e como *eco*	many
(antes de consonante + e final)	ei como en *peine*	fate
(entre consonantes)	ai como ei en *peine*	rain
	au similar a la a de *bata*	cause
B	como en *bomba*	boy
C (antes de a, o, u)	como en *cama*	cat
(antes de e,i)	como en *cena*	cereal
	ch como en *cheque*	check
D	como en *doble*	David
	dge como en ya	knowledge
E	entre "a" y "e"	thanks
	e como en *estar*	let
	i como en *cinco*	he, be
(final de monosílabo)	iu como en *diurno*	new, few
(final de la palabra)	(muda)	fine, live
(antes de t, d)	ea como i en *rival*	read, eat
	ea como ei en *rey*	great
	ea como e en *error*	sweater
(después de consonante)	ee como i en *kilo*	bee, see
	ei como i en *nido*	neither
	ei como ei en *peine*	eight
F	como en *fallo*	face
G (antes de a, o, u)	como en *gato*	game
(antes de e, i)	entre "ch" y "y"	George
(al final de palabra)	gh se pronuncia f como en *faro*	laugh
	gh (es muda)	ghost
H (como en *j* suave)	*gente, jaula*	home
I	i (pero más relajada)	sister
(final de la sílaba)	ai como en *vaina*	hi
	i como en *niño*	marine
	ie como i en *nido*	field
	ie como en ai en *vaina*	pie
J	como en *ya* (entre "ch" y "y")	jaguar
K (antes de n)	como en *cama*	keep
	(es muda)	known
L	como en *limón*	limb
	ll como "l" en *catálogo*	villa

M	como en *madre*	mail
N	como en *nada*	never
O (entre consonantes)	**a** como en *habla*	not
(después de **d, t**)	**u** como en *uso*	to, do
	au como en *Laura*	how
(final de la palabra)	**o** alargada "**ou**"	hello
(entre consonante y **t** final)	**oa** como **o** (pero más alargada)	coat
	oo como en **u** en *pulso*	food
	oo como en **u** en *pulso* (pero más relajada)	good
	ou como en **u** en *pulso*	you
	ou como **au** en *Laura*	round
	ou como en **a** (pero más relajada)	tough
P	como en *pobre*	stop
	ph como **f** en *foca*	telephone
Q	**qu** como en *cual*	quack
R	como en *raro*	race
S (principio o final de sílaba)	como en *siempre*	same
(entre vocales)	como en *zumbido*	rose
(antes de **ure**)	*¡shhh!*	sure
	sh como en *¡shhh!*	shoes
T (principio o final de sílaba)	como en *tarea*	top, correct
(antes de **ion**)	*¡shhh!*	condition
(antes de **ure**)	como en *mucho*	nature
(en verbos, sustantivos, etc.)	**th** como **z** en *zapato*	thanks
(en artículos como la, pronombres, etc.) **th** como **d** en lado		the
U (antes de consonante + **e** final)	**iu** como en *diurno*	excuse
	u como en *pulso* (más relajada)	put
	u como en *pulso*	attitude
	a (más relajada)	under
V	como en *vino*	valet
W	como en *huevo*	weapon
(antes de **o**)	**wh** como **j** en *jugo*	who
(antes de **a, i, e**)	**wh** como **w** en *whiskey*	white, where
X (al principio de palabra)	**z** como en *zinc*	xylophone
(cuando va entre vocales)	se pronuncia **gs**	exempt
(en los demás casos)	como en e*x*acto	box
Y (final de palabra después de consonante)	**ai** como en *vaina*	my, by
(principio de la palabra)	como en *ya* (muy suave)	yellow
Z	como en *zumbido*	zoo

Portugese Pronunciation Guide

A: (unstressed) **o** as in *mother*; (stressed) **a** as in *father*; **ão** as **own** in *town*; **ai** as **ie** in *pie*; **au** as **own** in *town*; **ã** as **an** in *anger*; **â** as the **a** in *cat*

B: as the **b** in *but*

C: before **e** or **i**, as the **s** in *safe*; before **a, o, u,** as the **c** in *come*

Ç: only before **a, o, u** as the **s** in *song*

CH: as the **ch** in *machine* or **sh** in *shoot*

D: as the **d** in *door*; before **i** or **e** as in *judge*

E: **ê** is closed; **é** is open, the **e** as in *net;* weak stress the **a** as in *about*; **ei** as **ay** in *day*

F: the **f** as in *first*

G: before **a, o, u,** as the hard **g** in *got*; before **e** and **i**, as the **s** in *pleasure*

H: the **h** is silent

I: the **i** as in *free*

J: as **dj** in *measure*

K: as the **k** in kite

L: as in *silver*; **lh** as **lli** in million

M: as in *mean*

N: as in *night*; **nh** as **ni** in *onion,* similar in Spanish to *año*

O: closed as **o** in *law; open* as **o** in *not*; **oi** as **oy** in *toy*; **ou** as **ow** in *slow*; **ô** as **oa** in *coal*

P: as in *people*

Q: before **a** or **o** the **qu** as the similar sound of the English word *quota.* before **e** and **i** the **qu** is pronounced like the **c** in the English word cat

R: as the first letter of a word, it is pronounced as an **h** as in *heat*, otherwise it is pronounce much like the English **h** as in *home*

S: at the beginning of a word or syllable, as the **s** in *sail*; between vowels, as the **s** in *rose*. The **sh** sound is like the **sh** in the English word *ship*

T: pronounced as the English **t** except when followed by **e** or **i** it is pronounced as **chee** as in the English word *cheese.*

U: as the las **u** in *kung fu*

V: as the English **v** in *Victor*

W: Brazilians tend to pronounce **w** as the **v** sound

X: as **sh** in *shoe*

Y: as **y** in yell

Z: as **z** in zero

There are 4 defined 'qualities' of Portuguese vowels, known as open, close, reduced, and nasal.

When the vowel has a circumflex over it ($\wedge$), close quality; with an acute accent over it ('), open quality, (usually the acute é is pronounced as more as 'ay'); a tilde (~) over a vowel has a nasal pronunciation as does the letter m or n after a vowel. When a word ends with a vowel, or starts with an 'e', you would normally use the reduced quality unless there is an accent to indicate otherwise. However, an 'e' at the end of a word, followed by a vowel at the start of the next word, normally requires the 'e' to become like the 'e' in 'people' (for ease of articulation).

Chinese Pronunciation Guide

The Chinese phonetic alphabet (Pinyin) is a system which converts Chinese characters into the Roman alphabet to be pronounced according to a combination of English sounds and tonal pitches.

The Pinyin pronunciations for each English letter or combinations of letters could vary because spoken Chinese has a variety of regional preferences. The following illustrates the most prevalent pronunciations:

1. The consonants **B, D, F, G, H, K, L, M, N, P, S, T W** and **Y** have the same sound as in English. But,

    c　like the English **ts** in **its/cats**
    j　like the English **j** in **j**eer/**j**erk/**j**ack/**j**ar
    q　like the English **ch** in **ch**eer/**chee**se/**ch**eat, with a strong puff of air
    r　like the English **ur** in leis**ur**e/s**ur**e, with the tongue rolled back
    x　like the English **ss/sh/se** as in **see/she/sea** (whole word), with a gentle hissing sound
    z　like the English **ds/dz** as in li**ds**/ki**ds**/be**ds**
    ch　like the English **ch** in **church**, with the tongue rolled back and a strong puff of air
    sh　like the English **sh** in **sh**oe/**sh**red, with the tongue rolled back
    zh　like the English **j**, with the tongue rolled back

2. The vowels have these sounds:

    a　like the English **ar/ah** as in f**ar**/**ah**
    e　like the English **er/eh/uh** as in h**er**/l**e**t/h**ur**t
    i　like the English **ee** as in s**ee**/f**ee**/b**ee**
    o　like the English **or/oh** as in f**or**
    u　like the English **ue/oo/ew** as in s**ue**/w**oo**/s**oo**n/p**ew**
    ü　like the French **u** as in **r**ue or the German **ü** as in **über**

Some additional sounds of importance are:

    chi　like the sound **chur** as in the English **churn**
    ci　like the sound **tsur** as in the English **surf**
    ei　like the sound **ay** as in the English say/may/hay
    ie　like the sound **yeh** as in the English **yellow**
    iu　like the sound **yo** as in the English **yoyo**
    ou　like the sound **oh** as in the English **oh/ought/owe**
    ri　like the sound **rur** as in the English **rural**
    shi　like the sound **shur** as in the English **shirt/shire/shirr/shirk**
    si　like the sound **sur** as in the English **surface/surf/absurd/surge**
    ui　like the sound **way** as in the English **way/sway/away**
    uo　like the sound **war** as in the English **war/warn**
    zh　like the sound **dj** as in the English **jar**
    zhi　like the sound **jur** as in the English **jury/injury**
    zi　like the sound as in the English **buzz**
    ou　like the sound **o** as in the English **so**
    ii　like the sound **I** as in the English machine

After letters such as **j, q, x, l, n, m**:

> **e** is pronounced **"eh"** (as in **"yes"**)
> **i** is pronounced **"eeee"** (as in **"peaches"** or **"green"**)
> **u** is pronounced **"oo"** like (as in **"you"**), except after **j, q,** and **x,** when it is pronounced like the German **ü**

After the following common consonants or groups of consonants such as **zh, ch, sh, r, z, c, s:**

> **e** is pronounced **"ur"** (as in **"shirt**)
> **i** is barely pronounced at all, but the consonant is pronounced is a slightly more long-drawn-out way (think of the **r** as in **"grrr"**)
> **u** is pronounced **"oo"** (as in **"you"**)

After **i** or **y, i** is pronounced as in the English yet

Chinese is a tonal language. A tone is a variation in pitch which indicates how a syllable is to be pronounced. There are four marked tones:

> First tone (**-**) high, level pitch
> Second tone (**´**) starting high and rising
> Third tone (**v**) falling first, then rising
> Fourth tone (**`**) starting high and falling

All tones are marked above the vowel of a syllable. Tones appear only in the Pinyin Romanization, not in the characters. Few syllables are toneless and do not have tone marks (neutral tone). In some instances the tone of syllable may change according to the syllable tone following or preceding it. For example:

1. The negative adverb **bù** (不) normally is pronounced in the fourth tone, but when it is followed by a fourth-tone syllable its tone then changes to the second tone.

2. The numeral **yī** (一) normally is pronounced in the first tone, but if it precedes a first-, second- or third-tone syllable its tone changes to the fourth tone. Also, if it precedes a fourth-tone syllable its tone changes to the second tone.

3. Whenever a third-tone syllable precedes another third tone it is pronounced in the second tone (with no change in the tone mark).

In this guide phonetic syllables are written as separate units. This is done intentionally to facilitate Chinese pronunciation for non-Chinese speakers.

The signs and symbols appearing in this guide are identified as follows:

(AERO) = aeronautics
(AGRIC) = agriculture
(ANAT) = anatomical
(ARCHIT) = architecture
(ARTE) = art, artistic
(ASTROL) = astrology
(ASTRON) = astronomy
(AUTO) = automotive
(BIOL) = biology
(BOT) = botany
(CINE) = cinema
(COM) = commercial
(DEP) = sports
(DER) = legal
(ECON) = economics
(ELECTR) = electrical
(FIN) = financial
(FIS) = physics
(FOTO) = photography

(GEN) = general meaning
(GEOG) = geography
(GEOL) = geology
(GRAM) = grammar
(INFORM) = inf. technology
(LITER) = literature
(MAT) = mathematics
(MECAN) = mechanical
(MED) = medical
(METEO) = meteorological
(MIL) = military
(MUS) = music
(NAUT) = nautical
(POL) = politics
(QUIM) = chemistry
(RELIG) = religion
(TECNOL) = technology
(ZOOL) = zoology

(A) = the feminine ending
(ab) = abbreviation
(adj) = adjective
(adv) = adverb
(am) = aspect marker
(at) = abstruse term
(attr) = attribute
(aux) = auxiliary verb
ó = or (Spanish)
(bf) = bound form
(coll) = Beijing colloquial
(cmp) = complement
(conj) = conjunction
(cov) = coverb
(f) = feminine
(fe) = fixed expression
(id) = idiomatic saying
(intj) = interjection
(lg) = language

(loan) = loan word
(m) = masculine
(mp) = modal particle
(n) = noun
(num) = number
(pej) = pejorative
(pref) = prefix
(pw) = place word
(suf) = suffix
(sv) = stative verb
(rv) = reflexive verb
(vp) verbal phrase
(wr) = writing
o = or (Portuguese)
os = oneself
s = plural
sb = somebody
sthg = something
ú = or (Spanish)

The following definitions are for symbols particular to the Chinese language:

(am) = an aspect marker is used to indicate the stage of completion of an action and generally are used suffixes to verbs.

> For example:
> For an action in progress (much like "ing" in English) the word "**zhe**" is attached to the verb.
> For a completed action "**le**" is used as the verbal suffix.

While the aspect of an action does not refer to tense (past, present and future) "le" is used as an aspect of an action in any tense. The aspect marker "**le**" is also a modal particle (mp) used to express attitude, opinion, feeling. Other model particles are: "**ba**" = supposition; "**a**" = warning; "**lou**" = exclamation.

(aux) = In the Chinese language auxiliary or "helping" verbs always precede the main verb. When an auxiliary verb and a coverb (cov) are used together the auxiliary verb always appears before the coverb.

(bf) = Bound forms are morphemes (single characters) and cannot act as a free word in a sentence nor function as a prefix, suffix, measure word or particle. Bound forms can be meaningful or meaningless (syllabic sound) words.

(fe) = Fixed expressions are those which allow little or no allowances for word substitutions.

(sv) = A stative verb is treated as an adjective in English and as a verb in Chinese. The sense of "to be" is incorporated into these verbs. "**shì**" should never precede a stative verb. A stative verb can be negated by "**bù**" and modified by adverbs of degree. Stative verbs may be used as adverbs.

(vp) = A verb phrase (phrasal verb) is a verb combined with a preposition or an adverb to form a particular meaning. Verb phrases include descriptive predicates that do not behave as stative verbs (sv) or as phrases containing a verb.

(suf) = A suffix it is always bound and usually is combined with a noun although verbal suffixes exist. Aspect markers can function as verbal suffixes.

(cov) = Coverb(s) which, in English are prepositions, directly precede nouns and immediately follow the main verb. Examples:

> **gēn:** 跟, *with;* **gěi:** 给, *for, for the benefit of to, from*
> **gēn** *is also a conjunction (and)*
> **gěi** *is also a suffix (to)*

(pref) = Prefixes are always bound and combine with nouns. Examples are:

> **lăo:** 老, *old*
> **fěi:** 非, *non, not*
> **hăo:** 好, *good.* **Hăo** *is also used as a suffix to show completion of an action*
> **nán:** 难, *difficult*

Pinyin is the Chinese phonetic alphabet. Pinyin is not a substitute for learning Chinese but acts as a guide for its pronunciation.

Written Chinese uses characters to represent syllables which have both meaning and sound. Although the meanings of the syllables are virtually constant for the various Chinese dialects there are syllables which are pronounced differently. This guide favors the toned versions. Examples of these pronunciation differences, as they appear in this guide, are:

chu (处) vs. **chù** (处) **po** (泼) vs. **pó** (泼)
dao (到) vs. **dào** (到) **qi** (气) vs. **qì** (气)
dǎo (倒) vs. **dào** (倒) **qing** (清) vs. **qīng** (清)
fa (发) vs. **fā** (发) **shi** (实) vs. **shí** (实)
fu (付) vs. **fù** (付) **shi** (师) vs. **shī** (师)
hū (糊) vs. **hú** (糊) **shi** (拾) vs. **shí** (拾)
hua (滑) vs. **huá** (滑) **su** (诉) vs. **sù** (诉)
huang (晃) vs. **huàng** (晃) **xia** (下) vs. **xià** (下)
kong (空) vs. **kōng** (空) **yi** (意) vs. **yì** (意)
ku (苦) vs. **kǔ** (苦) **zhu** (住) vs. **zhù** (住)
la (辣) vs. **là** (辣)

Also note that many Chinese characters have more than one pronunciation. The following is a list of the most prevalent shared character syllables appearing in this guide:

ái (挨) and **āi** (挨) **dǎo** (倒) and **dào** (倒)
bā (吧) and **ba** (吧) **dé** (得) and **děi** (得)
bā (扒) and **pá** (扒) **de** (地) and **dì** (地)
bāo (剥) and **bō** (剥) **de** (的) and **dí** (的)
báo (薄) and **bò** (薄) and **bó** (薄) **diào** (调) and **tiáo** (调)
bēi (背) and **bèi** (背) **dīng** (钉) and **dìng** (钉)
bié (别) and **biè** (别) **dōu** (都) and **dū** (都)
cáng (藏) and **zàng** (藏) **dǒu** (斗) and **dòu** (斗)
céng (曾) and **zēng** (曾) **è** (恶) and **wù** (恶)
chā (差) and **chà** (差) and **chāi** (差) **fā** (发) and **fà** (发)
cān (参) and **shēn** (参) **fēn** (分) and **fèn** (分)
chà (刹) and **shā** (刹) **gān** (干) and **gàn** (干)
cháng (长) and **zhǎng** (长) **gěi** (给) and **jǐ** (给)
cháo (朝) and **zhāo** (朝) **gēng** (更) and **gèng** (更)
chē (车) and **jū** (车) **gōng** (供) and **gòng** (供)
chēn (称) and **chèn** (称) and **chèng** (称) **guān** (冠) and **guàn** (冠)
chéng (盛) and **shéng** (盛) **hái** (还) and **huán** (还)
chōng (冲) and **chòng** (冲) **háng** (行) and **xíng** (行)
chóng (重) and **zhòng** (重) **háo** (号) and **hào** (号)
chǔ (处) and **chù** (处) **hǎo** (好) and **hào** (好)
chuán (传) and **zhuàn** (传) **hē** (喝) and **hè** (喝)
cì (伺) and **sì** (伺) **hé** (和) and **huó** (和)
dá (打) and **dǎ** (打) **hè** (吓) and **xià** (吓)
dàn (弹) and **tán** (弹) **héng** (横) and **hèng** (横)
dāng (当) and **dàng** (当) **hōng** (哄) and **hǒng** (哄) and **hòng** (哄)

hū (糊) and hú (糊) and hù (糊)
huá (划) and huà (划)
hái (还) and huán (还)
huǎng (晃) and huàng (晃)
hún (混) and hùn (混)
jī (几) and jǐ (几)
jī (奇) and qí (奇)
jì (系) and xì (系)
jiā (夹) and jiá (夹)
jiǎ (假) and jià (假)
jiāng (将) and jiàng (将)
jiàng (降) and xiáng (降)
jiàng (强) and qiáng (强) and qiǎng (强)
jiáo (嚼) and jué (嚼)
jiǎo (角) and jué (角)
jiào (校) and xiào (校)
jiào (觉) and jué (觉)
jiē (结) and jié (结)
jǐn (尽) and jìn (尽)
jìn (劲) and jìng (劲)
juān (圈) and juàn (圈) and quān (圈)
juǎn (卷) and juàn (卷)
kǎ (卡) and qiǎ (卡)
kān (看) and kàn (看)
kōng (空) and kòng (空)
là (落) and lào (落) and luò (落)
lè (乐) and yuè (乐)
le (了) and liǎo (了)
léi (累) and lěi (累) and lèi (累)
liáng (凉) and liàng (凉)
liáng (量) and liàng (量)
liù (陆) and lù (陆)
lóng (笼) and lǒng (笼)
lòng (弄) and nòng (弄)
lòu (露) and lù (露)
lǜ (率) and shuài (率)
mā (抹) and mǒ (抹)
má (吗) and ma (吗)
mái (埋) and mán (埋)
méi (没) and mò (没)
mēn (闷) and mèn (闷)
mēng (蒙) and méng (蒙)
mó (模) and mú (模)
nán (难) and nàn (难)
ne (呢) and ní (呢)
níng (宁) and nìng (宁)
pāo (泡) and pào (泡)
piān (片) and piàn (片)
piāo (漂) and piǎo (漂) and piào (漂)
pū (铺) and pù (铺)

qiē (切) and qiè (切)
qū (曲) and qǔ (曲)
sā (撒) and sǎ (撒)
sāi (塞) and sài (塞)
sǎn (散) and sàn (散)
sāng (丧) and sàng (丧)
sǎo (扫) and sào (扫)
shān (扇) and shàn (扇)
shǎo (少) and shào (少)
shé (折) and zhē (折) and zhé (折)
shě (舍) and shè (舍)
shéi (谁) and shuí (谁)
shén (什) and shí (什)
shěng (省) and xǐng (省)
shóu (熟) and shú (熟)
shǔ (数) and shù (数)
shuì (说) and shuō (说) and yuè (说)
sù (宿) and xiǔ (宿) and xiù (宿)
tiāo (挑) and tiǎo (挑)
wéi (为) and wèi (为)
xiān (鲜) and xiǎn (鲜)
xiāng (相) and xiàng (相)
xiāo (削) and xuē (削)
xiě (血) and xuè (血)
xīng (兴) and xìng (兴)
yā (呀) and ya (呀)
yān (烟) and yàn (烟)
yīng (应) and yìng (应)
yōng (佣) and yòng (佣)
yú (予) and yǔ (予)
yǔ (与) and yù (与)
yūn (晕) and yùn (晕)
zā (扎) and zhā (扎)
zǎi (载) and zài (载)
zāng (脏) and zàng (脏)
zhān (占) and zhàn (占)
zhǎng (涨) and zhàng (涨)
zháo (着) and zhào (着) and zhe (着)
and zhuó (着)
zhǎo (爪) and zhuǎ (爪)
zhè (这) and zhèi (这)
zhēng (症) and zhèng (症)
zhēng (挣) and zhèng (挣)
zhī (只) and zhǐ (只)
zhōng (中) and zhòng (中)
zhǒng (种) and zhòng (种)
zhuǎn (转) and zhuàn (转)
zuān (钻) and zuàn (钻)
zuō (作) and zuò (作)

These shared syllables also can have different meanings. As examples:

chā (n), **chà** (v) (sv) and **chāi** (v) (n), share the same character **(差)**.
chà: 差, *to differ from*
chāi: 差, *to dispatch, to send on an errant; job*
chā (n): 差, *difference (MAT); mistake*

chōng and **chòng** share the same character **(冲)**.
chōng (v) (n): 冲, *to push forward, to clash, to collide; important place, thoroughfare; opposition*
chòng (sv) (prep) (v): 冲, *vigorous, powerful; toward, on the basis of, according to; to punch*

dé and **děi** share the same character **(得)**.
dé (v) (adj) (aux): 得, *to get, to catch; to be suitable; to be equal, to be ready/finished; glad, satisfied, comfortable, cozy.* When used with **děi (**得**)**, *to need; must, to have to/ should*

dòu and **dǒu** share the same character **(斗)**.
dòu: 斗, *to fight, to struggle*
dǒu: 斗, *is a measure word*

è and **wù** share the same character **(恶)**.
è (v) (n): 恶, *fierce, ferocious; bad, evil, wicked; wickedness;*
wù: 恶, *to hate, to dislike, to loathe*

hǎo (好**)** and **hào (**好**)** share the same character
hǎo (sv) (adv) (v): 好, *good, fine; friendly; in order to, to that, very, such, so, quite a lot; to get well/be on good health*
hào is also a suffix indicating completion of an action. It is also used as a prefix to indicate "*good to*" to describe an act

hū, hú and **hù** share the same character **(糊)**.
hū: 糊, *to plaster*
hú (v) (n): 糊, *to smear, to paste; to overcook sthg; porridge*
hù (n): 糊, *paste*

kōng and **kòng** share the same character **(空)**.
kōng (sv) (n) (adv): 空, *empty, hollow; sky, air; for nothing*
kòng (v) (sv) (n): 空, *to leave blank; vacant, unoccupied; free time*

nán and **nàn** share the same character **(难)**.
nán (sv) (v): 难, *difficult, hard; impossible; to make things hard/difficult*
nàn (n): 难, *trouble, adversity, disaster, calamity, tragedy; tragedy, blame*

nòng and **lòng** share the same character **(弄)**.
lòng (n): 弄, *lane*
nòng: 弄, *to do, to get, to make, to manipulate, to play tricks on*

qiē and **qiè** share the same character **(切)**.
qiē (v): 切, *to cut, to slice, to chop*
qiè (v) (adv): 切, *to correspond to/be close to; absolutely, exactly*

Both **wù** and **è** share the same character (恶).
wù (v) (bf): 恶, *to loathe/hate; to dislike*
è (sv) (n): 恶, *fierce, ferocious; bad, evil, wicked; wickedness*

zhēng and **zhèng** share the same character (挣).
zhēng: 挣, *to struggle*
zhèng: 挣, *to earn; to get free, to break free*

But also note these variations among syllables and characters. As examples:

huì (汇) and **huì** (会) have different characters.
huì (v) (n): 汇, *to converge, to gather together; to collect, to transfer; collection, assemblage*
huì (v) (n): 会, *will, to be possible to/able to; to get together/assemble, conference, union, society*

shuì, shuō and **yuè** share the same character:
shuì: 说, *to persuade*
shuō (v) (n): 说, *to say/speak, to explain; doctrine*
yuè (sv): 说, *happy*

shú (sv) (adv) and **shóu** (sv) (adv) use the same character (熟) and have the same meanings: *skilled, experienced; ripe, cooked; deeply, thoroughly*

Both **xíng** and **háng** share the same character (行).
háng (n): 行, *row, line; profession, business; company*
xíng (sv) (bf): 行, *right, acceptable, capable, competent; go/walk/travel; be current; circulate; prevail*

Throughout this guide there will be words composed of the same syllables and tones but have different characters and meanings. As examples:

cè tīng (v) (n): (侧听), *to eavesdrop*
cè tīng (n): (侧厅), *side room*

xián rén (n): (贤人), *virtuous person; a worthy; a sage*
xián rén (n): (闲人), *unoccupied person; idler; an unconcerned person*

xiǎn yào (sv) (n): (显要), *powerful and influential; influential figure; VIP*
xiǎn yào (sv): (险要), *strategically located and difficult to access*

xiàn zhì (n): (限制), *restrict, confine, restriction, limit, confinement*
xiàn zhì (attr): (宪制), *constitutional*

yǐn huì (v): (隐讳), *to avoid mentioning sthg; to be taboo*
yǐn huì (sv): (隐晦), *obscure; veiled*
yǐn jiàn (v): (引见), *to introduce/present sb/sthg*
yǐn jiàn (v): (引荐/见), *to recommend sb/sthg*

yìng zhào (v): (应招), *to respond to a call*
yìng zhào (v): (映照), *to shine upon; to combine to make a pretty scene; to be bright and shining*

zhōng zhǐ (v) (n): (终止), *to stop/end sthg; termination, annulment, abrogation*
zhōng zhǐ (v): (中止), *to discontinue/suspend/break off/stop halfway*

zhòng shāng (n): (重伤), *serious wound; severe injury*
zhòng shāng (v): (中伤), *to slander/malign*
> NOTE: **zhòng shāng** also appears as **zhōng shāng** (v): (中伤), *to defame/discredit*

The reader, for further study, should note the following examples of syllable constructions/meaning variations that appear in this guide. There are no set rules for "word building" in the Chinese language.

xìng (性): (suf) -ty, -ness, -ism, -ity. For example **xìng** can be added at the end of an adjective to make a noun: **kě kào xìng**: 可靠性, *reliability*
dù (suf): 度, *is a measure word for "intensity"; -ness, -ity*

zi (子) and **zhě** (者) are nominalizers, *"one who"* (**-er**)
zi (子) generally is used after nouns
zhě (者) is used after verbs and adjectives

There are three ways to say "economist" ("ist") in Chinese:
jīng jì xué jiā: (经济学家)
jīng jì xué rén: (经济学人)
jīng jì xué zhě: (经济学者)

de (的) generally signals an adjective. Without it the syllable converts to a noun. As examples:

SYLLABLE	ADJECTIVE	SYLLABLE	NOUN
hēi 'an de: (黑暗的)	dark	**hēi 'an:** (黑暗)	darkness
xìng fú de: (幸福的)	happy	**xìng fù:** (幸福)	happiness
cū cāo de: (粗糙的)	rough/crude/coarse	**cū cāo:** (粗糙)	roughness/ rudeness/ coarseness
yán kù de: (严酷的)	harsh	**yán kù:** (严酷)	harshness
cū lǔ de: (粗鲁的)	rude	**cū lǔ:** (粗鲁)	rudeness
duǎn zàn de: (短暂的)	short	**duǎn zàn:** (短暂)	shortness
		duǎn xìng: (短性)	
shortness			
kuài lè de: (快乐的)	happy/	**kuài lè:** (快乐)	happiness/ cheerful cheerfulness
But:			
tiáo lǐ de: (条理的)	reasonable	**tiáo lǐ:** (条理)	orderliness
wú yòng (attr): (无用)	useless	**wú yòng xìng:** (无用性)	uselessness

yī (一) signifies *"one"* or *"a", "an", "each",* or *"per"*. As an adjective it means *"single", "alone", "only one"; "the same", "together"; "whole", "all", "throughout"*. When used as an adverb it indicates a brief or lightly taken action. As a conjunction it signifies *"once"*

or "as soon as". With the negative particle **bù** (不), **yī** (一), *not, not at all*.
Before a verb **yī** (一) indicates an action and its result; It is also used for emphasis.

When read alone, in counting, or in reading numbers **yī** (一) is pronounced in the first tone. When **yī** (一) precedes a 1st, 2nd or 3rd tone syllable its tone changes to the 4th tone. When **yī** (一) is followed by a 4th tone syllable its tone changes to the 2nd tone. These rules also apply to **yi** (unstressed or neutral tone) as seen in the above listing where it is shown as **yì**.

de 的 is a particle which is often used to modify a word, phrase or clause or a noun or noun clause. It is also used to change an adjective into a noun or a verb phrase into a noun phrase. It also is used to indicate possession; after an adjective to modify a noun; after an adjective to change it into a noun; after a clause to make it modify a noun; to change a verb phrase it into a noun phrase; and, for emphasis. In this guide both **de** (的) and (sv) are used interchangeably according to the author's preference to designate an adjective.

de (得) + **děi** (得) + **dé** (得) share the same character.
de (得) is used between two verbs to indicate "possibility"; between a verb and an adjective or a clause to show degree or extent; and, used in the negative as a warning or admonition. **dé** (v), *to have/get/obtain*; **děi** (v), *to have, must*.

de (地) is used after and adjective to form and adverb, the equivalent to "-ly" in English.

piàn zi: (骗子) and **piàn zi shǒu:** (骗子手) both mean swindler/cheat. The addition of **shǒu:** (手) emphasizes that the swindler/cheat is very adept/good at being a swindler, cheat. **shǒu:** (手) **=** a skilled hand, a cracker jack of a swindler/cheat.

dà (大) as an adjective gives the meaning of: big, large, major; heavy, strong. As an adverb **dà** means *"to a great extent", "to an extreme"*. When used after a negative it means *"not very", "not often"*.

bù (不), the negative adverb, normally is pronounced in the 4th tone. However, when it is followed by 4th tone syllable, its tone usually changes to the 2nd tone (/)
bù lì or **bú lì** (不利)

shàng: 上, is a verb meaning "go up"/ "ascend". When used to indicate getting on or into a vehicle, horse, motorcycle, bicycle, airplane, train, stage or platform it means "mount" , "board" or "get on". When used as a suffix: after verbs = *"up"*; after nouns = *"on,", "in", "with regards to"*, with the *"-ically"* ending. As an adjective it indicates *"up"*, *"upper"*, *"high"* (in grade or quality) and also can mean *"first", "preceding", "previous"*.

yǒu (有) means "to have", "to possess"; "there is" and "there are". It is also used to indicate or mean probability or comparison, or that something has happened or appeared to have happened.
yǒu (有) has the concept of: "much', "many", "advanced", etc.; and "somewhat" or "almost certain" (when estimating height, weight; distance, degree, age, etc.); and is used as a determiner or pronoun for "some" people, occasions, things, localities.
yǒu (有) is also used in certain set phrases to indicate politeness and with the noun to create the adjective.
yuán (员) indicates a person or persons engaged in some field of activity.

zhě (者**)** is used to indicate a person engaged in a particular profession.

shī dàng (vp): (失当), *inappropriate, improper*
shì dàng (sv): (适当), *suitable, proper*

The adverb suffix "-ly" is distinguishable from its adjective suffix. As examples:
easy **(róng yì de:** 容易的**)** - *easily, likely* **(róng yì de:** 容易地**)**;
rapid, quick **(xùn sù de:** 迅速的**)** - *quickly, rapidly* **(xùn sù de:** 迅速地**)**;
vague, blurred, dim **(mó hu de:** 模糊的**)** - *vaguely, blurry, dimly* **(mó hu de:** 模糊地 **)**;
vague, unclear **(hán hu de:** 含糊的**)** - *vaguely* **(hán hu de:** 含糊地**)**;
vague, evasive **(shǎn shuò qí cí de:** 闪烁其词的**)** - *vaguely, evasively* **(shǎn shuò qí cí de:** 闪烁其词地**)**;
slight, a little **(lüè wēi de:** 略微的**)** - *slightly* **(lüè wēi de:** 略微地**)**;
smooth **(guāng huá de:** 光滑的**)** - *smoothly* **(guāng huá de:** 光滑地**)**;
weak **(wēn shùn de:** 温顺的**)** - *weakly* **(wēn shùn de:** 温顺地**)**;
menacing threating **(kǒng hè de:** 恐吓的**)** - *menacingly* **(kǒng hè de:** 恐吓地**)**.

The adjectival suffix "-al" often involves adding *de* (的) to the syllable. As examples:
education **(jiào yù:** 教育**)** - *educational* **(jiào yù de:** 教育的**)**;
nature **(zì rán:** 自然**)** - *natural* **(zì rán de:** 自然的**)**;
recreation **(yú lè:** 娱乐**)** - *recreational* **(yú lè de:** 娱乐的**)**;
sensation **(hōng dòng:** 哄动**)** - *sensational* **(hōng dòng de:** 哄动 的**)**;
season **(jì jié:** 季节**)** - *seasonal* **(jì jié de:** 季节的/**jì jié xìng:** 季节性 **)**.

The "-al" noun forming suffix sometimes involves no changes. As examples:
to arrive **(dào dá:** 到达**)** - *arrival* **(dào dá:** 到达**)**;
to refuse **(jù jué:** 拒绝**)** - *refusal* **(jù jué:** 拒绝**)**.

To avoid excessive word repetition among the various Chinese definitions this guide cross references the Chinese to the Spanish. The Chinese language must be described by its word constructions and parts of speech to be appreciated and better understood by non-Chinese speakers. The Chinese language is characterized not only by its range of meanings for similar words but also as a language where concepts are cobbled. Additionally, its various parts of speech are often interchangeable. Nouns can be verbs and verbs can be nouns, adverbs or adjectives.

A

Interchangeable Spanish-Portuguese-English words and their Chinese equivalents
Palabras en Español-Portugués-Inglés y sus equivalentes en Chino
Palavras em Espanhol-Português-Inglês e seus equivalentes em Chinês
西班牙语，葡萄牙语，英语及中文的对等单词

ABDOMINAL; abdominal;
  fù bù de: 腹部的

ACNÉ; acne;
  fěn cì: 粉刺

ACRE; acre;
  yīng mǔ: 英亩, *acre*

AD HOC; ad hoc;
  tè (adv) (bf): 特, *especially; special, particular, exceptional*;
  tè shè: 特设, *ad hoc; for one particular purpose*;
  SEE (请查看**) ESPECIAL, ESPECIALIDAD**

ADVERBIAL; adverbial;
  fù cí de: 副词的

AGENDA; agenda; *work schedule; diary, directory*;
  yì chéng: 议程

AIRBAG; airbag;
  qì 'náng: 气囊

ÁLBUM; álbum; *(for stamps, photos)*;
jí yóu cè: 集邮册, *stamp, album*;
xiàng piàn bù: 相片簿, *photo album*;
yǐng jí: 影集, *photo/picture album*

ÁLGEBRA; álgebra;
  dài shù: 代数

ALTER EGO; alter ego;
  gǎi biàn zì wǒ: 改变自我

AMNESIA; amnésia;
  jiàn wàng zhèng: 健忘症

AMORAL; amoral;
  wú dào dé gan: 无道德感

ANAL; anal;
  gāng mén: 肛门

ANCESTRAL; ancestral;
  zǔ chuán de: 祖传的, *handed down*;
  zǔ xiān de: 祖先的, *ancestral*;
  zǔ zōng de: 祖宗的, *ancestral*

ANEMIA; anemia;
  pín xuě: 贫血

ANIMAL; animal;
  dòng wù (n): 动物, *animal*

ANTICLÍMAX; anticlímax;
  hǔ tóu shé wěi: 虎头蛇尾

ANTISOCIAL; anti-social;
  bù hé qún de: 不合群的, *unsociable*;
  bù shàn yú shè jiāo de: 不善于社交的, *unsocial*;
  bù xǐ huān jiāo jì de: 不喜欢交际的, *unsocial*;
  bù xǐ huān shè jiāo de: 不喜欢社交的, *unsocial*;
  fǎn shè huì de: 反社会的, *antisocial*;
  fǎn shè huì xìng gé: 反社会性格, *antisocial personality*;
  fǎn shè huì xíng wéi: 反社会行为, *antisocial behavior*;
  gū pì de (sv): 孤僻的, *antisocial and eccentric*;
  yàn wù shè jiāo de: 厌恶社交的, *antisocial*;
  SEE (请查看**) INSOCIABLE**

ÁREA; área;

fàn wéi: 范围, *area of activity/job/study*;
miàn jī: 面积, *area*;
SEE (请查看) REGIONAL

AROMA; aroma;
xiāng wèi: 香味, *of food, coffee, etc.*;
SEE (请查看) FRAGANTE

ART DECO; arte deco;
yì shù zhuāng shì: 艺术装饰

ARTERIAL; arterial;
zhǔ gàn dào de: 主干道的

ARTIFICIAL; artificial;
bù zhēn de: 不真的, *artificial*;
rén gōng (attr): 人工, *man-made; artificial*;
rén wéi (attr): 人为, *man-made; artificial*;

rén zào (attr) (n): 人造, *synthetic; imitation*;
SEE (请查看) SINTÉTICO

ATLAS; atlas;
dì tú jí: 地图集

AU PAIR; au pair;
hù huì shēng: 互惠生;
bāng gōng (n): 帮工, *helper; farm hand*

AUDIO; áudio;
lù yīn: 录音

AUDIOVISUAL; audiovisual;
shì tīng: 视听

AUTO; auto;
qì chē: 汽车;
SEE (请查看) AUTOMÓVIL

Easily recognizable Spanish-Portuguese-English nouns, adjectives and adverbs and their Chinese equivalents
Nombres, sustantivos, adjetivos y adverbios en Español-Portugués-Inglés y sus equivalentes en Chino
Nomes, substantivos, adjetivos e advérbios em Espanhol-Português-Inglês e seus equivalentes em Chinês
容易辨认的西班牙语，葡萄牙语，英语的名词，形容词和副词和他们的中文对等词

ÁBACO; abaco; *abacus*;
suàn pán: 算盘

ABANDONADO (A); abandonado (A);
abandoned, deserted; derelict;
bèi yí qì de: 被遗弃的, *abandoned*

ABATIDO (A); abatido (A); *drawn, weakened; downcast; depression (METEO) (ECON)* ... ABATIMIENTO;
abatimiento; *paleness, weakness; dejection; depression*;
cuì ruò (sv) (n): 脆弱, *fragile, weak, frail; frailty, weakness*;
xiāo chén (sv): 消沉, *downcast, dejected, depressed*;
xiāo tiáo (sv) (n): 萧条, *desolate, bleak; economic depression*;
xū ruò (sv): 虚弱, *weak, debilitated; weakness*;

yù mèn (vp): 郁闷, *gloomy, depressed*;
SEE (请查看) DESANIMADO, IMPOTENCIA

ABERRANTE; aberrante; *aberrant*;
yì cháng (sv) (adv) (n): 异常, *unusual, abnormal; unusually; abnormality*;
SEE (请查看) ANOMALÍA

ABISMAL; abissal; *deep; vast, enormous; irreconcilable*;
guǎng dà (sv): 广大, *wide, vast, large-scale*;
shēn (sv) (n) (adv): 深, *deep, penetrating, profound; depth; deeply*

ABNEGACIÓN; abnegação;
abnegation, self-denial;
kè kǔ de: 刻苦的, *assiduous, hardworking*;

kè zhì: 克制, *to exercise restraint, self-denial*

ABNEGADO (A); **abnegado** (A); *self-denying, self-sacrificing*;
  kè jǐ de: 克己的, *self-denying*;
  xiàn shēn de: 献身的, *self-sacrificing*

ABOLICIÓN; abolição; *abolition, elimination, termination*;
  fèi chú (v) (sv): 废除, *to abolish; to abrogate; abolition*;
SEE (请查看) ANULAR, REVOCAR

ABOMINACIÓN; abominação; *abomination*;
  yàn wù (v) (sv): 厌恶, *to loathe/detest; detestable*;
  zēng wù de: 憎恶的, *hateful*

ABORTO; aborto; *abortion; miscarriage*;
  liú chǎn (n) (v): 流产, *abortion, miscarriage; to miscarry/fall through*

ABRASIVO (A); **abrasivo** (A); *abrasive; grinding; harsh, hurtful*;
  cū bào de: 粗暴的, *an abrasive person/manner*;
  cū cào de: 粗糙的, *rough, coarse, crude, harsh, abrasive*;
  cū guǎng (sv): 粗犷, *rough, crude, boorish; straightforward and uninhibited*;
  cū guǎng de: 粗犷的, *rugged, rude, boorish*;
  cū huà (n): 粗话, *coarse language*;
  cū lòu de: 粗陋的, *coarse and crude*;
  cū lǔ de: 粗鲁的, *rude; boorish*;
  cū lüè de: 粗略的, *rough; sketchy*;
  cū yě de: 粗野的, *rude, boorish; uncouth*;
  yán cí (n): 严词, *in strong/stern language*;
  yán gé de: 严格的, *strict, rigorous, rigid*;
  yán jǐn de: 严谨的, *rigorous, strict*;
  yán jùn de: 严峻的, *stern, severe, rigorous*;
  yán kù de: 严酷的, *harsh, bitter, grim*;
  yán lì de: 严厉的, *stern, severe*;

yǒu hài de: 有害的, *harmful*;
SEE (请查看) IRRITANTE

ABRIL; abril;
  sì yuè: 四月

ABSCESO; abcesso; *abscess*;
  nóng zhǒng: 脓肿

ABSENTISMO; absentismo; *absenteeism*;
  kuàng gōng: 旷工

ABSOLUTAMENTE; absolutamente; *absolutely* ... **ABSOLUTO** (A); **absoluto;** *absolute, perfect, unqualified*;
  jué duì de (adv) (sv): 绝对地 , *absolutely; perfectly; absolute, perfect*
  què zuò de: 确凿的, *definite, conclusive*

ABSORVENCIA; absorvencia; *absorbency*... **ABSORBENTE; absorvente;** *absorbent; interesting, absorbing*;
  néng xī shōu de: 能吸收的, *absorbent, absorbing*;
  yǒu xī shōu néng lì de: 有吸收能力的, *absorbent*

ABSORTO; absorto; *absorbed, engrossed, involved, immersed*;
  zhǐ gù (sv): 只顾, *absorbed in*

ABSTENCIÓN; abstenção; *abstention*;
  qì quán (n) (v): 弃权, *abstention; to abstain from voting*

ABSTINENCIA; absténcia; *abstinence, self-denial, temperance*;
  jié zhì yǐn shí: 节制饮食**/ jiè jiǔ:** 戒酒, *abstinence from food/drink*;
  jié zhì (n) (v) (sv): 节制, *abstinence; to abstain from eating/drinking; abstemious*

ABSTRACTO (A); **abstrato;** *abstract (adj)*;
  chōu xiàng de: 抽象的, *abstract; theoretical*;
  tí yào: 提要, *summary, abstract, synopsis*;

wén zhāi: 文摘, *abstract, digest;*
zhāi yào (n) (v): 摘要, *summary,*
abstract; to summarize/abstract

ABSTRUSO (A); **abstruso;** *abstruse,*
obscure, profound;
  bù zhī míng (sv): 不知名, *little-known;*
  huì sè de: 晦涩的, *difficult to*
  understand;
  shēn bù kě cè (fe): 深不可测,
  fathomless; beyond comprehension;
  shēn dù (n): 深度, *depth, profundity,*
  sophistication;
  shēn qiǎn (n): 深浅, *depth,*
  seriousness;
  shēn shēn de (adv): 深深地,
  profoundly, keenly, deeply;
  shēn suì (sv): 深邃, *profound,*
  abstruse, recondite; deep and far;
  shèn tòu (sv): 渗透, *profound and*
  through, penetrating;
  shēn yōu (sv): 深幽, *deep and serene;*
  shēn zhǎn (vp): 伸展, *profound and*
  thorough;
SEE (请查看) **PROFUNDO, ANÓNIMO**

ABSURDO (A); **absurdo;** *absurd,*
ridiculous, nonsense;
  fèi huà (v) (n): 废话, *to talk nonsense;*
  nonsense;
  gǒu pì (fe): 狗屁, *nonsense;*
  guǐ huà (n): 鬼话, *lie, falsehood,*
  nonsense;
  hú shuō (n) (v): 胡说, *nonsense; to*
  drivel;
  hú shuō bā dào (n): 胡说八道,
  nonsense, rubbish;
  huāng dàn de: 荒诞的 , *absurd,*
  fantastic;
  huāng miù de: 荒谬的, *ridiculous,*
  absurd;
  huāng táng de: 荒唐的, *absurd,*
  fantastic, preposterous;
  kě xiào de: 可笑的, *ridiculous, funny;*
  absurd, laughable;
  pì huà (n): 屁话, *nonsense;*
SEE (请查看) **RIDÍCULO,**
DESCONCERTANTE

ABUNDANCIA; abundância;
abundance, plenty; affluent;

fēng fù (sv) (n): 丰富, *abundant;*
abundance;
  fù ráo de: 富饶的, *endowed, fertile,*
  abundant;
  fù yù de: 富裕的, *affluent;*
  fù zú de: 富足的, *rich, affluent,*
  plentiful, abundant

ABUSIVO (A); **abusivo** (A); *abusive,*
exorbitant, outrageous, improper; very
bad, appalling, unfair;
  bù gōng píng de: 不公平的, *unfair,*
  unjust;
  cán bào de: 残暴的, *outrageous,*
  ruthless, brutal;
  guò gāo de: 过高的, *exorbitant;*
  hài rén tīng wén (fe): 骇人听闻,
  appalling, shocking;
  màn mà de: 谩骂的, *abusive, insulting;*
  wú chǐ de: 无耻的, *shameless, brazen;*
  wú lǐ de: 无理的, *unreasonable;*
  yán zhòng de: 严重的, *appalling*
  (intense);
SEE (请查看) **INOPORTUNO**

ABUSO; abuso; *abuse, overuse,*
misuse;
  làn yòng (n) (v): 滥用, *abuse, misuse;*
  to abuse/ misuse;
  nüè dài (n) (v): 虐待, *physical abuse; to*
  abuse sb;
  rǔ mà (n) (sv) (v): 辱骂, *insults;*
  insulting, humiliating; to insult/abuse;
  wěi xiè: 猥亵, *sexual abuse;*
  wù yòng (n) (v): 误用, *misuse; to*
  misuse

ABYECTO (A); **abjeto** (A); *vile,*
wretched, abject;
  bēi cǎn de: 悲惨的, *wretched,*
  miserable;
  bēi jiàn de: 卑贱的, *lowly, wretched,*
  abject;
  è liè de: 恶劣, *bad, vile; of poor quality;*
  hán suān de: 寒酸的, *poverty-stricken,*
  wretched, shabby;
  jí huài de: 极坏的, *vile, unpleasant*
  weather/food, etc.; very bad, the worst;
  kě lián (sv) (v): 可怜, *pitiful, wretched;*
  to pity;

kě wù de: 可恶的, *vile, offensive language/ behavior*;
zāo gāo de: 糟糕的, *bad, wretched*

ACCESIBLE; acessível; *accessible; approachable; affordable;*
róng yì jiē
jìn de: 容易接近的, *accessible, approachable*

ACCESO; acesso; *access; entrance, entry; admittance;*
jìn chū kǒu (n) (v): 进出口, *entrance and exit, to import and export;*
jǐng kǒu: 井口, *opening of a well, entrance to a mine;*
mén kǒu: 门口, *entrance, doorway;*
rù kǒu chù (n): 入口处, *entrance;*
tōng lù: 通路, *thoroughfare, route, passageway*

ACCESORIO; acessório; *accessory, incidental, extra;*
bèi fèn: 备份, *back up, spare, extra;*
é wài (adv): 额外, *extra; in addition;*
fù jiā (n) (v): 附加, *supplementary; to add/attach;*
fù jiàn: 附件, *appendix, annex; accessory; enclosure; attachments/ accessories to sthg;*
pèi jiàn: 配件, *accessories, spare parts*

ACCIDENTADO (A); **acidentado;** *rough, uneven; troubled;*
bù píng tǎn de: 不平坦的, *uneven; not level, flat, smooth;*
cēn cī (sv) (n): 参差, *uneven, irregular; disparity, difference;*
cēn cī bù qí (fe): 参差不齐, *uneven, irregular;*
SEE (请查看) **ABRASIVO**

ACCIDENTALMENTE; acidentalmente; *accidentally, unintentionally;*
kě xī: 可惜, *unfortunate, regrettable;*
pèng qiǎo de (adv): 碰巧地, *accidentally;*
yì wài (sv) (adv): 意外, *accidental; accidentally;*

SEE (请查看) **ARBITRARIEDAD**

ACCIDENTE; acidente; *accident, chance; collision;*
shì gù: 事故, *vehicular accident;*
yì wài: 意外, *mishap, accident*

ACCIÓN; ação; *action, act;*
huó dòng (n): 活动, *activity, maneuver, act;*
xíng dòng (n) (v): 行动, *operation; action; to move; to be mobile;*
xíng wéi (n): 行为, *action; conduct; behavior; activity;*
SEE (请查看) **ACTUAR, AFECTAR**

ACELERADO (A); **acelerado;** *accelerated, rapid, quick;*
kuài (sv) (adv): 快, *fast, quick, soon; quickly;*
kuài jié (sv): 快捷, *speedy, fast, quick;*
xùn sù de: 迅速的, *swift, rapid, speedy;*
SEE (请查看) **RÁPIDO, ÁGIL**

ACENTO; acento; *accent, stress, emphasis;*
qiáng diào (n) (v): 强调, *accent; to stress/ emphasize*

ACEPTABLE; aceitável; *acceptable, passable;*
guò de qù (v) (sv): 过得去, *to be able to pass/go through; passable, so-so;*
hé yì de: 合意的, *suitable;*
kě jiē shòu de: 可接受的, *acceptable, permissible;*
lìng rén mǎn yì de: 令人满意的, *adequate*

ACEPTACIÓN; aceitação; *acceptance, approval; popularity;*
jiē shòu (v) (n): 接受, *to accept; acceptance;*
shòu huān yíng: 受欢迎, *acceptance;*
SEE (请查看) **ADMITIR**

ACERBO; acerbo; *bitter, sour; harsh;*
chén tòng (sv): 沉痛, *deeply grieved/ painful, bitter;*

kè bó (sv): 刻薄 , *harsh, unkind, mean*;
kǔ (sv) (n) (v) (adv): 苦, *bitter, excessive; hardship, suffering, pain; to suffer/cause sb to suffer; painstakingly*;
kǔ shuǐ: 苦水, *hard/bitter water; suffering, grievance; gripe; bile*;
sōu (sv): 搜, *sour, spoiled*;
suān de: 酸的, *sour, tart; sore, aching*;
xīn suān (sv) (n): 辛酸, *bitter, miserable; hardship*;
SEE (请查看) **SEVERIDAD**

ACLAMACIÓN; aclamação;
acclamation, applause;
chēng zàn: 称赞, *to praise/acclaim/ commend*;
gǔ zhǎng (n) (v): 鼓掌, *applause; to clap*;
hè cǎi (n) (v): 喝彩, *acclaim, cheer; to cheer*;
SEE (请查看) **APROBACIÓN**

ACOMODADIZO; acomodadiço;
accommodating, obliging; pliable;
hào kè de: 好客的, *hospitable*;
lè yú zhù rén de: 乐于助人的, *accommodating*;
rè xīn zhù rén de: 热心助人的, *obliging*;
róng yì wān de: 容易弯的, *pliable*;
yuàn yì bāng máng de: 愿意帮忙的, *obliging*

ACORDE; acorde; *in accord/agreement with; compliance*;
yī cóng (n) (v): 依从, *compliance; to comply*

ACTITUD; atitude, *response, attitude, position, feeling, view*;
tài dù: 态度, *manner; bearing; attitude; approach*

ACTIVIDAD; atividade; *activity*;
shēng huó: 生活, *activity; life*;
SEE (请查看) **ACCIÓN, AFECTAR, FUNCIÓN, ACTUAR**

ACTIVO (A); **ativo;** *active, hardworking, lively, energetic*;

huó pō (sv): 活泼, *lively; vivacious, vivid*;
huó yuè de: 活跃的, *active; vigorous*;
jī jí de: 积极的, *positive, enthusiastic, active, vigorous*;
láo lù mìng: 劳碌命, *workaholic*;
néng dòng de: 能动的, *active, dynamic*;
nǔ lì (v) (sv): 努力, *to make an effort/try hard; hardworking; diligent*;
yǒu lì de: 有力的, *strong, powerful, energetic*;
SEE (请查看) **ANIMOSO, ESTUDIAR, VITALIDAD**

ACTO; ato; *act, action*;
bàn yǎn: 扮演, *play the part of; act; the acting profession*;
xíng dòng (n) (v): 行动, *act, action, conduct; to move*;
SEE (请查看) **ACCIÓN, ACTUAR, AFECTAR, FUNCIÓN**

ACTUALIDAD; atualidade; *nowadays; currently, presently*;
liú xíng de: 流行的, *current, accepted idea/custom, etc.*;
mù qián de: 目前地, *presently; currently, at present*;
rú jīn: 如今, *today, now, nowadays*;
shí xià de (adv): 时下地, *at present, currently*;
xiàn jīn: 现今, *today; nowadays, now*;
xiàn zài: 现在, *now*;
SEE (请查看) **CONTEMPORÁNEO**

ACUMULACIÓN; acumulação;
accumulation, accretion;
jī lěi (n) (v): 积累, *accumulation; to accumulate*;
lěi jī de: 累积的, *cumulative, progressive*

ACUSACIÓN; acusação; *charge, accusation, indictment*;
qiǎn zé (n) (v): 谴责, *accusation, criticism; to denounce*;
zuì míng: 罪名, *a criminal charge; accusation*

ADAPTABILIDAD; adaptabilidade;

adaptability, versatility;
shì yìng xìng (n): 适应性, adaptability, flexibility

ADAPTACIÓN; adaptação;
adjustment, adaptation;
shì yìng (n): 适应, adaptation;
SEE (请查看) ALTERAR

ADHERENTE; aderente; adhesive, sticky;
jiāo nián de: 胶粘的, sticky, glutinous;
nián de: 粘的, sticky substance;
nián hu de: 黏糊的, sticky, glutinous; languid;
shī dù dà de: 湿度大的, high humidity (sticky);
zhān de: 粘的, sticky

ADHESIVO (A); **adesivo;** adhesive, adherent;
jiāo (n): 胶, glue, anything sticky;
jiāo nián jì: 胶粘剂, adhesive;
nián hé jì (n): 粘合剂, binder, adhesive;
nián zhuó jì: 粘着剂, adhesive agent

ADICIONAL; adicional; additional, extra;
bèi fèn: 备份, back up, spare, extra;
lìng wài: 另外, additional; in addition; besides; separate; other; moreover; furthermore;
SEE (请查看) ACCESORIO

ADICTIVO; viciador; addictive ...
ADICTO (A); **adicto;** addict;
ài hào zhě: 爱好者, an enthusiast for sports/jazz, etc.;
diàn shì mí: 电视迷, TV junkie/fan;
duì mǒu shì rù mí de: 对某事入迷的, to be addicted to food/TV, etc.;
duì mǒu shì shàng yǐn de: 对某事上瘾的, to be addicted to drugs/alcohol;
hǎi luò yīn chéng yǐn de rén: 海洛因成瘾的人, a drug/heroin addict;
lìng rén zháo mí de: 令人着迷的, compulsive
qiáng pò xìng de: 强迫性的, compulsive liar, gambler, etc.;
rù mí (sv) (n): 入迷的, compulsive; an

addiction to gambling/sports, etc.;
shàng yǐn de: 上瘾的, habit forming;
shǐ rén rù mí de: 使人入迷的, an addictive activity;
yì shàng yǐn de: 易上瘾的, an addictive drug;
yǐn: 瘾, an addiction to drugs, alcohol;
zú qiú mí: 足球迷, a TV/football addict

ADMIRACIÓN; admiração; admiration ... **ADMIRADOR** (A); **admirador;** admirer;
ài mù zhě: 爱慕者, suitor;
liǎo jiě: 了解, appreciation of (understanding);
mǒu rén de zàn shǎng zhě: 某人的赞赏者, admirer;
qīn pèi (n) (v): 钦佩, admiration; to like/respect/ admire;
xīn shǎng (n) (v): 欣赏, appreciation, enjoyment; to appreciate

ADMISIBLE; admissível; admissible ...
ADMISIÓN; admissão; acceptance;
jiē nà (n) (v): 接纳, acceptance (of a person); to admit;
rèn kě (v) (n): 认可, to accept (of sthg new); approval;
róng xǔ tí chū de: 容许提出的, allowable, acceptable, admissible;
zhí dé cǎi nà de: 值得采纳的, adoptable, acceptable;
zhǔn rù (vp): 准入, admission; access;
SEE (请查看) ACEPTABLE, ACEPTACIÓN

ADMONICIÓN; admonição; warning, reprimand;
jǐng gào (n) (v): 警告, warning; to warn;
yù zhào (n): 预兆, omen, sign, harbinger, warning;
SEE (请查看) ADVERTENCIA, ANUNCIAR

ADOLESCENCIA; adolescência; adolescence ... **ADOLESCENTE** (adj); **adolescente;** adolescent;
qīng chūn qī (n) (sv): 青春期, adolescence; adolescent;

qīng shào nián: 青少年, *teenager*

ADOPCIÓN; adopção; *adoption, acceptance, assumption;*
bèi shōu yǎng de: 被收养的, *adopted child;*
jiǎ dìng (v) (n): 假定, *to suppose/ assume; assumption, hypothesis;*
yí jū de: 宜居的, *adopted country, home, etc.*

ADQUISICIÓN; aquisição; *acquisition, purchase;*
gòu mǎi (n) (v): 购买, *purchase, to purchase;*
huò dé: 获得, *acquisition of property, goods, etc.;*
xí dé: 习得, *acquisition of a skill*

ADULACIÓN; adulação; *adulation, flattery;*
chǎn yú (v) (n): 谄谀, *to flatter; servility;*
ē yú fèng chéng: 阿谀奉承, *adulation;*
fèng chéng huà: 奉承话, *flattery*

ADULTERACIÓN; adulteração; *adulteration;*
chān jiǎ: 掺假, *adulteration*

ADULTERIO; adulterío; *adultery;*
tōng jiān: 通奸

ADÚLTERO (A); **adúltero;** *adulterer, adulteress;*
jiān fū: 奸夫, *adulterer;*
jiān fù: 奸妇, *adulteress*

ADULTO (A); **adulto** (A); *adult;*
chéng nián (n) (v) (adv): 成年, *adult, grown-up; to grow up; all year, year after year;*
chéng nián rén: 成年人, *an adult;*
chéng rén (n) (v): 成人, *adult, grown-up; accomplished person; to grow up*

ADVERSARIO (A); **adversário** (A); *adversary, opponent;*
dà dí: 大敌, *archenemy;*

dí guó: 敌国, *hostile power, enemy state;*
duì shǒu: 对手, *opponent; adversary;*
SEE (请查看) ENEMIGO

ADVERSIDAD; adversidade; *adversity, setback, mishap;*
bù xìng (sv) (n): 不幸, *unfortunate; misfortune, adversity;*
cuò zhé (n) (v): 挫折, *setback, reverse; to frustrate;*
fù fā: 复发, *setback in health;*
huàn nàn: 患难, *adversity;*
nàn (bf): 难, *calamity, disaster, adversity;*
nì jìng (n): 逆境, *adversity, adverse circumstances;*
zāi (bf): 灾, *disaster, calamity; misfortune;*
zāi huàn (n): 灾患, *calamity, disaster;*
SEE (请查看) AFLICCIÓN

ADVERSO (A); **adverso** (A); *adverse;*
bú lì de: 不利的, *unfavorable;*
bù yǒu hǎo de: 不友好的, *unfriendly;*
dí duì (attr): 敌对, *hostile, antagonistic;*
nì zhe de: 逆着的, *contrary, adverse;*
xiāng fǎn de: 相反的, *contrary, opposite;*
yǒu dí yì de: 有敌意的, *antagonistic, hostile*

ADVERTENCIA; advertência; *warning, word of advice;*
zhōng gào: 忠告, *advice; advise;*
SEE (请查看) ADMONICIÓN

AEROPUERTO; aeroporto; *airport;*
fēi jī chǎng: 飞机场

AFABLE; afável; *affable, genial;*
hé 'ǎi kě qīn de: 和蔼可亲的, *affable;*
qīn qiè de: 亲切的, *genial face, personality, etc.; warm, close*

AFAMADO (A); **afamado;** *famous, notable;*
yǒu míng (sv) (v): 有名, *well-known, famous; to be famous/well-known;*
zhù míng: 著名, *famous, celebrated*

AFECCIÓN (MED); **afecção**; *disease, complaint*;
  jí bìng: 疾病, *disease*;
SEE (请查看) **ENFERMEDAD**

AFECTADO (A); **afetado**(A); *affected, moved, touched; afflicted*;
  gǎn dòng (sv) (v): 感动, *moved (emotionally touched); to move/touch sb*;
  zuò zuò de: 做作的, *affected*

AFECTO; **afeto**; *affection, fondness; inclined*;
  gǎn qíng: 感情, *feeling; emotion; affection; sensation*;
  qíng gǎn: 情感, *emotion, feeling, friendship*;
  qíng yì: 情意, *affection, goodwill*;
  xǐ 'ài (n) (v): 喜爱, *fondness, affection; to like/love*

AFECTUOSO (A); **afetuoso** (A); *affectionate, loving, attached*;
  chōng mǎn gǎn qíng de: 充满感情的, *affectionate*;
  ēn 'ài: 恩爱, *affection, love*;
  qīn 'ài de: 亲爱的, *dear, beloved*;
  qīn mì de: 亲密的, *intimate, close*;
  wēn róu de: 温柔的, *gentle and soft*;
SEE (请查看) **AMOROSO, CORDIALIDAD, AFABLE**

AFILIACIÓN; **afilição**; *affiliation, membership*;
  huì yuán zhèng: 会员证, *membership card*;
  huì yuán zī gé: 会员资格, *membership*;
  huì yuán: 会员, *member*;
  jiā rù (vp): 加入, *to add/mix/put in; to join/accede to*;
  suǒ shǔ: 所属, *subordinate, affiliation*

AFÍN; **afín**; *similar, related*;
  lèi sì de (sv) (v) (n): 类似的, *be similar to; analogy*;
  lèi sì diǎn (n): 类似点, *similar points, similarities*;
  lèi tóng (vp): 类同, *identical, same; similar, alike; analogy*;

  tóng lèi (n): 同类, *same kind*;
  tóng yàng (attr) (sv): 同样, *same, equal; similar*;
  xiāng sì (sv) (v) (n): 相似, *resemble, to be similar/ alike; resemblance*;
  xiāng xiàng (sv) (v): 相像, *similar; to resemble, to be similar/alike*;
SEE (请查看) **ANÁLOGO**

AFIRMATIVO (A); **afirmativo** (A); *affirmative, positive*;
  kěn dìng (sv) (v) (adv): 肯定, *positive, affirmative; to affirm/approve/regard as positive; definitely*;
SEE (请查看) **AFIRMAR**

AFLICCIÓN; **aflição**; *affliction, suffering, sorrow*;
  jí kǔ: 疾苦, *suffering, hardship, difficulty*;
  kǔ chù: 苦处, *suffering, hardship*;
  kǔ chǔ: 苦楚, *suffering, misery*;
  kǔ tóu: 苦头, *suffering, hardship*;
  tòng kǔ (n) (sv): 痛苦, *pain, suffering; painful*;
  tòng yǎng: 痛痒, *suffering, difficulties*;
  zāi nàn: 灾难, *catastrophe, calamity, suffering*;
SEE (请查看) **ACERBO**

AFORTUNADAMENTE; **felizmente**; *fortunately, luckily*;
  duō kuī (v) (adv): 多亏, *to be lucky; luckily*;
  hǎo zài de (adv): 好在地, *fortunately, luckily*;
  qià qiǎo de (adv): 恰巧地, *by chance, luckily*;
  xìng kuī (adv): 幸亏, *fortunately, luckily*;
  zhèng hǎo de (adv): 正好地, *fortunately, exactly, just in time*

AFORTUNADO (A); **afortunado** (A); *fortunate, lucky*;
  còu qiǎo de: 凑巧的, *lucky*;
  jí lì (sv) (n): 吉利, *fortunate; favorable; good luck*;
  jí xiáng de: 吉祥的, *lucky, auspicious*;
  xìng yùn (sv) (n): 幸运, *lucky, fortunate; good luck*

AGENCIA; agência; *agency, office, bureau;*
  bàn shì chù: 办事处, *office; agency;*
  dài lǐ chù: 代理处, *agency*

AGENTE; agente; *agent;*
  dài lǐ rén: 代理人, *agent*

ÁGIL; ágil; *agile, quick, swift; dexterous; lively ...* **ÁGILMENTE; agilmente;** *nimbly, quickly, swiftly;*
  hěn kuài de (adv): 很快地, *quickly;*
  lì luo (sv): 利落, *agile, nimble, dexterous; neat, orderly; settled, finished;*
  líng huó de: 灵活的, *agile, flexible; nimble;*
  líng mǐn (sv): 灵敏, *sensitive, keen, agile, acute;*
  mǐn jié de: 敏捷的, *quick, nimble; agile;*
  mǐn ruì (adv) (adj): 敏锐, *nimbly; sharp, acute;*
SEE (请查看) BREVE, RÁPIDO

AGITACIÓN; agitação; *shaking, stirring, bustle;*
  dòng yáo (v) (sv): 动摇, *to shake/waver/vacillate; shaking;*
  fán máng de: 繁忙的, *busy, bustling;*
  hōng dòng (v) (sv): 哄动, *to stir up/cause a sensation; stirred up;*
  jī dòng (sv) (v): 激动, *stirred, stirring, exciting, agitated; to excite/stir/agitate;*
  jī dòng rén xīn (sv): 激动人心, *stirring*

AGITADO; agitado; *choppy, rough, turbulent, bumpy, agitated;*
  bō tāo (sv) (n): 波涛, *roaring, billowing; billows, great waves;*
  bō tāo xiōng yǒng de: 波涛汹涌的, *choppy;*
  diān bǒ (v) (sv): 颠簸, *to bump/toss/jolt; bumpy;*
  dòng dàng (v) (sv): 动荡, *to experience unrest/turmoil; turbulent, unstable;*
  hùn luàn (sv) (n): 混乱, *chaotic; chaos;*
  jiāo lǜ de: 焦虑的, *agitated person;*
  kēng kēng wā wā (fe): 坑坑洼洼, *full of bumps and holes; bumpy;*

  kuáng bào de: 狂暴的, *turbulent, violent;*
SEE (请查看) AGITACIÓN

AGOSTO; Agosto; *August;*
  bā yuè: 八月

AGRADABLE; agradável; *pleasant, nice, agreeable;*
  hǎo kàn (sv) (adv): 好看的, *nice; nicely;*
  hé ǎi kě qīn (fe): 和蔼可亲, *affable, genial;*
  lìng rén yú kuài de: 令人愉快的, *agreeable, pleasant, nice;*
  měi hǎo (sv): 美好, *fine, nice, happy;*
  shū shì (sv): 舒适, *cozy, comfortable, pleasant;*
  xiāng chǔ de: 相处的, *compatible, amicable;*
  yí rén (sv): 宜人, *pleasant, delightful, agreeable;*
  yú kuài de: 愉快的, *cheerful, delightful, pleasant;*
SEE (请查看) BUENO, AMIGABLE, AMABILIDAD, EDUCADO, FINO, LINDO, SIMPÁTICO

AGRAVANTE; agravante; *aggravating ...* **AGRAVIO; agravo;** *offense, insult, grievance;*
  bù mǎn de: 不满的, *resentful, discontented, dissatisfied;*
  fán nǎo de: 烦恼的, *worried, annoyed;*
  jiā jù (sv) (v): 加剧, *aggravate, intensify; to aggravate/make worse/exacerbate;*
  nǎo huǒ de: 恼火的, *angry, annoyed;*
  qì nǎo de: 气恼的, *sulky/sullen/ruffled;*
  shǐ qì nǎo de: 使气恼的, *aggravating;*
  xīn fán de: 心烦的, *irritated, annoyed;*
  yuàn qì: 怨气, *grievance, complaint, resentment;*
SEE (请查看) DESDÉN

AGRESIÓN; agressão; *aggression ...* **AGRESIVO (A); agressivo;** *aggressive ...* **AGRESOR (A); agressor;** *aggressor;*
  hào zhàn de: 好战的, *belligerent; warlike;*
  qīn lüè (n) (v) (sv): 侵略, *aggression; to*

invade; aggressive;
yǒu chuǎng jìn de: 有闯劲的,
forceful/aggressive person;
SEE (请查看) ASALTANTE, BÉLICO

AGUA; água; *water*;
shuǐ: 水

AGUADO; aguado; *watery, thin;*
watered down, weak;
dàn de: 淡的, *thin, light; tasteless,*
weak;
hán shuǐ guò duō de: 含水过多的,
watery;
xī de: 稀的, *watery soup/coffee, etc.*

AIRE; ar; *air;*
kōng qì: 空气

ALARMA; alarme; *alarm ...*
ALARMANTE; alarmante; *alarming ...*
ALERTA; alerta; *alert;*
gào jǐng dēng: 告警灯, *alarm,*
warning light;
hài rén tīng wén de: 骇人听闻的,
shocking;
jǐng bào: 警报, *a warning device*;
jīng huāng (sv) (n): 惊慌, *alarmed,*
scared; alarm, anxiety;
jǐng jué de: 警觉的, *alert, wide awake*;
jīng kǒng de: 惊恐的, *alarmed*
(person); alarming;
jīng rén de: 惊人的, *alarming,*
amazing;
jīng xiǎn de: 惊险的, *thrilling,*
alarming;
kě pà de: 可怕的, *frightful, dreadful*;
lìng rén hài pà de: 令人害怕的,
terrifying;
lìng rén kǒng jù de: 令人恐惧的,
frightening;
nào zhōng: 闹钟, *an alarm on a clock*;
zāo tòu le: 糟透了, *very bad; alarming,*
What a mess!

ALEGACIÓN; alegação; *allegation,*
declaration, statement;
xuān yán: 宣言, *declaration*;
SEE (请查看) ANUNCIAR

ALFABETO; alfabeto; *alphabet;*
zì mǔ biǎo: 字母表

ALIENACIÓN; alienação; *alienation;*
lí jiàn: 离间, *alienation*

ALTAMENTE (adv); **altamente;** *highly;*
gāo dù de: 高度地, *highly*

ALTERACIÓN; alteração; *alteration,*
change;
gǎi zào (v) (n): 改造, *to transform/*
reform/remake/ correct; change,
alteration;
gǎi zuò (vp) (n): 改作, *to change to;*
alteration;
zhuǎn biàn (n) (v): 转变, *changes; to*
transform;
SEE (请查看) ALTERAR

ALTERCADO; altercação; *altercation,*
argument;
zhēng biàn (n) (v): 争辩, *argument; to*
argue;
SEE (请查看) ARGUMENTAR

ALTERNATIVA; alternativa;
alternative, option, choice;
tì dài: 替代, *alternative*;
xuǎn xiàng: 选项, *option*;
xuǎn zé (n) (v): 选择, *preference; to*
select

ALTITUD; altitude; *altitude;*
gāo dù: 高度, *altitude, height; high*
degree; apogee;
hǎi bá: 海拔, *elevation, height above*
sea level;
SEE (请查看) ALTURA

ALTRUISMO; altruísmo; *altruism,*
selflessness, unselfish ... **ALTRUISTA;**
altruísta; *altruist, altruistic*;
lì tā zhǔ yì zhě: 利他主义者, *altruism*;
lì tā zhǔ yì: 利他主义, *altruism*;
wàng wǒ jīng shén: 忘我精神,
altruism;
wú sī (sv) (n): 无私, *unselfish,*
disinterested; selflessness

ALTURA; altura; *height, high, lofty, peak;*
  dǐng fēng: 顶风, *peak, crest; peak of a trend/era, etc.;*
  dǐng jiān: 顶尖, *top/best (in achievement); peak, highest point;*
  gāo 'ǎi: 高矮, *height;*
  gāo fēng: 高峰, *peak, height; summit;*
  gāo kōng: 高空, *high altitude;*
  gè zǐ: 个子, *height, stature; build;*
  gèr: 个儿, *size, height; stature;*
SEE (请查看) APOGEO, ALTITUD

AMABILIDAD; amabilidade; *kindness, courtesy* ... **AMABLE; amábel;** *kind, nice* ... **AMABLEMENTE; amavelmente;** *kindly;*
  bīn bīn yǒu lǐ de: 彬彬有礼的, *courteous;*
  cí de: 慈的, *kind, loving;*
  cí xiáng de: 慈祥的, *kind;*
  hào kè de: 好客的, *hospitable, friendly;*
  hǎo xīn (n) (sv): 好心, *kindness; kind;*
  hǎo yì: 好意, *kindness, good intentions;*
  kè tào (n) (v): 客套, *polite greeting, courtesy, civility; to exchange greetings;*
  lǐ jié (n): 礼节, *courtesy, etiquette, protocol;*
  lǐ yù (n):礼遇, *courteous treatment/ manners;*
  qiān gōng de: 谦恭的, *modest and courteous;*
  rén cí (sv) (n): 仁慈, *benevolent, kind; kindness;*
  yīn qín de: 殷勤的, *courteous request, etc.;*
  yǒu hǎo (n) (sv): 友好, *kind, friendly; close friend;*
SEE (请查看) AGRADABLE, EDUCADO, SIMPATÍA

AMBICIÓN; ambição; *ambition* ... **AMBICIOSO (A); ambicioso (A);** *ambitious;*
  bào fù: 抱负, *the desire, the ambition to achieve;*
  hào qiáng de: 好强的, *ambitious, eager to excel;*
  hào shèng de: 好胜的, *competitive, eager to excel;*
  hóng dà de: 宏大的, *ambitious idea, project, etc.;*
  xiōng jīn: 胸襟, *ambition;*
  xióng xīn (n): 雄心, *great ambition;*
  yě xīn (n): 野心, *wild ambition; careerism;*
  yuǎn dà de: 远大的, *long-range, ambitious, far-reaching;*
  zhì qi: 志气, *drive, ambition, resolve*

AMBIGÜEDAD; ambigüedade; *ambiguity* ... **AMBIGUO (A); ambíguo;** *ambiguous;*
  hán hú bù qìng (bf): 含糊不清, *vague and ambiguous;*
  hán hùn de: 含混的, *equivocal, evasive, ambiguous;*
  qí yì: 歧义, *ambiguity;*
SEE (请查看) ARCANO

AMBULANCIA; ambulância; *ambulance;*
  jiù hù chē: 救护车, *ambulance*

AMIGABLE; amigável; *friendly* ... **AMIGO; amigo;** *friend* ... **AMISTOSO; amigável;** *friendly, amiable, cordial, genial;*
  péng yǒu: 朋友, *friend;*
  suí he de: 随和的, *amiable, easygoing;*
  wēn hé de: 温和的, *amiable;*
  yǒu qíng: 友情, *friendship;*
  yǒu shàn de: 友善的, *friendly/amiable person;*
  yǒu yì: 友谊, *friendship;*
SEE (请查看) AGRADABLE, CORDIALIDAD, AFABLE, AMOROSO

AMNISTÍA; anistia; *amnesty, pardon, reprieve, commute;*
  dà shè: 大赦, *amnesty;*
  huǎn xíng: 缓刑, *reprieve;*
  shè miǎn: 赦免, *pardon*

AMOROSO (A); amoroso; *amorous, loving, affectionate;*
  biǎo shì ài de: 表示爱的, *loving relationship, etc.;*

chōng mǎn ài de: 充满爱的, *loving care, etc.*;
duō qíng de: 多情的, *susceptible*;
sè qíng (sv) (n): 色情, *amorous; sex, pornography*;
SEE (请查看) AFECTUOSO

AMPLIABLE; ampliável; *expandable*;
kuò zhǎn (sv) (v) (n): 扩展, *expandable; to expand/spread; expansion*

ANÁLISIS; análise; *analysis ...*
ANALISTA; analista; *analyst ...*
ANALÍTICO (A) (adj); **analítico** (A); *analytical, analytic*;
fēn xī (n) (v): 分析, *analysis; to analyze*;
fēn xī de: 分析的, *logical, analytical*
fēn xī zhě: 分析者, *analyst*

ANÁLOGO (A); **análogo;** *analogous, similar*;
xiāng jìn de: 相近的, *close, near, similar to*;
SEE (请查看) AFÍN

ANCESTRO; ancestral; *ancestor, predecessor*;
zǔ xiān: 祖先, *ancestor; forefather*

ANEXO (A); **anexo;** *connected, attached, enclosed*;
guān lián (v) (n): 关联, *to be interrelated/linked; connection, correlation attachment*;
SEE (请查看) ACCESORIO, CONEXIÓN

ANGULOSO (A); **anguloso** (A) (adj); *angular, sharp*;
jiān ruì: 尖锐, *sharp; intense; penetrating; pointed*;
yǒu jiǎo de: 有角的, *angular*

ANIMOSIDAD; animosidade; *animosity, ill will, antagonism, acrimony*;
chóu hèn (v) (n): 仇恨, *to hate bitterly/ intensely; animosity, hostility; hatred, enmity*;
dí yì: 敌意, *hostility, aggression, animosity*;

zēng hèn (n) (v): 憎恨, *animosity; to hate/detest*

ANIMOSO; animoso; *spirited, lively*;
qīng kuài (sv): 轻快, *brisk, lively, agile; light hearted*;
shēng dòng (sv): 生动, *lively, vivid*;
shēng qì bó bó de: 生气勃勃的, *animated person/ expression, etc.*;
SEE (请查看) ACTIVO

ANIVERSARIO; aniversário; *anniversary*;
zhōu nián: 周年, *annual; anniversary*

ANOMALÍA; anomalia; *anomaly, irregularity, oddity ...* **ANÓMALO; anômalo** (A); *anomalous, irregular, abnormal ...* **ANORMAL; anormal;** *abnormal, silly, cretinous ...*
ANORMALIDAD; anormalidade; *abnormality, strange, unnatural*;
biàn tài: 变态, *abnormal nature, abnormality*;
bù guī zé de: 不规则的, *irregular, unorthodox*;
fǎn cháng de: 反常的, *abnormal, unnatural*;
lí qí de: 离奇的, *strange, odd; bizarre*;
qí guài de: 奇怪的, *strange; odd; amazing, amazed*;
qí yì de: 奇异的, *strange, odd, bizarre; astonished*;
shī cháng de: 失常的, *abnormal, odd*;
xī qí de: 稀奇的, *strange, curious*;
SEE (请查看) ABERRANTE

ANÓNIMO; anônimo; *anonymous, unknown, undeclared*;
bù míng (sv) (v): 不明, *unknown; not clear; to fail to understand*;
bù zhī dào (sv): 不知道, *unknown*;
nì míng de: 匿名的, *anonymous letter/ gift/phone call, etc.*;
wú míng (attr): 无名, *unnamed, unknown, anonymous; indefinable, indescribable*;
SEE (请查看) ABSTRUSO

ANOTACIÓN; anotação; *note, entry,*

annotation;

bǐ jì (n) (v): 笔记, *notes; to take notes*;
jì lù (v) (n): 记录, *to take notes, keep minutes; notes, minutes*;
xiàng mù: 项目, *entry in a diary, etc.*;
zhù jiě (v) (n): 注解, *to annotate; annotation*;
zhù shì: 注释, *note in a book, article, etc.; annotation*

ANTAGÓNICO (A); **antagônico** (A); *antagonistic, hostile, opposing* ...
ANTAGONISMO; antagonismo; *antagonism, animosity, enmity, rancor* ... **ANTAGONISTA; antagonista;** *opponent, antagonist, rival, enemy;*
bù yǒu hǎo de: 不友好的, *hostile person/attitude, etc.*;
dí duì (sv) (n): 敌对, *hostile, antagonistic, belligerent; antagonism;*
duì shǒu: 对手, *opponent, adversary;*
SEE (请查看) **ANIMOSIDAD, ENEMIGO, AFRONTAR, ENEMISTAD, ABYECTO**

ANTECESOR (A); **antecessor;** *predecessor, ancestor;*
qián rèn: 前任, *predecessor;*
xiān bèi: 先辈, *ancestors, older generation;*
xiān rén: 先人, *ancestors;*
zǔ xiān: 祖先, *ancestor, forefather;*
SEE (请查看) **ANCESTRAL, ANCESTRO**

ANTENA; antena; *antenna;*
tiān xiàn: 天线, *antenna, aerial*

ANTERIORIDAD; anterioridade; *beforehand, prior, anterior* ...
ANTERIORMENTE; anteriormente; *previously, before* ... **ANTES; antes;** *before;*
cóng qián: 从前, *before, formerly;*
cóng tóu de (adv): 从头地, *from the beginning;*
guò qù (n) (v): 过去, *in the past, formerly, previously; to pass by;*
qián: 前, *former; previous;*
shàng wén de (adv): 上文地, *formerly;*
shì xiān (adv): 事先, *beforehand; in*

advance;
xiān qián de: 先前的, *past, previous, before;*
yǐ lái (n): 以来, *since;*
yǐ qián: 以前, *before, previously;*
yǐ wǎng: 以往, *before, in the past; previously;*
zài qián: 在前, *ago, prior to; before;*
zài xiān: 在先, *formerly, in the past, before;*
zǎo xiān: 早先, *previously, in the past; before;*
zhī qián: 之前, *before (in time), prior to, ago*

ANTIBIÓTICO; antibiótico; *antibiotic;*
kàng shēng sù: 抗生素, *antibiotic*

ANTICIPACIÓN; antecipação; *to be early, timely;*
àn qī de (adv): 按期地, *on schedule;*
àn shí de (adv): 按时地, *on time, on schedule;*
jí shí (sv) (adv): 及时, *timely, on time;*
rú qī de (adv): 如期地, *on time, as scheduled;*
zhǔn diǎn de (adv): 准点的, *punctual, on time, on the dot;*
zhǔn shí (sv) (adv): 准时, *on time, on schedule; punctually;*
SEE (请查看) **ANTERIORIDAD**

ANTICIPADAMENTE; anticipadamente; *in advance, beforehand* ... **ANTICIPADO; antecipado;** *early;*
tí qián (adv) (v): 提前, *in advance, before hand; to advance a date/time;*
zǎo (sv) (adv): 早, *early; early on, some time ago; in advance, beforehand;*
zǎo qī: 早期, *early/initial stage*

ANTÍDOTO; antidoto; *antidote;*
jiě dú jì: 解毒剂, *antidote to poison, medicine;*
jiě dú yào: 解毒药, *detoxification*

ANTIGUO (A); **antigo** (A); *old, vintage, antique; ancient;*
cāng lǎo: 苍老, *old, aged;*

gǔ dài: 古代, *ancient times, antiquity*;

gǔ dǒng (n): 古董, *antique*;

gǔ lǎo de: 古老的, *ancient, old*;

gǔ sè gǔ xiāng (fe): 古色古香, *antique, quaint*;

gǔ shí (n): 古时, *antiquity*;

gǔ wán (n): 古玩, *antiques, curios*;

guò shí (sv): 过时, *out-of-date; dated*;

lǎo (sv): 老, *old; aged*;

nián mài: 年迈, *old, aged*;

yuǎn gǔ: 远古, *antiquity, ancient times*

ANTIPATÍA; antipatia; *antipathy, dislike, aversion*;

fǎn gǎn (v) (n): 反感, *to be disgusted with/dislike; antipathy; bad reaction*;

tǎo yàn (sv) (v): 讨厌, *disagreeable, nasty, disgusting; to dislike/have an aversion to/for*;

SEE (请查看) ABOMINACIÓN

ANTISÉPTICO; anti-sêptico (A); *antiseptic*;

fáng fǔ jì: 防腐剂, *antiseptic*;

shā jūn jì (n): 杀菌剂, *germicide; fungicide*

ANTÍTESIS; antítese; *antithesis, opposite, contrasting, conflicting*;

duì fāng: 对方, *the other side; an adversary*;

duì lì miàn: 对立面, *opposite, antithesis*;

duì yú (n): 对于, *antithesis*;

duì zhào (n) (v): 对照, *antithesis, contrast, comparision; to compare*;

SEE (请查看) ADVERSO, ANIMOSIDAD, AFRONTAR

ANUAL; annual; *annual, yearly* **... ANUALMENTE; anualmente;** *annually, yearly*;

měi nián de: 每年地, *yearly*;

měi nián: 每年, *every year*;

nián dù de: 年度的, *annual*

ANVERSO; reverso, *reverse*; **contrapartida,** *opposite; obverse*;

bèi miàn (n): 背面, *back, reverse side*;

fǎn miàn (n) (sv): 反面, *reverse side;*

other side, back; opposite, negative;

xiāng duì (vp) (attr) (adv): 相对, *to be opposite, face to face; relative, corresponding; alternate*;

zhèng miàn (n) (attr) (adv): 正面, *obverse/right; front, facade; positive; directly, openly*;

SEE (请查看) ANTÍTESIS, AFRONTAR, CONTRARIO, ADVERSO

APARENTE; aparente; *apparent ...* **APARENTEMENTE; aparentemente;** *apparently*;

biǎo miàn kàn lái: 表面看来, *apparently*;

biǎo miàn shàng de: 表面上地, *superficially, apparently*;

kàn lái (conj): 看来, *apparently, it appears, it seems*;

míng míng de (adv): 明明地, *obviously, plainly, undoubtedly*;

míng xiǎn (sv) (adv): 明显, *clear, obvious, evident; apparent; clearly, obviously*;

sì hū de (adv): 似乎地, *apparently, as if*;

tū chū (sv) (v): 突出, *outstanding, obvious, noticeable; to stress/high light*;

xiǎn míng (sv): 显明, *obvious, distinct*;

xiǎn rán (adv) (sv): 显然, *obviously, apparently, evidently; clear, obvious, evident*

APARTAMENTO; apartamento; *apartment*;

gōng yù: 公寓, *apartment*

APARTE; à parte; *separated in space*; **separadamente,** *separately*; **distante,** *distant; aloof*; **aparte,** *aside; apart, separate, away, aside*;

bù tóng (sv) (n): 不同, *separate occasion/incident, etc.; different; difference*;

bù xiāng guān de: 不相关的, *separate issue/ question, etc.*;

dān dú (attr) (adv): 单独, *alone; solely, singly, individually; on one's own*;

dú lì (v) (n) (sv): 独立, *to stand alone;*

independence; independent;
fēn bié (v) (n) (adv): 分别, *to part/leave each other; to distinguish/differentiate; difference; separately, respectively, differently;*
fēn lí (v) (n): 分离, *to separate/sever; discreteness*

APATÍA; apatia; *apathy, indifference, lassitude, languor* **... APÁTICO** (A);
apático (A); *apathetic, unfeeling, lethargic;*
bù gǎn xìng qù de: 不感兴趣的, *uninterested; indifferent;*
bù guān xīn: 不关心, *indifference (no empathy);*
hūn shuì de: 昏睡的, *lethargic;*
lěng dàn (sv) (v): 冷淡, *indifferent; to treat coldly ;*
lěng mò: 冷漠, *apathy; unconcerned;*
má mù (n): 麻木, *numb; insensitive, apathetic;*
má mù bù rén de: 麻木不仁的, *apathetic, unfeeling, insensitive;*
méi xìng qù de: 没兴趣的, *uninterested;*
tuō lā de: 拖拉的, *dilatory, stalling;*
wú xìng qù (n): 无兴趣, *apathy (no interest), apathetic;*
SEE (请查看) **ATONÍA**

APÉNDICE; apêndice; *appendix, appendage;*
fù lù: 附录, *appendix;*
fù shǔ wù: 附属物, *accessory, appendage*

APENDICITIS; apendicite; *appendicitis;*
lán wěi yán: 阑尾炎, *appendicitis*

APETITO; apetite; *appetite* **...**
APETITOSO (A) (adj); **apetitoso** (A); *appetizing, tasty; tempting;*
hǎo chī de: 好吃的, *tasty, delicious;*
kāi wèi de: 开胃的, *appetizing;*
shí yòng de: 食用的, *edible;*
shí yù: 食欲, *appetite;*
wèi měi de: 味美的, *tasty;*
xiān měi de: 鲜美的, *delicious, tasty*

APLAUSO; aplauso; *applause, clapping;*
gǔ zhǎng: 鼓掌, *applause*
SEE (请查看) **ACLAMACIÓN**

APLICADO (A); **aplicado** (A); *diligent, conscientious, hardworking;*
gēng yún (n) (v): 耕耘, *diligence, hard work; farm work; to plow and weed, to cultivate;*
qín fèn (sv) (n): 勤奋, *diligent, hardworking; diligence;*
rèn zhēn (sv): 认真, *conscientious; serious, earnest;*
yòng xīn (sv) (n) (v): 用心, *careful, attentive, diligent; purpose, intention; to be diligent/ attentive/careful;*
SEE (请查看) **ACTIVO**

APLICADOR; aplicador; *applicator;*
tú mǒ qì: 涂抹器, *applicator*

APLOMO; compostura; *composure; assurance; confidence;*
bǎo xiǎn (n) (sv) (v): 保险, *insurance, assurance; secure, safe; to be bound/ sure to;*
chén wěn de: 沉稳的, *steady, staid, sedate; deep, profound;*
chén zhuó de: 沉着的, *cool-headed, composed; calm;*
tài rán de: 泰然的, *composed, calm;*
zhèn jìng (sv) (v): 镇静, *composed, calm, cool; to calm down;*
zì xìn xīn: 自信心, *self-confidence;*
SEE (请查看) **APREHENDER, CONVICCIÓN**

APOCALIPSIS; apocalípse; *calamity, disaster, tragedy, adversity;*
bēi jù: 悲剧, *tragedy;*
bēi jù xìng (n) (sv): 悲剧性, *tragedy; tragic nature;*
níng jìng: 宁静, *adversity;*
zāi (bf): 灾, *disaster, calamity; misfortune;*
zāi hài: 灾害, *disaster; calamity;*
zāi huò: 灾祸, *calamity; disaster;*
SEE (请查看) **AFLICCIÓN, ADVERSIDAD**

APÓCRIFO (A); **apócrifo** (A); *apocryphal, doubtful, unreliable, uncertain*;
  kě yí de: 可疑的, *doubtful*;
  wěi zào (sv) (v): 伪造, *apocryphal; to forge/ counterfeit*

APOGEO; apogeu; *apogee, height, peak*;
  dǐng diǎn (n): 顶点, *acme, zenith*;
  dǐng duān (n): 顶端, *top, peak, apex*;
  gāo dù (n): 高度, *altitude, height; apogee*;
  gāo fēn (attr): 高分, *high*;
SEE (请查看) ALTITUD, ALTURA

APRECIACIÓN; apreciação; *liking, appreciative*; **reconhecimento,** *recognition, understanding*; **gratidão,** *gratitude* ... **APRECIATIVO** (A); **apreciativo** (A); *appreciative*;
  gǎn jī (n) (v) (sv): 感激, *gratitude; to feel grateful; appreciative, grateful*;
  yǒu yǎn guāng (v) (sv): 有眼光, *to have good taste; appreciative*;
  zàn shǎng (sv) (v): 赞赏, *appreciative; to appreciate/ admire*;
SEE (请查看) ADMIRAR

APRENSIÓN; apreensão; *anxiety; fear, squeamishness, misgiving; apprehension* ... **APRENSIVO** (A); **apreensivo** (A); *apprehensive, overanxious, worried*;
  dān xīn (v) (sv) (n): 担心, *to worry; anxious; anxiety, worry*;
  gù lǜ (n): 顾虑, *worry, misgivings, apprehension*;
  hài pà (n) (v): 害怕, *fear; to fear*;
  xīn bìng: 心病, *worry, anxiety*;
  xīn jiāo de: 心焦的, *anxious, worried*;
  yōu lǜ (sv) (n): 忧虑, *worry, anxious; worry, anxiety*

APROBACIÓN; aprovação; *approval, approbation, endorsement* ... **APROBATORIO** (adj); **favorável;** *approving, favorable*;
  pī zhǔn (v) (n): 批准, *to approve/ endorse; approval, permission, sanction*;

zàn chéng (n) (v): 赞成, *approval, sanction; to approve/ endorse*;
SEE (请查看) CONFIRMACIÓN

APROPIACIÓN; apropriação; *appropriation*;
  bō kuǎn (v) (n): 拨款, *to allocate; appropriation, allocation*

APROPIADO (A); **apropiado** (A); *suitable, appropriate, fitting, right* ...
APTO; apto; *suitable, fit, apt*;
  hé shì (sv): 合适, *suitable, appropriate, right*;
  qià dàng (sv) (n): 恰当, *appropriate, proper, suitable; appropriateness*;
  shì hé (sv) (v): 适合, *suitable; to suit/fit*

APROXIMACIÓN; aproximação; *approximation* ... **APROXIMADO; aproximado;** *approximate*;
  dà gài (n): 大概, *general idea*;
  dà gài de (adv): 大概地, *approximately*;
  dà yuē de (adv): 大约地, *approximately; roughly*;
  jiē jìn (v) (sv) (n): 接近, *be close to/ near; to approach; approximation*

APTITUD (A); **aptidão;** *ability, aptitude, fitness*;
  cái (bf): 才, *talent, ability*;
  cái gàn (n): 才干, *ability, competence*;
  cái huá gài shì (fe): 才华盖世, *very gifted*;
  cái huá héng yì (fe): 才华横溢, *be full of wit and talent*;
  cái néng (n): 才能, *ability, talent; aptitude*;
  cái qì páng bó (fe): 才气磅礴, *tremendous talent*;
  cái qì yáng yì (fe): 才气洋溢, *have superb talent*;
  cái shí (n): 才识, *ability and insight*;
  cái shí guò rén (fe): 才识过人, *gifted with extraordinary talent and insight*
  cái sī (n): 才思, *creativeness*;
  cái xué (n): 才学, *scholarship, erudition*;
  cái yì (n): 才艺, *ability and art; talent and skill*;

cái zhì (n): 才智, *brilliance, ability and wisdom*;
cái zǐ (n): 才子, *gifted scholar*;
cái zī (n): 才资, *talent*;
néng lì (n): 能力, *ability, competence*

ARBITRARIEDAD; arbitrariedade; *arbitrariness* ... **ARBITRARIO** (A); **arbitrário;** *arbitrary;*
  ǒu rán de: 偶然地, *accidentally; occasionally*;
  rèn yì de: 任意地, *arbitrarily; willfully*;
  suí jī de (attr) (MAT): 随机的, *random arrangement, selection*;
  suí yì de xíng dòng: 随意的行动, *arbitrary, random*

ARBITRIO; arbítrio; *free will, discretion, volition, inclination, judgment*;
  zì jué zì yuàn de: 自觉自愿的, *of one's free will*;
  zì yóu yì zhì (fe) 自由意志, *carefree*;
SEE (请查看) **INCLINACIÓN, DISCRECIÓN**

ARCANO; desconhecido; *arcane, recondite, abstruse, obscure*;
  àn de: 暗的, *dark, dim, hidden, obscure/unclear*;
  bú zhù míng de: 不著名的, *obscure poet/writer, etc.*;
  fèi jiě de: 费解的, *hard to understand, obscure, unintelligible*;
  jiān sè de: 艰涩的, *involved and abstruse; intricate and obscure*;
  jiān shēn de: 艰深的, *difficult to understand, abstruse*;
  mì mì (sv) (n) (adv): 秘密, *secret, arcane; confidential; secretly*;
  mí mí de: 迷迷的, *unclear, arcane; stupid, ignorant*;
  mó hū (sv) (v): 模糊, *blurred, dim, obscure, fuzzy; to confuse/blur/obscure*;
  shén mì de: 神秘的, *mysterious; mystical, arcane*;
  yǐn huì de: 隐晦的, *obscure, veiled*
SEE (请查看) **DIFÍCIL, ARDUO, ABSTRUSO, AMBIGÜEDAD**

ARCHIVO; arquivo; *archive, file; archives, files*;

dàng 'àn: 档案, *file, archive; record*;
juàn zōng: 卷宗, *file, dossier; folder*

ARDOROSO; ardente; *ardent, fervent, eager, zealous, avid*;
  huǒ rè de: 火热的, *burning, hot, fervent*;
  rè liè de: 热烈的, *ardent, enthusiastic*;
  rè qiè de: 热切的, *avid, ardent, earnest*;
  rè qíng (n) (sv): 热情, *passion, zeal; enthusiastic, passionate*;
  rè xīn cháng (n): 热心肠, *ardent*

ARDUO; árduo; *arduous, hard, difficult, tough, onerous*;
  fán zhòng (sv): 繁重, *strenuous, onerous*;
  jiān jù (sv): 艰巨, *arduous, formidable, difficult*;
  jiān kǔ (sv): 艰苦, *arduous, Herculean*;
  jiān nán (sv) (n): 艰难, *difficult, hard; difficulty*;
  jiān xīn (sv) (n): 艰辛, *arduous, difficult; hardships*;
  kē (bf): 苛, *severe, exacting*;
  kùn kǔ (sv): 困苦, *difficult, hard; in hardship*;
  má fán (sv) (n) (v): 麻烦, *troublesome, bothersome; trouble, to bother/trouble*;
SEE (请查看) **DIFÍCIL, FATIGA, APLICADO**

ARGUMENTO; argumento; *argument, storyline, assertion, contention*;
  zhēng biàn: 争辩, *argument*;
SEE (请查看) **PROPOSICIÓN, CONTROVERSIA, ASEVERACIÓN**

ÁRIDO (A); **árido** (A); *dry, arid, parched, barren*;
  gān bā bā (sv) (adv): 干巴巴, *dry, arid; insipid; directly*;
  gān biě de: 干瘪的, *shriveled, dried; dry, dull*;
  gān hàn de: 干旱的, *arid*;
  gān kě de: 干渴的, *dry and thirsty*;
  gān kū de: 干枯的, *withered, dried up*;
  gān zào de: 干燥的, *dry, arid; dull*;
  huāng wú (sv) (v): 荒芜, *barren; to lie*

in waste/be uncultivated;
pín jí de: 贫瘠的, *barren and poor (of land)*

ARISCO (A); **arisco** (A); *surly, unfriendly, unsociable*;
  bù yǒu hǎo de: 不友好的, *unfriendly*;
  pí qì huài de: 脾气坏的, *unfriendly*;
SEE (请查看) **ABRASIVO**

ARITMÉTICA; aritmético; *arithmetic*;
  suàn shù: 算术, *arithmetic*

ARMONÍA; harmonia; *harmony ...*
ARMONIOSO (A); **harmonioso** (A);
harmonious;
  hé mù (n) (sv): 和睦, *harmony, accord; harmonious*;
  hé shēng: 和声, *harmony (MUS)*;
  hé xié de: 和谐的, *harmonious*;
  yuè 'ěr de: 悦耳的, *harmonious sound/ tune, etc.*;
SEE (请查看) **AMIGABLE**

AROMÁTICO; aromático; *aromatic, fragrant*;
  fāng xiāng de: 芳香的, *fragrant*;
  xiāng de: 香的, *aromatic*;
SEE (请查看) **FRAGANCIA**

AROMATIZADOR; purificador de ar; *air freshener*;
  kōng qì qīng xīn jì: 空气清新剂, *air freshener*

ARRESTO; prisão; *arrest; detention (MIL); confinement*;
  jū bǔ: 拘捕, *detention, arrest*

ARROGANCIA; arrogância; *arrogance ...* **ARROGANTE; arrogante;** *arrogant*;
  ào màn (sv) (n): 傲慢, *arrogant; arrogance*;
  fú kuā (sv) (v): 浮夸, *boastful; to be boastful, to exaggerate*;
  jiāo 'ào (sv) (n): 骄傲, *arrogant, proud; pride*;
  mù kōng yī qiè (fe): 目空一切, *to be arrogant/condescending*;

zì dà de: 自大的, *pompous, arrogant*

ARTEFACTO; artefato; *device, machine, appliance; artifact*;
  jī qì: 机器, *machine, engine, apparatus*;
  jī xiè: 机械, *machinery, mechanism*;
  qì jù: 器具, *appliance, device*;
  qì xiè: 器械, *equipment, instrument*;
  shè bèi: 设备, *device*;
  yòng jù: 用具, *tool, apparatus, appliance*

ARTERIA; artêria; *artery (MED); arterial street*;
  dòng mài: 动脉, *blood vessel*;
  yào dào: 要道, *route*

ÁRTICO (A); **ártico**(A); *Arctic* ;
  běi jí: 北极, *Artic*

ARTICULACIÓN; articulação; *fluent; articulation*;
  liú chàng (sv): 流畅, *easy and smooth*;
  liú lì de: 流利的, *fluent*;
  nián zhuó de: 粘着的, *coherent*;
  tōng shùn de: 通顺的, *coherent, smooth, polished*

ARTÍCULO; artigo; *article, item, thing; news article*;
  dōng xi (n): 东西, *thing; creature*;
  pǐn mù: 品目, *item, list of items*;
  tiáo kuǎn (n): 条款, *clause, article, provision*;
  wén zhāng (n): 文章, *news article*;
  wù pǐn (n): 物品, *object, item, thing*;
  xiàng mù (n): 项目, *item, article; clause, project*;
SEE (请查看) **ÍTEM, OBJETO**

ARTIFICIO; artificio; *device; artifice, trick; cunning, sly ...* **ARTIFICIOSO** (A); **arranjado** (A); *contrived*;
  bù zì rán de: 不自然的, *contrived*;
  diāo de: 刁的, *tricky, sly*;
  diāo huá de: 刁滑的, *cunning, crafty, artful, sly*;
  guǐ de: 诡的, *deceitful, tricky*;
  guǐ zhà de: 诡诈的; *crafty, cunning*;
  huá (sv) (bf) (v): 滑, *slippery, smooth; cunning, crafty; to slip/slide*;

jì liǎng: 伎俩, *deception*;
jiān (sv): 奸, *evil, treacherous*;
jiǎo (bf): 狡, *crafty, cunning*;
jiǎo huá de: 狡猾的, *cunning, crafty, tricky*;
jiǎo xiá de: 狡黠的, *sly, crafty, cunning*;
jiǎo zhà (n) (sv): 狡诈, *deceit; deceitful*;
jīng míng de: 精明的, *astute, shrewd, smart*;
kuāng piàn: 诓骗, *deceit*;
piàn shù: 骗术, *deceitful trick*;
SEE (请查看) FRAUDE, ESTRATAGEMA

ARTISTA; **artista**; *artist* ... **ARTÍSTICO** (A); **artístico** (A); *artistic*;
yì shù de: 艺术的, *artistic*;
yì shù jiā: 艺术家, *artist*

ASALTANTE; **agressor** (A); *attacker, assailant, raider*;
rù qīn zhě: 入侵者, *attacker*;
gōng jī zhě: 攻击者, *attacker, assailant*

ASALTO; **ataque**; *assault, robbery, attack*;
jìn gōng: 进攻, *attack, assault; to attack/assault*;
qiǎng jié: 抢劫, *robbery*;
xí jī: 袭击, *physical attack/assault on a person*;
SEE (请查看) ASALTAR

ASAMBLEA; **reunião**, *meeting*; **assembléia**, *law-making body*; *assembly, meeting, law body*;
jí huì (n): 集会, *assembly, rally, gathering*;
yì huì (n): 议会, *parliament, legislative assembly*;

ASCENDENTE; **ascendente**; *ascending, rising, increasing, ascendant*;
shàng shēng (n): 上升, *ascent*;
shàng shēng de: 上升的, *ascendant*;
yuè lái yuè dà de (adv): 越来越大地, *more and more, increasingly*;
SEE (请查看) AUMENTAR

ASCENSOR; **elevador**; *elevator*;
diàn tī: 电梯, *elevator*;
SEE (请查看) ELEVADOR

ASEVERACIÓN; **afirmação**, *affirmation*; **alegação**, *assertion*; **reivindicação**, *demand*; **argumentação**, *contention*; **assertiva**, *assertion*; **afirmação**, *assertion, declaration*;
duàn yán (v) (n) (sv): 断言, *to assert; assertion; assertive*;
biǎo míng (v) (n): 表明, *to indicate/make known; assertion*

ASFALTO; **asfalto**; *asphalt, blacktop*;
lì qīng: 沥青, *pitch, asphalt, bitumen*

ASFIXIA; **asfixia**; *suffocation, asphyxiation* ... **ASFIXIANTE**; **asfixiante**; *stifling, asphyxiating; suffocating*;
lìng rén zhì xī: 令人窒息, *stifling, suffocating*

ASIGNACIÓN; **atribuição**, *assignment of a task, responsibility*; **alocação**, *sharing money, resources, things*; **atribuição**, *sharing tickets, seats, places; assignment, allocation, allowance*;
fēn pèi (n) (v): 分配, *allocation; to dispense*;
pèi jǐ: 配给, *ration*;
rèn wù: 任务, *assignment of a task*

ASIMÉTRICO (A); **assimétrico**(A); *asymmetrical; asymmetric*;
fēi duì chèn (attr): 非对称, *asymmetric(ally); skewed*

ASIMILACIÓN; **assimilação**, *assimilation of ideas, facts*; **absorção**, *assimilation of people, food; assimilation, absorption*;
néng xī shōu: 能吸收, *absorption*;
tóng huà (v) (n): 同化, *to be assimilated; assimilation, convergence*;
SEE (请查看) ABSORBER

ASISTENTE; assistente; *helper; orderly (MIL); assistant, helper;*
  bāng shǒu: 帮手, *helper, assistant;*
  qín wù bīng: 勤务兵, *military orderly;*
  qín zá gōng: 勤杂工, *medical orderly;*
  yíng yè yuán: 营业员, *assistant (in a shop);*
  zhù jiào: 助教, *assistant; teaching assistant;*
  zhù shǒu: 助手, *helper, assistant*

ASOCIACIÓN; associação; *association, union, organization, society;*
  bāng huì: 帮会, *secret society;*
  bāng pài: 帮派, *gang, faction;*
  gōng huì: 工会, *trade union;*
  guā gé: 瓜葛, *association, connection;*
  jī gòu: 机构, *mechanism, organization, structure;*
  lián méng: 联盟, *alliance, coalition, league, union;*
  shè: 社, *organization, agency, society;*
  shè huì: 社会, *society, organization (GEN);*
  suǒ shǔ: 所属, *subordinate; affiliation;*
  tǐ xì: 体系, *system, setup;*
  tuán tǐ: 团体, *organization, team;*
  xié huì: 协会, *society, association, group;*
  zǔ zhī xì tǒng (n): 组织系统, *organization, system;*
  zǔ zhī: 组织, *organization; to organize;*
SEE (请查看**) ORGANISMO**

ASOCIADO (A); associado (A); *associated, affiliated, aligned, united;*
  lián jūn (n): 联军, *allied forces/troops; united forces;*
  tuán jié (sv) (v): 团结, *united; to unite/ join forces;*
SEE (请查看**) COHESIONAR**

ASPECTO; aspecto; *aspect, look; face; bearing; appearance;*
  jǔ zhǐ: 举止, *bearing, posture;*
  miàn mào: 面貌, *aspect, quality, appearance;*
  wài mào: 外貌, *appearance; exterior looks;*
SEE (请查看**) EXPRESIÓN, SIMULAR**

ASPIRANTE; aspirante; *aspiring; candidate, applicant;*
  hòu xuǎn rén: 候选人, *candidate;*
  qǐng qiú zhě: 请求者, *applicant, supplicant;*
  shēn qǐng rén: 申请人, *applicant;*
  yìng shì rén: 应试人, *examination applicant*

ASPIRINA; aspirina; *aspirin;*
  ā sī pī lín: 阿司匹林, *aspirin*

ASTUCIA; astúcia; *astuteness ...*
ASTUTO (A); astuto (A); *astute;*
  cóng míng (sv): 聪明, *clever, intelligent;*
  jī mǐn (sv): 机敏, *alert, resourceful, astute;*
  líng lì (sv): 伶俐, *clever, bright, quick-witted*

ATÁVICO; atávico; *atavistic;*
  gé dài yí chuán: 隔代遗传, *atavistic*

ATEMPORAL; imortal; *timeless, everlasting, immortal, endless;*
  bù xiǔ de: 不朽的, *immortal being; immortal;*
  liú fāng bǎi shì de rén: 流芳百世的人, *immortal (famous) person;*
  liú fāng bǎi shì de: 流芳百世的, *immortal words, poetry, etc.;*
SEE (请查看**) ETERNIDAD, INMORTAL**

ATENCIÓN; atenção; *attention ...*
ATENTAMENTE; atentamente; *attentively ...* **ATENTO (A); atento;** *attentive;*
  jǐng jué (n): 警觉, *alertness, vigilance;*
  jù jīng huì shén (fe): 聚精会神, *attentive;*
  tǐ tiē (sv): 体贴, *considerate, obliging;*
  zhōu dào (sv): 周到, *attentive, considerate, thoughtful;*
  zhōu mì (sv): 周密, *thoughtful, thorough, attentive;*
  zhù yì (n) (v): 注意, *attention; to pay attention to/ take note of;*
  zhuān xīn (sv) (v) (n): 专心, *attentive,*

watchful, alert, aware; to be absorbed in; intention;
SEE (请查看) **APLICADO**

ATESTADO; atestado; *affidavit, statement; packed/ stuffed with;*
  xuān shì shū: 宣誓书, *affidavit, written oath;*
  dān bǎo shū: 担保书, *affidavit*

ÁTICO; sótão, cobertura; *attic, penthouse;*
  gé lóu (n): 阁楼, *attic, loft*

ATÍPICO (A); **atípico;** *atypical, exceptional;*
  bù xún cháng (sv): 不寻常, *unusual;*
  dú tè (sv): 独特, *exceptional (unusual), unique, distinctive;*
  fēi cháng (sv) (adv): 非常, *exceptional; extraordinary; special, unusual; very extremely;*
  fēi fán (sv): 非凡, *outstanding, extraordinary;*
  jié chū (sv): 杰出, *exceptional, outstanding, remarkable;*
  yì hū xún cháng (fe): 异乎寻常, *unusual, exceptional;*
  yǔ zhòng bù tóng (fe): 与众不同, *distinctive*
SEE (请查看) **RARO, DIFERENTE, ESPECIAL**

ATLÁNTICO; Atlantico; *Atlantic (ocean, seaboard);*
  dà xī yáng: 大西洋, *Atlantic*

ATLÉTICO; atlético; *athletic;*
  yùn dòng de: 运动的, *athletic person*

ATONÍA; apatia; *lethargy, apathy, indifference;*
  juàn dài de (adv): 倦怠地, *listlessly;*
  méi jīng dǎ cǎi de: 没精打采的, *listless;*
  wú shēng qì: 无生气, *lethargy; inert;*
  wú xìng qù de: 无兴趣的, *lethargic;*
SEE (请查看) **APATÍA, LETÁRGICO**

ATRACCIÓN; atração; *attraction,*

attractiveness, charm ... **ATRACTIVO** (A); **atraente;** *attractive person, idea, offer; appeal;*
  xī yǐn lì, 吸引力, *attraction, affinity, appeal;*
  xī yǐn rèn (sv): 吸引人, *attractive/ interesting person;*
  yǒu mèi lì (sv): 有魅力, *attractive, exquisite*

ATRIBUTO; atributo; *attribute;*
  tè xìng (n): 特性, *attribute, characteristic;*
  shǔ xìng (n): 属性, *attribute*

ATROCIDAD; atrocidade; *atrocity ...* **ATROZ; atroz;** *atrocious;*
  bào xíng: 暴行, *atrocity, savage act, outrage;*
SEE (请查看) **FEROZ, CRUELDAD**

AUDAZ; audacioso; *bold, audacious, daring, intrepid;*
  dǎn (n) (v): 胆, *courage, audacity; to dare;*
  dǎn dà (sv): 胆大, *bold, audacious;*
  dǎn liàng (n): 胆量, *courage;*
  dǎn zi (n): 胆子, *courage, guts;*
  wú wèi (sv): 无畏, *fearless, dauntless;*
  yǒng gǎn (sv): 勇敢, *intrepid, brave, courageous;*
SEE (请查看) **TEMERIDAD, INTRÉPIDO**

AUDICIÓN; audição; *audition;*
  shì yǎn: 试演, *audition*

AUDIENCIA; audiência; *audience;*
  dú zhě: 读者, *public/outdoor audience;*
  guān zhòng: 观众, *audience (in a theater/room, etc.);*
  jiē jiàn: 接见, *audience with the pope/ the president, etc.;*
  tīng zhòng: 听众, *radio/TV audience*

AUDITORIO; auditório; *auditorium, hall;*
  lǐ táng: 礼堂, *auditorium*

AUGUSTO (A) (adj); **augusto;** *august, venerable, impressive;*

dé gāo wàng zhòng (fe): 德高望重, *noble character, high prestige*;
gāo guì de (sv): 高贵的, *noble, high; highly privileged, elitist*;
lìn rén zūn jìng (sv): 令人尊敬, *venerable*;
zūn guì (sv): 尊贵, *honorable, respected*;
zūn jìng (sv) (v): 尊敬, *distinguished; to respect/ honor*;
zūn yán (n) (sv): 尊严, *dignity; dignified; august*

AUSPICIOSO; promissor; *promising, encouraging, favorable;*
guāng míng (sv) (n): 光明, *bright, promising; light*;
hǎo gǎn (n): 好感, *favorable impression*;
lìng rén gǔ wǔ de: 令人鼓舞的, *encouraging; heartening*;
shì yí (sv): 适宜, *appropriate, favorable*;
yǒu qián tú (sv): 有前途, *auspicious, promising*;
yǒu xī wàng (sv): 有希望, *promising, hopeful*;
SEE (请查看) **BENÉFICO, PROPICIO**

AUSTERIDAD; austeridade; *austerity* **... AUSTERO** (A); **austero;** *austere;*
jiǎn pǔ (sv) (n): 简朴, *austere, simple and unadorned; plain*;
SEE (请查看) **SIMPLE, CONCISO, RIGOR, SERIEDAD**

AUTENTICIDAD; autenticidade; *authenticity* **... AUTÉNTICO** (A); **autêntico;** *authentic;*
zhēn (n) (sv) (adv): 真, *truth; true, real, genuine; really, truly, indeed*;
zhēn shí (sv): 真实, *authentic (true, real)*;
zhēn shí xìng: 真实性, *authenticity*;
zhēn zhèng (attr): 真正, *genuine, true, real*;
zhèng zōng (sv) (n): 正宗, *authentic, genuine; orthodox*

AUTOCOMPASIÓN; autocomiseração; *self-pity;*
zì lián (v): 自怜, *to be self-pitying*

AUTOCONTROL; autocontrole; *self-control;*
zì zhì lì : 自制力, *self-control*

AUTODEFENSA; legítima defensa; *self-defense;*
zì wèi: 自卫, *self-defense*

AUTODIDACTA; autodidata; *self-taught;*
zì xué: 自学, *self-taught*

AUTODISCIPLINA; autodisciplina; *self-discipline;*
zì lǜ: 自律, *self-discipline*

AUTOESTIMA; amor-próprio; *self-esteem;*
zì zūn (v): 自尊, *to have self-esteem, self-respect*;
zì zūn xīn (n): 自尊心, *self-esteem*;
zì xìn (sv) (v): 自信, *self-confident; to believe in oneself*

AUTÓGRAFO; autógrafo; *autograph;*
qīn bǐ qiān míng: 亲笔签名, *autograph*

AUTOMÓVIL; automóvel; *automobile, car;*
qì chē: 汽车, *auto, motor vehicle*;
SEE (请查看) **AUTO**

AUTORIDAD; autoridade; *authority* **... AUTORIZACIÓN; autorização;** *authorization;*
dāng jú: 当局, *governmental authority*;
mǒu fāng miàn de quán wēi: 某方面的权威, *an authority, an expert on sthg*;
quán (n) (adv) (v): 权, *power, authority, might, influence, right, entitlement; expediency, tentatively; to consider, for the time being*;
quán lì (n): 权利, *right, privilege, power*;
quán wēi (n): 权威, *power, authority; authoritativeness*;

xǔ kě (n) (v): 许可, *right, permission, authority; to allow, to permit*;
zhí quán (n): 职权, *authority*;
SEE (请查看) AUTORIZAR

AUXILIO; auxilio; *assistance, help; aid (MED)*;
　bāng zhù (v) (n): 帮助, *to help; assistance, aid; helper*;
　jiù mìng: 救命, *help (for sb in danger)*;
　yuán zhù: 援助, *assistance, aid*;
SEE (请查看) ASISTIR, SERVIR, SOSTÉN

AVANZADO; avançado; *advanced, increased, well-ahead*;
　dào wǎn qī de: 到晚期的, *an advanced level/stage*;
　fā dá de: 发达的, *an advanced country*;
　gāo děng (sv): 高等, *advanced, higher*;
　gāo jí (sv): 高级, *senior, advanced, high-level*;
　gāo yú (adv): 高于, *higher, greater*;
　xiān jìn (sv) (n): 先进 *advanced, highly developed; vanguard*;
　xiān qián (n) (sv): 先前, *before, previously; past, previous*;
　xiān tóu (sv) (n): 先头, *ahead, in front*

AVARICIA; avareza; *avarice ...*
AVARICIOSO (A); **avarento;** *avaricious ... AVARO* (A); **avarento;** *miserly*;
　lìn (sv): 吝, *stingy, tight, miserly*;
　sè (bf): 啬, *stingy*;
　tān lán (sv): 贪婪, *greedy, rapacious, avaricious, avid/eager for*;
　tān xīn (sv) (n): 贪心, *avaricious, insatiable; greed, rapacity*;
SEE (请查看) MÍSERO

AVENTURA; aventura; *adventure*;
　mào xiǎn (n) (v): 冒险, *adventure; to take risks/chances*;
　qí yù 奇遇, *happy encounter/adventure*

ÁVIDO; ávido; *avid*;
　jí qiè (sv) (adv): 急切, *eager, avid; eagerly*;
　kě wàng (v) (sv): 渴望, *to thirst/long for; avid*;
SEE (请查看) ARDOROSO, EFUSIVO

AVIÓN; aeroplane; *airplane*;
　fēi jī: 飞机, *airplane*

Easily recognizable verbs and their Portuguese and Chinese equivalents
Verbos fácilmente reconocibles en Español-Portugués-Inglés y sus equivalentes en Chino
Verbos facilmente reconhecível em Espanhol-Português-Inglês e seus equivalentes em Chinês
很容易辨认的西班牙语，葡萄牙语，英语动词和他们的中文对等词

ABANDONAR; abandonar; *to leave, to desert;* **desamparar;** *to abandon;* **negligenciar;** *to neglect;* **dexiar,** *to give up; to abandon;*
　bèi qì: 背弃, *to abandon/forsake*;
　dài màn: 怠慢, *to neglect/not pay attention to*;
　diū qì: 丢弃, *to abandon/discard*;
　fàng qì: 放弃, *to abandon/give up on sthg*;
　fèi qì: 废弃, *to abandon/discard*;
　hū (bf) (adv): 忽, *to neglect/overlook;*

suddenly;
　hū lüè: 忽略, *to neglect/not care for*;
　hū shì: 忽视, *to neglect/overlook sthg/sb*;
　lí qì: 离弃, *to abandon/desert*;
　pāo qì: 抛弃, *to leave/abandon/desert a person, family, etc.*;
　pāo shě: 抛舍, *to abandon*;
　pāo zhì: 抛掷, *to throw/cast; to throw away; to abandon*;
　piē: 撇, *to cast aside/abandon*;
　piē qì: 撇弃, *to cast away/abandon*;

piē xià: 撇下, *to cast away/abandon*;
rēng xià: 扔下, *to abandon*;
shě qì: 舍弃, *to give up/abandon*;
shū hū (v) (n): 疏忽, *to neglect work/ duty, etc.; negligence, carelessness*;
yí qì: 遗弃, *to abandon/desert a wife and children/forsake*

ABOLIR; abolir; *to abolish*;
fèi zhǐ: 废止, *to abolish/annul*;
gé chú: 革除, *to abolish/get rid of*;
SEE (请查看) ABOLICIÓN, ANULAR, INVALIDAR, REVOCAR

ABORTAR; abortar; *to abort*;
shǐ liú chǎn: 使流产, *to abort a child*;
shǐ zhōng zhǐ: 使终止, *to abort a mission*

ABREVIAR; encurtar; *to shorten*;
suō duǎn (v) (n): 缩短, *to shorten/ curtail/cut down/ reduce; abbreviation, curtailment*

ABSOLVER; absolver; *to absolve (RELIG)*;
miǎn chú: 免除, *to prevent/avoid; to remit*

ABSORBER; absorver; *to absorb*;
xī shōu (v) (n): 吸收, *to absorb/suck up; to assimiliate; absortion*

ABUSAR; insultar, *to insult*;
maltratar, *to maltreat*; **abusar**, *to misuse*; **exceder**, *to go too far*;
practicar, *to abuse sthg/sb*; **aproveitar**, *to take advantage of/make most of*; *to abuse sthg; to go too far*;
cuī cán: 摧残, *to abuse sexually*;
làn yòng: 滥用, *to misuse (abuse) power/drugs/alcohol*;
nüè dài: 虐待, *to abuse/mistreat physically*;
qī rǔ: 欺辱, *to bully and humiliate; to insult*;
rǔ mà (v) (sv): 辱骂, *to insult; insulting*;
wǔ rǔ (v) (n) (sv): 侮辱, *to insult, to humiliate, to defile; insult; insulting*

ACAMPAR; acampar, *to encamp/camp*;
shè yíng: 设营, *to camp*

ACCIONAR; ativar; *to set off; to activate*;
kāi dòng (v): 开动, *to activate/start/set in motion*;
SEE (请查看) OPERAR, REALIZAR, EJECUTAR

ACELERAR; acelerar; *to accelerate/ speed up*;
jiā sù (v): 加速, *to accelerate; to expedite*;
SEE (请查看) PRECIPITAR

ACEPTAR; aceitar, *to accept, to take, to receive*; **assentir**, *to agree, to follow*; **aprovar**, *to accept as satisfactory*; **assumir**, *to admit, accept as one's own; to accept*;
chéng jiē: 承接, *to undertake/accept/ continue*;
chéng rèn: 承认, *to admit to, to confess/accept responsibility*;
fú shū: 服输, *to concede/admit defeat*;
jiē nà: 接纳, *to be accepted (as into an organization, as a friend, etc.)*;
jiē shòu: 接受, *to accept an invitation/ advice, responsibility; or to accept, as true or valid or as inevitable*;
rèn shū: 认输, *to accept a loss/admit defeat*;
SEE (请查看) ADMITIR, CONFESAR

ACLAMAR; aclamar; *to acclaim*;
huān hū: 欢呼, *to hail/acclaim*;
SEE (请查看) APLAUDIR, GLORIFICAR

ACOMODAR; acomodar; *to oblige; to seat sb, to install/accommodate*;
róng nà: 容纳, *to accommodate; to tolerate*;
SEE (请查看) COMPELER

ACOMPAÑAR; acompanhar; *to go with/ accompany sb*;
bàn (n) (v): 伴, *company, companion; to accompany*;

bàn suí: 伴随, *to accompany; to follow;*

péi bàn: 陪伴, *to accompany/keep sb company;*

péi chī: 陪吃, *to accompany a guest at a dinner;*

péi chuáng: 陪床, *to keep sb company at a hospital;*

péi kè: 陪客, *to keep guests company;*

péi shì: 陪侍, *to accompany and attend to sb;*

péi: 陪, *to keep sb company; to accompany sb for help/assist;*

suí cóng (v) (n): 随从, *to accompany; retinue, entourage;*

xiāng bàn: 相伴, *to accompany sb; to be together/accompany each other;*

zuò bàn: 作伴, *to keep sb company, to accompany;*

SEE (请查看**) ASISTIR**

ACOSAR; atormentar; *to pester; to harass;*

fán rǎo: 烦扰, *to pester; to bother/disturb sb;*

jiū chán: 纠缠, *to pester; to nag/worry sb;*

kù rǎo (v) (sv): 困扰, *to trouble, to perplex, to annoy; perplexed;*

SEE (请查看**) MOLESTAR**

ACTIVAR; ativar; *to activate;*

jī huó: 激活, *to activate;*

qǐ dòng: 启动, *to activate, to start/switch on (a machine);*

SEE (请查看**) ACCIONAR**

ACTUAR; assumir; *to assume control; to act/ undertake;*

cāo chí: 操持, *to manage/handle;*

cāo zòng: 操纵, *to control; to operate sthg;*

chēng bàn: 承办, *to undertake; to host/sponsor;*

chéng nuò (v) (n): 承诺, *to undertake, to promise; undertaking, commitment;*

cóng shì: 从事, *to undertake;*

dān dāng: 担当, *to take on; to assume control;*

dòng zuò (n) (v) (suf): 动作, *movement, motion, action; to act/start moving; -ation;*

guǎn shù: 管束, *to restrain/control;*

guǎn zhì: 管制, *to control/watch;*

jià yù: 驾驭, *to control sthg; to drive/ pilot sthg;*

jiān chá: 监察, *to supervise; to control;*

jiān dū (v) (n): 监督, *to supervise; to control; supervisor;*

jiē guǎn: 接管, *to take control over a company;*

jǐn wò: 紧握, *to hold firmly; to control;*

kòng zhì (v) (n): 控制, *to control; to dominate; control, domination;*

rěn nài (v) (n): 忍耐, *to endure; to control oneself; patience;*

zhàn lǐng: 占领, *to take control of a country;*

zhǎng guǎn: 掌管, *to control/be in charge of;*

zhǎng quán: 掌权, *to be in power/ have control over;*

zhào bàn: 照办, *to act accordingly;*

zhī pèi: 支配, *to arrange; to allocate; to control;*

zūn xíng: 遵行, *to act on; to follow;*

SEE (请查看**) AFECTAR, FUNCIONAR, OPERAR**

ACUMULAR; acumular; *to accumulate;*

duī cún: 堆存, *to store up/accumulate;*

duī fàng: 堆放, *to stack/pile up;*

duī jī: 堆积, *to pile up/accumulate;*

duī jí: 堆集, *to accumulate/gather together;*

duī: 堆, *to pile up/heap up; to pack; to crowd;*

jī jù: 积聚, *to accumulate/gather/ assemble;*

jī lěi: 积累, *to accumulate;*

jī xù: 积蓄, *to accumulate; to save; to amass;*

jù: 聚, *to assemble; to gather; to get together; to amass;*

jù jí: 聚集, *to convene/gather together;*

lěi jī (v) (n): 累积, *to add up; accumulative;*

lěi jì: 累计, *to accumulate/add up;*

ACUSAR; acusar; *to accuse/charge;*

kòng sù (v) (n): 控诉, *to accuse/ denounce; complaint;*

zé bèi: 责备, *to blame/accuse;*
zé guài: 责怪, *to blame;*
zé wèn: 责问, *to call sb to account for sthg;*
SEE (请查看) CULPAR, INCRIMINAR, IMPUTAR

ADAPTAR; adaptar; *to adjust/adapt;*
gǎi biān: 改编, *to adapt; to rearrange; to revise;*
shǐ shì hé: 使适合, *to alter/change; to make suitable;*
shì yìng: 适应, *to adapt to/get used to;*
tiáo jì: 调剂, *to adjust/equalize; to regulate, to make up a prescription;*
tiáo jié: 调节, *to adjust/regulate;*
tiáo pín (v) (n): 调频, *to adjust the frequency; frequency modulation;*
tiáo zhěng: 调整, *to adjust; to regulate; to restructure; to balance;*
yìng biàn (v): 应变, *to adapt to change; to meet a contingency;*
SEE (请查看) AJUSTAR

ADHERIR; aderir; *to stick/adhere;*
fù zhuó: 附着, *to stick/adhere to sthg;*
tiē (v) (bf) (n): 贴, *to paste/stick/glue; to keep close to; allowance;*
zhān (v) (sv): 粘, *to stick/adhere to; to glue/paste; to cling to; sticky;*
zhān lián (v) (n): 粘连, *to adhere; adhesion (MED);*
zhān tiē: 粘贴, *to paste/stick*

ADJUDICAR; adjudicar; *to award/adjudicate;*
cái dìng: 裁定, *to judge/rule;*
cái duàn: 裁断, *to consider and decide;*
cái jué (v) (n): 裁决, *to judge/adjudicate/rule; ruling;*
cái pàn (v) (n): 裁判, *to judge/decide; umpire, judge, referee;*
jiǎng shǎng (n) (v): 奖赏, *reward; to reward, to award;*
pàn jué: 判决, *to pass judgment, to reach a verdict*

ADMINISTRAR; administrar; *to manage/run/ administer;*
bàn bào: 办报, *to run a newspaper;*

cāo zuò: 操作, *to operate;*
dāng jiā: 当家, *to manage a household;*
guǎn lǐ (v) (n): 管理, *to supervise/manage/run; supervision, management;*
guǎn xiá: 管辖, *to administer;*
jīng shǒu: 经手, *to handle/deal with personally;*
jīng yíng: 经营, *to manage/run/operate;*
jǔ bàn: 举办, *to hold/run/sponsor;*
lǐ cái: 理财, *to manage the finances;*
liào lǐ (v) (n): 料理, *to manage; to arrange; to take care of; Japanese cuisine;*
yíng yùn: 营运, *to operate/run;*
yùn xíng: 运行, *to move/run/operate;*
zhì lǐ: 治理, *to rule/govern/administer/manage;*
SEE (请查看) ACTUAR, GOBERNAR

ADMIRAR; admirar; *to admire;*
jìng pèi: 敬佩, *to admire, to esteem;*
xīn shǎng: 欣赏, *to enjoy; to admire; to appreciate;*
zàn yáng: 赞扬, *to praise/speak highly of;*
SEE (请查看) ADMIRACIÓN

ADMITIR; admitir; *to allow entry, to admit/let sb join; to acknowledge; to admit;*
jìn rù: 进入, *to enter, to go into;*
lù qǔ: 录取, *to admit; to enroll; to recruit;*
rèn cuò: 认错, *to admit a mistake; to apologize;*
rèn zhàng: 认账, *to acknowledge a mistake/ obligation/fault; to admit the truth;*
rù (v) (n): 入, *to enter; to join; to agree with; (bf) to enter; to receive; to take in; income;*
rù chǎng: 入场, *to be admitted; to enter;*
rù huǒ: 入伙, *to join a group/undertaking;*
yǔn xǔ jìn rù: 允许进入, *to admit sb;*
zhāo gòng: 招供, *to confess; to admit;*
SEE (请查看) ACEPTAR

ADOCTRINAR; doutrinar; *to instruct/*

indoctrinate;
  guàn shū: 灌输, *to indoctrinate; to teach; to impart*;
  jiào dǎo (n) (v): 教导, *guidance; to instruct*;
  zé chéng: 责成, *to instruct*;
  zé lìng: 责令, *to order; to instruct/guide*

ADOPTAR; adotar; *to adopt/pass/take;*
  cǎi qǔ: 采取, *to adopt a measure/ policy/method, etc.;*
  cǎi yòng: 采用, *to adopt a plan/ method, etc.;*
  lǐng yǎng: 领养, *to adopt a child;*
  shōu yǎng: 收养, *to adopt a child;*
  tōng guò: 通过, *to adopt/pass a law/ suggestion, etc.;*
SEE (请查看**) APROBACIÓN, ACEPTACIÓN**

ADORAR; adorar; *to worship/adore;*
  chóng bài: 崇拜, *to worship/adore*
SEE (请查看**) IDOLATRAR**

ADORNAR; adornar; *to decorate/ adorn;*
  zhuāng shì (v) (n): 装饰, *to adorn/ decorate; ornament*

ADULAR; adular; *to flatter;*
  chuī pěng: 吹捧, *to flatter;*
  fèng chéng: 奉承, *to flatter, to adulate;*
  pāi mǎ pì (v): 拍马屁, *to flatter/suck up to/fawn on/ butter up*

AFECTAR; afetar; *to affect; to upset; to sadden;*
  bō jí: 波及, *to involve, to affect;*
  gǎo chòu: 搞臭, *to shame/discredit sb;*
  gǎo kuǎ: 搞垮, *to undermine; to upset;*
  jiǎo luàn: 搅乱, *to disturb; to upset; to mess up;*
  qiān dòng: 牵动, *to affect; to touch sb;*
  qiān guà: 牵挂, *to worry; to be very concerned;*
  shāng xīn (v) (sv): 伤心, *to sadden sb; to be sad;*
  shǐ kǔ nǎo: 使苦恼, *to upset sb;*

  yǐng xiǎng (v) (n): 影响, *to influence sb/sthg, to affect; influence, impact, affect;*
  zuò yòng (n) (v): 作用, *action, impact, effect; motive; to affect;*
SEE (请查看**) AFECTADO**

AFIRMAR; afirmar; *to confirm/declare/ affirm;*
  shēn míng: 申明, *to declare;*
SEE (请查看**) ASEVERACIÓN, AFIRMATIVO**

AFRONTAR; enfrentar, *to face;* **confrontar,** *to compare; to face up to/ confront;*
  duì kàng (n) (v): 对抗, *confrontation; to confront/ oppose;*
  duì lì: 对立, *to oppose; to confront;*
  miàn duì: 面对, *to confront; to face*

AGITAR; agitar, *to shake; to stir/ agitate/wave;*
  cì jī (sv) (v): 刺激, *exciting, irritating; to provoke, to incite;*
  gǔ dòng: 鼓动, *to agitate; to arouse/ instigate/ incite;*
  jiǎo dòng: 搅动, *to mix, to stir; to disturb;*
  jiào suō: 教唆, *to instigate/incite;*
  shān dòng: 煽动, *to agitate/incite/ stir up;*
  tiǎo bō (v) (n): 挑拨, *to incite; to instigate; provocation;*
  tiǎo suō: 挑唆, *to incite; to instigate;*
  yáo dòng: 摇动, *to wave/sway/rock;*
  zhǐ shǐ: 指使, *to incite/provoke;*
SEE (请查看**) AGITACIÓN**

AGRANDAR; ampliar; *to enlarge;*
  fàng dà: 放大, *to enlarge/amplify/ magnify;*
  kuò dà (v) (sv) (n): 扩大, *to enlarge/ expand; spacious; expansion, enlargement;*
  kuò zhāng (v) (n): 扩张, *to expand/ extend/ enlarge/dilate; dilation*
SEE (请查看**) AMPLIAR, EXPANDIR**

AGRAVAR; agravar; *to make worse* **... IRRITAR,** *to annoy, irritate; to* aggravate;

jī nù (v) (sv): 激怒, *to provoke; to irritate; to enrage; irritable*;

jiā zhòng: 加重, *to aggravate*;

kùn rǎo (v) (sv): 困扰, *to trouble; to annoy; to disturb; vexed, annoyed*;

shǐ ' è huà: 使恶化, *to aggravate, to make worse*;

shǐ bù shū fu: 使不舒服, *to irritate the skin, eyes, etc.*;

shǐ fán zào (v) (sv): 使烦躁, *to irritate sb; peevish, agitated*;

SEE (请查看) **AGITAR, AGRAVANTE**

AGRAVIAR; insultar, *insult;* **ofender,** *to offend/insult;*

chù fàn: 触犯, *to offend; to violate*;

dé zuì: 得罪, *to offend, to displease; to break the law*;

shòu rǔ: 受辱, *to be insulted/ humiliated*;

SEE (请查看) **ABUSAR, HUMILLAR, OFENDER**

AGRUPAR; colher, *to collect (GEN);* **reunir,** *to collect; gather strength/ courage;* **ganhar,** *to gather speed, momentum;* **franzir,** *to gather into folds; to group together, group, to gather;*

cǎi jí: 采集, *to collect/gather; to put together*;

huì zǒng: 汇总, *to gather/collect; to pool*;

jí (v) (n): 集, *to collect/gather; market, anthology*;

jí hé: 集合, *to gather, to assemble*;

jí jié: 集结, *to build up; to concentrate*;

shōu jí: 收集, *to collect/gather*;

zǒng (v) (adv): 总, *to gather; to assemble; always, invariably, inevitable, surely*;

SEE (请查看) **ACUMULAR, CONCENTRAR**

AJUSTAR; ajustar; *to adjust/alter/ correct;* **adaptar-se,** *to adjust to sthg; to adjust, tighten, fit, regulate;*

biàn dòng (v) (n): 变动, *to change/ alter/modify; change, fluctuation*;

bō zhèng: 拨正, *to correct/make right*;

dìng zhèng: 订正, *to correct a text*;

gǎi zhèng: 改正, *to correct/amend*;

gēng gǎi: 更改, *to alter plans/a situation, etc.*;

jiū zhèng: 纠正, *to correct sthg/sb*;

pī gǎi: 批改, *to correct/mark*;

shān gǎi: 删改, *to revise/edit*;

tú gǎi: 涂改, *to alter*;

xiū gǎi (v) (n): 修改, *to amend/revise/ alter/modify; alteration, modification*;

SEE (请查看) **ADAPTAR, ACTUAR**

ALARMAR, alarmar, *to scare; to alarm, alert ...* **ALERTAR; alarma;** *to alert, to give the alarm;*

jīng dòng: 惊动, *to alarm; to disturb*;

shǐ jīng huāng: 使惊慌, *to alarm sb, to raise/ sound the alarm*;

shǐ jīng jué: 使警觉, *to alert sb; to give the alert*;

shǐ jīng kǒng: 使惊恐, *to frighten sb*

ALTERAR; alterar; *to change/modify/ alter;*

biàn huà: 变化, *to alter, to change*;

gǎi biàn (n) (v): 改变, *adaptation; to change/ reform*;

wāi qū (v) (n): 歪曲, *to distort/ misrepresent; distortion*;

zhuǎn huà: 转化, *to change/ transform*;

SEE (请查看) **ADAPTAR, AJUSTAR, MODIFICAR, VARIAR**

ALTERNAR; alternar; *to alternate; to mix/socialize;*

biàn huàn: 变换, *to vary/alternate/ convert*;

cān jiā shè jiāo: 参加社交, *to socialize*;

jiāo jì: 交际, *to socialize/interact socially*;

jiāo tán: 交谈, *to chitchat*;

jiāo tì (v) (adv): 交替, *to alternate/ replace; one after other, taking turns*;

lún liú: 轮流, *to alternate with/take turns*;

shè huì huà: 社会化, *to socialize*;

xiāng jiàn: 相间, *to alternate with*;

yìng chou (v) (n): 应酬, *to socialize*

with; social engagement;
zhōu xuán: 周旋, *to socialize/deal with*

ALUDIR; aludir, *to allude to sthg/refer to;*
  àn shì: 暗示, *to hint, to suggest;*
  àn zhǐ: 暗指, *to insinuate;*
  cān jiàn: 参见, *to refer to/reference;*
  cān kǎo (v) (n): 参考, *to consult/refer to; consultation, reference;*
  tán dào: 谈到, *to talk about/refer to;*
  tí dào: 提到, *to allude to sthg, to mention, to refer;*
  tí qǐ: 提起, *to mention/raise a topic;*
  yǐng shè: 影射, *to allude/insinuate; to cast aspersions*

AMERITAR; merecer; *to merit, deserve;*
  yīng dé: 应得, *to deserve;*
  zhí dé (v) (sv): 值得, *to merit/deserve; deserving*

AMPLIAR; expandir; *to expand/extend;*
  chuán dì: 传递, *to extend/transmit/ transfer; to deliver;*
  fā zhǎn (v) (n): 发展, *to develop/ expand; development, growth;*
  kuò chōng: 扩充, *to enlarge/expand/ increase/ strengthen;*
  shēn cháng: 深长, *to stretch/extend;*
  tí gòng: 提供, *to extend credit;*
  yán cháng (v) (n): 延长, *to prolong/ lengthen/ extend; extension;*
  yán shēn (v) (n): 延伸, *to extend/ stretch/elongate; to spread; extension;*
  yǐn shēn: 引申, *to extend;*
SEE (请查看) EXPANDIR,
AGRANDAR

AMPLIFICAR; amplificar; *to amplify;*
  xiáng shù: 详述, *to amplify on an idea, plan, etc.;*
  zēng dà: 增大, *to increase/enlarge on;*
SEE (请查看) AGRANDAR,
AUMENTAR

AMPUTAR; amputar; *to amputate/ cut off;*

jié zhī: 截肢, *to amputate;*
qiē chú: 切除, *to cut off*

ANALIZAR; analisar, *to examine; to analyze;*
  jiǎn chá: 检查, *to examine sthg;*
SEE (请查看) ANÁLISIS

ANEXAR; prender, *to fasten sthg to sthg;* **anexar,** *to attach sthg to a document;* **atribuir,** *to attach blame/ importance to sthg/sb; to attach/annex, append;*
  fù shàng: 附上, *to fasten, to join;*
  fù shè: 附设, *to add sthg to;*
  fù shǔ: 附属, *to attach sthg to;*
SEE (请查看) ADHERIR,
ACCESORIO

ANOTAR; notar, *to note, indicate;* **observar,** *to observe;* **apontar,** *to point out;* **mencionar,** *to mention;* **contemplar,** *to contemplate;* **comentar,** *to comment on; to note/make a note of/record;*
  biǎo míng: 表明, *to show; to indicate;*
  duì mǒu shì fā biǎo yì jiàn: 对某事 发表意见, *to comment on sthg;*
  jì xià: 记下, *to note down;*
  liú yì: 留意, *to note/observe;*
  zhǐ chū: 指出, *to point out;*
  zhǐ xiàng: 志向, *to point to/direct to;*
  zhù míng: 注明, *to indicate/note clearly;*
SEE (请查看) ALUDIR

ANTECEDER; preceder; *to precede;*
  xiān fā zhì rén (fe): 先发制人, *to preempt; to gain the initiative;*
  xiān xíng (v) (n): 先行, *to go ahead/ precede; forerunner*

ANTICIPAR; prever, *to expect;* **anticipar,** *to anticipate; to foresee;*
  děng hòu: 等候, *to expect/wait for;*
  liào dào: 料到, *to expect/foresee;*
  liào xiǎng: 料想, *to expect/presume;*
  qī dài: 期待, *to await/expect;*
  qī wàng: 期望, *to look forward to/ hope; hope, wish;*

xī wàng (v) (n): 希望, *to hope/dream/ expect; hope, wish;*
xiǎng dé dào: 想得到, *to think/expect/ imagine;*
yì liào (v) (n): 意料, *to anticipate/ expect; expectation;*
yì xiǎng: 意想, *to intend/expect;*
yù xiǎng (v) (n): 预想, *to expect/ anticipate; anticipation*

ANULAR; anular; *to cancel/annul/ revoke;* **sobrepujar,** *to cancel out; to cancel/annul/repeal/ rescind;*
dǎ xiāo: 打消, *to give up on/cancel;*
diào xiāo: 吊销, *to revoke/withdraw sthg;*
qǔ xiāo: 取消, *to cancel/abolish;*
zhù xiāo: 注销, *to cancel/write off;*
zuò fèi: 作废, *to cancel/nullify/become invalid;*
SEE (请查看) REVOCAR, ABOLICIÓN, RESCINDIR

ANUNCIAR; anunciar; *to announce/ advertise;*
biāo bǎng: 标榜, *to advertise/flaunt/ brag;*
fā biǎo: 发表, *to announce/make public;*
fā bù: 发布, *to issue a statement/ announce/ release;*
gōng bù: 公布, *to announce/publish;*
gōng gào (v) (n): 公告, *to give public notice; announcement;*
jiē shì (v) (n): 揭示, *to reveal/ announce; announcement;*
shēng míng (v) (n): 声明, *to state/ announce; statement, declaration;*
tōng gào (v) (n): 通告, *to announce; public notice;*
yù gào (v) (n): 预告, *to announce in advance/give advance notice/warning; foretelling, notice;*
zuò guǎng gào: 做广告, *to advertise*

APARTAR; apartar, *to split/break up; to move away/remove/separate;*
bān chū qù: 搬出去, *to move out;*
chāi chú: 拆除, *to dismantle/remove;*
chāi huǒ: 拆伙, *to dissolve a*

partnership;
chāi sàn: 拆散, *to break up/break apart;*
fēn huà: 分化, *to break up/become divided;*
fēn jiā: 分家, *to separate and live apart;*
fēn jū: 分居, *to live apart/be separated (of married persons);*
fēn kāi (v) (adv): 分开, *to split up (people/things); to move apart; separately;*
fēn liè: 分裂, *to split/divide/break up; to fragment;*
fēn shǒu: 分手, *to break up/say goodbye;*
gē liè: 割裂, *to cut apart/separate;*
gē zhì: 搁置, *to shelve, to put aside;*
jī pò: 击破, *to break up/destroy;*
jué jiāo: 绝交, *to break off relations/ break up;*
kāi zǒu: 开走, *to move off;*
lí kāi: 离开, *to move away (from a town/area, etc.); to depart; to deviate from;*
pò liè: 破裂, *to split/burst/break up;*
qǐ chéng qián wǎng: 启程前往, *to move on;*
zǒu kāi: 走开, *to move away (from a position from a door, window, etc.);*
zǔ gé: 阻隔, *to separate/cut off;*
SEE (请查看) APARTE

APELAR; apelar; *to appeal;*
āi qiú (v) (n): 哀求, *to beg/entreat/ implore; request, entreaty;*
hào zhào: 号召, *to call/appeal;*
hū: 呼, *to appeal/call on/plead for;*
qǐng qiú: 请求, *to ask/request/entreat;*
shàng fǎng: 上访, *to appeal to a higher authority;*
shàng sù: 上诉, *to appeal to a higher court;*
shēn sù: 申诉, *to appeal/complain;*
sù zhū: 诉诸, *to resort/appeal to*

APLANAR; aplanar; *to level/make even/flatten;*
nòng píng: 弄平, *to flatten/even/level;*
yā píng: 压平, *to flatten*

APLAUDIR; aplaudir; *to applaud/ welcome/ approve;*
  huān yíng: 欢迎, *to welcome; to greet;*
  pāi shǒu: 拍手, *to applaud;*
  yíng jiē: 迎接, *to welcome;*
SEE (请查看) ACLAMACIÓN, APLAUSO, ACLAMAR

APLICAR; aplicar; *to apply/give;*
  shēn qǐng (v) (n): 申请, *to apply, make an application; application;*
  shī jiā: 施加, *to exert (apply/impose) pressure, etc.;*
  shí jiàn (v) (n): 实践, *to put into practice; practice;*
  shí jìn: 使劲, *to exert (apply) oneself;*
  shí shī: 实施, *to apply; to implement; to carry out;*
  shí xíng: 实行, *to put into practice/ carry out;*
  shī yòng: 使用, *to use; to employ; to apply;*
  shī yòng: 施用, *suit/be applicable;*
  shī zhǎn: 施展, *to put to good use;*
  shī: 施, *to carry out; to apply; to use; to exert;*
  tào yòng: 套用, *to apply mechanically/ by rote;*
  yìng yòng: 应用, *to apply; to use;*
  yìng zhēng: 应征, *to apply for a job; to enlist;*
  yǔ yǐ: 予以, *to give/grant;*
  zhì cái: 制裁, *to apply; to impose;*
  zhì dòng: 制动, *to apply the brakes*

APRECIAR; apreciar; *to appreciate, be fond of, like;*
  kàn shàng: 看上, *to like, to favor;*
  kàn zhòng: 看中, *to choose; to fancy; to like/prefer;*
  shěn měi (v) (n): 审美, *to appreciate art/beauty, etc.; estheticism;*
  tǐ wèi (v) (n): 体味, *to appreciate, to savor; body odor;*
  xǐ hào: 喜好, *to like; to be fond of;*
  xǐ huān (v) (n): 喜欢, *to like/be fond of; happy;*
SEE (请查看) ADMIRAR, APRECIACIÓN

APREHENDER; deter, *to stop, to detain, to keep, to hold back;* **to** *apprehend, to arrest, seize, detain ...*
ARRESTAR; prender, *to arrest;* **deter,** *to stop;*
  bǎ wò (v) (n): 把握, *to grasp/seize; certainty, assurance;*
  bà zhàn: 霸占, *to occupy/seize;*
  bǔ zhuō: 捕捉, *to seize/capture/hunt down;*
  dǎi bǔ: 逮捕, *to arrest, to apprehend, to detain;*
  dòu liú: 逗留, *to stay/stop;*
  duó qǔ: 夺取, *to capture/seize; to strive for;*
  gōng kè: 攻克, *to capture/seize;*
  jiān jìn: 监禁, *to imprison;*
  jū jìn: 拘禁, *to restrain; to arrest;*
  kòu liú: 扣留, *to detain; to arrest; to confiscate;*
  kòu yā: 扣押, *to detain; to hold;*
  lán jié: 拦截, *to intercept and rob/mug;*
  lán lù: 拦路, *to block the way;*
  lán zhù: 拦住, *to stop/hold up;*
  lán zǔ: 拦阻, *to stop/hold up;*
  ná huò: 拿获, *to apprehend sb;*
  ná zhù: 拿住, *to arrest;*
  qiǎng duó: 抢夺, *to seize/grab;*
  qīn zhàn: 侵占, *to invade and occupy/ seize;*
  tíng dùn (v) (n): 停顿, *to stop/pause; stop, pause;*
  tíng zhǐ: 停止, *to stop/halt;*
  xiū zhǐ: 休止, *to stop/cease;*
  zhàn lǐng: 占领, *to capture/seize;*
  zhàn zhù (v) (n): 站住, *to stop/halt/ stand firm, pause;*
  zhì zhǐ: 制止, *to prevent/restrain/stop;*
  zhǐ zhù: 止住, *to stop/halt/desist;*
  zhōng zhǐ: 终止, *to stop/end/cease/ conclude;*
  zhù shǒu: 住手, *to stop/stay one's hand;*
  zhuā huò: 抓获, *to catch a criminal/ thief;*
  zǔ zhì (v) (n): 阻滞, *to clog/stop up; obstruction;*
SEE (请查看) ARRESTO

APROBAR; aprovar; *to approve/pass/ endorse;*

diǎn tóu: 点头, *to nod in approval; to agree/ approve*;

rèn kě: 认可, *to approve of/endorse; to accept; to confirm*;

zàn tóng: 赞同, *to approve of/agree with*;

SEE (请查看) ASENTIR, APROBACIÓN, ADOPTAR, AFIRMAR, PERMITIR

APROPIAR; apropiar; *to adapt, to appropriate, award, assign*;

gǎi biān (v) (n): 改编, *to adapt to TV/a movie; to reorganize; to rearrange; adaptation*;

shǐ shì hé: 使适合, *to adapt, to alter, to change*;

SEE (请查看) ADJUDICAR

APROVISIONAR; fornecer, *to supply sthg to sb*; **prover,** *to provide sthg to sb*; **abastecer,** *to supply with, to stock up; to supply; to provision*;

bǔ fā: 补发, *to reissue*;

bǔ jǐ: 补给, *to supply*;

chǔ bèi (mǒu wù): 储备(某物), *to stock up*;

fú yǎng: 抚养, *to provide for/bring up/foster*;

fú zhù: 扶助, *to support/help/assist*;

gōng diàn: 供电, *to supply electricity*;

gōng jǐ: 供给, *to supply/provide*;

gōng nuǎn: 供暖, *to provide/supply heat*;

gōng yìng wù: 供应物, *to stock*;

gōng yìng: 供应, *to supply; to provide/offer*;

gōng: 供, *to supply/provide/furnish*;

jù yǒu: 具有, *to have/be provided with*;

pèi bèi (v) (n): 配备, *to provide/allocate; equipment*;

sòng huò: 送货, *to supply (commercially)*;

tí gōng: 提供, *to provide, to supply (GEN)*;

tóu dì: 投递, *to deliver*;

zhào fā: 照发, *to issue/provide*;

zhào guǎn: 照管, *to provide for/look after*;

zhī chēng: 支撑, *to support/maintain*;

zhī yìng: 支应, *to supply/deal with*;

zhī yuán: 支援, *to support/assist/help/aid*

APROXIMAR; aproximar; *to bring nearer/to approximate; to move closer/bring nearer*;

huì jù: 汇聚, *to converge*;

jiē chù: 接触, *to come into contact with/come close to*;

jiē jìn yú: 接近于, *to approximate*;

jìn sì (v) (sv): 近似, *to be similar to; to approximate; similar*;

lín jiē: 邻接, *to border on*;

lín jìn (sv) (n): 临近, *to be close/nearby; vicinity*;

pò jìn: 迫近, *to approach; to get close to*;

SEE (请查看) APROXIMACIÓN

AQUIETAR; aquietar; *to calm down/allay*;

píng dìng: 平定, *to calm down; to suppress*;

shǐ píng jìng: 使平静, *to make/cause sb/sthg to be calm/quiet/tranquil*;

ARBITRAR; arbitrar; *to referee/umpire; to arbitrate*;

dāng cái pàn: 当裁判, *to referee a game*;

tiáo chù: 调处, *to mediate/arbitrate*;

tiáo tíng: 调停, *to mediate/intervene*;

zhòng cái: 仲裁, *to arbitrate*

ARGUMENTAR; discutir, *to quarrel* **argumentar,** *to argue one's case*; **alegar,** *to allege; to argue*;

chǎo jià: 吵架, *to quarrel*;

chǎo zuǐ: 吵嘴, *to bicker/quarrel/wrangle*;

chě pí: 扯皮, *to wrangle/argue back and forth/argue loudly/dispute over nothing*;

fān liǎn: 翻脸, *to quarrel*;

guǐ biàn: 诡辩, *to quibble*;

jì jiào: 计较, *to argue/dispute/discuss*;

jīn jīn jì jiào (fe): 斤斤计较, *to quibble; to complain/worry about everything; to be self-centered*;

rǎng rǎng: 嚷嚷, *to shout/yell/argue*

noisily;

shuō lǐ: 说理, *to argue/reason*;

xuān chēng: 宣称, *to allege*;

yìng shuō: 硬说, *to assert/allege*;

zhēng chǎo: 争吵, *to quarrel/wrangle*;

zhēng míng: 争鸣, *to contend*;

zhēng yì (v) (n): 争议, *to dispute; controversy*;

SEE (请查看) **ARGUMENTO**

ARRUINAR; **arruinar**, *to ruin/spoil/bankrupt*; **arrasar**, *to demolish*; **destruir**, *to destroy*; **estragar**, *to spoil/damage; to ruin/wreck*;

chāi huǐ: 拆毁, *to demolish*;

dǎ diào: 打掉, *to destroy*;

dǎ pò: 打破, *to break; to smash; to destroy sb's faith/confidence, etc.*;

huǐ huài (v) (n):: 毁坏, *to destroy/damage; damage*;

huǐ miè: 毁灭, *to destroy; to exterminate*;

huǐ sǔn: 毁损, *to damage*;

jī huǐ: 击毁, *to smash; to wreck; to attack and destroy*;

mái zàng: 埋葬, *to wreck; to destroy; to eliminate*;

nòng huài: 弄坏, *to ruin/spoil/make a mess of*;

nòng zāo (v) (sv): 弄糟, *to spoil/make a mess of; spoiled*;

pò chǎn: 破产, *to go bankrupt/fall through*;

pò huài: 破坏, *to destroy a building/an object; to vandalize*;

pò suì (v) (sv): 破碎, *to smash; to break into pieces; to fall apart; tattered, broken*;

shā sǐ: 杀死, *to destroy an animal*;

shāng hài: 伤害, *to hurt/damage/harm*;

sǔn hài (v) (sv): 损害, *to spoil/damage; to harm/ injure; harmful*;

sǔn huài (v) (sv): 损坏, *to ruin/damage sthg; worn*;

sǔn shāng (v) (n): 损伤, *to damage/harm; loss*;

zàng sòng: 葬送, *to ruin/jeopardize/endanger*;

zāo tà: 糟蹋, *to waste/ruin; to rape sb*;

to insult sb;

zuò jian: 作践, *to spoil/waste; to disparage sb*;

SEE (请查看) **APARTAR**

ASALTAR; **atacar**, *to attack*; **agredir**, *to attack sb physically/verbally*; **insultar**, *to insult sb*; **afetar**, *to offend sb; to attack, storm, assault*;

chōng fēng: 冲锋, *to assault; to charge*;

dǎ jī: 打击, *to hit; to strike; to attack*;

fā zuò: 发作, *an attack of an illness*;

gōng jī: 攻击, *to attack, to assault*;

gōng zhàn: 攻占, *to attack and occupy*;

pēng jī: 抨击, *to attack (criticize) a person, an idea, etc.*;

tū jī: 突击, *to assault; to do a rush job*;

xí jī: 袭击, *to attack sb physically/verbally*;

xíng xiōng: 行凶, *to assault; to murder*;

zhuó shǒu: 着手, *to attack (tackle) a job/a problem, etc.*;

SEE (请查看) **ABUSAR, AGRAVIAR, ASALTO**

ASCENDER; **ascender**; *to rise; to go up/climb*;

dēng shān: 登山, *to climb a mountain; mountaineering*;

dēng: 登, *to climb up a ladder, etc.*;

pá: 爬, *to climb up (GEN)*;

pá gāo: 爬高, *to climb*;

pān dēng: 攀登, *to climb a hill/mountain, etc.*;

shàng shēng: 上升, *to ascend/increase*;

shàng zhǎng (v) (sv): 上涨, *to rise/go up; rising tide*;

shēng gāo: 升高, *to raise/elevate*;

xīng qǐ: 兴起, *to rise/spring up/be on the upgrade*

ASENTIR; **concordar**; *to assent/agree*;

tóng yì (v) (n): 同意, *consenter; to agree/approve; to have the same opinion; constant rule/principle*;

tóu hé: 投合, *to get along/agree*;

yìng chèng: 应承, *to agree to/ promise/consent*;
yìng nuò: 应诺, *to agree to/promise*;
yuē dìng: 约定, *to agree on/promise*;
SEE (请查看) **APROBACIÓN, RESOLVER**

ASFIXIAR; asfixiar; *to asphyxiate/ suffocate*;
zhì xī: 窒息, *to stifle; to suffocate*

ASISTIR; auxiliar; *to assist sb; to attend to, to accompany sb*;
bāng máng: 帮忙, *to help/do a favor for*;
péi tóng: 陪同, *to accompany/guide*;
xié zhù: 协助, *to help/assist*;
zàn zhù (v) (n): 赞助, *to assist/aid/ sponsor; support, assistance*;
zhāng luo: 张罗, *to attend to*;
zuò měi: 作美, *to cooperate/help/make things easy*;
SEE (请查看) **APROVISIONAR, AUXILIO, ACOMPAÑAR**

ASUMIR; assumir; *to assume/take over/take on*;
chéng dān: 承担, *to assume power/ responsibility*;
chéng xiàn: 呈现, *to assume/adopt an appearance/an attitude*;
shè xiǎng: 设想, *to assume, to conceive*;
SEE (请查看) **ACTUAR**

ATENDER; cuidar de, *to deal with sb/ sthg*;
atender a, *to look after sb/sthg; to attend to/deal with/look after*;
chù lǐ: 处理, *to attend to needs/affairs*;
zhào liào: 照料, *to attend to a patient/ customer, etc.*

ATRAPAR; pegar, *to catch (GEN), to catch on fire;* **apanhar,** *to catch sthg;* **flagar,** *to discover/ surprise sb;* **compreender,** *to hear clearly;* **despertar,** *to catch sb's interest/ attention;* **prender,** *to catch on a hook/in a trap or door; to catch, trap*;

bǔ huò: 捕获, *to catch/trap/capture an animal*;
fā huǒ: 发火, *to catch fire; to lose one's temper; to flare up*;
fā lěng: 发冷, *to feel cold/catch a cold*;
gǎn shàng: 赶上, *to catch up with; to overtake*;
gēn shàng: 跟上, *to keep pace with; to catch up*;
kàn dào: 看到, *to catch sight of*;
kàn jiàn: 看见, *to see; to catch sight of*;
rǎn bìng: 染病, *to catch a disease*;
shāng fēng (v) (n): 伤风, *to catch a cold*;
shòu hán: 受寒, *to catch a chill*;
zháo liáng: 着凉, *to catch a cold/chill*;
zhuā zhù: 抓住, *to catch; to grab; to capture*;
SEE (请查看) **APREHENDER**

ATRIBUIR; atribuir; *to attribute to/ confer on*;
guī yīn: 归因, *attribute to/ascribe to*;
guī yú: 归于, *to belong to/be attributed to*;
guī yīn yú: 归因于, *to attribute to*

AUDITAR; auditorar; *to audit*;
shěn jì: 审计, *to audit*

AUGURAR; prever; *to predict, to foresee*;
yù bào (v) (n): 预报, *to forecast; forecast*;
yù gǎn (v) (n): 预感, *to have a presentiment; premonition*;
yù jì (v) (n): 预计, *to estimate, to predict; estimate*;
yù jiàn (v) (n): 预见, *to predict/foresee; foresight*;
yù liào (v) (n): 预料, *to expect; to predict; expectation, anticipation*;
yù qī: 预期, *to expect, to predict*;
yù shì: 预示, *to foretell, to predict; to portend*;
yù yán (v) (n): 预言, *to predict/fortell; prediction*;
SEE (请查看) **ANTICIPAR, ANUNCIAR**

AUMENTAR; aumentar; *to increase/*

augment/ magnify;

tí gāo: 提高, *to increase; to improve;*
tiān jiā: 添加, *to add; to increase;*
zēng bǔ: 增补, *to supplement;*
zēng chǎn: 增产, *to increase production/output;*
zēng duō: 增多, *to grow in number;*
zēng jiā (v) (n): 增加, *to augment; increment;*
zēng zhǎng (v) (n): 增长; *to grow; to increase; to grow; growth, increase;*
SEE (请查看) AGRANDAR, AMPLIAR

AUTOMATIZAR; automatizar; *to automate;*
shǐ zì dòng huà: 使自动化, *to automate*

AUTORIZAR; autorizar, *to authorize;*
permitir, *to permit; to allow/authorize/ empower;*
hé zhǔn: 核准, *to authorize;*
róng rěn (v) (n) (sv): 容忍, *to tolerate/ to condone; tolerance; tolerant;*
róng xǔ: 容许, *to permit; to condone; to tolerate;*
shòu quán: 授权, *to authorize; to license;*
tīng píng: 听凭, *to allow; to let; to permit;*
tīng rèn: 听任, *to allow; to let;*
yǔn xǔ: 允许, *to allow; to permit;*
SEE (请查看) AUTORIDAD, ACOMODAR, ADMITIR, CONSENTIR, PERMITIR

AVANZAR; adiantar, *to being forward in time, to advance;* **adiantar,** *to advance*

money to sb; **avançar,** *to go forward/ move forward;* **propor,** *to propose sthg; to advance/move/put forward;*
jiàn yì (v) (n): 建议, *to propose/suggest; proposal, suggestion;*
jìn bù (v) (sv) (n): 进步, *to improve; advanced; progress;*
jìn jūn: 进军, *to advance, to march (of troops);*
qián jìn: 前进; *to advance; to move forward;*
tí chū: 提出, *to advance (propose) sthg;*
yù fù: 预付, *to advance money;*
SEE (请查看) EVACUAR

AVISAR; aconselhar, *to give advice;*
assessorar, *to give professional advice;*
avisar, *to inform; to advise/warn; to catch sight of/notify;*
gào sù: 告诉, *to tell, to inform;*
quàn dǎo: 劝导, *to persuade; to advise;*
quàn gào (v) (n): 劝告, *to advise; advice;*
quàn shuō: 劝说; *to persuade; to advise;*
quàn zǔ: 劝阻, *to dissuade sb;*
shuō fú (v) (n): 说服, *to persuade; to convince; persuasion;*
shuō míng (v) (n): 说明, *to explain, to prove; explanation;*
zhōng gào (v) (n):忠告, *to advise; advice*

AVIVAR; avivar; *to revive (GEN), to rekindle; revive/brighten/intensify;*
diǎn rán: 点燃, *to rekindle;*
fù huó: 复活, *to revive;*
huàn qǐ: 唤起, *to revive hope/courage/ interest, etc.*

Interchangeable Spanish-Portuguese-English words and their Chinese equivalents
Palabras en Español-Portugués-Inglés y sus equivalentes en Chino
Palavras em Espanhol-Português-Inglês e seus equivalentes em Chinês
西班牙语，葡萄牙语，英语及中文的对等单词

BANANA; banana;
  xiāng jiāo: 香蕉, *banana*

BANAL; banal; *mundane; ordinary;*
  píng cháng (sv) (adv): 平常, *ordinary,*
common, normal; generally, usually,
ordinarily, as a rule;
  píng fán de: 平凡的, *ordinary,*
common, mediocre;
  píng yōng de: 平庸的, *mediocre,*
commonplace;
  pǔ tōng de: 普通的, *common,*
ordinary, average;
  rì cháng (attr): 日常, *day to day,*
everyday, ordinary;
  shì sú (n) (sv): 世俗, *common custom;*
secular, worldly;
  xún cháng de: 寻常的, *ordinary,*
usual, common

BESTIAL; bestial; *animal, brutal;*
tremendous;
  qín shòu: 禽兽, *a brute (pej);*
  shòu xíng: 兽行, *brutal act;*
SEE (请查看) **BRUTALIDAD, BESTIA**

BESTSELLER (s); best-seller, *book;*
  chàng xiāo shū: 畅销书, *best-seller*
  shū: 书, *book*

BÍCEPS; bíceps;
  èr tóu jī: 二头肌, *biceps*

BIKINI ó BIQUINI; biquíni;
  bǐ jī ní: 比基尼, *bikini*

BILATERAL; bilateral;
  shuāng biān de: 双边的, *bilateral*

BINGO; bingo; *bingo hall;*
  bīn guǒ: 宾果, *bingo hall*

BIT (INFORM); **bit;**
  wèi yuán: 位元, *bit*

BOOM; boom; *increase; growth,*
expansion;

  fán róng (sv): 繁荣, *brooming,*
prosperous;
  kuò zhǎn fǎ (n): 扩展法, *expansion;*
  shēng zhǎng (v) (n): 生长, *to grow/*
develop; to grow up/be brought up;
growth;
SEE (请查看) **AGRANDAR, AMPLIAR**

BRAILLE; Braille;
  máng wén: 盲文, *Braille*

BRIDGE; bridge; *the game;*
  qiáo pái: 桥牌, *bridge*

BRUNCH; brunch;
  zǎo wǔ cān: 早午餐, *brunch*

BRUTAL; brutal;
  bào nüè (sv) (n): 暴虐, *brutal, cruel; an*
abusive relationship;
  cán kù (sv) (n): 残酷, *cruel, brutal,*
ruthless; cruelty;
SEE (请查看) **ATROCIDAD**

BUFFER (INFORM); **buffer;**
  huǎn chōng qì: 缓冲器, *buffer*
(MECAN), bumper;
  huǎn chōng qū: 缓冲区, *buffer*
(INFORM)

BUFFET ó BUFÉ; bufê;
  zì zhù cān: 自助餐, *buffet, cafeteria*

BUG (INFORM); **bug;**
  bìng dù: 病毒, *bug (computer);*
  bìng jūn: 病菌, *virus;*
  chóng zi: 虫子, *insect*

BULIMIA; bulimia;
  bào shí zhèng: 暴食症, *bulimia*

BUNGEE; bungee; *jumping; bungee*
jumping;
  bèng jí tiào: 蹦极跳, *bungee jumping*

BYTE (INFORM); **byte;**
  zì jié: 字节, *byte*

Easily recognizable Spanish-Portuguese-English nouns, adjectives and adverbs and their Chinese equivalents
Nombres, sustantivos, adjetivos y adverbios en Español-Portugués-Inglés y sus equivalentes en Chino
Nomes, substantivos, adjetivos e advérbios em Espanhol-Português-Inglês e seus equivalentes em Chinês
容易辨认的西班牙语，葡萄牙语，英语的名词，形容词和副词和他们的中文对等词

BALCÓN; sacada; balcão; *balcony in a theatre/on a building*;
　lóu zuò: 楼座, *balcony in a theatre*;
　lù tái: 露台, *open balcony*;
　yáng tái: 阳台, *covered balcony*

BALOTA; voto; *ballot*;
　xuǎn piào: 选票, *ballot*

BÁLSAMO; bálsamo; *balsam, balm, ointment*;
　ruǎn gāo: 软膏, *ointment, paste*;
　xiāng gāo: 香膏, *balsam, balm*
　zhèn tòng (sv): 镇痛, *soothing ointment, analgesia; to relieve pain*

BAMBÚ; bambu; *bamboo*;
　zhú zi:竹子, *bamboo*

BANCO; banco; *bank; bench, pew*;
　àn: 岸, *river bank*;
　cháng yǐ: 长椅, *bench, seat*;
　gōng zuò tái: 工作台, *bench, table in a factory, laboratory*;
　kù: 库, *bank of data*;
　pái: 排, *bank of switches/dials, etc.*;
　xié pō: 斜坡, *earthen bank*;
　yín háng: 银行, *bank building, bank*

BANDA; bando, *gang; band*;
　qún: 群, *band, group of helpers, supporters, etc.*;
　yī bāng: 一帮, *gang of criminals*;
　yī huǒ: 一伙, *group of friends, youths*;
　yī zǔ: 一组, *gang of workmen*;
SEE (请查看) ASOCIACIÓN

BANDIDO (A); **bandido** (A); *bandit, outlaw*;
　dǎi tú: 歹徒, *gangster, thug*;
　dào fěi: 盗匪, *bandit, robber*;
　dào zéi: 盗贼, *thief, robber*;

hú zi: 胡子, *beard, mustache; bandit*;
qiáng dào: 强盗, *robber, bandit, thief; hijacker*;
qiáng rén: 强人, *robber, intrepid person*;
táo fàn: 逃犯, *escaped criminal, outlaw*;
tóu mù: 头目, *gang leader*;
tǔ fěi: 土匪, *bandit*

BANQUETE; banquete; *banquet, feast*;
　yàn huì: 宴会, *banquet, dinner party; feast*;
　yàn xí: 筵席, *banquet, feast*;
　shèng yàn: 盛宴, *grand banquet, feast*;

BARBERÍA; barbearia; *barbershop ...*
BARBERO (A); **barbeiro;** *barber*;
　lǐ fà shī: 理发师, *hairdresser*;
　lǐ fà tīng: 理发厅, *barbershop*;
　lǐ fà yuán: 理发员, *barber, hairdresser*

BARÓMETRO; barômetro; *barometer*;
　qì yā biǎo: 气压表, *barometer*

BARRICADA; barricada; *barricade*;
　lù zhàng: 路障, *barricade*

BARRIL; barril; *barrel (wine, beer, oil)*;
　dà tǒng: 大桶, *barrel, cask*;
　yī tǒng shuǐ: 一桶水, *a barrel of water*

BASE; base (GEN); *base (ARCHIT)*;
　dì jī: 地基, *foundations (of a building); base*;
　dǐ zuò: 底座, *the base of a cup/vase/ lamp, etc.*

BÁSICO (A); **básico** (A); *basic*;
　jī běn de: 基本的, *basic, essential*;

jī chǔ de: 基础的, *basic*

BASTARDO (A); **bastardo** (A);
bastard; mean, base;
  huài dàn: 坏蛋, *bad egg; scoundrel; bastard*;
  hún dàn: 混蛋, *bastard, wretch, scoundrel, skunk*;
  wáng bā dàn: 王八蛋, *illegitimate*;
  sī shēng zǐ: 私生子, *illegitimate off spring*;
  wáng bā: 王八, *tortoise, cuckold*;
  zá zhǒng: 杂种, *hybrid, bastard, son of a bitch*

BEBE (A); **bebê**; *baby*;
  bǎo bǎo: 宝宝, *darling; baby*;
  yīng 'ér: 婴儿, *infant; baby*

BEICON ó TOCINO; bacon; *bacon*;
  xián ròu (n): 咸肉, *salt meat, bacon*;
  xián zhū ròu: 咸猪肉, *salty preserved pork/ham/ bacon*;
  yān zhū ròu: 腌猪肉, *bacon*

BÉISBOL; beisebol; *baseball*;
  bàng qiú: 棒球, *baseball*

BÉLICO (A); **belico** (A); *war, warlike ...*
BELICOSO (A); **belicoso** (A); *bellicose*
... BELIGERANTE; beligerante;
belligerent;
  hào biàn (sv): 好辨, *contentious*;
  hào dòu (sv): 好斗, *aggressive, warlike; bellicose*;
SEE (请查看**) AGRESIÓN**

BENEFICIARIO (A); **beneficiário** (A);
beneficiary;
  huò yì zhě: 获益者, *beneficiary*

BENÉFICO (A); **favorável; benéfico** (A); *favorable, beneficial*;
  yōu huì (sv): 优惠, *preferential, favorable*;
  yǒu lì (v) (sv): 有力, *to be advantageous; beneficial, favorable*;
  yǒu yì (v) (sv): 有益, *to be profitable; beneficial, useful*;
  yǒu yì chù (v) (sv): 有益处, *to be advantageous; beneficial, useful, helpful*;
SEE (请查看**) AUSPICIOSO**

BESTIA; estúpido (A); **bruto** (A);
thickheaded, stupid person, brute;
  bèn (sv): 笨, *stupid; silly; clumsy; awkward*;
  bèn zhuō (sv): 笨拙, *clumsy; stupid; awkward*;
  chī dāi (sv): 痴呆, *dim-witted; stupid*;
  chǔn huò (n): 蠢货, *blockhead*;
  fàn tǒng (n): 饭桶, *rice container, stupid person*;
  shǎ zi (n): 傻子, *fool; simpleton*;
  yú bèn (sv): 愚笨, *dull-witted, stupid, foolish, clumsy*;
  yú dùn (sv): 愚钝, *slow-witted*;
  yú zhuō (sv): 愚拙, *clumsy and stupid*;
SEE (请查看**) BRUTALIDAD, BRUTO**

BICARBONATO; bicarbonato;
bicarbonate;
  xiǎo sū dǎ: 小苏打

BICICLETA; bicicleta; *bicycle, bike*;
  zì xíng chē: 自行车

BIGAMIA; bigamia; *bigamy*;
  chóng hūn: 重婚

BILINGÜE; bilíngüe; *bilingual*;
  shuāng yǔ de: 双语的, *bilingual*

BILIOSO (A); **bilioso** (A); *bilious; bad-tempered, peevish, irritable*;
  bào zào (sv): 暴躁, *irritable, hot-tempered*;
  fā pí qì: 发脾气, *to lose one's temper, to get angry*;
  fán zào (sv): 烦躁, *agitated, fretful; irritable and restless*;
  jí zào (sv): 急躁, *irritable, irascible; rash, impatient*;
  pí qì huài (sv): 脾气坏, *very bad-tempered*;
  yì jī nù (vp): 易激怒, *irritable, prone to anger*;
  yì nù (v) (sv): 易怒, *to be irascible/ peevish/prone to anger; irritable*;
SEE (请查看**) AGITADO**

BINOCULARES; binoculo; *binoculars;*
wàng yuǎn jìng: 望远镜, *binoculars*

BIOGRAFÍA; biografia; *biography*
... BIOGRÁFICO (A); biográfico (A);
biographical;
zhuàn jì (sv) (n): 传记, *biographical;*
biography

BIOLOGÍA; biologia; *biology ...*
BIOLÓGICO(A); biológico (A);
biological; organic ... **BIÓLOGO (A);**
biologista; *biologist;*
shēng wù de: 生物的, *biological*
warefare, etc.;
shēng wù xué jiā: 生物学家,
biologist;
shēng wù xué: 生物学, *biology;*
shēng wù xué de: 生物学的,
biological research, science, etc.

BOICOT; boicote; *boycott, embargo, ban;*
dǐ zhì (n) (v): 抵制, *boycott; to resist/*
boycott;
jìn zhǐ (n) (v) (sv): 禁止, *prohibition,*
ban; to prohibit; prohibitive

BOLETÍN; boletim; *bulletin; journal,*
review;
gōng gào: 公告, *bulletin, news update;*
gōng gào lán: 公告栏, *bulletin board;*
tōng bào (n) (v): 通告, *circular,*
bulletin; journal; to circulate a notice

BOLSA; saco; *bag ...* **BOLSO; bolsa;**
purse, handbag;
dài: 袋, *paper/plastic bag;*
hé bāo: 荷包, *small bag, pouch;*
qián bāo: 钱包, *money purse;*
shǒu bāo: 手包, *handbag purse;*
shǒu dài: 手袋, *handbag*

BOMBA; bomba; *bomb;*
zhà dàn: 炸弹, *bomb*

BOTA; bota; *boot;*
xié lèi: 鞋类, *footwear;*
xuē zi: 靴子, *footwear for winter*
xuē: 靴, *boots, galoshes*

BOTE; bote; *boat;*
chuán: 船, *small boat;*
dú mù zhōu: 独木舟, *canoe;*
lún chuán: 轮船, *ship*

BOTELLA; garraga; *bottle;*
nǎi píng: 奶瓶, *nursing bottle; milk*
bottle
píng zi: 瓶子, *bottle, flask, jar*

BOTÓN; botão; *button, knob;*
àn niǔ: 按钮, *button on a machine;*
push button;
bǎ shǒu: 把手, *grip, door knob, handle;*
kòu zi: 扣子, *knob, button;*
niǔ kòu: 纽扣, *button on clothes;*
xuán niǔ: 旋钮, *knob on a radio, TV*

BOYA; bóia; *buoy, float;*
fú biāo: 浮标, *buoy*

BRAVÍO (A); bravio (A); *wild country;*
savage, ferocious; wild/untamed animal;
impetuous person;
huāng yě: 荒野, *wilds;*
huāng yuán (n): 荒原, *wasteland,*
wilderness;
jí xìng zi (n) (sv): 急性子, *impetuous*
person, hothead; impetuous, having an
impatient disposition;
kuáng (sv) (n): 狂, *mad, crazy; violent,*
wild; insanity;
kuáng liè (sv): 狂烈, *violent, intense,*
angry;
kuàng yě (n): 旷野, *wilderness;*
xiōng (sv): 凶, *violent, ferocious, fierce,*
terrible;
xiōng měng (sv): 凶猛, *vicious, fierce;*
yě rén: 野人, *savage person;*
yě shēng (sv): 野生, *wild; uncultivated;*
feral;
yě shēng dòng wù: 野生动物, *wild*
animals;
yě shēng zhí wù: 野生植物, *wild*
plants;
yě shòu (n): 野兽, *wild animal;*
yě xīn: 野心, *wild ambition;*
yě xìng (n): 野性, *wild nature;*
savagery;
SEE (请查看) IMPACIENCIA, FEROZ

BRAVO (A) (adj); **bravo**; *brave*;
 hǎo hàn: 好汉, *brave man, hero*;
 yīng yǒng de: 英勇的, *brave attempt/ action, etc.*;
 yǒng gǎn de: 勇敢的, *brave person*;
 yǒng měng de: 勇猛, *valiant*;
 zhuàng liè de: 壮烈的, *heroic, brave*

BRAVO (n); **bravo** (A), **good!**; *Well done!*;
 hǎo de: 好的, *good, fine, alright*;
 bù cuò de: 不错的, *Not bad!, Pretty good!*

BREVE; **breve**; *short, brief, quick, concise*;
 duǎn (sv) (v) (n): 短, *short, brief; to lack; weakness*;
 duǎn cù (sv): 短促, *very brief*;
 duǎn xiǎo (sv): 短小, *short, concise*;
 duǎn zàn (sv) (n): 短暂, *short, brief; transient; shortness*;
 jiǎn (sv) (n): 简, *simple, brief; simplified; letter*;
 jiǎn jiè (n): 简介, *brief introduction, synopsis*;
 jiǎn liàn (sv): 简练, *succinct, terse*;
 kuài sù (sv): 快速, *fast, quick, high-speed*;
 sù xiào (n): 速效, *quick results*;
SEE (请查看) CONCISO, AUSTERIDAD

BRÓCOLI ó BRÉCOL; **broccoli**; *broccoli*;
 xī lán huā: 西兰花, *broccoli*

BRONCE; **bronze**; *bronze, brass*;
 qīng tóng xiàng: 青铜像, *the sculpture (bronze)*;
 qīng tóng: 青铜, *the metal (bronze)*;
 tóng qì: 铜器, *bronze/brass/copper ware*

BRONCO (A); **bronco** (A); *rude; rough, rugged, harsh*;
 duō yán shí (sv): 多岩石, *rugged*;
 qí qū de: 崎岖的, *rough terrain* ;
 wú lài (sv) (n): 无赖, *shameless; rascal*;
SEE (请查看) ABRASIVO,

GROSERO, VULGAR, HOSTIL, BRUSCO

BRONQUITIS; **bronquite**; *bronchitis*;
 zhī qì guǎn yán: 支气管炎, *bronchitis*

BRUSCO (A); **brusco** (A); *sudden; coarse; brusque, curt*;
 cǎo shuài (sv): 草率, *rash, curt, sloppy*;
 táng tū wú lǐ de: 唐突无理的, *curt reply/tone/ person*;
 tū rán de (adv) (sv): 突然地, *suddenly, abruptly; abrupt, short*;
SEE (请查看) BRONCO

BRUTALIDAD; **brutalidade**; *brutality*;
 shòu xìng: 兽性, *barbarity*;
 shòu xíng: 兽行, *brutal act/bestial behavior*;
SEE (请查看) BRAVÍO, BRUTAL, ATROCIDAD, BESTIAL, INCLEMENCIA

BRUTO(A); **bruto** (A); *uncut; crude*;
 cāo (sv): 糙, *rough, coarse; of poor workmanship; unskilled; careless, hasty*;
 jiǎn lòu de: 简陋的, *simple, crude*;
 wèi jiā gōng de: 未加工的, *unprocessed*;
 yě mán de: 野蛮的, *uncivilized*;
SEE (请查看) ABRASIVO, BRONCO, OBSCENO

BUCÓLICO (A); **bucólico** (A); *bucolic, pastoral; rural*;
 nóng chǎng: 农场, *farm*;
 tián yuán de: 田园的, *countryside*;
 xiāng cūn: 乡村, *village, countryside; rural*;
 xiāng xià: 乡下, *countryside, village*

BÚFALO; **búfalo**; *buffalo*;
 shuǐ niú: 水牛, *buffalo*

BULBO; **bulbo**; *bulb*;
 diàn dēng pào: 电灯泡, *electric bulb*

BULLICIOSO (A); **buliçoso** (A); *turbulent; lively; noisy, boisterous*;
 chǎo chǎo nào nào de: 吵吵闹闹的, *boisterous*

fā fēng (sv) (v): 发疯, *noisy, wild; to go mad/crazy*;
xuān nào (sv) (v): 喧闹, *noisy place/ crowd, rowdy; to make a noise/racket*

guān liáo zuò fēng: 官僚作风, *bureaucracy (pej)*;
guān liáo tǐ xì 官僚体系, *bureaucracy (as a system)*

BUROCRACIA; burocracia; *bureaucracy ...* **BURÓCRATA; burocrata;** *bureaucrat;*

BUSTO; busto; *bust, chest;*
xiōng wéi: 胸围, *bust; chest measurement*

Easily recognizable verbs and their Portuguese and Chinese equivalents
Verbos fácilmente reconocibles en Español-Portugués-Inglés y sus equivalentes en Chino
Verbos facilmente reconhecível em Espanhol-Português-Inglês e seus equivalentes em Chinês
很容易辨认的西班牙语，葡萄牙语，英语动词和他们的中文对等词

BENEFICIAR; beneficiar; *to benefit;*
yǒu yì yú: 有益于, *to benefit from/by; to be good for sb;*
zào fú: 造福, *to bring a benefit to sb/ sthg*

BLASFEMAR; blasfemar; *to blaspheme;*
xiè dú: 亵渎, *to blaspheme;*
zǔ zhòu: 诅咒, *to curse, to swear at*

BLOCAR; bloquear; *to surround; to block off/block; to tackle; to stop/trap (DEP);*
dǎng zhù: 挡住, *to block a view, etc.;*
dǔ sè: 堵塞, *to block an entrance/road, etc., to block up sthg;*
dǔ zhù: 堵住, *to block off sthg;*
SEE (请查看**) SOLUCIONAR, PREVENCIÓN**

BRILLAR; brilhar; *to shine;*
fā guāng: 发光, *to give out light; to shine/to be luminous;*
zhào yào: 照耀, *the sun/a light shines*

BURLAR; burlar; *to cheat/deceive; to defraud; to evade/flout/deceive/trick/ outwit;*

dòng hè: 恫吓, *to browbeat/bully; to threaten/intimidate;*
méng bì: 蒙蔽, *to deceive, to hoodwink;*
méng hùn: 蒙混, *to deceive, to muddle through (by deceit)*
mēng piàn: 蒙骗, *to deceive, to hoodwink, to delude;*
qī piàn: 欺骗, *to fool, to deceive sb;*
qī shēng: 欺生, *to take advantage of sb;*
qī yā: 欺压, *to tyrannize/ride roughshod over*
qī zhà: 欺诈, *to swindle sb;*
wēi bī: 威逼, *to coerce/intimidate;*
xíng piàn: 行骗, *to cheat/deceive/ swindle;*
zhà qǔ: 榨取, *to extort/squeeze/ exploit;*
zhà qǔ: 诈取, *to obtain sthg by cheating; to defraud;*
zì qī qī rén (fe): 自欺欺人, *to deceive oneself as well as others;*
zuò bì: 作弊, *to cheat in a game/on an exam, etc.;*
zuò jiǎ: 作假, *to fake sthg, to play tricks on sb*

C

Interchangeable Spanish-Portuguese-English words and their Chinese equivalents
Palabras en Español-Portugués-Inglés y sus equivalentes en Chino
Palavras em Espanhol-Português-Inglês e seus equivalentes em Chinês
西班牙语，葡萄牙语，英语及中文的对等单词

CABARET ó CABARÉ; cabaré;
 gē wǔ biǎo yǎn: 歌舞表演, *song and dance*

CANAL; canal; *also channel (GEOG), pipe; also T.V. channel;*
 hǎi xiá: 海峡, *channel; strait;*
 shuǐ qú: 水渠, *canal for irrigation;*
 yùn hé: 运河, *canal for ships/barges*

CÁNCER; câncer;
 ái zhèng: 癌症, *cancer*

CAPITAL; capital, *essential, capital city; money (ECON); capital city, money; essential;*
 zī běn jīn: 资本金, *financial, capital; principal;*
 shǒu dū: 首都, *capital city*

CARNAL; carnal;
 ròu tǐ (sv): 肉体, *the human body, flesh;*
 xìng yù: 性欲, *sexual desire; urge;*
SEE (请查看) ERÓTICO

CASSETTE ó CASETE; cassete;
 cí dài: 磁带, *cassette*

CELESTIAL; celestial;
 tiān de: 天的, *celestial*

CENSOR (POL)**; censor;**
 shěn chá yuán: 审查员, *censor*

CENTRAL; central;
 zhōng (bf) (suf) (n) (sv): 中, *center, middle, interior; middle; halfway; neutral; Ok! , All right!;*
 zhōng bù (n): 中部, *middle, central section;*

zhōng shù (sv) (n): 中数, *mean, median;*
zhōng tú (n): 中途, *halfway, midway;*
zhōng xīn (n): 中心, *center, heart, core;*
zhōng xīn de: 中心的, *central;*
zhōng yāng (sv) (n): 中央, *central; middle, center;*
SEE (请查看) MEDIA

CERCA; cerca de; *around; near, close, about;*
 chà bù duō (sv) (adv): 差不多, *almost, about; almost equal/the same; nearly;*
 fù jìn: 附近, *vicinity;*
 jī hū (adv): 几乎, *almost, nearly;*
 jìn: 近, *close, near; similar; to approach;*
 zhōu wéi (n): 周围, *vicinity; around; surrounding;*
SEE (请查看) APROXIMACIÓN, APROXIMADAMENTE, PRÓXIMO

CEREAL; cereal;
 gǔ lèi shí pǐn: 谷类食品, *breakfast cereal;*
 gǔ lèi liáng shi: 谷类粮食, *grain, cereals, food;*
 gǔ lèi shí wù: 谷类食物, *plant, crop*

CHIP (INFORM)**; chip;** *microchip;*
 jí chéng diàn lù: 集成电路, *microchip*

CHOCOLATE; chocolate;
 qiǎo kè lì: 巧克力, *chocolate*

CIRCULAR; circular;
 jiàn jiē de (attr) (adv): 间接地, *circular, circuitous, indirect; indirectly;*
 rào xíng (attr): 绕行, *circuitous, roundabout;*

tuán yuán (v) (sv): 团圆, *to reunite/ have a reunion; round, circular;*
yuán quān shì (n): 圆圈式, *circular shape;*
yuán xíng (n): 圆形, *circular shape/ type; round*

CLAMOR; clamor;
  chǎo rǎng (n) (v): 吵嚷, *racket; to make a racket;*
  xuān xiāo (sv) (v): 喧嚣, *noisy; to clamor;*
SEE (请查看) BULLICIOSO

CLERICAL; clerical (RELIG);
  jiào shì de: 教士的, *clerical;*
  jiào shì: 教士, *clergy*

CLÍMAX; clímax;
  gāo cháo: 高潮, *high tide; climax, upsurge;*
SEE (请查看) APOGEO

COLON; colon (ANAT);
  jié cháng: 结肠, *colon, large intestine*

COLONIAL; colonial;
  zhí mín de: 殖民的, *colonial*

COMA (MED); **coma;**
  hūn mí (n) (v): 昏迷, *coma, stupor; to faint*

CONSENSUAL; consensual; *agreed, consensual;*
  xié dìng (n) (v): 协定, *agreement, accord, pact; to reach an agreement;*
  xié shāng jiě jué (n): 协商解决, *compromise/ negotiated settlement;*
  xié yì (v) (n): 协议, *to agree on/discuss/ negotiate; agreement;*
SEE (请查看) COMPROMISO, PACTO

CONTINENTAL; continental (GEOL);
  dà lù: 大陆, *continent;*
  dà lù de: 大陆的, *continental*

CÓRNEA; córnea;
  jiǎo mó: 角膜, *cornea*

CRACK; crack; *cocaine; crack cocaine; top athlete;*
  chún kě kǎ yīn: 纯可卡因, *crack (cocaine);*
  jīng gàn (sv): 精干, *competent, crack;*
  jīng ruì (sv): 精锐, *crack, elite;*
  kě kǎ yīn: 可卡因, *cocaine*

CRÉPE ó CREPE; crepe; *pancake;*
  báo jiān bǐng: 薄煎饼, *pancake;*
  bó bǐng/báo bǐng: 薄饼/薄饼, *pancake;*
  bó kǎo bǐng: 薄烤饼, *pancake;*
  lào bǐng (n) (v): 烙饼, *pancake, baked wheat; to make a pancake*

CRESCENDO; crescendo;
  jiān qiáng (sv) (v) (n): 坚强, *strong, firm; to strengthen; crescendo (MUS);*
SEE (请查看) CLÍMAX

CRIMINAL; criminal (adj);
  fàn rén (n): 犯人, *criminal, convict, prisoner;*
  xíng shì (n): 刑事, *criminal; criminal law;*
  zuì fàn de: 罪犯的, *criminal offense, record;*
SEE (请查看) BANDIDO, BASTARDO, INFRACTOR

CROISSANT ó CRUASÁN; croissant ;
  yáng jiǎo miàn bāo: 羊角面包, *croissant*

CRUCIAL; crucial (GEN);
  guān jiàn xìng (sv): 关键性, *crucial;*
  guǒ duàn (sv): 果断, *decisive; resolute;*
  jǐn jí (sv): 紧急, *urgent, critical; pressing;*
  jǐn yào (sv): 紧要, *critical, crucial;*
  wēi jī (n): 危机, *crisis, critical moment;*
  wēi jí (sv) (v): 危急, *critical, in imminent danger; to endanger/imperil;*
  yào hài: 要害, *key part; crucial point*

CRUEL; cruel; *sadistic;*
  è dú (sv): 恶毒, *venomous; vicious; malicious;*

è yì (sv) (n): 恶意, *malicious, spiteful; malice, evil*;
nüè dài kuáng (n) (sv): 虐待狂, *sadist; sadism; sadistic*;
SEE (请查看) **ABUSIVO**

CULTURAL; cultural;
wén huà de: 文化的, *cultural*

CURSOR (INFORM); **cursor;**
guāng biāo: 光标, *cursor*

Easily recognizable Spanish-Portuguese-English nouns, adjectives and adverbs and their Chinese equivalents
Nombres, sustantivos, adjetivos y adverbios en Español-Portugués-Inglés y sus equivalentes en Chino
Nomes, substantivos, adjetivos e advérbios em Espanhol-Português-Inglês e seus equivalentes em Chinês
容易辨认的西班牙语，葡萄牙语，英语的名词，形容词和副词和他们的中文对等词

CABINA; cabine; *cabin (GEN); booth, telephone booth*;
gé kāi de xiǎo jiān: 隔开的小间, *telephone booth*;
tóu piào zhàn: 投票站, *voting booth*;
tān zi: 摊子, *booth at a fair*;
xiǎo mù wū: 小木屋, *cabin*

CABLEGRAMA; cabograma; *cablegram*;
diàn bào: 电报, *telegram*;
fā diàn bào: 发电报, *cablegram*

CAFÉ; café; *coffee*;
kā fēi: 咖啡, *coffee*

CAFEÍNA; cafeína; *caffeine*;
kā fēi yīn: 咖啡因, *caffeine*

CALAMIDAD; calamidade; *calamity, disaster* ... **CALAMITOSO** (A);
calamitoso (A); *calamitous, disastrous*;
bù dé liǎo de: 不得了的, *disastrous; desperately serious*;
hěn zāo de: 很糟的, *disastrous, awful*;
huò huàn: 祸患, *disaster, calamity*;
huò shì: 祸事, *disaster*;
wēi nàn: 危难, *danger, dire peril, calamity*;
zāi nàn xìng de: 灾难性的, *catastrophic, calamitous, disastrous; fatal*;
zāi qíng: 灾情, *disaster conditions, calamity*;
zāi qū (n): 灾区, *disaster area*;

SEE (请查看) **ADVERSIDAD, AFLICCIÓN, APOCALIPSIS**

CALCIO; cálcio; *calcium*;
gài: 钙, *calcium*

CALCULADORA; calculadora; *calculator*;
jì suàn qì: 计算器, *calculator*

CÁLCULO; cálculo; *calculus (MAT); calculation*;
jì: 计, *calculation*;
jì suàn: 计算, *calculation, plan, scheme*;
yù cè (n) (v): 预测, *estimate; to calculate*

CALENDARIO; calendário; *calendar*;
rì lì: 日历, *calendar*

CALIFICACIÓN; qualificação; *grade, mark; rating, standing*;
chéng jì: 成绩, *grade, score; success; achievement*;
děng jí: 等级, *grade, rank, social status*;
jí bié: 级别, *level, rank, grade*;
jì hao: 记号, *mark, sign*;
pǐn jí: 品级, *grade (of a product, etc.), workmanship*;
sù zhì: 素质, *skill*

CALIFICADO (A); **qualificado** (A); *skilled, qualified*;

gòu gé (vp): 够格, *to be qualified; qualified, presentable;*
gòu tiáo jiàn (vp): 够条件, *to be qualified; qualified, to reach the standard;*
hé gé (sv) (v): 合格, *qualified, trained; to qualify/ reach a standard/pass;*
jì gōng: 技工, *skilled worker, technician;*
jì shù gōng rén (n): 技术工人, *skilled worker;*
jù bèi: 具备, *to be qualified/have/ possess;*
shī zī: 师资, *qualified teachers;*
shú liàn (sv): 熟练, *skilled, practiced, proficient;*
shú liàn gōng rén: 熟练工人, *skilled, proficient worker;*
xiù cai: 秀才, *scholar, skillful writer;*
SEE (请查看) COMPETENTE, CAPAZ, APTITUD

CALMA; calmo; *calm (GEN); calm, lull; relaxed;*
ān níng de: 安宁的, *calm place;*
huǎn hé (sv) (v): 缓和, *relaxed; to relax;*
lěng jìng de: 冷静的, *calm person;*
píng jìng (sv) (n): 平静, *calm, quiet, tranquil; calmness;*
qīng sōng (sv): 轻松, *relaxed; relaxing;*
zhèn jìng de: 镇静的, *calm voice;*
SEE (请查看) TRANQUILO

CALORÍA; caloria; *calorie;*
kǎ lù lǐ: 卡路里, *calorie*

CALUMNIA; calúnia; *slander, calumny;*
fěi bàng (n) (v): 诽谤, *slander; to libel/ slander*

CÁMARA; câmera; *camera;*
shè yǐng jī: 摄影机, *camera for filming, TV;*
zhào xiàng jī: 照相机, *camera for photos*

CAMUFLAJE; camuflagem; *camouflage;*
wěi zhuāng: 伪装, *camouflage*

CANCELACIÓN; cancelamento; *cancellation;*
tuì piào (n): 退票, *cancellation of a holiday/ reservation, etc.;*
SEE (请查看) ANULAR

CANCEROSO (A); **canceroso** (A); *cancerous;*
ái: 癌, *carcinoma, cancer;*
ái de: 癌的, *cancerous;*
ái xì bāo: 癌细胞, *cancer cell;*
SEE (请查看) CÁNCER

CANTINA; cantina; *restaurant; cafeteria, snack bar, canteen;*
cān guǎn: 餐馆, *restaurant;*
shí táng: 食堂, *canteen;*
xiǎo chī bù: 小吃部, *snack bar;*
zì zhù cān tīng: 自助餐厅, *cafeteria*

CAOS; caos; *chaos ...* **CAÓTICO** (A); **caôtico** (A); *chaotic;*
dòng luàn (n): 动乱, *turmoil, upheaval, disturbance;*
fēn luàn (n) (sv): 纷乱, *confusion, disorder; numerous and disorderly; helter-skelter; chaotic;*
hú tu (sv): 糊涂, *muddled, confused, chaotic;*
hùn dùn (n) (sv): 混沌, *chaos; muddle-headed;*
luàn (sv) (n) (v): 乱, *disorderly, confused; chaos, unrest; to confuse;*
wěn luàn (sv): 紊乱, *chaotic*

CAPA; capa; *cape, cloak;*
pī fēng: 披风, *cloak;*
pī jiān: 披肩, *cape, shawl, scarf*

CAPACIDAD; capacidade; *capacity;*
chǎn liàng: 产量, *capacity of a factory;*
kě róng nà rén shù: 可容纳人数, *capacity of a theater/a stadium;*
kě zhuāng zǎi rén shù: 可装载人数, *capacity of an elevator;*
róng liàng: 容量, *capacity of a container/a ship*

CAPAZ; capaz; *capable, able;*
cōng yǐng (sv): 聪颖, *intelligent, bright, clever;*

néng nài (n): 能耐, *ability, capability, skill*;
néng rén (n): 能人, *able person*;
yǒu cái gàn (sv): 有才干, *(much/ many), abilities, much competence*;
yǒu néng lì (sv): 有能力, *competent; capable, able person*;
SEE (请查看) COMPETENTE, APTITUD

CAPITALISTA; capitalista; *capitalist*;
zī běn jiā: 资本家, *a capitalist*;
zī běn zhǔ yì de: 资本主义的, *capitalist system*

CÁPSULA; cápsula; *capsule (MED) (AERO)*;
jiāo náng: 胶囊, *capsule of medicine*;
tài kōng cāng: 太空舱, *spacecraft*

CAQUI ó KAKI ó KHAKI; cáqui; *kaki*;
kǎ qí bù: 卡其布, *the material*;
tǔ huáng sè: 土黄色, *the color*

CARABINA; carabina; *carbine, rifle*;
bù qiāng: 步枪, *rifle*

CARÁCTER; caractere; *character*;
tè xìng: 特性, *character of a person*;
xìng zhì: 性质, *character of an object, idea*;
míng yù: 名誉, *reputation*

CARACTERÍSTICO; característico
(A); *characteristic*;
tè diǎn (n): 特点, *characteristic/ distinguishing feature*;
tè sè (n): 特色, *distinguishing feature/ quality/ characteristic; special quality*;
tè yǒu (sv): 特有, *special/distinctive characteristic*;
tè zhēng (n): 特征, *characteristic feature/trait*;

CARBURANTE; combustível; *fuel*;
qì yóu: 汽油, *gasoline*;
rán liào: 燃料, *heating fuel*

CARGAMENTO; carregamento,
cargo, load;

huò wù: 货物, *goods, merchandise; cargo*

CARICATURA; caricature; *caricature*;
màn huà: 漫画, *caricature*

CARISMA; carisma; *charisma* ...
CARISMÁTICO (A); **carismático** (A);
charismatic;
hào zhào lì (sv) (v): 号召力, *charisma; to attract/appeal to*;
mèi lì (n): 魅力, *glamor, charm, enchantment*;
yǒu mèi lì de: 有魅力的, *charismatic*;
SEE (请查看) ATRACCIÓN

CARPINTERÍA; carpintaria;
carpentry; woodwork ... **CARPINTERO**
(A); **carpinteiro** (A); *carpenter; also a woodpecker*;
mù gōng yè: 木工业, *carpentry*;
mù gōng: 木工, *woodwork*;
mù jiàng: 木匠, *carpenter*

CARTA; carta; *letter*;
xìn: 信, *letter, mail*

CARTEL; cartel (COM); *sign, poster*;
hǎi bào: 海报, *poster*;
lù biāo: 路标, *sign post, road sign*;
shǒu shì: 手势, *a gesture, sign*;
zhǐ shì pái: 指示牌, *a sign, notice*;
zhǐ shì qì: 指示器, *indicator, sign*

CASTIDAD; castidade; *chastity, purity*;
chǔ nǚ (n): 处女, *virgin (female), maiden*;
chún (sv): 纯, *pure and unmixed; genuine*;
chún dù (n): 纯度, *purity, pureness*;
chún jié (sv): 纯洁, *pure; clean and honest; chaste*;
zhēn cāo (n): 贞操, *chastity; virginity (of a woman); loyalty; moral integrity*;
zhēn jié (n): 贞节, *chastity; virginity (of a woman); moral integrity (of men); loyalty*;
zhēn jié (sv): 贞洁, *chaste*

CASTIGO; castigo; *punishment*;

punishment; penalty (DEP);
  chéng fá (n) (v): 惩罚, *penalty; to punish/penalize*;
  chǔ fá (n) (v): 处罚, *punishment; to punish/penalize*;
  xíng fá (n): 刑罚, *penalty, punishment*

CASTO (adj); **casto** (A); *chaste, pure*;
  chún lǐ lùn de: 纯理论的, *pure (theoretical)*;
  wán quán de: 完全的, *pure (complete)*;
SEE (请查看) CASTIDAD

CATÁSTROFE; catástrofe;
catastrophe, disaster ...
CATASTRÓFICO; catastrófico (A);
catastrophic, disastrous;
  dà huò de: 大祸的, *catastrophic*;
  dà zāi nàn (n): 大灾难, *catastrophe*;
  è guǒ: 恶果, *disastrous result*;
  huò hài (n) (v): 祸害, *disaster; to damage/destroy*;
  huò huàn de: 祸患的, *disastrous*;
SEE (请查看) CAOS, CALAMIDAD, AFLICCIÓN

CATEGORÍA; categoria; *category ...*
CATEGÓRICO (A); **categórico** (A);
categorical; express order;
  wú tiáo jiàn de: 无条件的, *categorical*

CÁUSTICO (A); **cáustico** (A); *caustic*;
  jiān kè (sv): 尖刻, *acrimonious, caustic, biting*

CAVERNA; caverna, *cavern*; **gruta;**
grotto; cave, cavern;
  dà shān dòng: 大山洞, *cavern*;
  shān dòng: 山洞, *cave*

CAVERNOSO (A); **imenso** (A);
cavernous, deep;
  dà dòng xué shì de: 大洞穴式的, *cavernous*

CAVIDAD; cavidade; *cavity in an object/ structure/ body*; **cárie,** *cavity in a tooth; cavity; pit, hole*;
  dòng: 洞, *cavity in a wall, a tooth*

cavity; grotto;
  kēng wā: 坑洼, *pot hole*;
  kēng: 坑, *hole in a road/in the ground, etc.*;
  qiāng: 腔, *body cavity*

CELEBRACIÓN; celebração;
celebration;
  qìng diǎn (n): 庆典, *celebration*

CÉLEBRE; célebre, *celebrated*;
famoso, *famous; famous, noted, celebrated*;
  míng pái (n): 名牌, *famous brand/ designer*;
  míng wèi (n): 名位, *fame and position*;
  míng yōu (attr): 名优, *famous*;
  míng yù (n): 名誉, *fame, reputation*;
  zhī míng (sv): 知名, *noted, famous*;
  zhù chēng (sv): 著称, *celebrated, famous*;
SEE (请查看) FAMOSO, AFAMADO

CELEBRIDAD; celebridade; *celebrity, fame*;
  míng liú (n): 名流, *celebrities*;
  míng rén (n): 名人, *celebrity; notable/ famous/ eminent person*;
  míng wàng (n): 名望, *fame, prestige*;
  míng xīng (n): 明星, *star, celebrity*

CELULAR; cellular (adj) (n); *cellular, cell; cell phone*;
  shǒu jī: 手机, *cell phone*

CEMENTO; ciment, *cement*;
concreto, *concrete, cement*;
  hùn níng tǔ (n): 混凝土, *concrete*;
  shuǐ ní: 水泥, *cement*

CENSO; censo; *census*;
  rén kǒu diào chá: 人口调查, *census*

CENSURA; censura; *criticism, reprimand; censorship*;
  pī píng (n) (v): 批评, *censure, criticism; to criticize*;
  píng lùn: 评论, *criticism of a book, play, etc.*;
  shěn chá zhèng cè: 审查政策,

censorship of books, plays, etc.;
shěn chá: 审查, *censorship of news*

CENSURABLE; repreensível;
reprehensible;
  yīng shòu zhǐ zé de: 应收指责的,
  reprehensible

CÉNTRICO (adj); **central;** *crucial,
essential; central;*
  bì bù kě shǎo (fe): 必不可少,
  absolutely necessary, indispensable;
  bì xū (v) (sv) (aux): 必需, *to need;
  necessary, essential; to need/require;*
  bì yào (sv) (n): 必要, *necessary; need;*
  zuì guān jiàn de: 最关键的, *most
  important*
SEE (请查看) **CRUCIAL**

CENTRO; centro; *center;*
  zhōng shū (pw): 中枢, *center, pivot;
  control center;*
  zhōng zhóu (n): 中轴, *axis;*
SEE (请查看) **CENTRAL, CIRCULAR**

CENTURIA; século; *century;*
  shì jì: 世纪, *century*

CERÁMICA; cerâmica; *ceramics;*
  táo cí qì: 陶瓷器, *chinaware, porcelain;*
  táo cí: 陶瓷, *ceramics, pottery and
  porcelain;*
  táo qì: 陶器, *ceramic, earthenware,
  pottery*

CERCO; cerco; *siege; circle, ring,
enclosure;*
  huán lù: 环路, *beltway;*
  huán xíng: 环形, *ring-shaped, circle;*
  wéi chǎng: 围场, *enclosure of an area;*
  yuán huán: 圆环, *circle, ring;*
  yuán quān: 圆圈, *ring; traffic circle,
  rotary;*
SEE (请查看) **CIRCULAR**

CEREMONIA; cerimônia; *ceremony;*
  diǎn lǐ: 典礼, *event; ceremony,
  celebration;*
  lǐ yí: 礼仪, *ritual;*
  yí shì: 仪式, *ceremony; formality*

CERO; zero; *zero, nothing;*
  líng: 零, *zero (the number);*
  líng dù: 零度, *zero (MAT), a nullity;*
  lìng fēn: 零分, *zero, score of zero,
  scoreless;*
  méi yǒu dōng xi: 没有东西, *nothing*

CERTIFICADO; certificado;
certificate; certified, registered;
  zhèng jiàn: 证件, *certificate,
  credentials*

CESACIÓN; suspensão; *cessation,
suspension;*
  zàn lìng tíng zhǐ: 暂令停止,
  suspension from a job/ team, etc.;
  zàn qiě (adv): 暂且, *for the moment,
  temporarily;*
  zàn xíng (adv) (sv): 暂行, *provisionally,
  temporarily; interm;*
SEE (请查看) **COMPLETAR,
APREHENDER**

CHAMPÚ; xampu; *shampoo;*
  xǐ fà jì: 洗发剂, *shampoo*

CHIMENEA; chaminé; *chimney; funnel,
smokestack, fireplace;*
  bì lú: 壁炉, *fireplace;*
  dà yān cōng: 大烟囱, *smokestack;*
  yān cōng: 烟囱, *chimney, funnel*

CÍCLICO (A); **cíclico** (A); *cyclical;*
  xún huán de: 循环的, *cyclical*

CICLO; ciclo; *process, cycle; series,
season;*
  guò chéng: 过程, *process, course;*
  jì jié: 季节, *season;*
  jìn chéng: 进程, *course, process;
  progress;*
  lián zǎi: 连载, *series;*
  shí lìng: 时令, *season;*
  zhōu qī: 周期, *period, cycle, revolution*

CIGARRILLO; cigarro; *cigarette;*
  xiāng yān: 香烟, *cigarette*

CIGARRO; charuto; *cigar;*
  xuě jiā yān: 雪茄烟, *cigar*

CINE; cinema; *cinema;*
  diàn yǐng yuàn: 电影院, *cinema*

CIRCUITO; circuito (GEN); *circuit, track;*
  diàn lù: 电路, *electric circuit;*
  guǐ jì: 轨迹, *track, orbit;*
  quān dào: 圈道, *a lap; lecture circuit, etc.*

CIRCULACIÓN; circulação; *traffic/ money or blood circulation;*
  chuán yuè: 传阅, *circulation of a document;*
  liú tōng: 流通, *circulation of air;*
  xún huán: 循环, *circulation of blood*

CIRCUNSPECTO; circunspecto (A); *circumspect, prudent;*
  jié jiǎn de: 节俭的, *thrifty, frugal;*
  jǐn shèn xiǎo xīn de: 谨慎小心的, *circumspect;*
  shèn zhòng de: 慎重的, *prudent;*
SEE (请查看**) PRUDENCIA, PERSPICAZ**

CIRCUNSTANCIA; circunstância; *circumstance;*
  guāng jǐng (n): 光景, *circumstances, situation;*
  huán jìng (n): 环境, *environment, circumstances;*
  jìng kuàng (n): 境况, *conditions, circumstances, situation;*
  qíng jǐng (n): 情景, *circumstances;*
  qíng kuàng: 情况, *conditions, state of affairs, development, circumstances;*
  qíng xing (n): 情形, *situation, condition;*
  xíng shì (n): 形势, *situation, circumstances*

CIRCUNSTANCIAL; circunstancial; *chance, incidental, circumstantial;*
  cì yào (attr): 次要, *less important, secondary; minor;*
  jiàn jiē (attr) (adv): 间接, *indirect, secondhand; (sv) circumstantial;*
  líng xīng (attr): 零星, *fragmentary; scattered, piecemeal;*

  ǒu fā (sv): 偶发, *accidental, occasional*

CIVILIZACIÓN; civilização; *civilization;*
  wén huà (n): 文化, *culture, civilization; education;*
  wén míng (n) (sv): 文明, *civilization, culture; civilized*

CIVILIZADO (A); **civilizado** (A); *civilized;*
  yǒu jiào yǎng de: 有教养的, *civilized person/behavior*

CLAMOROSO (A); **clamoroso** (A); *clamorous; resounding, loud;*
  gāo shēng (adv): 高声, *loudly;*
  hóng dà (sv): 洪大, *loud;*
  xiǎng liàng (sv): 响亮, *loud, clear, resounding; resonant;*
SEE (请查看**) CLAMOR**

CLANDESTINIDAD; sigilo; *secrecy ...*
CLANDESTINO (A); **clandestino** (A); *clandestine, secret;*
  ào mì (n): 奥秘, *mystery, secret;*
  ào miào (n) (adj): 奥妙, *secret; profound, mysterious;*
  bǎo shǒu mì mì: 保守秘密, *clandestine, secrecy;*
  jī mì (sv) (n): 机密, *classified; secret; top-secret;*
  jī yào (sv): 机要, *confidential;*
  mì (sv): 秘, *secret, mysterious;*
  mì fāng (n): 秘方, *secret recipe/ formula;*
  sī xià de (adv): 私下地, *privately, in secret;*
  yǐn (v) (sv) (n): 隐, *to hide; hidden; secret;*
  yǐn mì (v) (sv) (n): 隐秘, *to hide; hidden, concealed; secret;*
SEE (请查看**) ARCANO**

CLARIDAD; claridade; *clearness, clarity, light;*
  qīng chè (sv): 清澈, *limpid, clear;*
  qīng xī (sv): 清晰, *distinct (sound), clear (view);*
  qīng xī dù: 清晰度, *clarity*

CLÁSICO (A); **classic** (A); *classical,*
classic; outstanding;
  chuán tǒng (sv) (n): 传统, *traditional,*
  conventional; tradition, convention,
  classic;
  diǎn xíng (sv): 典型, *classical,*
  outstanding; typical, representative;
  gǔ diǎn (sv) (attr): 古典, *classical,*
  classic; classics;
  gǔ diǎn shì (sv) (n): 古典式, *classical*
  model; standard;
  gǔ diǎn zuò jiā (n): 古典作家,
  classical writer, author;
  jié zuò (n): 杰作, *masterpiece*;
  jīng diǎn (sv) (attr) (n): 经典, *classical;*
  classics, scriptures; text;
SEE (请查看) **ATÍPICO, AFAMADO**

CLASIFICACIÓN; classificação;
classification;
  lèi bié: 类别, *category, class,*
  classification;
  lèi xíng: 类型, *type, category, typology*

CLAUSTROFOBIA; claustrofobia;
claustrophobia;
  yōu bì kǒng jù: 幽闭恐怖,
  claustrophobia

CLAVÍCULA; clavícula; *collarbone,*
clavicle;
  suǒ gǔ: 锁骨, *collarbone*

CLEMENCIA; clemência; *mercy,*
clemency ... **CLEMENTE; clemente;**
clement, indulgent, merciful;
  cí bēi (sv): 慈悲, *mercy, compassion*;
  kuān róng (sv) (v): 宽容, *tolerant,*
  lenient; to forgive;
  lián mǐn (n) (v): 怜悯, *mercy; to have*
  pity on/ compassion for;
  rén 'ài: 仁爱, *kindheartedness, charity*;
SEE (请查看) **COMPASIÓN**

CLIMA; clima; *climate*;
  qì hòu: 气候, *climate*

CLIMATIZADO (A); **climatizado** (A);
air conditioned;
  zhuāng yǒu kōng tiáo de:
  装有空调的, *air conditioned*

CLÍNICA; clínica; *hospital, clinic*;
  mén zhěn bù (pw): 门诊部, *clinic;*
  outpatient department;
  zhěn suǒ: 诊所, *clinic*

COCHE; coche; *coach, carriage; car,*
automobile;
  chē xiāng: 车厢, *railcar, carriage,*
  coach;
SEE (请查看) **AUTOMÓVIL**

COEXISTENCIA; coexistência;
coexistence;
  gòng chǔ (n) (v): 共处, *coexistence; to*
  coexist

COHERENTE; coerente; *coherent,*
consistent, in tune with;
  lián guàn (sv) (v): 连贯, *coherent,*
  consistent; connected, linked; to link up,
  to piece/hang together;
  tōng shùn (sv): 通顺, *coherent;*
  smooth; clear;
  yī guàn (sv) (attr): 一贯, *consistent,*
  persistent

COINCIDENCIA; coincidência;
coincidence;
  qiǎo hé (attr) (n): 巧合, *coincidental,*
  providential; coincidence, providence

COLABORACIÓN; colaboração;
collaboration;
  gōu jié: 勾结, *collaboration with the*
  enemy;
  hé zuò: 合作, *collaboration on a book/*
  research, etc.

COLAPSO; colapso; *collapse (GEN);*
breakdown (MED);
  bēng kuì (v) (n): 崩溃, *to collapse/fall*
  apart; collapse;
  dǎo tā (v): 倒塌, *to collapse, to topple*
  over, to cave in;
  kuǎ diào (v) (n): 垮掉, *to collapse from*
  hunger/ disease, etc.; exhaustion;
  wǎ jiě (v) (n): 瓦解, *to collapse of a*
  system, company, etc.; disintegration;
  xū tuō (v) (n): 虚脱, *to collapse;*
  exhaustion

CÓLERA; cólera (MED); *cholera; anger, rage;*
  fèn nù: 愤怒, *anger;*
  huò luàn: 霍乱, *cholera (MED);*
  kuáng nù: 狂怒, *rage;*
  shèng nù: 盛怒, *fury, rage, anger;*
  shēng qì: 生气, *anger; to take offense/ get angry;*
SEE (请查看) **FURIA**

COLESTEROL; colesterol; *cholesterol;*
  dǎn gù chún: 胆固醇, *cholesterol*

COLIFLOR; couve-flor; *cauliflower;*
  cài huā: 菜花, *cauliflower*

COLISIÓN; colisão; *collision, crash;*
  chē huò: 车祸, *crash (of a car);*
  pèng zhuàng: 碰撞, *collision;*
  zhuì jī: 坠机, *crash (of an airplane)*

COLONIA; colônia; *colony (GEN);*
  zhí mín dì: 殖民地, *colony*

COLOQUIAL; coloquial (adj); *colloquial;*
  kǒu yǔ: 口语, *colloquial speech; gossip*

COLOQUIO; coloquio; *symposium, conversation; discussion;*
  tǎo lùn: 讨论, *discussion, talk;*
SEE (请查看) **ALTERNAR**

COLOSAL; colosal (adj); *colossal, amazing, fantastic* ... **COLOSO; colosso;** *colossus;*
  jí hǎo de: 极好的, *fantastic, extremely good;*
  jiàn guī (fe): 见鬼, *fantastic, odd, absurd; preposterous; (intj) Damn it!*
  jīng qí (sv): 惊奇, *surprised, amazed;*
  jīng xīn dòng pò (fe): 惊心动魄, *horrifying, breathtaking;*
  jù dà de (attr): 巨大的, *huge, gigantic;*
  jù rén: 巨人, *giant, colossus;*
  liǎo bu dé (sv): 了不得, *terrific, extraordinary; awful;*
  liǎo bu qǐ (sv): 了不起, *amazing, extraordinary, terrific;*

  páng dà de: 庞大的, *colossal; gigantic;*
SEE (请查看) **ALARMA**

COLUMNA; coluna; *column;*
  háng liè (n): 行列, *ranks; procession; row or column;*
  yuán zhù (n): 圆柱, *cylinder (MAT), column;*
  zhī zhù: 支柱, *column (ARCHIT);*
  zhù xíng wù: 柱形物, *column of smoke;*
  zhuān lán: 专栏, *newspaper column;*
  zòng duì: 纵队, *column of people, trucks, etc.*

COLUMNISTA; colunista; *columnist;*
  zhuān lán zuò jiā: 专栏作家, *columnist*

COMBATE; combate; *fight, battle, combat* ... **COMBATIENTE; combatente;** *combatant, fighter*
  zhàn dòu (n) (v): 战斗, *battle, action; to fight;*
  zhàn dòu de: 战斗的, *combative, fighting, militant;*
  zhàn dòu zhě: 战斗者, *fighter, battler;*
  zhàn dòu yuán (n): 战斗员, *fighter, combatant*

COMEDIA; comêdia; *comedy;*
  xǐ jù: 喜剧, *comedy*

COMENTARIO; comentário; *comment; comment, remark; essay, commentary* ... **COMENTARISTA; comentarista;** *commentator;*
  jiě shuō yuán: 解说员, *sb who describes sthg;*
  píng lùn zhě: 评论者, *an expert on sthg;*
  píng lùn: 评论, *written or spoken comment;*
  shí kuàng jiě shuō: 实况解说, *commentary;*
  xiě zhào: 写照, *reflection on a situation/ development, etc.*

COMETA; cometa; *comet; kite;*
  fēng zheng: 风筝, *kite;*

huì xīng: 彗星, *comet*

COMISIÓN; comissão; *commission (GEN); to work on a commission basis (COM); task* ... **COMITÉ; comitê;** *committee;*
  shòu xián lìng: 授衔令, *military commission;*
  wěi tuō xiàng mù: 委托项目, *a commission for a piece of work;*
  wěi tuō: 委托, *a commission to an artist/musician, etc.;*
  wěi yuán huì: 委员会, *commission, committee;*
  yōng jīn: 佣金, *money commission*

COMPADRE; comarada; *friend; godfather; buddy, mate;*
  bāng tóu: 帮头, *godfather (gangster);*
  jiào fù: 教父, *godfather;*
  péng you: 朋友, *buddy, friend;*
SEE (请查看) COMPAŃERO

COMPACTO (A); compacto (A) (adj); *small and neat; compact, dense;*
  xiǎo qiǎo: 小巧, *compact in size/ design/shape;*
  xiù zhēn de: 袖珍的, *compact camera/ car, etc.*

COMPAÑERO (A); companheiro (A); *companion;*
  bàn lǚ: 伴侣, *mate, partner, companion;*
  bànr (n): 伴儿, *companion, partner;*
  péi bàn: 陪伴, *companionship;*
  tóng bàn (n): 同伴, *classmate;*
SEE (请查看) COMPADRE

COMPARACIÓN; comparação; *comparison;*
  bǐ fāng (n) (v): 比方, *analogy; to compare;*
  bǐ lì (n): 比例, *ratio, proportion;*
  bǐ lǜ (n): 比率, *ratio, rate, percentage;*
  bǐ nǐ (v) (n): 比拟, *to compare; comparison;*
  fǎn chā: 反差, *contrast;*
SEE (请查看) ANTÍTESIS

COMPÁS; bússola; *compass;*
  zhǐ nán zhēn (n): 指南针, *compass;*
  luó pán (n): 罗盘, *compass*

COMPASIÓN; compaixão; *compassion, pity* ... **COMPASIVO (A); compassivo (A);** *compassionate;*
  biǎo shì lián mǐn de: 表示怜悯的, *compassionate;*
  kě bēi de shì: 可悲的是, *pity;*
  tóng qíng xīn (n) (sv): 同情心, *compassion; compassionate;*
  tóng qíng: 同情, *compassion, pity;*
  yí hàn de shì: 遗憾的是, *pity;*
SEE (请查看) CLEMENCIA

COMPENSACIÓN; compensação; *compensation;*
  bǔ cháng (n) (v): 补偿, *compensation for disappointment, an adjustment; to compensate sb;*
  péi cháng jīn: 赔偿金, *money compensation*

COMPETENTE; competente; *competent;*
  gàn cái (n): 干才, *ability, capability;*
  gàn liàn (sv): 干练, *capable and skillful;*
  hǎo shǒu (n): 好手, *expert, professional;*
  jīng (sv) (n): 精, *refined, elegant, smart, skilled, clever, proficient; essence, energy;*
  jīng tōng (v) (sv): 精通, *to be proficient; expert/ proficient;*
  ná shǒu (sv): 拿手, *adept, good at;*
  néng (aux) (n): 能, *can, be able to; talent, ability, energy;*
  néng gàn (sv): 能干, *able, capable;*
  néng shǒu (n): 能手, *expert; master hand;*
SEE (请查看) APTITUD, CALIFICADO, CAPAZ, CRACK

COMPETITIVO (A); competitivo (A); *competitive;*
  jìng jì xìng de: 竞技性的, *competitive sports/activities, etc.;*
  jìng zhēng xìng de: 竞争性的, *competitive businesses/countries, etc.;*

qiú shèng xīn qiè de: 求胜心切的, *competitive person;*
yǒu jìng zhēng lì de: 有竞争力的, *competitive prices/products, etc.;*
SEE (请查看) **AMBICIÓN**

COMPLACIDO; complacente;
complacent; pleased, satisfied;
kāi xīn (sv): 开心, *pleased, happy, satisfied;*
kuài wèi (sv): 快慰, *pleased with;*
lè zī zī (sv): 乐滋滋, *contented, pleased;*
mǎn (v) (sv) (adv): 满, *to be satisfied; full, complete; completely;*
mǎn zú (v) (sv): 满足, *to satisfy; contented, satisfied;*
què xìn de: 确信的, *satisfied (convinced);*
rú yì (v) (sv): 如意, *to be satisfied; as one wishes;*
zì dé (sv): 自得, *self-satisfied, content;*
zì mǎn (sv): 自满, *self-satisfied, complacent;*
SEE (请查看) **DÓCIL**

COMPLETAMENTE; completamente
(adv); *completely, totally, entirely;*
chún cuì (sv) (adv): 纯粹, *pure; only, completely;*
gān jìng (sv) (adv): 干净, *clean, neat and tidy; completely, totally;*
quán (sv) (adv) (v): 全, *complete, whole, full, total, entire; completely, entirely; to make sthg whole/ intact; to make sthg perfect/complete;*
quán rán (adv): 全然, *completely, entirely, utterly;*
tǒng (v) (n) (adv): 统, *to unite; all; entirely;*
tǒng tǒng (adv): 统统, *completely, entirely, totally*

COMPLETO (A); **completo** (A);
complete, balanced; full, total;
chè dǐ (sv): 彻底, *thorough, complete;*
jiàn quán (sv) (v): 健全, *perfect, complete; to strengthen;*
qí quán (sv): 齐全, *complete;*
shí zú (sv): 十足, *100%; out-and-out, downright;*

wán bèi (sv): 完备, *complete;*
wán zhěng (sv): 完整, *complete, thorough, whole, entire;*
zhōu xiáng (sv): 周详, *comprehensive, complete*

COMPLICACIÓN; complicação;
complication ... **COMPLICADO** (A);
complicado (A); *complicated;*
bìng fā (v) (attr): 并发, *to be complicated by; concomitant;*
bìng fā zhèng: 并发症, *complication (MED);*
fù zá de: 复杂的, *complicated, complex;*
fù zá xìng: 复杂性, *complication; complexity;*
qū zhé de: 曲折的, *winding, tortuous, complicated*

CÓMPLICE; cúmplice; *accomplice;*
bāng xiōng (v) (n): 帮凶, *to be an accomplice/assist in a crime; accomplice, accessory;*
tóng móu (n) (sv): 同谋, *confederate, accomplice; to conspire*

COMPONENTE; componente;
component, constituent;
bù fèn: 部分, *part, section, share;*
bù jiàn: 部件, *components, parts for machinery, etc.;*
chéng fèn: 成分, *component;*
yuán jiàn: 元件, *element, component, part;*
yuán sù: 元素, *essential factor, element (QUIM);*
zǔ chéng bù fen: 组成部分, *component, part of a plan, etc.;*
zǔ chéng (n) (v): 组成, *component parts, elements; to form/compose/make into*

COMPULSIVO (adj); **compulsivo** (A);
compulsive; **envolvente,** *compelling; compulsive;*
lìng rén xìn fú (sv) (v): 令人信服, *compelling; to compel;*
qiáng liè de yù wàng: 强烈的欲望, *compulsion, desire, impulse;*
qiáng pò xìng de: 强迫性的, *compulsive behavior;*

SEE (请查看) MANDATO

COMPRENSIÓN; comprensão; *comprehension;*
lǐ jiě (v) (n): 理解, *to understand; comprehension;*
lǐng huì (v) (n): 领会, *to understand; uptake*

COMPROMISO; meio-termo; *commitment, agreement, compromise;*
xǔ nuò (n) (v): 许诺, *commitment; to promise;*
yì wù (sv) (n): 义务, *voluntary; duty, obligation;*
zé rèn (n): 责任, *duty, responsibility, obligation;*
SEE (请查看) ACTUAR, CONSENSUAL

COMPUTADOR; computador; *computer;*
diàn nǎo: 电脑, *computer;*
jì suàn jī: 计算机, *computer*

COMUNICACIÓN; comunicação; *communication;*
lái wǎng (v) (n): 来往, *to have dealing with; dealings, communication*

COMUNICADO; anuncio; *public statement; announcement, press release;*
fā yán (v) (n): 发言, *to speak; speech, statement;*
gōng bào (n): 公报, *bulletin, public announcement;*
proclamation; to give public notice;
mìng tí (n) (v): 命题, *statement, proposition, thesis; to assign sb a topic;*
qǐ shì (n): 启事, *notice, announcement;*
tán huà (v) (n): 谈话, *to discuss; statement;*
SEE (请查看) ANUNCIAR, BOLETÍN, ALEGACIÓN, COMUNICAR

CONCENTRACIÓN; concentração; *concentration, centralized ...*
CONCENTRADO (A); **concentrado** (A); *concentrated, centralized; extract, concentrate;*

cuì qǔ wù: 萃取物, *extract;*
jí zhōng (sv) (n) (v): 集中, *concentrated effort/ attempt, etc.; concentration; to concentrate;*
mì jí (sv): 密集, *concentrated, crowded together;*
nóng dù (n): 浓度, *concentration; strength, density;*
nóng suō guǒ zhī (n): 浓缩果汁, *condensed (fruit juices);*
nóng suō wù (n): 浓缩物, *concentrate;*
SEE (请查看) ATENCIÓN, CONCENTRAR

CONCEPTO; conceito; *concept, opinion;*
gài niàn (n): 概念, *concept, conception, notion;*
guān diǎn: 观点, *point of view, opinion;*
jiàn jiě: 见解, *opinion, view;*
kàn fǎ: 看法, *point of view, vision, opinion;*
shuō fǎ: 说法, *version, wording, opinion;*
xiǎng fǎ (n) (v): 想法, *idea, opinion; to think of a way to do sthg;*
yì jiàn (n): 异见, *objection, dissent;*
yì jiàn (n): 意见, *view, option, idea, suggestion;*
yì jìng: 意境, *creative concept, artistic view;*
yì si (n) (v): 意思, *meaning, idea, opinion; to mean*

CONCESIÓN; concessão; *concession;*
quán yì (n): 权益, *rights and interests;*
ràng bù (n) (v): 让步, *compromise; concession; to compromise;*
SEE (请查看) AUTORIDAD, CONFIRMAR

CONCIENCIA; consciência; *conscience;*
liáng xīn (n): 良心, *conscience;*
xīn gān (n): 心肝, *conscience; character, guts;*
xīn lǐ (n): 心理, *psychology, mentality;*
xīn lǐ huà (n): 心里话, *innermost*

thoughts/feeling;
xīn shì (n): 心事, *preoccupation*;
xīn xì (sv): 心细, *careful, scrupulous*

CONCISO (A); **conciso** (A); *concise, brief, succinct*;
 jiǎn dān (sv): 简单, *simple, uncomplicated*;
 jiǎn duǎn (sv) (adv): 简短, *brief, succinct, terse; briefly*;
 jiǎn jié (sv) (n): 简洁, *concise, succinct; terseness*;
 jiǎn míng (sv): 简明, *succinct, concise; simple and clear*;
 jiǎn yào (sv): 简要, *concise, brief; to the point*;
 jiǎn yuē (sv): 简约, *brief, concise; sketchy*;
SEE (请查看) AUSTERIDAD, BREVE

CONCRETAMENTE; concretamente;
really, actually; specifically; exactly;
 dàng zhēn (v) (adv) (n): 当真, *to take seriously; truly, really; serious/sincere person*;
 dí què (adv): 的确, *indeed, really, certainly*;
 guǒ rán (adv) (conj): 果然, *really, as expected*;
 guǒ zhēn (adv) (conj): 果真, *really, as expected; if indeed/really*;
 kě shì (conj) (adv): 可是, *but, yet, however; indeed, really, definitely*;
 qí shí (adv): 其实, *actually, really, in fact*;
SEE (请查看) EXACTAMENTE

CONCRETO (A); **concreto** (A);
concrete, specific;
 jù tǐ (sv): 具体, *concrete, specific, detailed*;
 míng què (sv) (v): 明确, *clear-cut, explicit, to clarify*;
 què záo (sv): 确凿, *conclusive, undeniable*;
 shí lì (n): 实例, *concrete example*

CONCUPISCENCIA;
concupiscência; *lustfulness, concupiscence; greed, avarice, cupidity,*

rapacity ... **CONCUPISCENTE;**
concupiscente; *materialistic; lustful, concupiscent; greedy, avaricious, selfish*;
 tān (v) (sv): 贪, *to be greedy, to covet; greedy, corrupt*;
 tān chī (sv) (v): 贪吃, *gluttonous; to be gluttonous*;
 tān duō wú yàn (fe): 贪多无厌, *insatiable*;
 tān fǔ (sv): 贪腐, *corrupted*;
 tān lìn (vp): 贪吝, *avaricious and miserly*;
 tān niàn (n): 贪念, *covetous thoughts*;
 tān sè (sv): 贪色, *lustful*;
 tān wū (v) (n): 贪污, *to be corrupt/ venal; corruption*;
 tān zuǐ (sv): 贪嘴, *gluttonous*;
 zì sī (sv): 自私, *selfish, self-centered*;
SEE (请查看) AVARICIA

CONDICIONAL; condicional;
conditional;
 yǒu tiáo jiàn (attr): 有条件, *conditional*

CONDIMENTO; condimentos;
seasoning, flavoring, dressing;
 tiáo liào: 调料, *salad dressing, condiment*;
 tiáo wèi pǐn: 调味品, *seasoning, flavoring*

CONDUCTA; conduta; *conduct, behavior*;
 biǎo (v) (n): 表, *to express/show/ indicate; feelings, attitude*;
 biǎo xiàn (v) (n): 表现, *to show/display feelings; conduct, behavior*;
 wéi rén (v) (n): 为人, *to behave; behavior*;
 yí tài (n): 仪态, *bearing, behavior*;
SEE (请查看) ACTIVIDAD, COSTUMBRE

CONEXIÓN; conexão; *connection*;
 jiē tóu (n) (v): 接头, *connection; to connect/join*;
 lián jiē (v) (adv) (n) (sv): 连接, *to join/ link; continuously; conjunction, linking; joint*;

lián xì (v) (n): 联系, *to link/relate/ integrate; relationship, connection*;
SEE (请查看) **ASOCIACIÓN, ANEXO**

CONFABULACIÓN; confabulação;
plot, conspiracy; intrigue;
  cè huà zhě (n): 策划者, *planner, plotter*;
  mì móu (v) (n): 密谋, *to conspire/plot; scheme, intrigue*;
  yīn móu zhě (n): 阴谋者, *plotter*;
SEE (请查看) **SIMULACIÓN, CONSPIRACIÓN**

CONFERENCIA; conferência;
conference, meeting;
  huì yì (n): 会议, *conference, meeting*

CONFIANZA; confiança; *confidence, trust; reliance*;
  xìn lài (sv) (n) (v): 信赖, *reliant; reliance; to trust*;
  xìn yòng (n): 信用, *trustworthiness, credit*;
SEE (请查看) **DEPENDER, CONVICCIÓN**

CONFIDENCIAL; confidencial;
confidential;
  àn (sv): 暗, *dark, dim, dull; (bf) hidden, secret, unclear*;
  àn cáng de (sv) (v): 暗藏的, *secret, undercover, hidden; to hide/conceal*;
  mì jué (n): 秘诀, *knack, secret of success*;
  xìn fù (attr): 信服, *confidential*
SEE (请查看) **RESERVADO, SECRETO, PRIVADO, ÍNTIMO, ARCANO, CLANDESTINIDAD**

CONFIDENTE; confidente; *confidant, intimate friend; informer*;
  mì yǒu: 密友, *confidant*;
  sī rén (n) (attr): 私人, *personal friend; confidant; private, personal*;
  zhī jǐ: 知己, *bosom/intimate friend*;
  zhī xīn rén: 知心人, *confidant*;
SEE (请查看) **ÍNTIMO**

CONFIGURACIÓN; configuração;

configuration, outline, layout;
  lún kuò: 轮廓, *outline, contour*;
  pèi zhì :配置, *configuration*;
  tān kāi (n) (v): 摊开, *layout; to layout/ spread out*

CONFINAMIENTO; confinamiento;
confinement;
  jìn bì (v) (n): 禁闭, *to confine sb; confinement*;
  xiáo xiǎo de: 狭小的, *confined*;
SEE (请查看) **APREHENDER**

CONFIRMACIÓN; confirmação;
confirmation;
  què rèn (n) (v): 确认, *confirmation of a date/an appointment, etc.; to confirm/ affirm*;
SEE (请查看) **APROBACIÓN, AFIRMAR**

CONFISCACIÓN; confisco;
confiscation;
  mò shōu (v) (n): 没收, *to confiscate/ expropriate; confiscation*

CONFLICTIVO (A); **controverso** (A);
controversial, troubled;
  duō shì (sv) (v): 多事, *troublesome; to be eventful*;
  fèi shì (sv) (v): 费事, *troublesome, difficult; to take the trouble to do sthg*;
  luàn shì: 乱世, *troubled times*;
  má fan (sv) (n) (v): 麻烦, *troublesome, problematic; trouble; to trouble/bother*;
  wéi nán de: 为难的, *embarrassed, troubled, awkward*;
SEE (请查看) **APRENSIÓN, CONTENCIOSO**

CONFLICTO; conflito; *conflict, problem*;
  chōng tū (v) (n): 冲突, *to conflict with/ clash; conflict, contradiction*;
  wèn tí (n): 问题, *problem, question*;
  zhēng duān (n): 争端, *conflict, dispute, controversy*;
SEE (请查看) **DIFÍCIL, ARGUMENTAR, CONTRADICCIÓN**

CONFORME; conforme; *in*

accordance, in agreement with;

fú hé (v) (n): 符合, *to conform with/to; coincidence*;

gēn jù (cov) (n) (v): 根据, *according to; basis, foundation, grounds; to lodge/ settle os*;

hé hū (v): 合乎, *to conform to/with; to accord with, to correspond with*;

yī zhào (cov) (prep): 依照, *to be based on; according to, in accordance with*;

SEE (请查看) UNIFICACIÓN

CONFORMIDAD; conformidade; *approval, agreement;*

xǔ kě (v) (n): 许可, *to permit/allow; permission*;

SEE (请查看) APROBACIÓN, ASENTIR

CONFORT; conforto; *comfort …*
CONFORTABLE; confortável; *comfortable;*

ān lè (sv): 安乐, *comfortable, carefree*;

ān wèi (sv) (v) (n): 安慰, *comforted, reassured; to comfort/console; comfort, relief, consolation*;

ān yì (sv): 安逸, *comfortable*;

kuān yù de (adv): 宽裕的, *(live) comfortably*;

qīng sōng (v) (sv): 轻松, *to relax; comfortable/ relaxed life/job, etc.*;

shǐ shēn tǐ shū fu de: 使身体舒服的, *comfortable chair/seat/bed/room, etc.*;

shū fu (sv): 舒服, *comfortable, well*;

shū fu de (adv): 舒服地, *(sit, settle) comfortably*;

shū tan (sv): 舒坦, *comfortable, at ease*;

shū xīn (sv): 舒心, *pleasant and agreeable; comfortable; happy*;

SEE (请查看) AGRADABLE

CONFRONTACIÓN; confrontação; *confrontation;*

duì zhì (v) (n): 对峙, *to confront; confrontation*;

SEE (请查看) AFRONTAR, CONFLICTO

CONFUSO (A) (adj); **confusso** (A);

confused, hazy, blurred;

hú li hú tu (fe) (vp): 糊里糊涂, *confused, muddleheaded; in a daze; thoughtless, slipshod*;

kùn huò (sv) (n) (v): 困惑, *bewildered, confused, puzzled; bewilderment, confusion; to be confused*;

mí hu (sv): 迷糊, *confused; blurred; dazed*;

mí máng (sv): 迷茫, *confused, perplexed, dazed*;

mí wǎng (sv) (v): 迷惘, *perplexed; be at a loss/ confused*;

SEE (请查看) CAOS

CONJETURA; confusão; *conjecture, surmise;*

cāi xiǎng (v) (n): 猜想, *to surmise, to suppose; guess, surmise*;

tuī cè (v) (n): 推测, *to infer; explanation*

CONJUNTO (A); **conjunto** (A); *joint, combined;*

gòng shí: 共识, *common understanding, consensus*;

gòng tóng (sv) (adv): 共同, *common, mutual; jointly, together*;

gòng yǒu (v) (sv): 共有, *to jointly possess; common, public*;

jiē hé (v) (n): 结合, *to combine/unite/ integrate; to associate; fusion*;

SEE (请查看) COHESIONAR, CONEXIÓN

CONMISERACIÓN; coniseração; *pity, commiseration;*

gòng míng (n): 共鸣, *sympathy; sympathetic response*;

SEE (请查看) COMPASIÓN

CONNOTACIÓN; conotação; *connotation;*

hán yì: 含义, *meaning, implication, connotation*;

nèi hán: 内涵, *connotation; intention; (attr) implied*;

yán wài zhī yì: 言外之意, *connotation*

CONQUISTA; conquista; *conquest …*
CONQUISTADOR (A); **conquistador**

(A); *conquering (adj), conqueror (n)*;
kè fú (v) (n): 克服, *to surmount/ conquer; conquest*;
tǒng zhì (v) (n) (sv): 统治, *to rule/ dominate; domination; dominant*;
zhēng fú (n) (v): 征服, *conquest; to conquer*;
zhī pèi (v) (n): 支配, *to control/govern; government*;
SEE (请查看) APREHENDER

CONSECUENCIA; conseqüência; *consequence …* **CONSECUENTE; consequente;** *consistent with, consequent*;
hòu guǒ (n): 后果, *consequence, aftermath*;
jié guǒ (n): 结果, *result, outcome, consequence*;
suí zhī fā shēng de : 随之发生的, *consequential, resulting*;
zhòng yào de: 重要的, *consequential, important*

CONSECUTIVO (A); **consecutive** (A); *consecutive*;
lián chuàn (sv): 连串, *consecutive*;
lián xù (attr): 连续, *consecutive, successive, running*

CONSENSO; consenso; *consensus, consent …* **CONSENSUAL; consensual;** *agreed, consensual*;
gòng shí: 共识, *consensus*;
hé yì (sv): 合意, *suitable; mutually agreeable*;
yī zhì (sv) (n): 一致, *unanimous; agreement; consensus*;
SEE (请查看) APROBACIÓN, DUPLICADO

CONSERVACIÓN; conservação; *conservation*;
bǎo cún (v) (n): 保存, *to preserve; to conserve; to keep; conservation, preservation*;
bǎo hù (v) (n): 保护, *to conserve; conservation (of the environment)*;
jié yuē (v) (n): 节约, *to economize; conservation (of energy), frugality*

CONSIDERACIÓN; consideração; *consideration*;
dù liàng (n) (v): 度量, *tolerance, consideration; to measure*;
kǎo lǜ (v) (n): 考虑, *to think over, to consider; deliberation*;
kǎo lǜ móu shì (v): 考虑某事, *to think over, to plan things*;
sī kǎo (v) (n): 思考, *to ponder over, to reflect on; reflection*

CONSIDERADO (A); **atencioso;** *thoughtful; considerate*;
zhōu zhì (sv): 周至, *thoughtful*;
SEE (请查看) ATENCIÓN

CONSOLACIÓN; consolação; *consolation*;
ān wèi: 安慰, *consolation*;
fǔ xù (n) (v): 抚恤, *consolation; to console/comfort*

CONSORCIO; consórcio; *consortium, syndicate*;
cái tuán: 财团, *financial group, consortium*;
guó jì cái tuán: 国际财团, *consortium*;
hé zuò (v) (n): 合作, *to cooperate/ collaborate; consortium*

CONSORTE; consorte; *spouse, consort*;
ài ren: 爱人, *spouse, husband, wife (in China)*;
lǎo bàn: 老伴, *husband, wife, spouse*;
pèi 'ǒu: 配偶, *spouse, husband, wife*

CONSPICUO (A); **conspícuo** (A); *conspicuous, famous, eminent*;
míng xiǎn (sv): 明显, *clear, obvious, evident, conspicuous*;
wén míng (sv) (v): 闻名, *famous; to know by reputation*;
xiǎn zhù (sv): 显著, *notable, marked, striking, outstanding, distinctive, conspicuous*;
zhuó yuè (vp): 卓越, *outstanding, brilliant, eminent*;
SEE (请查看) CÉLEBRE, CELEBRIDAD, ATÍPICO, AUGUSTO,

EGREGIO, FAMOSO, AFAMADO

CONSPIRACIÓN; conspiração; *conspiracy;*
 yīn xiǎn (sv): 阴险, *sinister, insidious, treacherous;*
SEE (请查看**) CONFABULACIÓN**

CONSTANTE; constante; *persistent, steadfast, constant* … **CONSTANCIA; constância;** *persistence, constancy, perseverance;*
 bù duàn (adv) (v): 不断, *unceasingly, constantly, continually; to continue;*
 bù sǐ xīn (fe): 不死心, *unwilling to quit/give up;*
 bù zhǐ (v) (adv): 不止, *to continue; continuously, incessantly, more than;*
 chí jiǔ (sv): 持久, *lasting, durable; persistent;*
 chí zhī yǐ héng (fe): 持之以恒, *to persevere; to act in a persistent manner;*
 chóng fù (sv): 重复, *persistent/ constant, interruptions, questions, etc.;*
 jiān jué (sv) (adv): 坚决, *resolute, determined, firmed; resolutely, firmly;*
 piān piān (adv): 偏偏, *persistently; just; only;*
SEE (请查看**) CONTINUADO, PERSEVERANCIA, INSISTENTE, CONTUMACIA**

CONSTERNACIÓN; consternação; *consternation, dismay;*
 huī xīn (sv): 灰心, *to lose heart/be discouraged;*
 jīng 'è (sv) (n): 惊愕, *to be stunned/ stupefied; dismay;*
 kǔ nǎo (sv): 苦恼, *distressed, worried;*
SEE (请查看**) DESANIMADO, DESILUSIÓN**

CONSTITUCIONAL; constitucional; *constitutional;*
 xiàn fǎ de: 宪法的, *constitutional;*
 xiàn zhèng: 宪政, *constitutional government*

CONSTRUCCIÓN; construção; *construction, building project;*

jiàn shè (v) (n): 建设, *to build; construction;*
jiàn zào (v) (n): 建造, *to build, to construct, to make; construction;*
jiàn zhù (v) (n): 建筑, *to build, to construct; building, structure;*
jié gòu (n) (v): 结构, *structure, construction; composition, texture; to make, to arrange, to organize;*
tǔ mù (n): 土木, *building, construction*

CONSTRUCTIVO (A); **construtivo** (A); *constructive;*
 jī jí (sv): 积极, *positive, constructive; energetic;*
 jiàn shè xìng (n): 建设性, *constructive nature;*
 yǒu bāng zhù: 有帮助, *constructive*

CONSULTOR (A); **consultor** (A); *consultant;*
 cān móu (n) (v): 参谋, *advisor, consultant; to advise;*
 gù wèn: 顾问, *consultant, advisor*

CONSUMADO (A); **consumado** (A); *consummate, thorough;*
 wán měi (sv) (n) (adv): 完美, *perfect; perfection, consummate; perfectly;*
SEE (请查看**) CASTO, COMPLETO**

CONTACTO; contato; *contact;*
 mén dào (n): 门道, *contacts, social contacts;*
SEE (请查看**) APROXIMAR**

CONTAGIO; contágio; *contagion; infection (MED); contamination* …
CONTAGIOSO (A); **contagiante; contagioso** (A); *infectious, catching, contagious;*
 chuán rǎn (n) (v) (sv):传染, *contagion; to infect/be contagious; infections, contagious, catching;*
 chuán rǎn bìng (n): 传染病, *infectious/contagious disease;*
 gǎn rǎn xìng de: 感染性的, *infectious, catching, contagious;*
 gǎn rǎn: 感染, *infection;*

jiē chù chuán rǎn de: 接触传染的, *contagious*

CONTAMINACIÓN; contaminação; *contamination, pollution* ... **CONTAMINANTE; poluente;** *pollutant*;
  wū rǎn (v) (n): 污染, *to pollute, to contaminate; pollution, contamination*;
  wū rǎn wù: 污染物, *pollutant, contaminant*

CONTEMPLACIÓN; contemplação; *contemplation* ... **CONTEMPLATIVO** (A); **contemplativo** (A); *contemplative*;
  chén sī (n) v) (sv): 沉思, *contemplation; to ponder; to meditate; to reflect on; contemplative*

CONTEMPORÁNEO (A); **contemporâneo;** *contemporary*;
  dāng dài (n): 当代, *present (time), contemporary period*;
  dāng jīn (n): 当今, *present (time), nowadays*;
  tóng yī shí dài: 同一时代, *contemporary (of the same time)*;
  tóng bèi rén (n): 同辈人, *a contemporary*;
  tóng dài rén: 同代人, *contemporary (with another person/persons)*;
  tóng qī (n): 同期, *corresponding period; same year/ period*;
  tóng shí (n) (adv) (conj): 同时, *living or occurring at the same time (contemporary); meanwhile, besides, in addition to*;
  tóng shí dài (n): 同时代, *at the same time; contemporary period/generation*;
  tóng shí qī (n): 同时期, *contemporary stage/period of time*;
  xiàn dài (n) (attr): 现代, *modern times; contemporary age*;
  zhè cì (pron) (attr): 这次, *this time; present, current*

CONTENCIOSO (A); **contencioso** (A); *contentious, quarrelsome*;
  hào zhēng lùn de: 好争论的, *contentious*;
  yǐn qǐ zhēng lùn de: 引起争论的, *contentious*;
  yǒu zhēng yì de: 有争议的, *controversial, contested, contentious*

CONTEXTO; contexto; *context*;
  shàng xià wén: 上下文, *context (of a word/phrase)*;
  yǔ jìng: 语境, *context; situation*

CONTIGUO (A); **contíguo** (A); *next to sthg; contiguous; adjacent*;
  biān (n) (adv): 边, *side, edge; next to, nearby; periphery, boarder*;
  biān jiè (n): 边界, *border, boundary*;
  biān yán (n): 边沿, *edge, fringe*;
  gé bì (adv): 隔壁, *next door*;
  lín (sv) (n): 临, *neighboring, adjacent; close, near*;
  páng biān (adv): 旁边, *next to, beside; side*;
SEE (请查看) CERCA

CONTINENTE; continent; *continent* (GEOG);
  dà lù: 大陆, *continent, mainland*;
  zhōu: 洲, *continent*

CONTINGENCIA; contingência; *eventuality, unpredictability, contingency, possibility* ... **CONTINGENTE;** **contingente;** *unforeseeable, contingent*;
  bù kě yù liào de: 不可预料的, *unpredictable, unexpected*;
  hěn kě néng (sv): 很可能, *likely*;
  kě néng (sv) (aux) (n) (adv): 可能, *possible, probable; probably, maybe; possibility; eventually*;
  kě néng xìng (n): 可能性, *possibility, probability, likelihood*;
  ǒu rán xìng (n) (attr): 偶然性, *contingency, fortuity, chance; occasional*;
  wàn yī (n) (conj): 万一, *contingency; just in case*;
  zuì hòu (sv) (n): 最后, *eventual; eventuality*;
SEE (请查看) CIRCUNSTANCIAL, POSIBLE, EVENTUALIDAD

CONTINUADO (A); **contínuo** (A); *continual* ... **CONTINUAMENTE;**

constantemente; *constantly* ...
CONTINUO (A); **contínuo** (A);
continuous;
  bù tíng (v) (adv): 不停, *to be nonstop;*
incessantly;
  bù zhǐ (v) (adv): 不止, *to continue;*
continuously, incessantly;
  chí xù bù duàn de: 持续不断地,
continuously;
  jì xù (v) (adv): 继续, *to continue; to go*
on and on;
  jīn cháng (adv): 经常, *every day, daily;*
frequently, constantly;
  lián xù (attr): 连续, *continuous,*
successive, running;
  lián xù bù duàn (adv): 连续不断,
continuously, incessantly;
  lián xù bù tíng (sv): 连续不停,
continuous;
  lù xù (adv): 陆续, *constantly;*
continually, successively;
  shí kè (n) (adv): 时刻, *time, moment;*
always, constantly;
  yī xiàng (adv): 一向, *constantly;*
  yī zài (adv): 一再, *again and again;*
repeatedly;
  yī zhí (adv): 一直, *continuously, always;*
SEE (请查看) CONSTANTE,
PERSEVERANCIA

CONTORSIÓN; contorção; *contortion;*
twist, tangle, distortion;
  chán jié (n) (v): 缠结, *entanglement; to*
be tangled up;
  jī xíng (n): 畸形, *deformity;*
  niǔ wāi (n): 扭歪, *distortion;*
  qū zhé (sv): 曲折, *winding, tortuous;*
complicated, intricate;
  wāi xié (sv): 歪斜, *crooked, askew;*
  wāi: 歪, *distortion*

CONTRABANDISTA;
contrabandista; *smuggler;*
  zǒu sī zhě: 走私者, *smuggler*

CONTRACCIÓN; contração;
contraction;
  shōu suō (v) (n): 收缩, *to contract, to*
shrink; contraction; constriction;
SEE (请查看) ABREVIAR

CONTRADICCIÓN; contradição;
contradiction .. **CONTRADICTORIO**
(A); **contraditório** (A); *contradictory;*
  máo dùn (n) (sv) (v): 矛盾, *conflict,*
contradiction; contradictory; to conflict

CONTRAPRODUCENTE;
contraproducente; *counter-productive;*
  chǎn shēng xiāng fǎn xiào guǒ de:
产生相反效果的, *counter-productive*

CONTRARIO (A); **contrário** (A);
opposite, contrary, opposing;
  duì cè (n): 对策, *countermeasure;*
  duì miàn (n): 对面, *opposite;*
  fǎn zhī (conj): 反之, *on the contrary,*
otherwise;
  hào yǔ rén zuò duì de: 好与人作对
的, *contrary, argumentative;*
  xiāng fǎn de: 相反的, *contrary,*
opposite, different;
SEE (请查看) CONTENCIOSO,
ANVERSO

CONTRATA (f) ó **CONTRATO** (m);
contrato; *contract, agreement;*
  hè tong (n) (v): 合同, *contract;*
SEE (请查看) ASENTIR

CONTRATIEMPO; contratempo;
setback; hurdle; upset; reverse;
  cuò bài (v) (n): 挫败, *to frustrate/*
defeat; setback;
  nán chù (sv) (n): 难处, *trouble,*
dilemma, misfortune;
  nán diǎn (n): 难点, *difficulty;*
  shī bài (n) (v): 失败, *defeat, reverse,*
loss; to be defeated;
  tuì bù (v) (n): 退步, *to step backward/*
retrogress; setback, leeway;
SEE (请查看) ADVERSIDAD, DIFÍCIL

CONTRIBUCIÓN; contribuição;
contribution;
  gōng jī (n): 功绩, *contribution;*
  gōng láo (n): 功劳, *contribution,*
credit;
  juān (v) (n): 捐, *to donate/contribute;*
tax;
  juān kuǎn (v) (n): 捐款, *to contribute;*

donation, contribution;
juān xiàn (n): 捐献, *contribution*;
SEE (请查看) **CONTRIBUIR**

CONTRICIÓN; contrição; *contrition, repentance, compunction* ... **CONTRITO** (A); **contrito** (A); *contrite*;
ào huǐ: 懊悔, *repentance*;
biǎo shì huǐ zuì de: 表示悔罪的, *showing contriteness*;
huǐ zuì de: 悔罪的, *contrite*;
tòng huǐ de: 痛悔地, *deeply regret, contritely*;
tòng huǐ: 痛悔, *contrition*

CONTROVERSIA; controvérsia; *controversy*;
zhēng lùn (n) (v): 争论, *dispute, argument, debate; to dispute/controvert/argue*;
SEE (请查看) **CONTRARIO, POLÉMICA**

CONTUMACIA; contumácia; *obstinacy, stubbornness*;
gù zhi (sv): 固执, *stubborn, obstinate*;
jué jiàng (sv): 倔强, *stubborn; unbending*;
niú pí qi (n): 牛脾气, *stubbornness*;
wán (sv) (bf): 顽, *stupid, foolish, stubborn, obstinate, mischievous*;
wán gù (sv): 顽固, *obstinate, stubborn; persistent*;
wán liè (sv): 顽劣, *stubborn and loud-mouthed*;
wán qiáng (sv): 顽强, *tenacious, indomitable*;
zhí yì (adv) (v): 执意, *stubbornly, obstinately; to insist*;
zuǐ yìng (sv): 嘴硬, *stubborn, reluctant*

CONVENCIÓN; convenção; *convention*;
dà huì (n): 大会, *convention, conference, rally, political convention*;
SEE (请查看) **CONFERENCIA**

CONVENCIONAL; convencional; *conventional*;
cháng guī (n): 常规, *normal practice,*

convention, rule, routine;
gōng yuē (n): 公约, *convention, pact; joint pledge*;
guàn lì (n): 惯例, *usual practice, convention*;
guàn lì de: 惯例的, *conventional*;
guàn yòng (v) (attr): 惯用, *to consistently use/practice; customary, habitual; conventional*
shè huì xí sú (n): 社会习俗, *convention (custom)*;
xí sú (n): 习俗, *custom, convention*;
SEE (请查看) **CONSENSUAL, CLÁSICO, NORMA**

CONVENIENTE; conveniente, *suitable*; **cômodo** (A), *handy; convenient, advisable*;
biàn lì (sv): 便利, *easy, convenient*;
biàn yú (vp): 便于, *to be convenient; easy to*;
fāng biàn (sv) (v): 方便, *convenient, appropriate; handy (useful), suitable; to go to the toilet*;
jiǎn biàn (sv): 简便, *convenient, handy*;
qīng biàn (sv): 轻便, *portable, handy, light*;
shì dàng de: 适当的, *suitable, proper*;
shì yòng (sv): 适用, *suitable, applicable*;
shì zhōng (sv): 适中, *appropriate, just right*;
shǒu biān de: 手边的, *handy (close at hand)*;
shùn shǒu (sv) (adv): 顺手, *smooth, handy; conveniently*;
tiē qiè (sv): 贴切, *suitable, appropriate, apt*;
zì zhǔ (v) (n): 自主, *to suit/help oneself; self-help*;
SEE (请查看) **APROPIADO, CUALIFICADO**

CONVENTO; convento; *convent, nunnery*;
xiū dào yuàn: 修道院, *monastery, convent*

CONVERSACIÓN; conversação; *conversation, talk*;
tán huà (v) (n): 谈话, *to talk; chat*;

SEE (请查看) **COLOQUIO, ALTERNAR**

CONVERSADOR (A); **conversador** (A); *talkative, conversationalist, chatty*;
 jiàn tán de: 健谈的, *talkative*;
 liáo tiān (v) (n): 聊天, *chat; gossip*;
 xián liáo de: 闲聊的, *chatty*;
 zuǐ suì (sv): 嘴碎, *garrulous, loquacious*

CONVEXO (A); **convexo** (A); *convex*;
 tū chū (sv) (v): 凸出, *convex; to protrude*

CONVICCIÓN; **convicção**; *conviction, certitude*; **condenação**; *jury conviction; conviction, certitude, confidence ...*
CONVINCENTE; **convincente**; *convincing*;
 fú qì: 服气, *to be convinced/won over*;
 jiān dìng de xìn yǎng (n): 坚定的信仰, *belief, conviction*;
 jiān xìn (sv) (n): 坚信, *to be convinced; conviction, certainty*;
 lìng rén xìn fú de: 令人信服的, *convincing*;
 shǐ rén shēn xìn de: 使人深信的, *convincing*;
 xìn xīn (n): 信心, *confidence, faith*;
 xìn yǎng (v) (n): 信仰, *to believe in sthg; faith, conviction*;
 yǒu shuō fú lì: 有说服力, *convincing; forceful; persuasive*;
 zhé fú: 折服, *to be convinced/astonished/filled with admiration*

CONVULSIVO (A) (adj); **convulsivo** (A); *convulsive*;
 chōu chù (v) (n) (sv): 抽搐, *to twitch; tic (MED); convulsive*;
 dòng luàn (v) (n) (sv): 动乱, *to have social turmoil/ unrest; disturbance; convulsive*;
SEE (请查看) **AGITADO, AGITAR, BRAVÍO, DRÁSTICO, VIOLENCIA**

COOPERACIÓN; **cooperação**; *cooperation ...* **COOPERATIVO** (A); **cooperativo** (A); *cooperative*;
 hé bàn de: 合办的, *jointly run*;

hé zuò de: 合作的, *cooperative (effort)*;
 hé zuò shè: 合作社, *a cooperative*;
 hé zuò suǒ: 合作所, *cooperation*;
 lè yì hé zuò de: 乐意合作的, *cooperative person*;
SEE (请查看) **COLABORACIÓN**

COORDINACIÓN; **coordenação**; *coordination*;
 xié tiáo (v) (sv): 协调, *to coordinate; coordinated, balanced*;
 xié tiáo xìng (n): 协调性, *harmony*;
 xié zuò (v) (n): 协作, *to collaborate; cooperation, coordination*;
 zuò biāo (n): 坐标, *coordination*

COPIA; **cópia**; *copy, duplicate ...*
COPIADORA; **copiadora**; *copier*; **printshop**; *photocopier*;
 fù yìn jiàn: 复印件, *copy, photocopy, duplicate*;
 yǐng yìn jī: 影印机, *photocopier*;
SEE (请查看) **DUPLICADO, DUPLICAR**

COPIOSO (A); **copioso** (A); *copious; abundant, heavy*;
 chōng fèn (sv): 充分, *enough, sufficient, full*;
 chōng pèi (sv): 充沛, *plentiful, abundant*;
 fù ráo (sv): 富饶, *fertile, abundant; richly endowed*;
 fù zú (sv): 富足, *affluent; plentiful, abundant*;
SEE (请查看) **ABUNDANCIA, OPULENCIA**

CORDIALIDAD; **cordialidade**; *warmth, cordiality ...* **CORDIALMENTE**; **cordialmente**; *warmly, cordially*;
 qīn qiè (sv): 亲切, *cordial, warm; close, dear*;
 rè liè chéng zhì de: 热烈诚挚的, *sincere, cordial*;
 zhōng xīn (attr): 忠心, *cordial, heartfelt; wholehearted*;
SEE (请查看) **GENTIL, AFABLE, AMIGABLE, RESPETUOSO,**

FAMILIAR, SIMPATÍA, SINCERO

CORPORACIÓN; corporação;
corporation … **CORPORATIVO** (A);
corporativista; *corporate;*
  gōng sī de: 公司的, *corporate;*
  gōng sī: 公司, *company, corporation;*
SEE (请查看**) ASOCIACIÓN**

CORPULENCIA; corpulência;
corpulence, burliness, stoutness …
CORPULENTO (A); **corpulento** (A);
corpulent, stout, burly; solid;
  féi chǔn (sv): 肥蠢, *fat and clumsy;*
  féi chǔn rú zhū (fe): 肥蠢如猪, *fat
  and stupid as a pig;*
  féi hòu (sv): 肥厚, *fat, plump, fleshy;*
  féi mǎn (sv): 肥满, *plump;*
  féi pàng (sv): 肥胖, *fat, corpulent,
  obese;*
  féi pàng zhèng (n): 肥胖症, *obesity;*
  féi tóu féi nǎo (fe): 肥头肥脑,
  corpulent;
  féi yú (vp): 肥腴, *fertile; stout; fat,
  plump;*
SEE (请查看**) OBESIDAD, GRANDE**

CORRECCIÓN; correção; emenda;
change; correction;
  dǐ xiāo: 抵消, *to offset, to neutralize;*
  jiǎo zhèng: 矫正, *to correct/rectify;*
  xiū gǎi zhī chù: 修改之处, *correction;*
SEE (请查看**) AJUSTAR, ALTERNAR,
MODIFICACIÓN**

CORRECTAMENTE; correctamente;
correctly … **CORRECTO** (A); **certo** (A);
correct, right; **adequadamente,** *suitably,
appropriately; completely; correctly,
accurately;*
  bù cuò (sv): 不错, *correct, right; pretty
  good, not bad;*
  dé tǐ (sv) (n): 得体, *proper;
  appropriateness;*
  duān zhèng (sv) (v): 端正, *upright,
  proper, correct; to rectify;*
  duān zhèng (adv): 端正, *correctly;*
  qià rú qí fèn (fe): 恰如其分,
  appropriate;
  qiè hé (sv) (v): 切合, *appropriate; to*

correspond to;
  shì dàng (sv): 适当 , *suitable, proper;*
  shì dù (n) (sv): 适度, *appropriate act;
  moderate;*
  tuǒ dang (sv): 妥当, *suitable,
  appropriate, proper;*
  tuǒ tiē (sv): 妥贴, *appropriate; fitting,
  properly done;*
  zài lǐ (sv): 在理, *right, reasonable,
  sensible;*
  zhèng què (sv) (adv): 正确, *right,
  correct, proper; correctly;*
SEE (请查看**) APROPIADO,
AUSPICIOSO, CONVENIENTE**

CORRESPONDENCIA;
correspondência; *correspondence,
mail;*
  tōng xùn (v) (n): 通讯, *to
  communicate; correspondence;*
  yóu jiàn: 邮件, *mail, post, postal items;*
  yóu zhèng: 邮政, *mail; postal service*

CORRESPONDIENTE;
correspondente; *corresponding,
respective, appropriate, suitable, proper;*
  duì yìng (v) (sv): 对应, *to relate to;
  corresponding, reciprocal;*
  gè zì (pron): 各自, *each, respective;*
  xiāng bàn wù (n): 相伴物,
  concomitant;
  xiāng chèn (sv): 相称, *agreeing,
  corresponding, matching, suitable;*
  xiāng dāng (vp) (adv) (sv): 相当, *to
  match/balance/ correspond to, be equal
  to, be equivalent to; be suitable, fit,
  appropriate; quite, fairly, considerably;
  fit, appropriate;*
  xiāng yí (sv): 相宜, *be suitable/
  appropriate;*
SEE (请查看**) APROPIADO,
CONTEMPORÁNEO**

CORROSIÓN; corrosão; *corrosion,
erosion (GEOL)* … **CORROSIVO** (A);
corrosivo (A); *corrosive;*
  fǔ shí (v) (n): 腐蚀, *to corrode;
  corrosion;*
  fǔ shí jì: 腐蚀剂, *caustic, corrosive
  agent;*

fǔ shí xìng de: 腐蚀性的, *corrosive, corruptive*;
liú shī (v) (n): 流失, *to erode, to run off; erosion*;
qīn shí (v) (n): 侵蚀, *to corrode, to erode; erosion*;
qīn shí zuò yòng: 侵蚀作用, *erosion*

CORRUPCIÓN; corrupção (GEN); **depravação**, *depravity; moral corruption, bribery; rot, decay ...*
CORRUPTO (A); **corrupto** (A); *corrupt*;
fǔ bài (v) (sv) (n): 腐败, *to decay; to rot; rotten, corrupt; corruption*;
fǔ bài de: 腐败的, *corrupt; rotten*;
fǔ chòu (attr) (v): 腐臭, *putrid; to decay*;
fǔ 'é (sv): 腐恶, *corrupt and evil*;
fǔ huà (sv) (v): 腐化, *degenerate, dissolute; to rot, to decay*;
fǔ huà duò luò de: 腐化堕落的, *depraved*;
fǔ huài (vp): 腐坏, *rotten, putrid, decayed*;
fǔ làn (sv): 腐烂, *putrid; corrupt, rotten*;
fǔ shí xìng (n): 腐蚀性, *corruption*;
fǔ xiǔ (v) (adj): 腐朽, *to rot; rotten, decayed, decadent*;
huì lù (n) (v): 贿赂, *bribery; to bribe*

COSMÉTICO (A); **cosmetico**; **superficial**, *superficial; cosmetic*;
huà zhuāng yòng de: 化妆用的, *cosmetic*;
SEE (请查看) **FRÍVOLO**

CÓSMICO (A); **cósmico** (A); *cosmic*;
yǔ zhòu (n) (adj): 宇宙, *cosmos; cosmic*

COSMONAUTA; cosmonauta; *cosmonaut*;
yǔ háng yuán: 宇航员, *cosmonaut*

COSTO; custo; *cost, price*;
chǎn pǐn chéng běn (n): 产品成本, *cost of goods*;
chéng běn (n): 成本, *cost of production*;
dài jià: 代价, *price/ cost of doing sthg*;
fèi (n) (v) (adv): 费, *expenses; to spend/ charge/cost; wasteful, expensive*;
fèi yòng: 费用, *cost, expenses, expenditures*;
huā fèi (v) (n): 花费, *to pay, to spend; cost, expense*

COSTOSO; oneroso (A), *expensive*; **dispendioso** (A), *involving loss or damage; costly*;
áng guì (sv): 昂贵, *costly, expensive*;
dài jià cǎn zhòng de: 代价惨重的, *expensive, costly*;
dài jià gāo de: 代价高的, *costly (mistake)*;
fèi qián (v) (sv): 费钱, *to be costly, expensive; costly*;
guì (sv): 贵, *expensive, costly*

COSTUMBRE; costume; *as a habit or tradition*; **preferência**, *trade (COM); customs and manners*;
fēng qì (n): 风气, *common practice*;
fēng sú (n): 风俗, *custom, mores*;
guī ju (sv) (n): 规矩, *custom, norm, established practice*;
xí (n) (v): 习, *habit, custom, practice; to practice, to study*;
xí guàn (n) (v): 习惯, *custom, habit; to be used to*;
SEE (请查看) **BANAL, CLÁSICO, CONVENCIONAL**

COTÓN; algoado, *fabric; plants*; **linha**, *thread; cotton fabric*;
fǎng zhī pǐn: 纺织品, *textile, fabric*;
mián huā: 棉花, *cotton*

CRASO (A); **crasso** (A); *crass; gross*;
fēi cháng pàng de: 非常胖的, *gross*;
yú dùn de: 愚钝的, *crass*

CRÉDITO; crédito; *credit, reputation; loan, on credit*;
dài fāng (n): 贷方, *credit*;
dài kuǎn (v) (n): 贷款, *to grant a loan; loan*;
xìn dài (n): 信贷, *credit, credit financing*;
xīn yù (n): 信誉, *prestige, credit, reputation*;

zhàng (bf): 帐, *accounts, account book; debt, credit, credit account*;
SEE (请查看) CONFIANZA

CREDULIDAD; credulidade; *credulity ... CRÉDULO* (A); **crédulo** (A); *credulous, gullible*;
  qīng xìn (v): 轻信, *to be credulous, gullible*;
  qīng xìn de (adv): 轻信地, *credulously*;
  róng yì shòu piàn de: 容易受骗的, *gullible*;
  yì shàng dàng de: 易上当的, *gullible*

CREÍBLE; crível; *credible, believable, plausible*;
  kě kào de: 可靠的; *credible person/ organization*;
  kě xìn de: 可信的, *credible claim/ statement*;
  yǒu xī wàng de: 有希望的, *credible idea/policy*

CREMA; creme; *cream*;
  nǎi yóu: 奶油, *cream, butter*

CREMOSO (A); **cremoso** (A); *creamy*;
  guāng huá xì nì de: 光滑细腻的, *smooth, creamy*

CRETINO (A); **cretino** (A); *cretin (n), cretinous (adj)*;
  bái chī: 白痴, *idiot, idiocy*;
  bèn dàn (n): 笨蛋, *cretin, idiot, fool*

CRIMEN; crime; *crime*;
  zuì 'è (n): 罪恶, *crime, evil*;
  zuì guò (n): 罪过, *fault, offense*;
  zuì xíng (n): 罪行, *crime, criminal acts, offense*

CRÍPTICO (A); **enigmático** (A); *cryptic, obscure, inscrutable*;
  lìng rén fèi jiě de: 令人费解的, *inscrutable*;
SEE (请查看) ARCANO

CRÍQUET; críquete, *(the game)*; **grilo,** *(the insect)*; *cricket*;
  bǎn qiú: 板球, *cricket (the game)*;

xī shuài: 蟋蟀, *cricket (the insect)*

CRISTAL; cristal; *glass, crystal*;
  bēi zi: 杯子, *cup; glass*;
  bō li (n): 玻璃, *glass; glasslike*;
  bō li bēi (n): 玻璃杯, *glass, tumbler*;
  jiǔ bēi (n): 酒杯, *wine cup/glass*;
  shuǐ jīng (n): 水晶, *crystal*;
  shuǐ jīng: 水晶, *crystal glass, vase*

CRITERIO; criterio; *criterion, standard, principal*;
  biāo zhǔn (n) (sv): 标准, *standard, criterion, norm; standard*;
  biāo zhǔn de: 标准的, *standard (practice, procedure, way, etc.)*;
  guī fàn de: 规范的, *standard (feature, model, etc.)*;
  pǔ tōng de: 普通的, *standard (size)*

CRÍTICA; crítica; *criticism, faultfinding, disapproval ... CRÍTICO* (A); **crítico** (A); **criterioso,** *selective; critic (n), critical (adj)*;
  pī píng jiā (n): 批评家, *critic*;
  pī píng xìng: 批评性, *criticism*;
  pī píng zhě (n): 批评者, *critic*;
  pī shì (v) (n): 批示, *to comment on; comments, critique*;
  pī yǔ: 批语, *criticism, commentary*;
  tiāo tì (v) (sv): 挑剔, *to nitpick/be hypercritical; picky, fastidious*;
SEE (请查看) CENSURA, DESAPROBACIÓN

CROMO; cromo; *chrome, chromium*;
  gè: 铬, *chromium, chrome*

CROMOSOMA; cromossomo; *chromosome*;
  rǎn sè tǐ: 染色体, *chromosome*

CRÓNICO (A); **crônico** (A); *chronic;* **inveterado,** *inveterate; ingrained; persistent, habitual*;
  jī xí nán gǎi (sv): 积习难改, *chronic liar/smoker, etc.*;
  màn xìng (sv): 慢性, *chronic illness*;
  xí guàn xìng (attr) (n): 习惯性, *habitual; inertia*;

yán zhòng (sv): 严重, *chronic, serious problem/ shortage, etc.*;
SEE (请查看) CONSTANTE, INVETERADO, PERSEVERANCIA

CRONOLÓGICO (A); cronológico (A); *chronological* ... CRONOLOGÍA; cronologia; *chronology*;
  àn shí jiān shùn xù de: 按时间顺序的, *chronological*;
  biān nián xué: 编年学, *chronology*;
  nián dài xué: 年代学, *chronology*

CRUDO; cru o crua, *raw; crude oil; crude, uncooked*;
  shēng de: 生的, *raw, uncooked*;
  shēng lěng: 生冷, *raw or cold food*;
  shēng shuǐ: 生水, *unboiled water*

CRUELDAD; crueldade; *cruelty*;
  cán rěn (sv): 残忍, *cruel, ruthless, cruelty*;
SEE (请查看) BRUTALIDAD, BRUTAL, BESTIA, ATROCIDAD

CUALIDAD; qualidade; *quality*;
  pǐn gé (n): 品格, *character; quality and style*;
  pǐn zhì: 品质, *character/quality of character; qualities*;
  tè xìng: 特性, *specific property/ characteristics*;
  tè zhì: 特质, *special qualities/ characteristics, peculiarities*;
  xìng zhì (n): 性质, *character, nature, quality*;
  zhì liàng: 质量, *quality; mass (FIS)*;
SEE (请查看) CALIFICACIÓN

CUALIFICADO; qualificado; *skilled, qualified*;
  lǎo liàn (sv): 老练, *experienced, skillful*;
  líng qiǎo (sv): 灵巧, *agile, nimble, skillful*;
  qīng qiǎo (sv): 轻巧, *skillful; handy*;
SEE (请查看) CALIFICADO

CUANTÍA; quantidade; *quantity; amount, extent*;
  dà liàng (n) (sv) (attr): 大量, *large*

quantity, mass; generous; voluminous;
  liàng: 量, *quantity*;
  shù mù: 数目, *number, amount*;
SEE (请查看) CUANTITATIVO

CUANTITATIVO (A); quantitativo (A); *quantitative*;
  dìng liàng (n) (v) (attr): 定量, *fixed quantity; to quantify; quantitative*;
  shù liàng (attr) (n): 数量, *quantitative; quantity, amount*

CUESTIÓN; questão; *question, matter* ... CUESTIONABLE; questionável; *questionable, debatable*;
  bù què dìng de: 不确定的, *questionable, indeterminate*
  kào bù zhù de: 靠不住的, *questionable, unreliable*;
  kě yí de: 可疑的, *questionable doubtful*;
SEE (请查看) DESCONFIANZA, DUDA, SUSPICACIA, PROBLEMÁTICO

CULPA; culpa; *fault, blame; guilt (DER)* ... CULPABILIDAD; culpabilidade; *guilt, culpability*;
  bù shì/bù shi (v) (n): 不是, *to not be; fault, blame*;
  cuò chù (n): 错处, *fault*;
  duǎn chù: 短处, *fault, weakness*;
  nèi jiù: 内疚, *guilt*;
  zuì jiù: 罪咎, *fault, error, offense*;
  zuì zé (n): 罪责, *guilt, responsibility*;
SEE (请查看) ACUSAR, DEFECTO, CRIMEN, FALACIA

CULTURA; cultura; *culture*;
  wén jiào (n): 文教, *culture and education*;
SEE (请查看) CIVILIZACIÓN, EDUCADO

CUOTA; cota; *quota, share*;
  dìng 'é (n) (v): 定额, *quota; to have a certain quantity*;
  fèn 'é (n): 份额, *share, portion*;
  míng 'é (n): 名额, *quota (of people)*;
  pèi 'é (n): 配额, *quota*;

xiàn 'é (n): 限额, *quota, ration; limit;*
zhǐ biāo (n): 指标, *target, quota;*
indicator; index

CUPÓN; cupon; *coupon, voucher;*
piào jù (n): 票据, *bill; receipt; voucher;*
píng dān (n): 凭单, *voucher;*
píng zhèng (n): 凭证, *evidence, proof;*
voucher

CÚPULA; cúpula; *dome, cupola;*
gǒng dǐng (n): 拱顶, *vault; dome;*
yuán dǐng (n): 圆顶, *dome;*
yuán wū dǐng (n): 圆屋顶, *dome*

CURACIÓN; cura; *treatment (MED);*
cure, healing;
liáo fǎ: 疗法, *medical cure;*
yào wū: 药物, *medicine;*
zhì liáo: 治疗, *cure, medical treatment*

CURIOSIDAD; curiosidade;
raridade, *a rarity; curiosity,*
inquisitiveness ... **CURIOSO** (A);
curioso (A); *curious, inquisitive; prying;*
ài dǎ ting (vp) (sv): 爱打听, *to be*
inquisitive; snoopy, nosy;
gǔ dǒng (n): 古董, *curios;*
hào qí (sv): 好奇, *curious, inquisitive;*
hào qí xīn (n): 好奇心, *curiosity;*
xī qí (sv): 稀奇, *strange, curious;*
xī shǎo (sv): 稀少, *few, rare, scarce;*

xī yǒu (sv) (n): 稀有, *rare, unusual;*
rarity

CURVATURA; curvatura; *curvature* ...
CURVA; curva; *bend, curve* ... **CURVO**
(A); **curvo** (A); *curved;*
qū xiàn (n):曲线, *curve, curvature;*
wān qū bù fen:弯曲部分, *curve in a*
road, bend in a pipe;
wān qū chù: 弯曲处, *bend in a road/*
pipe, etc.
wān qū (sv): 弯曲, *curved, bent;*
winding, meandering;
wān (sv) (v) (n): 弯, *bent, curved,*
crooked; to bend/flex; turn, curve;
wān (bf) (v): 湾, *bend in a stream/gulf/*
bay; to anchor/moor/tie up

CUSTODIA; custódia; *custody, care,*
safekeeping ... **CUSTODIO** (A); **guarda;**
custodian;
bǎo guǎn rén: 保管人, *custodian,*
trustee;
jiān hù: 监护 , *guardianship;*
kān guǎn (v) (n): 看管, *to guard/look*
after; custodian;
kān shǒu (v) (n): 看守, *to guard; jailer;*
mén wèi: 门卫, *guard, custodian;*
zhào gu (v) (n): 照顾, *to look after/care*
for; custody, safekeeping;
SEE (请查看**) DEFENSOR**

Easily recognizable verbs and their Portuguese and Chinese equivalents
Verbos fácilmente reconocibles en Español-Portugués-Inglés y sus
equivalentes en Chino
Verbos facilmente reconhecível em Espanhol-Português-Inglês e seus
equivalentes em Chinês
很容易辨认的西班牙语，葡萄牙语，英语动词和他们的中文对等词

CALCULAR; calcular; *to calculate/*
work out;
jì suàn (v) (n): 计算, *to count/calculate;*
consideration, planning

CALIBRAR; graduar; *to mark out;*
calibrar, *to adjust; to calibrate, gauge,*
measure;
jiào zhǔn: 校准, *to adjust/calibrate;*
liáng: 量, *to measure*

CANCELAR; cancelar; *to cancel/pay/*
settle/pay off;
fù qīng (rv): 付清, *to pay in full;*
huán qīng (rv): 还清, *to pay off, to pay*
in full;
SEE (请查看**) ANULAR**

CAPITALIZAR; capitalizar; *to*
capitalize, capitalize on;
lì yòng: 利用, *to use; to exploit; to take*
advantage of;

zì běn huà (v) (n): 资本化, *to capitalize; capitalization*

CAPTURAR; capturar; *to capture/ seize;*
  jiǎo huò: 缴获, *to capture/seize;*
  fǎn yìng: 反应, *to capture the mood;*
  fú lǔ: 俘虏, *to capture a person;*
  zhàn yǒu: 占有, *to capture market share; to own/ have;*
  SEE (请查看) ASALTAR, ATRAPAR

CARACTERIZAR; caracterizar; *to characterize;*
  miáo huì ... de tè zhēng: 描绘 ... 的 特征

CATEGORIZAR; categorizar; *to classify; to categorize;*
  fēn bān: 分班, *to divide into classes;*
  fēn biàn: 分辨, *to distinguish/ differentiate;*
  fēn duàn: 分段, *to segment;*
  fēn jí: 分级, *to sort/classify/grade;*
  fēn lèi: 分类, *to classify/sort;*
  guī lèi (v) (n): 归类, *to sort out/classify; categorization;*
  guī rù: 归入, *to classify/assign;*
  SEE (请查看) CLASIFICAR

CAUSAR; causar; *to cause/make;*
  dǎo zhì: 导致, *to produce/cause/lead to;*
  (shǐ) fā shēng: (使) 发生, *to happen/ occur/take place;*
  yǐn qǐ: 引起, *to give rise to, to lead to; to draw, attract*

CELEBRAR; celebrar; *to celebrate;*
  gē sòng: 歌颂, *to extol/eulogize;*
  qìng zhù: 庆祝, *to celebrate;*
  zàn měi: 赞美, *to praise/eulogize*

CENTRALIZAR; centralizar; *to centralize;*
  jí zhōng dào zhōng yāng: 集中到中 央, *to centralize;*
  SEE (请查看) AGRUPAR, CONCENTRACIÓN

CERTIFICAR; certificar; *to assure, to affirm; to certify;*
  zhèng míng (v) (n): 证明, *to prove/ testify/bear out; certificate, proof, identification, testimonial;*
  SEE (请查看) APROBACIÓN

CIVILIZAR; civilizar; *to civilize;*
  jiào huà (v) (n): 教化, *to enlighten / civilize people by education; culture;*
  kāi huà: 开化, *to become civilized*

CLAMAR; clamar; *to exclaim/clamor for/cry out;*
  chǎo chǎo nào nào de yāo qiú: 吵吵闹闹的要求;
  hǎn jiào: 喊叫, *to shout, to cry out;*
  hǎn yuān: 喊冤, *to cry out about a harm/wrong;*
  hū háo: 呼号, *to wail/cry out in distress;*
  hū jiù: 呼救, *to call for help;*
  jīng jiào: 惊叫, *to cry out in fear;*
  qiú jiù: 求救, *to ask/cry for help*

CLASIFICAR; classificar; *to classify, sort;*
  bá ... fēn lèi: 把 ...分类, *to sort;*
  SEE (请查看) CATEGORIZAR, CENTRALIZAR

COEXISTIR; coexistir; *to coexist (POL);*
  gòng cún: 共存, *to coexist*

COHESIONAR; unificar; *to unite/draw together;*
  lián hé (v) (n): 联合, *to unite/ally; alliance, union, coalition;*
  tuán jié (v) (n): 团结, *to unite/rally; agglomeration*

COINCIDIR; coincidir; *to coincide;*
  tóng shí fā shēng: 同时发生, *to coincide*

COLABORAR; colaborar; *to cooperate; to collaborate/contribute;*
  chuàn tōng: 串通, *to collaborate/ collude/conspire;*
  gōu jié: 勾结, *to collude/collaborate with;*

hé móu: 合谋, *to conspire/plot*;
hù lián: 互连, *to interconnect*;
hù zhù: 互助, *to cooperate/help each other*;
juān zhù: 捐助, *to offer assistance/ help; to contribute*;
SEE (请查看) ASISTIR, CONSORCIO

COLECCIONAR; colecionar; *to collect*;
cǎi fēng: 采风, *to collect folks songs*;
cáng shū (v) (n): 藏书, *to collect books; book collection*;
còu he: 凑合, *to gather together, to collect*;
huì biān: 汇编, *to compile, to collect*;
huì jí: 汇集, *to collect/compile; to converge, to come together*;
shōu cáng: 收藏, *to collect, to store*;
shōu fèi: 收费, *to collect fees*;
sōu jí: 搜集, *to collect/gather*;
tí qǔ: 提取, *to collect/pick up*;
zhēng jí: 征集, *to collect; to draft/call up; to recruit*;
SEE (请查看) AGRUPAR

COLISIONAR; colidir; *to collide*;
chù dòng: 触动, *to collide with*;
zhuàng chē: 撞车, *to collide (vehicles); to clash*;
SEE (请查看) CONFLICTO, COLISIÓN

COMBATIR; combater; *to struggle, to fight*;
dǎ jià: 打架, *to fight, to scuffle, to come to blows*;
fèn dòu: 奋斗, *to struggle, to fight, to strive for*;
zhēng dòu: 争斗, *to fight, to struggle*;
zhēng duó: 争夺, *to fight/struggle for*;
zhēng qǔ: 争取, *to strive/fight for*;
zhēng zhá: 挣扎, *to struggle*;
zuò zhàn: 作战, *to fight, to battle*;
SEE (请查看) DENUNCIAR

COMENTAR; comentar; *to comment on, discuss*;
píng lùn (v) (n): 评论, *to comment on, discuss; comment, commentary; review*;

yì lùn (v) (n): 议论, *to debate/discuss; discussion*

COMETER; cometer; *to commit/carry out*;
fàn zuì: 犯罪, *to commit a crime/ offense*;
jìn xíng: 进行, *to carry out, to conduct*;
luò shí: 落实, *to carry out, to make sure*;
nòng xū zuò jiǎ (fe): 弄虚作假, *to commit fraud*;
tuī xíng: 推行, *to carry out, to implement*;
zuò 'àn: 作案, *to commit an offense*;
SEE (请查看) ACTUAR, APLICAR, EJECUTIVO

COMISIONAR; comissionar; *to entrust; to commission*;
shòu tuō: 受托, *to be commissioned*;
tuō fù: 托付, *to entrust/commit to the care of*;
wěi rèn: 委任, *to appoint*;
xìn tuō: 信托, *to trust/entrust*;
SEE (请查看) DELEGAR, CONSIGNAR

COMPARAR; comparar; *to compare*;
bǐ jiào (v) (adv): 比较, *to compare, to contrast, relatively, comparatively; rather*;
bǐ nǐ (v) (n): 比拟, *to match, to compare; comparison, metaphor*;
bǐ zhào: 比照, *to contrast/base sthg on*;
duì bǐ: 对比, *to contrast, to balance*;
lèi bǐ: 类比, *to compare; analogy*;
qiè cuō: 切磋, *to compare notes/learn through discussion*;
xiāng bǐ: 相比, *to compare with, to contrast*;
SEE (请查看) ANTÍTESIS

COMPELER; compelir; *to force sb to do sthg; to compel*;
bèi pò: 被迫, *to be forced/compelled*;
pò shǐ: 迫使, *to oblige; to force/ compel*;
SEE (请查看) MANDATO

COMPENSAR; compensar; *to compensate*;
  péi cháng (v) (n): 赔偿, *to compensate, to pay for; to make amends; reparations*;
  péi kuǎn (v) (n): 赔款, *to pay reparations; reparations*;
  péi zhàng: 赔账, *to pay for a loss/ damage*;
SEE (请查看) **COMPENSACIÓN, REMEDIAR**

COMPETIR; competir; *to compete with or against*;
  bǐ sài (v) (n): 比赛, *to compete; game, match*;
  jiāo fēng: 交锋, *to compete, to combat*;
  jìng zhēng (v) (n): 竞争, *to compete; competition*;
  jìng: 竞, *to compete, to contend*;
  jué zhú: 角逐, *to compete, to contest*;
  kàng héng: 抗衡, *to compete, to contend with/ against*

COMPILAR; compilar; *to compile*;
  biān jí (v) (n): 编辑, *to edit/compile; editor, compiler*;
  biān xiě: 编写, *to compile*;
  biān zào: 编造, *to compile, to draw up; to invent, to fabricate*;
  biān zhù: 编著, *to compile*;
  biān zuǎn: 编纂, *to compile, to edit*;
  zhù shù: 著述, *to write, to compile*;
SEE (请查看) **ÍNDICE, COLECCIONAR**

COMPLETAR; completar; *to complete/finish*;
  jié shù: 结束, *to end, to finish*;
  sǎo wěi: 扫尾, *to finish, to wind up*;
  wán bì: 完毕, *to complete, to finish*;
  wán gōng: 完工, *to finish (doing sthg), to complete sthg*;
  wán jié: 完结, *to finish, to conclude*;
  wán shì: 万事, *to finish (doing sthg), to be done/ settled*;
SEE (请查看) **DECIDIR, CONCLUIR**

COMPLICAR; complicar; *to complicate/worsen; to involve/implicate*;
  bìng fā: 并发, *to be complicated by*;

(shǐ) fù zá huà (v): (使) 复杂化, *to make sthg complicated, to complicate*;
(shǐ) juǎn rù (vp): (使) 卷入, *to be drawn into; be involved in*;
(shǐ) qiān lián (vp): (使) 牵连, *to involve/implicate sb; to tie up with/ integrate with*;
  shǐ fù zá: 使复杂, *to entangle*;
SEE (请查看) **DETERIORAR**

COMPUTAR; computer; *to compute/ calculate*;
  dǎ suàn (v) (sv): 打算, *to plan, to calculate; to intend; intention, calculation*;
  huá suàn (v): 划算, *to calculate/weigh/ consider*;
  jì shù: 计数, *to count, to calculate*;
  jì suàn: 计算, *to compute, to calculate; to consider, to plot/plan*;
  tuī suàn: 推算, *to calculate/estimate/ reckon*;
  yǎn suàn: 演算, *to calculate (MAT), to work out*;
  yùn suàn: 运算, *to calculate*

COMUNICAR; comunicar; *to link; to convey/inform*;
  bào gào (v) (n): 报告, *to report, to inform; report*;
  biǎo dá: 表达, *to express sthg, to convey*;
  biǎo shì (v) (n): 表示, *to express, to show, to indicate; feelings/attitude/ emotions*;
  dǎ zhāo hu: 打招呼, *to inform/notify; to greet*;
  gào zhī: 告知, *to inform, to notify*;
  shū sòng: 输送, *to transfer, to convey*;
  sù yuān: 诉冤, *to inform*;
  tōng zhī (v) (n): 通知, *to notify, to inform; notice, circular*;
  zhuǎn dá: 转达, *to pass on, to convey*;
  zhuǎn gào: 转告, *to transmit, to pass on a message, etc.*;
  zhuǎn jiāo: 转交, *to transmit, to pass on*;
  zhuǎn shù: 转述, *to pass on a message/story/ account, etc.*;
SEE (请查看) **INFORMAR,**

NOTIFICAR, AVISAR, BOLETÍN, CONDUCTA

CONCENTRAR; concentrar; *to think/ concentrate; to assemble;*
  nóng suō: 浓缩, *to concentrate on, to center on; to enrich (QUIM);*
  quán shén guàn zhù (fe): 全神贯注, *to concentrate and be entirely engrossed in sthg; undivided attention;*
  xiǎng tōng: 想通, *to think things through;*
  xiǎng: 想, *to think;*
  yǐ wéi: 以为, *to think, to believe;*
  zhuān zhù: 专著, *to concentrate on;*
  zhuó xiǎng: 着想, *to consider, to think about;*
SEE (请查看) **AGRUPAR, CONSIDERACIÓN, CONCENTRACIÓN**

CONCERNIR; concernir; *to concern;*
  cāo xīn (v) (sv): 操心, *to worry about/ be concerned over; concerned;*
  guà niàn (v) (n): 挂念, *to be concerned/ worried about; concern;*
  guān huái (v) (n): 关怀, *to be concerned for; concern, care;*
  guān qiè (v) (sv): 关切, *to be deeply concerned; considerate, thoughtful;*
  guò wèn: 过问, *to be concerned with/ take an interest in;*
  xiāng gān (v) (n) (attr): 相干, *to be concerned with; to have to do with; relevance; relevant;*
  yǒu guān: 有关, *to concern, to be relevant;*
SEE (请查看) **APRENSIÓN**

CONCILIAR; conciliar; *to reconcile/ harmonize;*
  gān xīn: 甘心, *to be reconciled to; to be compensated/satisfied;*
  hé hǎo: 和好, *to reconcile/be at peace with;*
  pái jiě: 排解, *to reconcile; to intervene/ mediate;*
SEE (请查看) **DECIDIR, INTERMEDIAR**

CONCLUIR; concluir; *to conclude/ finish/complete;*
  duàn dìng: 断定, *to conclude, to determine;*
  guī jié: 归结, *to summarize, to conclude;*
  guī nà: 归纳, *to conclude, to sum up;*
  shōu chǎng (v) (n): 收场, *to wind up; to end up; ending;*
  shōu pán: 收盘, *to close (a deal); to declare an end to (a contest, etc.);*
  shōu wěi: 收尾, *to conclude/wind up;*
  tián xiě: 填写, *to complete;*
SEE (请查看) **COMPLETAR, FINALIZAR, ULTIMAR**

CONDENSAR; condenser; *to condense;*
  yā suō (v) (n): 压缩, *to condense/ reduce/compress; compression, shortening;*
SEE (请查看) **CONCENTRAR**

CONECTAR; conectar; *to connect;*
  jiē hé: 接合, *to connect, to assemble, to link;*
  xiāng lián: 相连, *to link, to connect;*
  xiāng tōng: 相通, *to be interlocked/ connected;*
SEE (请查看) **CONECCIÓN**

CONFERIR; conferir; *to confer;*
  shòu yǔ: 授予, *to confer sthg on sb;*
  xié shāng (v) (n): 协商, *to confer with; agreement*

CONFESAR; confessor; *to confess/ admit/ acknowledge;*
  gòng rèn: 供认, *acknowledge/accept;*
  zì gòng: 自供, *to confess;*
SEE (请查看) **ACEPTAR, ADMITIR**

CONFINAR; confinar; *to confine, to isolate; to banish, exile;*
  (shǐ) gé lí (sv) (v) (attr): (使) 隔离, *isolated; to isolate; isolating;*
  gé jué: 隔绝, *to isolate/completely cut off;*
  jú xiàn (sv) (v) (n): 局限, *limited; to confine; restriction;*

liú fàng (v): 流放, *to banish/exile*;
qū zhú (v): 驱逐, *to expel/get rid of*;
xiàn zhì (v) (n): 限制, *to confine/*
be confined/restrict; restriction,
confinement, limit;
SEE (请查看) APREHENDER,
CONFINAMIENTO

CONFIRMAR; confirmar; *to confirm*;
rèn kě: 认可, *to approve of/endorse; to*
confirm;
SEE (请查看) APROBACIÓN,
AFIRMAR, DETERMINAR

CONFISCAR; confiscar; *to confiscate*;
mò shōu (v) (n): 没收, *to confiscate;*
confiscation

CONFORMAR; conformar; *to*
conform/shape;
zūn zhào: 遵照, *to comply with/*
conform to;
zūn zhǒu: 遵守, *to comply/conform/*
abide by

CONGRATULAR; congratular; *to*
congratulate;
gōng xǐ (n) (fe): 恭喜, *congratulations*;
zhù hè (v) (n): 祝贺, *to congratulate;*
congratulations;
SEE (请查看) FELICITAR

CONGREGAR; congregar; *to*
assemble/congregate;
huì hé: 会合, *to meet, to congregate*;
SEE (请查看) AGRUPAR

CONJETURAR; conjeturar; *to guess/*
surmise; conjecture;
cāi cè: 猜测, *to guess/speculate*;
tuī cè: 推测, *to infer/surmise*;
tuī dǎo: 推导, *to infer/deduce*;
tuī lǐ: 推理, *to infer/reason*;
tuī xiǎng: 推想, *to imagine/guess*;
SEE (请查看) CONJETURA

CONSENTIR; consenter; *to allow/*
permit/tolerate;
gū xī: 姑息, *to indulge/appease/*
tolerate;

yīng yǔn (v): 应允, *to consent/assent*;
SEE (请查看) ACOMODAR,
ASENTIR, AUTORIZAR

CONSERVAR; conservar; *to preserve/*
sustain/retain;
bǎo cáng (v) (n): 保藏, *to store/*
preserve; preservation;
SEE (请查看) CONSERVACIÓN

CONSIDERAR; considerar; *to*
consider;
xiǎng: 想, *to think/consider*;
SEE (请查看) CONSIDERACIÓN

CONSIGNAR; consignar; *to consign/*
send;
jì shòu: 寄售, *to consign for sale*;
tuō mài: 托卖, *to consign sthg for sale*
to sb;
wěi tuō: 委托, *to trust/entrust/*
commission
yùn sòng: 运送, *to transport/convey*

CONSISTIR; *to consist*;
bāo kuò: 包括, *to include/ consist of; to*
comprise; to incorporate;
yóu ... zǔ chéng: 由...组成, *to consist*;
zài yú: 在于, *to consist in; to depend*
on;
SEE (请查看) CONTENER

CONSOLAR; consolar; *to console/*
comfort;
fǔ wèi: 抚慰, *to comfort/console/*
soothe;
SEE (请查看) CONSOLACIÓN,
COMFORT

CONSOLIDAR; consolidar; *to*
consolidate/strengthen;
gǒng gù: 巩固, *to consolidate/*
strengthen/solidify;
jiā qiáng: 加强, *to strengthen/*
augment/reinforce

CONSPIRAR; conspirer; *to conspire/*
plot;
mì móu: 密谋, *to conspire/plot/*
scheme;
tú móu (v) (n): 图谋, *to conspire; to*

plot/scheme

CONSTITUIR; constituir; *set up/ constitute;*
  chéng: 成, *to become/turn into; (bf) to accomplish/ succeed; result; developed; established; capable, able; whole*
  gòu chéng (v) (n): 构成, *to constitute/ form/ compose/make up; formation;*
SEE (请查看**) FORMATIVO**

CONSULTAR; consultar; *to look up/ consult/see;*
  chá yuè: 查阅, *to look sthg up;*
  qǐng jiào: 请教, *to consult*

CONSUMAR; consumar; *to complete/ consummate;*
  shí xiàn: 实现, *to realize (a goal)/ achieve sthg/ bring sthg about;*
SEE (请查看**) COMPLETAR, CONCLUIR**

CONSUMIR; consumer; *to consume;*
  xiāo fèi (v) (n): 消费, *to consume; consumption;*
  xiāo hào (v) (n): 消耗, *to consume/use up, to deplete*

CONTAMINAR; contaminar; *to contaminate/pollute;*
  zhān wū: 沾污, *to contaminate; to make dirty/soil;*
SEE (请查看**) CONTAMINACIÓN**

CONTEMPLAR; contemplar; *to contemplate/gaze at;*
  wán wèi: 玩味, *to ponder, to contemplate;*
  zhù shì: 注视, *to gaze at/watch attentively;*
SEE (请查看**) CONTEMPLACIÓN**

CONTENER; conter, *to control, to contain ...* **CONTROLAR; controlar;** *to control;*
  bǎ chí: 把持, *to dominate, to control, to monopolize;*
  bǎi bù: 摆布, *to arrange, to control, to order;*
  bāo hán (v) (n) (sv): 包含, *to contain/*

embody/ include; inclusion; inclusive;
  bāo róng: 包容, *to pardon/ forgive; to contain/hold;*
  jià yù: 驾驭, *to control/drive a car/ boat, etc.;*
  jié zhì: 节制, *to command, to control;*
  qiān zhì: 牵制, *to pin sb down, to control/restrain; to restrict;*
SEE (请查看**) ACTUAR, ADMINISTRAR**

CONTENTAR; contentar; *to please/ keep happy;*
  gāo xìng: 高兴, *to please*

CONTINUAR; continuar; *to continue/ carry on;*
  jì xù (v) (adv): 继续, *to continue/to go on; continually;*
SEE (请查看**) PERSEVERANCIA**

CONTRARRESTAR; neutralizer; *to counteract;*
  dǐ kàng: 抵抗, *to resist/stand up to;*
SEE (请查看**) CORRECCIÓN**

CONTRIBUIR; contribuir; *to contribute to or towards;*
  gòng xiàn (v) (n): 贡献, *to contribute/ dedicate/ devote; contribution*

CONVERGER; convergir; *to converge;*
  huì hé: 汇合, *to meet;*
SEE (请查看**) APROXIMAR, CONCENTRACIÓN**

CONVERSAR; converser; *to talk/ converse;*
  jiǎng huà (v) (n): 讲话, *to speak, to talk; speech;*
  shuō (v) (n): 说, *to say/speak; to explain; theory, doctrine;*
  shuō huà (v) (n): 说话, *to speak/talk; speech, conversation;*
  yán tán (v) (n): 言谈, *to speak, to talk; manner of speech;*
SEE (请查看**) ALTERNAR, COMENTAR, CONVERSACIÓN**

CONVERTIR; converter; *to convert (RELIG); transform sb/sthg;*
  shǐ gǎi biàn: 使改变, *to change, transform;*
  shǐ zhuǎn biàn: 使转变, *to convert (RELIG);*
SEE (请查看) **ALTERAR**

CONVIVIR; conviver; *to coexist; to live together;*
  gòng cún (v): 共存, *to coexist;*
  tóng fáng: 同房, *to have sex, to live together, to sleep together;*
SEE (请查看) **COEXISTENCIA**

CONVOCAR; convocar; *to convene/ call;*
  kāi huì (v): 开会, *to hold/attend a meeting;*
  zhào huàn: 召唤, *to summon/call;*
  zhào jí: 召集, *to convene/assemble/ summon*

COOPERAR; cooperar; *to cooperate with/collaborate;*
  hé zuò (n) (v): 合作, *cooperation, to cooperate;*
SEE (请查看) **COLABORAR, COLABORACIÓN**

COORDINAR; coordenar; *to coordinate;*
  jiē yìng: 接应, *to coordinate with sb; to back up sb;*
SEE (请查看) **COORDINACIÓN**

COPIAR; copier; *to copy/reproduce; to imitate;*

chāo xí: 抄袭, *to plagiarize;*
  chāo xiě: 抄写, *to copy by hand/ transcribe;*
  fǎng zào: 仿造, *to copy/be modeled on;*
  mó fǎng (v) (n): 模仿, *to imitate/copy; imitation;*
SEE (请查看) **DUPLICADO**

CORROBORAR; corroborar; *to corroborate;*
  zhèng shí: 证实, *to confirm, to verify;*
SEE (请查看) **APROBAR, CONFIRMAR, ASENTIR, RATIFICAR, APROBACIÓN, CONFIRMACIÓN**

CRITICAR; criticar; *to review/criticize;*
  píng lùn (v) (n): 评论, *to discuss/ comment on; comment, review, commentary;*
SEE (请查看) **CRÍTICO, CRÍTICA, CENSURA, COMENTAR**

CUALIFICAR; qualificar; *to qualify;*
  hé gé (v) (n): 合格, *to qualify; qualified;*
SEE (请查看) **CALIFICADO**

CUANTIFICAR; quantificar; *to quantify/assess;*
  liàng huà: 量化, *to quantify;*
SEE (请查看) **CUANTITATIVO**

CULPAR; culpar; *to blame;*
  fēi nàn: 非难, *to blame, to censure;*
  guī jiù: 归咎, *to blame;*
  mán yuàn: 埋怨, *to blame, to complain, to grumble;*
SEE (请查看) **ACUSAR**

Interchangeable Spanish-Portuguese-English words and their Chinese equivalents
Palabras en Español-Portugués-Inglés y sus equivalentes en Chino
Palavras em Espanhol-Português-Inglês e seus equivalentes em Chinês
西班牙语，葡萄牙语，英语及中文的对等单词

DEBATE; debate;
  biàn lùn (v) (n): 辩论, *to argue/debate; argument, debate;*
SEE (请查看**) CONTROVERSIA**

DEBUT ó DÉBUT; debut;
  shǒu cì yǎn chū: 首次演出, *debut*

DEBUTANTE; debutante; *rookie, beginner, novice;*
  chū xué zhě: 初学者, *beginner;*
  shēng shǒu: 生手, *sb new/unfamiliar to a job, tyro; beginner, novice*
  xīn shǒu: 新手, *rookie; new hand, raw recruit; novice*

DECIMAL; decimal;
  shí jìn xiǎo shù: 十进小数, *decimal;*
  xiǎo shù diǎn: 小数点, *decimal point;*
  xiǎo shù: 小数, *decimal*

DÉFICIT; déficit;
  bù zú de: 不足的, *deficiency, lacking;*
  chì zì: 赤字, *deficit;*
  kuī kōng (n) (v): 亏空, *deficit, debt; to be in debt;*
  qiàn zhài (v): 欠债, *to owe a debt;*
  quē fá (n) (v): 缺乏, *deficiency, deficiencies; to be short of/ lack;*
  quē shǎo de (v) (n): 缺少的, *to lack; be short of*
  zhài wù (n): 债务, *debt, liabilities*

DELTA; delta (GEOL); *the letter; also delta (GEOL);*
  sān jiǎo zhōu: 三角洲, *delta (GEOL)*

DETECTOR; detector;
  tàn cè qì: 探测器, *detector, probe*

DIABETES; diabetes;
  táng niào bìng: 糖尿病, *diabetes*

DIAGONAL; diagonal;
  duì jiǎo xiàn: 对角线, *diagonal (MAT);*
  qīng xié de: 倾斜的, *diagonally;*
  xié de: 斜的, *diagonal;*
  xié wén: 斜纹, *diagonal (weave, pattern, design)*

DIESEL; diesel;
  chái yóu: 柴油, *diesel oil;*
  nèi rán jī chē: 内燃机车, *diesel locomotive;*
  nèi rán jī: 内燃机, *diesel engine*

DIGITAL (INFORM)**; digital** (GEN)**;** *finger;*
  shù mǎ: 数码, *numeral, digital;*
  shù zì de: 数字的, *digital;*
  shù zì: 数字, *number, finger, digit*

DIPLOMA; diploma;
  bì yè zhèng shū: 毕业证书, *diploma;*
  wén píng: 文凭, *diploma*

DIVISOR (MAT)**; divisor** (A)**;**
  chú shù: 除数, *divisor (MAT)*

DÚO; duo;
  yī duì biǎo yǎn zhě: 一队表演者, *duo, twosome (in a play/act);*
  yī duì: 一对, *a twosome; duo;*
  yī shuāng: 一双, *two, twin, both*

DÚPLEX; duplex;
  fù shì gōng yù fáng: 复式公寓房, *duplex;*
  lián shi fáng wū: 联式房屋, *duplex*

Easily recognizable Spanish-Portuguese-English nouns, adjectives and adverbs and their Chinese equivalents
Nombres, sustantivos, adjetivos y adverbios en Español-Portugués-Inglés y sus equivalentes en Chino
Nomes, substantivos, adjetivos e advérbios em Espanhol-Português-Inglês e seus equivalentes em Chinês
容易辨认的西班牙语，葡萄牙语，英语的名词，形容词和副词和他们的中文对等词

DÁTIL; data; *date (the fruit);*
  hǎi zǎo (BOT): 海枣, *date palm, date*

DÉBIL; débil; *feeble, weak, faint;*
  dàn (sv): 淡, *tasteless, weak; thin, light; pale;*
  dān bó (sv): 单薄, *frail, weak;*
  méi jìn (sv): 没劲, *exhausted;*
  ruǎn ruò (sv): 软弱, *weak, feeble;*
  ruò xiǎo (sv): 弱小, *weak and small;*
  ruò zhì (sv): 弱智, *feeble mind;*
  shuāi lǎo (sv): 衰老, *old and feeble, decrepit;*
  wēi ruò (sv): 微弱, *faint, feeble, weak;*
  wú lì (vp) (sv): 无力, *incapable, powerless;*
  wú néng (sv): 无能, *unable, powerless;*
SEE (请查看) DEFICIENCIA, DEFICIENTE, ABATIDO

DEBILIDAD; debilidade; *weakness, feebleness;*
  bó ruò: 薄弱, *weakness of a system;*
  pí ruǎn: 疲软, *weakness of an economy;*
  quē diǎn: 缺点, *shortcoming, defect; weakness;*
  ruò diǎn (n): 弱点, *shortcoming; weakness; failing;*
SEE (请查看) ABATIDO

DEBILITACIÓN; debilitação; *weakening;*
  shǐ shuāi ruò de: 使衰弱的, *feeble, weakened;*
  shǐ xū ruò de: 使虚弱的 *debilitating;*
  shuāi (bf): 衰, *to decline/wane; feeble, declining*

DÉBITO; débito; *debit, debt;*
  qiàn kuǎn (v) (n): 欠款, *to owe money; debt;*

  zhài kuǎn (n): 债款, *loan, debt;*
SEE (请查看) DÉFICIT

DÉCADA; década; *decade;*
  shí nián: 十年, *decade*

DECADENCIA; decadência; *decline, decay, decadence;*
  tuí táng (vp): 颓唐, *decrepit, failing; dejected;*
SEE (请查看) CORRUPCIÓN

DECADENTE; decadente; *decadent, declining;*
  duò luò (v) (sv): 堕落, *to be corrupted; degenerate, decadent;*
  duò luò de: 堕落的, *degenerate;*
  tuí fèi de: 颓废的, *decadent*

DECENCIA; decência; *decency ...*
DECENTE; decente; *decent, upright, respectable;*
  shòu zūn zhòng de: 受尊重的, *decent, honest person;*
  tǐ miàn (n): 体面, *dignity, decent;*
  tǐ miàn de: 体面的, *decent;*
  zhèng pài (sv) (n): 正派, *upright, honest, decent; decency; original/real thing/brand;*
SEE (请查看) CORRECTAMENTE, CORRECTO, DIGNIDAD

DECEPCIÓN; decepção; *disappointment;*
  shī wàng (v) (n): 失望, *to lose hope/be disappointed; disappointment;*
  shī wàng de: 失望的, *disappointed;*
  sǎo xìng (v) (sv): 扫兴, *to be disappointed/ discouraged; disappointed, discouraged;*
  xiè qì (v) (sv): 泄气, *to lose heart/be disappointed; disappointing, frustrating;*

SEE (请查看) **FRUSTRACIÓN**

DECIBELIO; decibel; *decibel;*
  fēn bèi: 分贝, *decibel*

DECISIVO (A); **decisivo** (A); *decisive;*
  jiān dìng guǒ duàn de: 坚定果断的, *decisive manner;*
  jué dìng xìng (sv) (n): 决定性, *decisive battle/event, etc.; decisiveness;*
  jué zhàn (n): 决战, *decisive battle;*
  SEE (请查看) **CRUCIAL**

DECLARACIÓN; declaração; *written declaration; declaration;*
  xuān yán: 宣言, *declaration; manifesto; public announcement;*
  SEE (请查看) **ANUNCIAR, COMUNICADO**

DECLIVE; declive; *slope; incline, gradient; decline;*
  xié miàn (n): 斜面, *inclined plane;*
  xié pō (n): 胁迫, *slope, gradient*

DECORACIÓN; decoração; *decoration;*
  jiǎng zhāng: 奖章, *medal, decoration;*
  xūn zhāng: 勋章, *a medal;*
  SEE (请查看) **ADORNAR**

DECORO; decoro; *decorum, decency, dignity ...* **DECOROSO** (A); **decoroso** (A); *decent; decorous, dignified;*
  duān zhuāng (sv) 端庄, *elegant, dignified;*
  yōu yǎ (sv): 优雅, *in good taste;*
  zūn guì de: 尊贵的, *respected;*
  SEE (请查看) **DECENCIA, DECENTE, AUGUSTO**

DECRÉPITO (A); **decrépito** (A); *decrepit; declining;*
  lǎo ruò de: 老弱的, *decrepit;*
  shuāi lǎo: 衰老, *senile;*
  SEE (请查看) **DECADENCIA, DECADENTE, SENIL**

DEDICACIÓN; dedicação; *dedication, devotion, commitment;*

xiàn shēn: 献身, *dedication;*
  yì wū: 义务, *duty, obligation;*
  zhōng chéng (sv) (n): 忠诚, *devotion, loyal; loyalty, faithfulness*

DEDUCCIÓN; dedução; *deduction, conclusion ...* **DEDUCTIVO** (A); **dedutivo** (A); *deductive;*
  jié lùn (n): 结论, *deduction;*
  jié shù (v) (n): 结束, *to define; definition, explanation;*
  jié wěi (n): 结尾, *conclusion, end of sthg;*
  yǎn yì (n) (v): 演绎, *deduction; to deduce;*
  yǎn yì de: 演绎的, *deductive;*
  SEE (请查看) **DEDUCCIÓN**

DEFECTO; defeito; *defect, lack, fault, shortcoming ...* **DEFECTUOSO** (A); **defeituoso** (A); *defective, faulty;*
  guò cuò: 过错, *fault;*
  máo bìng: 毛病, *defect;*
  quē xiàn: 缺陷, *flaw, shortcoming;*
  yǒu quē diǎn de: 有缺点的, *defective;*
  SEE (请查看) **DEFICIENCIA, DEBILIDAD**

DEFENSIVO (A); **defensivo** (A); *defensive, justified, protective; excuse;*
  fáng wèi de: 防卫的, *defensive behavior;*
  fáng wèi yòng de: 防卫用的, *defensive;*
  fáng yù de: 防御的, *defensive weapons/measures;*

DEFENSOR (A); **defensor** (A); *defender, champion; defense attorney;*
  bǎo hù rén: 保护人, *a protector;*
  fáng yù zhě: 防御者, *defender;*
  wèi shì: 卫士, *bodyguard*

DEFERENCIA; deferência; *deference, respect;*
  jìng zhòng: 敬重, *respect, honor;*
  tīng cóng: 听从, *obedience;*
  zūn cóng: 遵从, *deference;*
  SEE (请查看) **AUGUSTO**

DEFICIENCIA; deficiência; *deficiency, shortcoming, defect* ... **DEFICIENTE; deficiente;** *deficient, lacking, inadequate;*
  bú gòu gé de: 不够格的, *inadequate;*
  quē fá zhèng (n): 缺乏症, *medical deficiency;*
  quē qiàn (n): 缺欠, *shortage, lack; defect; shortcoming;*
  quē shǎo (v) (n): 缺少, *to be short of; lack;*
SEE (请查看**) DÉBIL, DÉBITO, DECADENCIA, DEBILIDAD, DÉFICIT, DEFECTO**

DEFINICIÓN; definição; *explanation, decision, definition;*
  dìng yì (n) (v): 定义, *definition; to define;*
SEE (请查看**) DEDUCCIÓN**

DEFINIDO (A); **definido** (A); *defined, definite, clear; clearly defined;*
  míng què de: 明确的, *clear-cut, explicit; unequivocal;*
  qīng chè de: 清澈的, *clear;*
  què qiè de: 确切的, *definite;*
  wú yí (adv) (n): 无疑, *beyond a doubt; certainty;*
  wú yí de: 无疑的, *clear (obvious);*
  yī dìng (attr): 一定, *fixed, specified, definite, regular; certainly, surely, necessarily; given, particular, certain;*
  yī dìng de: 一定的, *definite;*
SEE (请查看**) DECISIVO, CONCRETO**

DEFINITIVO (A); **definitive** (A); *permanent; definitive, final, decisive;*
  chí jiǔ de: 持久的, *permanent relationship/ feature/solution;*
  jiǔ cháng (attr): 久长, *lasting, permanent, enduring;*
  yǒng jiǔ de: 永久的, *permanent, perpetual;*
  zuì hòu (vp) (adv): 最后, *last, final, ultimate; finally, ultimately;*
SEE (请查看**) DECISIVO, CONSTANTE**

DEGRADANTE; degradante; *demeaning; degrading, humiliating;*
  bēi liè (sv): 卑劣, *base, mean, despicable;*
  diū rén (sv): 丢人, *disgraceful;*
  ké chǐ (sv): 可耻的, *disgraceful, shameful;*
  pǐn zhì dī liè de: 品质低劣的, *degrading;*
  shǐ diū liǎn (sv): 使丢脸, *to be shamed, disgraced*

DELEITE; deleite; *delight, pleasure;*
  gāo xìng (sv): 高兴, *glad, happy;*
  lè qù (n): 乐趣, *delight, pleasure, joy;*
  lè shì: 乐事, *pleasure;*
SEE (请查看**) COMPLACIDO**

DELIBERACIÓN; deliberação; *deliberation, consideration, discussion;*
  shěn yì (n): 审议, *deliberation, consideration;*
SEE (请查看**) COLOQUIO, COMENTAR**

DELIBERADO (A); **deliverado** (A); *deliberate, considered; intentional;*
  cún xīn (v) (adv): 存心, *to intend; deliberately, intentionally;*
  gù yì (adv) (n): 故意, *deliberately, intentionally, on purpose; intention;*
  màn tiáo sī lǐ (fe): 慢条斯理, *deliberately, slowly and methodically;*
  xù yì (adv): 蓄意, *deliberately;*
SEE (请查看**) BENÉFICO**

DELICADO (A); **delgado** (A); *slim, slender; delicate, fine; exquisite; dainty;*
  jiāo nèn (sv): 娇嫩, *delicate;*
  jiāo yàn (sv): 娇艳, *delicate and charming;*
  jīng měi (sv): 精美, *exquisite, delicate;*
  jīng zhì (sv): 精致, *fine, exquisite, delicate;*
  měi wèi (attr): 美味, *dainty;*
  miáo tiáo (sv): 苗条, *slim, willowy;*
  qīng qiǎo (sv): 轻巧, *dainty, light, portable;*
  wēi miào (sv): 微妙, *delicate;*
  xì cháng (sv): 细长, *slender; long and thin;*

xì nì (sv): 细腻, *exquisite, fine and smooth*;

yōu měi (sv): 优美, *exquisite, graceful*;

SEE (请查看) ATENTO, AFABLE, CONSIDERADO

DELICIOSO (A); deleitoso (A); *delicious; delightful*;

hǎo chī (sv): 好吃, *tasty, delicious*;

SEE (请查看) DELEITE, DELICADO

DEMARCACIÓN; demarcação; *demarcation, area, district*;

jiè xiàn: 界限, *boundary; limits, bounds*

DEMOCRACIA; democracia; *democracy* ... DEMÓCRATA; democrata; *democratic (adj), Democrat (n)* ... DEMOCRÁTICO (A); democrático (A); *democratic*;

mín zhǔ: 民主, *Democracy*;

Mín zhǔ dǎng rén: 民主党人, *Democrat*;

mín zhǔ de: 民主的, *democratic*

DEMOLICIÓN; demolição; *demolition*;

bào pò (v) (n): 爆破, *to blow up, to demolish; demolition*;

cuī huǐ (n) (v): 摧毁, *demolition; to destroy, to wreck*;

SEE (请查看) ARRUINAR

DEMONIO; demônio; *devil, demon*;

è mó: 恶魔, *demon, evil*

DENIGRANTE; degradante; *degrading, insulting, denigrating*;

qīng miè de: 轻蔑的, *scornful, contemptuous*;

wǔ rǔ de: 侮辱的, *insulting*;

SEE (请查看) DEGRADANTE

DENSIDAD; densidade; *density, thickness*;

hòu dù: 厚度, *thickness*;

mì dù: 密度, *density, thickness*;

SEE (请查看) CONCENTRACIÓN

DENSO (A); denso (A); *thick trees, undergrowth; dense, heavy, thick*;

chóu mì (sv) (n): 稠密, *crowded, dense; density*;

cū (sv): 粗, *thick, coarse, crude; wide*;

hòu (sv): 厚, *thick*;

mào mì (sv): 茂密, *dense, thick (of vegetation)* ;

mì (sv) (bf): 密, *dense, thick; intimate, close; fine, meticulous; secret*;

mì jí de: 密集的, *dense*;

nóng (sv): 浓, *dense, thick, concentrated*;

nóng de: 浓的, *dense, thick*;

nóng yù: 浓郁, *dense (of a forest, etc.); rich (in color, fragrance, etc.)*;

SEE (请查看) DENSIDAD, CONCENTRACIÓN

DENTISTA; dentista; *dentist*;

yá chǐ de: 牙齿的, *dental*;

yá xiàn: 牙线, *dental floss*;

yá yī: 牙医, *dentist*

DENUNCIA; denúncia; *accusation, denunciation, condemnation*;

chì zé (n) (v): 斥责, *denunciation; to denounce, to rebuke*;

zhǐ kòng (n) (v): 指控, *accusation; to accuse sb, to charge sb*;

SEE (请查看) ACUSACIÓN

DEPARTAMENTO; departamento; *department, compartment*;

bù: 部, *department*;

chē xiāng: 车厢, *compartments*;

fēn gé jiān: 分隔间, *compartment*;

fēn zhī (n): 分支, *subdivision, branch*;

gé háng rú gé shān (fe): 隔行如隔山, *to be compartmentalized*;

gé jiān (n): 隔间, *partition; compartment*

DEPENDIENTE; dependente; *reliant; addicted; dependent, subordinate*;

shǔ dì (n): 属地, *dependency*;

shǔ yú (v) (n): 属于, *to belong to/be part of; dependent*;

suō shǔ (n): 所属, *subordinate, affiliation*;

xìn rèn (v) (n): 信任, *to trust/have confidence in; dependence*;

yī fù (v) (n) (sv): 依附, *to rely on/submit to/attach os to; dependence; dependent;*
yī lài (v) (n): 依赖, *to rely on/depend on; dependence*

DEPÓSITO; depósito; *deposit; depository; storage, warehouse, tank;*
  cāng kù: 仓库, *storage, warehouse;*
  dà róng qì: 大容器, *tank;*
  dìng jīn: 定金, *deposit, up front money;*
  kù fáng: 库房, *warehouse, storeroom*

DEPRAVADO (A); **depravado** (A): *depraved; corrupt; degenerate;*
  fū huà duò luò de (fe): 腐化堕落的, *become corrupt and degenerate;*
  shāng fēng bài sú (fe): 伤风败俗, *decadent customs;*
  tuí fèi (vp): 颓废, *dispirited, decadent, ruined, weakened;*
  tuí fèi qī (n): 颓废期, *decadence;*
  tuí fèi zhǔ yì (n): 颓废主义, *decadence;*
  tuì huà biàn zhì (fe): 蜕化变质, *become morally degenerate; transmutation;*
  tuì huà de (v) (n): 退化的, *to degenerate/atrophy/ deteriorate; deterioration, degeneration, atrophy*
  tuí sàng (sv): 颓丧, *dispirited, listless; decadent;*
SEE (请查看**) DECADENCIA, DECADENTE, CORRUPCIÓN, INMORAL**

DEPRECIACIÓN; depreciação; *depreciation;*
  zhé jiù: 折旧, *depreciation (ECON)*

DEPREDADOR (A); **depredador** (A): *predatory (adj), predator (n);*
  lüè duó zhě: 掠夺者, *plunderer, robber;*
  lüè duó: 掠夺, *to plunder, to rob, to pillage;*
  shí ròu de: 食肉的, *predatory;*
  shí ròu dòng wù: 食肉动物, *predator (animal)*

DESACOSTUMBRADO (A);

desacostumado (A); *unaccustomed, unusual;*
  bù xí guàn de: 不习惯的, *unaccustomed;*
  bù píng cháng de: 不平常的, *unusual*

DESAFORTUNADO (A); **desafortunado** (A): *unfortunate, unlucky;*
  bù jí lì (sv): 不吉利, *unlucky (things, event, etc.);*
  bù xìng yùn (sv): 不幸运, *unlucky (person);*
  kě xī (sv): 可惜, *regrettable, unfortunate;*
SEE (请查看**) ADVERSIDAD**

DESAGRACIADO (A); **deselegante**: *graceless, unattractive;*
  bù yōu měi: 不优美, *graceless;*
  měi yǒu mèi lì: 没有魅力, *unattractive person*

DESAGRADABLE; desagradável; *unpleasant, disagreeable;*
  bù yú kuài de: 不愉快的, *unpleasant person;*
  lìng rén bù kài de: 令人不快的, *disagreeable experience/smell;*
  lìng rén tǎo yàn (sv): 令人讨厌, *unpleasant person/ manner;*
  nán xiāng chǔ de: 难相处的, *disagreeable person;*
  shǐ rén bù yú kuài de: 使人不愉快的, *unpleasant job/experience;*
  tǎo xián (sv): 讨嫌, *disagreeable, annoying;*
SEE (请查看**) ANTIPATÍA**

DESAGRADO; desagrado; *displeasure;*
  bù kuài: 不快, *unhappy;*
  bù mǎn (n) (sv): 不满, *dissatisfaction; resentful, dissatisfied;*
SEE (请查看**) CÓLERA**

DESAMOR; desamor; *antipathy; coldness, indifference, apathy;*
  bù zài hu (sv) (v): 不在乎, *indifferent, uncaring; to not mind/care;*

bù zài yì (sv): 不在意, *to not mind; to slight; to pass over; to take no notice*;
dàn mò (sv): 淡漠, *indifferent, apathetic*;
dī xī (n): 低息, *low interest*;
lěng bǎn dèng (n): 冷板凳, *cold-shoulder, cold reception; a job/post of no consequence*;
lěng bīng bīng (sv): 冷冰冰, *cold in manner; ice-cold, icy, frosty*;
lěng kù (sv): 冷酷, *cruel and cold, unfeeling, callous*;
SEE (请查看) **ATONÍA, ANTIPATÍA, APATÍA**

DESANIMADO (A); **desanimado** (A); *despondent; downhearted, dejected*;
chuí tóu sàng qì (fe): 垂头丧气, *to be chest fallen/ dejected*;
chuí xià (v): 垂下, *to hang down*;
dī luò (vp): 低落, *low, downcast, depressed*;
jǔ sàng (sv): 沮丧, *despondent, dejected; depressed*;
qì něi (sv): 气馁, *discouraged, despondent*;
sàng qì (v) (sv): 丧气, *dejected; disheartened*;
shī hún luò pò (fe): 失魂落魄, *to be despondent*;
xiāo jí (sv): 消极, *negative, pessimistic; passive*;
yì yù (sv): 抑郁, *depressed, despondent*;
SEE (请查看) **ABATIDO, DECEPCIÓN**

DESAPASIONADO (A); **desapaixonado** (A); *impartial, dispassionate*;
chí píng (sv) (v): 持平, *unbiased, fair, impartial, just; to keep a balance, to stay level*
gōng dào (sv): 公道, *fair; impartial, reasonable*;
gōng píng (sv): 公平, *fair, impartial, just*;
gōng zhèng (sv) (n): 公正, *impartial, just, fair; impartiality*;
SEE (请查看) **CALMA**

DESAPROBACIÓN; desaprovação; *disapproval*;
bù tóng yì (n) (v): 不同意, *disapproval; to disapprove*;
bù zàn chéng (n) (v): 不赞成, *disapproval; to disapprove/not endorse*

DESARME; desarmento; *disarmament*;
cái jūn (n) (v): 裁军, *disarmament; to disarm*

DESASTRE; desastre; *accident, disaster ... ***DESASTROSO** (A);
desastroso (A); *disastrous, calamitous*;
chà zi (n): 岔子, *accident, trouble*;
chū shì (v) (n): 出事, *to have an accident; accident*;
huò hai (n) (v): 祸害, *disaster, to destroy/damage*;
huò hài (n): 祸害, *calamity*;
huǒ zāi (n): 火灾, *disastrous fire*;
shì gù (n): 事故, *mishap, accident*;
SEE (请查看) **CALAMIDAD, CALAMITOSO, AFLICCIÓN, APOCALIPSIS, CATÁSTROFE**

DESATENCIÓN; descortesia; *discourtesy; inattention ... ***DESATENTO** (A); **desatento** (A); *inattentive; heedless, careless, discourteous, unobservant, unmindful*;
bù kè qi de: 不客气的, *discourteous,*
bù lǐ mào (n) (sv): 不礼貌, *discourtesy; discourteous, impolite*;
bù zhù yì de: 不注意的, *inattentive, heedless*;
cǎo shuài de: 草率的, *careless, rash; sloppy*;
cū xīn de: 粗心的, *careless, thoughtless*;
dà yì (vp): 大意, *careless*;
diào yǐ qīng xīn de: 掉以轻心地, *heedlessly*;
hú luàn (adv): 胡乱, *carelessly, casually*;
lǎn sǎn (sv): 懒散, *lazy, careless*;
mǎ dà hā (fe): 马大哈, *scatterbrained, careless*;
mǎ hu (sv): 马虎, *careless, negligent, sloppy*;

màn bù jīn xīn (fe): 漫不经心, *careless, casual, negligent, absentminded*;
shū hu (v) (n) (sv): 疏忽, *to be careless/negligent; carelessness, negligence, oversight; negligent, careless*;
sōng xiè (sv) (v): 松懈, *inattentive, lax; to slacken*;
wú yōu wú lǜ: 无忧无虑, *insouciance, unconcern, carefree*;
xīn bù zài yān (fe): 心不在焉, *absentminded, inattentive*;
SEE (请查看) **DESAMOR, ATONÍA**

DESCARTABLE; descartável;
disposable;
yī cì xìng de: 一次性的, *disposable razor, lighter, diaper, etc.*

DESCENDENTE; decrecente;
descending; downward, diminishing;
jiǎn shǎo: 减少, *to reduce, to decrease*;
xiàng xià de: 向下地, *downward (s)*

DESCENSO; descida; *descent, drop*;
xià jiàng: 下降, *of an aircraft*;
xià pō (n) (v): 下坡, *of a mountain/hill, downhill path; to go downhill*;
SEE (请查看) **BANCO**

DESCONCERTANTE; desconcertante; *disconcerting*;
huāng (sv): 慌, *nervous, flustered, confused*;
huāng luàn (sv): 慌乱, *flustered, bewildered*;
huāng zhāng (sv): 慌张, *nervous, flustered*;
jiāo zào (sv): 焦躁, *fretful, impatient*;
xīn huāng (v) (sv): 心慌, *to be nervous; flustered*
SEE (请查看) **AGITACIÓN, AGITAR, BILIOSO, CONSTERNACIÓN, CONFUSO**

DESCONFIADO (A); **desconfiado** (A);
distrustful; suspicious, incredulous;
bù xiāng xìn de: 不相信的, *incredulous*;
huái yí (sv) (n) (v): 怀疑, *distrustful, skeptical; doubt, distrust; to doubt/distrust/suspect*;
qǐ yí de: 起疑的, *suspicious*

DESCONFIANZA; desconfiança;
distrust; mistrust; doubt, question;
bú xìn rèn: 不信任, *distrust, mistrust*;
yí lǜ (v) (n): 疑虑, *to doubt; doubt, misgivings*;
yí tuán (n): 疑团, *a maze of doubts/suspicions*;
yí yì (n): 疑义, *doubt; doubtful point/word*;
yí yún (n): 疑云, *misgivings, suspicions*;
SEE (请查看) **DESCONFIADO**

DESCONSIDERACIÓN;
indelicadeza; *thoughtlessness*;
bú tì bié rén zhuó xiǎng de: 不替别人着想的, *inconsiderate*;
bù tǐ tiē de: 不体贴的, *thoughtless*;
SEE (请查看) **DESATENTO, NEGLIGENCIA**

DESCONTENTO (A); **descontente;**
discontented, unhappy, dissatisfied;
bù kuài lè de: 不快乐的, *unhappy*;
bù mǎn qíng xù (n): 不满情绪, *feeling of dissatisfaction*;
bù mǎn yì de: 不满意的, *discontented, dissatisfied*;
bù zhòng yì (sv): 不钟意, *not to one's liking*;
chóu chàng (sv): 惆怅, *disconsolate*;
SEE (请查看) **DESAGRADO**

DESCONTROL; caos; *lack of control, chaos*;
luàn (sv) (n) (v): 乱, *disorderly, confused; chaos, riot, unrest; to confuse, to mix up*;
luàn hōng hōng (adj) (sv): 乱哄哄, *chaotic; noisy and disorderly*;
luàn zāo zāo (adv) (sv): 乱糟糟, *chaotic; in a mess*;
luàn zi (n): 乱子, *disturbance, trouble, disorder*;
SEE (请查看) **CAOS, CONFUSO**

DESCRÉDITO; descrédito; *discredit, disrepute*;
diū liǎn (v) (sv) (n): 丢脸, *to lose face*;

shame; shameful act;
huài míng (n): 坏名, *bad reputation*;
huài míng shēng (n): 坏名声, *disrepute*;
kě chǐ (sv): 可耻, *disgraceful, shameful, ignominious*;
sāng shī xìn yù (v) (n): 丧失信誉, *to bring discredit on sb; discredit*;
SEE (请查看) INSULTAR

DESCRIPCIÓN; descrição; *description* ... **DESCRIPTIVO** (A); **descritivo** (A); *descriptive*;
miáo shù (v) (n): 描述, *to describe; characterization*;
miáo xiě (v) (n) (sv): 描写, *to describe, to depict; description; descriptive*

DESDÉN; desdém; *distain, scorn, contempt; disgust; hatred*;
bēi bǐ (sv): 卑鄙, *contemptible*;
bēi xià (sv): 卑下, *base, menial*;
bǐ shì (v) (n): 鄙视, *to despise; disdain*;
miè (bf): 蔑, *disdain, scorn*;
miè shì (n) (v): 蔑视, *disdain, contempt; to ignore/ scorn/ despise; to flout*;
nǎo hèn: 恼恨, *to resent, to hate*;
ròu má (sv): 肉麻, *disgusting, sickening*;
zēng wù (v) (n): 憎恶, *to loathe/abhor; phobia*;
SEE (请查看) ABOMINACIÓN, DEGRADANTE, ANTIPATÍA, DENIGRANTE, ANIMOSIDAD

DESERCIÓN; deserção; *desertion (MIL), defection (POL)*;
bèi pàn zhě: 背叛者, *defection*;
táo bīng: 逃兵, *army deserter*

DESESPERACIÓN; desesperança; *despair, desperation* ... **DESESPERADO** (A); **desesperado** (A); *desperate, irritated; intense; hopeless; furious* ...
DESESPERO; desespero; *despair, despondency; desperation*;
jué wàng (v) (sv) (n): 绝望, *to give up all hope; to feel desperate; hopeless; desperation, despair*;
SEE (请查看) DECEPCIÓN,

DESANIMADO

DESFAVORABLE; desfavorável; *unfavorable*;
bù lì (sv): 不利, *unfavorable, detrimental*
liè shì (n): 劣势, *unfavorable situation*

DESHABITADO (A); **desabitado** (A); *uninhabited; empty, vacant*;
kōng (sv): 空, *empty, hollow*;
kōng dàng dàng (sv): 空荡荡, *absolutely empty, deserted, void*;
kōng dòng (sv): 空洞, *cavity, empty*;
kòng xì (n): 空隙, *gap, empty space, void, loophole*;
kōng xū (sv): 空虚, *empty, hollow, void*;
wú rén jū zhù de:无人居住的, *uninhabited*

DESHONESTO (A); **desonesto** (A); *dishonest*;
bù chéng shí de: 不诚实的, *dishonest person*;
bù zhèng dāng de: 不正当的, *dishonest, improper behavior*;
bù zhèng zhí: 不正直, *dishonest behavior/ practices*

DESHONRA (f); **desonra;** *dishonor; disgrace* ... **DESHONROSO** (A); **desonroso** (A); *dishonorable, shameful*;
bù duān (vp): 不端, *improper, dishonorable*;
bù guāng cǎi de: 不光彩的, *dishonorable person, behavior*;
SEE (请查看) DESCRÉDITO

DESIGNACIÓN; designação; *designation, appointment*;
rèn mìng: 任命, *appointment with a doctor, etc.*;
yuē huì: 约会, *appointment to a meeting*;
zhí wù: 职务, *appointment to a post/ position*

DESIGNIO; desígnio; *plan, design*;
shè jì (n) (v): 设计, *design, plan; to*

design/plan;
tú (bf): 图, *scheme, plan; attempt; intention*;
tú 'àn (n): 图案, *pattern, design*;
tú yàng (n): 图样, *pattern, design, draft*;
SEE (请查看) PLANIFICAR, PROPÓSITO, INTENCIÓN

DESIGUAL; desigual; *different; irregular; unfair; unequal, uneven ...*
DESIGUALDAD; desigualdade; *inequality*;
bù bǐ (vp): 不比, *to be unlike*;
bù děng (vp): 不等, *different, unequal*;
bù děng jià (n) (vp): 不等价, *unequal values*;
bù děng liàng (n): 不等量, *unequal quantity*;
bù gōng (sv): 不公, *unjust, unfair*;
bù gōng zhèng (n): 不公正, *injustice*;
bù guī zé (sv) (n): 不规则, *irregular, incorrect; irregularity*;
bù lèi (vp): 不类, *different; discrete*;
bù píng děng (n): 不平等, *inequality*;
bù tóng (sv): 不同, *unequal lengths, amounts, etc.; not alike, different; difference*;
liǎng yàng (sv): 两样, *different, distinct*;
yuān qū (n): 冤屈, *unfair treatment, injustice*;
yuān wang (v) (sv): 冤枉, *to be treated unfairly; to be falsely charged; not worthwhile*;
yuān yù (n) (v): 冤狱, *unjust charge/ verdict; to wrong sb*;
SEE (请查看) DISTINCIÓN, INCORRECTO

DESILUSIÓN; desapontamento; *disillusion, disappointment*;
huàn xiǎng (n) (v): 幻想, *disillusion; to be disillusioned*;
huī xīn sàng qì (fe): 灰心丧气, *to be disheartened; become discouraged*;
kǔ mèn (sv): 苦闷, *depressed, discouraged*;
lìng rén shī wàng de: 令人失望的, *disappointing*;

xǐng wù (n) (v): 醒悟, *disillusion; to wake up to reality*;
yōu yù (sv): 忧郁, *depressed, sullen*;
SEE (请查看) DECEPCIÓN, DESANIMADO, CONSTERNACIÓN

DESINFECTANTE; desinfetante; *disinfectant*;
xiāo dú jì: 消毒剂, *disinfectant*

DESINFORMACIÓN; desinformação; *misinformation, disinformation*;
jiǎ qíng bào: 假情报, *disinformation*

DESINTEGRACIÓN; desintegração; *disintegration, breakup*;
gù zhàng (n): 故障, *malfunction, breakdown*;
zhōng jié (n): 终结, *end, final stage; dissolution*;
SEE (请查看) COLAPSO

DESINTERÉS; desinteresse; *disinterest, impersonal ...*
DESINTERESADO (A); **desinteressado** (A); *unselfish, disinterested, indifferent*;
kè guān (n): 客观, *objectivity; objective, impersonal*;
kè guān de: 客观的, *impersonal*;
lěng mò de: 冷漠的, *indifferent*;
méi xìng qū: 没兴趣, *unconcerned, disinterest*;
wú sī de: 无私的, *disinterested, unselfish*;
SEE (请查看) DESAMOR

DESMEDIDO (A); **desmedido** (A); *immense; excessive; boundless*;
guǎng kuò (sv): 广阔, *vast, broad*;
guò duō (sv): 过多, *excessive*;
guò fèn (sv): 过分, *excessive, undue*;
jí duān (sv): 极端, *extreme*;
jù dà (sv) (n): 巨大, *immense, enormous, huge, tremendous; immensity*;
wú biān (vp): 无边, *boundless*;
wú xiàn (attr): 无限, *infinite, limitless, boundless*

DESMOTIVADO (A); **desmotivado**

(A); *unmotivated, uninspired, apathetic*;
  lěng dàn de: 冷淡的, *cold (to)*;
  quē fá gǎn qíng de: 缺乏感情的,
  apathetic;
**SEE (请查看) DESINTERÉS, APATÍA,
DESAMOR**

DESNUTRICIÓN; desnutrição;
malnutrition, undernourishment;
  yíng yǎng bù liáng (n) (vp): 营养不
  良, *malnutrition, undernourishment*;
  yíng yǎng bù zú (n) (vp): 营养不足,
  undernourishment, malnutrition

DESOBEDIENCIA; desobediência;
disobedience ... **DESOBEDIENTE;
desobediente;** *disobedient*;
  bù fú cóng (sv) (n): 不服从,
  disobedient; disobedience

DESOCUPADO (A); **desocupado** (A);
*idle; available; empty; free, unemployed;
unoccupied, vacant, unrestricted*;
  kòng xián (sv) (n): 空闲, *free; free/
  leisure time*;
  lǎn duò (sv): 懒惰, *lazy*;
  lǎn hàn (n): 懒汉, *lazybones, idler*;
  lǎn yáng yáng (sv): 懒洋洋, *lazy,
  lethargic*;
  méi yǒu yì yì (v) (sv): 没有意义, *to be
  meaningless*;
  shī yè (sv): 失业, *unemployed*;
  shī yè zhě: 失业者, *the unemployed*;
  xián (sv) (n): 闲, *not busy, idle; not in
  use; irrelevant; free/spare time*;
  xián sǎn (sv): 闲散, *idle, free*;
**SEE (请查看) DESHABITADO,
DESEMPLEADO, VACANTE,
DESOCUPADO**

DESODORANTE; desodorante;
deodorant;
  chú chòu jì: 除臭剂, *deodorant*

DESOLACIÓN; desolação; *sadness;
devastation; desolation, distress, grief* ...
DESOLADO (A); **desolado** (A); *sad;
devastated; desolate; shattered*;
  āi chóu (sv): 哀愁, *sad, sorrowful*;
  āi shāng (sv): 哀伤, *sad, heartbroken*;

āi sī (n): 哀思, *grief*;
bēi fèn (sv): 悲愤, *grief and anger*;
bēi kǔ (sv) (n): 悲苦, *sad and painful;
bitterness, grief*;
bēi liáng (sv) (n): 悲凉, *desolate,
forlorn; desolation*;
bēi qī (sv): 悲戚, *plaintive, mournful*;
bēi qiè (sv) (wr): 悲切, *mournful*;
bēi shāng (sv): 悲伤, *sad, sorrowful*;
bēi tòng (sv): 悲痛, *grieved, sorrowful*;
gǎn dào zhèn hàn de: 感到震撼的,
shattered, overwhelmed;
gū jì de: 孤寂的, *desolate, lonely*;
jí dù bēi 'āi: 极度悲哀, *grief-stricken*;
shāng (n) (sv) (v): 伤, *injury; sad, to
injure/harm/ hurt*;
shāng xīn de: 伤心的, *unhappy, sad*;
xīn suān (sv) (v): 心酸, *sad; to grieve*;
yōu chóu (sv): 忧愁, *worried, sad,
depressed*;
**SEE (请查看) DESILUSIÓN,
AFLICCIÓN, AFECTAR,
ADVERSIDAD, CONSTERNACIÓN,
APRENSIÓN, MELANCOLÍA**

DESORBITANTE; excesivo (A);
excessive; overwhelming;
  guò fèn de: 过分的, *excessive*;
  yā dǎo xìng de: 压倒性的,
  overwhelming (victory, majority, etc.);
  jí qí qiáng liè de: 极其强烈的,
  overwhelming (desire, sense of, etc.)

DESORDEN; desordem; *mess,
disorder, chaos* ... **DESORDENADO**
(A); **desarrumado** (A); *untidy; messy,
jumbled*;
  bù qí (sv): 不齐, *not neat, untidy*;
  bù zhěng jié de: 不整洁的, *untidy*;
  lā ta de: 邋遢的, *untidy person*;
  líng luàn de: 凌乱的, *untidy place*;
  líng luàn: 凌乱, *mess, untidiness*;
  luàn (sv) (n) (v): 乱, *disorderly,
  confused; chaos, riot; to confuse*;
  sǎn luàn (sv): 散乱, *messy, in disorder*;
  zá luàn (sv) (adv): 杂乱, *disorderly;
  pell-mell*;
**SEE (请查看) CAOS,
DESCRONTROL, CONFLICTIVO**

DESORIENTACIÓN; desorientação;
disorientation, confusion;
  hú li bā tū (vp): 糊理八涂, *confused, muddle-headed;*
SEE (请查看) **CAOS, CONFUSO, DESCONTROL**

DESPENSA; despensa; *pantry; larder, storeroom;*
  shí pǐn shì: 食品室, *pantry*

DESPREOCUPADO (A);
despreocupado (A); *carefree; unworried, unconcerned;*
  bù gǎn xìng qù de: 不感兴趣的, *unconcerned;*
  wú yōu wú lǜ de: 无忧无虑的, *carefree person*

DESPRESTIGIO; descrédito;
discredit, loss of prestige;
  sàng shī xìn yù: 丧失信誉, *discredit*

DESTILERÍA; destilaria; *distillery;*
  jiǔ chǎng: 酒厂, *brewery, winery, distillery*

DESTINO; destino; *destiny; fate; destination;*
  mìng yùn: 命运, *fate, destiny*

DESTRUCTIVO (A) (adj); **destrutivo**
(A); *destructive;*
  pò huài xìng de: 破坏性的, *destructive force, capacity;*
  yǒu wēi hài de: 有危害的, *destructive person*

DETALLADO (A); **detalhado** (A);
detailed, thorough ... **DETALLE;**
detalhe; *detail;*
  tòu chè (sv): 透彻, *penetrating, thorough;*
  xì jié: 细节, *details, particulars;*
  xiáng (bf): 详, *detailed, minute; clear, known;*
  xiáng jiě (v) (n): 详解, *explain in detail; detail;*
  xiáng jìn (sv): 详尽, *detailed, exhaustive;*

  xiáng qíng: 详情, *details, particulars; detailed information;*
  xiáng xì (sv): 详细, *detailed, minute;*
SEE (请查看) **COMPLETO**

DETECCIÓN; detecção; *perception, detection;*
  gǎn zhī néng lì: 感知能力, *perception;*
  fā xiàn: 发现, *detection of disease;*
  zhēn chá: 侦查, *detection of a secret*

DETENCIÓN; detenção; *arrest, detention; holdup, delay;*
  yán huǎn (v) (n): 延缓, *to delay/ postpone; delay;*
SEE (请查看) **APREHENDER**

DETERGENTE; detergente;
detergent;
  qīng jié jì: 清洁剂, *detergent;*
  qù gōu jì: 去垢剂, *detergent;*
  xǐ dí jì: 洗涤剂, *detergent;*
  xǐ yī fěn: 洗衣粉, *laundry detergent*

DETERMINACIÓN; determinação;
determination, decision;
  jué dìng (v) (n): 决定, *to decide, to resolve; decision, resolution;*
  jué xīn (n) (v): 决心, *determination, resolution; to be determined;*
  jué yì (n): 决议, *resolution*

DETERMINADO (A); **determinado**
(A); *certain, definite, determined;*
  bì rán (sv) (n): 必然, *inevitable, certain;*
  què qiè (sv): 确切, *definite, certain;*
SEE (请查看) **DEFINIDO, AFIRMAR, CONCRETO, CONFIRMAR**

DETERMINANTE (adj); **determinante;**
determinant (MAT); decisive; determinant;
  guǒ duàn (adj) (sv): 果断, *resolute, decisive;*
SEE (请查看) **DEFINIDO, DECISIVO**

DETONACIÓN; detonação;
detonation, explosion;
  bào zhà shēng: 爆炸声, *explosion (sound);*
  bào zhà: 爆炸, *explosion of a bomb*

DETRIMENTO; detrimento; *detriment*;
 sǔn hài: 损害, *detriment*

DEVALUACIÓN; desvalorização;
devaluation;
 biǎn zhí: 贬值, *devaluation*

DEVASTACIÓN; desvastação;
devastation;
 pò huài xìng: 破坏性, *destruction,
 devastation; destructiveness*;
 shǐ huáng liáng: 使荒凉, *devastation*;
SEE (请查看) **DEMOLICIÓN**

DEVOTO (A); **devoto** (A); *devout;
devotional*;
 qián chéng (sv) (n): 虔诚, *pious,
 devout; piety*

DIABÉTICO (A); **diabético** (A);
diabetic;
 táng niào bìng de: 糖尿病的,
 diabetic;
SEE (请查看) **DIABETES**

DIABLO; diabo; *devil*;
 mó guǐ: 魔鬼, *demon, monster, devil*;
 mó guài: 魔怪, *fiends, demons and
 monsters*

DIABÓLICO (A); **diabólico** (A);
diabolical;
 xiōng bào de: 凶暴的, *diabolical;
 fierce and brutal*;
SEE (请查看) **ABUSIVO, BRAVÍO**

DIÁFANO (A); **diáfano** (A); *diaphanous;
transparent, clear, crystal clear*;
 tòu míng (sv): 透明, *transparent, open,
 public*;
SEE (请查看) **CLARIDAD**

DIAGNÓSTICO; diagnóstico;
diagnosis;
 zhěn duàn: 诊断, *diagnosis*

DIAGRAMA; diagrama; *diagram*;
 tú jiě: 图解, *diagram*

DIALECTO; dialeto; *dialect*;

fāng yán: 方言, *dialect*

DIÁLISIS; diálise; *dialysis*;
 xuè yè tòu xī: 血液透析, *dialysis*

DIÁLOGO; diálogo; *dialogue (POL)*;
 duì huà: 对话, *dialogue*

DIAMANTE; diamante; *diamond*;
 líng xíng: 菱形, *diamond shape*;
 zuàn shí: 钻石, *a diamond*

DIÁMETRO; diâmetro; *diameter*;
 zhí jìng: 直径, *diameter*

DIARIO (A); **diário** (A); *daily, everyday*;
 měi rì de (adj): 每日的, *daily*;
 měi tiān de (adv): 每天地, *daily*;
 rì cháng de (adv): 日常地, *every day*

DIARREA; diarréia; *diarrhea*;
 fù xiè: 腹泻, *diarrhea*

DICCIÓN; dicção; *diction*;
 cuò cí: 措辞, *wording, diction*;
 wén cí: 文辞; *diction, language*

DICCIONARIO; dicionário; *dictionary*;
 cí diǎn: 词典, *dictionary*

DICIEMBRE; dezembro; *December*;
 shí èr yuè: 十二月, *December*

DICTADO; ditado; *dictation*;
 kǒu shù: 口述, *dictation*;
SEE (请查看) **DICTAR**

DICTADOR (A); **ditador** (A); *dictator*;
 dú cái zhě: 独裁者, *dictator, ruler;
 overbearing person*

DICTADURA; ditadura; *dictatorship*;
 dú cái guó jiā: 独裁国家, *dictatorship
 of a country*;
 dú cái zhèng fǔ: 独裁政府,
 dictatorship of a government

DIETA; dieta; *diet*;
 rì cháng yǐn shí: 日常饮食, *daily diet*;
 yǐn shí: 饮食, *diet*

DIFAMACIÓN; difamação, *slander; libel, defamation* ... **DIFAMATORIO** (A); **difamatorio** (A); *defamatory, slanderous;*
  chán bàng: 谗谤, *to defame, slander, calumniate;*
  fěi bàng wén (n): 诽谤文, *libel;*
  fěi bàng zhě (n): 诽谤者, *libeler, slanderer;*
  zhòng shāng (n) (v): 中伤, *defamation; to defame/ discredit; to slander;*
SEE (请查看) CALUMNIA, DIFAMAR

DIFERENCIA; diferença; *difference* ... **DIFERENTE; diferente;** *different, unlike, unique, dissimilar;*
  bù chéng bǐ lì (vp): 不成比例, *be disproportional;*
  bù xiàng (sv): 不像, *unlike;*
  bù xiāng róng (sv): 不相容, *incompatible;*
  chā (n): 差, *difference; deviation; mistake;*
  chā bié (n): 差别, *difference, contrast;*
  chā 'é (n): 差额, *difference/discrepancy (in a sum/quota, etc.);*
  chā jù (n): 差距, *difference, disparity, gap;*
  dú yī wú 'èr (fe): 独一无二, *unique, unparalleled;*
  fēn qí (n): 分歧, *difference, divergence;*
  lìng lèi (n) (adv): 另类, *different, special; out of the ordinary;*
  qū bié (v) (n): 区别, *to distinguish, to differentiate; difference;*
SEE (请查看) DESIGUAL, ATÍPICO, DESIGUAL, ANOMALÍA, DIVERGENCIA

DIFÍCIL; difícil; *difficult, hard* ... **DIFICULTAD; dificuldade;** *problem (GEN); difficulty, complexity; obstacle;*
  biè niu (n): 别扭, *awkward, difficult; uncomfortable;*
  fèi jiě (sv): 费解, *hard to understand; obscure;*
  fèi jìn (sv): 费劲, *needs great effort, strenuous;*
  fēng làng (n): 风浪, *hardships, difficulties;*

  kùn kǔ (sv): 困苦, *hard, difficult; in hardship;*
  kùn nan (sv) (n): 困难, *hard, difficult; poverty, problem, difficulty;*
  kùn nán: 困难, *difficult job, etc.;*
  nán (sv) (v): 难, *difficult, hard, troublesome; to be difficult/hard/ disagreeable/unpleasant; (pref) difficult, disagreeable; to make difficult/ difficulties;*
  nán 'áo (sv): 难熬, *difficult to endure;*
  nán bàn (sv): 难办, *hard to handle;*
  nán chán (sv): 难缠, *demanding;*
  nán chī (sv): 难吃, *unpalatable;*
  nàn chǔ (sv): 难处, *hard to get along with, hard to manage;*
  nán dòu (sv): 难斗, *difficult (of a person); tough;*
  nán duì fu de: 难对付的, *difficulty;*
  nán guān (n): 难关, *difficulty, crisis;*
  nán miǎn (sv): 难免, *hard to avoid;*
  nán nài (vp): 难耐, *hard to endure;*
  xīn láo (sv): 辛劳, *hard, laborious;*
  yí nán (sv) (n): 疑难, *difficult; problem;*
SEE (请查看) ARDUO, DESCONCERTANTE, AFLICCIÓN, CONTRATIEMPO

DIFUSO (A); **difuso** (A); *diffuse, widespread;*
  fēn bù (v) (n): 分布, *to be distributed; distribution;*
  fēn bù guǎng de: 分布广的, *widespread use/ practice/belief, etc.;*
  kuò sàn (v) (n): 扩散, *to spread, to scatter; diffusion;*
  kuò sàn de: 扩散的, *widespread;*
  pǔ biàn de: 普遍的, *widespread support/opposition, etc.;*
  sàn kāi de: 散开的, *diffuse*

DIGNATARIO (A); **dignitário** (A); *dignitary;*
  zhí wèi gāo de rén: 职位高的人, *dignitary*

DIGNIDAD; dignidade; *dignity, decency;*
  hé yí (n) (sv): 合宜, *decency, suitable, appropriate;*

SEE (请查看) AUGUSTO, CORRECTAMENTE, CORRECTO, DECENCIA, SOLEMNE

DIGNO (A); **digno** (A); *dignified, praiseworthy*;
  wěn zhòng: 稳重, *unruffled, calm and steady*;
SEE (请查看) AUGUSTO

DIGRESIÓN; digressão; *digression, deviation, detour*;
  piān chā: 偏差, *deviation, error*;
  piān xiàng (v) (n): 偏向, *to be partial to; deviation*;
  xián huà: 闲话, *gossip, digression*;
SEE (请查看) DIFERENCIA

DILATADO (A); **dilatado** (A); *dilated; extensive*;
  cū fàng (sv): 粗放, *extensive*;
  guǎng fàn (sv): 广泛, *extensive, wide-ranging*;
  kuān guǎng (sv): 宽广, *extensive, broad, vast*;
  kuān kuò (sv): 宽阔, *wide, broad; open-minded*;
  liáo kuò (sv): 辽阔, *vast, extensive*;
  màn cháng (sv): 漫长, *extensive, endless*;
SEE (请查看) COLOSAL, ESPACIOSO

DILEMA; dilema; *dilemma, predicament, quandary; impasse*;
  kùn: 困, *to surround, (bf) stranded, hard-pressed*;
  kùn jú (n): 困局, *predicament, difficult situation*;
  liǎng nán (vp): 两难, *unable to decide, be in a dilemma*;
  sǐ hú tòng: 死胡同, *impasse, dead end*;
  yóu yù bù dìng: 犹豫不定, *hesitate, remain undecided*
SEE (请查看) DIFÍCIL, ARDUO, CONFUSO, DESCONCERTANTE, DIFÍCIL

DILETANTE; amador; *amateur; dilettante, dabbler*;

wài háng (n) (sv): 外行, *amateur, layman, non-professional*;
yè yú ài hào zhě: 业余爱好者, *non-professional*;
yè yú de: 业余的, *amateur person*;
yì shù ài hào zhě: 艺术爱好者, *dilettante*

DILIGENCIA; diligência; *diligence ... DILIGENTE; diligente;* *diligent, attentive, careful, scrupulous*;
  jiǎn diǎn (sv): 检点, *careful/diligent in study; cautious/restrained in conduct*;
  qín fèn de: 勤奋的, *diligent worker*;
  tǐ tiē de: 体贴的, *polite, helpful person*;
  xì zhì (sv): 细致, *fastidious, meticulous, scrupulous; precise, intricate*;
  xiǎo xīn (v) (sv): 小心, *to be careful; careful*;
  zī zī bù juàn: 孜孜不倦, *diligently; assiduously*;
SEE (请查看) ATENCIÓN, APLICADO, CONCIENCIA

DIMINUTO (A); **diminuto** (A); *minute; tiny, minuscule, teeny, little*;
  wēi guān (sv): 微观, *microscopic*;
  wēi hū qí wēi: 微乎其微, *very little*;
  wēi xiǎo (sv): 微笑, *tiny, small, little*;
  wēi xíng: 微型, *mini, tiny*;
  xì xiǎo (sv): 细小, *tiny, minute; trivial, petty*;
SEE (请查看) PARTÍCULA

DINÁMICO (A); **dinâmico** (A); *dynamic, vigorous, lively, spirited*;
  huó yuè (sv) (v): 活跃, *brisk, active, dynamic; to enliven/animate/invigorate*;
  néng dòng (sv) (attr): 能动, *active, dynamic*;
SEE (请查看) VIVACIDAD

DINAMITA; dinamite; *dynamite*;
  gān yóu zhà yào: 甘油炸药, *dynamite*;
SEE (请查看) EXPLOSIVO

DINOSAURIO; dinossauro; *dinosaur (ZOOL)*;
  kǒng lóng: 恐龙, *dinosaur*

DIÓCESIS; diocese; *diocese*;

zhǔ jiào guǎn qū de: 主教管区的, *diocese*

DIPLOMACIA; diplomacia; *diplomacy;* **wài jiāo:** 外交, *diplomacy*

DIRECCIÓN; direção, *direction;* **endereço,** *address; domicile; direction;* **dì zhǐ:** 地址, *address;* **fāng xiàng:** 方向, *direction*

DIRECTO; direto (A) (GEN); *direct, straight, straightforward;* **bǐ zhǐ de:** 笔直的, *direct, straight;* **jiǎn dān de:** 简单的, *straightforward;* **SEE (请查看) INMEDIATAMENTE**

DIRECTOR (A); **diretor** (A); *governing, guiding;* **fāng zhēn:** 方针, *policy, guiding principle;* **tǒng zhì de:** 统治的, *governing;* **zhǐ dǎo** (v) (n) (sv): 指导, *to guide/ direct; direction, guidance; guiding*

DISCAPACIDAD; deficiência; *disability* ... **DISCAPACITADO** (A); **incapacitado** (A); *disabled, incapacitated;* **cán jí** (sv): 残疾, *disabled;* **cán jí rén:** 残疾人, *the disabled;* **shāng cán** (n): 伤残, *disability; (attr) wounded and disabled;* **SEE (请查看) IMPOSIBILITADO**

DISCIPLINA; disciplina; *discipline;* **fēng jì** (n): 风纪, *conduct and discipline;* **jì lǜ:** 纪律, *discipline of children, pupils;* **yuē shù** (n) (v): 约束, *control, restraint, domination; to control/restrain/bind/ dominate*

DISCÍPULO (A); **discípulo** (A); *disciple;* **mén tú:** 门徒, *disciple; follower;* **xìn tú:** 信徒, *believer; disciple; follower*

DISCONFORME (adj); **discordante; dissonante** (MUS); *incompatible, discordant;*

bù xiāng róng de: 不相容的, *incompatible;* **SEE (请查看) CONTRADICCIÓN**

DISCORDANCIA; discordância; *discord, disagreement* ... **DISCORDIA; discordia;** *discord, strife, dissension, clash;* **bù hé** (aux) (v) (n): 不和, *should not, ought not; does not conform to, is not compatible; discord* **jiū fēn** (n): 纠纷, *dispute, issue;* **lìng rén bù kuài de** (sv) (n): 令人不快的, *discord, displeasure;* **zhuàng jī** (v) (n): 撞击, *to ram, to dash against/ strike; clash;* **SEE (请查看) ARGUMENTAR, CONFLICTO, DIFERENCIA**

DISCOTECA; discoteca; *discotheque, disco;* **dí sī kē wǔ tīng:** 迪斯科舞厅, *disco*

DISCRECIÓN; discrição; *discretion* ... **DISCRETAMENTE; discretamente;** *discreetly, cautiously, prudently* ... **DISCRETO** (A); **discreto** (A); *discreet, sober; modest;* **jǐn shèn** (adv) (sv) (n): 谨慎, *cautiously; cautious, circumspect; discretion;* **shèn zhòng** (sv) (adv): 慎重, *cautious, discreet; cautiously, discreetly;* **zhèng zhòng** (sv): 郑重, *sober, serious;* **SEE (请查看) PRUDENCIA, DILIGENCIA**

DISCREPANCIA; discrepância; *difference, discrepancy;* **xiāng chà** (v) (n): 相差, *to differ; discrepancy* **SEE (请查看) DIFERENCIA, DIFERENTE**

DISCULPA; desculpa; *reason, explanation; excuse, apology;* **dào qiàn:** 道歉, *apology;* **SEE (请查看) EXCUSA**

DISENTERÍA; disenteria; *dysentery*;
lì jí: 痢疾, *dysentery*

DISERTACIÓN; discurso; *discourse*;
disertação, *dissertation*; *discourse*;
　lùn wén (n): 论文, *thesis, dissertation*;
　yǎn shuō (n) (v): 演说, *speech,*
　address; to deliver a speech

DISIDENTE; dissidente (n); *dissident*
(adj), dissenter (n);
　yì jǐ: 异己, *alien, outsider; dissident*

DISOLUTO (A); **dissoluto** (A);
dissolute, corrupt, degenerate;
　fàng dàng de: 放荡的, *dissolute*;
　làng dàng de: 浪荡的, *dissolute,*
　dissipated;
SEE (请查看) **DECADENCIA,**
DECADENTE, CORRUPCIÓN,
DEGENERAR

DISOLVENTE; solvente; *solvent*;
　róng jì: 溶剂, *chemical solvent*

DISPARIDAD; disparidade; *disparity*;
　xuán shū (sv): 悬殊, *greatly disparate,*
　different;
SEE (请查看 **DESIGUAL,**
DIFERENCIA

DISPENSARIO; dispensário;
dispensary, clinic;
　yào fáng: 药房, *dispensary*;
SEE (请查看) **CLÍNICA**

DISPERSO (A); **disperse** (A);
scattered; dispersed; unfocused;
　fēn (v) (n): 分, *to divide/separate/split;*
　separation;
　fēn suì (v) (sv): 粉碎, *to smash/crush/*
　scatter; broken to pieces, scattered;
　lí sàn (v) (attr): 离散, *to be dispersed/*
　scattered about;
　qī líng bā luò (fe): 七零八落, *to be*
　scattered here and there;
　sàn luàn (sv): 散乱, *scattered,*
　disordered;
　shū sàn (sv) (v): 疏散, *sparse,*
　scattered; to scatter;
　xī shū de: 稀疏的, *few and scattered,*
sparse;
SEE (请查看) **DESORDENADO,**
DISPERSAR

DISPOSICIÓN; disposição;
arrangement; layout, disposition;
　ān pái (v) (n): 安排, *to arrange/plan/fix*
　up; plan, arrangement;
　bù jú: 布局, *overall arrangement,*
　distribution;
　tiáo lǐ (n) (sv): 条理, *order,*
　arrangement, method; reasonable;
SEE (请查看) **ASENTIR**

DISPUTA; disputa; *dispute, argument*;
　lùn diǎn (n): 论点, *argument, thesis,*
　point at issue;
　zhēng zhí (n) (v): 争执, *dispute; to*
　dispute;
SEE (请查看) **CONFLICTO,**
ARGUMENTO, CONTROVERSIA,
ARGUMENTAR

DISTANCIA; distância; *distance*;
　jù lí: 距离, *distance between two*
　different places;
SEE (请查看) **REMOTO**

DISTANTE; distante; *distant*;
　jiǔ yuǎn: 久远, *distant past*;
　piān yuǎn (sv): 偏远, *remote, faraway*;
　yáo yáo (sv): 遥遥, *distant, faraway*;
　yuǎn de: 远的, *distant place*;
　yuǎn fāng de: 远方的, *distant relative*;
SEE (请查看) **DESMOTIVADO,**
REMOTO

DISTINCIÓN; distinção; *distinction,*
difference;
　gè bié (sv) (adv) (attr): 各别, *out of*
　the ordinary, peculiar, eccentric, distinct,
　different; separately,
　individually; individual, specific;
　gè bié (sv) (attr): 个别, *very few,*
　exceptional; specific, individual;
SEE (请查看) **DIFERENCIA,**
DIFERENTE, ATÍPICO, CLARIDAD,
CONCRETO, DESIGUAL,
DETERMINADO, APARENTE

DISTRACCIÓN; distração (GEN);

distraction; pastime, hobby;
  jīng shén huàn sàn: 精神涣散, *diversion*;
SEE (请查看**) HOBBY, RECREACIÓN**

DISTRIBUCIÓN; distribuição;
distribution, delivery;
  fēn fā: 分发, *distribution of food/ newspapers/ supplies, etc.;*
SEE (请查看**) DIFUSO**

DISTRITO; distrito; *district, precinct;*
  guǎn xiá qū: 管辖区, *various areas of a city;*
  qū yù: 区域, *administrative area;*
SEE (请查看**) ÁREA**

DISTURBIO; distúrbio; *riot, disturbance;*
  gān rǎo: 干扰, *upheaval, upset;*
  sāo luàn: 骚乱, *violent incident, disturbance;*
SEE (请查看**) CAOS, REBELIÓN**

DIVERGENCIA; divergência;
divergence; divide, fork, split;
  chā yì: 差异, *difference, divergence, discrepancy;*
SEE (请查看**) DIFERENCIA**

DIVERGENTE; divergente; *divergent; deviate, wander, digress;*
  piān xī (n): 偏析, *deflection, deviation;*
  qí tú: 歧途, *wrong path;*
SEE (请查看**) DIGRESIÓN, AMBIGÜEDAD**

DIVERSIDAD; diversidade; *diversity, difference, disparity;*
  duō yàng xìng (n): 多样性, *variety, diversity;*
SEE (请查看**) DIFERENCIA**

DIVERSO (A)**; diverso** (A)**;** *different, varied, diverse;*
  bù tóng de: 不同的, *distinct;*
  duō jí de: 多极的, *multipolar;*
  duō yàng (n): 多样, *many styles/kinds/ types;*
  duō yuán lùn (n): 多元论, *pluralism;*

duō zhǒng (n): 多种, *many kinds;*
  duō zhǒng duō yàng de: 多种多样的, *varied, diverse, manifold;*
  gè zhǒng (n): 各种, *various kinds/ types;*
SEE (请查看**) MULTILATERAL, VARIADO**

DIVERTIDO (A)**; divertido** (A)**;**
entertaining, enjoyable, amusing;
  dòu lè (sv) (v): 逗乐, *amusing; to seek pleasure/ amuse os/clown around;*
  fēng qù (n) (sv): 风趣, *humor, wit; interesting, funny, humorous;*
  hǎo xiào (sv): 好笑, *funny, laughable;*
  yǒu lè qù de: 有乐趣的, *enjoyable;*
  yǒu yì si (sv) (v): 有意思, *significant, meaningful, interesting, enjoyable, amusing; to have the intention to do sthg;*
  yú lè (n) (sv): 娱乐, *amusement, entertainment, recreation; entertaining*

DIVIDENDO; dividendo; *dividend;*
  hóng lì: 红利, *dividend*

DIVORCIADO (A)**; divorciado** (A)**;**
divorced;
  lí yì de: 离异的, *divorced*

DIVULGACIÓN; divulgador (A)**;**
revelation, disclosure;
  jiē fā (n) (v): 揭发, *disclosure; to disclose;*
  jiē lù (n) (v): 揭露, *disclosure, revelation; to expose/ unmask/ferret out;*
  xiǎn lù (n) (v): 显露, *disclosure, revelation; to appear/reveal/unveil;*
  xiè lù (n) (v): 泄露, *disclosure; to leak/ divulge;*
SEE (请查看**) INTERPRETAR**

DÓCIL; dócil; *docile, obedient ...*
DOCILIDAD; docilidade; *obedience, docility;*
  fú cóng (v) (n): 服从, *to obey; obedience;*
  fú tiē (sv): 服贴, *docile, submissive;*
  tīng huà (v) (sv): 听话, *to obey;*

obedient;
xùn fú (sv) (v): 驯服, *docile, tractable, to tame*

DOCUMENTACIÓN; documentação; *documentation* ... **DOCUMENTAL; documentário;** *documentary* ... **DOCUMENTO; documento;** *document*;
 jì lù piàn: 纪录片, *documentary*;
 wén jiàn: 文件, *document*;
SEE (请查看) **CERTIFICADO**

DOGMÁTICO (A); **dogmático** (A); *dogmatic*;
 jiào tiáo (sv) (n): 教条, *dogmatic; dogma, doctrine*;

DÓLAR; dólar; *dollar*;
 yuán: 圆, *dollar*

DOMICILIO; domicilio; *home, residence, address*;
 tōng xùn chù: 通讯处, *address*;
 zhù zhái: 住宅, *residence*;
 zhù zhǐ: 住址 *address*

DOMINANTE; dominante; *dominant, prevailing*;
 shèng qì líng rén de: 盛气凌人的, *domineering*;
 yōu shì (n): 优势, *superiority, dominance*;
 zhàn yōu shì (sv) (v): 占优势, *preponderant, prevailing; to gain the upper hand*;
 zhàn zhǔ dǎo dì wèi: 占主导地位, *dominant person/role, etc.*;
 zhī pèi de: 支配的, *dominant*;
 zhǔ dǎo de: 主导的, *prevailing view, opinion, etc.*;
SEE (请查看) **PREDOMINAR, CONQUISTA, PRINCIPAL, PREPOTENCIA**

DRAMÁTICO (A); **dramático** (A); *exciting; dramatic*;
 xì jù xìng de: 戏剧性的, *dramatic*;
SEE (请查看) **AGITACIÓN, AGITAR, DESCONCERTANTE, INSPIRAR**

DRÁSTICO (A); **drástico** (A); *drastic*;
 guò jī (sv) (n): 过激, *drastic, extreme; extremist*;
 jù liè (sv): 剧烈, *drastic, violent, fierce*;
 měng liè (sv): 猛烈, *fierce, violent, drastic*;
SEE (请查看) **RIGOR**

DROGA; droga; *illegal substance*;
 dú pǐn: 毒品, *narcotics, drugs*

DUDA; dúvida; *doubt*;
 huái yí lùn (n): 怀疑论, *skepticism*;
 huái yí pài (n): 怀疑派, *doubter, unbeliever*;
 yí wèn (n): 疑问, *doubt; question*;
 yí xīn (n) (v): 疑心, *suspicion; to suspect*;
SEE (请查看) **DESCONFIADO, DESCONFIANZA, CUESTIÓN**

DUELO; duelo; *duel*;
 jué dòu: 决斗, *duel*

DUNA; duna; *dune*;
 shā qiū: 沙丘, *sand dune*

DUPLICADO (A); **duplicata;** *duplicate, identical, matching*;
 chóng fù (v) (n): 重复, *to duplicate/repeat sthg; repetition, reduplication*;
 fù zhì (v) (n): 复制, *to duplicate, to reproduce; clone*;
 fù zhì pǐn: 复制品, *replica, reproduction*;
 léi tóng (v) (sv): 雷同, *to echo, to duplicate; identical*;
 tóng yī (sv): 同一, *same, identical*;
 wán quán xiāng tóng: 完全相同, *identical*;
 wěn hé (sv) (v): 吻合, *identical; to coincide*;
 xiāng tóng (v) (attr) (n): 相同, *to be alike/identical/ equivalent; homo-; identity, similarity*;

DUPLICIDAD; duplicidade; *duplicity, deceitfulness, deceptiveness*;
 kǒu shì xīn fēi (fe): 口是心非, *hypocritical*;

qī piàn xìng: 欺骗性, *duplicity, fraudulent nature*;
wěi shàn (sv): 伪善, *hypocritical*;
xū nǐ (v) (sv): 虚拟, *to be invented; fictitious*;
SEE (请查看) HIPÓCRITA, BURLAR, HIPOCRESÍA, INSIDIOSO

DURABILIDAD; durabilidade; *durability*;
nài yòng de: 耐用的, *durable*

DURACIÓN; duração; *length (time), duration*;
chì xù shí jiān: 持续时间, *process, course*;
qī jiān (n): 期间, *time, period, duration*

DURADERO (A); **duradouro** (A); *lasting; long-lasting, hard-wearing ...*
DURO; duro (GEN), *harsh, hard, tough; stiff, firm, stale*;

bù xīn xiān de: 不新鲜的, *stale*;
cháng qī (n): 长期, *long-lasting; long-term*;
cū cāo de: 粗糙的, *harsh*;
jiān gù de: 艰巨的, *tough, firm, solid, sturdy*;
jiān gù: 坚固, *sturdy*;
jiān shí de: 坚实的, *solid substantial*;
láo gù de: 牢固的, *firm, secure, durable*;
nài jiǔ de: 耐久的, *durable, long-lasting*;
yìng bāng bāng de: 硬邦邦的, *rock hard*;
yìng (sv) (adv): 硬, *hard, stiff, firm; doggedly*;
yìng dù: 硬度, *hardness*;
SEE (请查看) DEFINITIVO, DURABILIDAD

DURANTE; durante; *during*;
zài ... qī jiān: 在期间, *during*

Easily recognizable verbs and their Portuguese and Chinese equivalents
Verbos fácilmente reconocibles en Español-Portugués-Inglés y sus equivalentes en Chino
Verbos facilmente reconhecível em Espanhol-Português-Inglês e seus equivalentes em Chinês
很容易辨认的西班牙语，葡萄牙语，英语动词和他们的中文对等词

DATAR; datar; *to date/date back/date from*;
gěi ... zhù míng rì qī: 给...注明日期, *to date a letter/check, etc.*;
què dìng ... de nián dài: 确定...的年代, *to date an event/object*

DEBATIR; debater; *to debate/discuss*;
shāng liang: 商量, *to discuss, to consult*;
SEE (请查看) ARGUMENTAR, ARGUMENTO, COLOQUIO, CRITICAR, COMUNICADO, COMENTAR, CONSIDERACIÓN

DECIDIR; decidir; *to decide/settle/resolve*;
chǔ lǐ: 处理, *to solve (a problem), to handle, to deal with*;
hé jiě: 和解, *to settle differences*;

jié qīng: 结清, *to settle, to square up*;
jié suàn: 结算, *to settle up*;
jué duàn (v) (n): 决断, *to decide, to resolve; resolution*;
liǎo què: 了却, *to settle, to solve*;
pàn dìng: 判定, *to decide, to determine*;
pàn duàn: 判断, *to judge, to determine; judgment*;
píng pàn: 评判, *to judge, to decide*;
qīng suàn: 清算, *to settle, to resolve; to expose*;
qīng zhàng: 清账, *to settle an account*;
SEE (请查看) ASENTIR, BLOCAR, DETERMINACIÓN

DECLARAR; declarar; *to declare*;
xuān bù (v) (n): 宣布, *to declare/proclaim/ announce; statement*;
SEE (请查看) ANUNCIAR

DECLINAR; declinar; *to decline;*
 xiè jué (v) (adv): 谢绝, *to refuse/
decline; politely*

DECORAR; decorar; *to decorate;*
 zhuāng shì (v) (n): 装饰, *to decorate/
adorn; ornament;*
**SEE (请查看) ADORNAR,
ORNAMENTAR**

DEDICAR; dedicar; *to dedicate;*
 fèng xiàn: 奉献, *to dedicate*

DEFENDER; defender; *to defend/
champion;*
 fáng yù (v) (n): 防御, *to defend/guard;
defense*

DEFINIR; definir; *to define, describe;*
 miáo huì: 描绘, *to draw, to describe;*
 xiě zhēn (v) (n): 写真, *to describe
accurately; portrait;*
 xíng róng (v) (n): 形容, *to describe;
look, appearance;*
**SEE (请查看) DEFINICIÓN,
DESCRIPCIÓN, INTERPRETAR,
DELIMITAR**

DEFORMAR; deformar; *to deform/
distort;*
 biàn xíng (v) (n): 变形, *to
become deformed/be out of shape;
transformation, modification;*
 niǔ qū (v): 扭曲, *to distort;*
 wāi qū shì shí (v): 歪曲事实, *to distort
the facts;*
SEE (请查看) ALTERAR

DEFRAUDAR; defraudar; *to defraud;
to disappoint, cheat, defraud;*
 hǒng piàn: 哄骗, *to cheat;*
 hù nòng: 糊弄, *to fool;*
 piàn qǔ: 骗取, *to worm away into sb's
trust/cheat by false pretenses;*
 piàn: 骗, *to deceive/fool/hoodwink/
cheat;*
 zhà piàn: 诈骗, *to swindle;*
SEE (请查看) DUPLICIDAD, BURLAR

DEGENERAR; degenerar; *to
degenerate;*

shuāi tuì (v) (n): 衰退, *to fail/decline;
recession;*
 tuì huà (v) (n): 退化, *to degenerate/
deteriorate; atrophy*

DELEGAR; delegar; *to delegate;*
 wěi pài: 委派, *to appoint/delegate;*
SEE (请查看) COMISIONAR

DELIBERAR; deliberar, *to decide,
to ponder over; to deliberate/debate/
discuss;*
 shāng yì: 商议, *to confer/discuss;*
 sī lǜ: 思虑, *to consider carefully;*
 zǐ xì kǎo lǜ: 仔细考虑, *to ponder over/
deliberate;*
**SEE (请查看) DECIDIR,
ARGUMENTO, CONTEMPLACIÓN,
CONSIDERACIÓN, CONTEMPLAR**

DELIMITAR; delimitar; *to define, set
limits, delimit;*
 xiàn dìng: 限定, *to prescribe/limit/
restrict*

DELINEAR; delinear; *to outline/
delineate;*
 kè huà: 刻画, *to depict/portray/
characterize;*
 kè huà chū (rv): 刻画出, *to depict/
portray;*
**SEE (请查看) DESCRIPCIÓN,
INTERPRETAR , GENERALIZAR**

DEMANDAR; demandar; *to sue,
demand;*
 qǐ sù: 起诉, *to sue;*
 yāo qiú (v) (n): 要求, *to demand sthg;
demand, request*

DEMOSTRAR; demonstrar; *to prove/
demonstrate/ show;*
 lùn zhèng (v) (n): 论证, *to expound/
prove; argument, demonstration, proof*

DENOTAR; denotar; *to indicate/
denote/show;*
 biāo zhì (n) (v): 标志, *sign, symbol; to
symbolize, to indicate;*
 shì ... de fú hào: 是...的符号, *to
denote;*

shì lì (v) (n): 示例, *to give an example; example;*
shì yì: 示意, *to signal, to hint, to indicate;*
zhǐ míng: 指明, *to show clearly, to indicate;*
zhǐ shì (v) (n): 指示, *to indicate, to point out; directive, instructions;*
SEE (请查看) COMUNICAR

DENUNCIAR; denunciar; *to report/ expose/denounce;*
chì (bf): 斥, *to scold/reprimand; to loudly rebuke;*
dòu zhēng: 斗争, *to denounce, to accuse; to fight, to strive for;*
kòng zuì: 控罪, *to charge, to accuse;*
qiǎn (bf): 谴, *to denounce/censure;*
shēng tǎo: 声讨, *to condemn, to denounce;*
wèn zuì: 问罪, *to denounce;*
zé mà: 责骂, *to scold/rebuke;*
zhǐ chì: 指斥, *to denounce, to rebuke;*
SEE (请查看) ACUSAR, DENUNCIA, ACUSACIÓN, REPRIMENDA

DEPENDER; depender; *to depend;*
píng zhàng: 凭仗, *to rely on;*
zhǐ kào: 指靠, *to depend on;*
SEE (请查看) CONSISTIR, INDICAR, DEPENDIENTE

DEPLORAR; deplorar; *to lament; to deplore/regret;*
hòu huǐ: 后悔, *to regret/repent;*
qiàng liè fǎn duì: 强烈反对, *to deplore;*
tòng xī: 痛惜, *to deeply regret, deplore;*
yī liàn: 依恋, *to regret/be reluctant to leave;*
zhuī huǐ: 追悔, *to regret, to repent*

DEPORTAR; deportar; *to deport;*
qū zhú chū jìng (fe): 驱逐出境, *to expel/drive away/ deport*

DEPOSITAR; depositar; *to deposit/ place; to settle;*
chén diàn (v) (n): 沉淀, *to settle; sediment;*

chén jī (v) (n): 沉积, *to deposit; sediment;*
cún fàng: 存放, *to deposit sthg; to leave sthg in the care of sb;*
cún kuǎn (v) (n): 存款, *to deposit money; deposit;*
cún xiàn: 存现, *to deposit cash;*
fàng xià: 放下, *to put down;*
jì cún: 寄存, *to deposit, to leave with sb, to check;*
tuō guǎn: 托管, *to deposit, to entrust*

DERIVAR; derivar; *to derive;*
dé dào: 得到, *to succeed in obtaining sthg, to gain from sthg, to receive sthg from sb/sthg;*
pài shēng: 派生, *to derive;*
qǔ dé: 取得, *to gain/acquire/obtain; to aim at/seek*

DESACTIVAR; desativar; *to defuse/ deactivate/ neutralize;*
guān bì: 关闭, *to close/shut down;*
shǐ wú xiào: 使无效, *to neutralize/ invalidate; to make/be useless*

DESARMAR; desarmar; *to dismantle/ disarm/take away;*
jiǎo xiè: 缴械, *to disarm*

DESAUTORIZAR; desautorizar; *to deny/deprive/ discredit;*
bō duó: 剥夺, *to deprive/strip away/ expropriate;*
fǒu dìng (v) (sv): 否定, *to negate, to refute; negative;*
fǒu jué: 否决, *to veto, to overrule;*
fǒu rèn: 否认, *to deny, to repudiate*

DESCONCERTAR; desconcertar; *to confuse/upset; to disconcert/agitate/ fluster;*
hùn tóng: 混同, *to confuse, to mix up;*
mí huò: 迷惑, *to confuse, to puzzle, to mislead;*
shǐ bù 'ān: 使不安, *to disconcert;*
shǐ huāng zhāng: 使慌张, *to fluster sb;*
shǐ jiāo lǜ: 使焦虑, *to agitate;*
zháo huāng: 着慌, *to become*

flustered;
SEE (请查看) DESCONTROL

DESCONECTAR; desconectar; *to disconnect/unplug/ switch off*;
  bá qù ... de chā tóu: 拔去...的插头, *to unplug*;
  chāi kāi: 拆开, *to disconnect*

DESCONTENTAR; descontentar; *to displease; to upset/make unhappy*;
  shǐ kǔn rǎo: 使困扰, *to upset sb, to make sb unhappy*;
SEE (请查看) AGRAVIAR

DESCRIBIR; descrever; *to describe/ outline/delineate*;
  gài kuò: 概括, *to outline*;
SEE (请查看) DESCRIPCIÓN, DELINEAR

DESENCANTAR; desencantar; *to disappoint/ disenchant/disillusion*;
  gū fù: 辜负, *let down; fail to live up to; disappoint*;
  shǐ shī wàng: 使失望, *to let down*;
  hán xīn (sv) (v): 寒心, *disillusioned, bitterly disappointed; to tremble with fear*;
SEE (请查看) DECEPCIÓN

DESENROLLAR; desenrolar; *to progress; to unfold* ... **DESENVOLVER; desenvolver;** *to develop/improve; to unwrap; to manage*;
  gǎi jìn: 改进, *to improve*;
  zhǎn kāi: 展开, *to develop*;
  zhǎng jìn (v) (n): 长进, *to progress, to improve; improvement, progress*

DESERTAR; desertar; *to desert/give up/leave/ abandon*;
  diū qì: 丢弃, *to desert*;
SEE (请查看) ABANDONAR

DESHONRAR; desonrar; *to dishonor/ disgrace/insult*;
  diū miàn zi (fe): 丢面子, *to lose face*;
  wū rǔ: 污辱, *to insult, to humiliate; to rape*;

SEE (请查看) HUMILLACIÓN, AGRAVIAR, DEGRADANTE, DESCRÉDITO

DESIGNAR; designar; *to appoint, designate*;
  rèn mìng: 任命, *to appoint*;
  zhǐ dìng: 指定, *to appoint*;
  zhǐ pài: 指派, *to designate*

DESINFECTAR; desinfetar; *to disinfect*;
  shā jūn: 杀菌, *to disinfect*;
SEE (请查看) PASTEURIZAR

DESINTEGRAR; desintegrar; *to disintegrate*;
  jiě tǐ: 解体, *to disintegrate/fall apart*;
  tǔ bēng wǎ jiě (fe): 土崩瓦解, *to disintegrate, to crumble, to fall apart*;
SEE (请查看) COLAPSO

DESMEMBRAR; desmembrar; *to divide up; to dismember*;
  fēn: 分, *to mark off*;
  huà fēn: 划分, *to divide*;
  zhī jiě: 支解, *to dismember*;
SEE (请查看) APARTAR, PARCELAR

DESMONTAR; desmontar; *to dismantle; to take apart, to strip down*;
  chāi: 拆, *to tear open/take apart; to pull down; dismantle*;
  chāi qiáng: 拆墙, *to demolish walls*;
  chāi qù: 拆去, *to dismantle/pull down*;
  chāi xià: 拆下, *to detach/take away*;
  chāi xiè: 拆卸, *to dismantle; to dismount*;
  chāi yòng: 拆用, *to dismantle and use; to cannibalize; to borrow for use*;
  chè chú: 撤除, *to remove, to dismantle*;
SEE (请查看) APARTAR, ARRUINAR, DESCONECTAR

DESMORALIZAR; desmoralizar; *to demoralize*;
  shǐ xiè qì (v) (sv): 使泄气, *to lose heart; disappointing, frustrating, weak, sissified*;

SEE (请查看) DESENCANTAR

DESOCUPAR; desocupar; *to empty;*
to vacate, to clear out;
  bān chū: 搬出, *to move out; to bring*
  out; to come up with;
  cí qù: 辞去, *to vacate/leave a job/*
  position, etc.;
  kòng chū: 空出, *to vacate a seat/*
  house, etc.;
  téng chū: 腾出, *to clear out/vacate;*
  zǒu kāi: 走开, *to get away; to clear off*

DESORGANIZAR; desorganizar;
to throw into confusion; to disorganize
... DESORIENTAR; desorientar; *to*
disorient/confuse;
  dǎ luàn: 打乱, *to throw into confusion;*
  nòng cuò: 弄错, *to confuse;*
  shǐ mí shī fāng xiàng: 使迷失方向,
  to disorient;
SEE (请查看) DESCONCERTAR,
CONFUSO

DESPACHAR; despacher; *to*
dispatch/sell/finish off;
  chī guāng: 吃光, *to finish off/eat up*
  (all the food);
  chū shòu: 出售, *to sell/offer for sale;*
  gàn diào (coll): 干掉, *to kill/get rid of/*
  liquidate/ finish off;
  hē guāng: 喝光, *to finish off a drink, to*
  drink up;
  mài: 卖, *to sell; to betray/ sell out;*
SEE (请查看) ARRUINAR,
DEDUCCIÓN, ERRADICAR,
CONCLUIR

DETECTAR; detectar; *to detect/*
discover/perceive;
  fā jué: 发觉, *to discover/to find;*
  gǎn jué (v) (n) (sv): 感觉, *to feel, to*
  sense, to perceive; perception, sensation;
  perceptive;
SEE (请查看) DETECCIÓN

DETENER; deter; *to stop, to detain, to*
keep, to delay; arrest;
  dài bǔ: 逮捕, *to arrest;*
  dān ge: 耽搁, *to stop over/stay; to*

delay
  tíng (v) (bf): 停, *to stop/pause; to stop*
  over; to park; berth; ready, settled;
  zhàn (v) (n): 站, *to take a stand, to*
  stop/halt; station, stop;
SEE (请查看) DETENCIÓN,
APREHENDER, BLOCAR

DETERIORAR; deteriorar; *to spoil, to*
damage; to damage, deteriorate;
  biàn huài: 变坏, *to degenerate;*
  è huà: 恶化, *to worsen; to grow*
  corrupt;
  jiāo guàn (sv): 浇灌, *pamper, coddle*
  (spoil);
  nì 'ài: 溺爱, *to spoil/dote on (a child);*
  sǔn huǐ: 损毁, *to ruin;*
  sǔn shī (v) (n): 损失, *to lose; loss;*
SEE (请查看) ARRUINAR,
DEGENERAR

DETERMINAR; determinar; *to*
determine/settle/ assess;
  què dìng: 确定, *to determine/discover/*
  find from the facts;
SEE (请查看) DETERMINACIÓN

DETESTAR; detestar; *to detest/hate/*
loathe;
  bù xǐ huān: 不喜欢, *to have/feel a*
  strong dislike for sb/sthg;
  wù (v) (bf): 恶, *to loathe; hate;*
  xián: 嫌, *to dislike;*
  yàn (v) (bf): 厌, *to detest/loathe, to be*
  disgusted/ bored with sb/sthg;
  yuàn (v) (bf): 怨, *to blame; resentment,*
  grudge, enmity;
  yuàn hèn (v) (n): 怨恨, *to hate; a*
  grudge;
  zēng (v) (bf): 憎, *to hate/dislike/loath;*
SEE (请查看) ABOMINACIÓN,
ANIMOSIDAD, DESDÉN

DETONAR; detonar; *to detonate/*
explode;
  yǐn bào: 引爆, *to ignite/detonate;*
SEE (请查看) DETONACIÓN

DEVALUAR; desvalorizar; *to devalue/*
devaluate;

shǐ biǎn zhí (ECON): 使贬值, *to devalue, to devaluate; to depreciate*

DEVASTAR; devastar; *to devastate/ destroy/ overwhelm*;
  cuī huǐ: 摧毁, *to destroy/smash/wreck*;
SEE (请查看) **ARRUINAR**

DEVOLVER; devolver; *to give back/ return/send back*;
  huí lái (v) (n): 回来, *to return, to come back/be back; return*

DEVORAR; devorar; *to consume/to devour/wolf down*;
  hào jìn: 耗尽, *to exhaust/use up*;
  láng tūn hǔ yàn: 狼吞虎咽, *to devour/ wolf down*

DIAGNOSTICAR; diagnosticar; *to diagnose*;
  zhěn bìng: 诊病, *to diagnose a disease*;
  zhěn chá: 诊察, *to examine a patient*;
  zhěn liáo: 诊疗, *to diagnose and treat*;
  zhěn zhì: 诊治, *to diagnose and treat*;
SEE (请查看) **DIAGNÓSTICO**

DICTAR; ditar; *to dictate, to pronounce, to issue*;
  tīng xiě (v) (n): 听写, *to dictate; dictation*

DIFAMAR; difamar; *to slander*;
  huǐ bàng (v) (n): 毁谤, *to slander, to libel; slander*;
  wū miè (v) (n): 污蔑, *to slander, to vilify, to tarnish; slander*;
SEE (请查看) **DIFAMATORIO, CALUMNIA**

DIFERENCIAR; diferenciar; *to distinguish/ differentiate*;
  fēn qīng: 分清, *to distinguish/draw a clear line between things*;
  huà qīng: 划清, *to distinguish clearly*;
  pàn bié: 判别, *to differentiate, to distinguish*;
  shí bié: 识别, *to distinguish, to recognize, to identify*;

SEE (请查看) **APARTAR, DIFERENCIA, CATEGORIZAR**

DIFICULTAR; dificultar; *to complicate; to make difficult, to hinder, to obstruct*;
  fáng (bf): 妨, *to hinder/impede/ obstruct*;
  fáng 'ài: 妨碍, *to hamper, to impede, to obstruct*;
  fù zá (sv): 复杂, *complicated, complex*;
  fù zá huà: 复杂化, *to complicate; to make sthg complicated*;
  zhàng bì: 障壁, *to block/obstruct/ screen*;
  zǔ 'ài (v) (n): 阻碍, *to hinder/block/ impede/bar; to frustrate a plan/ an attempt; obstruction, obstacle, hindrance, friction, resistance, stricture*;
  zǔ dǎng: 阻挡, *to stop/resist/obstruct/ stem*;
  zǔ lán (v) (n): 阻拦, *to stop/obstruct; inhibition*;
  zǔ náo: 阻挠, *to obstruct/thwart/ prevent*;
  zǔ sè (v) (n): 阻塞, *to block up/ obstruct/clog; traffic jam*;
SEE (请查看) **DIFÍCIL, COMPLICACIÓN, COMPLICADO, BLOCAR, COMPLICAR**

DILUIR; diluir; *to dilute/water down*;
  chōng dàn: 冲淡, *to dilute/water down*;
  jiǎn ruò: 减弱, *to weaken/abate*;
  jiǎn: 减, *to subtract; to reduce/ decrease; to cut, to lessen/diminish/ deduct*;
  shǐ biàn dàn: 使变淡, *to dilute*;
  (shǐ) biàn ruò: (使)变弱, *to weaken, to make inferior*

DISCIPLINAR; disciplinar; *to discipline*;
  xùn dǎo: 训导, *to discipline*;
SEE (请查看) **CASTIGO**

DISCRIMINAR; discriminar; *to discriminate*;
  qū bié duì dài: 区别对待, *to give different treatment to*;

qí shì: 歧视, *to discriminate (against)*

DISCULPAR; desculpar; *to excuse/ forgive; to apologize;*
  ráo shù: 饶恕, *to forgive;*
  yuán liàng: 原谅, *to excuse/pardon/ forgive*

DISEMINAR; disseminar; *to scatter, to disseminate, to spread;*
  biàn jí: 遍及, *to spread all over;*
  chuán bō: 传播, *to disseminate, to spread; to transmit, to broadcast;*
  fàn làn: 泛滥, *to overflow, to spread unchecked;*
  liú chuán: 流传, *to hand down, to circulate, to spread;*
  pǔ jí (v) (sv): 普及, *to spread, to popularize; universal, popular;*
  sàn bō: 散播, *to spread;*
  sàn bù: 散步, *to disseminate, to scatter, to diffuse;*
SEE (请查看) AMPLIAR, DIFUSO, DISPENSAR

DISOLVER; dissolver; *to dissolve/ break up/liquidate;*
  chú diào: 除掉, *to liquidate;*
  róng jiě: 溶解, *to dissolve in a liquid, etc.;*
  yè huà: 液化, *to dissolve;*
SEE (请查看) DESINTEGRACIÓN, APARTAR

DISPENSAR; dispensar; *to dispense with sthg; to grant; to excuse;*
  bāo hán: 包涵, *to excuse, to forgive;*
SEE (请查看) APLICAR, CLEMENCIA, DISCULPAR, APROBAR, PERMITIR

DISPERSAR; dispersar; *to scatter, disperse, break up;*
  fēn sàn: 分散, *to disperse/scatter/ decentralize;*
  sàn kāi: 散开, *to spread out, to disperse;*
SEE (请查看) DISEMINAR

DISTRIBUIR; distribuir; *to distribute/ deliver/allocate;*

fēn fā: 分发, *to distribute/hand-out/ issue;*
SEE (请查看) DISEMINAR, ASIGNACIÓN, DIFUSO

DIVERGIR; divergir; *to branch off; to disagree; to diverge/ differ; to deviate;*
  bèi lí: 背离, *to depart/deviate from;*
  chū piān chā: 出偏差, *to deviate;*
  fēn chà: 分叉, *to diverge, to fork/ branch;*
  piān lí: 偏离, *to deviate, to diverge;*
  tuō lí cháng guī: 脱离常规, *to deviate;*
  zǒu yàng: 走样, *to deviate from;*
SEE (请查看) DESAPROBACIÓN, DESIGUAL

DIVERSIFICAR; diversificar; *to diversify;*
  duō yàng huà (v) (n): 多样化, *to diversify/make varied; diversity*

DIVIDIR; dividir; *to divide/split up;*
  fēn chéng: 分成, *to divide;*
  fēn chū: 分出, *to separate/divide;*
  fēn gē wéi: 分割为, *cut apart/break up;*
  fēn gē: 分割, *to cut apart/break up;*
  fēn gé: 分隔, *to separate/divide;*
  fēn zǔ: 分组, *to divide into groups;*
SEE (请查看) APARTAR, DESMEMBRAR, DISOLVER

DIVORCIAR; divorciar; *to divorce;*
  lí hūn: 离婚, *to divorce;*
  lí yì: 离异, *to divorce;*
SEE (请查看) APARTAR

DIVULGAR; divulgar; *to publicize, to spread, to disclose; to divulge;*
  xiè lòu: 泄漏, *to leak, to divulge;*
  tòu lù: 透露, *to divulge/leak/reveal*

DOCUMENTAR; documentar; *to document/check/ research;*
  hé duì: 核对, *to check figures, to prove;*
  jiǎn chá (v) (n): 检查, *to check/inspect/ examine; self-criticism; examination;*
  tàn tǎo: 探讨, *to inquire into/explore;*

yán jiū (v) (n): 研究, *to study/research; to consider; discussion, deliberation*;
SEE (请查看) **INVESTIGAR**

DOMESTICAR; domesticar; *to domesticate, to tame*;
  xùn huà: 驯化, *to tame/domesticate*;
  xùn yǎng: 驯养, *to raise and train animals, to domesticate*

DOMINAR; dominar; *to dominate/control*;
  zhī pèi: 支配, *to dominate, to control, to govern*;
SEE (请查看) **ACTUAR, DESIGNAR**

DONAR; doar; *to give, to donate sthg*;
  huán lǐ: 还礼, *to give a gift in return; to return a salute*;
  juān xiàn: 捐献, *to donate blood*;
  juān zèng: 捐赠, *to donate money/clothes, etc.*;
  shī shě: 施舍, *to give alms; to give in charity*;
SEE (请查看) **APLICAR**

DOPAR; dopar; *to dope, drug*;

shǐ má zuì: 使麻醉, *to sedate*;
xīng fèn jì: 兴奋剂, *doping, stimulus*

DORMIR; dormir; *to sleep*;
  shuì: 睡, *to sleep*;
  jìng zhǐ (v) (n): 静止, *to be static; motionless*;
  mèng jiàn: 梦见, *to dream about sb/sthg*;
  shuì jiào: 睡觉, *to sleep, go to bed*;
  shuì mèng (v) (n): 睡梦, *to dream; sleep, dream*;
  zuò mèng: 做梦, *to dream/have a pipe dream*;
SEE (请查看 **DESILUSIÓN, ÁVIDO**

DUPLICAR; duplicar; *to double; to copy, to duplicate*;
  fù běn: 副本, *to duplicate/make a transcript/copy*;
  fù xiě: 复写, *to duplicate; to make carbon copies*;
  shǐ jiā bèi: 使加倍, *to double/redouble*;
SEE (请查看) **DUPLICADO**

Interchangeable Spanish-Portuguese-English words and their Chinese equivalents
Palabras en Español-Portugués-Inglés y sus equivalentes en Chino
Palavras em Espanhol-Português-Inglês e seus equivalentes em Chinês
西班牙语，葡萄牙语，英语及中文的对等单词

ECLIPSE; eclipse;
  rì shí: 日食, *solar eclipse*;
  yuè shí: 月食, *lunar eclipse*

ECZEMA ó ECCEMA; eczema;
  shī zhěn: 湿疹, *eczema*

EDITOR (A); **editor** (A); *publisher; publishing*;
  zhǔ biān:主编, *chief editor/editor-in-*

chief; editorial writer;
SEE (请查看) **COMPILAR**

EDITORIAL; editorial; *editorial, leading article*;
  shè lùn: 社论, *editorial*

EGO; ego;
  zì wǒ (n): 自我, *ego; (pr) self, oneself*

ÉLITE ó ELITE; elite;
 jīng yīng: 精英, elite

E-MAIL; e-mail;
 diàn zǐ yóu jiàn: 电子邮件, e-mail

EMBARGO; embargo; seizure;
 jìn yùn (attr): 禁运, embargoed;
SEE (请查看) APREHENDER

ENIGMA; enigma;
 mí (n): 谜, enigma;
 mí yī yàng de (sv) (adv): 谜一样地,
 enigmatic; enigmatically

ERA; era;
 shí dài: 时代, age, period

EURO; euro; the euro;
 ōu yuán: 欧元, the euro

EVENTUAL; eventual; chance;
 zhōng yú (adv): 终于, eventually;
 zuì zhōng de (adj): 最终的, eventual

EXPERIMENTAL; experimental;
 shì yàn xìng (attr): 试验性, trial,
 experimental

EXTERIOR; exterior;
 shì wài (n): 室外, outdoor, exterior,
 outside;
 wài bian (n): 外边, outside, outer
 surface; exterior;
 wài bù (n): 外部, exterior, external;
 wài guān (n): 外观, appearance,
 exterior

Easily recognizable Spanish-Portuguese-English nouns, adjectives and adverbs and their Chinese equivalents
Nombres, sustantivos, adjetivos y adverbios en Español-Portugués-Inglés y sus equivalentes en Chino
Nomes, substantivos, adjetivos e advérbios em Espanhol-Português-Inglês e seus equivalentes em Chinês
容易辨认的西班牙语，葡萄牙语，英语的名词，形容词和副词和他们的中文对等词

EBRIO; ébrio; intoxicated, drunk;
 hē zuì (v) (sv): 喝醉, to get drunk;
 drunk;
 jiǔ guǐ (n): 酒鬼, drunkard, alcoholic;
 zuì (sv): 醉, drunk, tipsy;
 zuì hàn (n): 醉汉, drunkard;
 zuì jìnr (n): 醉劲儿, drunkenness;
 zuì māor (n): 醉猫儿, addled drunkard;
 zuì tài (n): 醉态, drunkenness;
 zuì wēng (n): 醉翁, old drunkard;
 zuì wò: 醉卧, to lie in a drunken stupor;
 zuì yǎn (n) vp): 醉眼, pie-eyed; bleary-
 eyed from drink;
 zuì yǎn méng lóng (fe): 醉眼朦胧,
 drunk and bleary-eyed;
 zuì yì (n): 醉意, tipsy feeling

ECONOMÍA; economia; economy
... ECONÓMICO (A); **econômico**
(A); economic **... ECONOMISTA;**
economista; economist;
 jīng jì (n) (sv): 经济, economy; financial

condition; income; economical, thrifty; of
economical value;
 jīng jì de: 经济的, economic;
SEE (请查看) ASOCIACIÓN

EDUCACIÓN; educação; education,
teaching **... EDUCACIONAL;**
educacional; educational;
 jiào xué: 教学, teaching;
 jiào yù de: 教育的, educational;
SEE (请查看) FORMATIVO

EDUCADO (A); educado (A); polite,
well mannered, cultured;
 kè qi (sv) (v): 客气, polite, courteous; to
 be polite;
 kè qi de: 客气的, polite, courteous;
 kě qīn (sv): 可亲, kindly, amiable;
 lǐ mào (n): 礼貌, courtesy, politeness,
 manners;
 wén (sv): 文, literary, bookish;

wén yǎ (sv): 文雅, *elegant, refined, graceful*;
wén yǎ de: 文雅的, *refined, graceful*;
xiù měi (sv): 秀美, *graceful, elegant*;
xiù qi (sv): 秀气, *delicate, elegant, refined (of manners)*;
xiù yì (sv): 秀逸, *elegant and graceful*;
yǒu lǐ mào de: 有礼貌的, *polite person*;
SEE (请查看**) AMABILIDAD, DELICADO, REFINADO, AGRADABLE, CORRECTO, AMABLE, GENTIL**

EDUCADOR (A); **educador** (A); *instructor; teacher, educator*;
dǎo shī: 导师, *tutor, mentor*;
jiào yuán: 教员, *instructor, teacher*

EFECTIVIDAD; efetividade; *effectiveness* ... **EFECTIVO; efetivo** (A); *effective; real; cash* ... **EFECTO; efeito;** *effect; result* ... **EFICIENCIA; eficácia;** *efficiency* ... **EFICIENTE; eficaz;** *efficient*;
duì xiàn: 兑现, *cash*;
gōng xiào: 功效, *efficiency, efficacy*;
guǎn shì (v) (sv): 管事, *to be in control/charge; useful, effective*;
líng tōng (sv): 灵通, *well-informed, effective (reliable)*;
líng yàn (sv): 灵验, *effective, accurate (foresight)*;
shí jì (n) (sv): 实际, *reality, practice, praxis; practical, real, actual, concrete*;
xiào (bf): 效, *effect, result; efficiency; imitate*;
xiào guǒ: 效果, *effect, result, impression*;
xiào lǜ (n): 效率, *efficiency, productivity*;
xiào lǜ gāo (sv): 效率高, *efficient*;
xiào néng: 效能, *efficacy, effectiveness*;
xiào yì: 效益, *benefit, effectiveness, efficiency*;
xiào yìng: 效应, *effect*;
xiào yòng: 效用, *usefulness, effectiveness*;
yǒu xiào (sv) (v): 有效, *successful;*

effective, valid; to be effective;
SEE (请查看**) AFECTAR, BENÉFICO**

EFUSIVO (A); **efusivo** (A); *effusive, enthusiastic, exuberant*;
hěn gǎn xìng qù de (adv): 很感兴趣地, *enthusiastically*;
jī jí xìng (n): 积极性, *zeal, initiative, enthusiasm*;
jī qíng (sv): 激情, *effusive*;
mào shèng (sv) (n): 茂盛, *exuberant; exuberance*;
rè liè (sv): 热烈, *ardent, enthusiastic*;
rè qiè (sv): 热切, *fervent, earnest*;
rè xīn (sv) (n): 热心, *enthusiastic, ardent; warm-hearted, zeal, ardor*;
wàng shèng (sv): 旺盛, *vigorous, exuberant, thriving*;
SEE (请查看**) ENTUSIASMO, ARDOROSO, CONSTRUCTIVO**

EGOCÉNTRICO (A); **egocêntrico;** *egocentric, self-centered*;
kuáng wàng (sv): 狂妄, *egotistical, arrogant, insolent*;
lì jǐ (sv): 利己, *selfish*;
lì jǐ zhǔ yì: 利己主义, *egotism*;
zì sī zì lì (sv): 自私自利, *self-centered*;
zì wǒ zhōng xīn (sv): 自我中心, *egocentric*;
zì wǒ zhǔ yì zhě (n): 自我主义者, *egocentric person*;
SEE (请查看**) EGO**

EGREGIO (A); **egregio** (A); *illustrious, eminent, distinguished*;
chū míng (v) (sv): 出名, *to become famous; well-known for*;
zhuó zhù (sv): 卓著, *distinguished, outstanding, eminent*;
SEE (请查看**) CÉLEBRE, EMINENTE, ATÍPICO, AFAMADO, FAMOSO**

EJECUTIVO (A); **executivo** (A); *executive*;
zhí xíng (v) (attr): 执行, *to carry out; executive*;
zhí xíng de: 执行的, *executive role*;
zhǔ guǎn (v) (n): 主管, *to be in charge/responsible for; boss, chief*;

zhǔ guǎn rén yuán: 主管人员, *an executive*;
zhǔ guǎn rén: 主管人, *boss*

EJEMPLO; exemplo; *example*;
  bǎng yàng: 榜样, *example, model (of good behavior, etc.);*
  biāo běn: 标本, *example, sample, specimen;*
  diǎn fàn: 典范, *model, example;*
  lì tí: 例题, *example;*
  lì zi: 例子, *example, instance, case;*
  yàng bǎn (n): 样板, *model, prototype; sample; template, example;*
SEE (请查看) CLÁSICO, DENOTAR

ELÁSTICO (A); **elástico** (A); *elastic, flexible, springy;*
  jī dòng líng huó (fe): 机动灵活, *flexible;*
  jī dòng xìng (n): 机动性, *flexibility;*
  líng huó (sv): 灵活, *nimble, agile; flexible, elastic, adaptable*
  líng huó xìng (n): 灵活性, *flexibility of ideas, approach, etc.*
  róu rèn (vp): 柔韧, *pliable and tough;*
  róu rèn xìng (n): 柔韧性, *flexibility of an object, materials, etc.;*
  xiàng pí: 橡皮, *elastic material;*
  yǒu tán lì de: 有弹力的, *elasticity;*
  yǒu tán xìng de: 有弹性的, *elastic, stretchy*

ELECTRICIDAD; electricidade; *electricity ...* **ELECTRICISTA; electricista;** *electrician (n); electrical (adj) ...* **ELÉCTRICO** (A); **elétrico** (A); *electric;*
  diàn dēng: 电灯, *electric light/lamp;*
  diàn dòng (sv): 电动, *electric, power;*
  diàn gōng: 电工, *electrician; electrical engineering;*
  diàn jī: 电机, *electrical machinery;*
  diàn lǎn: 电缆, *electric cable;*
  diàn lì: 电力, *electric power, electricity;*
  diàn liú: 电流, *electric current, circuitry;*
  diàn qì: 电器, *electric devices/appliances;*
  diàn qì: 电气, *electricity;*

  diàn yā: 电压, *voltage;*
  diàn yuán: 电源, *electric power source/supply;*
  diàn zhàn: 电站, *electrical generating plant*

ELECTRÓNICA; eletrônica; *electronics;*
  diàn zǐ xué: 电子学, *electronics*

ELECTRODO; eletrodo; *electrode;*
  diàn jí: 电极, *electrode*

ELEFANTE (A); **elefante** (A); *elephant;*
  dà xiàng: 大象, *elephant*

ELEGANCIA; elegância; *elegance, gracefulness, tastefulness ...*
ELEGANTE; elegante; *elegant, stylish, smart, fashionable;*
  fēng cǎi (n): 风采, *writing talent, elegance;*
  fēng yǎ (sv): 风雅, *elegant, refined;*
  gāo yǎ (n): 高雅, *elegance, gentility;*
  xiù qì (sv): 秀气, *delicate, elegance, fine;*
  yǎ zhì (sv) (n): 雅致, *refined, tasteful; refinement;*
SEE (请查看) DECORO, DELICADO, EDUCADO

ELEVADO (A); **elevador** (A); *high; noble; lofty, great; elevated;*
  gāo jié de: 高洁的, *noble;*
  gāo shàng de: 高尚的, *lofty;*
SEE (请查看) EGREGIO

ELEVADOR; elevador; *elevator, hoist;*
  diàn tī: 电梯, *elevator;*
SEE (请查看) ASCENSOR

ELOCUENCIA; eloqüência; *eloquence;*
  kǒu cái: 口才, *eloquence;*
  xióng biàn (sv) (n): 雄辩, *convincing, eloquent; convincing argument/eloquence*

ELUSIVO (A); **evasivo** (A); *evasive, elusive, slippery; indirect;*

bù yì zhǎo dào (sv): 不易找到, *elusive*;

huá tóu (sv): 滑头, *slippery, cunning, foxy*;

táo bì (sv) (n) (v): 逃避, *evasive, elusive; evasion; to escape/evade*

EMBARAZOSO (A); **embaracoso** (A); *awkward, embarrassing*;
  jiǒng kuàng: 窘况, *difficult situation*;
  lìng rén gān gà de: 令人尴尬的, *embarrassing*;
  wéi nán (sv): 为难, *embarrassed*;
  yáng xiàng: 洋相, *awkward behavior*;
SEE (请查看) **DIFÍCIL**

EMBLEMA; emblema; *emblem; badge, symbol*;
  xiàng zhēng (n) (v): 象征, *emblem; to symbolize/ signify*;
SEE (请查看) **INSIGNIA**

EMERGENCIA; emergência; *emergency*;
  jí zhěn: 急诊, *emergency treatment*;
  jǐn jí (sv): 紧急, *urgent, critical*;
  jǐn jí huì yì: 紧急会议, *emergency meeting*;
  jǐn jí qíng kuàng: 紧急情况, *a crisis*;
  jǐn jí shì jiàn: 紧急事件, *emergency*;
  lín jiè diǎn: 临界点, *crisis, critical point*;
SEE (请查看) **CRUCIAL, DIFÍCIL**

EMERGENTE; emergente; *emergent; emerging*;
  chū xiàn (v) (n): 出现, *to appear, to emerge; emergence*;
  fā zhǎn de: 发展的, *emerging*;
  xīn chū xiàn de: 新出现的, *emergent*

EMIGRANTE (adj); **emigrante** (n); *emigrant, migrant*;
  qiáo mín: 侨民, *alien residents*;
SEE (请查看) **EMIGRAR**

EMINENTE; eminente; *eminent, high, outstanding*;
  xiǎn hè de: 显赫的, *illustrious, celebrated, famous*;

SEE (请查看) **CÉLEBRE, EGREGIO, ATÍPICO, CONSPICUO, AFAMADO**

EMOCIÓN; emoção; *emotion, excitement*;
  qíng xù: 情绪, *emotions, feelings, mood*;
  rén qíng: 人情, *human feelings, emotion*;
SEE (请查看) **EFUSIVO, AFECTO, DESCONCERTANTE**

ENDÉMICO (A); **endêmico**; *endemic (MED); rife, chronic*;
  lǎo máo bìng: 老毛病, *chronic problem, bad habit*;
  liú xíng: 流行, *endemic, rife*;
  liú xíng (v) (sv): 流行, *to spread, to rage (a disease); prevalent, popular, fashionable; rife, endemic*;
  màn xìng (sv) (attr): 慢性, *chronic; slow (in taking effect)*;
SEE (请查看) **PERSEVERANCIA, UNIVERSALIDAD**

ENEMIGO (A); **inimigo** (A); *enemy, hostile*;
  chóu dí: 仇敌, *enemy, foe*;
  dí jūn: 敌军, *enemy troops, hostile forces*;
  dí rén: 敌人, *enemy, opponent*;
  duì tou: 对头, *enemy, opponent, adversary*;
  jiān xi: 奸细, *spy, enemy agent*;
  nèi jiān: 内奸, *hidden traitor, enemy*;
  yuān jia: 冤家, *enemy, foe*

ENEMISTAD; inimizade; *enmity, animosity*;
  yuān chóu: 冤仇, *enmity, rancor*;
SEE (请查看) **ANIMOSIDAD**

ENERGÍA; energia; *energy, drive*;
  jīng hàn de (sv): 精悍的, *capable, vigorous, intrepid*;
  jīng lì (n): 精力, *energy, vigor*;
  jīng lì chōng pèi (fe): 精力充沛, *full of vigor*;
  lì (n): 力, *power, strength, ability; physical strength/energy*;

néng chǎn (sv) (attr): 能产, *productive*;
néng dòng xìng (n): 能动性, *dynamic role, initiative*;
néng shì: 能士, *capable/talented persons*;
SEE (请查看) APTITUD, CAPAZ, DINÁMICO, ÍMPETU, VITALIDAD

ENÉRGICO (A); **enérgico** (A); *energetic, vigorous*;
  chōng mǎn huó lì de: 充满活力的, *energetic, vigorous*;
  gāng jìng (sv): 刚劲, *bold, vigorous*;
  jīng lì wàng shèng de: 精力旺盛的, *energetic*;
SEE (请查看) BENÉFICO, EFUSIVO, ESPÍRITU, POTENTE

ENERVANTE; enervante; *annoying; draining, exasperating*;
  kǔn rǎo de: 困扰的 , *vexed*;
  yàn fán (n) (v): 厌烦, *annoyance; to be fed up with*;
SEE (请查看) ANTIPATÍA, IRRITANTE

ÉNFASIS; ênfase; *emphasis; insistence* ... **ENFÁTICO** (A); **enfático**; *emphatic; insistent*;
  bù duàn de: 不断的, *insistent (continual)*;
  jiān chí bù xiè (fe): 坚持不懈, *persistent, unremitting*;
  jiān jué de (adv): 坚决地, *firmly, resolutely*;
  jiān jué zhǔ zhāng: 坚决主张, *insistence*;
  qiáng diào (n) (sv): 强调, *emphasis; emphatic*;
SEE (请查看) INSISTIR

ENFERMEDAD; enfermidade; *illness, disease*... **ENFERMO** (A); **enfermo** (A); *ill, sick*;
  bìng (n) (v): 病, *disease; to become sick; (bf) fault, defect*;
  bìng hào: 病号, *person on a sick list; patient*;
  bìng wēi (sv): 病危, *to be critically ill*;
  bìng zhèng (n): 病症, *illness, disease*;
  bù jiàn kāng de: 不健康的, *unwell, ill*;

è liè de: 恶劣的, *ill, (feel) nasty/poor*;
ě xin (v) (sv): 恶心, *to feel nauseated/ turn sick; disgusting, nauseous*;
huài de: 坏的, *ill*;
shēng bìng de: 生病的, *sick, ill*;
yǒu bìng (sv) (v): 有病, *sick, unwell; to be sick*;
zhèng hòu (n): 症候, *disease, symptom*;
zhēng/zhèng (n): 症/症, *disease, illness; symptoms*

ENFISEMA; enfisema; *emphysema*;
  fèi qì zhǒng: 肺气肿, *emphysema*

ENIGMÁTICO (A); **enigmático** (A); *enigmatic, mysterious*;
  guǐ mì (sv): 诡秘, *secretive, furtive*;
  mí (n): 谜, *riddle, conundrum; enigma, mystery*;
  mò cè gāo shēn (fe): 莫测高深, *unfathomable, enigmatic*;
  shén mì (sv): 神秘, *mysterious, mystical*;
SEE (请查看) ENIGMA

ENORME; enorme; *enormous, huge ...* **ENORMIDAD; enormidade**; *enormity, immensity; tremendous, great*;
  dà liàng de (adv): 大量地, *enormously*;
  fēi cháng (sv) (adv): 非常, *tremendous; tremendously, immensely*;
  páng dà (sv): 庞大, *huge, immense*;
  qióng xiōng jí 'è (fe): 穷凶极恶, *extremely vicious*;
  wú biān jì de: 无边际的, *boundless*;
SEE (请查看) COLOSAL, DESMEDIDO, CUANTÍA

ENTRADA; entrada; *entrance*;
  mén hù: 门户, *door, entrance; strategic gateway*

ENTUSIASMO; entusiasmo; *enthusiasm...* **ENTUSIASTA; entusiasta**; *enthusiastic (adj), enthusiast (n)*;
  rè qíng bēn fàng (fe): 热情奔放, *bubbling with enthusiasm*;
  rè qíng yáng yì (fe): 热情洋溢, *glowing with enthusiasm*;

rè re nào nao: 热热闹闹, *lively, buzzing with excitement*;
rè xīn rén (n): 热心人, *enthusiastic person*;
rè xīn yú (v): 热心于, *to be enthusiastic about sthg*;
rè zhōng (v) (n): 热衷, *to hanker after/ be fond of; deep commitment*;
SEE (请查看) EFUSIVO, ARDOROSO

EQUILIBRADO (A); **equilibrado** (A); *level-headed, sensible*;
míng lǐ (sv): 明礼, *sensible, reasonable*;
míng zhì (sv): 明智, *sagacious, wise, good sense*;
shí bié lì qiáng de: 识别力强的, *intense discernment*;
tōng qíng (sv): 通情, *reasonable, showing good sense*;
tōng qíng dá lǐ de: 通情达理的, *sensible*;
tóu nǎo lěng jìng (vp): 头脑冷静, *have a cool head; level-headed*;
tóu nǎo qīng chǔ (vp): 头脑清楚, *clear-headed with an alert mind*;
tóu nǎo qīng xǐng (vp):头脑清醒 , *keep a cool head*

EQUILIBRIO; equilíbrio; *balance, equilibrium*;
píng héng: 平衡, *equilibrium*;
shǐ píng héng: 使平衡, *balance*

EQUIVALENTE; equivalente; *equivalent*;
tóng děng (sv): 同等, *equivalent*;
xiāng děng (v) (n): 相等, *to be equal; equivalent*

EQUIVOCADO (A) (adj) **equivocado** (A); *mistaken, wrong; misplaced ...*
ERRÓNEO (A); **errôneo** (A); *incorrect, wrong, erroneous, untrue, false*;
bú dào dé de: 不道德的, *wrong*;
bù hǎo de: 不好的, *wrong (unsatisfactory)*;
bù hé shì de: 不合适的, *wrong (person/job/part/ etc.)*
bù qià dàng de: 不恰当的, *wrong (inappropriate)*;

bù zhēn shí (n) (sv): 不真实, *untruth; untrue*;
cuò wù de (adv): 错误地, *wrongly, erroneously, mistakenly*;
dào dé de: 道德的, *wrong (morally bad)*;
huǎng yán (n) (sv): 谎言, *lie, falsehood; lying*;
jiǎ (sv): 假, *false, fake; phony; artificial; conditional/tentative (DER)*;
kuǎng yán (n): 谎言, *false words, lie*;
miù wù (n): 谬误, *falsehood, error*;
xié 'è: 邪恶, *wrong (evil); vicious, wicked*;
yī ge cuò wù (n): 一个错误, *a mistake*;
SEE (请查看) INOPORTUNO, CULPA, DESIGUAL

ERÓTICO (A); **erótico** (A); *erotic*;
yǐn qǐ xìng yù de: 引起性欲的, *erotic dream, experience*;
sè qíng de: 色情的, *erotic*;
sè qíng (n): 色情, *sex, pornography*

ERRÁTICO; errante; *wandering; erratic*;
bù guī zé de: 不规则的, *irregular, not fixed*;
guài pì de: 怪癖的, *erratic, eccentric*;
wú guī lǜ de: 无规律的, *erratic, irregular*;
SEE (请查看 DESIGUAL

ERUDITO (A); **erudito** (A); *erudite, learned, scholarly*;
bǎo xué (attr): 饱学, *learned, erudite*;
yǒu xué wèn de: 有学问的, *erudite*

ESCÁNDALO; escândalo; *scandal, outrage; racket, din ...* **ESCANDALOSO** (A); **escandaloso** (A); *scandalous, outrageous; rowdy*;
chǒu shì (n): 丑事, *scandal*;
chǒu wén (n): 丑闻, *scandal*;
chū chǒu de: 出丑的, *shameful, scandalous*;
diū liǎn de: 丢脸的, *scandalous, shameful*;
hài rén de:害人的, *shocking, outrageous, frightening*;

SEE (请查看**) ABUSIVO, ATROCIDAD, CLAMOR, DESCRÉDITO**

ESCRUTINIO; escrutínio; *scrutiny/ examination; count;*
  kào shì: 考试, *examination;*
  xì chá: 细查, *scrutiny;*
SEE (请查看**) DOCUMENTAR**

ESENCIAL;essencial; *essential;*
  bì xū de: 必须的, *essential, indispensable;*
  bì yào de: 必要的, *necessary, vital, indispensable;*
  bì yào qián tí (n): 必要前提, *prerequisite; precondition;*
  bì yào tiáo jiàn (n): 必要条件, *essential condition; prerequisite;*
SEE (请查看**) BASE, CÉNTRICO**

ESNOB (adj); **esnobe;** *snobbish, stuck-up; snob;*
  shì lì de rén: 势利的人, *snobbish;*
  shì li yǎn: 势利眼, *snob; snobbery*

ESPACIOSO (A); **espaçoso** (A); *spacious, roomy;*
  guǎng kuò de: 广阔的, *spacious, vast, broad;*
  kuān chǎng de: 宽敞的, *spacious, roomy*

ESPECIAL; especial; *special ...*
ESPECIALIDAD; especialidade; *specialty;*
  tè shū de: 特殊的, *special, particular, outstanding, extraordinary;*
  tè bié de: 特别的, *special, particular;*
  zhuān yè: 专业, *specialty, discipline/ field of research*

ESPECIFICACIÓN; especificação; *specification;*
  guī fàn (n) (v) (sv): 规范, *specification, norm, standard; to standardize; standard, normal;*
SEE (请查看**) NORMA**

ESPECÍFICO (A); **específico** (A); *specific, definite, precise, exact;*
  jīng mì (sv): 精密, *accurate, precise;*
  jīng què (sv) (n): 精确, *accurate, exact, precise; accuracy;*
  jù tǐ (sv): 具体, *concrete, specific, particular, detailed;*
  tè dìng (sv): 特定, *specific, specified; specially designated;*
  zhǔn què (sv): 准确, *accurate, precise, exact;*
SEE (请查看**) CONCRETO, CONFIRMAR, DETERMINADO, DILIGENCIA, EXACTAMENTE**

ESPÉCIMEN; espécime; *specimen;*
  yàng pǐn: 样品, *specimen; sample (of a product)*

ESPECTACULAR; espetacular; *spectacular;*
  zhuàng guān (sv) (n): 壮观, *spectacular, magnificent; magnificent sight;*
SEE (请查看**) ESPLÉNDIDO**

ESPECTADOR (A); **espectador;** *spectator, onlooker, viewer;*
  páng guān zhě: 旁观者, *onlooker, bystander, spectator;*
SEE (请查看**) AUDIENCIA**

ESPIONAJE; espionagem; *espionage, spying;*
  jiàn dié huó dòng: 间谍活动, *espionage;*
  tè wu (n): 特务, *special agent, spy;*
  tè wù huó dòng: 特务活动, *espionage*

ESPIRAL; espiral; *spiral;*
  luó xuán: 螺旋, *spiral, helix;*
  luó xuán xíng de: 螺旋形的, *spiral*

ESPÍRITU; espírito; *spirit;*
  guǐ hún: 鬼魂, *ghost, spirit;*
  guǐ shén: 鬼神, *supernatural beings;*
  hún pò: 魂魄, *soul, psyche;*
  jīng shén: 精神, *spirit, mind; consciousness;*
  líng hún: 灵魂, *soul, spirit;*
  qì gài: 气概, *spirit, mettle;*

xīn líng: 心灵, *mind; soul, spirit*;
yì qì: 意气, *spirit, temperament*;
yōu líng: 幽灵, *ghost, spirit*

ESPLÉNDIDO (A); **esplêndido**
(A); *splendid, magnificent, lovely ...*
ESPLENDOR; esplendor; *splendor, greatness, magnificence*;
  guāng cǎi (n) (sv): 光彩, *splendor, brilliance, luster, radiance; glorious, brilliant*;
  guāng huī (n) (sv): 光辉, *radiance, brilliance; bright, magnificent*;
  hóng wěi (sv) (n): 宏伟, *magnificent, grand; magnificence*;
  huá lì (sv) (n): 华丽, *magnificent, resplendent, gorgeous; magnificence*;
  huá měi (sv): 华美, *magnificent, resplendent*
  kě 'ài de: 可爱的, *lovely*;
  měi lì de: 美丽的, *lovely, beautiful*;
  qì zhuàng shān hé (fe): 气壮山河, *magnificent, inspiring*;
  xuàn làn (sv): 绚烂, *splendid, gorgeous*;
  xuàn lì (sv): 绚丽, *gorgeous, magnificent*;
  zhuàng lì (vp): 壮丽, *majestic, magnificent*;
SEE (请查看**) COLOSAL, ESPECTACULAR, EXCELENCIA**

ESPONTÁNEO (A); **espontâneo** (A);
spontaneous, instinctive, automatic;
  běn néng (n) (sv): 本能, *instinct; instinctive*;
  běn xìng (n): 本性, *nature, instincts*;
  quán zì dòng (sv): 全自动, *automatic*;
  zì dòng (sv): 自动, *voluntary, automatic; of one's own act*;
  zì fā (sv): 自发, *spontaneous; unconscious, without thinking*;
  zì rán ér rán de: 自然而然的, *unplanned, spontaneous*

ESPORÁDICO (A); **esporádico** (A);
sporadic, scattered, occasional;
  ǒu 'ěr (sv) (adv): 偶尔, *occasional, occasionally*;
  ǒu 'ěr fā shēng de: 偶尔发生的, *occasional*;

SEE (请查看**) CIRCUNSTANCIAL**

ESTABILIDAD; estabilidade; *stability, firmness ...* **ESTABLE; estável** (GEN);
stable, permanent, regular, steady;
  ān dìng (sv) (v): 安定, *stable, settled; to stabilize*;
  wěn dāng (sv): 稳当, *reliable, secure, steady*;
  wěn dìng (v) (sv): 稳定, *to stabilize; steady, stable*;
  wěn dìng xìng de: 稳定性的, *stability of an object*;
  wěn gù (sv) (v): 稳固, *firm, stable; to stabilize*;
  wěn jiàn (sv): 稳健, *steady, firm*;
SEE (请查看**) DIGNO**

ESTACIÓN; estação (GEN); *station*;
  chē zhàn: 车站, *a railway station*;
  diàn tái: 电台, *broadcasting station*;
  jǐng chá: 警察, *a police/rail station*

ESTADIO; estádio; *stadium; stage*;
  lù tiān yùn dòng chǎng: 露天运动场, *stadium*;
  tǐ yù chǎng: 体育场, *stadium*;
  wǔ tái: 舞台, *stage, arena*

ESTILO; estilo; *style*;
  fāng shì: 方式, *way/style/manner of life*;
  fēng gé (n): 风格, *style, manner, mode; personality, bearing*;
  fēng mào (n): 风貌, *style; scene*;
  kuǎn shì (n): 款式, *style, design*;
  pài tóu (n): 派头, *style, manner, air*;
  shí shàng (n): 时尚, *fashion, fad*;
  wén tǐ (n): 文体, *style in art/sports/recreation*;
  yàng shì (n): 样式, *design, pattern, style, type, form*

ESTILOSO (A); **estilístico** (A); *stylish*;
  shí máo de: 时髦的, *stylish, fashionable, in vogue*;
  piào liang de: 漂亮的, *splendid, smart*

ESTIMA; estima; *esteem, respect*;
  jìng yì: 敬意, *respect; tribute*;

shàng mian: 上面, *respect, regard; higher authorities; above*;
zūn zhòng: 尊重, *esteem*

ESTIMATIVO (A); **estimativo**; *approximate, rough*;
cū bào (sv): 粗暴, *crude, rough*;
cū cāo (sv): 粗糙, *coarse, rough*;
yuē (adv): 约, *about, around, approximately*;
SEE (请查看) APROXIMACIÓN, DECIDIR

ESTIPULACIÓN; estipulação; *stipulation; condition*;
tiáo jiàn: 条件, *condition, factor, requirement*;
xū qiú: 需求, *requirement, demand*

ESTOICO (A); **estóico** (A); *stoical, stoic*;
jìn yù zhǔ yì zhě (n): 禁欲主义者, *asceticism, stoic*;
jìn yù zhǔ yì de (adv): 禁欲主义地, *stoically*

ESTRATAGEMA; estratagema; *stratagem; trick, ruse*;
bǎ xì (n): 把戏, *cheap trick; acrobatics*;
è zuò jù (n): 恶作剧, *prank; hazing; mischief*;
guǐ jì (n): 诡计, *trick, ruse, crafty plot, cunning scheme*;
jì cè (n): 计策, *stratagem, plan*;
jì liǎng (n): 伎俩, *trick, intrigue; maneuver; skill, dexterity, craft*;
qiào mén (n): 窍门, *knack; trick of the trade*

ESTRATEGIA; estratégia; *strategy*;
xíng dòng jì huà: 行动计划, *plan*;
SEE (请查看) CONTRARIO, TÁCTICA

ESTRATÉGICO (A); **estratégico** (A); *strategic*;
guān jiàn de: 关键的, *strategic position*;
yǒu zhàn lüè yì yì de: 有战略意义的, *strategic site, plan*;
zhàn lüè de: 战略的, *strategic weapons*

ESTRÉS; estresse; *stress, tension, pressure; burden*;
yā lì: 压力, *mental stress, strain*;
zhòng yā: 重压, *stress, force, pressure*

ESTRESADO (A); **estressado** (A); *stressed, stressed-out*;
jǐn zhāng de: 紧张的, *nervous, keyed up; tense, strained*

ESTRIDENTE; estridente; *strident; shrill, raucous, noisy*;
cáo zá (sv): 嘈杂, *noisy (place)*;
cì 'ěr (sv): 刺耳, *jarring; ear-piercing; strident; shrill*;
cū lì de: 粗砺的, *strident, raspy*;
jiān ruì (sv): 尖锐, *sharp, penetrating; keen, intense; acute; shrill*;
jiān shēng (n): 尖声, *sharp/high-pitched sound/ voice*;
jù liè de: 剧烈的, *intense*;
mǐn ruì (sv): 敏锐, *quick, sharp, acute, keen*;
qiáng liè (sv): 强烈, *strong, keen, sharp, intense*;
shā yǎ (sv): 沙哑, *raucous; hoarse, husky*;
SEE (请查看) ABRASIVO

ESTUDIANTE; estudante; *student, pupil*;
dà xué shēng: 大学生, *at a university*;
zhōng xué shēng: 中学生, *at a school*

ESTUDIOSO (A); **estudioso** (A); *studious*;
hào xué (sv): 好学, *studious, fond of learning*

ESTUPEFACCIÓN; estupefação (A); *astonishment, amazement …*
ESTUPEFACTO (A); **estupefato** (A); *astonished, amazed, shocked*
… ESTUPENDO (A); **estupendo** (A); *wonderful, great, stupendous …*
ESTUPOR; estupor; *dazed, amazed; stupor (MED)*;
gǎn dào jīng yà: 感到惊讶, *to feel amazed/ astounded*;

jīng cǎi (sv): 精彩, *brilliant, splendid, wonderful*;

jīng rén (sv): 惊人, *astonishing, amazing, surprising*;

jīng yà (sv): 惊讶, *amazed, astounded; astounding*;

jīng yà de: 惊讶的, *amazing, astounding*;

liǎo bù qǐ de: 了不起的, *amazing, terrific, extraordinary*;

lìng rén jīng yà de: 令人惊讶的, *amazing*;

mù dèng kǒu dāi (fe): 目瞪口呆, *dumbstruck, stupefied*;

qí yì (sv): 奇异, *strange, queer; astonished, astounded*;

shǐ chī jīng: 使吃惊, *amazement*;

SEE (请查看) **COLOSAL**

ESTUPIDEZ; **estupidez**; *stupidity, stupid thing to do* ... **ESTÚPIDO** (A); **estúpido** (A); *stupid, idiot*;

bái chī (n): 白痴, *idiot*;

bèn de: 笨的, *stupid; stupid person*;

chī (sv): 痴, *silly, idiotic*;

chí dùn (sv): 迟钝, *slow (thought/ action); stupid*;

chī kuáng (sv): 痴狂, *nonsensical, idiotic; infatuated*;

chǔn cái: 蠢材, *fool, idiot*;

chǔn de: 蠢的, *stupid, foolish*;

chǔn lǘ: 蠢驴, *idiot, donkey, ass*;

chǔn shì: 蠢事, *stupidity, folly, lunacy*;

chǔn tóu chǔn nǎo de: 蠢头蠢脑的, *stupid-looking*;

chǔn zhū: 蠢猪, *idiot*;

shǎ (sv): 傻, *stupid, muddle-headed; stunned*

shǎ guā (n): 傻瓜, *fool*;

shǎ zi (n) (sv): 傻子, *fool; stupid, muddle-headed*;

wú liáo (sv): 无聊, *bored, boring; senseless, silly, stupid*;

yú bù kě jí (ff): 愚不可及, *height of folly; hopelessly stupid*;

yú chǔn (sv) (n): 愚蠢, *stupid, foolish, silly; stupidity; foolishness; silliness*;

SEE (请查看) **IDIOTA, BESTIA, CRETINO**

ETERNIDAD; **eternidade**; *eternity...*
ETERNO; **eterno**; *eternal, everlasting*;

wàn gǔ (adv): 万古, *forever, eternally*;

wú qióng (vp): 无穷, *infinite, endless; inexhaustible*;

yǒng (adv): 永, *perpetually, forever, always*;

yǒng héng (sv): 永恒, *eternal, perpetual, everlasting*;

yǒng jiǔ (attr): 永久, *permanent, perpetual, everlasting*;

yǒng jiù xìng (sv) (n): 永久性, *perpetual; eternity, perpetuity*;

yǒng shēng (n) (v) (attr): 永生, *eternal life; to be immortal; forever; immortal*;

yǒng shì (n): 永世, *forever; the whole lifetime*;

yǒng shì bù xiǔ (fe): 永世不朽, *last forever, be everlasting*;

yǒng wú xiū zhǐ (fe): 永无休止, *be endless, last forever, boundless*

EUFORIA; **euforia**; *euphoria, elation* ... **EUFÓRICO** (A); **eufórico** (A); *exuberant, euphoric*;

chōng pèi de jīng lì (n): 充沛的精力, *exuberant*;

fēng fù (sv): 丰富, *exuberant*;

gāo xìng de: 高兴地, *gleefully*;

jīng lì chōng pèi de (adv): 精力充沛地, *exuberantly*;

kuài lè de: 快乐的, *joyful, happy*;

kuáng xǐ (sv): 狂喜, *ecstatic, exultant*;

xīn kuài (sv): 欣快, *happy, pleased; glad, joyful*;

xìng gāo cǎi liè (fe): 兴高采烈, *in high spirits, jubilant; elation*;

yì cháng gāo xìng de: 异常高兴的, *euphoric*;

yì cháng xīng fèn de: 异常兴奋的, *euphoric*;

SEE (请查看) **EFUSIVO**

EVASIÓN; **evasão**; *escape, evasion* ... **EVASIVO** (A) (adj); **evasivo** (A); *evasive, noncommittal*;

bù biǎo tài de: 不表态的, *noncommittal*;

hán hu qí cí (fe): 含糊其辞, *equivocate*;

huí bì (n) (sv): 回避, *evasion; evasive;*
shǎn shuò (sv): 闪烁, *evasive, vague, noncommittal;*
táo shuì (n) (v): 逃税, *evasion; to evade taxes;*
SEE (请查看) ELUSIVO

EVENTO; evento; *event; contingency* **... EVENTUALIDAD; eventualidade;** *eventuality, contingency;*
shì jiàn: 事件, *event, incident; occurrence;*
shì qián: 事前, *before the event; in advance;*
SEE (请查看) ESTIPULACIÓN, CONTINGENCIA

EVIDENCIA; evidência; *evidence, proof; obviousness;*
gēn jù: 根据, *proof;*
wù zhèng: 物证, *material evidence;*
zhèng jù: 证据, *legal evidence;*
zhèng yán: 证言, *testimony*

EVIDENTE; evidente; *evident, obvious, clear;*
míng bai (sv) (v): 明白, *obvious, clear; to understand/realize;*
míng lǎng (sv): 明朗, *bright and clear; obvious, clear-cut;*
míng liǎo (sv) (v): 明了, *clear, plain; to be clear about;*
tū chū (sv) (v): 突出, *obvious, noticeable; to stress/ highlight;*
SEE (请查看) OBVIAMENTE, OBVIO, CONCRETO

EVOLUCIÓN; evolução; *evolution, development;*
jìn huà (v) (n): 进化, *to evolve; evolution;*
SEE (请查看) AMPLIAR

EXACTAMENTE; exatamente; *exactly, precisely;*
jiù shì (adv): 就是, *exactly;*
qià qià (adv): 恰恰, *just, precisely;*
què qiè de (adv): 确切地, *precisely;*
SEE (请查看) PRECISAMENTE

EXAGERACIÓN; exagero; *exaggeration, overstatement ...*
EXAGERADO (A) **exagerado** (A); *exaggerated, flamboyant, excessive;*
guò duō de: 过多的, *excessive;*
kuā dà qí cí (fe): 夸大其词, *exaggerate;*
kuā dà zhī cí (n): 夸大之词, *exaggeration;*
kuā zhāng (sv) (v) (n): 夸张, *exaggerated; to overstate; hyperbole, exaggeration;*
SEE (请查看) DESMEDIDO

EXAMEN; exame; *exam, examination;*
kǎo shì (n) (v): 考试, *exam; to take an exam;*
SEE (请查看) DOCUMENTAR

EXCELENCIA; excelência; *excellence...* **EXCELENTE; excelente;** *excellent, superb, splendid* **... EXCEPCIONAL; excepcional;** *exceptional, special, uncommon, rare ...* **EXCEPCIONALMENTE; excepcionalmente;** *exceptionally;*
bá jiān (sv) (v): 拔尖, *outstanding, superb; to excel;*
dà hǎo (sv): 大好, *excellent;*
gāo chāo (sv): 高超, *excellent, superb;*
gé wài (adv): 格外, *exceptionally;*
lì wài (n) (sv): 例外, *exception; exceptional;*
lì wài (n): 例外, *exception;*
tài bàng le (fe): 太棒了, *Excellent!;*
tài hǎo le: 太好了, *very good;*
tè bié (sv) (adv): 特别, *peculiar, unusual, special, particular; especially, particularly;*
tè děng: 特等, *special /top quality/ grade;*
tè jí (attr): 特级, *superfine, superior grade;*
tè yì (sv): 特异, *excellent, exceptionally good, unique, distinctive;*
tè zhǒng (sv): 特种, *special, particular;*
yōu yì (vp): 优异, *outstanding, excellent;*
zhuō yuè (vp): 卓越的, *outstanding, brilliant;*

SEE (请查看) **ATÍPICO, COLOSAL**

EXCEPCIÓN; exceção; *exception, oddity, quirk, rarity*;
  chú wài (n) (v): 除外, *exception; to except, to not count/include*;
  guài pǐ: 怪癖, *distortion, quirk*;
  lì wài (n): 例外, *exception, irregularity*

EXCESIVO (A); **excessivo** (A); *excessive ...* **EXCESO; excesso;** *excess*;
  chāo liàng: 超量, *excess*;
  duō yú (sv): 多余, *excessive, unnecessary*;
  guò (sv): 过, *drastic, extreme*;
  guò dù (sv): 过度, *excessive, immoderate*;
  guò tóu (sv): 过头, *excessive, too much*;
SEE (请查看) **EXAGERACIÓN, DESMEDIDO**

EXCITANTE; exitante; *exciting, arousing*;
  jī fèn (sv) (v): 激奋, *exciting; indignant; to be forced to act*;
SEE (请查看) **AGITACIÓN, AGITAR, DESCONCERTANTE, INSPIRAR**

EXCLUSIVO (A); **exclusivo** (A); *exclusive, sole*;
  dú jiā (attr): 独家, *exclusive, sole*;
  dú jiā de: 独家的, *exclusive story/ interview, etc.*;
  dú yǒu de: 独有的, *exclusive (possession, rights)*;
  quán bù de: 全部的, *exclusive (entirely)*;
  gāo jí de: 高级的, *exclusive club, district, etc.*;
  jǐn jǐn (adv): 仅仅, *only*;
  pái chì de: 排斥的, *exclusive (restrictive)*;
  pái chú zài wài (n): 排除在外, *exclusion of a person, fact, etc.*;
  pái wài de: 排外的, *exclusive (barring, discriminatory)*;
SEE (请查看) **COMPLETO, DISCIPLINA, CONFINAR**

EXCUSA; desculpa; *reason for, explanation; excuse; apology*;
  chén shù (v) (n): 陈述, *to state; formulation, statement; (attr) indicative, declarative*;
  jiě dá (v) (n): 解答, *to answer, to explain; resolution*;
  jiè kǒu (n) (v): 借口, *justification, excuse, pretext; to use as an excuse/ pretext*;
  lǐ yóu (n): 理由, *reason, grounds, argument*;
  shuō fa: 说法, *version, wording, opinion, justification*;
SEE (请查看) **ANUNCIAR, AVISAR**

EXHAUSTIVO (A); **exaustivo** (A); *exhaustive, thorough, complete*;
  chè tóu chè wěi (fe): 彻头彻尾, *through-and-through; from the top to bottom*;
  quán mào (n): 全貌, *complete picture; full view*;
SEE (请查看) **ATENCIÓN, COMPLETO, DETALLADO**

EXHAUSTO (A); **exausto** (A); *exhausted, tired, fatigued, weary*;
  fá lì (sv) (v): 乏力, *fatigued, exhausted; to be incapable of doing sthg*;
  jīn pí lì jìn (fe): 筋疲力尽, *exhausted, tired-out*;
  kū jié (sv): 枯竭, *exhausted, spent; dried-up*;
  kùn fá (sv): 困乏, *tired*;
  láo lèi (sv) (v): 劳累, *overworked, tired; to cause trouble for sb*;
  pí bèi (sv): 疲惫, *weary, exhausted*;
  pí fá (sv): 疲乏, *weary, fatigued*;
  pí juàn (sv): 疲倦, *tired and sleepy*;
  pí láo (sv) (n): 疲劳, *tired, weary; fatigue*;
  pí láo guò dù (vp): 疲劳过度, *to be excessively fatigued*;
  wěi dùn (sv): 萎顿, *exhausted, weary*;
SEE (请查看) **DÉBIL**

EXHIBICIÓN; exibição; *show, display, exhibition*;
  bó lǎn huì: 博览会, *exhibition, fair, exposition*;

chén liè guǎn: 陈列馆, *museum, exhibition hall*;
chén liè shì: 陈列室, *exhibition/show room*;
chén liè suǒ: 陈列所, *museum; exhibition hall; permanent exhibition*;
zhǎn lǎn huì: 展览会, *exhibition*;
zhǎn pǐn: 展品, *exhibit, item on display*

EXILIO; exílio; *exile*;
liú wáng (v) (n): 流亡, *to go into exile; exile*

EXISTENCIA; existência; *existence*;
cún zài (v) (n): 存在, *to exist; existence, reality*

EXISTENTE; existente; *existing, in existence*;
xiàn yǒu (sv): 现有, *currently, available, existing*

EXORBITANTE; exorbitante; *exorbitant, extreme, outrageous*;
guò gāo (sv): 过高, *exorbitant*;
guò tóu (sv): 过头, *excessive, too much*;
jīng rén (sv): 惊人, *outrageous, appalling (behavior), astonishing, amazing, alarming*
wú chǐ (sv): 无耻, *outrageous (price, cost); shameless, brazen*;
zuì yuǎn (vp): 最远, *furthest, extreme*;
SEE (请查看) EXCESIVO, EXTREMADO, EXTREMO, ATROCIDAD, DESMEDIDO, DRÁSTICO

EXÓTICO (A); **exótico** (A); *exotic, unique, extraordinary*;
bù xún cháng de: 不寻常的, *unusual*;
dú dào (sv): 独到, *original, unique*;
dú yì wú 'èr (fe): 独一无二, *unique, unparalleled*;
hǎn yǒu (vp) (v): 罕有, *unique, rare, unusual, exceptional; to rarely have*;
yì guó qíng diào (n): 异国情调, *exotic atmosphere/ touch/food/place*;
SEE (请查看) EXCEPCIÓN, ATÍPICO, COLOSAL, DISTINCIÓN

EXPECTACIÓN; expectativa; *expectation, excitement*;
xīng fèn (v) (n) (sv): 兴奋, *to be excited; excitement; exciting*;
SEE (请查看) ANTICIPAR, AUGURAR, EMOCIÓN

EXPEDITIVO (A); **expedito** (A); *expeditious, efficient, ready, fast*;
quán yí (sv): 权宜, *expedient*;
SEE (请查看) EFECTIVIDAD

EXPERIENCIA; experiência; *experience*... **EXPERIMENTADO** (A); **experiente;** *experienced*;
gǎn shòu (n) (v): 感受, *experience, impression; to feel, to sense*;
jiàn shi (v) (n): 见识, *to enlarge one's knowledge/ experiences; knowledge, experience*;
jīng guò (v) (n): 经过, *to pass/go through; experience*;
jīng yàn (n) (v): 经验, *experience; to experience*;
lǎo chéng (sv): 老成, *mature, experienced*;
lǎo liàn (sv): 老练, *experienced, skillful*;
yǒu jīng yàn (sv): 有经验, *experienced, practiced*;
yuè lì (n) (v): 阅历, *experience; to experience*

EXPERIMENTACIÓN; experimentação; *experimentation* ... **EXPERIMENTO; experimento;** *experiment*;
shí yàn: 实验, *scientific, experiment*;
shì yòng: 试用, *trial, experiment*

EXPERTO (A); **especializado** (A); *specialist; expert*;
gāo shǒu (n): 高手, *expert*;
lǎo shǒu (n): 老手, *expert*;
nèi háng (n) (sv): 内行, *expert, specialist; knowledgeable about sthg*;
yī shēng : 医生, *specialist (doctor)*;
zhuān jiā (n): 专家, *expert, specialist*;
SEE (请查看) COMPETENTE

EXPLÍCITO(A); **explícito** (A); *explicit*;
zhí shuài (sv):直率, *frank, candid,*

explicit;
SEE (请查看) CONCRETO

EXPLOSIVO (A); **explosivo** (A);
explosive;
  bào zào de: 暴躁的, *explosive person/ temper*;
  bào zhà de: 爆炸的, *explosive device/ effect*;
  bào zhà xìng de: 爆炸性的, *explosive situation/issue*;
  zhà yào: 炸药, *explosive substance; dynamite*

EXPRÉS; expresso; *urgent; express*;
  huǒ jí (sv): 火急, *urgent, pressing*;
  tè jí (sv): 特级, *especially urgent; top priority*;
  tè kuài (sv): 特快, *express (mail, service, etc.)*;
SEE (请查看) EMERGENCIA

EXPRESAMENTE; expressamente;
expressly, explicitly, specifically;
  jù tǐ (sv) (adv): 具体, *concrete, specific, particular*;
  jù tǐ de (adv): 具体地, *specifically*;
  míng què de: 明确地, *exactly*;
  tè bié de: 特别地, *specifically, expressly*;
  tè dìng de: 特定地, *exclusively*;
  zhuān mén (sv) (adj): 专门, *specialized, special*;
  zhuān mén de (adv): 专门地, *specifically*

EXPRESIÓN; expressão; *expression*;
  biǎo qíng: 表情, *gesture, expression*;
  liǎn sè (n): 脸色, *facial expression; complexion*;
  miàn sè (n): 面色, *facial expression*;
  qì sè (n): 气色, *look, expression*;
  shén sè (n): 神色, *expression, look*;
  yán cí (n): 言辞, *words, wording, expression*

EXTENSAMENTE; extensivamente;
extensively, widely **... EXTENSO** (A);
extenso (A); *in area; extensive (long, lengthy)*;
  dà guī mó (adv): 大规模, *extensively, large-scale*;
  kuān kuàng (sv): 宽旷, *extensive, vast*;
SEE (请查看) DESMEDIDO, DILATADO

EXTERNO (A); **externo** (A); *external, outside*;
  duì wài (sv) (v): 对外, *external, foreign; to resist foreign, aggression*;
  wài biǎo (n): 外表, *outward appearance; exterior; surface*;
  wài lái (sv): 外来, *outside, external, foreign*;
  wài mian (n): 外面, *outside, exterior*;
  wài tou (n): 外头, *outside, outdoors*;
  wài zài (sv): 外在, *external, extrinsic*;
SEE (请查看) EXTERIOR

EXTINCIÓN; extinção; *extinction, loss, termination* **... EXTINTO; extinto** (A);
extinct;
  miè jué: 灭绝, *extinction (of a species, etc.)*;
  xī miè le (sv): 熄灭了, *extinct*;
SEE (请查看) DETERIORAR

EXTRAORDINARIO (A);
extraordinário (A); *extraordinary; special, outstanding*;
  chū zhòng (sv): 出众, *outstanding*;
  fēi cháng (sv) (adv): 非常, *special, extraordinary, unusual; extremely, highly*;
  mào jiān (sv): 冒尖, *outstanding*;
  xī yǒu (sv): 稀有, *rare*;
  tè bié (sv) (adv): 特别, *unusual, special; especially*;
  tè zhǒng (sv): 特种, *special, particular*;
SEE (请查看) ESTUPEFACCIÓN, EXÓTICO, ATÍPICO, COLOSAL, EGREGIO, EXCEPCIONAL

EXTREMADO (A) (adj); **excessivo** (A); *excessive, extreme* **... EXTREMO** (A); **extremo** (A); *extreme; furthest, outermost*;
  jí diǎn: 极点, *the limit, the extreme, furthest point, extremity*;
  jí dù (n) (adv): 极度, *extreme point*;

extremely, ultimately;
mò duān: 末端, *extreme point; tip, end;*
piān jī (sv): 偏激, *extreme, radical;*
zhuó jué (sv): 卓绝, *unsurpassed, extreme;*
SEE (请查看) EXCESIVO, DESMEDIDO, DRÁSTICO

EXTROVERTIDO (A); **extrovertido** (A); *extrovert; outgoing;*
wài xiàng (sv) (n) (attr): 外向, *open, frank; extroverted; extroversion; exocentric;*
wài xiàng de: 外向的, *exocentric;*
wài xiàng xìng: 外向性, *outgoing personality;*

xìng gé wài xiàng zhě: 性格外向者, *extroverted*

EXUBERANCIA; exuberância; *exuberance* … **EXUBERANTE; exuberante,** *exuberant; exuberant;*
huó pō de: 活泼地, *lively;*
SEE (请查看) ENTUSIASMO, ARDOROSO, EFUSIVO

EXULTANTE; exultante; *exultant, elated, overjoyed;*
huān xǐ: 欢喜, *overjoyed, happy, delighted; to like, to be fond of;*
huān xīn (sv) (n): 欢心, *elated; joy;*
kuáng xǐ (sv): 狂喜, *ecstatic, exultant*

Easily recognizable verbs and their Portuguese and Chinese equivalents
Verbos fácilmente reconocibles en Español-Portugués-Inglés y sus equivalentes en Chino
Verbos facilmente reconhecível em Espanhol-Português-Inglês e seus equivalentes em Chinês
很容易辨认的西班牙语，葡萄牙语，英语动词和他们的中文对等词

ECLIPSAR; eclipsar; *to eclipse, to outshine, to surpass;*
chāo yuè: 超越, *to exceed, to surmount, to surpass*

EDUCAR; educar; *to educate, bring up, train;*
fǔ yǎng: 抚养, *to rear a child;*
xùn liàn: 训练, *to train;*
SEE (请查看) FORMAR, FORMATIVO

EFECTUAR; efetuar; *to carry out, to go on, to take place;*
jìn xíng: 进行, *to carry out an attack/ an investigation, etc.;*
SEE (请查看) APLICAR, EJECUTIVO

EJECUTAR; executar; *to execute/ perform/carry out;*
shí xíng: 实行, *to perform a ceremony;*
SEE (请查看) CONCLUIR, EJECUTIVO

ELABORAR; elaborar; *to prepare; to make, to draw up, to produce;*
cǎo nǐ: 草拟, *to draw up a plan, etc.;*
chéng wéi: 成为, *to be, to become sthg;*
cù shǐ mǒu rén: 促使某人 … *to make (force) sb do sthg;*
fàn: 犯, *to make a mistake;*
jiāng mǒu rén: 将某人 … *to make sthg into sthg;*
jié jiāo: 结交, *to make a friend/enemy;*
shēng chǎn: 生产, *to manufacture sthg;*
shǐ chéng gōng: 使成功, *to cause (make) … , to succeed;*
shǐ: 使 , *to make/cause/enable; to use/ employ/ apply;*
zhèng: 挣, *to make money; to struggle/ strive;*
zhì zào: 制造, *to make/manufacture/ create;*
SEE (请查看) FABRICAR, MANUFACTURAR, PRODUCIR

ELIMINAR; eliminar; *to eliminate/ remove/get rid of*;
jiè chú: 戒除, *to stop smoking*;
táo tài: 淘汰, *to eliminate a candidate*;
xiāo chú (v) (n): 消除, *to eliminate poverty, to eliminate; elimination*

ELUCIDAR; elucidar; *to elucidate, explain*;
chǎn míng: 阐明, *to give reasons for sthg*;
SEE (请查看) INTERPRETAR

EMANAR; emanar; *to emanate/come from*;
fā shè (v): 发射, *to launch/project; to emit/transmit*;
lái zì (vp): 来自, *to come/stem/ originate from*

EMBARCAR; embarcar; *to embark/ board*;
chéng zuò: 乘坐, *to ride in a boat*;
cóng shì: 从事, *to embark on a career/ journey, etc.*;
dēng jī: 登机, *to board a plane*;
dēng lún: 登轮, *to board a steamship*;
dēng shàng: 登上, *to embark on/to board a ship/ train/plane*;
shàng chuán: 上船, *to board a ship/ boat; to embark*

EMIGRAR; emigrar; *to emigrate/ move/relocate/ resettle*;
liú dòng: 流动, *to flow, to move, to go from place to place*;
liú làng: 流浪, *to wander, to roam about*;
nuó dòng: 挪动, *to move/shift sthg*;
qiān chū: 迁出, *to move out*;
qiān jìn: 迁进, *to move in*;
qiān xǐ: 迁徙, *to move, to migrate*;
qiān yí: 迁移, *to move/migrate; to transfer/shift*;
qiáo jū: 侨居, *to emigrate*;
yí dòng: 移动, *to move/shift sthg*;
yí jū guó wài: 移居国外, *to emigrate abroad/ overseas*;
yí jū: 移居, *to shift/move*;
yí mín (v) (n): 移民, *to emigrate/*

immigrate; settler, immigrant; hermit, recluse

EMITIR; emitir; *to emit/issue*;
fā biǎo chū lai: 发表出来, *to publish/ issue*;
fā chòu: 发臭, *to release a bad odor*;
fā chū: 发出, *to issue/send/give out sthg; to deliver; to give an order/ instructions, etc.*;
fā gěi: 发给, *to issue/distribute*;
fā hào shī lìng (fe): 发号施令, *to issue orders/ order people about*;
fā rè: 发热, *to give out/generate/emit heat*;
fā shēng: 发生, *to produce/emit sound*;
fā sòng: 发送, *to transmit*;
fā xiè: 发泄, *to let off/give vent to*;
fā xíng: 发行, *to issue/publish/ distribute*;
fā zì (vp): 发自, *to evolve from/issue from*;
fàng shè: 放射, *to radiate, to emit*;
sàn: 散, *to break up/distribute/let out*;
sàn fā: 散发, *to send out/diffuse/ distribute/issue*;
shū chū: 输出, *to send out/emit (a signal, etc.); to export*;
SEE (请查看) ANUNCIAR

ENTRAR; entrar; *to go in, to come in, to enter*;
cān jiā bǐ sài: 参加比赛, *to enter a competition*;
cān jiā: 参加, *to enter; to take part in*;
cān yù: 参与, *to come in on a deal*;
cān zhàn: 参战, *to enter a war/take part in a battle*;
chéng bāo: 承包, *to enter into a contract*;
chū chǎng: 出场, *to appear on stage; to enter an arena*;
dào dá: 到达, *to enter a plane/a train; to go in*;
dēng chǎng: 登场, *to go on stage; to enter*;
dēng lù: 登录, *to make an entry in a book, etc.*;
jìn rù: 进入, *to enter/go into a room/ building*;

jìn chǎng: 进场, *to enter an arena*;
jìn lái: 进来, *to enter, to come in, to get in*;
jìn qù: 进去, *to enter*;
jìn rù: 进入, *Come in!*;
jìn zhàng: 进账, *to come into money*;
kāi shǐ jìn rù: 开始进入, *to enter a new stage/phase*;
rù jìng: 入境, *to enter a country*;
rù: 入, *to enter a profession*;
shū chū: 输出, *to enter (data, etc.); to import, to introduce sthg*;
shū rù: 输入, *to enter into a computer; to import; to introduce sthg*;
SEE (请查看) ADMITIR

ENUMERAR; enumerar; *to list/ enumerate/specify/ count*;
biāo míng: 标明, *to list, to show*;
liè chū: 列出, *to list/record*;
luó liè: 罗列, *to list, to enumerate; to set out, to display*

EQUIPAR; equipar; *to equip/fit out*;
pèi bèi: 配备, *to equip (furnish) a car, room, etc.; to prepare sb for sthg*;
zhuāng bèi: 装备, *to equip sb/sthg*

EQUIVALER; equivaler; *to be equal to/equivalent/ rank with*;
bǐ de shàng: 比得上, *can compare with/compare favorably with*;
děng jià (n): 等价, *equal in value, equivalence*;
děng tóng duì dài: 等同对待, *to equate*;
děng tóng: 等同, *to equate, to be equal to*;
děng yú: 等于, *to be equal/equivalent to; to be the same as*;
pǐ dí: 匹敌, *to be equal to, to be well-matched*;
shǐ xiāng děng: 使相等, *to equalize*;
xiāng fú: 相符, *to conform to, to match*;
zhé hé: 折合, *to convert into; to amount to; to be equivalent to*;
SEE (请查看) EQUIVALENTE

ERRADICAR; erradicar; *to eradicate/*
root out/ remove;
bá chú: 拔除, *to pull out, to remove*;
chǎn chú: 铲除, *to root out, to eradicate*;
gǎi diào: 改掉, *to remove, to give up*;
gēn chú: 根除, *to root out, to eliminate, to eradicate*;
xiāo miè: 消灭, *to eliminate, to eradicate, to perish, to die out*;
gēn jué: 根绝, *to root/stamp out; to eradicate*;
gōu xiāo: 勾销, *to expunge, to erase, to remove*;
jiě chú: 解除, *to remove, to get rid of*;
pái chì: 排斥, *to reject, to exclude, to remove*;
qīng chǔ: 清楚, *to remove a stain*;
tuō xià: 脱下, *to remove clothing/ bandage, etc.*;
yí zǒu: 移走, *remove an object*;
zhāi chú: 摘除, *to excise, to remove*;
SEE (请查看) APARTAR, DESMONTAR

ESCAPAR; escapar; *to escape/run away*;
táo pǎo: 逃跑, *to run away/flee*;
táo tuō: 逃脱, *to succeed in escaping*;
táo zǒu: 逃走, *to get away, to run away/flee*

ESPECULAR; especular; *to speculate/consider; to guess, gamble*;
dǔ bó: 赌博, *to gamble*;
rèn wéi: 认为, *to think/believe sthg about sb/sthg*;
SEE (请查看) OPORTUNISTA, AVENTURA, CONSIDERACIÓN, CONJETURAR

ESTUDIAR; estudar; *to study*;
dú shū: 读书, *to study, to attend school*;
gōng dú: 攻读, *to study a subject*;
liú xué: 留学, *to study abroad*;
niàn shū: 念书, *to read, to recite, to study*;
qiú xué: 求学, *to go to school/college; to study*;
xué xí: 学习, *to study, to learn, to learn from*;

yòng gōng (v) (sv): 用功, *to study, to work hard; hardworking, diligent*;
zhì xué: 治学, *to do scholarly research, to study*;
zǐ xì chá kàn: 仔细查看, *to study evidence/sb's face*;
zì xí: 自习, *to study alone*

EVACUAR; evacuar; *to evacuate/ move/relocate/ transfer*;
bān jiā: 搬家, *to relocate*;
chè bīng: 撤兵, *to withdraw*;
chè lí: 撤离, *to leave/evacuate*;
chè tuì: 撤退, *to retreat (withdraw)*;
jìn zhǎn (v) (n): 进展, *to make progress/headway; progress, advance*;
shū sàn: 疏散, *to evacuate people*;
tuì bì: 退避, *to withdraw and stay away*;
tuì chū: 退出, *to withdraw from, to quit*;
tuì xiū: 退休, *to retire*;
zhuǎn xué: 转学, *to transfer to another school (of a student)*;
SEE (请查看**) EMIGRAR**

EVADIR; evadir; *to evade/avoid/ escape*;
bì miǎn: 避免, *to avoid/dodge*;
duǒ bì: 躲避, *to evade, to shun*;
fáng zhǐ: 防止, *to prevent (trouble, danger, etc.)*;
SEE (请查看**) ESCAPAR**

EVAPORAR; evaporar; *to evaporate/ vanish/ disappear*;
jué jì: 绝迹, *to be eradicated, to vanish*;
miè jué: 灭绝, *to cease, to exit*;
sàn shī: 散失, *to lose, to evaporate*;
shī zōng: 失踪, *to disappear, to be missing*;
xiāo shī: 消失, *to vanish, to disappear, to be missing*;
yǐn tuì: 隐退, *to live in seclusion, to disappear, to retire*;
zhēng fā: 蒸发, *to evaporate*

EVOLUCIONAR; evoluir; *to evolve/ develop*;
fā yù: 发育, *to develop, to grow*;

jìn huà (v) (n): 进化, *to evolve; evolution*;
kāi fā: 开发, *to develop/open up*;
yǎn biàn: 演变, *to develop, to evolve*;
SEE (请查看**) AMPLIAR, BOOM**

EXASPERAR; exasperar; *to exasperate/infuriate*;
jī nù: 激怒, *to exasperate/infuriate*;
SEE (请查看**) AGRAVAR**

EXCAVAR; escavar; *to dig/dig out/ excavate*;
fā jué: 发掘, *to excavate, to unearth*;
wā jué: 挖掘, *to dig, to excavate*;
wā: 挖, *to dig, to excavate*

EXCEDER; exceder; *to exceed/ surpass*;
chāo chū: 超出, *to exceed/overstep*;
chāo 'é: 超额, *to exceed a quota*;
chāo guò: 超过, *to exceed (more than)*;
chāo yuè: 超越, *to exceed/surpass*;
sài guò: 赛过, *to overtake, to surpass*

EXCEPTUAR; excetuar; *to except, exclude*;
bù bāo kuò: 不包括, *to exclude, eliminate*;
chú diào: 除掉, *to except/eliminate*;
chú wài: 除外, *to exclude*;
pái chì: 排斥, *to reject, to exclude, to reject*

EXISTIR; existir; *to exist*;
shēng cún: 生存, *to subsist/exist/live*;
SEE (请查看**) EXISTENCIA**

EXPANDIR; expandir; *to spread; to expand/extend/enlarge*;
péng zhàng: 膨胀, *to expand/swell/ inflate*;
shēn cháng: 伸长, *to stretch, to extend*;
shēn suō: 伸缩, *to expand and contract; to be flexible*;
shēn zhǎn (v) (n): 伸展, *to spread/ extend; extension*;
shū zhǎn (v) (sv): 舒展, *to spread, to*

stretch out; comfortable, pleasant;
tuò zhǎn: 拓展, to expand;
yán xù: 延续, to continue, to last, to extend;
zhāng kāi: 张开, to open/spread;
zhuàng dà (v) (sv): 壮大, to expand; to grow in strength; well-built;
SEE (请查看) AGRANDAR, AMPLIAR, DISEMINAR

EXPLORAR; explorar; *to explore/ examine; to reconnoiter (MIL);*
chá kàn: 查看, *to look sthg over, to examine a situation; to check up/go over/ferret out;*
chá kǎo: 查考, *to examine, to do research on;*
hé suàn: 核算, *to assess, to examine and calculate;*
kān tàn: 勘探, *to explore for sthg in particular;*
kǎo chá: 考查, *to examine, to check;*
kǎo hé: 考核, *to examine, to check, to assess sb's capabilities;*
kǎo wèn: 考问, *to examine orally, to question;*
shěn dìng: 审定, *to examine and approve, to finalize;*
shěn hé: 审核, *to examine and verify, to check;*
shěn pàn: 审判, *to examine and decide (a case), to sentence;*
shěn pī: 审批, *to examine and approve;*
tàn cè: 探测, *to explore, to probe;*
tàn chá: 探查, *to explore with the hands;*
tàn jiū: 探究, *to explore an idea;*
tàn suǒ: 探索, *to explore a place, to probe;*
tàn xiǎn: 探险, *to look around, to explore;*
zhěn shì: 诊室, *to examine a patient;*
SEE (请查看) CENSURA, DELIBERACIÓN, DIAGNOSTICAR, DOCUMENTAR

EXPRESAR; expressar; *to express/ voice;*
biǎo dá (v) (n): 表达, *to express/ convey/voice/act; expression;*
SEE (请查看) FORMULAR, COMUNICAR

EXPULSAR; expulsar; *to expel/send off/reject;*
gǎn zǒu: 赶走, *to expel/drive away;*
kāi chú: 开除, *to expel, to discharge, to fire;*
SEE (请查看) CONFINAR

Interchangeable Spanish-Portuguese-English words and their Chinese equivalents
Palabras en Español-Portugués-Inglés y sus equivalentes en Chino
Palavras em Espanhol-Português-Inglês e seus equivalentes em Chinês
西班牙语，葡萄牙语，英语及中文的对等单词

FACIAL; facial;
miàn bù (n): 面部, *facial; face*

FACSÍMILE; fac-simile;
chuán zhēn: 传真, *facsimile*

FAMILIAR; familiar;
cháng jiàn (sv): 常见, *commonly seen,*

familiar;
SEE (请查看) CORDIALIDAD

FAST FOOD; fast-food;
kuài cān: 快餐, *fast food; snack*

FATAL; fatal; *awful, terrible; mortal;*

jí huài (sv) (vp): 极坏, *very bad, the worst*;
kě pà (sv): 可怕, *fearful, terrible, awful*;
zāi nàn xìng (attr): 灾难性, *disastrous*;
zhì mìng (attr): 致命, *fatal, mortal, deadly*

FAUNA; fauna;
dòng wù qún: 动物群, *fauna*

FAVOR; favor;
zhī chí: 支持, *favor*

FEBRIL (MED); **febril;** *hectic, feverish*;
kuáng rè (sv): 狂热, *feverish, fanatical*

FECAL; fecal;
fèn biàn: 粪便, *excrement and urine, night soil*

FEDERAL; federal;
lián bāng de: 联邦的, *federal*;
lián bāng zhì: 联邦制, *federalism*

FERVOR (RELIG); **fervor;**
chì rè (n) (sv): 炽热, *fervid, ardent; red heat*;
SEE (请查看**) ENTUSIASMO, ARDOROSO**

FESTIVAL (RELIG); **festival;**
jié rì: 节日, *festival, holiday*

FEUDAL; feudal;
fēng jiàn de: 封建的, *feudal*;
fēng jiàn zhì dù: 封建制度, *feudalism*

FIASCO; fiasco;
cán bài (n): 残败, *fiasco; wipeout*

FILM ó FILME; filme; *movie, film*;
yǐng piàn: 影片, *film*

FINAL; final;
zhōng duān: 终端, *terminal*;
zhōng jí: 终极, *final, ultimate*;
zhōng jú: 终局, *end, outcome*;
zuì zhōng 最终, *last, final, ultimate*;
SEE (请查看**) DEFINITIVO, TERMINAL**

FLASH; flash; *flash, photo flash,*

inspiration; newsflash, *inspiration*;
dēng: 灯, *photo flash*;
gǔ wǔ: 鼓舞, *inspiration*

FLORA; flora;
zhí wù qún: 植物群, *flora*

FLORAL; floral;
huā (n) (v) (sv): 花, *flower, blossom; fireworks; essence; to spread, expend; flowery, florid*;
huā de: 花的, *floral, florid*

FÓRCEPS; fórceps;
qián zi: 钳子, *forceps, clamp, pliers, tongs*;
chǎn qián: 产钳, *obstetrics forceps*

FORMAL; formal;
zhèng shì de: 正式的, *formal offer/ approval/ occasion/dinner*;
shǒu xù (n): 手续, *procedure, formality*

FÓRMULA; fórmula;
chéng shì: 程式, *formula, pattern, program, form*;
fāng zi: 方子, *prescription, formula*;
gōng shì (MATH): 公式, *formula*

FREELANCE; freelance;
zì yóu zhí yè zhě: 自由职业者, *freelance person*

FREEZER ó CONGELADOR; freezer;
bīng guì: 冰柜, *refrigerator, ice box*;
bīng xiāng: 冰箱, *refrigerator, freezer*

FRONTAL; frontal;
zhèng miàn (n) (attr) (adv): 正面, *obverse/right side; front, facade; positive; directly, openly*;
zhèng miàn de: 正面的, *frontal*

FRUGAL; frugal;
jié jiǎn: 节俭, *frugal, thrifty, economical*;
SEE (请查看**) AUSTERIDAD, ECONOMÍA**

FUNDAMENTAL; fundamental;
gēn běn (n) (sv) (adv): 根本, *base, foundation; basic, fundamental,*

essential; thoroughly;
jī běn (n) (sv) (adv): 基本, *basics, fundamental, elementary; essential; basically*

FUNERAL; funeral;
　hòu shì: 后事, *funeral;*
　sāng zàng (v) (n): 丧葬, *to conduct a funeral; burial, funeral;*

zàng lǐ: 葬礼, *funeral ceremony, burial rights*

FUROR; furor; *fury, rage;*
　bào nù: 暴怒, *violent rage, fury;*
　nù huǒ: 怒火, *anger, fury;*
　nù qì: 怒气, *anger, rage;*
SEE (请查看) CÓLERA

Easily recognizable Spanish-Portuguese-English nouns, adjectives and adverbs and their Chinese equivalents
Nombres, sustantivos, adjetivos y adverbios en Español-Portugués-Inglés y sus equivalentes en Chino
Nomes, substantivos, adjetivos e advérbios em Espanhol-Português-Inglês e seus equivalentes em Chinês
容易辨认的西班牙语，葡萄牙语，英语的名词，形容词和副词和他们的中文对等词

FABRICANTE; fabricante; *manufacturer;*
　zhì zào yè zhě: 制造业者, *manufacturer;*
　zhì zào shāng: 制造商, *manufacturer*

FABULOSO (A); **fabuloso** (A); *fabulous, incredible;*
　gé wài de: 格外的, *fabulous beauty/ wealth/success;*
SEE (请查看) COLOSAL

FACETA; faceta; *facet, aspect, characteristic, feature;*
　céng miàn: 层面, *scope, range, aspect;*
　fāng miàn: 方面, *aspect, facet; side;*
　jú miàn: 局面, *situation, phase, aspect;*
　yàng zi: 样子, *aspect; appearance, shape, manner, air;*
　zhǎng xiàng: 长相, *looks, features, appearance;*
SEE (请查看) CARACTERÍSTICO

FÁCIL; fácil; *easy, simple, uncomplicated, basic;*
　róng yì de: 容易的, *easy;*
SEE (请查看) BÁSICO, DIRECTO

FACTIBLE; factível; *feasible, viable, practicable;*

　kě xíng (sv): 可行, *feasible, workable, practicable;*
SEE (请查看) POSIBLE

FALACIA; falácia; *fallacy, deceit, mistake, error ... FALLO; erro; mistake, error;*
　chā cuò: 差错, *mistake, error;*
　cuò wù (n) (sv): 错误, *mistake, error, wrong, incorrect;*
　guò shī: 过失, *mistake, error;*
　miù lùn: 谬论, *fallacy;*
　wù chā: 误差, *error;*
　xié shuō: 邪说, *heresy; fallacy;*
SEE (请查看) DESINTEGRACIÓN, DIGRESIÓN

FALIBLE; falível; *fallible, deceitful, misleading, erroneous ... FALSEDAD; falsidade;* *hypocrisy; falseness, falsity;*
　cuò wù de: 错误的, *erroneous;*
　jiǎ zhuāng (sv): 假装的, *insincere person/smile/ promise;*
　shǐ rén wù jiě de: 使人误解的, *misleading;*
SEE (请查看) HIPÓCRITA, DUPLICIDAD

FALSIFICACIÓN; falsificação; *falsification, forgery;*

wěi zào pǐn: 伪造品, *forged document/painting, etc.*;
wěi zào zuì: 伪造罪, *forgery (the crime)*;
yàn pǐn: 赝品, *a fake*

FALSO (A); **falso** (A); *false, untrue; fake, counterfeit; spurious*;
huǎng huà: 谎话, *lie, falsehood*;
jiǎ huò: 假货, *fake*;
rén gōng de: 人工的, *artificial; man-made*;
xū jiǎ (sv): 虚假, *false, phony*;
SEE (请查看) FALIBLE, EQUIVOCADO, APÓCRIFO

FALTA; falta; *lack, need, absence; shortcoming, fault*;
xū qiú: 需求, *need, demand, requirement*;
xū yào (v) (n): 需要, *to need; needs, necessities*;
SEE (请查看) CÉNTRICO, DEBILIDAD, DÉFICIT, DEFECTO, DEFICIENCIA

FAMA; fama; *fame, glory*;
guāng róng de: 光荣的, *glorious*;
róng yù: 荣 誉, *glory*;
shēng yù: 声誉, *fame*

FAMILIA; família; *family*;
jiā tíng: 家庭, *family, household*;
jiā: 家, *family, household, home*;
rén jiā: 人家, *household, family*

FAMOSO (A); **famoso** (A); *famous person, celebrity*;
yào rén (n): 要人, *important person, VIP*;
SEE (请查看) CÉLEBRE, CELEBRIDAD, AFAMADO, EGREGIO

FANÁTICO (A); **fanatico** (A); *fanatic; fanatical, compulsive, rabid ...*
FANATISMO; fanatismo; *fanaticism, hysteria, frenzy*;
fā kuáng shì de: 发狂似的, *frantic*;
kuáng luàn (sv): 狂乱, *frantic, frenzied, mad*;

kuáng luàn de (adv): 狂乱地, *frantically*;
kuáng rè (sv): 狂热, *crazed, fanatical; feverish, delirious*;
kuáng rè zhě: 狂热者, *fanatic*;
qiú mí: 球迷, *fan (sports enthusiast)*

FANTÁSTICO (A); **fantástico** (A); *fantastic, extraordinary, marvelous, spectacular, wonderful*;
jiàn guǐ (fe): 见鬼, *fantastic, absurd*;
měi miào (sv): 美妙, *marvelous, wonderful*;
piāo liang (sv): 漂亮, *pretty, beautiful, wonderful*;
qí miào (sv): 奇妙, *wonderful, marvelous, fantastic*;
SEE (请查看) ESTUPOR, ESPECTACULAR

FARMACÉUTICO (A); **farmacêutico** (A); *pharmaceutical ...* **FARMACIA; farmácia;** *pharmacy*;
yào diàn (pw): 药店, *drugstore, pharmacy*;
zhì yào (v) (n) (sv): 制药, *to make/manufacture medicines; pharmacy; pharmaceutical*;
SEE (请查看) DISPENSARIO

FASCINANTE; fascinante; *fascinating, intriguing, beguiling, engrossing, enthralling, spellbinding*;
mí rén de: 迷人的, *fascinating person/place/thing*;
rù mí de: 入迷的, *be fascinated, be enchanted*;
yǐn rén rú shèng (fe): 引人入胜, *intriguing, fascinating, absorbing*;
SEE (请查看) FASCINAR

FASE; fase; *phase, stage*;
jiē duàn: 阶 段, *stage, phase*

FATALISMO; fatalismo; *fatalism ...* **FATALISTA; fatalista;** *fatalistic (adj), fatalist (n); pessimist*;
bēi guān (sv): 悲 观, *pessimistic*;
bēi guān zhǔ yì zhě: 悲观主义者, *pesimist*;

bēi guān zhǔ yì: 悲观主义, *pessimism*;
sù mìng lùn zhě: 宿命论者, *fatalist*;
sù mìng lùn: 宿命论, *fatalism, determinism*

FATIGA; fadiga; *fatigue, weariness, tiredness ...* **FATIGADO** (A); **fatigado** (A); *tired, weary, worn out ...*
FATIGOSO (A); **fatigoso** (A); *tiring, fatiguing;* **exaustivo** (A); *exhausting; tiring*;
  kùn rén de: 困人的, *tiring*;
  lèi de: 累 的, *tired of doing sthg*;
  pí bèi bù kān de: 疲惫不堪的, *tired out, exhausted*;
  pī fá: 疲乏, *tired of sb/sthg; weary; fatigued*;
  pí láo qiáng dù (n): 疲劳强度, *tiredness*
  pò jiù: 破 旧, *worn out or damaged article/object*;
  pò làn (sv): 破烂, *worn out, tattered, ragged*;
  shǐ rén pí láo de: 使人疲劳的, *tiring, tiresome*;
SEE (请查看**) EXHAUSTO**

FATUO (A); **fátuo** (A); *fatuous, foolish, conceited*;
  zì fù: 自负, *conceited*;
  zì gāo zì dà (fe): 自高自大, *conceited, self-important*;
SEE (请查看**) BURLAR, COMPLACIDO**

FAVORITISMO; favoritismo; *favoritism, bias, prejudice, partiality*;
  piān 'ài: 偏 爱, *favoritism, favorite*;
  piān jiàn: 偏 见, *bias, prejudice*;
  piān xīn (sv): 偏心, *bias, partiality*

FAVORITO (A); **favorito** (A); *favorite, best-liked, most-liked* ;
  piān 'ài: 偏爱, *favorite thing/person*;
  yōu xiān de: 优先的, *preferential*;
  zuì xǐ huān de: 最喜欢的, *favorite food/book/author, etc.*;
SEE (请查看**) DIGRESIÓN**

FEDERACIÓN; federeção; *federation*;
  lián bāng: 联邦, *federation, union, commonwealth*

FELONÍA; felonia; *treachery, betrayal; felony*;
  bèi pàn: 背叛, *betrayal*;
  wēi xiǎn: 危险, *treachery*;
  zhòng zuì: 重罪, *felony*

FEMENINO (A); **feminino** (A); *feminine, female (BOT) (ZOOL) ...* **FÉMINA; fêmea;** *female, woman ...* **FEMINIDAD** ó **FEMINEIDAD; feminilidade;** *femininity ...* **FEMINISMO; feminismo;** *feminism ...* **FEMINISTA; feminista;** *feminist*;
  cí xìng: 雌性, *female*;
  nǚ quán zhǔ yì zhě (n): 女权主义者, *feminist*
  nǚ quán zhǔ yì: 女权主义, *feminism*;
  nǚ xìng de: 女性的, *femininity*;
  nǚ xìng: 女性, *female sex, woman*;
  nǚ zǐ: 女子, *woman, female*

FENOMENAL; fenomenal; *fantastic, phenomenal*;
  fēi fán de: 非 凡 的, *phenomenal*;
  jí hǎo de: 极 好 的, *fantastic*;
SEE (请查看**) FANTÁSTICO**

FEROZ; feroz; *fierce; ferocious, cruel, savage, brutal, frenzied; intense, truculent, barbaric*;
  cán kù de: 残酷的, *cruel, brutal ruthless*;
  cán rěn de: 残忍的, *cruel and ruthless*;
  è dú de: 恶 毒的, *cruel treatment, behaviour*;
  xiōng cán de: 凶残的, *savage and ruthless*;
  xiōng 'è de: 凶恶的, *ferocious and vicious; fiendish*;
  xiōng hěn de: 凶狠的, *fierce and malicious*;
  xiong xiǎn de: 凶险的, *dangerous and dreadful*;
  yě màn de: 野蛮的, *uncivilized; savage; atrocious; brutal*;
SEE (请查看**) ABUSIVO, BRAVÍO,**

DIABÓLICO, DRÁSTICO
FESTIVO (A); **festivo** (A); *festive, cheerful, merry*;
  huān kuài de: 欢快的, *cheerful*;
  huān lè (sv) 欢乐, *happy, joyful, delighted; happy and gay; merry*;
  huān xǐ (sv) (v): 欢喜, *joyful, happy, delighted; to be fond of*;
  kuài lè (sv): 快乐, *happy, cheerful*;
  lè hā ha (vp): 乐哈哈, *joyful, cheerful*;
  lè hē hē (vp): 乐呵呵, *happy and buoyant*;
  lè tiān: 乐天, *to be carefree*;
  lè yì (v) (sv): 乐意, *to love to (do sthg); happy, pleased*;
  lè yú: 乐于, *to be happy, to take delight in*;
  shū chàng (sv): 舒畅, *happy, carefree*;
  tòng kuai (sv): 痛快, *happy, joyful*;
  xǐ qìng de: 喜庆的, *festive*;
  xìng fú (sv) (n): 幸福, *happy; happiness*;
SEE (请查看) **APRECIAR, COMPLACIDO, DELEITE**

FETICHE; fetiche; *fetish, obsession, mania, compulsion*;
  mí liàn: 迷恋, *to be obsessed/infatuated with*;
  zháo mí: 着迷, *obsession, spellbound*;
SEE (请查看) **COMPULSIVO**

FÉTIDO; fétido (A); *fetid, stinking, foul smelling*;
  chòu (sv): 臭, *smelly, stinky, foul, disgusting*;
  chòu hōng hōng (fe): 臭烘烘, *stinky*;
  chòu qì: 臭气, *stench*;
  è chòu (adj) (n): 恶臭, *stench*;
  è liè (sv): 恶劣, *vile, nasty, of very poor quality*;
  nán wén: 难闻, *stinking, malodorous*

FETO; feto; *fetus*;
  tāi 'er: 胎儿, *fetus*

FEUDALISMO; feudalismo; *feudalism*;
  fēng jiàn de: 封建的, *feudal society/system*;
SEE (请查看) **FEUDAL**

FICTICIO (A); **ficticio** (A); *fictitious, imaginary, fabricated*;
  dù zhuàn de: 杜撰的, *made up, fictitious*;
  xū gòu de: 虚构的, *fictitious*

FIDELIDAD; fidelidade; *fidelity, loyalty; accuracy*;
  zhōng chéng: 忠诚, *fidelity of spouse/dog*;
  jīng què: 精确, *fidelity of a report/translation*

FILTRACIÓN; filtragem; *filtration; leak, seepage*;
  liè xì: 裂隙, *leak of liquid/gas*;
  lòu dòng: 漏洞, *leak in the roof/pipe, etc.*;
  shèn chū (v) (n): 渗出, *to seep/ooze out; seepage*

FILTRO; filtro; *filter, screening*;
  guò lǜ qì: 过滤器, *filter of water/oil*

FIN; final; último (A); *end, extreme limit; purpose, aim*;
  mò wěi: 末尾, *end*;
SEE (请查看) **DEFINITIVO, TERMINADO, FUNCIÓN**

FINALISTA; finalista; *finalist*;
  jué sài xuǎn shǒu 决赛选手, *finalist*

FINALIZACIÓN; finalização; *termination, conclusion, completion*;
  jié shù: 结束, *end of a book/meeting/film*;
SEE (请查看) **APREHENDER, TERMINADO**

FINALMENTE; finalmente; *finally, in the end*;
  zuì zhōng de: 最终的, *finally*;
SEE (请查看) **DEFINITIVO**

FINITO (A); **finito** (A); *finite, bounded, restricted, delimited*;
  xiàn dìng de: 限定的, *finite*;
  yǒu xiàn de: 有限的, *limited, finite*

FINO (A); **fino** (A); *fine, thin, slim*;
  báo de: 薄的, *slim book/wallet, etc.*;
  miáo tiáo de: 苗条的, *slim figure*;
  shòu de: 瘦的, *thin person*;
  xì de: 细的, *fine in texture*;
  xī de: 稀的, *thin soup/sauce, etc.*;
  xì wēi chā bié (n): 细微差别, *a fine distinction, subtle difference*;
  xì wēi de (adj) (sv): 细微的, *slight, fine, subtle*

FINURA; exelência; *high-quality; fineness, excellence; refinement, politeness*;
  jīng liáng: 精良, *excellent, superior, of the best quality*;
  jīng zhàn: 精湛, *exquisite*;
SEE (请查看) DELICADO

FIRME; firme; *firm (GEN); stable, secure, solid, compact; resolute, determined, steadfast; resolved, purposeful ...*
FIRMEMENTE; firmemente; *securely, firmly, solidly, rigidly ...* **FIRMEZA; firmeza;** *firmness, stability, resolution, strength*;
  jiān (bf): 坚, *hard, solid; firm, strong; stronghold, fortification; (adv) firmly, resolutely*;
  jiān chí bù yú (fe): 坚持不渝, *persistent, preserving*;
  jiān dìng (sv) (v):坚定, *firm, staunch, steadfast; to strengthen*;
  jiān dìng bù yí (fe): 坚定不移, *resolute, unflinching, unswerving*;
  jiān dìng bù yú (fe): 坚定不渝, *steadfastly, unremittingly*;
  jiān dìng xìng (n): 坚定性, *firmness, staunchness*;
  jiān hòu (sv): 坚厚, *firm*;
  jiān láo (sv): 坚牢, *firm and fast*;
  jiān láo dù: 坚牢度, *firmness, fastness*;
  jiān qiáng (sv) (v): 坚强 , *strong, firm, staunch; to strengthen*;
  jiān qiáng bù qū (fe): 坚强不屈, *adamant; firm and inflexible*;
  jiān rèn (sv): 坚韧, *firm and tenacious*;
  jiān rèn bù bá (fe): 坚韧不拔, *dauntless*;
  jiān wěn (sv): 坚稳, *stable, steady*

(prices, costs) ;
  jiān yìng (sv): 坚硬, *hard, solid*;
  jiān zhēn (sv): 坚贞, *faithful, constant*;
  jiē shí (sv): 结实, *solid, sturdy, durable; strong*;
  wěn gù (sv) (v): 稳固, *firm, stable; to stabilize*;
SEE (请查看) ÉNFASIS, CONSTANTE, SUBSTANCIOSO

FLAGRANTE; flagrante; *flagrant, glaring, notorious, scandalous, blatant*;
  chū chǒu: 出丑, *scandalous*;
  gōng rán (adv): 公然, *openly, brazenly*;
  hòu yán (vp): 厚颜, *brazen, shameless*;
  hòu yán wú chǐ (fe): 厚颜无耻, *impudent; shameless*;
  míng mù zhāng dǎn (fe): 明目张胆, *brazenly, flagrantly, openly and boldly*;
SEE (请查看) ATROCIDAD, BRONCO, APARENTE, EVIDENTE

FLAMA; flama; *flame*;
  huǒ guāng: 火光, *flame, blaze*

FLEXIBILIDAD; flexibidade; *flexibility, suppleness, pliancy*;
  róu rèn xìng: 柔韧性, *flexibility of an object*;
SEE (请查看) ELÁSTICO

FLUCTUACIÓN; fluctuação; *fluctuation ...* **FLUCTUANTE; flutuante,** *floating, fluctuating; wavering*;
  dòng yáo yóu yù (vp): 动摇犹豫, *irresolute and wavering*;
  liú zhuǎn (attr): 流转, *fluctuating*

FLUIDEZ; fluência; *fluency; fluidity, smoothness ...* **FLUIDO** (A); **fluido** (A); *fluid, flowing; fluent; smooth; free flowing*;
  ān wěn (sv): 安稳, *steady, smooth*;
  guāng huá (sv): 光滑, *smooth, glossy, sleek*;
  huá rùn (sv): 滑润, *smooth*;
  liú chàng (sv): 流畅, *easy and smooth*;
  liú lì (sv) (n): 流利, *fluent, smooth; fluency*;

liú zhì (n): 流质, *fluid*;
shùn kǒu (sv): 顺口, *smooth (to taste/ preference)*;
shùn lì (sv): 顺利, *smooth, successful*;
tōng shāng (sv): 通商, *coherent, smooth, polished*;
yóu qiāng huá diào (fe): 油腔滑调, *glib, unctuous*;
yuán huá (sv): 圆滑, *smooth, slick, tactful*;
SEE (请查看) CONVENIENTE

FLUORESCENTE; flourescente; *fluorescent*;
fā yíng guāng de: 发荧光的, *fluorescent material, color*;
rì guāng dēng: 日光灯, *florescent light/lamp*;
yíng guāng: 荧光, *fluorescence*

FOBIA; fobia; *phobia, aversion, dread, dislike*;
dān xīn de: 担心的, *worried*;
kǒng bù (sv) (n): 恐怖, *fearful; terror*;
kǒng bù bìng: 恐怖病, *phobia*;
tǎo yàn de rén: 讨厌的人, *aversion to/dread of people*;
SEE (请查看) DESAGRADABLE, ANTIPATÍA, DESDÉN

FOCO; foco; *focus (MED) (MAT); center, focal point, spotlight*;
jiāo diǎn: 焦点, *focal point, central, issue, focus*;
jù guāng dēng (n): 聚光灯, *spotlight*;
SEE (请查看) CENTRAL

FORMA; forma; *form (GEN); shape, way*;
mó shì: 模式, *form, shape of a plan/ idea, etc.*;
xíng zhuàng: 形状, *form, circle/ triangle, etc.*

FORMAL; formal; *formal (GEN), official; well behaved, serious or reliable person; dependable*;
hé lǐ yí de: 合礼仪的, *formal speech, behaviour*;
yǒu tiáo lǐ de: 有条理的, *formal*

approach/style;
zhèng guī de: 正规的, *formal education, qualifications*;
zhèng shì de: 正式的, *formal offer/ approval/ occasion/dinner*

FORMALIDAD; formalidade; *formality, seriousness, correctness*;
lǐ jié: 礼节, *politeness, etiquette, ceremony, protocol*;
xíng shì: 形式, *formality*;
SEE (请查看) FORMAL

FORMATIVO (A); **formativo** (A); *formative, educational, instructive, developmental*;
chéng zhǎng de: 成长的, *developmental, formative*;
jiào yǎng (n) (v): 教养, *breeding, upbringing; education, culture; to bring up, to train, to educate*;
jiào yù (v) (n): 教育, *to teach, to educate, to inculcate; education*;
xíng chéng (n) (v): 形成, *formation; to take shape/form*;
SEE (请查看) AFECTAR

FORMATO; formato; *shape, format* (INFORM);
xíng tài: 形态, *form, shape*;
SEE (请查看) FORMA

FORTUNA; fortuna; *fortune, luck, destiny*;
hǎo yùn: 好运, *good fortune*;
huài yùn: 坏运, *bad fortune*;
shí yùn (n): 时运, *luck, fortune*;
yùn qi (n): 运气, *fortune, luck*;
SEE (请查看) DESTINO

FÓSFORO; fósforo; *phosphorus; match*;
huǒ chái: 火柴, *match*;
lín: 磷, *phosphorous*

FOTO; foto; *photo, picture*;
tú piàn: 图片, *picture, photograph*;
xiàng piàn: 相片, *image, photograph*;
zhào piàn: 照片, *photograph, picture*

FOTOCOPIA; fotocópia; *photocopy, print;*
  yǐng yìn běn: 影印本, *facsimile, photo-offset;*
  yǐng yìn (v) (n): 影印, *to photocopy; photocopy*

FOTOCOPIADORA; fotocopiadora; *photocopier;*
  yǐng yìn jī: 影印机, *photocopier*

FOTOGÉNICO (A); **fotogénico** (A); *photogenic;*
  shàng xiàng (sv) (v): 上相, *photogenic, to be photographed*

FOTOGRAFÍA; fotografia; *photography;*
  shè yǐng (n) (v): 摄影, *photography; to take a photograph, to shoot a film;*
  shè yǐng shù: 摄影术, *photography*

FOTOGRÁFICO (A); **fotográfico** (A); *photographic;*
  shè yǐng de: 摄影的, *photographic equipment*

FOTÓGRAFO (A); **fotógrafo** (A); *photographer;*
  shè yǐng shī: 摄影师, *photographer, cameraman;*
  shè yǐng zhě: 摄影者, *photographer, cameraman*

FRACTURA; fratura (MED); *fracture (MED); break, separation, division, breach, rupture; fault (GEOL);*
  duàn céng (n): 断层, *fault, crack (GEOL)*
  duàn liè (n): 断裂, *fracture of a bone;*
  pò liè (n): 破裂, *a rupture (MED)*

FRAGANCIA; fragância; *fragrance;*
  xiāng qì: 香气, *fragrance*

FRAGANTE; fragrante; *fragrant, scented;*
  fāng xiāng (sv) (n): 芳香, *fragrant, balmy, aromatic; fragrance;*
  fēn fāng (sv): 芬芳, *fragrant, sweet-smelling;*

  xiāng qì (n): 香气, *fragrance, aroma; incense;*
SEE (请查看**) AROMA**

FRÁGIL; frágil; *breakable, delicate, fragile;*
  ruò bù jīn fēng (sv): 弱不禁风, *fragile, extremely delicate;*
SEE (请查看**) DELICADO, ELEGANCIA**

FRAGMENTARIO (A); **fragmentário** (A); *fragmentary ... **FRAGMENTO; fragmento;** fragment, piece, chip;*
  piàn duàn (n): 片段, *part, fragment, extract;*
  suì piàn (n) (sv): 碎片, *fragment, chip; fragmentary*

FRANCO (A); **franco** (A); *frank, open, direct;*
  shuài zhí (sv): 率直, *frank, blunt;*
  tǎn chéng (sv): 坦诚, *frank and honest;*
  tǎn shuài (sv): 坦率, *frank, candid;*
  zhí jié liǎo dàng (sv): 直截了当, *straight forward, blunt;*
  zhí shuài (sv): 直率, *frank, candid;*
  zhí xìng zi (n): 直性子, *straightforward/forthright person*

FRATERNIDAD; fraternidade; *brotherhood, fraternity ... **FRATERNO** (A); **fraterno** (A); fraternal, brotherly;*
  gēr men: 哥儿们, *brothers, pals, buddies;*
  lián yì huì: 联谊会, *fraternity;*
  shè huì: 社会, *society;*
  tóng rén: 同人/仁, *group;*
  xiōng dì bān de: 兄弟般的, *fraternal;*
  xiōng dì de: 兄弟的, *fraternal, brotherly;*
SEE (请查看**) ASOCIACIÓN**

FRAUDE; fraude; *fraud, deception, hoax, swindle, scam ... **FRAUDULENTO** (A); **fraudulento** (A); fraudulent, dishonest;*
  guǐ jì: 诡计, *deceitful act, scam;*
  jiǎ 'àn (n): 假案, *frame-up, fabricated case;*

jiǎ xiàng (n): 假象, *false/deceptive appearance*;
piàn jú: 骗局, *fraud, hoax, scam*;
piàn qǔ (n) (v): 骗取, *swindle; to defraud/swindle*;
piàn zi: 骗子, *cheater, swindler*;
xì nòng: 戏弄, *hoax*;
SEE (请查看) HIPÓCRITA, BURLAR, DUPLICIDAD, FALSO, DEFRAUDAR

FRECUENCIA (adv); **freqüência**; *frequency* ... **FRECUENTE; freqüênte**; *often, frequent* ... **FRECUENTEMENTE**; **freqüêntemente**; *frequently, often*;
cháng cháng (adv): 常常, *frequently, usually*;
dòng bu dòng (adv): 动不动, *easily, frequently*;
jīng cháng (adv): 经常, *frequently, often; regularly*;
měi měi (adv): 每每, *often, frequently*;
pín (adv): 频, *frequently, repeatedly; (bf) frequency*;
pín dù (n): 频度, *frequency*;
pín fán (sv): 频繁, *frequent, often*;
pín fán xìng (n): 频繁性, *frequency*;
pín lǜ (n): 频率, *frequency*;
shí cháng (adv): 时常, *often*;
wǎng wǎng (adv): 往往, *often, frequently*

FRENESÍ; frenesi; *frenzy; wildness*;
fēng kuáng (sv): 疯狂, *crazy, wild*;
SEE (请查看) BRAVÍO, CÓLERA, FANÁTICO, FUROR

FRENÉTICO (A); **furioso** (A), *furious*; **frenetico** (A), *frantic, mad, frenzied*;
dà fā léi tíng: 大发雷霆, *furious (person)*;
qiáng jìng: 强劲, *furious (effort)*;
fā fēng (sv): 发疯, *frantic; frenzied*;
kuáng luàn (sv): 狂乱, *frantic place, etc.*;
SEE (请查看) FRENESÍ

FRESCO (A); **fresco** (A); *fresh, cool; clean, clear*;
fēng liáng (sv): 风凉, *cool*;

liáng (sv) (v): 凉, *cold, cool; to make cool*;
liáng kuài (sv): 凉快, *nice and cool*;
qīng chéng (sv): 清澄, *limpid, clear*;
qīng liáng (sv): 清凉, *cool and refreshing*;
xīn (sv): 新, *new, fresh, up-to-date*;
yīn liáng (sv): 阴凉, *shady and cool*;
SEE (请查看) CLARIDAD, COMPLETAMENTE

FRÍGIDO (A); **frigido** (A); *frigid, frosty, frozen, wintery, cold* ... **FRÍO** (A); **frio** (A); *cold*;
bīng liáng (sv): 冰凉, *ice-cold*;
dòng tǔ: 冻土, *tundra, frozen ground*;
hán lěng de: 寒冷的, *frigid*;
lěng de: 冷的, *cold weather/ temperature, etc.*;
shuāng dòng (n): 霜冻, *frost*;
SEE (请查看) DESAMOR, DESMOTIVADO

FRIVOLIDAD; frivolidade; *frivolity, frivolousness, insouciance*;
ān xián (sv): 安闲, *carefree, leisurely*;
qīng bó (sv) (v): 轻薄, *frivolous, flippant, flirtatious; to insult*;
qīng fú (sv): 轻浮, *frivolous*;
qīng fú de: 轻浮的, *frivolous conduct, person, etc.*;
qīng shuài (sv): 轻率, *rash, hasty, thoughtless*;
qīng tiāo (sv): 轻佻, *frivolous, capricious*;
qīng tiǎo (sv): 轻窕, *frivolous, capricious, playful*;
wú suǒ wèi de: 无所谓的, *frivolous activity*;
SEE (请查看) NEGLIGENCIA, INDIFERENCIA

FRÍVOLO (A); **frívolo** (A); *frivolous, superficial, trivial, insignificant*;
biǎo miàn xìng de: 表面性的, *superficial knowledge, etc.*;
ér xì (n): 儿戏, *trivial matter*;
fū qiǎn (sv): 肤浅, *superficial, skin-deep*;
fū qiǎn de: 肤浅的, *superficial person*;

jī máo suàn pí (fe): 鸡毛蒜皮, *trifle, trivial matter*;
qiǎn bó (sv) (adv) (n): 浅薄, *shallow, superficial; meager; superficiality; shallowness*;
qiǎn jiàn (n): 浅见, *superficial view; humble opinion*;
qiǎn lòu (sv): 浅陋, *shallow, meager*;
suǒ suì de: 琐碎的, *trivial*;
wú zú qīng zhòng de: 无足轻重的, *insignificant*;
SEE (请查看) DIMINUTO

FRONTERA; fronteira; *border area; frontier*;
guó jiè: 国界, *frontier between countries*;
biān jiè: 边界, *border of country*

FRUGALIDAD; frugalidade; *frugality*;
jiǎn pǔ (sv): 简朴, *thrifty and simple, economical*;
jié jiǎn (sv): 节俭, *frugal, thrifty*;
SEE (请查看) ECONOMÍA

FRUSTRACIÓN; frustração; *frustration, disappointment, discontentment* ... **FRUSTRADO** (A); **frustrado** (A); *frustrated, failed; disappointed, discontented* ... **FRUSTRANTE; frustrante;** *frustrating, disappointing, discouraging*;
huī lěng (sv): 灰冷, *downhearted, discouraged*;
huī sè (n): 灰色, *melancholy*;
huī xīn sàng qì (fe): 灰心丧气, *be utterly disheartened; become discouraged; lose heart*;
shī luò (sv) (v): 失落, *discouraged; to be dejected*;
xīn hán: 心寒, *bitterly disappointed*;
SEE (请查看) AGRAVANTE, DECEPCIÓN, DESAGRADO, DESANIMADO, CONSTERNACIÓN, DESILUSIÓN

FRUTA; fruta, fruto; *fruit*;
guǒ zhī: 果汁, *fruit juice*;
shuǐ guǒ: 水果, *fruit*

FUGITIVO (A); **fugitivo** (A); *fugitive, escapee, runaway*;
táo wáng zhě: 逃亡者, *fugitive*

FUNCIÓN; função; *function, duty, task, chore; purpose, aim* ... **FUNCIONAL; funcional;** *functional, working, running, operational*;
fā huī jī néng: 发挥机能, *functional*;
gōng yòng: 公用, *function; use*;
jī néng: 机能, *function*;
mù biāo: 目标, *target, aim, goal*;
shí yòng de: 实用的, *functional furniture/design, etc.; practical, pragmatic*;
xìng néng: 性能, *function, performance*;
yòng chǎng: 用场, *use, purpose; usefulness*;
yòng tú: 用途, *use, application, purpose*;
zài yùn zhuǎn de: 在运转的, *functional or working equipment/device*;
zōng pài: 宗派, *function*;
zòng zhǐ: 宗旨, *aim, purpose*;
SEE (请查看) OPERACIONAL, PROSPECTO, RESPONSABILIDAD, INTENCIÓN

FUNDACIÓN; fundação; *foundation; founding, establishment*;
chéng lì: 成立, *foundation of organization/ company/ city*;
jī chǔ: 基础, *foundation of belief/way of life*;
SEE (请查看) BASE

FURIA; fûria; *fury; anger, rage* ... **FURIBUNDO** (A) ó **FURIOSO** (A); **furioso** (A); *furious, frenzied, unrestrained, savage, wild, violent*;
dà fā léi tíng de: 大发雷霆的, *furious person*;
kuáng yán (n): 狂言, *ravings*;
qì chōng chōng (fe): 气冲冲, *furious, enraged*;
qì fèn (sv): 气愤, *angry, furious*;
SEE (请查看) CÓLERA, FRENESÍ, FRENÉTICO, BRAVÍO, FUROR, DRÁSTICO, VIOLENCIA, VIGOROSO

FURTIVO (A); **furtivo** (A); *furtive, poacher; secretive; cunning, foxy, crafty*;
　guǐ guǐ suì suì de: 鬼鬼祟祟的, *furtive glance/ manner*;
　jiǎo zhà de: 狡诈的, *shifty, crafty, cunning*;
　tōu tōu mō mō de: 偷偷摸摸的, *furtive*;
　SEE (请查看) **ARTIFICIO**

FÚTIL; fútil; *futile*;
　tú láo (n): 徒劳, *futile, fruitless*;
　wú wèi (sv): 无谓, *meaningless, pointless*;
　wú xiào (sv) (v): 无效, *futile, ineffective; to be ineffective*;
　wú yì yì (sv): 无意义, *meaningless, pointless*;
　wú yòng (sv): 无用, *unnecessary, useless*

FUTURO (A); **futuro** (A); *intended; future*;
　chū lù: 出路, *prospects, a way out of problems/worries, etc.*;
　chū xi: 出息, *future prospects, promise*;
　hòu huàn: 后患, *future trouble, seeds of future danger*;
　hòu shì: 后事, *future event, later developments*;
　jiāng lái (n) (adv): 将来, *future; in the future*;
　qián chéng: 前程, *future, prospects, career*;
　qián tú: 前途, *future, career, prospects*;
　wèi lái: 未来, *future, tomorrow, time to come*;
　SEE (请查看) **COMPUTAR**

Easily recognizable verbs and their Portuguese and Chinese equivalents
Verbos fácilmente reconocibles en Español-Portugués-Inglés y sus equivalentes en Chino
Verbos facilmente reconhecível em Espanhol-Português-Inglês e seus equivalentes em Chinês
很容易辨认的西班牙语，葡萄牙语，英语动词和他们的中文对等词

FABRICAR; fabricar; *to make/ manufacture/fabricate*;
　chū chǎn (v) (n): 出产, *to produce/ manufacture; output*;
　liàn gāng: 炼钢, *to make steel*;
　liàn yóu: 炼油, *to refine oil*;
　zhì zuò: 制作, *to fabricate*;
　SEE (请查看) **ELABORAR, PRODUCIR, MANUFACTURAR**

FALSIFICAR; falsificar; *to forge/ falsify*;
　cuàn gǎi: 篡改, *to falsify*

FAMILIARIZAR; familiarizar; *to familiarize/acquaint*;
　rèn shi: 认识, *to understand/be acquainted with*;
　shú xī mǒu shì: 熟悉某事, *to familiarize os with sthg*

FASCINAR; fascinar; *to fascinate/ captivate*;

　rù mí: 入迷, *to be fascinated*;
　shǐ zháo mí: 使着迷; *to fascinate (intrigue/interest)*;
　zháo mó: 着魔, *to be possessed/ obsessed*;
　SEE (请查看) **FANÁTICO, FASCINANTE**

FATIGAR; fatigar; *to tire/weary/wear out*;
　shǐ pí láo: 使疲劳, *to tire*;
　yàn juàn: 厌倦, *to be weary of/tired of*;
　SEE (请查看) **COLAPSO, EXHAUSTO**

FELICITAR; felicitar; *to congratulate, be glad about*;
　zhù hè: 祝贺, *to congratulate*;
　SEE (请查看) **CONGRATULAR**

FILMAR; filmar; *to film*;

bǎ ... pāi chéng yǐng piàn: 把 ... 拍成影片, *to film a person/scene, book*;
SEE (请查看) **FOTOGRAFÍA**

FINALIZAR; finalizar; *to finish, complete, conclude, end*;
  wán shì: 完事, *to finish doing sthg, to be settled*;
SEE (请查看) **DEDUCCIÓN, CONCLUIR, COMPLETAR**

FINANCIAR; financiar; *to finance*;
  wèi ... tí gōng zī jīn: 为 ... 提供资金, *to finance*

FLEXIONAR; flexionar; *to bend/flex/limber*;
  wān zhé: 弯折, *to bend, to buckle*;
SEE (请查看) **INCLINAR, EXPANDIR**

FLUIR; fluir; *to flow; to derive from; to run*;
  chuān liú bù xī: 川流不息, *to flow*;
  liú dòng: 流动, *to flow, to move, to go from place to place*;
  zhōu zhuǎn: 周转, *to circulate, to turn over*;
SEE (请查看) **BOLETÍN, CIRCULACIÓN, DERIVAR, DISEMINAR**

FOMENTAR; fomentar; *to promote/encourage*;
  cù shǐ: 促使, *to induce, to urge, to promote*;
  dǎ qì: 打气, *to inflate, to pump up, to encourage*;
  gǔ lì: 鼓励, *to urge, to encourage*;
  gǔ wǔ: 鼓舞, *to inspire, to encourage*;
  pěng chǎng: 捧场, *to boost, to cheer on, to encourage*;
  shēng gé: 升格, *to promote, to upgrade*;
  shēng qiān: 升迁, *to promote*;
  tí chàng: 提倡, *to promote, to encourage/advocate*;
  tí shēng: 提升, *to promote, to upgrade; to hoist*;
  tí xié: 提携, *to guide/support/promote*;

tuī dòng: 推动, *to encourage, to promote, to motivate*;
  zhī chí: 支持, *to encourage*;
  zhù zhǎng: 助长, *to encourage, to promote; to foster*;
SEE (请查看) **PROMOCIONAR**

FORMALIZAR; formalizar; *to formalize, put in order*;
  dìng diào: 定调, *to set the tone*;
  dìng gǎo (v) (n): 定稿, *to finalize sthg; final version*;
  dìng jú (n) (v): 定局, *foregone conclusion; to be decisive*;
  dìng xíng: 定型, *to finalize, to standardize*

FORMAR; formar; *to form/train/educate/make*;
  chuán jiào: 传教, *to do missionary work*;
  chuán shòu: 传授, *to teach, to pass on skills/ knowledge, etc.*;
  jiǎng jiě: 讲解, *to explain*;
  jiǎng kè: 讲课, *to teach, to lecture*;
  jiǎng shòu: 讲授, *to teach, to lecture, to instruct*;
  jiāo shū: 教书, *to teach school/teach for a living*;
  shēn jiào: 身教, *to teach by example*;
  tiáo jiào: 调教, *to educate children; to train animals*;
  xùn liàn: 训练, *to train*;
SEE (请查看) **EDUCAR, ADOCTRINAR, FORMATIVO, INSTRUCCIÓN**

FORMULAR; formular; *to formulate/get an opinion/ draw up/express/make*;
  gòu xiǎng chū: 构想出, *to formulate a plan/ proposal*;
  nǐ dìng: 拟订, *to formulate, to draw up*;
  zhì dìng: 制定, *to formulate, to establish, to draw up*;
SEE (请查看) **EXPRESAR**

FOTOCOPIAR; fotocopiar; *to photocopy*;

fù yìn: 复印, *to copy, to photocopy; to print/duplicate*;
yǐng yìn: 影印, *to photocopy*

FOTOGRAFIAR; fotografar; *to photograph*;
  gěi...pāi zhào: 给 ... 拍照, *to photograph a person/ object/place*;
  zhào xiàng: 照相, *to take a photograph*;
SEE (请查看) FILMAR

FRACCIONAR; fracionar; *to fragment; to divide/ break up/split up*
... FRAGMENTAR; fragmentar; *to fragment, divide*;
  fēn céng: 分层, *to stratify, to divide into different layers*;
  guā fēn: 瓜分, *to divide, to carve off*;
  liè chéng suì piàn: 裂 成 碎 片, *to fragment*;
  liè kāi: 裂开, *to split open*;
  pò liè: 破裂, *to split up, to break up, to burst*;
  zhī lí: 支离, *to be fragmented/broken*;
SEE (请查看) ARRUINAR, DIVIDIR, APARTE, APARTAR, DESMEMBRAR, CATEGORIZAR

FRACTURAR; fraturar; *to fracture/ break/force*;
  duàn liè: 断裂, *to crack/break apart/ fracture*;
  gǔ zhé: 骨折, *to fracture*;
  zhé duàn: 折断, *to snap/break*;

FRECUENTAR; freqüentar; *to frequent/haunt/hang out*;
  cháng qù: 常去, *to frequent a pub/ restaurant, etc.*

FRUSTRAR; frustar; *to frustrate/ thwart*;
  shǐ jǔ sàng: 使沮丧, *to frustrate a person*;

yǒu 'ài: 有碍, *to obstruct*;
zhàng 'ài (v) (n)**:** 障碍, *to hinder; barrier*;
zǔ jī: 阻击, *to block*;
SEE (请查看) APREHENDER, BLOCAR, DIFICULTAR, PREVENIR

FUMAR; fumar; *to smoke*;
  chōu yān: 抽烟, *to smoke a cigarette/ cigar/a pipe, etc.*;
  mào yān: 冒烟, *to belch smoke*;
  xī yān: 吸烟, *to smoke*

FUNCIONAR; funcionar; *to work/ function*;
  cāo zuò: 操 作, *to operate a machine*;
  gōng zuò (v) (n)**:** 工作, *to work; job; (suf) -ation*;
  qǐ zuò yòng: 起作用, *to have an effect/function as*;
  yùn zhuàn: 运转, *to work, to run, to operate; to evolve*;
SEE (请查看) FUNCIONAL, ACTUAR, ADMINISTRAR, AFECTAR

FUNDAR; fundar; *to found, set up, establish*;
  chéng lì: 成立, *to set up, to establish, to found*;
  chuàng bàn: 创办, *to found, to establish, to launch*;
  chuàng jiàn: 创建, *to establish, to found, to create*;
  jiàn lì: 建立, *to build, to establish, to set up*;
  shè lì: 设立, *to establish, to set up, to found*;
  shù lì: 树立, *to establish, to set up*;
  zhì dìng: 制定, *to establish, to draw up; to institute*;
  zhì dìng: 制订, *to work out/map out/ formulate*

G

Interchangeable Spanish-Portuguese-English words and their Chinese equivalents
Palabras en Español-Portugués-Inglés y sus equivalentes en Chino
Palavras em Espanhol-Português-Inglês e seus equivalentes em Chinês
西班牙语，葡萄牙语，英语及中文的对等单词

GÁNGSTER; gângster;
 bào tú: 暴徒, *ruffian, thug*;
 yào fàn: 要犯, *chief offender, main criminal*;
 zhǔ fàn: 主犯, *main culprit, principal criminal*;
SEE (请查看) BANDIDO

GENERAL; general (GEN); *overall, widespread, universal; general (MIL)*;
 dà jú (n): 大局, *overall situation*;
 quán guó xìng (n): 全国性, *nationwide*;
 quán miàn (n) (sv): 全面, *overall, general, comprehensive*;
 quán pán (sv): 全盘, *overall complete*;
 zǒng tǐ (n): 总体, *overall, general*;
SEE (请查看) COMPLETAMENTE, UNIVERSALIDAD

GIGABYTE; gigabyte;
 qiān zhào zì jié: 千兆字节, *gigabyte*

GLAMOR ó GLAMOUR; glamor;
 měi lì (sv): 美丽, *beautiful*;
 mí rén (sv): 迷人, *enchanting, charming, attractive*;

SEE (请查看) CARISMA

GLOBAL; global; *overall, total*;
 quán qiú de: 全球的, *worldwide, global*;
 zōng hé de: 综合的, *overall, comprehensive*
SEE (请查看) GENERAL, TODO

GOURMET ó GURMET; gourmet;
 jīng měi de: 精美的, *gourmet food/cooking*;
 měi shí jiā (n): 美食家, *gourmet, gastronome*

GRADUAL; gradual;
 jiàn jiàn: 渐渐, *gradually, little by little*

GRAVE; grave; *serious, heavy*;
 chén tòng (sv): 沉痛, *severe, grave*;
 lì hài (sv): 利害, *terrible, devastating; tough, capable; severe, serious, fierce*;
 rèn zhēn (sv) (v): 认真, *serious, earnest; to take seriously*;
SEE (请查看) CRUCIAL, CALAMIDAD, GRAVE, SERIEDAD

Easily recognizable Spanish-Portuguese-English nouns, adjectives and adverbs and their Chinese equivalents
Nombres, sustantivos, adjetivos y adverbios en Español-Portugués-Inglés y sus equivalentes en Chino
Nomes, substantivos, adjetivos e advérbios em Espanhol-Português-Inglês e seus equivalentes em Chinês
容易辨认的西班牙语，葡萄牙语，英语的名词，形容词和副词和他们的中文对等词

GALA; festival; *celebration; ceremony, show, event; elegance*;
 jié rì: 节日, *festival*;

SEE (请查看) CELEBRACIÓN, CEREMONIA, CEREMONIA

GALANTE; galante; *gallant (only to describe men)*;
  zhuàng liè (sv): 壮烈, *heroic, brave*;
SEE (请查看) **AUDAZ, BRAVO**

GARAJE; garagem; *garage, a parking space*;
  cún chē chù: 存车处, *parking lot*;
  tíng chē chǎng: 停车场, *parking area/lot*

GARANTÍA; garantia; *guarantee, warranty*;
  bǎo dān: 保单, *warranty*;
SEE (请查看) **GARANTIZAR**

GASOLINERA; posto de gasolina; *gas station*;
  jiā yóu zhàn: 加油站, *gas/filling station*

GASTADO; gasto (A); *worn, old, stale, hackneyed*;
  chén fǔ (sv): 陈腐, *hackneyed, stale, trite*;
SEE (请查看) **ANTIGUO**

GENERALMENTE; generalidade; *generally, widely*;
  dà tǐ shang (adv): 大体上, *generally, on the whole; in general*;
SEE (请查看) **BANAL, UNIVERSALIDAD, EXTENSAMENTE**

GÉNERO; gênero, *genus;* **tipo,** *sort, type; genus; sort*;
  lèi bié: 类别, *classification, class, category*;
  shì yàng: 式样, *style, type; pattern, design*;
  zhǒng lèi: 种类, *type, kind, sort, class*;
SEE (请查看) **CLÁSICO, CLASIFICACIÓN, MODELO, ESTILO**

GENEROSIDAD; generosidade; *generosity ...* **GENEROSO** (A), **generoso** (A); *generous, unstinting, bountiful*;
  dà dù: 大度, *generosity, magnanimity*;
  dà fāng (sv): 大方, *generous*;

fēng shèng (sv): 丰盛, *rich, sumptuous*;
  kāng kǎi (n) (v): 慷慨, *generosity; to be generous*;
SEE (请查看) **ABUNDANCIA**

GENIO; genio; *genius, person of special ability*;
  tiān cái: 天才, *talent, genius*

GENTIL; gentil; *kind; nice ...*
GENTILEZA; gentileza; *courtesy, kindness, elegance*;
  hé 'ǎi (sv): 和蔼, *kind, nice, affable*;
  hé qi (sv) (n): 和气, *polite, kind, gentle*;
  hòu dào (sv): 厚道, *kind, generous*;
SEE (请查看) **ARMONÍA, EDUCADO, AMABILIDAD, CLEMENCIA**

GENUINO (A); **genuino** (A); *genuine, authentic, real, legitimate*;
  míng fù qí shí de: 名副其实的, *worthy*;
  shí huì (n) (sv): 实惠, *reality, tangible*;
  shí shí zài zài de: 实实在在的, *real, sincere interest, emotion*;
SEE (请查看) **AUTENTICIDAD, EFECTIVIDAD, SINCERO, PRÁCTICO**

GIGANTESCO (A); **gigantesco** (A); *gigantic, towering, immense, huge, massive, enormous*;
  gāo dà (sv): 高大, *huge, tall and big*;
  hào dà (sv): 浩大, *huge, vast*;
  hào fán (sv): 浩繁, *vast, many and varied*;
  jù (sv): 巨, *huge, enormous, gigantic*;
  jù xíng (sv): 巨型, *giant, enormous*;
  páng dà (sv): 庞大, *huge*;
SEE (请查看) **GRANDE, ENORME, DESMEDIDO, MONSTRUO**

GLAMOROSO; glamoroso (A); *glamorous, elegant, charming*;
  diǎn yǎ: 典雅, *elegance*;
  fù yǒu mèi lì de: 富有魅力的, *glamorous*;
  kǎo jiu (sv) (v): 考究, *tasteful, elegant; to investigate carefully, to be particular*;

mèi lì: 魅力, *charm of a place; glamor;*
mí rén de tè xìng: 迷人的特性, *charm of a person;*
shàng chéng (sv): 上乘, *elegant;*
xī yǐn rén: 吸引人, *charming place;*
SEE (请查看) GLAMOR, DECORO, DELICADO, ELEGANCIA

GLOBO; **globo;** *globe, Earth, sphere; balloon;*
dì qiú: 地球, *Earth*

GLORIA; **glória;** *glory, delight ...*
GLORIOSO (A); **glorioso** (A); *glorious;*
guāng róng (sv) (n): 光荣, *glorious, honorable; kudos;*
guāng yào (n) (v) (sv): 光耀, *glory; to glorify; glorious, honorable;*
róng (n) (sv): 荣, *glory; prosperous, glorious;*
róng huá fù guì (fe): 荣华富贵, *glory, splendor;*
róng yào (n) (sv): 荣耀, *glory, honor; glorious*

GLOTONERÍA; **gula;** *gluttony, greed, greediness;*
chán (sv): 馋, *greedy, gluttonous;*
chán zuǐ (n) (sv): 馋嘴, *glutton; gluttonous, greedy;*
tān (v) (sv): 贪, *to covet, to crave; greedy, corrupt;*
zuǐ chán (sv): 嘴馋, *gluttonous, fond of good food;*
SEE (请查看) AVARICIA

GORILA; **gorila;** *gorilla or bodyguard, bouncer, thug;*
bǎo biāo (n): 保镖, *bodyguard; armed escort;*
hù wèi (v) (n): 护卫, *to protect, to guard; bodyguard;*
shì wèi (n): 侍卫, *military bodyguard;*
wèi bīng (n): 卫兵, *guard, bodyguard;*
SEE (请查看) DEFENSOR

GRADUALMENTE; **gradualmente;** *gradually;*
zhú jiàn (adv): 逐渐, *gradually, by degrees*

SEE (请查看) GRADUAL, PROGRESIVO

GRANDE; **grande;** *big, large;*
dà de: 大的, *big (in size);*
dà hào: 大号, *large size;*
dà liàng de: 大量的, *large number, amount;*
dà pī (sv): 大批, *large number/ quantity of;*
dà xíng (sv): 大型, *large-scale;*
féi dà (sv): 肥大, *loose, large; baggy (of clothing);*
gāo de: 高的, *tall;*
wěi dà (sv): 伟大, *great, large, magnificent;*
SEE (请查看) ABISMAL

GRANDIOSO (A); **grandioso** (A); *grandiose; splendid, impressive;*
fú kuā (sv): 浮夸, *grandiose;*
qì zhuàng shān hé (fe): 气壮山河, *magnificent, inspiring;*
xióng wěi (sv): 雄伟, *imposing magnificent;*
xióng wēi (sv): 雄威, *majestic;*
yōu yì (sv): 优异, *outstanding, excellent;*
zhuàng kuò (vp): 壮阔, *glorious, magnificent; vast, grand;*
zhuàng lì (sv): 壮丽, *majestic, magnificent, glorious;*
SEE (请查看) ESPECTACULAR, IMPONENCIA, EXCELENCIA, ESPLÉNDIDO

GRATIFICACIÓN; **gratificação;** *recompense, reward;*
chóu jīn (n): 酬金, *monetary reward, remuneration;*
huí bào: 回报, *reward, satisfaction;*
jiǎng jīn: 奖金, *bonus, dividend;*
jiǎng lì (v) (n): 奖励, *to encourage and reward; award;*
jiǎng pǐn: 奖品, *award, prize, trophy;*
jiǎng zhuàng: 奖状, *certificate of merit;*
shǎng jīn: 赏金, *reward for capture of a criminal;*
SEE (请查看) DECORACIÓN

GRATIFICANTE; gratificante;
gratifying, rewarding, satisfying;
  yǒu jià zhí (sv): 有价值, *worthwhile cause, etc.*;
  zhí dé zuò (sv): 值得做, *rewarding/ worthwhile experience, etc.*

GRATIS; gratis; *free, for nothing*;
  miǎn fèi (sv): 免费, *to be free of charge*;
  wú cháng (sv): 无偿, *freely, gratis*

GRATITUD; gratidão; *gratitude, appreciation, thanksgiving*;
  gǎn jī de: 感激的, *grateful*;
SEE (请查看) APRECIACIÓN

GRAVEDAD; gravidade; *seriousness, gravity*;
  yán zhòng xìng: 严重性, *seriousness, gravity*;
  zhòng dà (sv): 重大, *grave concern/ danger, etc.*;
SEE (请查看) GRAVE

GRAVOSO; estressante; *stressful; costly, burdensome, oppressive*;
  jǐn zhāng (sv): 紧张, *stressful job/ situation, etc.*;

SEE (请查看) ONEROSO

GREGARIO (A); gregário (A);
gregarious, sociable;
  hào jiāo jì de: 好交际的, *sociable, gregarious*

GROSERO; grosa; *gross; coarse, rude, vulgar*;
  cū bào (sv): 粗暴, *crude, rough*;
  cū bǐ (sv): 粗鄙, *vulgar, coarse*;
  cū cāo (sv): 粗糙, *coarse, rough*;
  cū yě (sv): 粗野, *crude, rude, boorish*;
  táng tū (sv): 唐突, *brusque, rude*;
SEE (请查看) VULGAR, BRONCO

GROTESCO (A); grotesco (A);
grotesque;
  huāng táng (sv): 荒唐, *grotesque, shocking*;
  chǒu lòu (sv): 丑陋, *ugly*

GRUPO; grupo; *group*;
  bān zi: 班子, *organized group, team; operatic company*;
  bān zǔ: 班组, *group/team (in a factory, a school)*;
  pài bié: 派别, *group*

Easily recognizable verbs and their Portuguese and Chinese equivalents
Verbos fácilmente reconocibles en Español-Portugués-Inglés y sus equivalentes en Chino
Verbos facilmente reconhecível em Espanhol-Português-Inglês e seus equivalentes em Chinês
很容易辨认的西班牙语，葡萄牙语，英语动词和他们的中文对等词

GARANTIZAR; garantir; *to guarantee, vouch for*;
  bǎo zhèng (v) (n): 保证, *to guarantee, to safeguard; pledge*;
  dǎ bāo piào (fe): 打包票, *to vouch for/ guarantee*;
  dān bǎo: 担保, *to guarantee; to be responsible for*;
SEE (请查看) ACTUAR

GENERALIZAR; generalizar; *to generalize*;

  gài kuò (v) (adv) (n): 概括, *to summarize/generalize; briefly, in broad outline; generalization*;
SEE (请查看) DELINEAR

GLORIFICAR; glorificar; *to glorify/ dignify*;
  měi huà: 美化, *to beautify, to glorify*;
  sòng yáng: 颂扬, *to glamorize, to glorify*;
  tí gāo: 提高, *to enhance a reputation*;
SEE (请查看) ADULAR, AUMENTAR,

CELEBRAR, GLORIA

GOBERNAR; governor; *to govern/ administer*;
  shī zhèng: 施政, *to govern/administer*

GRADUAR; graduar; *to adjust/ regulate/calibrate*;
  jiào yàn: 交验, *to check, to calibrate*;
SEE (请查看) ADAPTAR

Interchangeable Spanish-Portuguese-English words and their Chinese equivalents
Palabras en Español-Portugués-Inglés y sus equivalentes en Chino
Palavras em Espanhol-Português-Inglês e seus equivalentes em Chinês
西班牙语，葡萄牙语，英语及中文的对等单词

HABITUAL; habitual; *regular*;
  cháng tài (n): 常态, *normal state (of affairs)*;
  cháng wù (sv): 常务, *routine, day-to-day*;
  gù dìng (sv) (v): 固定, *fixed, regular; to set, to fix*;
  zhèng cháng de: 正常的, *normal, usual, regular*;
SEE (请查看) NORMAL, NORMALIDAD

HALL; hall; *entrance hall, foyer*;
  mén tīng: 门厅, *foyer of a hotel, theater, etc.; hallway, vestibule*

HIPPY ó HIPPIE; hippie;
  xī pí shì: 嬉皮士, *hippy, hippie*;
  xī pí: 嬉皮, *hippy*

HOBBY; hobby;
ài hào: 爱好, *interest, hobby*

HORIZONTAL; horizontal;
  shuǐ píng (attr): 水平, *horizontal level*;

HORROR; horror (GEN);

jí qí kě pà (sv): 极其可怕, *horrific*;
jí qí kǒng bù (sv): 及其恐怖, *horrifying*;
jí zāo (sv): 极糟, *horrid*;
kǒng bù (sv) (n): 恐怖, *fearful, horrible, horrendous; horror*;
lìng rén kǒng jù (sv): 令人恐惧, *horrible (dream/ experience, etc.)*;
shòu jīng xià (sv): 受惊吓, *horrified*;
zāo tòu (sv); 糟透, *horrible (color/food, etc.)*;
SEE (请查看) HORROR

HOSPITAL; hospital;
  yī yuàn: 医院, *hospital*

HOTEL; hotel;
  bīn guǎn: 宾馆, *hotel*;
  kè diàn: 客店, *hotel, inn*;
  lǚ diàn: 旅店, *hotel, motel, inn*;
  lǚ guǎn: 旅馆, *hotel; inn*;
  zhāo dài suǒ: 招待所, *hostel*

HUMOR; humor; *mood, temperament*;
  qì zhì: 气质, *disposition, temperament*;
  xìng qíng: 性情, *disposition, temperament*;
  yì qì: 意气, *spirit, temperament*

Easily recognizable Spanish-Portuguese-English nouns, adjectives and adverbs and their Chinese equivalents
Nombres, sustantivos, adjetivos y adverbios en Español-Portugués-Inglés y sus equivalentes en Chino
Nomes, substantivos, adjetivos e advérbios em Espanhol-Português-Inglês e seus equivalentes em Chinês
容易辨认的西班牙语，葡萄牙语，英语的名词，形容词和副词和他们的中文对等词

HABITANTE; habitante; *inhabitant;*
  jū mín: 居民, *resident, inhabitant*

HÁBITO; hábito; *habit; religious clothing (RELIG);*
  zōng páo: 宗袍, *religious clothing (RELIG);*
SEE (请查看**) COSTUMBRE**

HAMBURGUESA; hambúrguer; *hamburger;*
  hàn bǎo bāo: 汉堡包, *hamburger*

HEGEMONÍA; hegemonia; *dominance, hegemony;*
  bà dào de: 霸道的, *overbearing;*
  bà quán: 霸权, *hegemony;*
  zhī pèi: 支配 , *dominance*

HELICÓPTERO; helicóptero; *helicopter;*
  zhí shēng fēi jī: 直升飞机, *helicopter*

HEMISFERIO; hemisfério; *hemisphere;*
  bàn qiú (GEOG)**:** 半球, *hemisphere*

HERMÉTICO (A)**; hermético** (A)**;** *airtight, hermetic, watertight;*
  dī shuǐ bù lòu (fe)**:** 滴水不漏, *watertight; with no loopholes;*
  fáng shuǐ de: 防水的, *waterproof;*
  mì fēng de: 密封的, *airtight, sealed;*
  yán mì: 严密, *tight*

HETERODOXIA; heterodoxo (A)**;** *unorthodox nature, heterodoxy;*
  yāo yán: 妖言, *heresy;*
  yì duān: 异端, *heresy, heterodoxy;*
SEE (请查看**) FALACIA, DESIGUAL**

HIATO; hiato; *hiatus, interval, break, interruption;*
  jiàn gé: 间隔, *break, pause;*
  zàn tíng: 暂停, *pause, rest;*
  jiàn xiē: 间歇, *pause, interval;*
SEE (请查看**) APREHENDER**

HIGIENE; higiene; *hygiene ...*
HIGIÉNICO; higiênico (A)**;** *hygienic,*

sanitary, clean;
  gān jìng de: 干净的, *clean, neat, neat and tidy; complete, total;*
  wèi shēng yuán: 卫生员, *sanitary*

HILARANTE; hilariante; *hilarious, uproarious, hysterical ...* **HILARIDAD; hilaridade;** *hilarity, exuberance, jubilation, glee;*
  fēi cháng yǒu qù de: 非常有趣的, *hilarious;*
  huá jī de: 滑稽的, *hilarious (account/ adventure, etc.); funny, amusing;*
  xǐ de: 喜的, *happy joyful;*
  xiē sī dǐ lǐ de: 歇斯底里的, *hysterical laughter;*
  xiē sī dǐ lǐ: 歇斯底里, *hilarious;*
  xīn xǐ de: 欣喜的, *joyful;*
SEE (请查看**) DIVERTIDO, RIDÍCULO**

HIPOCRESÍA; hipocrisia; *hypocrisy, deceit, duplicity, insincerity;*
  jiǎ yì (n) (adv)**:** 假意, *hypocrisy; hypocritically, insincerely;*
SEE (请查看**) BURLAR**

HIPÓCRITA; hipócrita; *hypocrite;*
  jiǎ de: 假的, *false;*
  wěi jūn zǐ: 伪君子, *hypocrite;*
  xū wěi (sv)**:** 虚伪, *deceptive, hypocritical;*
SEE (请查看**) DUPLICIDAD**

HIPÓTESIS; hipótese; *hypothesis;*
  jiǎ shè: 假设, *hypothesis*

HISTÉRICO (A)**; histérico** (A)**;** *hysterical, frantic;*
  bù 'ān (sv)**:** 不安, *worried, uneasy, anxious;*
  bù 'ān xīn (sv)**:** 不安心, *unable to settle down, anxious;*
  kuáng luàn de: 狂乱的, *frantic pace, search, etc.;*
SEE (请查看**) HILARANTE, FANÁTICO, BRAVÍO, BULLICIOSO, FURIA**

HISTORIA; história; *history; story, excuse;*

lì shǐ: 历史, *history of sb/sthg*;
SEE (请查看) DESCRIPCIÓN

HISTÓRICO (A); **histórico** (A);
historical; historic;
　lì shǐ de: 历史的, *historical*;
　lì shǐ xìng de: 历史性的, *historic*

HOMICIDIO; homicídio; *murder,*
homicide;
　shā rén: 杀人, *murder, homicide*

HOMOGÉNEO (A); **homogêneo** (A);
homogeneous, uniform;
　tóng yī de: 同一的, *uniform in length*;
　xiāng tóng de: 相同的, *similar*;
　yī zhì: 一致, *uniform growth/rise/*
　result, etc.

HONESTIDAD ú HONRADEZ;
honradez; *honesty, modesty, decency,*
fairness; honor ... **HONESTO** (A);
honesto (A); *trustworthy; honest,*
modest, decent;
　chéng shí (sv) (n): 诚实, *honest, true;*
　honesty, truth, integrity;
　kě xìn (sv): 可信, *trustworthy; reliable,*
　credible;
　lǎo shí (sv): 老实, *honest, frank; naive*;
　lián jié (sv): 廉洁, *honest; incorruptible*;
　shòu zūn zhòng : 受尊重, *honest,*
　decent person;
　zhèng dà (sv): 正大, *honest*;
　zhèng zhí (sv) (n): 正直, *honest,*
　upright, fair-minded; integrity;
　zhōng hòu (sv): 忠厚, *honest and*
　considerate;
　zhōng shí (sv): 忠实, *faithful and*
　trustworthy;
SEE (请查看) DECENCIA, AUGUSTO,
SINCERIDAD, FIDELIDAD

HONRA; honra; *honor; pride, toast of,*
proud of;
　zì háo: 自豪, *dignity*;
　zì zūn xīn qiáng de: 自尊心强的, *self-*
　respect

HORRENDO (A); **horrendo (A)**;
horrendous, horrific, ghastly, shocking,
appalling;

jí qí kě pà de: 极其可怕的, *horrific*;
kě pà de: 可怕的, *dreadful; ghastly*;
kǒng bù de: 恐怖的, *horrendous*;
zāo gāo de: 糟糕的, *awful*;
SEE (请查看) HORROR, ABUSIVO

HOSPITALIDAD; hospitalidade;
hospitality;
　hào kè (n): 好客, *hospitality (of host)*;
　hào kè de: 好客的, *hospitable (person,*
　etc.);
　wēn qíng (n): 温情, *warmheartedness,*
　tenderness;

HOSTIL; hostil; *hostile*;
　dí fāng de: 敌方的, *hostile enemy*;
SEE (请查看) ANTAGONISTA,
ANIMOSIDAD

HUMANIDAD; humanidade;
humanity, mankind ... **HUMANO** (A);
humano (A); *human; human, humane*;
　rén cí: 仁慈, *humanity, benevolence*;
　rén dào de: 人道的, *humane*
　treatment, etc.;
　rén de: 人的, *human*;
　rén lèi: 人类, *the human race,*
　mankind;
　rén xìng: 人性, *human nature,*
　humanness; humanity

HUMEDAD; umidade; *humidity,*
moisture, dampness;
　cháo shī (sv): 潮湿, *humid*;
　shī dù: 湿度, *humidity*;
　shī qì: 湿气, *moisture, dampness*;
　shī rùn (sv): 湿润, *damp, moist*

HUMILDAD; humildade; *humility,*
meekness ... **HUMILDE; humilde;**
humble, modest, meek, self-effacing,
deferential; lowly, inferior, mean, low-
born;
　pǔ shí: 朴实, *simplicity*;
　qiān bēi (sv): 谦卑, *humble*;
　qiān gōng (sv) (n): 谦恭, *polite and*
　modest; humility, modesty;
　qiān xū de: 谦虚的, *modest person*;
　qiān xùn: 谦逊, *humble, modest*;
　wēn shùn de: 温顺的, *docile, meek*;

SEE (请查看) ABYECTO

HUMILLACIÓN; humilhação; *humiliation* ... HUMILLANTE; humilhante; *humiliating, humbling*;
   diū liǎn de: 丢脸的, *humiliating experience, etc.*;

qū rǔ (n) (sv): 屈辱, *humiliation, disgrace; to be humiliated*;
SEE (请查看) DESHONRAR, DESCRÉDITO

Easily recognizable verbs and their Portuguese and Chinese equivalents
Verbos fácilmente reconocibles en Español-Portugués-Inglés y sus equivalentes en Chino
Verbos facilmente reconhecível em Espanhol-Português-Inglês e seus equivalentes em Chinês
很容易辨认的西班牙语，葡萄牙语，英语动词和他们的中文对等词

HABITAR; habitar; *to live in/inhabit/occupy*;
   jū zhù: 居住, *to live*;
   zhàn yòng: 占用, *to occupy/use/take over*

HIBERNAR; hibernar; *to hibernate*;
   dōng mián (v) (n): 冬眠, *to hibernate; hibernation*

HONRAR; honrar; *to be honored*;
   xiàng ... biǎo shì jìng yì: 向…表示敬意, *to honor sb*

HORRORIZAR; horripilar; *to horrify/terrify*;
   shǐ jù pà: 使惧怕, *to terrify*

HUMILLAR; humillar; *to humiliate/humble*;
   (shǐ) qū rǔ (sv) (n): 屈辱, *to be humiliated/insulted; disgrace, humiliation*;
   SEE (请查看) DESCRÉDITO, DESHONRAR

Interchangeable Spanish-Portuguese-English words and their Chinese equivalents
Palabras en Español-Portugués-Inglés y sus equivalentes en Chino
Palavras em Espanhol-Português-Inglês e seus equivalentes em Chinês
西班牙语，葡萄牙语，英语及中文的对等单词

IDEAL; ideal;
   lǐ xiǎng (sv) (n): 理想, *ideal; aspiration*;
   zhì xiàng: 志向, *aspiration, ideal, goal*

IMPASSE ó IMPASE; impasse;
   jiāng jú: 僵局, *deadlock, stalemate, impasse*;
   SEE (请查看) DILEMA

IMPERIAL; imperial;

cháo tíng: 朝廷, *imperial government*;
   gù gōng: 故宫, *Imperial Palace*;
   huáng quán: 皇权, *imperial power*;
   huáng shì: 皇室, *imperial family, royalty*

IMPOSTOR (A); impostor (A);
   mào míng dǐng tì zhě: 冒名顶替者, *impostor*

INCLUSIVE; inclusive;
 bāo kuò (sv) (v): 包括, *inclusive; to include/ comprise;*
 SEE (请查看) **CONTENER**

INCÓGNITO (A)**; incógnito** (A)**;** *unknown;*
 wèi zhī shù: 未知数, *unknown fact, quantity;*
 bù zhī dào (sv): 不知道, *unknown;*
 huà míng (v) (n): 化名, *to use an alias; alias;*
 yǐn xìng mái míng (sv): 隐姓埋名, *unidentified, unknown, covert, unrecognized;*
 yǐn xìng mái míng zhě: 隐姓埋名者, *in disguise, anonymous, undercover;*
 SEE (请查看) **ANÓNIMO**

INDIVIDUAL; individual (GEN)**;** *single;*
 gè rén zhǔ yì: 个人主义, *individualism;*
 gè rén: 个人, *individual. personal;*
 gè tǐ: 个体, *individual;*
 SEE (请查看) **DESIGUAL, SOLITARIO, UNIPERSONAL**

INDUSTRIAL; industrial;
 chǎn yè de (adj) (n): 产业的, *industrial; industry;*
 gōng yè de: 工业的, *industrial plant/ society, etc.;*
 háng yè: 行业, *industry, business; trade, profession*

INFERIOR; inferior;
 chà (sv) (v): 差, *inferior, poor; wrong, false; to be short of/lack sthg; to differ;*
 dī děng (sv): 低等, *lower, humble;*
 dī jiàn (sv): 低贱, *lowly, humble;*
 dī lián (sv): 低廉, *cheap; inexpensive;*
 dī sān xià sì (fe): 低三下四, *lowly, mean, servile;*
 liè děng (sv): 劣等, *low-grade, of poor quality;*
 liè děng pǐn: 劣等品, *inferior goods;*
 liè děng shēng: 劣等生, *unworthy, inferior;*
 liè zhì: 劣质, *of poor quality;*

xià jí (sv) (n): 下级, *inferior, subordinate;*
 zhuō liè (sv): 拙劣, *clumsy, inferior, botched;*
 SEE (请查看) **SECUNDARIO, MEDIOCRIDAD**

INFINITESIMAL; infinitesimal;
 wēi xiǎo (attr): 微小, *small, little, infinitesimal;*
 SEE (请查看) **GIGABYTE**

INFORMAL; informal; *unreliable, informal;*
 fēi zhèng guī (sv): 非正规, *informal (rule/regulation; etc.);*
 fēi zhèng shì (attr): 非正式, *informal, unofficial;*
 kào bù zhù (sv): 靠不住, *to be unreliable, undependable*

INSIGNIA; insígnia; *badge, decoration, flag;*
 huī zhāng: 徽章, *badge, insignia;*
 mào huī: 帽徽, *cap/helmet insignia;*
 qí zhì: 旗帜, *flag, banner;*
 qì zǐ: 妻子, *banner, flag;*
 SEE (请查看) **DECORACIÓN**

INSPECTOR (A)**; inspector** (A)**;**
 jiǎn chá yuán: 检查员, *inspector; supervisor, controller;*
 shì chá zhě: 视察者, *inspector*

INTERIOR; interior (adj)**;** *inner;*
 guó nèi (attr): 国内, *interior, internal;*
 nèi bù: 内部, *inside, interior, within;*
 nèi dì (pw): 内地, *inland, interior;*
 nèi zài (sv): 内在, *internal, inherent, intrinsic*

INTERNET; internet;
 hù lián wǎng: 互联网, *the Internet;*
 wǎng bā: 网吧, *Internet café;*
 yīn tè wǎng: 因特网, *the Internet*

ITEM; item;
 jié mù: 节目, *item on a program;*
 SEE (请查看) **ARTÍCULO**

Easily recognizable Spanish-Portuguese-English nouns, adjectives and adverbs and their Chinese equivalents
Nombres, sustantivos, adjetivos y adverbios en Español-Portugués-Inglés y sus equivalentes en Chino
Nomes, substantivos, adjetivos e advérbios em Espanhol-Português-Inglês e seus equivalentes em Chinês
容易辨认的西班牙语，葡萄牙语，英语的名词，形容词和副词和他们的中文对等词

IDEALISTA; **idealista**; *idealistic, idealist*;
  lǐ xiǎng de (adv): 理想地, *ideally*;
  lǐ xiǎng zhǔ yì zhě (sv) (n): 理想主义者, *idealistic; idealist*;
  lǐ xiǎng zhǔ yì: 理想主义, *idealism*;
  wéi xīn zhǔ yì zhě (n): 唯心主义者, *idealist*

ÍDEM; **idem**; *ditto*;
  tóng yàng de (adv) (attr): 同样地, *same as equal, similar*

IDÉNTICO (A); **idêntico** (A); *identical, duplicate, twin, same ...* **IDENTIDAD; identidade**; *identity*;
  qīng yī sè (sv) (n): 清一色, *identical; monotone*;
  shuāng shēng (n): 双生, *twin*;
  shēn fèn: 身份, *identity, status, position*;
SEE (请查看) **DUPLICADO, DIFERENCIAR**

IDENTIFICACIÓN; **identificação**; *identification, computer password*;
  kǒu lìng: 口令, *password*;
  mì mǎ: 密码, *password, code*;
SEE (请查看) **CERTIFICAR**

IDÍLICO; **idílico**; *idyllic, peaceful, blissful, pastoral*;
  ān dùn (v) (sv): 安顿, *to settle down; peaceful, undisturbed*;
  tài píng (sv): 太平, *peaceful*;
SEE (请查看) **CALMA, FRIVOLIDAD, PACÍFICO**

IDIOTA; **idiota**; *idiotic; stupid; idiot*;
  cǎo bāo: 草包, *straw bag; idiot*;
  dāi zi: 呆子, *fool, blockhead, idiot*;
SEE (请查看) **BESTIA, CRETINO,**

ESTUPIDEZ, ESTÚPIDO

IGNICIÓN; **ignição**; *ignition*;
  fā huǒ zhuāng zhì: 发火装置, *ignition mechanism*

IGNOMINIA; **ignominia**; *ignominy, disgrace, dishonor ...* **IGNOMINIOSO** (A); **ignominoso** (A); *ignominious, disgraceful*;
  chǐ rǔ (n): 耻辱, *shame, disgrace, ignominy, dishonor*;
  kě hèn (sv): 可恨, *detestable, hateful, abominable*;
  xiū cán (sv): 羞惭, *ashamed*;
SEE (请查看) **DESCRÉDITO, HUMILLACIÓN**

IGNORADO; **ignorado** (A); *unknown; (LITER) unknown, obscure*;
  wèi xiáng (vp): 未详, *to be unknown/ unclear*;
  wèi zhī shù: 未知数, *unknown number*;
SEE (请查看) **ARCANO, CRÍPTICO**

IGNORANCIA; **ignorância**; *ignorance, unawareness, inexperience ...* **IGNORANTE; ignorante**; *ignorant; rude; ignoramus, unaware*;
  méng mèi (sv): 蒙昧, *uncivilized, ignorant*;
  quē fá jīng yàn: 缺乏经验, *inexperience*;
  wú zhī (sv) (n): 无知, *ignorant, stupid; ignorance*;
  yú mèi (sv): 愚昧, *ignorant, fatuous*;
SEE (请查看) **INEXPERIENCIA, MALEDUCADO**

IGUAL; **igual**; *the same (as), similar to; identical ...* **IGUALMENTE**;

igualmente; *also, likewise; equally*;
  bìng qiě (conj): 并且, *and, also, besides, furthermore*;
  děng jià (n): 等价, *equivalence*;
  děng shì (n): 等式, *equality*;
  děng zhí (n): 等值, *equivalence, equal value*;
  píng děng (sv): 平等, *equal*;
  píng jūn (v) (sv): 平均, *to even, to average; equal*;
  xiāng děng de (adv): 相等地, *equally*;
  xiāng jì (sv): 相继, *close, similar to*;
  xiāng sì (sv): 相似, *similar, alike*;
SEE (请查看**) IDÉNTICO, DUPLICADO**

IGUALADO (A); **nivelado** (A); *level, evenly matched* ... **IGUALDAD**; **igualdade**; *equality, equal rights*;
  gōng zhèng de: 公正的, *just, fair, impartial*;
  jūn héng de: 均衡的, *balanced, even*;
  jūn yún de: 均匀的, *even, homogeneous*

ILEGAL; **ilegal**; *illegal, unlawful* .. **ILEGÍTIMO** (A); **ilegítimo** (A); *illegitimate, illegal* ... **ILÍCITO** (A); **ilícito** (A); *illicit, illegal, forbidden, unlawful*;
  bù zhèng dàng (sv): 不正当, *improper, immoral, illegal*;
  fēi fǎ (sv): 非法, *illegal, unlawful*;
  fēi fǎ de: 非法的, *illegal*;
  jìn zhǐ de: 禁止的, *forbidden*;
  wéi fǎ (v) (sv): 违法, *to break the law/ be illegal; illegitimate*;
  wéi fǎ de: 违法的, *illicit*

ILEGIBLE; **ilegível**; *illegible, unreadable, scrawled, scribbled*;
  nán biàn rèn (sv): 难辨认, *blurred, illegible*;
  nán yǐ biàn rèn de: 难以辨认的, *illegible*;
  zì jì mó hu (sv): 字迹模糊, *illegible handwriting*

ILETRADO (A); **iletrado** (A); *illiterate, uncultured, uneducated*;
  bì sè (sv): 闭塞, *unenlightened*;

  wén máng: 文盲, *illiterate*;
  yǔ yán cuò wù de: 语言错误的, *illiterate (as to writing)*;
SEE (请查看**) ABRASIVO**

ILIMITADO (A); **ilimitado** (A); *unlimited, limitless*;
  wú biān wú jì (fe): 无边无际, *limitless, boundless*;
  wú xiàn zhì: 无限制, *unlimited*

ILÓGICO (A); **ilógico** (A); *illogical, unreasonable, absurd*;
  bù tōng (v) (sv): 不同, *to be blocked up/won't work; illogical*;
  huāng dàn (sv): 荒诞, *absurd*;
  huāng miù (sv): 荒谬, *absurd, ridiculous*;
  huāng táng (sv): 荒唐, *absurd, preposterous*;
SEE (请查看**) RIDÍCULO**

ILUMINADO (A); **iluminado** (A); *enlightened; illuminated*;
  kāi míng (sv) (n): 开明, *enlightened, open-minded; enlightenment*;
  liàng tang (sv): 亮堂, *bright, enlightened*;
  míng: 明, *illumination, enlightenment*;
  qǐ shì (v) (n): 启示, *to enlighten; inspiration*;
  shǐ bǎi tuō piān jiàn: 使摆脱偏见, *to be enlightened*;
SEE (请查看**) AUSPICIOSO, RAYO, LÁMPARA, LUZ, AUSPICIOSO**

ILUSIÓN; **ilusão**; *hope, illusion* ... **ILUSORIO** (A); **ilusório** (A); *illusory; empty*;
  huàn jìng: 幻境, *fairyland; illusion*;
  huàn jué: 幻觉, *illusion, delusion*;
  huàn mèng: 幻梦, *illusion, dream*;
  huàn xiàng: 幻象, *phantom*;
  huàn yǐng: 幻影, *mirage, phantom*;
  mèng huàn: 梦幻, *illusion, dream*;
  mèng jìng: 梦境, *dreamland*;
  mèng xiǎng (v) (n): 梦想, *to dream; daydream, illusion*;
  xū huàn (sv): 虚幻, *unreal, illusory*;
SEE (请查看**) DESCONCERTANTE,**

DESILUSIÓN, EUFORIA, INTERÉS ILUSTRACIÓN; ilustração;
illustration, instance, example; sample
... ILUSTRADO (A); **ilustrado** (A);
illustrated, explained, depicted; erudite;
  chā tú: 插图, *illustration, diagram; illustration by example*;
  lì zhèng: 例证, *illustration, instance*;
  shì lì: 事例, *example, instance*;
  shí lì: 实例, *illustration (picture, chart, etc.)*;
  shuō míng de: 说明的, *explanatory*;
  tú shì (v) (n): 图示, *to illustrate with pictures; illustration*;
  yàng pǐn: 样品, *sample, swatch*;
SEE (请查看) **ANTICIPAR, DESCRIPCIÓN, DENOTAR, EJEMPLO**

IMAGEN; imagen; *image, TV picture*;
  biǎo xiàng: 表象, *image, appearance, idea*;
  diàn shì: 电视, *television, TV*;
  xiàng piàn: 相片, *photograph; image*;
  xíng xiàng (n) (sv): 形象, *image, form, figure*;
  yíng guāng píng: 荧光屏, *television screen*;
SEE (请查看) **PRESENTACIÓN**

IMAGINACIÓN; imaginação;
imagination **... IMAGINARIO**
(A); **imaginário** (A); *imaginary* **...**
IMAGINATIVO (A); **imaginatico** (A);
imaginative;
  jiǎ xiǎng de: 假想的, *imaginary*;
  jiǎ xiǎng: 假想, *imagination, hypothesis*;
  xiǎng xiàng lì: 想象力, *imagination*;
  xīn yǐng de: 新颖的, *imaginative idea, approach, solution*;
  xū gòu de: 虚构的, *imaginative, fictitious, imaginary*;
  jù yǒu xiǎng xiàng lì de: 具有想象力的, *imaginative*;
SEE (请查看) **IMAGINAR**

IMBATIBLE; imbatível; *unbeatable*;
  dǎ bu kuǎ de: 打不垮的, *unbeatable*;

wú yǔ lún bǐ (fe): 无与伦比, *incomparable, unique*

IMITACIÓN; imitação; *imitation, copy, counterfeit, fake*;
  chāo jiàn: 抄件, *duplicate, copy*;
  fān bǎn: 翻版, *copy, reproduction, reprint*;
  fǎng zhì pǐn: 仿制品, *imitation, replica; copy, duplicate*;
  fǔ zhì pǐn: 复制品, *copy*;
  wěi zào (n) (v): 伪造, *counterfeit (money, goods, etc.); to forge/counterfeit*

IMPACIENCIA; impaciência;
impatience, abrupt, testy, curt, short
... IMPACIENTE; impaciente;
impatient, restless, eager, intolerant
... IMPACIENTEMENTE;
impacientemente; *impatiently*;
  bù nài fán de: 不耐烦的, *irritable*;
  bù nài fán: 不耐烦, *impatience, irritation*;
  jí qiè: 急切, *impatience, eagerness*;
  jí zào: 急躁, *impatience, annoyance*;
  mào shi (sv): 冒失, *abrupt, rash, indiscreet*;
  xīn jí (sv): 心急, *impatient, quick-tempered*;
SEE (请查看) **DESCONCERTANTE**

IMPACTO; impacto; *impact, collision, crash*;
  bào diē: 暴跌, *stock market/business crash*;
  zhuàng jī: 撞击, *crash of a car*;
SEE (请查看) **COLISIÓN**

IMPARCIAL; imparcial; *impartial, fair, equitable, unbiased, evenhanded, disinterested* **... IMPARCIALIDAD;**
imparcialidade; *impartiality*;
  bù piān bù yǐ: 不偏不倚, *impartial, exact, just*;
  chí píng (sv) (v): 持平, *unbiased, fair, impartial; to balance interests*;
  zhōng lì xìng: 中立性, *impartiality, neutrality*;
SEE (请查看) **DESAPASIONADO, IGUALDAD**

IMPECABLE; impecável; *impeccable, faultless;*
  wú xiá cī de: 无瑕疵的, *impeccable; flawless;*
SEE (请查看) CONSUMADO, INFALIBLE

IMPEDIDO (A); **incapacitado** (A); *disabled;*
  cán jí (n): 残疾, *deformity, physical disability;*
SEE (请查看) DISCAPACITADO

IMPEDIMENTO; impedimento; *obstacle, impediment, hindrance;*
  zhàng 'ài (v) (n): 障碍, *to hinder, to obstruct; obstacle, barrier;*
  zhàng 'ài wù: 障碍物, *obstacle, barrier*

IMPENITENTE; impenitente; *impenitent, unrepentant;*
  bù ào huǐ (sv): 不懊悔, *unrepentant, not remorseful, without any regret;*
  wán gù bù huà (sv): 顽固不化, *incorrigibly obstinate*

IMPENSABLE; impensável; *unthinkable;*
  bù kě néng (sv); 不可能, *unreal, impossible;*
  bù kě xiǎng xiàng (sv): 不可想象, *unimaginable, inconceivable;*
  nán yǐ xiǎng xiàng (sv): 难以想象, *unimaginable;*
  nán yǐ xiāng xìn (fe): 难以相信, *hard to believe*

IMPERDONABLE; imperdoável; *unforgivable, inexcusable;*
  biàn hù bù liǎo (sv): 辩护不了, *unjustifiable, inexcusable, indefensible;*
  bù kě yuán liàng (sv): 不可原谅, *unforgivable, unpardonable, inexcusable;*
  nán wàng (sv): 难忘, *unforgettable;*
  wú fǎ fáng yù (sv): 无法防御, *indefensible;*
SEE (请查看) INJUSTO

IMPERFECCIÓN; imperfeição; *imperfection, flaw, fault;*

  pò zhàn: 破绽, *flaw, weak spot;*
SEE (请查看) CULPA, DESINTEGRACIÓN, CRIMEN

IMPERFECTO (A); **imperfeito** (A); *imperfect, flawed, defective;*
  bù wán měi de: 不完美的, *imperfect system/ understanding/world;*
  yǒu xiá cī de: 有瑕疵的, *imperfect goods;*
SEE (请查看) DEBILIDAD, DEFECTO

IMPERIOSO (A); **imperioso** (A); *imperious;*
  dú cái (v) (n): 独裁, *to dictate/ make arbitrary decisions; dictatorship, autocratic rule;*
SEE (请查看) PREPOTENCIA

IMPERTINENCIA; impertinência; *impertinence;*
IMPERTINENTE; impertinente; *impertinent, impudent;*
  bù kè qi (fe): 不客气, *impolite, rude, blunt;*
  bù qiè tí (sv): 不切题, *impertinent, irrelevant;*
  bù zūn jìng (sv) (n): 不尊敬, *disrespectful; disrespect;*
  lǔ mǎng (sv): 鲁莽, *crude and rash;*
  mǎng zhuàng (sv): 莽撞, *impetuous, rash, uncultured;*
SEE (请查看) BRONCO, DESATENCIÓN, GROSERO

ÍMPETU; impeto; *force, impetus;*
  dòng lì: 动力, *power, force, impetus;*
SEE (请查看) GROSERO

IMPETUOSIDAD; impetuosidade; *impetuosity, rashness ...* **IMPETUOSO** (A); **impetuoso** (A); *violent, impulsive, impetuous, rash;*
  jí zào (n): 急躁, *impetuosity;*
  lǔ mǎng (sv): 鲁莽, *impetuous, crude, rash;*
SEE (请查看) BRAVÍO, DRÁSTICO, INSTIGACIÓN

IMPLANTE; implante; *implant;*

zhí rù wù (n): 植入物, *implant (MED)*;
SEE (请查看) ADOCTRINAR

IMPLEMENTO; implemento;
implement, tool;
  qì jù: 器具, *tool, instrument, utensil, implement*;
SEE (请查看) ARTEFACTO

IMPLICACIÓN; implicação;
involvement, implication ...
IMPLÍCITAMENTE; implicitamente;
implicitly ... **IMPLÍCITO** (A); **implícito**
(A); *implicit, implied*;
  hán xù de: 含蓄的, *implicit (implied)*;
  hán yì: 含义, *meaning, implication, indifference*;
  jué duì de: 绝对的, *implicit (absolute)*;
  nèi hán de: 内含的, *implicit (inherent)*;
  qiān lián: 牵连, *involvement*;
  yán wài zhī yì (fe): 言外之意, *implication*;
SEE (请查看) CONSECUENCIA

IMPOLUTO (A); **impoluto** (A);
unpolluted, pure, unblemished;
  chún zhèng (sv): 纯正, *pure*;
  dì dào (sv): 地道, *pure; genuine, real*;
  qīng bái (sv): 清白, *pure, clean; innocent*;
SEE (请查看) COMPLETAMENTE

IMPONENCIA; impotência;
impressiveness ... **IMPONENTE;**
imponente; *imposing, impressive, stunning*;
  gǎn rén (sv): 感人, *impressive, touching, moving*;
  lìng rén qīn pèi (sv): 令人钦佩, *impressive, admirable*;
  qì pò: 气魄, *imposing manner; daring*;
  táng huáng (sv): 堂皇, *stately, grand*;
  táng táng (sv): 堂堂, *imposing, dignified*;
  wēi yán (sv): 威严, *imposing (person, manner)*;
  zhuàng guān: 壮观, *imposing (building, etc.)*

IMPOPULAR; impopular; *unpopular* ...
IMPOPULARIDAD; impopularidade;
unpopularity;
  bù liú xíng de: 不流行的, *unpopular*;
  bù shòu huān yíng de: 不受欢迎的, *unpopular person, decision*

IMPORTANCIA; importância;
importance ... **IMPORTANTE;**
importante; *important, significant, major*;
  yào jiàn (n): 要件, *key/important document/ condition*;
  yào jǐn (sv): 要紧, *important, serious, vital, essential*;
  yào wén (n): 要闻, *important news*;
  zhòng dà (sv): 重大, *great, major, significant, important*;
  zhòng dì (n): 重地, *important place/ location*;
  zhòng rèn (n): 重任, *important task/ responsibility*;
  zhòng yào (sv): 重要, *important, significant, critical, vital*;
SEE (请查看) CELEBRIDAD,
FAMOSO, DIVERTIDO, PETULANCIA

IMPOSIBILIDAD; impossibilidade;
impossibility ... **IMPOSIBLE;**
impossível; *impossible*;
  bù kě néng (sv) (n): 不可能, *unreal, impossible; impossibility*;
  nán duì fù (sv): 难对付, *impossible/ hard to believe/ understand*;
  nán yǐ duì fù (sv): 难以对付, *impossible/hard/ difficult to believe/ understand*;
  nán yǐ zhì xìn (fe): 难以置信, *impossible/difficult to believe*;
  nán yǐ zhì xìn de (adv): 难以置信地, *impossibility*;
  wú fǎ rěn shòu (sv): 无法忍受, *impossible/difficult to bear/endure*;
  zuò bù dào (sv): 做不到, *impossible to comply/ conform*

IMPOSIBILITADO (A);
impossibilitado (A); *disabled, impeded, prevented*;
  cán fèi (v) (n): 残废, *to be handicapped; disabled person*

IMPOTENCIA; impotência; *impotence, incapable* **... IMPOTENTE; impotente;** *impotent, powerless, helpless*;
　yáng wěi (n): 阳萎, *impotence (MED)*;
SEE (请查看) **ABATIDO**

IMPRECISO (A); **impreciso** (A); **vago** (A); *vague, imprecise*;
　bù jīng què (sv) (n): 不精确, *inaccurate, imprecise; inaccuracy*;
　bù zhǔn què (sv) (n): 不准确, *imprecise, inaccurate, impreciseness*;
　hán hùn (sv): 含混, *ambiguous; vague*;
　yǐn yuē (sv): 隐约, *indistinct, vague*;
SEE (请查看) **ARCANO, CRÍPTICO**

IMPREDECIBLE; imprevisível; *unpredictable, unforeseeable*;
　bù kě yù jiàn de: 不可预见的, *unforeseeable*;
　bù qī ér zhì de: 不期而至的, *unprepared*;
　cuò shǒu bù jí (fe): 措手不及, *be caught unaware/ unprepared*;
　méi yǒu zuò zhǔn bèi de: 没有作准备的, *unprepared*;
　yì liào bù dào de: 意料不到的, *unpredictable, unforeseeable*;
　yì wài (sv): 意外, *unexpected, unforeseen*;
SEE (请查看) **CONTINGENCIA**

IMPREMEDITADO (A); **acidental;** *unpremeditated, inadvertent*;
　fēi gù yì: 非故意, *inadvertently*;
　màn bù jīng xīn (fe): 漫不经心, *careless, negligent*;
　ǒu 'ěr (adv): 偶尔, *occasionally, by chance; accidentally*;
　pèng qiǎo (adv): 碰巧, *accidentally*;
　shù hu (n) (v): 疏忽, *carelessness, negligence; to be careless/negligent*;
　wú xīn (sv): 无心, *unintentionally*;
　yīn shū hu zào chéng de: 因疏忽造成的, *careless, negligent, unpremeditated*;
SEE (请查看) **BRUSCO, CIRCUNSTANCIAL, DESATENCIÓN, NEGLIGENCIA**

IMPRESCINDIBLE; imprescindível; *indispensable, essential*;
　bì bu kě shǎo de: 必不可少的, *indispensable, absolutely necessary*;
SEE (请查看) **CÉNTRICO, FUNDAMENTAL, COMPONENTE, NECESARIAMENTE**

IMPRESIÓN; impressão; *impression, imprint*;
　yìn (n) (v): 印, *seal, stamp; to print, to engrave*;
　yìn jì: 印记, *mark of stamp/seal/foot; imprint*;
　yìn zhāng: 印章, *seal, stamp*;
SEE (请查看) **CARACTERÍSTICO, DENOTAR**

IMPRESIONABLE; impressionável; *impressionable*;
　gǎn rén de: 感人的, *touching, moving*;
　yì shòu yǐng xiǎng de: 易受影响的, *susceptible*;
　yǐng xiǎng de: 影响的, *impressionable*;
SEE (请查看) **EXPERIENCIA, PROPENSIÓN**

IMPROBABILIDAD; improbabilidade; *improbability, unlikelihood*;
　bù dà fā shēng: 不大发生, *unlikely, improbable*;
　bù dà kě néng de: 不大可能的, *improbable, impossible; unlikely*;
　bù dà kě néng: 不大可能, *improbability*

IMPRODUCTIVO (A); **improdutivo** (A); *unproductive, unprofitable*;
　tú láo de: 徒劳的, *futile, fruitless effort/plan, etc.*
　wú jì (vp): 无际, *be unprofitable, useless*;
　wú yì: 无益, *unprofitable, useless*

IMPROPERIO; impropério; *insult, offense*;
　rǔ mà de: 辱骂的, *insulting*;

SEE (请查看) ABUSAR

IMPROPIO (A); imprópio (A); improper, unfitting, inappropriate;
  bù chéng tǐ tǒng de: 不成体统的, downright outrageous;
  bù shì dàng de: 不适当的, inappropriate, improper;
  bù tǐ miàn de: 不体面的, undignified, improper;
  bù xiāng chèn de: 不相称的, unsuitable, inappropriate;
  qiàn tuǒ (sv) (v): 欠妥, improper; to be improper;
  shī dàng (vp): 失当, inappropriate, improper;
SEE (请查看) INOPORTUNO

IMPROVISACIÓN; improvisação; improvisation ... IMPROVISADO (A); improvisado (A); improvised, makeshift;
  jí xìng (attr) (adv): 即兴, impromptu, extemporaneous

IMPROVISO; improviso; unexpectedly, suddenly;
  yì xiǎng bu dào (adv) (sv): 意想不到, unexpectedly; unexpected;
SEE (请查看) BRUSCO

IMPRUDENCIA; imprudência; imprudence, carelessness, indiscretion, rashness, inattentiveness ...
IMPRUDENTE; imprudente; careless, rash, imprudent;
  hòu yán (vp): 厚颜, brazen, shameless;
  hòu yán wú chǐ de (fe): 厚颜无耻的, imprudent, shameless;
  mào mèi wú lǐ de: 冒昧无礼的, presumptuous, impertinent;
  mào mèi wú lǐ: 冒昧无礼, impudent;
  wú lǐ: 无礼, impertinence

IMPULSIVO (A); impulsivo (A); impulsive, hothead ... IMPULSO; impulso, stimulus; urge; impulse;
  chōng dòng (sv) (n): 冲动, urge, impulse; impulsive person;
SEE (请查看) BRAVÍO

IMPUNE; impune; unpunished;
  méi shòu chéng fá de: 没受惩罚的, unpunished

IMPUNIDAD; impunidade; impunity;
  bù shòu chéng fá: 不受惩罚, with impunity

IMPUTACIÓN; imputação; accusation, imputation;
  zuì zhuàng (n): 罪状, charges/ allegations of a crime/offense;
SEE (请查看) ACUSACIÓN

INACCESIBLE; inacessível; inaccessible, aloof;
  dá bu dào de: 达不到的, aloof, inaccessible;
  nán dé dào de: 难得到的, inaccessible, unattainable;
  nán jiē chù dào de: 难接触到的, inaccessible, unreachable;
  nán jiē jìn de: 难接近的, inaccessible, unapproachable

INACEPTABLE; inadmissível; unacceptable;
  bù kě jiē shòu (sv) (n): 不可接受, unacceptable; unacceptability

INACTIVIDAD; inactividade, retirement, inactivity, unemployment ...
INACTIVO (A); inactivo (A); retired, idle; inactive, dormant, jobless;
  tuì xiū de: 退休的, retired;
  wú suǒ shì shì de (fe): 无所事事的, have nothing to do; idle away time;
  xián sǎn de: 闲散的, inactive;
SEE (请查看) DESOCUPADO

INADAPTADO (A); inadaptado (A); maladjusted (adj), misfit (n);
  xīn lǐ shī tiáo de: 心理失调的, maladjusted

INADMISIBLE; inadmissível; inadmissible, unacceptable;
  bù néng chéng rèn de: 不能承认的, inadmissible;
  bù néng jiē shòu de: 不能接受的, unacceptable;

bù xǔ kě de: 不许可的, *inadmissible (DER)*

INANIMADO (A); **inanimado** (A); *inanimate;*
  wú shēng mìng de: 无生命的, *inanimate;*
  wú shēng qì de: 无生气的, *inert*

INAPLICABLE; inaplicável; *inapplicable;*
  bù shì yòng de: 不适用的, *impractical, dysfunctional, inapplicable;*
  bù xiāng gān de: 不相干的, *irrelevant, immaterial, inapplicable*

INATENCIÓN; inanteção; *inattention;*
  bù zhù yì (sv) (n): 不注意, *inattentive; inattention;*
SEE (请查看**) DESATENCIÓN**

INCANDESCENTE; incandescente; *incandescent;*
  bái chì: 白炽, *incandescence, incandescent lamp, white heat;*
  bái rè (n): 白热, *incandescence, white heat;*
  càn làn (sv): 灿烂, *brilliant, sparkling; radiant, bright*

INCAPACIDAD; incapacidade; *inability, incompetence, incapacity*
... INCAPAZ; incapaz; *incapable; incompetent;*
  bù gòu gé: 不够格, *incompetence;*
  bù hé gé de: 不合格的, *unqualified;*
  bù huì de: 不会的, *incapable;*
  bù néng shèng rèn: 不能胜任, *incompetence, unqualified;*
  bù shèng rèn de: 不胜任的, *incompetent, unqualified;*
  méi néng lì de: 没能力的, *incompetent;*
  wú néng (sv) (n): 无能, *incompetent, incapable; incapability, incompetence;*
SEE (请查看**) INCOMPETENCIA, IMPOTENCIA**

INCENDIARIO (A); **incendiário** (A); *incendiary, inflammatory* **... INCENDIO;**

incêndio; *fire;*
  huǒ: 火, *flames;*
  lú huǒ: 炉火, *fire in a fireplace/hearth, etc.;*
  shān dòng xìng de: 煽动性的, *inflammatory;*
  zòng huǒ de: 纵火的, *incendiary;*
SEE (请查看**) DESASTRE**

INCENTIVO; incentivo; *incentive, motivation, inducement;*
  dǎo zhì: 导致, *inducement;*
  dòng jī: 动机, *motivation; motive, intention;*
  gǔ lì: 鼓励, *encouragement, inducement;*
  yǐn qǐ: 引起, *inducement; attraction;*
SEE (请查看**) AGITAR**

INCESANTE; incessante; *incessant, unceasing, continual;*
  chí xù bù duàn de: 持续不断的, *incessant;*
SEE (请查看**) CONSTANTE, CONTINUADO, FREQUENTE**

INCESTO; incesto; *incest;*
  luàn lún: 乱伦, *incest*

INCIDENTE; incidente; *incident, episode, happening;*
  chā qǔ: 插曲, *episode; interlude;*
  shì duān: 事端, *disturbance, incident;*
  shì jiàn: 事件, *incident, event;*
SEE (请查看**) DESASTRE**

INCIPIENTE; incipiente; *incipient, early;*
  gǎng kāi shǐ de: 刚开始的, *incipient, early;*
  kāi shǐ (n): 开始, *initial stage, beginning;*
  zǎo qī de: 早期的, *incipient*

INCISIVO (A); **incisivo** (A); *sharp, cutting, incisive;*
  jiān ruì de: 尖锐的, *sharp-pointed, penetrating, incisive; piercing*

INCLEMENCIA; inclemência,

ruthlessness; harshness, inclemency ...
INCLEMENTE; inclemente, *ruthless,*
merciless; harsh/inclement weather;
  kè bó (sv): 刻薄, *harsh, unkind*;
  kǔ shuǐ: 苦水, *misery, bitterness*;
  rěn xīn (v) (n): 忍心 , *to be hard*
  hearted enough to ...; cruelty;
  xīn hěn (sv): 心狠, *cruel, ruthless*;
SEE (请查看**) ATROCIDAD,**
ABRASIVO, BRUTAL, AFLICCIÓN,
CRUELDAD, GRAVE

INCLINACIÓN; fondness; *preference*;
inclinação; *slant, inclination; propensity*
... **INCLINADO** (A)**; inclinado** (A)**;**
inclined, sloping; inclined to do sthg;
  piān 'ài (n) (v): 偏爱, *preference; to be*
  partial;
  qīng xiàng (n) (v): 倾向, *tendency,*
  inclination, deviation; to prefer, to be
  inclined/have a tendency;
  qǐng xiàng yú zuò mǒu shì: 倾向
  于做某事 , *to tend to/be inclined to do*
  sthg;
  yōu xiān quán (n): 优先权, *priority,*
  preference;
SEE (请查看**) BANCO, BENÉFICO,**
DECLIVE, COSTUMBRE

INCLUSO (A) (adj)**; incluso** (A)**;**
enclosed, included ... **INCLUSO** (adv)**;**
inclusive; *inclusively, including*;
  bāo kuò (v) (n) (sv): 包括, *to include/*
  consist of; to comprise; inclusion;
  inclusive;
  bāo kuò zài nèi de: 包括在内的,
  included;
SEE (请查看**) CONTENER**

INCOHERENCIA; incoerência;
incoherence ... **INCOHERENTE;**
incoerente; *illogical; incoherent;*
inconsistent, disconnected;
  bù hé luó ji de (v) (sv): 不合逻辑的,
  illogical;
  bù lián guàn (sv) (n): 不连贯,
  incoherent; incoherence;
  yǔ wú lún cì (fe): 语无伦次, *speak*
  incoherently/ irrationally;
  yǔ wú lún cì de: 语无伦次的,
  incoherent;

SEE (请查看**) IRRACIONAL**

INCOLORO (A)**; incolor;** *colorless*;
  cāng bái (sv): 苍白, *pale, dull,*
  colorless;
  wú sè (vp): 无色, *colorless*

INCÓMODO (A)**; incômodo** (A)**;**
uncomfortable, boring; inconvenient
place;
  bù shū fu de: 不舒服的,
  uncomfortable; unwell;
  bù shū shì de: 不舒适的,
  uncomfortable chair, room, journey;
  bù zì zai (sv): 不自在, *uncomfortable*;
  nì fán (sv): 腻烦, *to be bored/fed up*
  with;
  wú liáo (sv): 无聊, *bored, boring*;
SEE (请查看**) DIFÍCIL**

INCOMPATIBILIDAD;
incompatibilidade; *incompatibility*;
  bù jiān róng de: 不兼容的,
  incompatible computers/software;
  bù xiāng pèi de: 不相配的,
  incompatible, ill-suited;
  bù xié tiáo de: 不协调的,
  incompatible; uncoordinated;
  hé bù lái de: 合不来的, *incompatible*
  people;
SEE (请查看**) DISCONFORME,**
CONTRADICCIÓN

INCOMPETENCIA; incompetência;
incompetence ... **INCOMPETENTE;**
incompetente; *incompetent*;
  bù gòu gé: 不够格, *incompetent*;
  bù néng shèng rèn: 不能胜任,
  incompetence;
  dī néng (sv): 低能, *incompetent;*
  mentally deficient;
SEE (请查看**) IMPOTENCIA,**
INCOMPETENCIA, INCAPACIDAD,
INEPTO

INCOMPLETO (A)**; incompleto** (A)**;**
incomplete;
  bù wán quán de: 不完全的,
  incomplete;
  bù wán shàn de: 不完善的, *imperfect,*

unconsummated; incomplete;
méi wán chéng de: 没完成的,
unaccomplished, incomplete

INCOMPRENDIDO (A);
incompreendido (A); *misunderstood;*
wěi qu (v) (sv): 委屈, *to feel wronged,*
to be misunderstood; unjustly treated;
wù huì (v) (n): 误会, *to misunderstand;*
misunderstanding;
wù jiě (v) (n): 误解, *to misread/*
misunderstand; misunderstanding

INCOMPRENSIBLE;
incompreensível; *incomprehensible*
... INCONCEBIBLE; inconcebível;
inconceivable, unthinkable; unimaginable;
bù kě xiǎng de: 不可想的,
unthinkable;
bù kě xiǎng xiàng (vp): 不可想象,
unimaginable;
wèi bì kě xìn de: 未必可信的,
improbable, unreliable, incredible;
SEE (请查看) **IMPROBABILIDAD,**
IMPOSIBILIDAD

INCONCLUSO (A); **inconcluso** (A);
unfinished;
fēi jié lùn xìng de: 非结论性的,
inconclusive;
wèi wán chéng de: 未完成的,
unfinished, incomplete;
wú jié guǒ de: 无结果的, *inconclusive;*
SEE (请查看) **COMPLETO**

INCONCRETO (A); **imprecise** (A);
imprecise, inexact, inaccurate;
bù jīng què de: 不精确的, *inaccurate,*
inexact, imprecise;
bù yán jǐn de: 不严谨的, *imprecise;*
bù zhèng què de: 不正确的,
incorrect, inaccurate;
SEE (请查看) **INEXACTITUD**

INCONDICIONAL; incondicional;
unconditional, complete;
jué duì (sv) (adv): 绝对, *absolute,*
unconditional; definitely;
wú tiáo jiàn (adv): 无条件,
unconditionally, without preconditions;
SEE (请查看) **CATEGORÍA**

INCONEXO (A); **desconexo** (A);
unconnected, disjointed, unrelated;
bù lián guàn de: 不连贯的,
disconnected, disjointed;
sǎn màn (sv): 散漫, *unorganized;*
careless and sloppy;
SEE (请查看) **DISPERSO**

INCONFORMISTA; inconformista;
nonconformist;
pàn nì (v) (n): 叛逆, *to rebel;*
nonconformist

INCONGRUENTE; incongruente;
incongruous, inconsistent;
bù xié tiáo de: 不协调的, *incongruous,*
discordant, contradictory, paradoxical;
SEE (请查看) **IMPROPIO**

INCONSCIENTE; inconsciente;
unconscious, thoughtless ...
INCONSIDERADO (A); **impensado**
(A); *inconsiderate, thoughtless;*
bù tì tā rén zhuó xiǎng de: 不替他人
着想的, *inconsiderate;*
bù zūn jìng de: 不尊敬的,
disrespectful;
qīng shuài de: 轻率的, *inconsiderate,*
neglectful, disrespectful;
shī qù zhī jué de: 失去知觉的, *not*
awake, unconscious;
wèi chá jué de: 未察觉的, *not*
conscious/aware of;
SEE (请查看) **NEGLIGENCIA,**
IMPRUDENCIA

INCONSECUENTE; inconsistente;
inconsistent;
bù yī zhì de: 不一致的, *inconsistent;*
máo dùn (sv) (n): 矛盾, *contradictory,*
inconsistent; contradiction,
inconsistency;
qián hòu máo dùn de: 前后矛盾的,
inconsistent statements

INCONSTANTE; inconfíavel,
unreliable; **fraco,** *weak; unreliable;*
bù kě kào de: 不可靠的, *unreliable*
machine, method;
bù kě xìn lài de: 不可信赖的,
unreliable person, firm;

kào bu zhù (sv): 靠不住, *unreliable, undependable*

INCONTABLE; inumerável; incontável; inúmeros (A) (adj); *countless, innumerable;*
  lěi lěi (sv) (adv): 累累, *countless; again and again;*
  shǔ bu qīng (attr): 数不清, *countless;*
  wú shù (sv): 无数, *countless, numberless*

INCONTENIBLE; inevitável; *inevitable; uncontainable, unstoppable;*
  bù kě bì miǎn de shì wù (sv) (n): 不可避免的事物, *inevitable; inevitability;*
  bù kě bì miǎn de: 不可避免的, *inevitable outcome/ result/ consequence;*
SEE (请查看**) DETERMINADO**

INCONTROLABLE; incontrolável; *uncontrollable;*
  bù shòu guǎn shù de: 不受管束的, *uncontrollable person;*
  kòng zhì bù liǎo (sv) (adv): 控制不了, *uncontrollable temper, laughter, etc.; uncontrollably*

INCONVENIENTE; inapropiado (A); *inappropriate;*
  bù xiāng chèn (sv) (adv) (n): 不相称, *inappropriate; unsuitable; inappropriately; inappropriateness;*
  bù xiāng yí de: 不相宜的, *improper remark/behaviour;*
SEE (请查看**) IMPROPIO**

INCORRECTO (A); **incorreto** (A); *incorrect, wrong;*
  bù duì (sv): 不对, *incorrect, wrong;*
  bù shì dàng de: 不适当的, *incorrect posture/diet;*
SEE (请查看**) FALACIA, EQUIVOCADO**

INCORREGIBLE; incorrigível; *incorrigible;*
  bù kě jiù yào de: 不可救药的, *incorrigible;*

nán yǐ gǎi zhèng de: 难以改正的, *incorrigible*

INCREDULIDAD; incredulidade; *incredulity ... INCRÉDULO* (A); **incrédulo** (A); *skeptical, incredulous;*
  bào huái yí tài du de rén: 抱怀疑态度的人, *skeptic;*
  biǎo shì huái yí (adv) (n): 表示怀疑, *incredulously; incredulity;*
  bù xiāng xìn: 不相信, *incredulity;*
  chí huái yí tài du de: 持怀疑态度的, *skeptical;*
SEE (请查看**) DESCONFIADO**

INCREÍBLE; incrível; *incredible, unconvincing, unbelievable;*
  bù kě sī yì de: 不可思议的, *inconceivable, incredible, unbelievable; enigma;*
  fēi cháng de (sv) (adv): 非常地, *unusual, extraordinary, special; very, extremely, highly;*
  nán yǐ zhì xìn de (adv) (fe): 难以置信地, *surprisingly; difficult/hard to believe*
  qí wén (n): 奇闻, *incredible story*

INCREMENTO; incremento; *increase, increment;*
  zēng zhí liàng: 增值量, *increment, value added, increase;*
SEE (请查看**) AUMENTAR**

INCUESTIONABLE; inquestionável; *irrefutable, unquestionable, indisputable;*
  bù kě fǒu rèn de: 不可否认的, *irrefutable;*
  háo wú yí wèn de: 毫无疑问的, *unquestionable;*
  wú kě biàn bó de: 无可辩驳的, *irrefutable;*
SEE (请查看**) INDISCUTIBLE**

INCULTO (A); **inculto** (A); *uneducated;*
  méi shòu guo jiào yù de: 没受过教育的, *uneducated*

INDECENTE; indecente; *indecent, shameless, obscene;*
  āng zāng de: 肮脏的, *dirty, filthy; indecent;*

xià liú de: 下流的, *indecent behaviour*;
SEE (请查看) BRONCO,
DESATENCIÓN

INDECIBLE; indescritível;
indescribable, unspeakable;
  nán yǐ xíng róng de: 难以形容的,
  indescribable

INDECISO (A); **indeciso** (A); *indecisive,
undecided, irresolute*;
  fēi jué dìng xìng de: 非决定性的,
  indecisive;
  wèi jué dìng de: 未决定的,
  undecided;
  yōu róu guǎ duàn de: 优柔寡断的,
  indecisive, irresolute;
  yóu yù bù jué de: 犹豫不决的,
  indecisive

INDECOROSO (A); **indecoroso** (A);
indecorous, unseemly;
  bù shì yí de: 不适宜的, *unseemly*

INDEFECTIBLE; infalível; *unfailing*;
  wú qióng wú jìn de: 无穷无尽的,
  inexhaustible;
SEE (请查看) CREÍBLE

INDEFENDIBLE; indefensável;
indefensible;
  bù kě yuán liàng de: 不可原谅的,
  inexcusable, indefensible, unpardonable;
  bù néng fáng yù de: 不能防御的,
  indefensible;
  zhàn bu zhù jiǎo (vp): 站不住脚,
  indefensible; not have a leg to stand on

INDEFINIBLE; indefenível;
indefinable, uncertain;
  bù què dìng de: 不确定的, *uncertain
  future/ outcome*

INDEFINIDO (A); **indefinido** (A);
indefinite, vague, undefined;
  bù dìng (sv) (adv): 不定, *uncertain,
  indefinite*;
SEE (请查看) ARCANO, CRÍPTICO,
IMPRECISO

INDELEBLE; indelével; *indelible,
permanent, enduring*;

cháng qī de: 长期的, *permanent
state/job/position*;
cháng rèn (sv): 常人, *permanent,
standing*;
cháng zhù (sv): 常驻, *resident,
permanent*;
qù bu diào: 去不掉, *indelible (won't
come off)*;
xǐ bu diào: 洗不掉, *indelible (won't
wash off)*;
SEE (请查看) DEFINITIVO,
IMMORTAL

INDEMNIDAD; indenização;
compensation; indemnity;
  péi cháng (v) (n): 赔偿, *to compensate,
  to make amends/atone for; reparations*;
  bǎo zhàng (v) (n): 保障, *to ensure, to
  guarantee; to safeguard; indemnity*;
SEE (请查看) COMPENSACIÓN

INDEPENDENCIA; independência;
independence ... **INDEPENDIENTE;
independente;** *independent*;
  dú lì (sv) (n): 独立, *independent;
  independence*;
  zì lì de: 自立的, *independent
  (financially)*;
  zì zhì (v) (n): 自治, *autonomy;
  independence; self-discipline*

INDESCRIPTIBLE; indescritível;
indescribable, inexpressible;
  nán yǐ xíng róng de: 难以形容的,
  indescribable; beyond description

INDESEABLE; indesejável;
undesirable, unwanted; repugnant;
  bù hé yì de: 不合意的, *unsuitable,
  unwanted*;
  bù xiǎng yào de: 不想要的,
  unwanted;
SEE (请查看) ABOMINACIÓN

INDETERMINADO (A);
indeterminado (A); *indeterminate,
indecisive*;
  bù míng què de: 不明确的,
  indeterminate;

yōu róu guǎ duàn (fe): 优柔寡断, *indecisive*;
yóu yù (sv) (v): 犹豫, *indecisive, hesitating; to hesitate/be irresolute*;
SEE (请查看) CUESTIÓN, INDECISO

INDICACIÓN; indicação; *sign, signal, indication* ... **INDICIO; indício;** *sign, clue, trace, indication* ... **INDIRECTA; indireta;** *hint, suggestion; clue* ... **INDIRECTAMENTE; indiretamente;** *indirectly* ... **INDIRECTO** (A); **indireto** (A); *indirect, oblique, veiled*;
  biāo jì (n): 标记, *label, tab, mark, symbol*;
  biāo qiān (n): 标签, *label, tag*;
  biāo shì (v) (n): 表示, *to designate, to highlight; mark, label, sign*;
  fú hào (n): 符号, *symbol, mark, sign*;
  jì hào (n): 记号, *mark, sign*;
  jiàn jiē (sv) (adv): 间接, *indirect result/effect, etc.; indirectly, responsible*;
  pái zi (n): 牌子, *tag, sign; brand, trademark*;
  qù xiàng (n): 去向 , *trace*;
  shǒu shì (n): 手势, *gesture, sign*;
  shǒu yǔ (n): 手语, *sign language*;
  wěi wǎn (sv): 委婉, *indirect (in speaking); tactful*;
  xiàn suǒ (n): 线索, *clue, lead; thread; trail*;
  xìn hào (n): 信号, *signal*;
  xìn hào dēng (n): 信号灯, *signal light*;
  yū huí de: 迂回的, *indirect route/method, etc.*;
  zhǐ zhēn (n): 指针, *indicator; pointer; guiding principle, guide*;
SEE (请查看) AUGURAR, DENOTAR, INSINUACIÓN

INDICADO (A); **indicado** (A); *recommended; advisable, indicated, suitable, specified*;
  hé shì de: 合适的, *suitable*;
  kě qǔ de: 可取的, *advisable, desirable*;
  míng zhì de: 明智的, *advisable, good*;
  shì yí de (adj) (sv): 适宜的, *suitable, appropriate*

ÍNDICE; índice; *index, catalog*;
  biān mù (v) (n): 编目, *to catalogue;*

catalogue;
  mù lù (n): 目录, *catalogue, list*;
  shū mù (n): 书目, *catalogue, book list*;
  suǒ yǐn (n) (v): 索引, *index; to bring together*;
  zhǐ shù: 指数, *index number; indicator (ECON)*

INDIFERENCIA; indiferença; *indifference, apathy, disregard* ... **INDIFERENTE; indiferente;** *indifferent, impartial, unconcerned*;
  bù lǐ cǎi (sv): 不理睬, *inattentive, disrespectful*;
  bù zūn zhòng (sv): 不尊重, *disrespectful*;
  dàn mò de: 淡漠的, *indifferent, unconcerned*;
  méi xìn qù de: 没兴趣的, *uninterested*;
  miè shì de: 蔑视的, *disdainful, scornful, spiteful, contemptful*;
  mò shì: 漠视, *disregard*;
  wú suǒ wèi (attr): 无所谓, *to be indifferent*;
SEE (请查看) DESAMOR, APATÍA

INDÍGENA; indígena; *indigenous, native*;
  běn tǔ de: 本土的, *indigenous*;
  gù tǔ: 故土, *native land, homeland, birthplace*;
  gù yǒu de: 固有的, *indigenous*;
  tǔ shēng tǔ zhǎng: 土生土长, *locally born and bred*;
  tǔ zhù rén: 土著人, *native; aborigine*;
  xiāng tǔ: 乡土, *native land; hometown*;
  zǔ guó: 祖国, *native land, motherland*

INDIGENTE; indigente; *destitute, poor, indigent*;
  kùn kǔ (sv): 困苦, *hard, difficult, in hardship*;
  pín fá (sv) (n): 贫乏, *poor, impoverished; deficient, lacking*;
  pín hán (sv): 贫寒, *poverty-stricken*;
  pín kùn (sv): 贫困, *poor, impoverished*;
  pín mín (n): 贫民, *poor people, paupers, indigents*;
  pín qióng de: 贫穷的, *poor person*;

qióng guāng dàn (fe): 穷光蛋, *pauper*;
qióng kǔ (sv): 穷苦, *impoverished, poverty-stricken*;
qióng kùn (sv): 穷困, *poor, poverty-stricken*;
qióng rén (n): 穷人, *poor people, the poor*;
SEE (请查看) DIFÍCIL

INDIGESTO (A); **indigesto** (A); *indigestible*;
  nán xiāo huà de: 难消化的, *indigestible*;
  xiāo huà bù liáng: 消化不良, *indigestion*

INDIGNACIÓN; indignação; *indignation, anger ...* **INDIGNADO** (A); **indignado** (A); *indignant, angry*;
  fèn hèn (sv): 愤恨, *resentful, embittered*;
  fèn kǎi (sv): 愤慨, *be indignant (at an injustice)*;
  fèn nù (n) (sv): 愤怒, *indignation, wrath, angry; furious, indignant*;
  huǒ qì (n): 火气, *anger, temper*;
  yì fèn: 义愤, *resentful; righteous/moral indignation*;
SEE (请查看) BRONCO, FUROR, DESAGRADO, DETESTAR, DESHONRAR, IRA

INDIGNANTE; ultrajante, *shocking, offensive*; **enfurecedor** (A); *outrageous, infuriating*;
  chū chǒu de: 出丑的, *scandalous*;
  dà dǎn de: 大胆的, *outrageous, daring, flamboyant*;
  jīng rén de: 惊人的, *outrageous, appalling*;
  lìng rén tǎo yàn de: 令人讨厌的, *infuriating*;
  lìng rén zhèn jīng de: 令人震惊的, *shocking, amazing, astonishing*;
  yǐn qǐ yì fèn de shì: 引起义愤的是, *scandal, outrage*;
SEE (请查看) FURIA, ATROCIDAD, ESCANDALOSO, INDIGNACIÓN

INDIGNO (A); **indigno** (A); *unworthy; despicable*;
  bù pèi (sv): 不配, *lack of qualifications for/to; not worthy of; unworthy; unqualified*;
  bù zhí de (sv): 不值得, *not worth it; unworthy of; unworthy; undeserving*;
  kě bǐ (sv): 可鄙, *despicable, mean*;
  wú jià zhí de: 无价值的, *unworthy*;
SEE (请查看) DESDÉN

INDISCRECIÓN; indiscrição; *indiscretion ...* **INDISCRETO** (A); **indiscreto** (A); *indiscreet, tactless*;
  bù dé tǐ (sv): 不得体, *tactless*;
  bù jiǎn (fe): 不检, *be indiscreet/careless*;
  bù qīng shuài de: 不轻率的, *rash, hasty, indiscreet*;
  bù shèn zhòng (sv) (n): 不慎重, *indiscreet, careless; indiscretion*;
  bù shèn zhòng de: 不慎重的, *indiscreet, careless*;
  qīng shuài (sv) (v): 轻率, *rash, hasty, indiscreet; to neglect, to slight, to ignore*

INDISCRIMINADO (A); **indiscriminado** (A); *indiscriminate*;
  bù jiā qū bié de: 不加区别的, *indiscriminate*;
  rèn yì de: 任意的, *indiscriminate*

INDISCUTIBLE; inquestionável; *indisputable, irrefutable*;
  bù tí chū yí wèn de: 不提出疑问的, *unquestioning*;
  wú kě zhēng yì de: 无可争议的, *indisputable*

INDISOLUBLE; insolúvel; *insoluble*;
bù róng jiě de: 不溶解的, *insoluble*

INDISPUESTO (A); **indisposto** (A); *indisposed, unwell; unwilling*;
  bù yuàn yì de: 不愿意的, *unwilling*;
  xiǎo bìng: 小病, *indisposition*;
  yǒu bìng de: 有病的, *unwell, indisposed*

INDIVIDUO; individual (adj);

individuo (n), *a person*;
individual, character;
  dān dú de: 单独地, *individually, alone*;
  dān gè de: 单个的, *particular*;
  dú tè de: 独特的, *unique*;
  gè bié de: 个别地, *individually, separately*;
  gè rén de: 个人的, *individual person*;
  gè rén: 个人, *single person*;
  gè xìng: 个性, *individuality, personality*

INDOLENCIA; indolência; *laziness, indolence ...* **INDOLENTE; indolente;** *indolent, lazy*;
  lǎn duò de: 懒惰的, *indolent*;
  lǎn sǎn de: 懒散的, *negligent, indolent*;
SEE (请查看) **DESOCUPADO**

INDOMABLE; indomável (adj); **indômito** (A); *untamable, rebellious, unruly, indomitable*;
  bù qū bù náo de: 不屈不挠的, *indomitable*;
  bù qū fú de: 不屈服的, *indomitable, unyielding*;
  jiān qiáng de: 坚强的, *unyielding; firm, staunch*;
  nán yǐ kòng zhì de: 难以控制的, *unruly, disorderly, unmanageable*;
  rèn xìng de: 任性的, *unruly child*;
  wán gù de: 顽固的, *obstinate, stubborn; head strong*

INDUDABLE; indubitável; *undoubted, unquestionable*;
  kěn dìng de: 肯定的, *undoubted*;
  wú kě zhì yí de: 无可置疑的, *unquestionable, undoubted*
  wú yōng zhì yí (adv) (fe): 毋庸置疑, *without doubt, doubtless, unquestionable, undoubtedly*;
SEE (请查看) **REALMENTE**

INDULGENCIA; indulgência; *leniency; indulgence; clemency ...* **INDULGENTE; indulgente;** *indulgent*;
  kuān hòu: 宽厚, *leniency*;
  kuān róng de: 宽容的, *tolerant, lenient*;
  nì 'ài (n) (sv): 溺爱, *overindulgence; indulgent, doting*;
  róng rěn de: 容忍的, *tolerant*;
  zòng róng (v) (n): 纵容, *to connive, to wink at; indulgence*;
  zòng róng: (n) (adj): 纵容, *allowance, acceptance; indulgent*

INEFABLE; inenarrável; *inexpressible; ineffable ...* **INEXPRESIVO** (A); **inexpressivo** (A), *expressionless; inexpressive, unutterable*;
  huài tòu le de: 坏透了的, *rotten to the core; unutterable*;
  nán yǐ yán chuán de: 难以言传的, *inexpressible*;
  wú fǎ xíng róng de: 无法形容的, *inexpressible*

INEFICIENCIA; ineficiência; *inefficiency, incompetence ...*
INEFICIENTE; ineficiente; *inefficient*;
  bù chèn zhí de: 不称职的, *inefficient; less than qualified/competent*;
  dī xiào lǜ: 低效率, *inefficiency*;
  méi yǒu xiào lǜ de: 没有效率的, *inefficient*;
  wú xiào (vp): 无效, *ineffective; useless*;
  wú xiào lǜ: 无效率, *inefficient*;
  xiào lǜ dī (sv) (n): 效率低, *inefficient; inefficiency*

INELUDIBLE; inevitável; *inevitable; unavoidable, inescapable*;
  bì rán de (adv): 必然地, *inevitably*;
  bù kě bì miǎn de:不可避免的 , *inevitable outcome, result, consequence*;
SEE (请查看) **DETERMINADO**

INEPTO (A); **inepto** (A); *inept, incompetent*;
  bù qià dàng de: 不恰当的, *inept; unsuitable*;
  bù shèng rèn (sv) (n): 不胜任, *incompetent; incompetence*;
  wú néng de: 无能的, *incompetent, incapable, inept*;
SEE (请查看) **ESTUPIDEZ, INEFICIENCIA**

INEQUÍVOCO (A); **inequívoco** (A);

unmistakable; unequivocal;
bù hán hu de: 不含糊的,
unambiguous, unequivocal;
què qiè wú yí de: 确切无疑的,
*beyond all doubt, quite certain,
unmistakable;*
SEE (请查看) OBVIO

INERCIA; inércia; *inertia, immobility;
apathy ...* **INERTE; inerte;** *inert, lifeless,
motionless;*
guàn xìng (n): 惯性, *inertia;*
wú shēng wù (n): 无生物, *inanimate
object, nonliving matter;*
SEE (请查看) DESAMOR

INESCRUTABLE; inescrutável;
inscrutable, mysterious;
guǐ mì (sv): 诡秘, *surreptitious,
secretive;*
guǐ mì de: 诡秘的, *mysterious,
secretive;*
SEE (请查看) ARCANO, DIFÍCIL,
INDOMABLE, ENIGMÁTICO

INESTABILIDAD; instabilidade;
instability, unpredictability;
bù wěn dìng xìng: 不稳定性,
instability (of a place/ situation/person)

INESTABLE; instável, *unstable;*
inseguro (A), *unsteady person, voice,
step; unstable, unsteady;*
bù kě kào de: 不可靠的, *unsteady,
unreliable;*
bù láo gù de: 不牢固的, *unstable
(thing);*
bù píng wěn de: 不平稳的, *unsteady,
uneven;*
bù wěn de: 不稳的, *unsteady,
unstable;*
bù wěn dìng de: 不稳定的, *unstable
(QUIM) (FIS);*
bù wěn gù de: 不稳固的, *unsteady,
unstable;*
fǎn fù wú cháng de: 反复无常的,
unstable person;
yáo huàng (adj) (v): 摇晃, *unsteady,
shaky; to rock/sway/shake;*
SEE (请查看) AGITADO

INEXACTITUD; imprecisão;
inaccuracy ... **INEXACTO** (A);
impreciso (A), *inaccurate;* **inexato**
(A), *inexact; inaccurate, incorrect, wrong,
inexact;*
bù zhǔn què de: 不准确的,
inaccurate, inexact, imprecise;
SEE (请查看) FALACIA, IMPRECISO,
INCORRECTO

INEXISTENTE; inexistente;
nonexistent ;
bù cún zài de: 不存在的, *nonexistent*

INEXPERIENCIA; inexperiência;
inexperience ... **INEXPERTO** (A);
inexperiente; *inexperienced, unskilled ;*
bù shú liàn de: 不熟练的, *unskilled,
unskillful;*
bù xū yào jì néng: 不需要技能,
unskilled, untrained, inexperienced;
quē fá jì néng: 缺乏技能, *unskilled,
inexperienced;*
quē fá jì qiǎo: 缺乏技巧, *unskilled,
untrained;*
wú jīng yàn de: 无经验的,
inexperienced;
SEE (请查看) IGNORANCIA

INFALIBLE; infalível; *infallible;*
bù huì cuò de: 不会错的, *infallible;*
juè duì kě kào de: 绝对可靠的,
infallible;
shí quán shí měi (fe): 十全十美,
perfect in every way;
wú xiè kě jī de: 无懈可击的, *faultless;*
SEE (请查看) COMPLETO

INFAME; infame; *shameful; odious ...*
INFAMIA; infâmia; *discredit; infamy,
slur, disgrace, shame, ignominy;*
chǐ (n) (sv): 耻, *shame, disgrace,
humiliation; shameful, disgraceful;*
chòu míng zhāo zhù (sv) (n): 臭名
昭著, *of ill repute, infamous, notorious;
notoriety;*
è xíng (n): 恶行, *evil/wicked conduct,
infamous;*
kě wù (sv): 可恶, *detestable,
abominable, obnoxious;*

SEE (请查看) DESCRÉDITO,
IGNOMINIA

INFANCIA; infância; *infancy;*
  chū qī (n): 初期, *initial stage, early days;*
  yīng 'ér de: 婴儿的, *infantile;*
  yīng 'ér qī (n): 婴儿期, *infant;*
  yòu zhì de: 幼稚的, *childish, puerile; naive*

INFATIGABLE; incansável,
indefatigable, tireless; tireless, untiring;
  bù juàn de: 不倦的, *tireless, indefatigable;*
  zī zī bù juàn de: 孜孜不倦的, *untiring;*
SEE (请查看) INDOMABLE

INFECCIÓN; infecção; *infection, disease* ... **INFECTO** (A); **infecto** (A), *contaminated; putrid, foul; infected, tainted;*
  āng zāng de: 肮脏的, *dirty, filthy;*
  è liè de: 恶劣的, *vile, nasty;*
  nán wén de: 难闻的, *stinking, foul smelling;*
SEE (请查看) CONTAGIO,
CONTAMINACIÓN, CORRUPTO

INFERIORIDAD; inferioridade;
inferiority;
  dī děng de: 低等的, *lower in hierarch, humble;*
  liè děng (attr): 劣等, *low-grade, poor; inferior;*
  zì bēi: 自卑, *inferiority*

INFÉRTIL; infértil; *infertile;*
  bù néng shēng yù de: 不能生育的, *infertile (man/ woman/animal);*
  bù yù zhèng: 不育症的, *infertility (man/woman animal);*
  pín jí: 贫瘠, *infertility (soil, land);*
SEE (请查看) ÁRIDO

INFESTADO; infestado (A); *infested;*
  bèi qīn rǎo de: 被侵扰的, *infested (plant/animal/ thing);*
SEE (请查看) INFECTO

INFIDELIDAD; infidelidade; *infidelity;*
  bèi xìn: 背信, *infidelity;*
  bù zhōng (vp) (n): 不忠, *to be disloyal, unfaithful, perfidious; infidelity;*
  bù zhōng chéng (vp): 不忠诚, *disloyal, unfaithful; infidelity, dishonesty*

INFINITO (A); **infinito** (A); *infinite, limitless, boundless, endless;*
  màn cháng de: 漫长的, *extensive, endless;*
  wú qióng de: 无穷的, *infinite, endless;*
  wú xiàn de: 无限的, *infinite, limitless;*
SEE (请查看) ENORME, ILIMITADO

INFLACIÓN; inflação; *inflation;*
  tōng huò péng zhàng: 通货膨胀, *inflation*

INFLAMABLE; inflamável;
inflammable;
  yì jī dòng de: 易激动的, *inflammable;*
  yì rán de: 易燃的, *flammable, inflammable, combustible*

INFLABLE; inflável; *inflatable;*
  kě chōng qì de: 可充气的, *inflatable;*
  kě péng zhàng de: 可膨胀的, *inflatable*

INFLAMACIÓN; inflamação;
inflammation (MED);
  fā yán (n) (v) (MED): 发炎, *inflammation; to become inflamed;*
  hóng zhǒng (sv): 红肿, *inflamed; red and swollen;*
  yán zhèng: 炎症, *inflammation*

INFLAMATORIO (A); **incendiante;**
inflammatory;
  shān dòng xìng de: 煽动性的, *inflammatory*

INFLUENCIA (n); **influência;** *influence, sway, control;*
  jù rén: 巨人, *influential figure;*
  míng jiā: 名家, *influential family;*
  quán guì: 权贵, *influential figure;*
  quán shì (n): 权势, *power and influence;*

shì lì (n): 势力, *force, power, influence*;
yǐng xiǎng lì (n): 影响力, *influence*;
yǒu quán shì de: 有权势的, *influential*;
yǒu yǐng xiǎng lì de: 有影响力的, *influential*;
SEE (请查看) AFECTAR

INFLUENCIABLE; influenciável; *easily influenced, impressionable*;
bù chéng shú de: 不成熟的, *immature*;
SEE (请查看) INOCENTÓN, CREDULIDAD

INFORMACIÓN; informação; *information; news, data*;
xìn xī (n): 信息, *information, news, message*;
xìn xī jì shù: 信息技术, *information, technology*

INFORMATIVO (A); **informativo** (A); *informative*;
yǒu jiàn shi de: 有见识的, *informed*;
zēng zhǎng jiàn wén de: 增长见闻的, *informative*

INFORTUNIO; infortúnio; *misfortune; mishap*;
è yùn (n): 厄运, *misfortune, adversity*;
nì jìng (n): 逆境, *adversity*;
SEE (请查看) DESASTRE

INFRACCIÓN; infração; *infringement, violation, infraction*;
wéi fǎn (n) (v): 违反, *violation of agreement/ law, infringement; to violate, to transgress, to infringe*

INFRACTOR (A); **infrator** (A); *infringer; offender*;
zuì fàn: 罪犯, *criminal, offender*;
SEE (请查看) CRIMINAL

INFRECUENTE; infreqüente; *infrequent, occasional, rare, seldom*;
ǒu 'fā de: 偶发的, *accidental, chance*;
ǒu 'rán (sv) (adv): 偶然, *accidental, chance; casual; accidentally, by chance*;

shǎo yǒu de: 少有的, *seldom, rare, exceptional*;
xī shǎo de: 稀少的, *infrequent; few, rare, scarce*;
SEE (请查看) IMPREMEDITADO

INGENIO; engenhosidade, *ingenuity*
... INGENIOSO; engenhoso (A): *ingenious; clever, resourceful*;
qiǎo miào de: 巧妙的, *clever, smart, ingenious*;
qiǎo miào: 巧妙, *ingenuity*;
zú zhì duō móu (id): 足智多谋, *to be resourceful, ingenuity*

INGENUO (A); **ingênuo** (A); *ingenuous; candid*;
dān chún (sv) (adv): 单纯, *simple, plain, artless, naive; purely, merely*;
tǎn shuài (sv): 坦率, *candid, frank*;
tiān zhēn (sv): 天真, *innocent, artless, naive*

INGRATITUD; ingratidão; *ingratitude*
... INGRATO (A); **ingrato;** *ungrateful, thankless*;
bù gǎn jī de: 不感激的, *ungrateful*;
wàng 'ēn fù yì: 忘恩负义, *ingratitude, thankless, ungrateful*

INGREDIENTE; ingrediente; *ingredient, constituent, component*;
pèi liào (n): 配料, *ingredients in a recipe*;
yào sù (n): 要素, *essential factor, key element*;
yīn sù (n): 因素, *factor, element*;
SEE (请查看) COMPONENTE

INHABITADO (A); **desabitado** (A); *uninhabited*;
bù shì yú jū zhù de: 不适于居住的, *uninhabitable*;
SEE (请查看) DESHABITADO

INHABITUAL; insólito (A) (adj), *unusual*; **raro** (A); *unusual, rare, uncommon; exceptional*;
bù dà (adv): 不大, *not very, not too, not often*;

fǎn cháng: 反常, *unusual, abnormal*;
hǎn jiàn (sv): 罕见, *rare, seldom seen*;
qí tè (sv): 奇特, *strange, odd, peculiar, unusual*;
tè bié (sv) (adv): 特别, *peculiar, unusual, special, particular; especially, particularly*;
xī yǒu (sv): 稀有, *rare, unusual*;
SEE (请查看) **UNUSUAL**

INHERENTE; inherente; *inherent, inborn, innate, intrinsic, implicit*;
àn shì: 暗室, *implicit*;
běn zhì (n): 本质, *essence, nature*;
gù yǒu (attr): 固有, *intrinsic, inherent, innate; proper; characteristic*;
hán xù (v) (sv): 含蓄, *to contain/embody; implicit, veiled; reserved*;
tiān fù (v) (n): 天赋, *to be naturally endowed; inborn/natural gifts, talent*;
tiān shēng (sv): 天生, *innate, inborn*;
xiān tiān (sv): 先天, *congenital, innate*;
SEE (请查看) **INTERIOR**

INHIBICIÓN; inibição; *inhibition, repression*;
yì zhì (v) (n): 抑制, *to restrain/control; inhibition (MED)*

INHÓSPITO (A); **inospitaleiro** (A); *inhospitable, unsociable, bleak*;
bù hào kè de: 不好客的, *inhospitable*;
SEE (请查看) **DESMOTIVADO**

INHUMANO (A); **inumano** (A); **desumano** (A); *cruel; inhuman*;
fēi rén lèi de: 非人类的, *inhuman*;
méi yǒu rén xìng de: 没有人性的, *inhuman*;
yě mán de: 野蛮的, *uncivilized, savage; barbarous, cruel*;
SEE (请查看) **CRUEL, CRUELDAD**

INICIACIÓN; início, *start*; **iniciação,** *introduction; initiation, beginning, commencement*;
dǎo yán (n): 导言, *introduction (to a writing)*;
gài lùn (n): 概论, *introduction; general discussion; outline*;

jì yuán (n): 纪元, *beginning of an era*;
kāi duān (n): 开端, *start, beginning*;
kāi shǒu (n): 开首, *start, beginning; (attr) initial*;
kāi tóu (n): 开头, *beginning, start*;
lì chūn (n): 立春, *beginning of spring*;
lì dōng (n): 立冬, *beginning of winter*;
lì qiū (n): 立秋, *beginning of autumn*;
lì xià (n): 立夏, *beginning of summer*;
qián yán (n): 前言, *forward, preface, introduction*;
shǒu wěi (n): 首尾, *beginning and end; from start to finish*;
xù mù (n): 序幕, *prelude*;
xù yán (n): 序言, *forward, preface*;
yuè chū (n): 月初, *beginning of the month*;
SEE (请查看) **INTRODUCCIÓN**

INIMAGINABLE; inimaginável; *unimaginable*;
nán yǐ xiǎng xiàng de: 难以想象的, *unimaginable*

ININTELIGIBLE; incompreensível; *unintelligible*;
bù qīng chǔ de: 不清楚的, *unintelligible, unclear*;
nán lǐ jiě de: 难理解的, *unintelligible*

ININTERRUMPIDO (A); **ininterrupto** (A); *uninterrupted, continuous*;
yán xù (sv): 延续, *constant, persistent, steady*;
SEE (请查看) **INCESANTE, CONTINUADO**

INJUSTO (A); **injusto** (A), *unfair*; **injusticia,** *injustice; unfair, unjust*;
bù gōng píng (sv): 不公平, *unfair, unjust*;
bù hé lǐ (sv): 不合理, *unjustifiable, inequitable*;
bù zhèng dàng (vp): 不正当, *unfair/improper behavior; unjustified*;
wěi qū (v) (sv): 委屈, *to feel wronged/unjustly treated*;
SEE (请查看 **DESIGUAL**

INMATERIAL; irrevalante; *immaterial*;
bù zhòng yào de: 不重要的, *immaterial*

INMEDIATAMENTE; imediatamente;
immediately, at once ... **INMEDIATO**
(A); **imediato** (A); *immediate, instant,*
prompt, spontaneous, instantaneous;
  dāng jí (adv): 当即, *immediately, right*
  away;
  dùn shí (adv): 顿时, *immediately;*
  jí kè (adv): 即刻, *immediately,*
  instantaneously;
  jí shí (adv): 即时, *immediately;*
  lì jí (adv): 立即, *immediately;*
  lì kè (adv): 立刻, *immediately,*
  promptly;
  zhí jiē (sv): 直接, *direct, straight,*
  immediate;
SEE (请查看**) BRUSCO**

INMENSIDAD; imensidão; *immensity,*
vastness ... **INMENSO** (A); **imenso**
(A); *immense, vast, enormous* ...
INMENSAMENTE; imensamente;
immensely, vastly;
  cāng máng (sv): 苍茫, *vast, boundless;*
  jí dà (adv): 极大, *enormously;*
  jí dà de: 极大的, *immense, enormous,*
  vast;
  wú biān jì de: 无边际的, *vast,*
  boundless;
SEE (请查看**) EXTENSO,**
DESMEDIDO, DILATADO, ABISMAL,
GIGANTESCO, GRANDIOSO

INMIGRACIÓN; imigração;
immigration... **INMIGRANTE;**
imigrante; *immigrant;*
  qiān jū: 迁居, *immigration;*
SEE (请查看**) EMIGRANTE**

INMINENCIA; iminência; *imminence*
... **INMINENTE; iminente;** *imminent,*
impending, looming, threatening;
  bī jìn de: 逼近的, *impending/imminent*
  disaster/ misfortune, etc.;
  jí jiāng fā shēng de: 即将发生的,
  threatening, impending
  jì jiāng lái lín de: 即将来临的,
  impending war/ marriage, etc.;
  jí pò (sv): 急迫, *urgent pressing,*
  imperative;
SEE (请查看**) CRUCIAL**

INMODERADO (A); **imoderado** (A);
immoderate, extreme, exorbitant;
  wú jié zhì de: 无节制的, *immoderate;*
  guò dù (adv) (v): 过度, *excessive,*
  undue, hyper; to overdo

INMODESTIA; imodéstia;
immodesty, indecency ... **INMORAL;**
imoral; *immoral, depraved, dissolute*
... **INMORALIDAD; imoralidade;**
immorality;
  bù dào dé (sv) (n): 不道德, *wicked,*
  immoral; inmorality;
  xià liú de: 下流的, *mean, obscene,*
  dirty;
  xié qì (n): 邪气, *depravity;*
  yín dàng de: 淫荡的, *immoral,*
  lascivious, lewd;
SEE (请查看**) DECADENTE,**
DEPRAVADO, CORRUPCIÓN,
DISOLUTO, SINIESTRO

INMORTAL; imortal; *immortal, eternal,*
everlasting;
  shén xiān (n): 神仙, *immortal being;*
  immortal;
  yǒng héng (sv): 永恒, *eternal,*
  perpetual, everlasting;
  yǒng jiǔ (sv): 永久, *permanent, eternal,*
  forever;
  yǒng shì (adv): 永世, *forever;*
  yǒng yuǎn (adv): 永远, *forever,*
  eternally

INMUNE; imune (MED); **isento**
(A); *immune (MED), exempt* (n) ...
INMUNIDAD; imunidade; *immunity;*
  huò miǎn de: 豁免的, *immune,*
  exempt;
  miǎn chú de: 免除的, *immune;*
  miǎn yì lì: 免疫力, *immunity;*
  yǒu miǎn yì lì de: 有免疫力的,
  immune (MED)

INMUTABLE; imutável; *immutable,*
unchanging;
  bù biàn: (sv): 不变, *unchanging,*
  unchanged

INNECESARIO (A); **desnecessário** (A); *unnecessary*;
  bù bì yào de: 不必要的, *unnecessary*

INNOBLE; ignóbil; *ignoble, dishonorable; mean, base*;
  kě wù (sv): 可恶, *detestable, abominable, obnoxious*;
SEE (请查看) DESCRÉDITO, DESDÉN, IGNOMINIA

INNOVACIÓN; inovação; *innovation*;
  chuàng xīn (v) (n): 创新, *to innovate, to create; creation, innovation*;
  gé xīn (v) (n): 革新, *to innovate, to reform; innovation, renovation*

INNOVADOR (A); **inovador** (A) (n); *innovative (adj), innovator (n)*;
  fù yǒu chuàng xīn jīng shén de: 富有创新精神的, *innovative person, innovator*;
  xīn yǐng de: 新颖的, *innovative product/design, etc.*

INOCENCIA; inocência; *innocence, ingenuous, virtuous* ... **INOCENTE; inocente;** *innocent, trusting, naive*;
  dān chún (sv) (adv): 单纯, *simple, plain, artless, naive; purely, merely*;
  qīng bái (sv) (DER): 清白, *not guilty, innocent*;
  tiān zhēn (sv) (n): 天真, *innocent, artless, naive; human nature*;
  wú zuì (vp): 无罪, *innocent; not guilty, guiltless*;
  xián huì (sv): 贤惠, *virtuous woman*;
  xián rén (n): 贤人, *virtuous person*;
  xìn rén (n): 信任, *honest/sincere/ trustworthy person*;
SEE (请查看) CASTIDAD

INOCENTÓN (A); **ingênuo** (A); *gullible; simpleton*;
  bèn dàn (n): 笨蛋, *simpleton, fool, idiot*;
SEE (请查看) INSENSATEZ, INFLUENCIABLE, BESTIA, CREDULIDAD

INOCUO (A); **inócuo** (A); *innocuous, harmless, inoffensive* ... **INOFENSIVO** (A); **inofensivo** (A); *inoffensive, harmless*;
  wú hài de: 无害的, *harmless, safe*;
  wú è yì de: 无恶意的, *inoffensive*;
  bù shāng rén de: 不伤人的, *inoffensive*;
  wú guān tòng yǎng de: 无关痛痒的, *harmless; innocuous*

INODORO (A); **inodoro** (A); *odorless*;
  méi qì wèi de: 没气味的, *odorless*

INOPERANTE; inoperante; *ineffective, inoperative, useless*;
  bù líng (sv): 不灵, *not working; not effective; inoperable, ineffective*;
  méi bāng zhù de: 没帮助的, *useless*;
  méi yòng de: 没用的, *useless*;
  wú yòng (attr): 无用, *useless; unusable*;
SEE (请查看) INÚTIL, INEFICAZ

INOPORTUNO (A); **inoportuno** (A); *inopportune, inconvenient time*;
  bù biàn (sv) (v): 不便, *inconvenient; to be inappropriate*;
  bù fāng biàn de: 不方便的, *inconvenient*;
  bù hé shì de: 不合适的, *inopportune*;
  bù hé shí yí de: 不合时宜的, *inopportune, inconvenient time, moment, etc.*;
SEE (请查看) CONFLICTIVO

INORGÁNICO (A); **inorgánico** (A); *inorganic*;
  wú jī (attr): 无机, *inorganic*

INQUIETO (A) (adj); **inquieto** (A); *worried, anxious* ... **INQUIETUD; inquietude;** *restlessness; worry, anxiety, concern; interest*;
  bù 'ān (sv): 不安, *worried, uneasy, anxious*;
  fán nǎo (sv) (n): 烦恼, *vexed, worried; worry, vexation*;
  jí yú (sv): 急于, *anxious, eager*;
  yōu chóu (sv): 忧愁, *worried, sad, depressed*;

yōu fèn (sv): 忧愤, *worried and indignant*;
yōu mèn (sv): 忧闷, *depressed*;
yōu shāng (sv): 忧伤, *worried, depressed*;
yōu xīn (v) (n): 忧心, *to worry; anxiety*;
yōu yù (sv): 忧郁, *depressed, sullen*;
zháo jí (sv): 着急, *worried, anxious*;
SEE (请查看) BILIOSO, DESCONCERTANTE, CONSTERNACIÓN, APRENSIÓN

INSACIABLE; insaciável; *insatiable, unsatisfied; extremely greedy*;
tān dé wú yàn (fe): 贪得无厌, *be insatiably greedy; extremely greedy*;
wú fǎ mǎn zú de: 无法满足的, *unsatisfied, insatiable, uncontended*

INSATISFACCIÓN; insatisfação; *dissatisfaction ...* **INSATISFACTORIO** (A); **insatisfatório** (A); *unsatisfactory ...* **INSATISFECHO** (A); **insatisfeito** (A); *dissatisfied; unacceptable*;
bù kě jiē shòu de: 不可接受的, *unacceptable*;
bù mǎn yì: 不满意, *dissatisfied*;
bù néng lìng rén mǎn yì de: 不能令人满意的, *unsatisfactory*;
shǐ bù gāo xìng: 使不高兴, *dissatisfaction*;
shǐ bù mǎn: 使不满, *dissatisfied*;
SEE (请查看) DESAGRADO

INSECTICIDA; inseticida; *insecticide ...* **INSECTO; inseto;** *insect*;
kūn chóng: 昆虫, *insect*;
shā chóng jì: 杀虫剂, *insect repellent*

INSEGURO (A); **inseguro** (A); *unsafe, insecure*;
bù ān quán de: 不安全的, *unsafe, dangerous*;
wēi xiǎn de: 危险的, *dangerous*

INSENSATEZ; insensatez; *foolishness, stupidity ...* **INSENSATO** (A); **insensato** (A), *foolish;* **insensível,** *insensitive, unfeeling; thoughtless*;
bù mǐn gǎn de: 不敏感的, *insensitive*;

chǔn shì (n): 蠢事, *folly, stupidity, lunacy*;
má mù bù rén (fe): 麻木不仁, *numbed, paralyzed; apathetic; insensitive*;
SEE (请查看) INGENUO, INSENSATO, APATÍA, IDIOTA, ESTUPIDEZ

INSIDIOSO (A); **insidioso** (A); *insidious, deceptive, treacherous*;
àn zhōng jiā hài de: 暗中加害的, *insidious*;
bèi pàn de: 背叛的, *treacherous*;
jiān zhà (sv): 奸诈, *crafty, treacherous*;
kào bu zhù de: 靠不住的, *deceptive*;
piàn rén (sv) (v): 骗人, *deceptive; to deceive/ defraud others*;
SEE (请查看) CONSPIRACIÓN

INSIGNIFICANCIA; insignificância; *insignificance ...* **INSIGNIFICANTE; insignificante;** *insignificant, unimportant, trifling*;
bù zhòng yào de: 不重要的, *unimportant, trifling*;
wú guān jǐn yào de: 无关紧要的, *insignificant*;
wú yì yì de: 无意义的, *insignificant*;
wú zú qīng zhòng: 无足轻重, *insignificant*

INSINCERO (A); **insincero** (A); *insincere, dishonest, deceitful*;
bù chéng kěn de: 不诚恳的, *insincere person*;
bù lǎo shi de: 不老实的, *dishonest*;
bù zhèn dāng de: 不正当的, *improper, illegitimate, dishonest*;
qí piàn xíng wéi de: 欺骗行为的, *deceitful*;
xū jiǎ de: 虚假的, *insincere*;
xū wěi de: 虚伪的, *insincere, false*;
SEE (请查看) DESHONESTO

INSINUACIÓN; insinuação; *insinuation, suggestion, hint, intimation ...* **INSINUANTE; insinuante;** *suggestive, insinuating*;
àn shì (v) (n): 暗示, *to hint, to suggest*;

suggestion, hint
tí xǐng: 提醒, *reminder*;
tiǎo dòu de: 挑逗的, *suggestive*;
SEE (请查看) AVANZAR,
IMPLICACIÓN, SUGESTIÓN

INSÍPIDO (A); **insípido** (A); *insipid,
tasteless; dull person*;
  dàn 'ér wú wèi (fe): 淡而无味,
  tasteless, insipid;
  kū zào de: 枯燥的, *dull and dry;
  uninteresting*;
  wú wèi de: 无味的, *tasteless; dull,
  insipid*

INSISTENCIA; insistência; *insistence,
compelling attention, demanding* ...
INSISTENTE; insistente; *insistent,
emphatic, firm, assertive*;
  chí xù de: 持续的, *demanding,
  persisting*;
  duàn rán de: 断然的, *emphatic/
  absolute/categoric statement/denial,
  etc.*;
  jiān chí de: 坚持的, *insistent,
  determined*;
  jiān jué yāo qiú: 坚决要求, *insistence*;
  jiān jué zhǔ zhāng (sv): 坚决主张,
  insistent, emphatic;
  qiáng diào (sv): 强调, *emphatic*;
  qiáng yìng (sv): 强硬, *tough,
  intransigent; emphatic*;
  yāo qiú gāo de: 要求高的,
  demanding;
SEE (请查看) ÉNFASIS,
CONSTANTE, CONTUMACIA,
COMPULSIVO

INSOCIABLE; insociável; *antisocial;
unsociable, introverted; shy*;
  yǔ shì wú zhēng (fe): 与世无争, *to be
  aloof/ antisocial*;
SEE (请查看) ANTISOCIAL

INSOLENCIA; insolência; *insolence,
disrespect, impertinence* ... **INSOLENTE;
insolente;** *insolent, haughty, rude*;
  bù zūn jìng: 不尊敬, *disrespect*;
  màn hèng wú lǐ de: 蛮横无礼的,
  overbearing, insolent, rude;

SEE (请查看) IMPRUDENCIA,
ARROGANCIA, BRONCO,
EGOCÉNTRICO

INSOLVENCIA; insolvência;
insolvency, bankruptcy ...
INSOLVENTE; insolvente; *insolvent,
bankrupt*;
  pò chǎn de: 破产的, *bankrupt*;
SEE (请查看) ARRUINAR

INSOMNE; insone; *sleepless; insomniac
...* **INSOMNIO; insônia;** *insomnia*;
  shī mián (sv): 失眠, *sleepless; insomnia*

**INSOPORTABLE; insuportável;
intolerável;** *unbearable, intolerable*;
  nán yǐ rěn shòu de: 难以忍受的,
  unbearable;
  wú fǎ rěn shòu de: 无法忍受的,
  intolerable

INSPECCIÓN; inspeção; *inspection,
examination*;
  jiǎn chá: 检查, *examination, inspection*

INSPIRACIÓN; inspiração; *inspiration,
revelation, vision*;
  hǎo zhǔ yi (n) (intj): 好主意,
  inspiration; great idea;
  líng gǎn (n): 灵感, *inspiration*

INSTALACIÓN; instalação;
installation;
  zhuāng zhì: (v) (n): 装置, *to install/fit;
  installation, unit, device*;
SEE (请查看) ARTEFACTO,
INSTALAR

INSTANTÁNEO (A); **instantâneo** (A),
*instant; instantaneous, immediate, direct,
instantly, unhesitatingly, spontaneous* ...
INSTANTE; instante; *moment, instant*;
  chà nà (n): 刹那, *instant, split-second*;
  jí kè de (adv): 即刻地, *at once,
  immediately*;
  lì jí de (adv): 立即地, *immediately, at
  once, promptly*;
  shùn jiān de (adv): 瞬间地, *in a
  twinkling*;
  shùn xī (adv) (n) (attr): 瞬息, *in a flash*;

instant; ephemeral;
sù róng (attr): 速溶, quick-dissolving, instantly-ready; instant;
SEE (请查看) INMEDIATAMENTE, EMERGENCIA

INSTIGACIÓN; instigação; instigation, encouragement, persuasion;
chōng dòng (n) (v): 冲动, impulse, encouragement; to get excited;
shān dòng zhě: 煽动者, instigator;
SEE (请查看) AGITAR

INSTINTIVO (A); **instintivo** (A); instinctive, tendency ... **INSTINTO; instinto;** instinct, intuition;
běn néng (sv) (n): 本能, instinctive; instinct;
zhí jué (n) (sv): 直觉, intuition; intuitive

INSTITUCIÓN; instintuição; institution;
fēng sú (n): 风俗, custom, institution, tradition;
jī gòu xìng de: 机构性的, institutional;
jī zhì: 机制, mechanism; system, institution;
xié huì (n): 协会, professional institute/organization;
xué yuàn: 学院, college, academy; educational institution;
yán jiū suǒ (n): 研究所, research institute;
SEE (请查看) FUNDAR

INSTRUCCIÓN; instrução; education, teaching, instruction ... **INSTRUCTIVO** (A); **instrutivo** (A); instructive, educational ... **INSTRUIDO** (A); **instruído** (A); educated;
jiào xué (n) (v): 教学, teaching, education; to teach;
jiào yuán (n): 教员, instructor;
wén huà jiè (n): 文化界, cultured people; educated circles;
xué wen (n): 学问, learning, knowledge;
yǒu jiào yù yì yì de: 有教育意义的, instructive;
SEE (请查看) CIVILIZACIÓN,

FORMATIVO, DIRECTOR, CULTURA

INSTRUMENTO; instrumento; instrument (GEN); musical instrument;
qì cái (n): 器材, equipment, materials;
yí qì (n): 仪器, instrument, apparatus;
SEE (请查看) ARTEFACTO

INSUBORDINACIÓN; insubordinação; insubordination ... **INSUBORDINADO** (A); **insubordinado** (A); insubordinate, unruly;
rèn xìng de: 任性的, willful, headstrong;
wéi kàng de: 违抗的, disobedient, defiant;
SEE (请查看) DESOBEDIENCIA

INSUFICIENCIA; insuficiência; lack, shortage, insufficiency ... **INSUFICIENTE; insuficiente;** insufficient, inadequate;
bù gòu (sv): 不够, insufficient; not enough;
bù zú (sv) (aux): 不足, not be enough; can not, should not;
SEE (请查看) FALTA, DÉFICIT

INSULINA; insulina; insulin;
yí dǎo sù: 胰岛素, insulin

INSULTANTE; insultuoso (A); insulting, offensive ... **INSULTO; insulto;** insult, abuse;
mà rén huà (n): 骂人话, abusive language;
mào fàn: 冒犯, affront;
rǔ mà de: 辱骂的, abusive, insulting, humiliating;
SEE (请查看) ABUSAR, DENIGRANTE, CRIMEN

INSURGENTE; insurgente; insurgent, rebel;
fǎn pàn zhě (v) (n): 反叛者, to rebel against society/parents; rebel;
qǐ yì zhě: 起义者, insurgent;
SEE (请查看) RENEGADO

INSUSTITUIBLE; insubstituível; *irreplaceable, invaluable, priceless*;
  bù néng tì dài de: 不能替代的, *irreplaceable*;
SEE (请查看) DIFERENCIA

INTACTO (A); **intacto** (A); *untouched, intact*;
  wán hǎo (vp): 完好, *intact, whole; in good condition, perfect*;
  wán hǎo wú sǔn (fe): 完好无损, *excellent and undamaged, intact*;
  wán zhěng de: 完整的, *complete, integrated, intact*;
  xián zhì de: 闲置的, *unused, unoccupied*;
  xīn de: 新的, *new, fresh; unused*

INTEGRIDAD; integridade; *integrity, wholeness* ... **ÍNTEGRO** (A); **íntegro** (A); *whole, entire; upright, honest*;
  gāng zhèng (sv): 刚正, *upright, principled*;
  lǎo shi (sv): 老实, *honest, frank; naive, simple-minded*;
  lián chǐ: 廉耻, *integrity; sense of honor/shame*;
  zhěng gè (attr): 整个, *entire, whole*;
SEE (请查看) INTACTO, DECENCIA, HONESTIDAD

INTELECTO; intelecto; *intellect, insight, intelligence* ... **INTELECTUAL; intelectual;** *intellectual, insightful, analytical* ... **INTELIGENCIA; inteligência;** *intelligence* ...
INTELIGENTE; inteligente; *intelligent, logical, bright, brilliant, smart, astute, quick, wise*;
  běn shi: 本事, *skill, ability*;
  cōng huì (sv): 聪慧, *smart, bright*;
  cōng ming (sv): 聪明, *clever, bright*;
  gāo míng (sv) (n): 高明, *brilliant; expert*;
  jī ling (sv): 机灵, *clever, smart, sharp*;
  lǐ zhì (n) (sv): 理智, *intellect, reason; rational*;
  líng gǎn: 灵感, *insight, inspiration*;
  nǎo lì: 脑力, *brains, intellect, an intellectual*;

qiǎo miào (sv): 巧妙, *clever, ingenious, smart*;
  zhì huì: 智慧, *wisdom, intelligence*;
  zhì lì: 智力, *intelligence, intellect*;
  zhì néng: 智能, *intelligence and ability*;
SEE (请查看) APTITUD, PERSPICAZ, COMPETENTE, EGREGIO

INTENCIÓN; intenção; *intention, motive, design, goal, aim* ...
INTENCIONAL (adj); **intencional;** *intentional* ... **INTENCIONADO** (A); **intencionado** (A), *intentional; deliberate, premeditated* ... **INTENTO; intento;** *intent, aim; attempt*;
  běn yì: 本意, *intention*;
  cóng róng (sv): 从容, *deliberate, unhurried*;
  gù yì de (adv): 故意地, *deliberately, willfully*;
  mù biāo: 目标, *target, goal, aim, objective*;
  mù dì: 目的, *purpose, aim, goal, objective*;
  niàn tou: 念头, *thought, intention, ideal, goal*;
  qǐ tú (n) (v): 企图, *plan, intention; to try/attempt*;
  shěn shèng de (adj): 审慎的, *careful, deliberate, cautious, circumspect*;
  shěn shèng (sv): 审慎, *deliberately, cautiously*;
  xīn cháng: 心肠, *heart, intention, state of mind*;
  xīn huái (n) (v): 心怀, *intention, purpose; to harbor*;
  xīn si: 心思, *thought, idea*;
  xīn yì: 心意, *purpose, intention, inclination*;
  xù yì de (adv): 蓄意地, *premeditatedly, deliberately*;
  yì tú: 意图, *intention*;
  yòng yi: 用意, *intention, purpose*;
  yǒu yì (v) (adv) (sv): 有意, *to intend to do sthg; on purpose, intentionally; deliberate*;
  zhǐ yì: 旨意, *design, purpose, aim, intention*;
  zōng zhǐ: 宗旨, *aim, purpose*;
SEE (请查看) PRUDENCIA, ATENCIÓN, DELIBERADO, ÍMPETU,

CONSTANTE, COMPUTAR, IDEAL, PREMEDITADO, INCENTIVO

INTENSIDAD; intensidade; *intensity, force, strength* ... **INTENSIVO** (A); **intensivo** (A); *intensive, thorough, concentrated, rigorous, dynamic* ... **INTENSO** (A); **intenso** (A); *intense, strong, vehement*;
 jí dù (adv) (n): 极度, *extremely, exceedingly, intensely; limit*;
 jiā qiáng (v) (sv): 加强, *to strengthen/ reinforce; intense*;
 liè dù: 烈度, *intensity*;
 qiáng dù: 强度, *intensity, strength*;
 qiáng liè (sv): 强烈, *strong, intense, violent*;
 shēng jí (v) (n): 升级, *to intensify; intensification*;
SEE (请查看**) AGRAVANTE, DETALLADO, DRÁSTICO, GRAVE**

INTERDICTO; interdição; *ban; prohibition*;
 jìn lìng: 禁令, *prohibition, ban*

INTERÉS; interesse; *interest (GEN); interest, concern; attraction, appeal* ... **INTERESADO** (A) (adj); **interessado** (A); *interested* ... **INTERESANTE; interessante;** *interesting; attractive*;
 dòng rén (sv): 动人, *inviting*;
 gǔ quán: 股权, *(business) interests*;
 guān xīn (sv): 关心, *interested (in sthg/ sb)*;
 guān zhù: 关注, *interest (in sthg/sb)*;
 hǎo gǎn: 好感, *attraction*;
 qù (n) (sv): 趣, *interest, inclination; interesting, entertaining*;
 qù wèi: 趣味, *interest, taste, delight*;
 xī yǐn rén (sv): 吸引人, *inviting*;
 xìng qù: 兴趣, *interest in sthg/sb*;
 xìng tóu: 兴头, *enthusiasm, interest*;
 xìng zhì: 兴致, *interest, in the mood*;
 yǒu guān (sv): 有关, *interested*;
 yǒu qù (sv) (v): 有趣, *interested, fascinated; to be interested in/fascinated with*;
SEE (请查看**) HOBBY**

INTERLUDIO; interlúdio; *interlude, interval, pause*;
 guò chǎng: 过场, *interlude*;
 jiàn gé (n) (v): 间隔, *interval, intermission; to be separated*;
 jiàn xiē: 间歇, *intermission, pause*;
SEE (请查看**) DESHABITADO, INCIDENTE**

INTERMITENTE; intermitente; *intermittent, sporadic, random*;
 duàn duàn xù xù de: 断断续续的, *intermittent*;
 líng xīng de: 零星的, *sporadic*;
 rèn yì (adv): 任意, *arbitrarily, willfully*;
 suí jī (adv) (attr): 随机, *randomly, pragmatically; random*

INTERNACIONAL; internacional; *international*;
 guó jì (sv) (n): 国际, *international*

INTERNO (A); **interno** (A); *internal, domestic*;
 guó nèi de: 国内的, *domestic, interior, internal*;
 nèi bù (n): 内部, *inside, internal, interior, within*;
 nèi lì (n): 内力, *internal force*;
 nèi lù (n): 内陆, *inland, interior of a country*;
 nèi wù (n): 内务, *internal affairs; domestic/family affairs*;
SEE (请查看**) INTERIOR**

INTERROGATORIO; interrogação; *interrogation, questioning*;
 pán wèn (v) (n): 盘问, *to interrogate; questioning, interrogation*;
 shěn wèn (v) (n): 审问, *to interrogate/ question; interrogation, questioning*;
 shěn xùn (n) (v): 审讯, *interrogation, trial; to try/interrogate*

INTERRUPCIÓN; interrupção; *interruption, disruption, suspension*;
 dǎ rǎo: 打扰, *interruption*

INTERSECCIÓN; interseção;

intersection;
jiāo chā kǒu: 交叉口, *intersection (of roads)*;
jiāo diǎn: 交点, *intersection*;
lù kǒu: 路口, *intersection, crossing*;
shí zì lù kǒu: 十字路口, *intersection, crossroads*

INTERVENCIÓN; intervenção;
intervention, hindrance, interruption;
gān shè: 干涉, *military intervention*;
gān yù: 干预, *intervention, interference (by a person)*

INTESTINO; intestino; *intestine*;
cháng dào: 肠道, *intestines*;
cháng wèi: 肠胃, *stomach and intestines*;
cháng zi: 肠子, *intestines*

INTIMIDACIÓN; intimidação;
intimidation, scare, terrify, unnerve;
bèi xié pò de: 被胁迫的, *intimidated*;
kě pà de: 可怕的, *intimidating person*;
kǒng bù de: 恐怖的, *intimidating atmosphere/ place/experience*;
kǒng hè (v) (n): 恐吓, *to threaten/ intimidate; threat*

ÍNTIMO (A); **íntimo** (A); *private, intimate; personal*;
mì qiè (sv) (adv) (v): 密切, *close, intimate; carefully; to establish close relations*;
mò nì (sv): 莫逆, *very friendly, intimate*;
qīn mì (sv): 亲密, *intimate, close*;
qīn rè (sv): 亲热, *affectionate, intimate*;
tiē xīn (sv): 贴心, *intimate, confidential*;
zhī xīn (sv): 知心, *intimate*;
zhī yīn: 知音, *intimate friend*

INTOLERANCIA; intolerância;
intolerance, impatience, bias, bigotry
... INTOLERANTE; intolerante;
intolerant, inflexible, biased;
bù kuān róng (n) (sv): 不宽容, *intolerant; intolerance*;
bù róng rěn de: 不容忍的, *intolerant attitude, etc.*;
wú fǎ rěn shòu de: 无法忍受的,

intolerable

INTRANSIGENTE; intransigente;
intransigent, stubborn, obstinate;
bù ràng bù de: 不让步的, *intransigent, unyielding*;
bù tuǒ xié de: 不妥协的, *intransigent*

INTRASCENDENCIA; insignificância; *insignificance, pointlessness* **... INTRASCENDENTE; insignificante;** *insignificant, paltry, trivial*;
bù yào jǐn (sv): 不要紧, *unimportant, not serious*;
bù zhòng yào (sv): 不重要, *unimportant, insignificant*;
suǒ shì (n): 琐事, *trifle, trivial matter*;
suǒ suì (sv) (n): 琐碎, *trifling, trivial; slight indisposition*;
wēi bù zú dào de: 微不足道的, *unimportant, not worth mentioning*;
SEE (请查看) **IMPORTANTE**

INTRÉPIDO (A); **intrépido** (A); *intrepid, unafraid; valiant; daring*;
wú wèi de: 无畏的, *fearless, dauntless, intrepid*;
SEE (请查看) **BANDIDO, BRAVO**

INTRIGA; intriga; *curiosity, intrigue, plot, scheme*;
fāng 'àn: 方案, *scheme, plan; program, project*;
SEE (请查看) **CONSPIRACIÓN, INTRIGAR**

INTRÍNSECO (A); **intrínsico** (A);
intrinsic, inherent, implicit, basic;
gù yǒu de: 固有的, *intrinsic, inherent, innate*;
nèi zài de: 内在的, *inherent, intrinsic; internal*

INTRODUCCIÓN; introdução;
introduction **... INTRODUCTORIO** (A);
introdutorio (A); *introductory*;
chū bù de: 初步的, *introductory, the first stages, beginning of sthg*;
dǎo yán: 导言, *introduction to a book*;

jiè shào xìng de: 介绍性的, *introductory remarks/ course, etc.;*
jiè shào: 介绍, *introduction to a book/ talk, etc.;*
shì xiāo de: 试销的, *introductory price/offer;*
xù yán: 序言, *foreword, introduction, preface;*
yǐn jìn: 引进, *introduction of new idea/ plan, etc.;*
yǐn yán (n): 引言, *foreword, introduction*

INTROVERTIDO (A); **introvertido** (A); *introverted, bashful, coy, withdrawn;*
gū dú (sv): 孤独, *lonely, solitary, lonesome, single, reclusive;*
nèi xiàng (sv) (n): 内向, *introverted; introversion;*
niǔ niē (sv): 扭捏, *coyly bashful;*
xìng gé nèi xiàng de: 性格内向的, *introverted;*
SEE (请查看) **TIMIDEZ**

INTUICIÓN; intuição; *intuition, instinct, presentiment* ... **INTUITIVO** (A); **intuitivo** (A); *intuitive;*
běn néng de: 本能的, *instinctive;*
zhí jué de: 直觉的, *intuitive;*
zhí jué: 直觉, *instinct, intuition;*
SEE (请查看) **INSTINTO**

INUTILIDAD; inutilidade; *uselessness;*
tú láo (n): 徒劳, *futile/fruitless/labor/ effort;*
wú yòng (sv): 无用, *unusable, useless;*
wú yòng xìng (n): 无用性, *uselessness;*
SEE (请查看) **INCAPACIDAD**

INVÁLIDO (A); **inválido** (A); *unacceptable; an ill person; invalid; disabled (MED);*
bìng ruò zhě: 病弱者, *invalid, sick and weak person;*
wú xiào (sv) (v): 无效, *invalid document/procedure, etc.; to be invalid/ ineffective;*
yào bu de: 要不得, *to be no good; to be unacceptable/ intolerable;*

SEE (请查看) **INADMISIBLE**

INVECTIVA; invectiva; *invective, tirade, insulting/ abusive language;*
mà rén de huà: 骂人的话, *abusive language;*
tòng chì (v) (n): 痛斥, *to bitterly attack; to reprimand/scold severely/inveigh; reprimand, invective;*
SEE (请查看) **ASALTAR**

INVENCIBLE; invencível; *invincible, indomitable, unbeatable;*
bù bài zhī dì (fe): 不败之地, *invincible/ impregnable position;*
bù qū bù náo (fe); 不屈不挠, *unyielding, indomitable;*
bù qū fú de: 不屈服的, *indomitable, unyielding;*
nán yǐ zhàn shèng de: 难以战胜的, *unbeatable person/team, etc.;*
wèi bèi jī bài de: 未被击败的, *unbeaten;*
wú dí de: 无敌的, *unmatched, invincible;*
zhàn wú bù shèng (fe): 战无不胜, *invincible;*
SEE (请查看) **IMBATIBLE**

INVENCIÓN ó INVENTO; invenção; *invention; fabrication;*
fā míng jiā: 发明家, *inventor;*
fā míng: 发明, *invention of a product, etc.*

INVENTARIO; inventário; *inventory;*
cún huò: 存货, *existing stock, inventory;*
kù cún: 库存, *supply, stock;*
qīng dān: 清单, *inventory of a house/ ship, etc.*

INVERSO (A); **inverso** (A); *opposite, inverse;*
fǎn xiàng de: 反向的, *opposite, reverse, inverse;*
SEE (请查看) **CONTRARIO**

INVETERADO; inveterado (A); *inveterate;*
gēn shēn dì gù de: 根深蒂固的,

inveterate;
guàn cháng de: 惯常的, *customary, usual, habitual*;
xí guàn xìng de: 习惯性的, *habitual*

INVITACIÓN; convite; *invitation*;
yāo qǐng (n) (v): 邀请, *invitation; to invite*

INVOLUNTARIO (A); **involuntário** (A); *involuntary*;
fēi běn yì de: 非本意的, *involuntary*;
shēn bù yóu jǐ (fe): 身不由己, *involuntarily*;
wú yì (v) (adv) (n): 无意, *to have no intention to do sthg; inadvertently; nonsense (lg)*;
wú yì de: 无意的, *involuntary, inadvertent*;
SEE (请查看) **ARBITRARIEDAD**

IRA; ravia, *anger;* **furia,** *rage; anger, ire*;
gān huǒ: 肝火, *anger, irascibility*;
SEE (请查看) **CÓLERA**

IRIDISCENTE; iridiscente; *iridescent*;
cǎi hóng sè de: 彩虹色的, *iridescent*;
wǔ guāng shí sè de: 五光十色的, *multicolored; multifarious*

IRONÍA; ironia; *irony, ridicule; satire*;
cháo xiào (v) (n): 嘲笑, *to ridicule/ deride/laugh at; raillery*;
fǎn yǔ (n): 反语, *irony; prevarication*;
fěng cì (v) (n): 讽刺, *to satirize/mock; satire, sarcasm*;
fěng cì wā kǔ (n) (sv): 讽刺挖苦, *satire, irony; ironic*;
SEE (请查看) **SÁTIRA**

IRRACIONAL; irracional;
unreasonable; irrational number (MAT); unreasonable;
bù hé lǐ de: 不合理的, *unreasonable decision/ price/amount, etc.*;
méi yǒu dào lǐ de: 没有道理的, *irrational, unreasonable; untrue*;
quē fá lǐ xìng de: 缺乏理性的, *irrational, unreasonable*;
SEE (请查看) **ABSURDO,**

IMPRUDENCIA

IRREAL; irreal; *unreal*;
jiǎ de: 假的, *fake, false, phony, artificial*;
lí pǔ de: 离谱的, *unreal, bizarre*;
xū jiǎ de: 虚假的, *false, phony*

IRRECONCILIABLE; irreconciliável;
irreconcilable;
bù néng hé jiě de: 不能和解的, *irreconcilable*;
bù néng xié tiáo de: 不能协调的, *irreconcilable*;
shì bù liǎng lì de: 势不两立的, *irreconcilable, incompatible*

IRRECUPERABLE; irreparável,
irretrievable loss; **irrecuperável,**
irrecoverable; hopeless, irreparable;
bù néng mí bǔ de: 不能弥补的, *irretrievable*;
bù néng wǎn huí de: 不能挽回的, *irreparable, irremediable*;
wú fǎ mí bǔ de: 无法弥补的, *irreparable*;
wú fǎ wǎn jiù de: 无法挽救的, *irretrievable*;
wú kě wǎn jiù de: 无可挽救的, *irreparable*;
SEE (请查看) **INCORREGIBLE, IRREPRODUCILE**

IRREGULARIDAD; irregularidade;
irregularity;
bù dìng qī de: 不定期的, *irregular hours/ times, etc.*;
bù zhèng dàng de: 不正当的, *irregular behavior*;
bù zhěng qí de: 不整齐的, *irregular surface/pattern, etc.*;
wú guī lǜ: 无规律, *irregularity*;
SEE (请查看) **ANOMALÍA, DESIGUAL**

IRRELEVANTE; irrelevante;
irrelevant, inapplicable;
bù shì yòng de: 不适用的, *inapplicable, unsuitable*;
bù xiāng guān de: 不相关的, *unrelated*;
wú guān (v) (n): 无关, *to be irrelevant*;

irrelevant;
SEE (请查看) **INAPLICABLE**

IRREPRIMIBLE; irreprimível;
irrepressible, incorrigible;
  bù néng yì zhì de: 不能抑制的,
  irrepressible;
SEE (请查看) **INCORREGIBLE**

IRREPRODUCIBLE; irreparável;
irreparable;
  bù kě mí bǔ de: 不可弥补的,
  irreparable;
SEE (请查看) **INCORREGIBLE**

IRRESOLUTO (A); **irresoluto** (A);
irresolute, indecisive, uncertain;
  chí yí bù jué (fe): 迟疑不决, *to be*
  irresolute/ uncertain/ undecided;
  chí yí bù jué de: 迟疑不决的,
  uncertain, irresolute, hesitant, undecided;
  nán yù liào de: 难预料的, *uncertain*;
  yōu róu guǎ duàn (fe): 优柔寡断,
  indecisive, irresolute;
  yōu yù bù jué (fe): 犹豫不决, *shilly-*
  shally;
  yóu yù de: 犹豫的, *hesitant*;
SEE (请查看) **CUESTIÓN**

IRRESPETUOSO (A); **desrespeitoso**
(A); *disrespectful*;
  wú lǐ de: 无礼的, *disrespectful,*
  impertinent

IRRESPONSABLE; irresponsável;
irresponsible;
  bù fù zé rèn de: 不负责任的,
  irresponsible attitude/behavior;
  wú zé rèn gǎn de: 无责任感的,

irresponsible person/driver

IRREVERENTE; irreverente;
irreverent, impious, profane;
  bù qián chéng de: 不虔诚的,
  irreverent ;
  xiè dú de: 亵渎的, *profane*;
SEE (请查看) **INCONSIDERADO**

IRRITABILIDAD; irritabilidade;
irritability; irascible, testy, touchy;
  mǐn gǎn (sv): 敏感, *sensitive, touchy;*
  susceptible;
  nǎo huǒ (sv): 恼火, *annoyed, angry*;
  nǎo rén (sv): 恼人, *irritated*;
  xīn fán (sv): 心烦, *irritated, annoyed*;
  xīn jí (sv): 心急, *impatient, quick-*
  tempered;
  yì nù (vp): 易怒, *irascible, irritable,*
  touchy;
SEE (请查看) **BILIOSO,**
IMPACIENCIA

IRRITACIÓN; irritação; *irritation*;
  nǎo nù: 恼怒, *feeling of annoyance*;
  nǎo rén de shì: 恼人的事, *annoying*
  thing;
SEE (请查看) **AGITAR**

IRRITANTE; irritante; *irritating,*
maddening, exasperating;
  fán rén (v) (sv): 烦人, *to annoy;*
  annoying, vexing, troubling

ITINERARIO; itinerário; *route,*
itinerary;
  lǚ xíng jì huà: 旅行计划, *itinerary*;
  xíng chéng: 行程, *itinerary*

Easily recognizable verbs and their Portuguese and Chinese equivalents
Verbos fácilmente reconocibles en Español-Portugués-Inglés y sus
equivalentes en Chino
Verbos facilmente reconhecível em Espanhol-Português-Inglês e seus
equivalentes em Chinês
很容易辨认的西班牙语，葡萄牙语，英语动词和他们的中文对等词

IDEAR; idear; *to plan; to think up/ devise/conceive*;
   ān pái: 安排, *to arrange/plan*;
   dǎ liàng: 大量, *to size up/to measure sb/sthg; to suppose/think*;
   gòu xiǎng (v) (n): 构想, *to conceive/ conceptualize; proposition, concept*;
   guī huà: 规划, *to program/plan*;
   xiǎng chū: 想出, *to come up with an idea/plan/ solution*;
   yǒu jì huà: 有计划, *to plan*;
   SEE (请查看) ASUMIR, CÁLCULO, DESIGNIO, CONSIDERACIÓN, CONCENTRAR, COMPUTAR

IDENTIFICAR; identificar; *to identify* ;
   shí bié (v) (n): 识别, *to distinguish/ discern; identification, recognition*

IDOLATRAR; idolatrar; *to worship/ idolize*;
   jìng 'ài: 敬爱, *to revere/respect/love*;
   jìng yǎng: 敬仰, *to revere/venerate*;
   SEE (请查看) ADORAR

IGNORAR; igonorar; *to ignore*;
   bù gù: 不顾, *to ignore sthg*;
   bù lǐ: 不理, *to ignore a person*;
   sā shǒu: 撒手, *to ignore; to give up/ let go*;
   zhì zhī bù lǐ (fe): 置之不理, *to ignore; to wave/ brush aside*;
   SEE (请查看) ABANDONAR

ILUMINAR; iluminar, *to light up; to illuminate/ enlighten*;
   guāng zhào: 光照, *to illuminate, to shine, to beam*;
   qǐ fā (v) (n): 启发, *to enlighten/ stimulate; enlightenment, stimulations*;
   zhào míng: 照明, *to illuminate a room/ street, etc.*;
   zhào shè: 照射, *to light up, to illuminate*;
   SEE (请查看) INTERPRETAR

ILUSTRAR; ilustrar; *to illustrate, to enlighten; to illustrate*;
   xiǎn shì (v) (n): 显示, *to show/display/ demonstrate/ manifest; show, display, demonstration*

IMAGINAR; imaginar; *to imagine/ suppose*;
   xiǎng xiàng (v) (n): 想象, *to imagine/ visualize; picture, imagination*;
   SEE (请查看) ASUMIR

IMPACTAR; impactar; *to shatter, to hit; to have an impact on/strike*;
   chóng jī mǒu rén/mǒu wù: 冲击某人/某物, *to have an impact on sb/sthg*;
   SEE (请查看) DISOLVER

IMPEDIR; impedir; *to obstruct; to prevent/stop*;
   fáng 'ài (v) (n): 妨碍, *to hamper, to impede, to obstruct; obstruction*;
   SEE (请查看) DIFICULTAR

IMPELER; impelir, *to thrust; to propel/ drive/urge*;
   jī lì (v) (n): 激励, *to encourage; to impel/ urge; drive, excitation*;
   tuī dòng: 推动, *to propel/drive a vehicle/boat/ machine/person*

IMPLANTAR; implantar, *to establish; to introduce, impose/bring in ...*
IMPLEMENTAR; implementar; *to implement/introduce/install*;
   guàn chè: 贯彻, *to carry out/ implement*;
   jiè shào: 介绍, *to introduce/present; to recommend/suggest*;
   SEE (请查看) APLICAR, FUNDAR

IMPLICAR; implicar; *to involve/ implicate*;
   lián lèi: 连累, *to implicate/involve*;
   qiān chě (v) (n): 牵扯, *to involve/ implicate/drag in; to impede/hinder; impediment, hinderance*;
   qiān lián: 牵连, *to implicate/involve*;
   qiān shè: 牵涉, *to be involve/drag in*;
   shè jí: 涉及, *to involve/touch upon*

IMPLORAR; implorer; *to implore, beg*;
   kěn qiú: 恳求, *to implore/entreat*;
   qǐ tǎo: 乞讨, *to beg/go begging*;
   SEE (请查看) APELAR

IMPORTUNAR; importunar; *to annoy;*
to bother/ pester;
  shǐ fán nǎo: 使烦恼, *to annoy/drive up*
  the wall;
SEE (请查看) **ACOSAR**

IMPOSIBILITAR; impossibilitar; *to*
make impossible/ prevent;
  zǔ dǎng: 阻挡, *to stem/stop/resist/*
  obstruct;
SEE (请查看) **BLOCAR**

IMPREGNAR; impregnar; *to*
impregnate/pervade/ soak;
  jìn pào: 浸泡, *to soak;*
  mí màn: 弥漫, *to pervade;*
  shǐ huái yùn: 使怀孕, *to impregnate*

IMPRESIONAR; impressionar; *to*
impress/be impressed;
  qiān dòng: 牵动, *to touch, to affect, to*
  influence;
SEE (请查看) **INFLUENCIAR**

IMPROVISAR; improviser; *to*
improvise/ad-lib;
  còu he: 凑合, *to gather together, to*
  collect, to improvise; to get by;
  còu shù: 凑数, *to make do with, to*
  improvise

IMPUGNAR; impugnar; *to refute;* *to*
challenge, contest;
  bó chì: 驳斥, *to refute/rebut;*
  bó huí: 驳回, *to reject/turn down;*
  fǎn bó: 反驳, *to refute/retort/negate;*
  pī bó: 批驳, *to refute/rebut;*
  pī pàn: 批判, *to criticize/repudiate;*
  tiǎo zhàn: 挑战, *to challenge by battle/*
  contest;
  zhì yí: 质疑, *to challenge/call into*
  question;
SEE (请查看) **DESAUTORIZAR**

IMPULSAR; impulsionar; *to propel; to*
drive; to promote;
  cù xiāo: 促销, *to promote a record/*
  film/ book/product;
  dài dòng: 带动, *to spur on/drive/*
  power;

jìn shēng: 晋升, *to promote an*
employee;
SEE (请查看) **ASISTIR**

IMPUTAR; imputar; *to attribute sthg to*
sb; to accuse/impute/attribute;
  guī gōng: 归功, *to give credit to; to*
  attribute success to sb;
  guī jiù: 归咎, *to blame; to attribute a*
  fault to sb;
  guī zuì: 归罪, *to impute;*
  zé nàn: 责难, *to blame/censure;*
SEE (请查看) **ACUSAR, ATRIBUIR,**
DENUNCIA, COMBATIR,
DENUNCIAR

INAUGURAR; inaugurar; *to open;* *to*
inaugurate, open;
  dǎ kāi: 打开, *to open, to expand; to*
  turn on;
  guà pái: 挂牌, *to open an office/*
  business;
  jiē kāi: 揭开, *to uncover; to open;*
  kāi chuàng: 开创, *to inaugurate a*
  system/measure; to start/initiate/found;
  kāi fā: 开发, *to develop, to open up;*
  kāi mù: 开幕, *to open, to inaugurate;*
  kāi shǐ: 开始, *to begin/start;*
  kāi yè: 开业, *to open a business;*
  kāi zhǎn: 开展, *to develop, to launch;*
  qǐ shǐ (v) (n): 起始, *to originate/initiate;*
  origin

INCITAR; incitir; *to urge on; to incite/*
stir up;
  cuī cù: 催促, *to urge/press;*
  diǎn huǒ: 点火, *to ignite; to stir up*
  trouble;
  gǔ wǔ: 鼓舞, *to inspire/encourage;*
  miǎn lì: 勉励, *to encourage/urge;*
  qǐ hòng: 起哄, *to heckle/stir up trouble;*
  rě huò: 惹祸, *to court disaster/stir up*
  trouble;
  rě shì: 惹事, *to stir up trouble;*
  tiǎo dòng: 挑动, *to provoke/stir up;*
  tiǎo dòu: 挑逗, *to provoke/tantalize;*
SEE (请查看) **INFLAMAR, INSPIRAR,**
AGITAR, INCENTIVO, FOMENTAR

INCLINAR; inclinar; *to bend/tilt/*
persuade/lean;

quàn dǎo: 劝导, *to induce/advise/admonish*;
SEE (请查看) **AVISAR, CURVATURA**

INCORPORAR; incorporar; *to incorporate*;
  guī bìng: 归并, *to incorporate/merge into*;
  huài guì: 划归, *to incorporate/subsume*;
SEE (请查看) **CONTENER**

INCREMENTAR; incrementar; *to increase*;
  zēng zhí: 增值, *to increase/grow; to appreciate in value*;
SEE (请查看) **AGRANDAR, AMPLIAR, AUMENTAR**

INCRIMINAR; incriminar; *to accuse/incriminate*;
  kòng gào (v) (n): 控告, *to incriminate; to accuse/ charge; accusation*;
  qiān lián: 牵连, *to involve (in trouble), to implicate; to incriminate*;
SEE (请查看) **IMPUTAR**

INCUBAR; incubar; *to incubate*;
  fū huà: 孵化, *to hatch, to incubate*;
  fū: 孵, *to incubate*

INCULCAR; inculcar; *to inculcate/instill*;
  fú zhí: 扶植, *to cultivate/foster/instill*;
  hù yǎng: 护养, *to cultivate*;
  zāi péi: 栽培, *to grow, to cultivate, to foster, to educate, to inculcate*;
  zào jiù (v) (n): 造就, *to cultivate; achievements*

INDEXAR; indexer; *to index, to file*;
  biān suǒ yǐn: 编索引, *to index a book/information*;
  guī dàng: 归档, *to file*;
SEE (请查看) **CATEGORIZAR**

INDICAR; indicar; *to indicate/register/show*;
  àn shì: 暗示, *to mention*;
  biāo míng: 标明, *to write a note, to mark/indicate*;
  zhǐ xiǎng (attr) (v): 指向, *directional; to point to, to direct to*;
  zhǐ yǐn: 指引, *to guide, to point the way*;
  zhǐ zhèng: 指正, *to point out*;
SEE (请查看) **SIMPLIFICAR, ANOTAR, COMUNICAR, DENOTAR**

INDIGNAR; indignar; *to anger/infuriate/outrage*;
  hán nù: 含怒, *to be angered*;
SEE (请查看) **AGRAVAR**

INDULTAR; indultar; *to pardon/reprieve*;
  shè miǎn (v) (n): 赦免, *to pardon a prisoner; pardon*;
  yuán liàng: 原谅, *to pardon; to forgive/excuse*;
SEE (请查看) **CLEMENCIA, DISPENSAR**

INDUSTRIALIZAR; industrializar; *to industrialize*;
  gōng yè huà (v) (n): 工业化, *to industrialize; industrialization*

INFESTAR; infester; *to infest/corrupt*;
  bài huài (v) (sv): 败坏, *to corrupt/undermine/ruin; rotten*;
  fǔ shí: 腐蚀, *to corrode/corrupt*;
SEE (请查看) **CORRUPCIÓN, DECADENTE, CORRUPTO**

INFILTRAR; infiltrar; *to penetrate; to inject/infiltrate*;
  shēn rù (v) (adv): 深入, *to penetrate; deeply, thoroughly*;
  shí pò: 识破, *to penetrate/see through*;
  zhù shè: 注射, *to inject*

INFLAMAR; inflamer; *to inflame/arouse/ignite*;
  diǎn huǒ: 点火, *to ignite/start a fire; to stir up trouble*;
  jī fā: 击发, *to ignite, to start*;
SEE (请查看) **INCITAR, DETONAR**

INFLUENCIAR; influenciar; *to*

influence/persuade/motivate;
 gǎn yìng: 感应, *to induce; to respond/ react*;
 shuō fū: 说服, *to persuade/convince*;
 SEE (请查看) AFECTAR, AVISAR, CONTAGIO, FOMENTAR

INFORMAR; informar; *to inform/ plead*;
 qǐ qiú: 乞求, *to plead/beg for*;
 shuō qíng: 说情, *to plead/intercede for*;
 tǎo qǐ: 讨乞, *to beg (for food, etc.)*;
 tǎo qíng: 讨情, *to plead fo sb*;
 tǎo ráo: 讨饶, *to ask for mercy/ask forgiveness*;
 yāng gào: 央告, *to plead/ask for earnestly*;
 yāng qiú: 央求, *to beg/plead/ask*;
 SEE (请查看) AVISAR, COMUNICAR

INFRINGIR; infringer; *to infringe/ contravene*;
 qīn fàn: 侵犯, *to infringe/encroach on*;
 qīn hài: 侵害, *to violate*;
 wéi fǎn: 违反, *to violate/transgress/ infringe*;
 SEE (请查看) AFRONTAR, AGRAVIAR, CONFLICTO

INOCULAR; inocular; *to inoculate*;
 dǎ zhēn: 打针, *to give/get an injection*;
 jiē zhòng: 接种, *to inoculate/ vaccinate*

INSINUAR; insinuar; *to insinuate/ imply*;
 àn hán: 暗含, *to imply*;
 yì wèi zhe: 意味着, *to signify/imply*;
 SEE (请查看) ALUDIR, INSINUACIÓN

INSISTIR; insister; *to insist/persist*;
 jiān chí: 坚持, *to go on/persist in*;
 zhí yì (sv) (v): 执意, *stubborn, obstinate; to insist on*;
 SEE (请查看) PERSEVERANCIA

INSPIRAR; inspirer; *to inspire*;
 gǎn zhào: 感召, *to inspire*;
 gǔ wǔ: 鼓舞, *to inspire/hearten/ encourage*;

qǐ fā: 启发, *to arouse/inspire/enlighten*;
 qū shǐ: 驱使, *to prompt/urge on/spur on*;
 zhèn fèn (v) (sv): 振奋, *to inspire/ stimulate; stimulating*;
 SEE (请查看) ILUMINADO, IMPELER

INSTALAR; instalar; *to install/fit*;
 ān zhuāng: 安装, *to install equipment/ software, etc.*;
 shè zhì: 设置, *to set up/install*;
 zhuāng pèi: 装配, *to assemble; to put/ fit together*;
 zhuāng zhì (v) (n): 装置, *to install/ equip; installation, equipment*

INSTIGAR; instigar; *to encourage; to instigate/incite*;
 dǎ qì: 打气, *to inflate/pump up/ encourage/bolster*;
 tí xié: 提携, *to promote, to guide and support*;
 tuī dòng: 推动, *to promote/encourage/ motivate*;
 SEE (请查看) INFLAMAR, INDIGNAR, INCITAR, INSPIRAR, EXCITANTE, FOMENTAR, GRATIFICACIÓN

INSTILAR; instilar; *to instill*;
 guàn shū: 灌输, *to instill into/imbue with*;
 SEE (请查看) INCULCAR, ADOCTRINAR

INSTITUIR; instituir; *to institute; to establish/found/ set up/create*;
 chuàng lì: 创立, *to establish/found/ create/originate*;
 SEE (请查看) IMPLANTAR, FUNDAR

INSULTAR; insultar; *to insult*;
 xiū rǔ (v) (n): 羞辱, *to humiliate/ shame/dishonor; humiliation*;
 SEE (请查看) ABUSAR

INTEGRAR; integrar; *to integrate/ incorporate/blend in*;
 dǎ chéng yī piàn (fe): 打成一片, *to become one, to merge, to integrate*;
 jié hé: 结合, *to combine, to integrate*;

to become a couple;
jié méng: 结盟, *to ally, to align;*
zhěng hé: 整合, *to integrate/conform;*
SEE (请查看) **INCORPORAR, UNIFICACIÓN**

INTENSIFICAR; intensificar; *to intensify/heighten;*
jī huà: 激化, *to intensify, to sharpen;*
jī zēng: 激增 , *to increase sharply, to shoot up;*
jiā jǐn: 加紧, *to speed up/intensify;*
jiā kuài: 加快, *to accelerate/speed up;*
SEE (请查看) **ACELERAR**

INTERCEDER; interceder; *to intercede/plead;*
shuō qīng: 说清, *to straighten out (a matter);*
SEE (请查看) **INFORMAR**

INTERCEPTAR; interceptar; *to cut off, to stop; to intercept/hold up;*
jié duàn: 截断, *to cut-off;*
jié huò: 截获, *to intercept; to cut off and capture;*
jié jī: 截击, *to intercept;*
jié qù: 截去, *to cut off/intercept;*
jié zhu: 截住, *to obstruct/intercept;*
SEE (请查看) **IMPEDIR, APREHENDER**

INTERFERIR; interferer; *to interfere;*
dǎo rǎo: 打扰, *to disturb/trouble;*
gān rǎo: 干扰, *to disturb/interfere;*
gān shè (v) (n): 干涉, *to interfere/ intervene/meddle; interference;*
SEE (请查看) **MOLESTAR, INTERCEPTAR, IMPEDIR**

INTERMEDIAR; intermediar; *to mediate;*
tiáo hé (v) (sv): 调和, *to mediate, to compromise; harmonious;*
SEE (请查看) **ARBITRAR, CONCILIAR**

INTERPRETAR; interpretar; *to interpret;*
jiě shì (v) (n): 解释, *to expound/ explain/interpret/ analyze; analysis, explanation, interpretation;*
kǒu yì: 口译, *to interpret (orally);*
SEE (请查看) **AVISAR, EXCUSA**

INTERROGAR; interrogar; *to question/interrogate;*
xùn wèn: 讯问, *to question/inquire/ interrogate;*
zhì wèn: 质问, *to question/interrogate;*
zhì xún: 质询, *to question/inquire/ask for an explanation;*
SEE (请查看) **INTERROGATORIO**

INTIMAR; intimidar; *to become intimate/very friendly;*
àn shì: 暗示, *to be intimate*

INTRIGAR; intrigar; *to intrigue/ scheme/plot;*
hé móu: 合谋, *to conspire/plot together;*
mì móu (v) (n): 密谋, *to plot/conspire; intrigue;*
SEE (请查看 **DESIGNIO, CONSPIRACIÓN, CONSPIRAR**

INTRODUCIR; introduzir; *to put in/ insert;*
ān chā: 安插, *to install/insert/place;*
chā rù (v) (n): 插入, *to insert/plug in; insertion;*
chuān chā: 穿插, *to weave in, to insert*

INVADIR; invadir; *to invade, violate, enter;*
qīn rù: 侵入, *to invade/violate;*
rù qīn: 入侵, *to invade/intrude;*
SEE (请查看) **AGRESIÓN, APREHENDER**

INVALIDAR; invalidar; *to invalidate;*
shǐ zuò fèi (vp): 使作废, *to invalidate/ cancel/ delete/nullify;*
SEE (请查看) **DESACTIVAR**

INVENTAR; inventor; *to invent;*
dú chuàng: 独创, *to invent;*
niē zào: 捏造, *to concoct/trump up;*
shǒu chuàng (v): 首创, *to initiate/*

originate/pioneer;
xū gòu: 虚构, *to fabricate/make up*;
SEE (请查看) **DUPLICIDAD, INVENCIÓN**

INVERTIR; inverter; *to reverse*;
fǎn bó: 反驳, *to refute*;
fǎn xiàng: 反向, *to reverse*

INVESTIGAR; investigar; *to research/investigate*;
diào chá (v) (n): 调查, *to investigate/survey; investigation, survey*;
kǎo chá: 考查, *to inspect/investigate*;
kǎo zhèng: 考证, *to verify/confirm by research*;
qīng chá: 清查, *to investigate/check*;
shěn hé: 审核, *to examine and verify, to check*;
shěn yuè: 审阅, *to check/review*;
tàn cè: 探测, *to explore/probe*;
tàn jiū: 探究, *to probe, to inquire into, to investigate*;
tàn míng: 探明, *to ascertain/verify*;

zhuī chá: 追查, *to investigate/trace*;
zhuī jiū: 追究, *to investigate*;
SEE (请查看) **CENSURA, DOCUMENTAR**

INVOCAR; invocar; *to invoke*;
qí qiú (v) (n): 祈求, *to supplicate; imperative, urgent, desperate*;
shàng fǎng: 上访, *to appeal for help to higher authority*;
SEE (请查看) **APELAR, CLAMAR**

IRONIZAR; ironizar; *to mock; to ridicule*;
cháo fěng: 嘲讽, *to sneer at/taunt/mock*;
chǐ xiào: 耻笑, *to mock/sneer at/ridicule*;
SEE (请查看) **IRONÍA**

IRRITAR; irritar; *to irritate*;
qiāo dǎ: 敲打, *to beat/irritate*;
SEE (请查看) **AGITAR, AGRAVAR**

Interchangeable Spanish-Portuguese-English words and their Chinese equivalents
Palabras en Español-Portugués-Inglés y sus equivalentes en Chino
Palavras em Espanhol-Português-Inglês e seus equivalentes em Chinês
西班牙语，葡萄牙语，英语及中文的对等单词

JADE; jade;
yù diāo: 玉雕, *jade carving*;
yù qì: 玉器, *jade object*;
yù shí: 玉石, *jade*

JAGUAR; jaguar;
měi zhōu hǔ: 美洲虎, *jaguar*

JAZZ; jazz;
jué shì yuè: 爵士乐, *jazz (MUS)*;
shǐ yǒu qù: 使有趣, *to jazz up food/an event, etc.*

JEANS; jeans;
niú zǎi kù: 牛仔裤, *jeans*

JET LAG; jet lag;
shí chā fǎn yìng : 时差反应, *jet lag; time difference*

JOGGING; jogging;
màn pǎo: 慢跑, *jogging*

JOVIAL; jovial;
kuài huo de: 快活的, *happy, cheerful, jovial; thrilled*;
SEE (请查看) **AGRADABLE**

JUDAS; judas; *a traitor*;
pàn tú: 叛徒, *traitor, renegade, turncoat*

JUDICIAL; judicial;
  fǎ yuàn de: 法院的, *judicial proceedings, courts, judicial centers, etc.*;
  míng duàn (n) (v): 明断, *justice; to be fair/impartial in judgment/conduct*;
  míng zhì de: 明智的, *judicious*;
  sī fǎ (sv) (n): 司法, *judicial; administration of justice, judicature*;
  yǒu jiàn shi de: 有见识的, *judicious*;
  SEE (请查看) DESAPASIONADO

JUDO ó YUDO; judô;
  róu dào: 柔道, *judo*;
  róu shù: 柔术, *jujitsu*

JUNIOR; júnior;
  hòu bèi: 后背, *younger generation; offspring*;
  hòu jìn (n) (sv): 后进, *juniors, next generation; less advanced, lagging behind*;
  jí bié dī: 级别低, *junior in rank/scale/level/grade*;
  nián shào de: 年少的, *young (of age)*;
  nián shào zhě: 年少者, *young person, junior*;
  nián yòu de: 年幼的, *young, underage*;
  shī dì: 师弟, *junior (male) apprentice*;
  shī mèi: 师妹, *junior (female) apprentice*;
  wǎn bèi (n): 晚辈, *younger generation, juniors*;
  xià jí: 下级, *lower level, subordinate*

Easily recognizable Spanish-Portuguese-English nouns, adjectives and adverbs and their Chinese equivalents
Nombres, sustantivos, adjetivos y adverbios en Español-Portugués-Inglés y sus equivalentes en Chino
Nomes, substantivos, adjetivos e advérbios em Espanhol-Português-Inglês e seus equivalentes em Chinês
容易辨认的西班牙语，葡萄牙语，英语的名词，形容词和副词和他们的中文对等词

JOCOSO (A); **jocoso** (A); *jocular*;
  huá ji (sv) (n): 滑稽, *funny, amusing; comic talk*

JOVIALIDAD; jovialidade; *joviality ...*
JÚBILO; júbilo; *elation; joy, jubilation ...* **JUBILOSO** (A); **jubiloso** (A), *elated; joyous, jubilant*;
  gāo xìng de: 高兴的, *glad, happy; willing*
  huān lè de: 欢乐的, *happy, joyful, delighted*;
  huān xǐ (sv) (v): 欢喜, *overjoyed; happy, delighted; to be fond of*;
  kuài huo rén: 快活人, *joviality; happy-go-lucky person*;
  kuài lè (n) (sv): 快乐, *happiness, joy, cheerfulness; happy, cheerful*;
  lè hē hē (fe): 乐呵呵, *happy and gay; joyful*;
  xīn xǐ (sv): 欣喜, *glad, happy, joyful*;
  yú yuè (sv): 愉悦, *delighted, cheerful*;
  SEE (请查看) AGRADABLE,
EUFORIA, JOVIAL

JUNTA; junta; *committee, council, military junta*;
  jūn rén jí tuán: 军人集团, *military junta/bloc/ groups/clique/circle*;
  zhèng quán: 政权, *political/state power; regime*;
  SEE (请查看) COMISIÓN, CONFERENCIA

JURADO (A); **jurado** (A); *sworn, jury; juror*;
  péi shěn tuán: 陪审团, *jury*;
  péi shěn yuán: 陪审员, *juror*;

JURISDICCIÓN; jurisdição; *jurisdiction*;
  cái pàn quán: 裁判权, *jurisdiction*;
  guǎn xiá quán: 管辖权, *jurisdiction*;
  quán xiàn: 权限, *jurisdiction, limits of power*;
  sī fǎ quán: 司法权, *judicial power, jurisdiction*

JURISPRUDENCIA; jurisprudência; *jurisprudence;*
  fǎ lǐ xué: 法理学, *jurisprudence*

JURISTA; jurista; *jurist;*
  fǎ xué jiā (n): 法学家, *jurist;*
  lǜ shī (n): 律师, *jurist, attorney, counsel, counselor, solicitor*

JUSTAMENTE; justamente; *rightly, precisely; justly, exactly;*
  gāng hǎo (adv): 刚好, *just, exactly;*
  jiù shì (adv) (conj) (aux): 就是, *exactly, quite, right; only, just; even if;*
  qià hǎo (adv): 恰好, *exactly, just right;*
  zhèng (adv): 正, *precisely, punctually;*
SEE (请查看) EXACTAMENTE

JUSTICIA; justiça; *justice, equity, fairness ...* **JUSTICIERO** (A); **justiceiro** (A); *righteous, just;*
  duì děng (sv): 对等, *equity, equality;*
  zhèng yì (n) (attr): 正义, *justice; just, righteous;*
SEE (请查看) DESAPASIONADO

JUSTIFICACIÓN; justificação; *justification ...* **JUSTO** (A); **justo** (A); *fair (GEN), just, deserved;*
  lǐ xìng (n) (sv): 理性, *reason, rationality, justification; reasonable;*
  lǐ yóu (n): 理由, *reason/grounds; argument, justification;*
  rèn wéi yǒu lǐ: 认为有理, *justification;*
  shuō fa (n): 说法, *version, wording, justification, opinion;*
  yǒu lǐ yóu (sv) (n): 有理由, *justifiable; justification;*
  yǒu lǐ (sv): 有理, *reasonable, justified;*
  zhèng dàng lǐ yóu: 正当理由, *justification;*
  zhí dé de: 值得的, *deserved*

JUVENIL; juvenil; *teenage; youthful (DEP) ...* **JUVENTUD; juventude;** *youth;*
  miào líng (n): 妙龄, *young, youthful;*
  nián qīng (sv): 年青, *teenage;*
  nián qīng de: 年青的, *youthful, young, puerile;*
  nián qīng rén: 年青人, *youngster;*
  qīng chūn (n): 青春, *youth, youthfulness;*
  yòu zhì (sv): 幼稚, *young, childish, naive*

Easily recognizable verbs and their Portuguese and Chinese equivalents
Verbos fácilmente reconocibles en Español-Portugués-Inglés y sus equivalentes en Chino
Verbos facilmente reconhecível em Espanhol-Português-Inglês e seus equivalentes em Chinês
很容易辨认的西班牙语，葡萄牙语，英语动词和他们的中文对等词

JURAR; jurar; *to swear/pledge;*
  fā shì: 发誓, *to pledge/vow/swear;*
  shǐ yán (n) (v): 失言, *oath, vow; to make a vow;*
  shì yán (n): 誓言, *oath, pledge;*
  xuān shì: 宣誓, *to swear/take an oath; to vow*

JUSTIFICAR; justificar; *to justify;*
  zhèng míng ... shì yǒu lǐ yóu: 证明...是有理由, *to justify*

K

Interchangeable Spanish-Portuguese-English words and their Chinese equivalents
Palabras en Español-Portugués-Inglés y sus equivalentes en Chino
Palavras em Espanhol-Português-Inglês e seus equivalentes em Chinês
西班牙语，葡萄牙语，英语及中文的对等单词

KARAOKE; karaokê;
  kǎ lā ōu kèi: 卡拉, *karaoke*

KÉTCHUP; ketchup;
  fān qié jiàng: 番茄酱, *tomato ketchup®*

KIT; kit; *also means assembly kit;*
  chéng tào yòng pǐn: 成套用品, *equipment kit;*

  fú zhuāng: 服装, *clothing kit;*
  pèi tào yuán jiàn: 配套元件, *assembly kit;*
  yòng pǐn bāo: 用品包, *kit set;*
  zhuāng bèi: 装备, *military kit*

KIWI; kiwi; *the fruit;*
  mí hóu táo: 猕猴桃, *kiwi fruit*

Easily recognizable Spanish-Portuguese-English nouns, adjectives and adverbs and their Chinese equivalents
Nombres, sustantivos, adjetivos y adverbios en Español-Portugués-Inglés y sus equivalentes en Chino
Nomes, substantivos, adjetivos e advérbios em Espanhol-Português-Inglês e seus equivalentes em Chinês
容易辨认的西班牙语，葡萄牙语，英语的名词，形容词和副词和他们的中文对等词

KILOGRAMO ó QUILIGRAMO;
  quilograma; *kilogram;*
  gōng jīn: 公斤, *kilogram*

KILÓMETRO ó QUILÓMETRO;
  quilômetro; *kilometer;*
  gōng lǐ: 公里, *kilometer*

L

Interchangeable Spanish-Portuguese-English words and their Chinese equivalents
Palabras en Español-Portugués-Inglés y sus equivalentes en Chino
Palavras em Espanhol-Português-Inglês e seus equivalentes em Chinês
西班牙语，葡萄牙语，英语及中文的对等单词

LABIAL; labial; *of the lips;*
  zuǐ chún: 嘴唇, *lips;*
  zuǐ jǐn (sv): 嘴紧, *tight-lipped;*
  zuǐ pí zi: 嘴皮子, *lips, gift of gab;*

LARVA; larva;
  yòu chóng: 幼虫, *larva;*
  yòu tǐ: 幼体, *young larva*

LÁSER; laser;
 jī guāng: 激光, *laser*;
 léi shè: 镭射, *laser*

LATERAL; lateral; *lateral*;
 cè miàn (sv) (n): 侧面, *lateral; side, flank*;
 héng xiàng (sv) (n): 横向, *lateral; crosswise, horizontal*

LÁTEX; látex;
 jiāo rǔ: 胶乳, *latex (BOT)*;
 xiàng jiāo: 橡胶, *rubber*

LAVA; lava;
 róng yán: 熔岩, *lava*;
 huǒ shān yán: 火山岩, *lava, volcanic rocks*

LEASING; leasing;
 zū lìn yè wù: 租赁业务, *charter business, leasing*;
 zū lìn zhì (n): 租赁制, *leasing system*

LEGAL; legal;
 fǎ dìng de: 法定的, *legal, statutory*;
 fǎ lǜ: 法律, *law, statute*;
 fǎ rén (n): 法人, *legal/corporate, entity*;
 hé fǎ de: 合法的, *legal, lawful, legitimate*

LIBERAL; liberal;
 dà fang (sv) (n): 大方, *generous/liberal (use, amount); experts, connoisseurs*;
 kāi míng de: 开明的, *tolerant, liberal*;
 kāng kǎi de: 慷慨的, *vehement, fervent; liberal, generous*;
 zì yóu dǎng: 自由党, *liberal (POL)*

LIBIDO; libido;
 xìng yù: 性欲, *libido*

LIMBO; limbo;
 chǔ yú bù dìng zhuàng tài:
 处于不定状态, *to be in limbo*

LITERAL; literal;
 wén zì de: 文字的, *literal*;
 zhí yì de: 直译的, *literal translation*;
 zì miàn de: 字面的, *literal sense, meaning*;
 zì miàn shàng de: 字面上的, *literal*

LOBBY; lobby (POL); *pressure group*;
 dà tīng: 大厅, *lobby of a building*;
 yóu shuì tuán: 游说团, *lobby, pressure group*

LOCAL; local;
 běn dì (n): 本地, *this locality;* (attr) *local*;
 běn dì rén (n): 本地人, *native, a local*;
 dāng dì (n) (attr): 当地, *locality, locality place*;
 dāng dì rén: 当地人, *the locals*;
 dì diǎn (n): 地点, *locale, place; site*;
 jú bù (n): 局部, *part;* (attr) *partial, local*;
 zài dì fāng (adv): 在地方, *locally*

LONGITUDINAL; longitudinal;
 jīng dù: 精度, *longitude*;
 jīng xiàn: 经线, *meridian, line of longitude*

LUMBAGO; lumbago;
 yāo téng: 腰疼, *lumbago*;
 yāo tòng: 腰痛, *lumbago*

LUNAR; lunar;
 yuè de: 月的, *lunar*

Easily recognizable Spanish-Portuguese-English nouns, adjectives and adverbs and their Chinese equivalents
Nombres, sustantivos, adjetivos y adverbios en Español-Portugués-Inglés y sus equivalentes en Chino
Nomes, substantivos, adjetivos e advérbios em Espanhol-Português-Inglês e seus equivalentes em Chinês
容易辨认的西班牙语，葡萄牙语，英语的名词，形容词和副词和他们的中文对等词

LABORATORIO; laboratório; *laboratory;*
  shí yàn shì: 实验室, *laboratory in school;*
  yán jiū shì: 研究室, *laboratory for analysis/ research*

LABORIOSO (A); **laborioso** (A); *industrious;*
  qín láo (sv): 勤劳, *industrious, hardworking;*

LACÓNICO (A); **lacônico** (A); *laconic, terse, precise, concise;*
  jiǎn jié de: 简洁的, *concise; succinct, to-the-point;*
  jīng liàn de: 精炼的, *terse, succinct*

LACRIMOSO (A); **lacrimoso** (A); *tearful, sorrowful ... LÁGRIMA;* **lágrima;** *tear;*
  bēi 'shāng (sv) (n): 悲伤, *sad, sorrowful; sorrow, grief;*
  kū qì (v) (sv): 哭泣, *to cry/weep/sob; tearful;*
  lèi shuǐ: 泪水, *tear, teardrop;*
  lèi zhū: 泪珠, *teardrop;*
  yǎn lèi (n): 眼泪, *tears, crying;*
  SEE (请查看**) DESOLACIÓN**

LAGUNA; laguna; *lagoon, pool;*
  huán jiāo hú: 环礁湖, *lagoon;*
  huán jiāo: 环礁, *atoll;*
  xiè hú: 泻湖, *lagoon*

LAMENTO; lament; *lament; moan, cry of pain;*
  āi dào: 哀悼, *lament for sb's death;*
  wǎn gē: 挽歌, *dirge, elegy;*
  SEE (请查看**) DESOLACIÓN**

LAMINADO (A); **laminado** (A); *laminated;*
  jiāo hé mù: 胶合木, *laminated wood*

LÁMPARA; lâmpada, *light; lamp;*
  dēng biāo: 灯标, *beacon;*
  dēng guāng: 灯光, *light, stage lighting, lamp light;*
  dēng huǒ: 灯火, *lights;*

dēng jù: 灯具, *lighting; lamps and lanterns;*
  dēng long: 灯笼, *lantern, lamp;*
  dēng pào: 灯泡, *light bulb;*
  dēng tǎ: 灯塔, *lighthouse, beacon;*
  dēng: 灯, *lamp, lantern, light; electric light;*
  guāng liàng (sv) (n): 光亮, *bright, shiny; light;*
  guāng xiàn: 光线, *light; beamy, ray;*
  liàng guāng: 亮光, *light beam, shaft of light;*
  tái dēng: 台灯, *reading lamp;*
  yóu dēng: 油灯, *oil lamp*

LAPSO; lapso; *mistake; lapse; space, interval; omission;*
  shī wù (v) (n): 失误, *to slip/make a mistake; mistake;*
  xiǎo cuò (n): 小错, *small mistake, slip;*
  SEE (请查看**) FALACIA, CULPA, OMISIÓN**

LASCIVIA; lascívia; *lust, lewdness, lecherous, salacious;*
  hào sè (sv) (n): 好色, *lustful; lust, lechery;*
  huáng sè (attr): 黄色, *decadent, obscene, pornographic;*
  ròu yù (n): 肉欲, *lust;*
  sè qíng de: 色情的, *lecherous;*
  xià liú (sv) (n): 下流, *low-down, mean; obscene, dirty, lewdness;*
  xìng yù (vp) (n): 性欲, *sexual desire/ urge;*
  yín dàng (n) (vp): 淫荡, *lasciviousness, lewdness; lecherous, lascivious, lewd;*
  SEE (请查看**) SALAZ**

LÁSTIMA; lástima; *pathetic, disgrace; pity, shame ... LASTIMERO* (A); **lastimoso** (A); *pitiful, pathetic;*
  kě bēi (sv): 可悲, *lamentable, pitiful, pathetic, sad;*
  kě lián (sv) (v): 可怜, *pathetic, poor, lamentable, pitiful; to pity;*
  SEE (请查看**) COMPASIÓN, CONSTERNACIÓN, DESCRÉDITO**

LATENTE; latente; *latent, concealed, dormant;*

qián fú: 潜伏, *latent, hidden, concealed*;
qián zài (attr): 潜在, *latent, potential*;
xiū mián: 休眠, *dormancy*

LATITUD; latitude; *latitude*;
wěi dù: 纬度, *latitude (GEOG)*;
zì yóu (n) (sv): 自由, *freedom, liberty, latitude; free, unrestrained*

LAXANTE; laxante; *laxative*;
xiè yào: 泻药, *laxative*

LEGALIDAD; legalidade; *legality*;
hé fǎ xìng: 合法性, *legitimacy, legality*

LEGENDARIO (A); **legendário** (A);
legendary;
chuán qí bān de: 传奇般的,
legendary, very famous

LEGÍTIMO (A); **legítimo** (A); *legitimate, rightful*;
hé fǎ (sv) (n): 合法, *lawful, rightful, legitimate; correct, right*;
zhèng dàng (vp): 正当, *proper, legitimate*;
SEE (请查看) **RAZONABLE**

LENTO (A); **lento** (A); *slow*;
chí dùn (sv): 迟钝, *slow/dull person*;
chí huǎn (sv): 迟缓, *slow, sluggish*;
chí zhì (sv): 迟滞, *slow moving*;
dāi zhì (sv): 呆滞, *slow; lack of circulation*;
huǎn màn (sv): 缓慢, *slow, tardy*;
màn (sv) (adv): 慢, *slow, indifferent, gradually*;
màn jìng tóu: 慢镜头, *slow motion*;
SEE (请查看) **ENDÉMICO, LETÁRGICO**

LEPRA; lepra; *leprosy ...* **LEPROSO** (A); **leproso** (A); *leprous (adj), leper (n)*;
má fēng bìng de: 麻风病的, *leprous*;
má fēng bìng huàn zhě: 麻风病患者, *leper*;
má fēng bìng: 麻风病, *leprosy*

LETAL; letal; *lethal, deadly, mortal, fatal*;

zhì mìng (v) (attr): 致命, *to be fatal/lethal; fatal, mortal, deadly*

LETÁRGICO (A); **letárgico** (A); *lethargic, sluggish, slow, dull, lazy*
... LETARGO; letargia; *lethargy, indolence, indifference, sloth*;
hūn shuì (n) (sv): 昏睡, *lethargy; lethargic*;
lǎn (sv): 懒, *lazy, lethargic*;
lěng kù (sv): 冷酷, *cold-hearted, callous*;
tuō lā (sv): 拖拉, *dilatory, stalling*;
tuō tà (sv): 拖沓, *dilatory, sluggish*;
SEE (请查看) **LENTO, DESAMOR, APATÍA, DESATENCIÓN, DESOCUPADO, INDIFERENCIA**

LEUCEMIA; leucemia; *leukemia*;
bái xuè bìng: 白血病, *leukemia*

LIBELO; libelo; *lampoon (GEN); libel*
fěi bàng xìng wèn: 诽谤行为, *liber and slander*;
fěi bàng zuì: 诽谤罪, *slander*;
wā kǔ xìng zuò pǐn: 挖苦性作品, *lampoon*;
SEE (请查看) **DIFAMACIÓN**

LICENCIA; licença; *license, permit*;
jià shǐ zhí zhào: 驾驶执照, *driver's license*;
tè xǔ: 特许, *commercial/special permission license*;
xǔ kě zhèng: 许可证, *license, permit*;
zhí zhào: 执照, *license, permit*

LICENCIOSO (A); **licencioso** (A);
licentious, immoral, promiscuous;
fàng dàng (sv): 放荡, *dissolute*;
SEE (请查看) **DEPRAVADO, PRESUNCIÓN**

LICOR; licor; *liquor*;
jiǔ: 酒, *wine, liquor, spirits*

LIFTING; lifting; *face-lift*;
zhěng róng (n) (v): 整容, *face-lift; to spruce up, to have a haircut/face-lift*

LIMITACIÓN; limitação; *limitation, limit, minimal* ... **LIMITADO** (A); limitado (A); *scant, limited, restricted, curbed* ... **LÍMITE; limite;** *maximum, limit, fixed, end*;
  jí diǎn: 极点, *farthest point, limit, utmost*;
  jí xiàn: 极限, *limit, maximum*;
  quán xiàn: 权限, *jurisdiction, limits of power*;
  xiàn dù: 限度, *limit, limitation*;
  xiàn qī: 限期, *deadline, time limit*;
  xiàn sù: 限速, *speed limit*;
  yǒu xiàn (v) (sv): 有限, *limited, finite*;
  zhǐ jìng: 止境, *end, limit*;
SEE (请查看**) DEFINIR, CONFINAR, MARGEN**

LIMONADA; limonada; *lemonade*;
  níng méng qì shuǐ: 柠檬汽水, *lemonade*

LÍMPIDO (A); límpido (A); *limpid, clear, transparent*;
  tòu míng (sv): 透明, *transparent, open, public*;
SEE (请查看**) CLARIDAD**

LIMUSINA; limusine; *limousine*;
  háo huá jiào chē: 豪华轿车, *limousine*

LIQUIDEZ; liquidez; *liquidity* ... **LÍQUIDO** (A); líquido (A); *liquid*;
  yè tǐ de: 液体的, *liquid*;
  yè tǐ: 液体, *liquid, fluid*

LISTA; lista (GEN); *list, register, inventory, index*;
  dān zi: 单子, *list*

LITERALMENTE; literalmente; *literally*;
  què shí de (adv): 确实地, *literally (for emphasis)*;
  zhú zì de (adv): 逐字地, *literally translated*;
SEE (请查看**) LITERAL**

LITERATURA; literatura; *literature*;

wén shǐ: 文史, *literature and history*;
wén xiàn: 文献, *publications, literature*;
wén xué: 文学, *novels, plays, poetry; literature*;
wén yì: 文艺, *literature and art*;
zuò pǐn: 作品, *works of literature/art*

LITORAL; litoral; *littoral, seacoast*;
  hǎi 'àn: 海岸, *seacoast, seashore*;
  hǎi bīn: 海滨, *seashore, seaside*

LITURGIA; liturgia; *liturgy (RELIG)*;
  lǐ bài yí shì: 礼拜仪式, *liturgy*

LÍVIDO (A); lívido (A); *pallid; livid, ashen, pale*;
  cāng bái (sv): 苍白, *pale, pallid, wan; lifeless, flat; gray, graying (of hair)*;
  dàn sè (n): 淡色, *pale/light color*;
  huī bái (sv) (attr): 灰白, *grayish white, ashen, pale*;
  huī sè (n): 灰色, *grey, ashy; pessimistic, gloomy; obscure, ambiguous*;
  tiě qīng (sv): 铁青, *ashen, livid, ghastly pale*;
  tǔ sè (n): 土色, *ashen, pale*

LÓBULO; lóbulo; *lobe (ANAT)*;
  ěr chuí: 耳垂, *earlobe*;
  féi yè: 肺叶, *lobe of a lung*

LOCALIDAD; localidade; *place, town, locality*;
  běn dì: 本地, *locality*;
  bù wèi: 部位, *position, place, location*;
  chǎng suǒ: 场所, *location, place*;
  chéng shì: 城市, *city, town*;
  chéng zhèn: 城镇, *town*;
  dì fāng: 地方, *locality; local administration*;
  xiāng zhèn: 乡镇, *village, town*;
SEE (请查看**) LOCAL**

LOCOMOCIÓN; locomoção; *locomotion*;
  yí dòng: 移动, *movement, shift*;
  yùn dòng: 运动, *movement, locomotion*

LOCOMOTORA; locomotiva; *engine, locomotive;*
  huǒ chē tóu: 火车头, *railway engine, locomotive;*
  huǒ chē: 火车, *a train*
  jī chē: 机车, *locomotive*

LOCUACIDAD; loquacidade;
loquacious, garrulous; verbose, wordy;
  dié dié bù xiū (vp): 喋喋不休, *jabber on and on;*
  duō huà (sv): 多话, *loquacious;*
  jiàn tán (sv): 健谈, *loquacious, verbose, talkative, brilliant in conversation;*
  luō suo (sv): 罗嗦, *long-winded, wordy; troublesome;*
  rǒng cháng (sv): 冗长, *long and tedious; redundant, verbose (of writing)*

LOGARITMO; logaritmo; *logarithm;*
  duì shù: 对数, *logarithm (MAT)*

LÓGICO (A); **lógico** (A); *logical, natural, rational, credible, believable, reasonable, plausible;*
  hé hū qíng lǐ de: 合乎情理的, *logical course of action;*
  hé lǐ de: 合理的, *rational, reasonable, equitable;*
  hé luó ji de: 合逻辑的, *logical conclusion/result;*
  luó ji (sv) (n): 逻辑, *logical argument, analysis; logic;*
  luó jì shàng de: 逻辑上的, *logical;*
  yǒu luó ji de: 有逻辑的, *logical*

LOGÍSTICA; logística; *logistics;*
  hòu qín: 后勤, *logistics (MIL)*

LONGEVIDAD; longevidade;
longevity;
  cháng shòu: 长寿, *longevity*

LONGEVO (A); **longevo** (A), *elderly; long-lived;*
  cháng shòu (sv): 长寿, *long-lived;*
  lǎo líng (n): 老龄, *old age, elderly people*

LOTE; lote, *parcel; batch, share, lot, piece of land;*

  bù fen: 部分, *part, section;*
  dì pí: 地皮, *building lot, land;*
  fèn 'é: 份额, *share, portion, part;*
  pī liàng: 批量, *lot, batch,*
SEE (请查看) COMPONENTE

LOTERÍA; loteria o loto; *lottery;*
  cǎi piào: 彩票, *lottery ticket;*
  jiǎng quàn: 奖券, *lottery coupon, raffle ticket*

LUBRICACIÓN; lubrificação;
lubrication ... LUBRICANTE;
lubrificante; *lubricant;*
  rùn huá jì: 润滑剂, *lubricant;*
  shǐ rùn huá: 使润滑, *lubrication*

LUCIDEZ; lucidez; *lucidity, clarity ...*
LÚCIDO (A); **lúcido** (A); *lucid, clear;*
  liǎo rán (sv): 了然, *understandable, clear;*
  míng bǎi zhe (vp): 明摆着, *obvious, clear, plain;*
  míng jìng: 明净, *clarity;*
  míng liàng (sv) (v): 明亮, *bright, well-lit; loud and clear; to become clear;*
  míng qiè (sv) (v): 明切, *definite, clear cut, explicit; to clarify;*
  qīng chǔ (sv) (v) (n): 清楚, *clear, distinct, without ambiguity; to know/be aware of; clarity;*
SEE (请查看) CLARIDAD, APARENTE, OBVIO, EVIDENTE, SINCERIDAD

LUCRATIVO (A); **lucrativo** (A);
lucrative, profitable;
  yǒu lì de: 有利的, *lucrative;*
SEE (请查看) RENTABLE

LUCRO; lucro; *profit;*
  lì rùn: 利润, *profit*

LUMINOSIDAD; luminosidade;
brightness, luminosity ... LUMINOSO (A); **luminoso** (A); *luminous, bright, illuminated;*
  fā liàng (sv) (v): 发亮, *luminous; to shine;*

guāng tǐ: 光体, *luminous body; luminary;*

guāng xiān (sv): 光线, *bright and new, fresh and bright;*

guāng zhào (n): 光照, *illumination, beam;*

liàng (sv) (v): 亮, *bright; light; to shine;*

liàng dù: 亮度, *brightness, luminosity (FIS);*

míng shì (n): 明室, *a well-lit room;*

míng yào (vp): 明耀, *bright and dazzling;*

SEE (请查看) BRILLAR, LUCIDEZ

LUNÁTICO (A); **lunático** (A); *lunatic, madman; mad, foolish;*

jīng shén shī cháng zhě: 精神失常者, *mentally ill;*

fēng zi: 疯子, *madman, lunatic;*

fēng de: 疯的, *mad*

LUSTRE; **lustre;** *polish; luster, gloss, brilliance* ... LUSTROSO (A); **lustroso** (A); *shiny, glossy;*

guāng yóu yóu (vp): 光油油, *glossy, shiny;*

guāng zé: 光泽, *luster, gloss, sheen;*

SEE (请查看) GLORIA, LÁMPARA, ESPLÉNDIDO

LUZ; **luz;** *light;*

dēng: 灯, *light, lamp, lantern, lighting;*

guāng yuán: 光源, *light source;*

guāng: 光, *light from sun/moon/lamp/fire;*

SEE (请查看) LUMINOSIDAD, LÁMPARA

Easily recognizable verbs and their Portuguese and Chinese equivalents
Verbos fácilmente reconocibles en Español-Portugués-Inglés y sus equivalentes en Chino
Verbos facilmente reconhecível em Espanhol-Português-Inglês e seus equivalentes em Chinês
很容易辨认的西班牙语，葡萄牙语，英语动词和他们的中文对等词

LAMENTAR; **lamentar;** *to regret; to lament/bemoan;*

āi dào (v) (n): 哀悼, *to lament/mourn sb's death; condolences;*

āi tàn: 哀叹, *to lament/sigh;*

bēi tàn: 悲叹, *to sigh mournfully; to lament, to bemoan;*

zhuī dào: 追悼, *to mourn;*

SEE (请查看) DEPLORAR

LAPIDAR; **lapidar;** *to polish/buff* ...
LUSTRAR; **lustrar;** *to polish/shine;*

cā guāng: 擦光, *to polish/buff; to rub;*

cā liàng: 擦亮, *to polish; to be more vigilant;*

pāo guāng: 抛光, *to polish/buff;*

shàng guāng: 上光, *to polish furniture/a floor; to glaze;*

SEE (请查看) LUSTRE, LUSTROSO

LEGALIZAR; **legalizar;** *to legalize/ authenticate* ... LEGITIMAR; **legitimar;** *to legitimize;*

hé fǎ huà: 合法化, *to legalize/ legitimize;*

rèn zhèng: 认证, *to authenticate, to attest to, to notarize; to approve;*

rèn zhī: 认知, *to acknowledge, to recognize;*

SEE (请查看) CONFIRMAR

LEGISLAR; **legislar;** *to legislate;*

lì fǎ chǎn shēng: 立法产生, *to legislate*

LEVANTAR; **levantar;** *to raise/lift, hoist; to build up;*

bái shǒu qǐ jiā (fe): 白手起家, *to build up from nothing, to start from scratch;*

jù jī: 聚积, *to build up/accumulate;*

tái gāo: 抬高, *to raise;*

SEE (请查看) AUMENTAR

LEVITAR; **levitar;** *to levitate;*

fú dòng: 浮动, *to float/fluctuate;*

piāo dàng: 飘荡, *to drift/float/wander;*

piāo fú (v) (vp): 漂浮, *to float; superficial, showy*;
piāo sǎ: 飘洒, *to drift/float*;
shēng kōng: 升空, *to levitate*

LIBERAR; liberar; *to liberate/set free/ release; to exempt*;
jiě fàng: 解放, *to liberate a city/ country; to emancipate*;
jiě jiù: 解救, *to save/rescue*;
shì fàng: 释放, *to liberate/set free*

LIMITAR; limitar; *to limit/restrict*;
qióng jìn: 穷尽, *to limit/end*;
SEE (请查看) DISCIPLINA, DEFINIR, CONFINAR

LINCHAR; linchar; *to lynch*;
guà: 挂, *to hang/hang up/put up/ execute*;
xuán guà (v) (n): 悬挂, *to hang a criminal; to fly a flag; car suspension*

LITIGAR; litigar; *to litigate/dispute*;
dǎ guān si: 打官司, *to file a lawsuit, to go to court*;
kàng yì: 抗议, *to protest*;
sù sòng (v) (n): 诉讼, *to litigate; lawsuit*;
zhēng duàn (v) (n): 争端, *to litigate; dispute, conflict*;
SEE (请查看) ARGUMENTO, ARGUMENTAR, COMPETIR

LOCALIZAR; localizar; *to find, to site; to locate/track/ down/find*;
chá huò: 查获, *to track down*;
dìng wèi (v) (n): 定位, *to locate/orient; orientation*;
xún zhǎo: 寻找, *to look for/seek*;
zhǎo dào: 找到, *to find/seek out*;
zhǎo xún: 找寻, *to look for/seek*;
zhuī xún: 追寻, *to track down*;
SEE (请查看) DETECCIÓN

Interchangeable Spanish-Portuguese-English words and their Chinese equivalents
Palabras en Español-Portugués-Inglés y sus equivalentes en Chino
Palavras em Espanhol-Português-Inglês e seus equivalentes em Chinês
西班牙语，葡萄牙语，英语及中文的对等单词

MACHETE; machete;
dà kǎn dāo: 大砍刀, *machete*

MACHISMO; machismo;
dà nán zǐ qì: 大男子气, *machismo*

MACRO; macro;
dà de: 大的, *macro; big, great*;
hóng guān de: 宏观的, *microscopic*

MAESTRO (A); **maestro (trina)**; *teacher*;
jiào shī: 教师, *teacher, instructor*;
yì shù dà shī: 艺术大师, *maestro (ART)*;
yīn yuè dà shī: 音乐大师, *maestro (MUSIC)*

MAFIA; mafia … MAFIOSO (A); **mafioso** (A);
fěi tú: 匪徒, *gangster, bandit*;
hēi shè huì: 黑社会, *criminal underworld*;
hēi shǒu dǎng: 黑手党, *mafia, gang*;
SEE (请查看) GÁNGSTER

MAIL; e-mail; *e-mail*;
diàn zǐ yóu jiàn: 电子邮件, *e-mail, email*;
SEE (请查看) E-MAIL

MALARIA; malária;
nüè ji: 疟疾, *malaria*;
nüè wén: 疟蚊, *malaria mosquito*

MANÍA; mania;
  kuáng zào (sv): 狂躁, *manic*
  pǐ hào: 癖好, *mania, favorite hobby*;
  zào kuáng (n) (vp): 躁狂, *mania;*
  irritable and unrestrained;
SEE (请查看**) FANÁTICO**

MANUAL; manual;
  shǒu cè (n): 手册, *handbook, manual*;
  shǒu gōng de: 手工的, *manual*
  (labor);
  tǐ lì de: 体力的, *manual/physical*;
  zhǐ nán (n): 指南, *guide, guidebook*

MARITAL; marital ... MATRIMONIAL;
matrimonial;
  hūn jià: 婚嫁, *marriage*;
  hūn lǐ (n) (sv): 婚礼, *wedding*
  ceremony; matrimonial;
  hūn yīn (n) (sv): 婚姻, *marriage,*
  matrimony; marital;
  hūn yuē: 婚约, *engagement*

MATERIAL; material;
  bù liào: 布料, *cloth*;
  cái liào: 材料, *material, data, stuff,*
  ingredients;
  liào (bf) (v): 料, *raw material, stuff,*
  makings; to expect/anticipate; to infer/
  foresee;
  sù cái: 素材, *source material*;
  wù zhì (n) (attr): 物质, *matter,*
  substance, material; materialistic;
  yī liào: 衣料, *material for clothing*;
  yuán liào: 原料, *raw material*;
  zhuī qiú shí lì (sv): 追求实利,
  materialistic;
  zī liào: 资料, *material, raw materials*

MATERNAL; maternal;
  mǔ qin de: 母亲的, *maternal*;
  mǔ qin: 母亲, *mother*;
  mǔ xì (n) (attr): 母系, *maternal side,*
  matriarchal

MATINÉE ó MATINÉ; matinê;
matinee;
  rì chǎng: 日场, *matinee*

ME; me; *as the personal pronoun: my,*
mine;

  wǒ de: 我的, *mine, my*;
  wǒ: 我, *me*

MEDICINAL; medicinal;
  yào cái: 药材, *medicinal, herbs*;
  yào cǎo: 药草 , *medicinal herbs*;
  yào fāng: 药方, *prescription*;
  yào jì: 药剂, *medicine, drug*;
  yào yòng (attr): 药用, *for medicinal*
  purposes/uses;
  yǒu liáo xiào de: 有疗效的, *medicinal*
  qualities/effects

MEDIEVAL; medieval;
  zhōng shì jì de: 中世纪的, *medieval*

MEDIOCRE; medíocre;
  zhōng děng de: 中等的, *middling;*
  secondary;
SEE (请查看**) ORDINARIO, BANAL**

MEGABYTE; megabyte;
  zhào zì jié: 兆字节, *megabyte*

MELODRAMA; melodrama;
  chuán qí jù: 传奇剧, *melodrama*;
  nào jù (n): 闹剧, *farce, slapstick comedy*

MEMORIAL; memorial;
  jì niàn bēi: 纪念碑, *monument,*
  memorial;
  jì niàn wù: 纪念物, *memorial, object,*
  souvenir

MENSTRUAL; menstrual;
  lì jià: 例假, *menstrual period; legal/*
  official holiday;
  yuè jīng qī: 月经期, *menstrual period*

MENTAL; mental; *intellectual;*
  zhī shi fèn zǐ: 知识分子, *intellectual,*
  intelligentsia;
SEE (请查看**) INTELECTO**

MENTOR (A); mentor (A);
  dǎo shī: 导师, *mentor*;
  liáng shī yì yǒu: 良师益友, *mentor*;
  zhǐ dǎo zhě: 指导者, *mentor*

MENÚ; menu;

cài dān: 菜单, *menu*

MINERAL; mineral;
 kuàng cáng: 矿藏, *mineral resources*;
 kuàng shí: 矿石, *ore*;
 kuàng wù: 矿物, *mineral*

MINI; mini; *miniskirt*;
 chāo duǎn kù: 超短裤, *minipants, hotpants*;
 chāo duǎn qún: 超短裙, *miniskirt*;
 mí nǐ qún: 迷你裙, *miniskirt*

MINISTERIAL; ministerial;
 bù zhǎng (sv) (n): 部长, *ministerial; minister (government)*;
 nèi gé (sv) (n): 内阁, *ministerial; (government) cabinet*;
 xíng zhèng (sv) (n): 行政, *ministerial; administration, executive branch of government*

MÓDEM; modem;
 tiáo zhì jiě tiáo qì: 调制解调器, *modem*

MODULAR; modular;
 dān yuán de: 单元的, *modular*

MOLAR; molar; *tooth; grinding*;
 mó yá (n) (v): 磨牙, *molar; to grind*

MOLECULAR; molecular;
 fēn zǐ de: 分子的, *molecular*

MONUMENTAL; monumental;
monumental, tremendous;
 bù xiǔ de: 不朽的, *monumental; immortal fame*;
SEE (请查看) ENORME, HISTÓRICO

MORAL; moral (s);
 dào dé: 道德, *moral, ethics, morality*;
 gǔ qì: 骨气, *strength of character, moral integrity*;
 měi dé: 美德, *moral excellence; virtue*;
 pǐn dé: 品德, *moral character, morality*;

pǐn xìng: 品性, *moral character*;
 xīn dì: 心地, *character; moral nature; mind*;
 yǒu dào dé de: 有道德的, *moral*;
SEE (请查看) PERSONALIDAD

MORTAL; mortal;
 fán rén de: 凡人的, *mortal (ordinary) person*;
 fēi yǒng shēng de: 非永生的, *mortal*;
SEE (请查看) FATAL

MOTEL; motel;
 qì chē lǚ guǎn: 汽车旅馆, *motel*

MULTILATERAL; multilateral;
 duō biān de: 多边的, *multilateral*;
 duō fāng miàn de: 多方面的, *many sided*;
 duō gōng néng de: 多功能的, *multifunction, all-purpose*

MUNICIPAL; municipal;
 shì (n) (v): 市, *city, municipality; to buy/ sell*;
 shì zhèng: 市政, *municipal administration*

MURAL; mural;
 bì huà: 壁画, *mural*

MUSCULAR; muscular;
 jī ròu de: 肌肉的, *muscular*

MUSICAL; musical;
 yīn fú: 音符, *musical note*;
 yīn yuè (sv) (n): 音乐, *musical; music*;
 yīn yuè jù: ,音乐剧 *musical drama*;
 yīn yuè piàn: 音乐片, *musical (film/ movie)*;
 yīn yuè xìng (attr): 音乐性, *musical*;
 yīn yuè yǎn zòu: 音乐演奏, *musical performance*;
 yuè pǔ: 乐谱, *musical score, musical*;
 yuè qǔ: 乐曲, *musical composition, music*

Easily recognizable Spanish-Portuguese-English nouns, adjectives and adverbs and their Chinese equivalents
Nombres, sustantivos, adjetivos y adverbios en Español-Portugués-Inglés y sus equivalentes en Chino
Nomes, substantivos, adjetivos e advérbios em Espanhol-Português-Inglês e seus equivalentes em Chinês
容易辨认的西班牙语，葡萄牙语，英语的名词，形容词和副词和他们的中文对等词

MACABRO (A); **macabro** (A); *macabre*;
  kě pà (sv): 可怕, *fearful, terrible, gruesome, macabre*;
SEE (请查看) ANTIPATÍA, HORROR

MAGISTRADO (A); **magistrado** (A);
judge, magistrate;
  dì fāng fǎ guān: 地方法官, *magistrate*;
  fǎ guān: 法官, *judge, justice*

MAGNÁNIMO (A); **magnânimo** (A);
magnanimous;
  kāng kǎi (sv): 慷慨, *magnanimous, generous; fervent, vehement*;
  kuān hóng dà liàng (fe): 宽宏大量, *magnanimous*

MAGNESIO; **magnésio**; *magnesium*;
  měi: 镁, *magnesium*

MAGNÉTICO (A); **magnético**
(A); *magnetic* ... **MAGNETISMO**;
magnetismo; *magnetism*;
  cí de: 磁的, *magnetic*;
  cí xìng (n) (sv): 磁性, *magnetism; magnetic (FIS)*;
  cí xìng de: 磁性的, *magnetism*;
SEE (请查看) CARISMA

MAGNIFICENCIA; **magnificência**;
magnificence ... **MAGNÍFICO** (A);
magnífico (A); *wonderful, magnificent*;
  piào liang (sv): 漂亮, *pretty, beatiful, wounderful*;
  zhuàng lì (vp) (n): 壮丽, *majestic, magnificent; magnificence*;
SEE (请查看) FANTÁSTICO, DELICADO, CLAMOROSO, ESPLÉNDIDO

MAGNITUD; **magnitude**; *magnitude, extent, immensity; significance*;

dà xiǎo (n): 大小, *size, magnitude, extent*;
  guī mó: 规模, *scale, scope, dimension*;
  yì wèi: 意味, *significance, implication*;
  zhòng yào xìng: 重要性, *importance, significance*;
SEE (请查看) DESMEDIDO, ÁREA, IMPORTANTE

MAL; **mal**; *evil (GEN); harm, wrong*;
  bù dàng (sv): 不当, *improper*;
  hài chù (n): 害处, *harm, evil*;
  huài (sv) (adv) (v) (n): 坏, *bad, evil, harmful; awfully; to go bad/spoil; evil idea, dirty trick*;
  huài chù (n): 坏处, *harm*;
  xié 'è (sv): 邪恶, *evil, wicked, vicious*;
SEE (请查看) CULPA, DESIGUAL, CRIMEN

MALEDUCADO (A); **mal-educado** (A);
uneducated, ill-mannered; rude;
  jǔ zhǐ cū lǔ (sv): 举止粗鲁, *ill-mannered*;
  yě mán (sv): 野蛮, *uncivilized, cruel, brutal*;
SEE (请查看) ASPECTO, GROSERO, BRONCO, IGNORANCIA, IMPERTINENTE

MALHUMORADO (A); **mal-humorado**
(A); *sullen, grumpy; bad-tempered*;
  mèn mèn bù lè (fe): 闷闷不乐, *in low spirits, depressed, sullen*;
  pí qi (n): 脾气, *temperament, bad temper*;
  pí qi huài (sv): 脾气坏, *grumpy, bad-tempered*;
SEE (请查看) DESANIMADO, DESILUSIÓN

MALICIA; **malícia**; *malice, spite*

... **MALICIOSO** (A); **malicioso**
(A); *malicious, spiteful, vicious*;
  dǎi dú (sv): 歹毒, *vicious*;
  è xìng (n) (sv): 恶性, *viciousness;
  malignancy, pernicious*;
  è yì de: 恶意的, *malicious; spiteful
  action/conduct*;
  hěn dú (sv): 狠毒, *vicious, cruel*;
  huái hèn de: 怀恨的, *spiteful person*;
  jiā xiǎn (sv): 艰险, *malicious, wicked,
  wily*;
  kè dú (sv): 刻毒, *malicious, spiteful*;
  xiǎn 'è (sv): 险恶, *dangerous, vicious*;
  xiōng hěn (sv): 凶狠, *vicious,
  malicious*;
SEE (请查看) **CRUEL, DETESTAR,
MAL, INTENCIONADO**

MANDATO; mandato; *mandate*;
  mìng lìng (v) (n): 命令 *to order/
  command; directive*;
  qiáng zhì (v) (attr) (sv): 强制, *to force/
  compel/ coerce; obligatory*;
  xùn lìng (n): 训令, *instructions, order,
  directive*;
SEE (请查看) **AUTORIZAR**

MANDÍBULA; mandíbula; *jaw,
mandible* ... **MAXILAR; maxilar;**
maxillary, jaw;
  hé: 颌, *jaw, mandible, maxillary*

MANICURA; manicure; *manicure*;
  xiū zhǐ jia (n): 修指甲, *manicure*

MANIFIESTO (A); **manifesto** (A);
evident, clear, manifest;
  míng bai (sv) (v): 明白, *clear, obvious,
  plain, manifest; to understand/realize/
  know*;
SEE (请查看) **OBVIO, OBVIAMENTE**

MANUFACTURA; manufatura;
product;
  yòng pǐn: 用品, *goods, products;
  appliances*;
  zhì pǐn: 制品, *product, merchandise*;
SEE (请查看) **RESULTA, PRODUCTO**

MANUSCRITO (A) (adj); **manuscrito**
(A); *handwritten*;
  bǐ jì de: 笔记的, *handwritten*;
  bǐ jì: 笔记, *a person's handwriting*;
  shǒu xiě tǐ: 手写体, *handwritten,
  script*;
  shǒu xiě: 手写, *handwritten*

MANUSCRITO (n); **manuscrito;**
manuscript;
  shǒu gǎo: 手稿, *manuscript*;
  yuán gǎo: 原稿, *original manuscript*

MAPA; mapa; *map*;
  dì tú: 地图, *map, atlas*

MARAVILLOSO (A); **maravilhoso** (A);
marvelous, wonderful;
  měi miào (sv): 美妙, *marvelous,
  wonderful, splendid*;
SEE (请查看) **ESTUPENDO,
MAGNIFICENCIA**

MARCA; marca; *mark*;
  biāo jì: 标记, *label, tab, mark, symbol*;
  biāo zhì wù: 标志物, *sign, mark,
  symbol*;
  biāo zhì: 标志, *sign, mark, emblem*;
  fú hào: 符号, *symbol, mark, sign*;
SEE (请查看) **CALIFICACIÓN,
DENOTAR, VESTIGIO**

MARCIAL; marcial; *martial (MIL)*;
  jūn fǎ: 军法, *martial law*;
  wǔ shù: 武术, *martial arts*

MARGARINA; margarina; *margarine*;
  rén zào huáng yóu: 人造黄油,
  margarine

MARGEN; margem; *margin*;
  biān jì: 边际, *limit, margin*;
  biān yuán (n): 边缘, *verge, edge,
  fringe, brink; margin, borderline*;
  yú dì: 余地, *margin, leeway, room*;
SEE (请查看) **DIFERENCIA**

MÁSCARA; máscara; *mask*;
  kǒu zhào: 口罩, *antiseptic/surgical/
  breathing mask*;
  miàn jù: 面具, *mask*;

SEE (请查看) CAMUFLAJE

MASCOTA; mascote; *mascot*;
jí xiáng wù: 吉祥物, *mascot*

MASCULINO (A); **masculino** (A);
male, manly, masculine;
　nán xìng: 男性, *male sex, man, virile*;
　nán zǐ hàn: 男子汉, *real/true man*;
　nán zǐ: 男子, *male, man*

MATERIALISMO; materialismo;
materialism ... **MATERIALISTA;**
materialista; *materialistic*;
　shí lì zhǔ yì (sv) (n): 实力主义,
　materialistic; materialism;
　wéi wù zhǔ yì zhě: 唯物主义者,
　materialist

MATERNIDAD; maternidade;
motherhood, maternity;
　mǔ qīn (sv) (n): 母亲, *maternal;*
　mother;
　mǔ qīn shēn fèn: 母亲身份,
　motherhood;
　yùn fù de: 孕妇的, *pregnant woman*

MATRIMONIO; matrimônio; *marriage,*
matrimony;
　hūn yīn: 婚姻, *matrimony*;
SEE (请查看) MARITAL

MÁXIMO (A) (adj); **máximo** (A); *highest,*
maximum;
　dǐng diǎn de: 顶点的, *maximum*;
　dǐng diǎn: 顶点, *acme, zenith,*
　pinnacle;
　duō de: 多的, *excessive; many*;
　jí xiàn: 极限, *limit, maximum*;
　zuì dà (vp): 最大, *biggest, biggest,*
　largest, greatest; maximum

MECANISMO; mecanismo;
mechanism, way of working;
　jī xiè zhuāng zhì: 机械装置,
　mechanism;
SEE (请查看) ARTEFACTO,
ASOCIACIÓN

MECANIZACIÓN; mecanização;
mechanization;

shǐ jī xiè huà: 使机械化,
mechanization

MEDIA; **médio** (A); *middle, medium;*
average;
　xún cháng (sv): 寻常, *usual, ordinary,*
　average, common;
　zhōng céng: 中层, *middle level*;
　zhōng jiān: 中间, *center, middle, core*;
SEE (请查看) BANAL, CENTRAL,
SECUNDARIO

MEDICACIÓN; medicação;
medication, treatment ...
MEDICAMENTO; medicamento;
medicine ... **MÉDICO** (A); **médico** (A);
medical;
　yào liáo fǎ: 药疗法, *medication*
　yào pǐn: 药品, *drugs, medicines*;
　yào wù: 药物, *pharmaceuticals*;
　yào yòng de: 药用的, *medicinal*;
　yào: 药, *medicine, drug, remedy*;
　yī liáo: 医疗, *medical treatment, care*;
　yì xué: 医学, *medicine, medical science*

MEDIOCRIDAD; mediocridade;
mediocrity; indifferent, ordinary;
　dī liè (sv): 低劣, *inferior, low-grade*;
　píng yōng (sv): 平庸, *mediocre,*
　commonplace;
　píng yōng de rén: 平庸的人,
　mediocrity (person);
SEE (请查看) MEDIA

MEGÁFONO; megafone; *megaphone*;
　kuò yīn qì: 扩音器, *megaphone*

MELANCOLÍA; melancolia;
melancholy, sadness;
　bēi 'āi (sv) (n): 悲哀, *grieved, sorrowful;*
　sorrow, sadness;
SEE (请查看) ADVERSIDAD,
DESILUSIÓN

MELODÍA; melodia; *melody* ...
MELÓDICO (A); **melódico** (A); *melodic*;
　gē qǔ: 歌曲, *song*;
　qǔ diào (n) (sv): 曲调, *tunes, melodies;*
　melodic;
　xuán lǜ: 旋律, *melody, tune*

MEMBRANA; membrana; *membrane;*
 bó mó: 薄膜, *membrane, film;*
 mó (bf): 膜, *membrane*

MEMORIA; memória; *memory;*
 huí yì (v) (n): 回忆, *to recall; recollection;*
 jì yì (v) (n): 记忆, *to remember/recall; memory, memorization;*
 jì yì lì: 记忆力, *ability to remember*

MENDICANTE; mendicante; *mendicant; beggar;*
 qǐ gài: 乞丐, *beggar;*
 yào fàn (v) (n): 要饭, *to beg for food/ money; beggar*

MENSUAL; mensalmente; *monthly;*
 měi yuè (sv) (adv): 每月, *monthly, every month;*
 yuè bào: 月报, *monthly magazine/ report, etc.;*
 yuè kān: 月刊, *monthly magazine, monthly;*
 yuè lì: 月历, *monthly interest;*
 yuè piào: 月票, *monthly bus pass;*
 yuè xīn: 月薪, *monthly pay/salary*

MENTALIDAD; mentalidade; *mentality;*
 sī xiǎng fāng fǎ: 思想方法, *method/ mode/way of thinking;*
 xīn tài: 心态, *psychology, mentality;*
SEE (请查看) INTELIGENCIA

MERCANTE; mercante; *merchant ...*
MERCANTIL; mercantil; *mercantile, commercial ...* **MERCANTILISMO; mercantilismo;** *mercantilism;*
 mào yì de: 贸易的, *mercantile;*
 mào yì zhǔ yì: 贸易主义, *mercantilism*
 shāng rén: 商人, *merchant;*
 shāng yè (sv) (n): 商业, *mercantile; commerce, business*

MERCURIO; mercúrio; *mercury; Mercury (ASTROL);*
 gǒng: 汞, *mercury;*
 shuǐ yín: 水银, *mercury, quicksilver*

MÉRITO; mérito; *merit, worth;*
 gōng dé: 功德, *merits, charitable acts;*
 jià zhí (n) (v): 价值, *value, worth; to cost;*
 yǒu gōng de: 有功的, *meritorious;*
 yōu diǎn: 优点, *merit*

MERO (A); **mero** (A); *mere, simple, bare, basic;*
 jī chǔ (n) (attr): 基础, *base, foundation; basis; basic, fundamental;*
SEE (请查看) FUNDAMENTAL

METABOLISMO; metabolismo; *metabolism;*
 xīn chén dài xiè: 新陈代谢, *metabolism*

METÁFORA; metáfora; *metaphor ...*
METAFÓRICO (A); **metafórico** (A); *metaphorical;*
 àn yù: 暗喻, *metaphor;*
 bǐ yù (n) (v): 比喻, *analogy, metaphor; to compare/ draw an analogy;*
 yǐn yù (sv) (n): 隐喻, *metaphorical; metaphor*

METALIZADO; metálico; *metallic;*
 hán jīn shǔ de: 含金属的, *metallic taste;*
 jīn shǔ xìng de: 金属性的, *metallic;*
 jīn shǔ zhì de: 金属质的, *made of metal, metallic;*
 jīn shǔ: 金属, *metals (in general)*

METALURGIA; metalurgia; *metallurgy;*
 yě jīn shù: 冶金术, *metallurgy;*
 yě jīn xué: 冶金学, *metallurgy*

METANO; metano; *methane;*
 jiǎ wán: 甲烷, *methane;*
 zhǎo qì: 沼气, *methane, marsh gas*

METEÓRICO (A); **meteórico** (A); *meteoric, brief, temporary, transient;*
 zàn shí (adv) (attr): 暂时, *temporarily; temporary, transient;*
SEE (请查看) BREVE, TEMPORAL

METEORITO; meteorito; *meteorite ...*
METEORO; meteoro; *meteor;*
  liú xīng: 流星, *meteor, shooting star;*
  yǔn xīng: 陨星, *meteorite*

METICULOSIDAD; meticulosidade;
meticulousness ... **METICULOSO** (A);
meticuloso (A); *meticulous, fastidious;*
thorough;
  jīng xì (sv): 精细, *meticulous, fine;*
  jīng xīn (sv): 精心, *meticulous,*
  elaborate;
  wú wēi bù zhì (fe): 无微不至,
  meticulously; in every possible way;
  xì zhì (sv): 细致, *fastidious, meticulous,*
  careful, scrupulous; precise, intricate;
  zǐ xì (sv) (v): 仔细, *careful, attentive; to*
  be careful;
SEE (请查看) **ATENCIÓN,**
COMPLETO, DILIGENCIA, CRÍTICA,
EXHAUSTIVO

METÓDICO (A); **metódico** (A);
methodical, organized, systematic;
  jǐng jǐng yǒu tiáo (fe): 井井有条,
  shipshape, methodical;
  jǐng rán (sv) (wr): 井然, *tidy,*
  methodical;
  jǐng rán yǒu xù (fe): 井然有序,
  orderly;
  yǒu tiáo bù wěn (fe): 有条不紊,
  methodical, systematical;
  yǒu tiáo lǐ (fe): 有条理, *systematic,*
  orderly;
  yǒu xì tǒng (sv): 有系统, *systematic;*
  yǒu zǔ zhī de (adv): 有组织地,
  systemically, in an organized way

MÉTODO; método; *method, way,*
means, manner, approach;
  fāng fǎ: 方法, *method, way, means,*
  device, manner, mode, principle;
  shǒu duàn: 手段, *method, means;*
SEE (请查看) **DISPOSICIÓN**

MÉTRICO (A); **métrico** (A); *metric;*
  gōng zhì de: 公制的, *metric*

METRO; metro; *meter;*
  biǎo (n): 表, *table, form, list; meter;*

watch; (bf) surface, exterior; model,
example; indicate
  mǐ: 米, *unit (a meter);*
  tíng chē jì shí qì: 停车计时器,
  parking meter;
  yí biǎo: 仪表, *meter for gas/water, etc.;*

METRÓPOLI; metrópole;
metropolis ... **METROPOLITANO** (A);
metropolitano (A); *metropolitan;*
  dà dū shì (n) (sv): 大都市, *metropolis;*
  metropolitan

MICROBIO; micróbio; *microbe;*
  wēi shēng wù: 微生物, *microbe*

MICROSCOPIO; microscópio;
microscope;
  xiǎn wēi jìng: 显微镜, *microscope*

MIGRACIÓN; migração; *migration;*
  yí jū: 移居, *migration of people;*
  qiān xǐ: 迁徙, *migration of birds*

MILITAR (adj); **militar;** *military;*
  jūn duì de: 军队的, *military;*
  jūn duì: 军队, *armed forces; army,*
  troops;
  jūn rén: 军人, *soldier, serviceman;*
  jūn shì: 军事, *military affairs, the*
  military;
  jūn yòng (attr): 军用, *for military use;*
  military

MINA; mina; *mine, strip mine;*
  kuàng jǐng: 矿井, *mine, pit;*
  kuàng shān: 矿山, *mine;*
  kuàng: 矿, *mine, mineral, deposit, ore*

MINIATURA; miniatura; *miniature,*
small, tiny, diminutive, little;
  wēi bó (sv): 微薄, *meager, scanty;*
  xiǎo xíng (attr): 小型, *small-sized,*
  small-scale, miniature;
SEE (请查看) **DIMINUTO**

MÍNIMO (A); **mínimo** (A); *minimum,*
minimal, least, slightest;
  jí xiǎo (adv): 极小, *minimum/least;*
  qǐ mǎ (adv): 起码, *minimum; at least;*

zuì dī (adv): 最低, *lowest, minimum*;
zuì dī de: 最低的, *lowest, smallest*;
zuì shǎo de: 最少的, *little*;
zuì xiǎo: 最小, *least*

MINISTRO (A); **ministro** (A); *minister*;
dà chén: 大臣, *high officials, cabinet ministers*;
mù shi: 牧师, *(religious) minister, pastor, priest, clergyman*;
SEE (请查看) **MINISTERIAL**

MINÚSCULO (A); **minúsculo** (A); *minuscule, minute, tiny*;
jí xiǎo de: 极小的, *minuscule*;
shǎo de: 少的, *minuscule; few, little*

MINUTO; **minuto**; *minute of time*;
fēn zhōng: 分钟, *minute*;
piàn kè: 片刻, *a moment, a short while*

MIOPÍA; **miopia**; *myopia*;
jìn shì (sv) (n): 近视, *myopic; short-sighted, myopia*

MISCELÁNEA; **miscelânea**; *miscellany*;
dà zá huì: 大杂烩, *hodgepodge*;
hùn hé wù: 混合物, *mixture, miscellany*

MISERIA; **miséria**; *poverty, destitution*;
hán suān: 寒酸, *poverty-stricken; shabby, wretched*;
pín hán (sv): 贫寒, *poverty-stricken*;
pín kùn (sv): 贫困, *poor, impoverished*;
pín qióng (sv): 贫穷, *poor, needy*;
SEE (请查看) **DIFÍCIL, AFLICCIÓN, INDIGENTE**

MÍSERO (A); **mísero** (A); *miserly; wretched, stingy, mean*;
lìn sè (sv): 吝啬, *stingy, tight, miserly*;
lìn sè guǐ (n): 吝啬鬼, *miser, skinflint*;
shǒu cái nú: 守财奴, *scrooge, miser*

MISIONERO (A); **missionário** (A); *missionary*;
chuán jiào shì: 传教士, *missionary*

MISTERIO; **mistério**; *mystery, puzzle, enigma, riddle, conundrum* ...
MISTERIOSO (A); **misterioso** (A); *mysterious* ... **MÍSTICO** (A); **místico** (A); *mystical (adj), mystic (n)*;
mí (n): 谜, *riddle, conundrum; enigma; mystery*;
mí yǔ (n): 谜语, *riddle, conundrum*;
shén mì xìng (attr) (n): 神秘性, *mystical, mysterious*;
shén mì zhǔ yì zhě: 神秘主义者, *mystic*;
shén qí (sv): 神奇, *magical, mystical, miraculous*;
xuán miào (sv): 玄妙, *mysterious, abstruse*;
yí 'àn (n): 疑案, *suspicious matter, mystery*;
SEE (请查看) **CLANDESTINIDAD, ENIGMÁTICO, PROBLEMA**

MODELO; **modelo**; *model, brand, design, replica*;
kuān shì (n): 款式, *style, design*;
mó shì (n): 模式, *model, pattern*;
mú jù (n): 模具, *mold, pattern*;
mú zi (n): 模子, *matrix, mold, pattern*;
shāng biāo (n): 商标, *brand, logo, trademark*;
xíng hào (n): 型号, *model, type, version*;
SEE (请查看 **DESIGNIO, EJEMPLO, GÉNERO**

MODERADO (A); **moderado** (A); *moderate, reasonable* ... **MÓDICO** (A); **módico** (A); *moderate; modest, reasonable*;
bù guò fèn (sv): 不过分, *not excessive*;
wēn hé (sv): 温和, *calm, quiet, moderate*;
yǒu lǐ (sv): 有理, *reasonable; justified*;
SEE (请查看) **CORRECTAMENTE, RAZONABLE, PACÍFICO, LIMITADO**

MODERNISMO; **modernismo**; *modernism* ... **MODERNIZACIÓN**; **modernização**; *modernization* ...
MODERNO (A); **moderno** (A); *modern*;
xiàn dài zhǔ yì: 现代主义, *modernism*;

xiàn dài huà: 现代化, *modernization*;
xīn shì (attr) (sv): 新式, *new style, modern*;
jìn dài (n): 近代, *recent, modern times*;
shí máo (sv): 时髦, *fashionable, in vogue, modern*;
SEE (请查看) **CONTEMPORÁNEO**

MODESTIA; modéstia; *modesty ...*
MODESTO (A); **modesto** (A); *modest, restrained, diffident; humble*;
pǔ sù (sv): 朴素, *simple, plain, frugal, thrifty, modest*;
qiān xū (v) (sv): 谦虚, *to speak modestly; modest, unassuming*;
xiū qiè (v) (sv): 羞怯, *to be shy/ timid/sheepish; modest*;
SEE (请查看) **DECORO, EDUCADO, CORRECTO, CORRECTAMENTE, HUMILDAD, RESERVADO**

MODIFICACIÓN; modificação;
modification, alteration, change;
biàn gēng (v) (n): 变更, *to change/ modify; modification*;
SEE (请查看) **AJUSTAR**

MODO; modo; *way, manner, procedure, method*;
bàn fǎ: 办法, *way, means*;
chéng xù: 程序, *procedure, program*;
fāng shì: 方式, *way of life; style/ pattern of life*;
SEE (请查看) **FÓRMULA, COSTUMBRE, MÉTODO, ESTILO, NORMA**

MODOS; modos; *manners, behavior*;
biǎo shuài: 表率, *model, good example*;
wéi rén (v) (n): 为人, *to behave; behavior*;
xíng wéi: 行为, *behavior, conduct*;
yí tài: 仪态, *bearing, behavior*;
SEE (请查看) **ASPECTO, COMUNICAR, EDUCADO, COSTUMBRE**

MOLÉCULA; molécula; *molecule*;
fēn zǐ: 分子, *molecule (QUIM)*

MOLESTIA; moléstia; *ailment; nuisance, inconvenience, bother; trouble*;
bù fāng biàn: 不方便, *inconvenient*;
dǎ rǎo (v) (n): 打扰, *to disturb/trouble; trouble, inconvenience*;
má fan de rén: 麻烦的人, *nuisance (person)*;
má fan de wù: 麻烦的物, *nuisance (sthg)*;
shāng nǎo jīn (sv): 伤脑筋, *bothersome, to be a headache*;
tǎo rén xián (sv): 讨人嫌, *disagreeable, annoying*;
SEE (请查看) **DESAGRADABLE, DESASTRE, INOPORTUNO, CONFLICTIVO**

MOMENTO; momento; *moment ...*
MOMENTÁNEO (A); **momentâneo** (A); *momentary, temporary, brief*;
piàn kè: 片刻, *moment, a short while*;
shí hou: 时候, *duration of time, moment, a point in time*;
zàn shí de (adv) (attr): 暂时地, *temporarily; temporary, transient*;
SEE (请查看) **BREVE, CONTINUADO, INSTANTÁNEO**

MONETARIO (A); **monetário** (A); *monetary*;
huò bì (sv) (n): 货币, *monetary; money*;
qián de: 钱的, *monetary*

MONOLÍTICO (A); **monolítico** (A); *monolithic, massive, huge*;
jiān rú pán shí de (fe): 坚如磐石的, *solid as a rock*;
zhěng kuài shí tou de: 整块石头的, *solid block, entire piece; (attr) monolithic*;
SEE (请查看) **COLOSAL**

MONÓLOGO; monólogo; *monologue, soliloquy*;
dú bái: 独白, *monologue, soliloquy*

MONOPOLIO; monopólio; *monopoly*;
lǒng duàn: 垄断, *monopoly*;
zhuān mài quán: 专卖权, *patent, monopoly right, monopoly*

MONOTONÍA; monotonia; *monotony, tedious, dull, routine* **... MONÓTONO** (A); **monótono** (A); *monotonous, dreary, humdrum*;
  cāng bái (sv): 苍白, *dull, bland, wan; pale, pallid*;
  dān diào (sv): 单调, *monotonous, dull; drab, humdrum*;
  píng dàn (sv): 平淡, *flat, dull, ordinary*;
  qiān piān yī lǜ (fe): 千篇一律, *be stereotyped, follow the same pattern*;
  qiān piān yī lǜ de: 千篇一律的, *monotonous*;
SEE (请查看**) CONVENCIONAL, UNIPERSONAL**

MONSTRUO; monstro; *huge, enormous, monster; superstar...* **MONSTRUOSIDAD; monstruosidade;** *monstrosity; gigantic; outrageous ...* **MONSTRUOSO** (A); **monstruoso** (A); *monstrous; disfigured; absurd*;
  cán rěn de rén: 残忍的人, *monster*;
  chāo jí míng xīng: 超级明星, *superstar*;
  duō duō guài shì (fe): 咄咄怪事, *monstrosity, absurdity*;
  guài mú guài yàng (fe): 怪模怪样, *grotesque*;
  guài wu (n): 怪物, *monster, freak; eccentric person*;
  guài yì (sv): 怪异, *monstrous, strange*;
  jī xíng (n) (sv): 畸形, *deformity (MED); giant, enormous*;
  jù xíng (sv) (n): 巨型, *giant, enormous; deformity (MED)*;
  páng rán dà wù (fe): 庞然大物, *colossus, giant, monster*;
  pò xiàng (n) (v): 破相, *disfigurement; to be afraid*;
SEE (请查看**) ENORME, MONOLÍTICO, ATROCIDAD, DESMEDIDO, DIABLO, GROTESCO, GIGANTESCO**

MONUMENTO; monumento; *monument, memorial*;
  jì niàn bēi: 纪念碑, *memorial, monumental*;
  pái wèi: 牌位, *memorial tablet/plaque*

MONTAÑERO (A); **montanhista; alpinista;** *mountaineer ...* **MONTAÑOSO** (A) (adj); **montanhoso** (A); *mountainous*;
  dēng shān yùn dòng: 登山运动, *mountaineering*;
  duō shān (attr): 多山, *mountainous*;
  pá shān jiā: 爬山家, *mountaineer*;
  shān dì: 山地, *mountainous region*;
  shān mài: 山脉, *mountain range*;
  shān qū: 山区, *mountainous area*

MORATORIA; moratória; *moratorium, halt, delay*;
  zàn jìn (n) (v): 暂禁, *moratorium; to prohibit/arrest*;
  zàn tíng (v) (n): 暂停, *to suspend; time out (DEP)*

MORBO; mórbido (A); *morbid pleasure, illness; macabre ...* **MORBOSIDAD; morbidez;** *morbidity, disordered, unsound*;
  bìng tài (n): 病态, *morbid/abnormal state (MED)*;
  bìng tài xīn lǐ: 病态心理, *morbidity (MED); morbid psychology/mentally*;
SEE (请查看**) DESILUSIÓN**

MORDAZ; mordaz; *caustic, biting, scathing*;
  fěng cì (sv): 讽刺, *caustic, biting*;
  jiān suān (sv): 尖酸, *acrimonious, tart*;
SEE (请查看**) CÁUSTICO**

MORFINA; morfina; *morphine*;
  mǎ fēi: 吗啡, *morphine*

MORTALIDAD; mortalidade; *mortality*;
  sǐ wáng lǜ: 死亡率, *mortality*;
  zhì mìng xìng: 致命性, *vulnerability*

MOSAICO; mosaico; *mosaic*;
  mǎ sài kè: 马赛克, *mosaic (loan)*;
  xiāng qiàn huà: 镶嵌画, *mosaic*

picture/design, mosaic;
xiāng qiàn xì gōng: 镶嵌细工, *inlaid work, mosaic*

MOSTAZA; mostarda; *mustard;*
jiè mo: 芥末, *mustard*

MOTIVACIÓN; motivação; *motivation, motive;*
dòng jī: 动机, *motive;*
SEE (请查看**) EFUSIVO, ÍMPETU, INTENCIÓN**

MOTIVO; motivo; *reason, cause;*
chéng yīn: 成因, *origin, factor, cause;*
gēn yóu: 根由, *cause;*
gēn yuán: 根源, *source, origin, cause;*
qǐ yīn: 起因, *cause, origin;*
yuán yīn: 原因, *cause, reason;*
SEE (请查看**) INAUGURAR, JUSTIFICACIÓN**

MUCOSA; muco; *mucus;*
bí ti: 鼻涕, *nasal mucus;*
nián yè: 粘液, *mucus*

MUDO (A)**; mudo** (A)**;** *mute;*
wú shēng (vp) (attr)**:** 无声, *noiseless, silent; voiceless;*
yǎ (v) (sv) (bf)**:** 哑, *to be mute/dumb; hoarse; dud;*
yǎ ba (n) (v)**:** 哑巴, *dumb/mute person; to be dumb/mute; to keep quiet/mum;*
SEE (请查看**) RETICENCIA**

MULATO (A)**; mulato** (A)**;** *mulatto;*
hēi bái hùn xuè 'ér: 黑白混血儿, *mulatto*

MULTICOLOR; multicolor; *multicolored;*
cǎi sè (n)**:** 彩色, *color, variegation;*
wǔ cǎi (n)**:** 五彩, *multicolored*

MULTIPLICACIÓN; multiplicação; *multiplication;*
chéng fǎ: 乘法, *multiplication (MAT)*

MULTIPLICIDAD; multiplicidade; *multiplicity ...* **MÚLTIPLO** (A)**; múltiplo**
(A)**;** *multiple;*
bèi (m) (bf)**:** 倍, *times, -fold; twice, double;*
bèi shù: 倍数, *multiple (MAT);*
duō (sv) (prep)**:** 多, *many, much, more; poly-, multi-*
duō bèi (attr)**:** 多倍, *multiple;*
duō chóng (attr)**:** 多重, *multiple; diversified, multiple;*
fù hé: 复合, *multiple;*
SEE (请查看**) DIVERSO**

MULTIUSO; multiuso; *multi-purpose;*
duō gōng néng: 多功能, *multi-function, all-purpose;*

MUNICIPIO; município; *municipality;*
shì: 市, *municipality, city; market*

MURMULLO; murmúrio; *whisper, murmur;*
ěr yǔ (n) (v)**:** 耳语, *whisper; to whisper in sb's ear;*
qiāo shēng (adv)**:** 悄声, *in a low voice, quietly*

MÚSCULO; músculo; *muscle ...*
MUSCULOSO (A)**; musculoso** (A)**;** *muscular;*
jī ròu (sv) (n)**:** 肌肉, *muscular; muscle;*
qiáng zhuàng (sv)**:** 强壮, *muscular, strong, sturdy*

MUSEO; museu; *museum;*
bó wù guǎn: 博物馆, *museum*

MÚSICA; música; *music ...* **MÚSICO**
(A)**; músico** (A)**;** *musician (n), musical (adj);*
yīn yuè jiā: 音乐家, *musician;*
yīn yuè: 音乐, *music;*
yuè qǔ: 乐曲, *score, musical composition*

MUTANTE; mutante; *mutant;*
tū biàn tǐ: 突变体, *mutant*

MUTILACIÓN; mutilação; *mutilation; defacement, ruination, destruction;*
cán quē (vp)**:** 残缺, *incomplete, fragmentary;*
SEE (请查看**) ARRUINAR,**

DEMOLICIÓN, DESFAVORABLE

MUTILADO (A); **mutilado** (A); *mutilated; disabled; mangled, maimed*;
 shǐ cán fèi: 使残废, *to be maimed*;
SEE (请查看) **IMPOSIBILITADO, DISCAPACITADO**

MUTUO (A); **mútuo** (A); *mutual, joint*;
 gòng tóng de: 共同的, *mutual benefit, interest*;
 gòng yǒu de: 共有的, *mutual feeling, attraction*

Easily recognizable verbs and their Portuguese and Chinese equivalents
Verbos fácilmente reconocibles en Español-Portugués-Inglés y sus equivalentes en Chino
Verbos facilmente reconhecível em Espanhol-Português-Inglês e seus equivalentes em Chinês
很容易辨认的西班牙语，葡萄牙语，英语动词和他们的中文对等词

MANIFESTAR; manifestar, *to express/ display; to show/declare/demonstrate*;
 biǎo dá: 表达, *to express/convey ideas/ thoughts, etc.*;
 biǎo shì: 表示, *to express/show/ indicate an attitude/feelings, etc.*;
 chén liè: 陈列, *to display/exhibit*;
 chū shì: 出示, *to display/show*;
 luó liè: 罗列, *to list/enumerate/display*;
 shēn shù: 申述, *to state/express/ explain; demonstration; example*;
 xiàn chū: 现出, *to reveal/display*;
 xuān gào: 宣告, *to declare/proclaim*;
 yǎn shì: 演示, *to demonstrate*;
 zhǎn chū: 展出, *to exhibit/put on display*;
 zhǎn lǎn: 展览, *to exhibit/show*;
 zhǎn shì: 展示, *to reveal/show*;
 zhǎn xiāo: 展销, *to display for sale*;
SEE (请查看) **DECLARAR, DEMOSTRAR, COMUNICAR, DENOTAR, ILUSTRAR**

MANIPULAR; manipular; *to operate/ manipulate*;
 cāo zuò: 操作, *to operate equipment/ machinery*;
 qiān xiàn: 牵线, *to pull strings/ manipulate*;
 shǒu shù (n) (v): 手术, *surgery; to operate*;
SEE (请查看) **ACTUAR, ADMINISTRAR**

MANUFACTURAR; manufaturar; *to manufacture ...*

MATERIALIZAR; materializar; *to produce, bring into being, carry out, materialize*;
 chǎn shēng : 产生, *to produce/ emerge/come into bring*;
 chū chǎn (v) (n): 出产, *to produce/ manufacture; output, production*;
 niē zào: 捏造, *to fabricate/concoct/ trump up*;
 shēng chǎn: 生产, *to produce/ manufacture; to give birth*;
 shēng chéng: 生成, *to be born/ produced; to form/grow*;
SEE (请查看) **EMERGENTE, ELABORAR**

MATRICULAR; matricular; *to register/ enroll*;
 bào kǎo: 报考, *to sign up for/register for*;
 dēng jì: 登记, *to register a birth/death/ marriage; to register/check in*;
 guà hào: 挂号, *to register/take a number to be called*;
 lì 'àn: 立案, *to register/put on record; to file a matter for investigation/prosecute*;
 lì hù: 立户, *to register for a residence; to open a bank account*;
 zhāo shēng: 招生, *to enroll students*;
 zhù cè: 注册, *to enroll/register*;
SEE (请查看) **ADMITIR**

MECANIZAR; mecanizar; *to mechanize*;
 jī xiè huà: 机械化, *to mechanize*

MEDITAR; refletir; *to ponder/meditate on/think about;*
  gū liáng: 估量, *to appraise, estimate, assess; to reckon/figure;*
  héng liáng (v) (n): 衡量, *to weigh/ measure/judge/ evaluate; evaluation;*
  kǎo lǜ: 考虑, *to think over/consider;*
  sī liang: 思量, *to consider/turn sthg over in one's mind;*
  sī suǒ: 思索, *to think deeply/ponder;*
  yǎng shén: 养神, *to rest/meditate;*
SEE (请查看) CONTEMPLACIÓN, CONSIDERACIÓN, DELIBERAR, CONTEMPLAR, CONCENTRAR

MEMORIZAR; memorizar; *to memorize;*
  jì zhu: 记住, *to learn by heart; to keep in mind;*
  shú jì: 熟记, *to memorize/learn by heart*

MENCIONAR; mencionar; *to mention;*
  tán qǐ: 谈起, *to mention/speak of;*
  zhān biān: 沾边, *to mention briefly/ touch on;*
SEE (请查看) ALUDIR

MODELAR; modelar; *to mold/shape;*
  sù zào: 塑造, *to model/mold/shape;*
  zào xíng (n): 造型, *model/mold; modeling, mold making*

MODERNIZAR; modernizar; *to modernize/bring up to date;*
  shǐ xiàn dài huà: 使现代化, *to modernize*

MODIFICAR; modificar; *to alter/ modify/adapt;*
  xiū shì: 修饰, *to modify; to decorate;*
SEE (请查看) ADAPTAR, AJUSTAR, ALTERAR, MODIFICACIÓN

MOLESTAR; molestar; *to annoy/ bother;*
  dǎ jiǎo: 打搅, *to disturb/trouble/annoy;*
  láo shén: 劳神, *to bother/trouble;*
  sāo rǎo: 骚扰, *to harass/molest; to be agitated/troubled;*

SEE (请查看) ACOSAR, AGRAVAR, PERTURBAR

MONITORIZAR; monitorar; *to monitor;*
  jiān cè: 监测, *to monitor/supervise;*
  jiān kǎo: 监考, *to monitor/proctor an exam;*
  jiān kòng: 监控, *to monitor/inspect and control;*
  jiān shì: 监视, *to monitor, to keep watch on, to keep a lookout over;*
  jiān tīng: 监听, *to monitor*

MONOPOLIZAR; monopolizar; *to monopolize;*
  bāo bàn: 包办, *to monopolize/take sole charge of;*
SEE (请查看) CONTROLAR, MONOPOLIO

MOTIVAR; motivar; *to cause/motivate;*
  chǎng shēng: 产生, *to cause/bring about;*
  shǐ de: 使得, *to make/cause;*
  zhāo rě: 招惹, *to provoke/cause;*
  zào chéng: 造成, *to cause/bring about;*
SEE (请查看) CAUSAR, IMPELER

MOVER; mover; *to move/drive/ provoke/rouse;*
  dài dòng: 带动, *to spur on/drive/ power;*
SEE (请查看) AGITAR, PROVOCAR, FOMENTAR

MULTIPLICAR; multiplicar; *to multiply, increase; multiply (MAT);*
  zēng jiàn: 增建, *to extend/expand;*
  zēng shè: 增设, *to add/add on;*
  zēng shēng: 增生, *to proliferate, multiply;*
SEE (请查看) MULTIPLICACIÓN, MULTIPLICIDAD, AUMENTAR

MURMURAR; murmurar; *to murmur/ whisper/gossip;*
  dī yǔ: 低语, *to whisper/murmur;*
  xián tán: 闲谈, *to gossip with sb, to engage in chitchat*

N

Interchangeable Spanish-Portuguese-English words and their Chinese equivalents
Palabras en Español-Portugués-Inglés y sus equivalentes en Chino
Palavras em Espanhol-Português-Inglês e seus equivalentes em Chinês
西班牙语，葡萄牙语，英语及中文的对等单词

NASAL; nasal;
 bí de: 鼻的, *nasal passage/cavity; nasal congestion*

NATURAL; natural;
 chū yú běn xìng de: 出于本性的, *natural/innate aptitude/talent, etc.*;
 dà zì rán de: 大自然的, *natural disaster*;
 qīn shēng de: 亲生的, *natural/ biological father/ parent/sister*;
 tiān rán de: 天然的, *natural material/ product/food, etc.*;
 zhèng cháng de: 正常的, *normal/ natural*;
 zì rán de: 自然的, *natural/unaffected person/ manner*

NÁUSEA; náusea;
 ě xīn: 恶心, *nausea*

NAVAL; naval;
 chuán bó de: 船舶的, *naval boats, ships; shipping*;
 hǎi jūn: 海军, *navy*;
 jūn jiàn: 军舰, *warship, naval vessel*

NÉCTAR; néctar;
 huā mì: 花蜜, *nectar*

NEUTRÓN; nêutron;
 zhōng zǐ: 中子, *neutron*

NICK; nick; *internet nickname*;
 chuò hào: 绰号, *nickname*

NIRVANA; nirvana;
 niè pán: 涅磐, *nirvana*

NOMINAL; nominal;
 míng yì shàng de: 名义上的, *nominal leader/head, etc.*;
 wēi bù zú dào de: 微不足道的, *nominal fee/sum/ amount*

NORMAL; normal;
 duì tóu (vp): 对头, *correct, on the right tract; normal, right*;
 zhèng cháng de: 正常的, *normal life/ behaviour/ circumstances/person*;
 zì rán (n) (sv) (adv): 自然, *natural world; natural, normal; naturally, of course*

NOSTALGIA; nostalgia;
 huái jiù (sv): 怀旧, *nostalgic; to reminisce*;
 liàn jiù (v) (n): 恋旧, *to yearn for the past/old friends; nostalgia*

NUCLEAR; nuclear;
 hé dòng lì: 核动力, *nuclear power*;
 hé néng: 核能, *nuclear fission/physics/ weapon/ power/energy*;
 hé xīn: 核心, *nuclear reactor/core*

Easily recognizable Spanish-Portuguese-English nouns, adjectives and adverbs and their Chinese equivalents
Nombres, sustantivos, adjetivos y adverbios en Español-Portugués-Inglés y sus equivalentes en Chino
Nomes, substantivos, adjetivos e advérbios em Espanhol-Português-Inglês e seus equivalentes em Chinês
容易辨认的西班牙语，葡萄牙语，英语的名词，形容词和副词和他们的中文对等词

NACIONAL; nacional; *national, domestic* ... **NACIONALIDAD; nacionalidade;** *nationality* ... **NACIONALISMO; nacionalismo;** *nationalism* ... **NACIONALISTA; nacionalista;** *nationalistic;*

  guó cè: 国策, *national policy;*
  guó chǎn (sv): 国产, *domestic, domestically produced;*
  guó fáng: 国防, *national defense;*
  guó gē: 国歌, *national anthem;*
  guó gé: 国格, *national character/ honor; prestige;*
  guó guāng (attr): 国光, *national glory;*
  guó hún: 国魂, *national spirit/genius;*
  guó jí: 国籍, *nationality; national identity, citizenship;*
  guó jiā biāo zhǔn: 国家标准, *national standard;*
  guó jiā dà shì: 国家大事, *national/ state affairs;*
  guó jiā: 国家, *national interest;*
  guó kù: 国库, *national/state treasury;*
  guó mín: 国民, *citizen, national;*
  guó qí: 国旗, *national flag;*
  guó yǒu de: 国有的, *national, state-owned;*
  mín zú fú zhuāng: 民族服装, *national dress;*
  mín zú guó jiā: 民族国家, *nation-state; national interest;*
  mín zú sè cǎi: 民族色彩, *national style;*
  mín zú tè diǎn: 民族特点, *national characteristics;*
  mín zú zhǔ yì de (adj): 民族主义的, *nationalistic;*
  mín zú zhǔ yì zhě (n): 民族主义者, *nationalist;*
  mín zú zhǔ yì: 民族主义, *nationalism;*
  mín zú: 民族, *nationality, ethnic group;*
SEE (请查看**) INTERIOR**

NADA; nada; *nothing;*
  ér yǐ (aux): 而已, *that's all, nothing more, nothing but, only;*
  méi yǒu (n) (v): 没有, *nothing; to not have; there is not; to be without;*
  méi yǒu dōng xi: 没有东西, *nothing (person/thing);*
  méi yǒu shén me (v): 没有什么, *nothing the matter, nothing wrong;*
  méi yǒu shì qing: 没有事情, *nothing wrong/ doing/going on;*
  shén me yě méi yóu: 什么也没有, *not anything (nothing)*

NARCISISMO; narcisismo; *narcissism* ... **NARCISISTA; narcisista;** *narcissistic (adj), narcissist (n);*
  zì liàn (sv) (n): 自恋, *narcissistic; narcissism (MED);*
  zì wǒ táo zuì: 自我陶醉, *narcissist*

NARCÓTICO (A); **narcótico** (A); *narcotic;*
  má zuì de: 麻醉的, *narcotic drugs/ effects;*
  má zuì jì (n): 麻醉剂, *anesthesia, narcotic;*
  má zuì yào (n): 麻醉药, *anesthetic, narcotic, chloroform;*
SEE (请查看**) DROGA**

NARRACIÓN; narração, *story, narrative; narration, account* ... **NARRADOR** (A); **narrador;** *narrator* ... **NARRATIVO** (A) (adj); **narrativo** (A); *narrative;*
  gù shi: 故事, *story, tale, narrative; plot;*
  jì xù wén (n): 记叙文, *narration, narrative;*
  jiǎng shù (v) (n): 讲述, *to tell about/ narrate; narration;*
  jiě shuō (v) (n): 解说, *to explain orally; narration;*
  jiě shuō yuán: 解说员, *narrator in TV/ radio/movie;*
  xù shì tǐ (n): 叙事体, *descriptive style;*
  xù shù (n): 叙述, *narrative;*
  xù shù zhě: 叙述者, *narrator in a novel/play*

NATAL (adj); **natal;** *native of a country, locality, etc.* ... **NATIVO** (A); **nativo** (adj) (n); *native;*
  běn dì rén: 本地人, *native, a local person;*
  běn guó de: 本国的, *native country;*
  běn guó: 本国, *native of a place*

gù tǔ: 故土, *native land, motherland;*
jí guàn: 籍贯, *native place, ancestral home;*
mǔ yǔ de: 母语的, *native language/ tongue;*
tǔ shēng de: 土生的, *native plant/ species;*
tǔ shēng tǔ zhǎng (fe): 土生土长, *locally born and bred;*
tǔ zhù rén: 土著人, *native, aborigine;*
zǔ guó: 祖国, *native land, motherland*

NATURA; naturaleza; *nature;*
dà zì rán: 大自然, *nature;*
sù xìng: 素性, *nature;*
tiān xìng: 天性, *nature; natural instincts;*
zì rán jiè: 自然界, *natural world, nature;*
SEE (请查看) CARÁCTER, NORMAL

NATURALIDAD; naturalidade; *naturalness;*
tiān rán (attr): 天然, *natural;*
zào huà: 造化, *nature; Creator, Mother Nature;*
zì rán de: 自然的, *natural person, manner;*

NÁUTICO (A); **náutico** (A); *nautical ... NAVEGABLE;* **navegável;** *navigable, seaworthy ... NAVEGACIÓN;* **navegação;** *navigation ...* **NAVEGADOR; navegador;** *navigator on a ship; surfer on a computer; browser on internet;*
háng hǎi de: 航海的, *nautical;*
háng hǎi jiā: 航海家, *navigator; seafarer;*
háng hǎi zhě: 航海者, *navigator;*
kě tōng háng de: 可通航的, *navigable;*
lǐng háng (v) (n): 领航, *to pilot/ navigate; navigation;*
lǐng háng yuán: 领航员, *navigator, pilot;*
liú lǎn qì: 浏览器, *browser on internet*

NEBLINA; neblina; *mist, mistiness, haze ... NEBULOSO* (A); **nebuloso** (A); *nebulous; cloudy; vague, misty, obscure;*
àn (sv) (bf): 暗, *dark, dim, dull; hidden, secret, unclear;*
bó wù (n): 薄雾, *mist, haze, light fog;*
méng lóng (sv): 朦胧, *dim, hazy; obscure; half asleep, drowsy;*
mó hu (sv) (v): 模糊, *blurred, dim, nebulous, vague, fuzzy; to blur/obscure/ confuse;*
xīng yún (n) (sv): 星云, *nebula; nebulous*

NECESARIAMENTE; necessariamente; *necessarily;* **NECESARIO** (A); **necessário** (A); *necessary ...* **NECESIDAD; necessidade;** *need for sthg/to do sthg;*
bì rán (adj) (adv) (n): 必然, *inevitable, certain; certainly; necessity;*
bì rán xìng (n): 必然性, *necessity, certainty, inevitability;*
bì rán zhī shì (n): 必然之事, *a matter of necessity;*
bì xū (aux): 必须, *must/to have to;*
bì xū pǐn (n): 必需品, *necessities, necessaries, necessity;*
bì yào xìng (n): 必要性, *necessity;*
SEE (请查看) CÉNTRICO, DETERMINADO

NECESITADO (A); **necessitado** (A); *to be needy, in need of ...* **NECESITADOS; necessitados;** *the needy;*
pín kǔ (sv): 贫苦, *poverty-stricken;*
pín kùn (sv): 贫困, *poor, impoverished;*
pín kùn de rén: 贫困的人, *the needy;*
pín kùn hù: 贫困户, *destitute family;*
pín mín: 贫民, *poor people, the poor;*
qióng kǔ (sv): 穷苦, *impoverished, poverty-stricken;*
qióng rén: 穷人, *poor people, the poor;*
SEE (请查看) MISERIA

NECTARINA; nectarine; *nectarine;*
yóu táo: 油桃, *nectarine*

NEFASTO (A); **nefasto** (A); *ominous; ill-fated, unlucky, unfortunate;*
bù xiáng (attr): 不祥, *ominous, inauspicious;*

bù xiáng de: 不祥的, *ominous sign/ event/silence;*
dǎo méi (sv) 倒霉, *be out of luck;*
xiān zhào: 先兆, *omen;*
zhù dìng (adv): 注定, *to be doomed/ destined;*
zhù dìng dǎo méi (sv): 注定倒霉, *ill-fated, doomed;*
SEE (请查看) ADVERSIDAD, AUGURAR, PRESENTIMIENTO

NEGACIÓN; negação; *denial, refusal, negation* ... **NEGATIVA; negativa;** *refusal;*
  jù jué (n) (v): 拒绝, *refusal; to refuse; to reject/decline;*
SEE (请查看) DESAUTORIZAR

NEGATIVO; negativo; *photo negative; negative (MAT)* ... **NEGATIVO** (A) (adj); **negativo** (A); *negative;*
  dǐ piàn: 底片, *photo negative;*
  fù de: 负的, *negative (MAT);*
  fù jí: 负极, *negative electric charge;*
  fù miàn de: 负面的, *negative effect/ news;*
  xiāo jí de: 消极的, *negative person/ attitude/view; pessimistic;*
  yīn xìng de: 隐性的, *negative test/ result*

NEGLIGENCIA; negligência; *negligence* ... **NEGLIGENTE; negligente;** *negligent, careless;*
  cū xīn (sv) (n): 粗心, *careless, thoughtless; carelessness;*
  cū xīn dà yì (fe): 粗心大意, *negligent, inadvertent , careless;*
  wán hū zhí shǒu: 玩忽职守, *carelessness;*
SEE (请查看) DESATENCIÓN

NEGOCIACIÓN; negociação; *negotiation;*
  qià tán (v) (n): 洽谈, *to negotiate; discussions, negotiations;*
  tán pàn: 谈判, *negotiations, talks; bargaining*

NEGOCIANTE; negociante; *businessman or woman, dealer;*
  fàn zi: 贩子, *dealer;*
  kè shāng: 客商, *business people;*
  nǚ shāng rén: 女商人, *business woman;*
  shāng rén: 商人, *businessman, merchant, trader*

NEGOCIO; negocio; *business;*
  jiāo yì (n) (v): 交易, *deal, trade, business; to bargain;*
  mǎi mai: 买卖, *business, deal;*
  shāng jī: 商机, *business, opportunities;*
  shāng jiā: 商家, *businessman; enterprise, business firm;*
  shāng jiè: 商界, *business circles;*
  shāng wù: 商务, *business, affairs;*
  shāng yè mì mì: 商业秘密, *business secrets;*
  shāng yè: 商业, *business, commerce, trade;*
  shēng yì: 生意, *business, trade;*
  shì qing: 事情, *matter, affair, business;*
  yè wù: 业务, *business;*
SEE (请查看) INDUSTRIAL

NEGRO (A); **negro** (A); *black color/ person; pessimistic;*
  hēi rén:黑人, *black person;*
  hēi sè: 黑色, *black;*
SEE (请查看) FATALISMO, LÍVIDO

NEÓFITO (A); **neófito** (A); *neophyte;*
  jiàn xí xiū shì: 见习修士, *novice, beginner;*
  jīng yàn (n) (v): 经验, *experience; to go through sthg; to experience sthg;*
  wú jīng yān (sv): 无经验, *inexperienced;*
SEE (请查看) NOVATO, DEBUTANTE

NEOLÍTICO (A); **neolítico** (A); *Neolithic (period);*
  xīn shí qì shí dài de: 新石器时代的, *Neolithic*

NEPOTISMO; nepotismo; *nepotism;*
  qún dài guān xi: 裙带关系, *nepotism;*
  rèn rén wéi qīn: 任人唯亲, *favoritism*

NERVIO; nervo; *nerve (ANAT)* ...
NERVIOSISMO (adj); **nervosismo;**
nervousness ... **NERVIOSO** (A);
nervoso (A); *nervous (ANAT); excitable;*
  shén jīng zhì: 神经质, *nervousness;*
  shén jīng: 神经, *nerve;*
  yǒng qì: 勇气, *courage, nerve (MED);*
SEE (请查看) **DESCONCERTANTE,**
TENSO

NEUMÁTICO (A); **pneumático** (A);
pneumatic;
  kě chōng qì (sv): 可充气, *pneumatic*

NEUMOMÍA; pneumonia; *pneumonia;*
  fèi yán: 肺炎, *pneumonia*

NEUROLOGÍA; neurologia; *neurology*
... **NEURÓLOGO** (A); **neurologista;**
neurologist;
  shén jīng bìng xué: 神经病学,
  neurology;
  shén jīng bìng xué jiā: 神经病学家,
  neurologist

NEURÓTICO (A); **neurótico** (A);
neurotic;
  shén jīng zhì (sv): 神经质, *neurotic;*
  shén jīng zhì zhě (n): 神经质者,
  neurotic

NEUTRALIDAD; neutralidade;
neutrality;
  zhōng lì: 中立, *neutrality*

NEVADA; nevada; *snowfall;*
  bào fēng xuě: 暴风雪, *snowstorm,*
  blizzard;
  xià xuě (n) (v): 下雪, *snow; to snow;*
  xià xuě le: 下雪了, *it is snowing;*
  xuě: 雪, *snow*

NEVADO (A); **nevado** (A); *snow covered*
or capped;
  xuě bái (vp): 雪白, *snow-white; snowy*
  white;
  xuě chǎng: 雪场, *snow pack;*
  xuě dì: 雪地, *snowfield;*
  xuě dǐng de: 雪顶的, *snowcapped;*
  xuě dǐng: 雪顶, *snowcap;*

  xuě jǐng: 雪景, *snow scene;*
  xuě pō: 雪坡, *snow bank;*
  xuě qū: 雪区, *snow patch/region;*
  xuě xiàn: 雪线, *snow line;*
  xuě yuán: 雪原, *snowfield*

NEXO; nexo; *link, connection, nexus;*
  guān jié: 关节, *join (BIOL), key/crucial*
  link;
  huán jié: 环节, *segment (BIOL), link;*
SEE (请查看) **ASOCIACIÓN**

NICHO; nicho; *niche;*
  bì kān: 壁龛, *niche for a statue; niche*
  in a wall;
  kòng bái: 空白, *niche/place in market/*
  organization/field

NICOTINA; nicotina; *nicotine;*
  ní gǔ dīng: 尼古丁, *nicotine*

NIEBLA; neblina; *fog;*
  wù qì: 雾气, *fog, mist;*
  dà wù: 大雾, *fog;*
SEE (请查看) **NEBLINA**

NIMBO; nimbo; *nimbus (METEO), halo;*
  guāng huán: 光环, *ring of light, halo*
  (RELIG);
  guāng lún: 光轮, *halo of saint, angel;*
  rì yùn: 日晕, *solar halo;*
  yuè yùn: 月晕, *lunar halo;*
  yǔ yún: 雨云, *nimbus*

NINFÓMANA; ninfomaníaca;
nymphomaniac;
  nǚ sè qíng kuáng: 女色情狂,
  nymphomania;
  sè qíng kuáng (n): 色情狂, *sex mania;*
  sè qíng kuáng rén: 色情狂人,
  nymphomaniac

NITRATO; nitrato; *nitrate* ... **NÍTRICO**
(A); **nitrato** (A); *nitric;*
  xiāo shí: 硝石, *nitric (QUIM); niter,*
  saltpeter;
  xiāo suān yán: 硝酸盐, *nitrate (QUIM)*

NITRÓGENO; nitrogênio; *nitrogen;*
  dàn: 氮, *nitrogen*

NOBLEZA; nobreza; *nobility;*
 gāo shàng: 高尚, *quality of nobility;*
 guì zú: 贵族, *the nobility*

NOCTURNO (A); **noturno** (A);
notívago (A); *nocturnal; night;*
 wǎn jiān: 晚间, *in the evening, at night;*
 wǎn shang: 晚上, *evening;*
 yè jiān: 夜间, *at night;*
 yè lǐ: 夜里, *at night, nighttime;*
 yè wǎn: 夜晚, *evening, night;*
 zài yè jiān huó dòng de: 在夜间活动
 的, *nocturnal*

NÓDULO; nódulo; *nodule;*
 jié: 节, *joint, knot, node;*
 xiǎo liú: 小瘤, *nodule*

NÓMADA; nômade; *nomadic (adj),*
nomad (n);
 liú làng zhě de: 流浪者的, *nomadic;*
 liú làng zhě: 流浪者, *vagrant;*
 yóu mù bù luò de rén: 游牧部落的
 人, *nomadic*

NOMBRE; nome; *name;*
 míng shēng: 名声, *name, reputation,*
 image;
 míng zi: 名字, *name of a person/thing*

NORMA; norma; *rule, norm, standard;*
regulation;
 běn wèi: 本位, *standard;*
 chéng xù: 程序, *procedure, order,*
 course, sequence;
 fǎ diǎn: 法典, *legal code;*
 guī chéng: 规程, *rules, regulations;*
 guī dìng (v) (n): 规定, *to stipulate/fix/*
 formulate; rule, regulation, stipulation;
 guī gé: 规格, *specifications, norms,*
 standards;
 guī zé: 规则, *rule, regulation;*
 guī zhāng: 规章, *rules, regulations;*
 shǒu zé: 守则, *rule, regulation;*
 tiáo lì: 条例, *regulations, rules,*
 ordinance;
 tiáo lìng: 条令, *regulations;*
 zhāng chéng: 章程, *regulation,*
 constitution;
 zhǔn zé: 准则, *standard, norm,*
 criterion;

SEE (请查看) CRITERIO

NORMALIDAD; normalidade;
normality, normalcy ...
NORMALMENTE; normalmente;
normally, usually;
 àn lǐ (adv): 按理, *normally, in principle,*
 theoretically;
 cháng cháng (adv): 常常, *frequently,*
 usually, often;
 cháng tài: 常态, *normality, normal*
 behavior/ conditions; (attr) normal;
 chéng guī: 成规, *established practice,*
 set rules; rut;
 chǐ dù: 尺度, *scale, dimension,*
 standard, measure;
 jié zòu: 节奏, *rhythm, beat; pattern;*
 sù lái (adv): 素来, *usually, always;*
 tōng cháng (adv): 通常, *usually,*
 ordinarily;
 tōng cháng de (adv): 通常地,
 normally, usually;
SEE (请查看) NORMAL, BANAL,
DISCIPLINA, COSTUMBRE,
CRITERIO, RUTINA

NORMATIVO (A) (adj); **normativo** (A);
normative, prescriptive;
 bù biàn: 不变, *fixed; (attr) fixed,*
 constant;
 guī zé (n) (sv): 规则, *rule, regulation;*
 regular, fixed;
 yuē dìng sú chéng (fe): 约定俗成,
 established by usage, customary,
 conventional, prescriptive;
 zhǐ dìng (v) (n) (sv): 指定, *to appoint/*
 assign; specification; prescriptive;
SEE (请查看) FIRME, HABITUAL,
NORMA

NOROESTE; noroeste; *northwestern*
(direction), northwest (region);
 xī běi (sv) (n): 西北, *northwestern;*
 northwest;
 xiàng xī běi de (adv): 向西北地,
 northwesterly

NORORIENTAL; nordeste;
northeastern (direction), northeast
(region);

dōng běi (sv) (n): 东北, *northeastern; northeast*

NORTE (adj); **norte**; *north, northern;*
 běi fāng (sv) (n): 北方, *northern; north*

NOSTÁLGICO (A); **nostálgico** (A); *nostalgic; homesick;*
 huái niàn: 怀念, *to cherish a memory;*
 lìng rén huái jiù de: 令人怀旧的, *nostalgic trip/ memory/ song/book*

NOTA; nota; *note;*
 bèi zhù: 备注, *notes;*
 yīn fú: 音符, *written/printed musical note;*
SEE (请查看) **ANOTACIÓN**

NOTACIÓN; notação; *notation;*
 fú hào: 符号, *notation, symbol, mark, code;*
 biāo jì: 标记, *sign, mark, symbol, token; notation*

NOTARIO (A); **notário** (A); *notary, notary public*
 gōng zhèng rén: 公证人, *notary*

NOTICIA; notícia; *the news ...*
NOTICIERO; noticiário; *news bulletin;*
 bào dào (v) (n): 报道, *to report the news; news report;*
 jiǎn bào: 简报, *bulletin, brief report; briefing;*
 jiǎn xùn: 简讯, *news in brief;*
 tōng xùn (v) (n): 通讯, *to communicate; news report, dispatch, correspondence, newsletter;*
 xiāo xi: 消息, *news, information;*
 xīn wén jiǎn bào: 新闻简报, *news bulletin;*
 xīn wén: 新闻, *news on TV/radio;*
 xìn xī: 信息, *information, news, message*

NOTORIO (A); **notório** (A); *famous; obvious, widely-known;*
 chòu míng yuǎn yáng (fe): 臭名远扬, *notorious;*
 chòu míng zhāo zhù (n) (sv): 臭名昭

著, *notoriety; notorious;*
 zhù chēn (sv): 著称, *celebrated, famous;*
SEE (请查看) **CÉLEBRE, EGREGIO, AFAMADO, CONSPICUO**

NOVATO (A); **novato** (A); *inexperienced, novice, beginner;*
 xīn shǒu: 新手, *beginner*
SEE (请查看) **NEÓFITO, DEBUTANTE**

NOVELA; novela; *soap opera; story; novel;*
 féi zào jù: 肥皂剧, *soap opera;*
 gù shi: 故事, *tale, story, plot;*
 xiǎo shuō: 小说, *novel, fiction*

NOVELISTA; novelista; *novelist;*
 xiǎo shuō jiā: 小说家, *novelist*

NOVICIO (A); **noviço** (A); *novice (RELIG);*
 jiàn xí xiū nǚ: 见习修女, *female religious, novice;*
 jiàn xí xiū shì: 见习修士, *male religious novice;*
 xiū nǚ: 修女, *nun, sister;*
 xiū shì: 修士, *brother, friar*

NOVÍSIMO (A); **novíssimo** (A); *newest, latest, brand new;*
 zhǎn xīn (sv) (attr): 崭新, *brand-new;*
 zuì jìn (adj) (vp): 最近, *recent, latest; recently, lately, in the near future;*
 zuì xīn (sv) (attr): 最新, *the newest, the latest; most recent;*
 zuì xīn shì (sv): 最新式, *most up-to-date (fashion)*

NUBLADO (A) (adj); **nublado** (A); *cloudy, overcast;*
 duō yún (vp): 多云, *cloudy;*
 huī mēng mēng (sv): 灰蒙蒙, *overcast, dusky;*
 yīn chén (sv): 阴沉, *overcast, somber, gloomy;*
 yīn tiān: 阴天, *cloudy day, overcast sky;*
 yīn yǔ (vp): 阴雨, *overcast and rainy*

NÚCLEO; núcleo; *nucleus; center, hub;*
hé xīn rén wù: 核心人物, *nucleus of a group;*
hé xīn xiǎo zǔ: 核心小组, *core group;*
hé zǐ: 核子, *nucleus, nucleon (FIS);*
hé: 核, *nucleus of atom, cell;*
SEE (请查看) CENTRO, CENTRAL

NUDISMO; nudismo; *nudism ...*
NUDISTA; nudista; *nudist;*
chì luǒ (n) (vp): 赤裸, *nudity; nude, bare;*
luǒ tǐ huà: 裸体画, *nude painting;*
luǒ tǐ xiàng: 裸体像, *nude statute/ figure;*
luǒ tǐ yíng: 裸体营, *nudist colony;*
luǒ tǐ zhǔ yì zhě: 裸体主义者, *nudist;*

luǒ tǐ zhǔ yì: 裸体主义, *nudism;*
luǒ tǐ: 裸体, *nudity; (attr) naked*

NUPCIAL; nupcial; *wedding; nuptial (adj);*
hūn yīn: 婚姻, *marriage, matrimony;*
xǐ shì: 喜事, *happy event, joyous occasion, wedding;*
SEE (请查看) MARITAL

NUTRICIONAL; nutriente; *nutritional, nutrient; nutritional ...* **NUTRITIVO** (A);
nutritivo (A); *nourishing; nutritious;*
yǎng fèn: 养分, *nutrient;*
yíng yǎng: 营养, *nutrient, nutrition;*
yǒu yíng yǎng de: 有营养的, *nutritious, nourishing*

Easily recognizable verbs and their Portuguese and Chinese equivalents
Verbos fácilmente reconocibles en Español-Portugués-Inglés y sus equivalentes en Chino
Verbos facilmente reconhecível em Espanhol-Português-Inglês e seus equivalentes em Chinês
很容易辨认的西班牙语，葡萄牙语，英语动词和他们的中文对等词

NACIONALIZAR; nacionalizar; *to nationalize;*
shǐ guó yǒu huà: 使国有化, *to nationalize*

NARCOTIZAR; narcotizar; *to drug;*
má zuì: 麻醉, *to drug a person/animal*

NARRAR; narrar; *to recount/tell/ narrate;*
jiǎng gù shi: 讲故事, *to narrate;*
jiǎng: 讲, *to speak/say/tell;*
xù shì: 叙事, *to narrate/recount;*
xù shù: 叙述, *to narrate/recount/relate*

NATURALIZAR; naturalizar; *to naturalize/become naturalized;*
guī huà: 归化, *to be naturalized, to submit to a rule of ...;*
rù jí: 入籍, *to become naturalized*

NAVEGAR; navegar; *to pilot, to sail;*
háng hǎi: 航海, *to sail/navigate;*

jià shǐ: 驾驶, *to drive a vehicle; to pilot a ship/plane;*
SEE (请查看) TRAVESÍA

NECESITAR; necessitar; *to need/ want; to need to do sthg;*
bì xū: 必须, *must; to have to;*
děi: 得, *to need; should do (could do with); (aux) must;*
xiǎng yào (aux) (n): 想要, *to want sthg; to wish/intend;*
SEE (请查看) NECESARIO, CÉNTRICO, FALTA

NEGAR; negar; *to deny/refuse;*
jù jué: 拒绝, *to refuse/reject/decline;*
SEE (请查看) DECLINAR, DESAUTORIZAR

NEGOCIAR; negociar; *to do business, negotiate, deal;*
jiā huò: 交货, *to deliver goods;*
jiāo fù: 交付, *to pay/deliver/consign;*
jiāo huàn: 交换, *to exchange/swap/*

trade;
jiāo shè: 交涉, *to negotiate*;
qià tán: 洽谈, *to hold trade talks/ negotiate*;
shāng tán: 商谈, *to discuss/negotiate*;
wǎng lái (v) (n): 往来, *to come and go; to contract/deal with; deal, contract*;
yíng yè: 营业, *to do business/trade*;
SEE (请查看) CONSENSUAL

NORMALIZAR; normalizar; *to standardize/normalize*;
biāo zhǔn huà: 标准化, *to standardize*;
zhèng cháng huà: 正常化, *to normalize*

NOTAR; notar; *to notice/point out*;
diǎn míng: 点明, *to point out, to put one's finger on, to clarify*;
tí shì (v) (n): 提示, *to point out/prompt; to hint; cue*;
zhǐ zhèng: 指正, *to point out/note*

things needing correction;
SEE (请查看) ANOTAR

NOTIFICAR; notificar; *to notify/ inform*;
zhāo hu: 招呼, *to call/notify/tell/greet/ look after*;
SEE (请查看) AVISAR, BOLETÍN, DECLARAR, COMUNICAR

NUBLAR; nublar; *to blur/cloud/mar*;
mí huò: 迷惑, *to confuse/puzzle/ mislead*;
SEE (请查看) NEBULOSO, DESCONTROL, DESCONCERTAR

NUMERAR; numerar; *to number*;
biān hào (v) (n): 编号, *to number; serial number*;
gěi...biān hào: 给... 编号, *to number sthg*;
zǒng gòng yǒu: 总共有, *to number/ put together*

Interchangeable Spanish-Portuguese-English words and their Chinese equivalents
Palabras en Español-Portugués-Inglés y sus equivalentes en Chino
Palavras em Espanhol-Português-Inglês e seus equivalentes em Chinês
西班牙语，葡萄牙语，英语及中文的对等单词

¡OH!; oh!;
ā: 啊, *interjection of surprise, Ah!, Oh!*

OASIS; oásis;
lǜ zhōu: 绿洲, *oasis (desert)*

OBOE; oboé;
shuāng huáng guǎn: 双簧管, *oboe*

ORDINAL; ordinal;
xù shù: 序数, *ordinal number*

ORIENTAL; oriental;
dōng fāng de: 东方的, *oriental*

ORIGINAL; original;

dú chuàng de: 独创的, *original artist/ idea*;
yuán zuò de: 原作的, *original art/ writing/music*;
yuán zuò: 原作, *not a copy*

ORNAMENTAL; ornamental;
zhuāng shì de: 装饰的, *ornamental*

OVAL ú OVALADO ú ÓVALO; *oval, oval, curve*;
tuǒ yuán (n) (sv): 椭圆, *oval; ellipse (MAT); elliptic, elliptical*;
tuǒ yuán xíng de: 椭圆形的, *oval, ellipse*

Easily recognizable Spanish-Portuguese-English nouns, adjectives and adverbs and their Chinese equivalents
Nombres, sustantivos, adjetivos y adverbios en Español-Portugués-Inglés y sus equivalentes en Chino
Nomes, substantivos, adjetivos e advérbios em Espanhol-Português-Inglês e seus equivalentes em Chinês
容易辨认的西班牙语，葡萄牙语，英语的名词，形容词和副词和他们的中文对等词

OBEDIENCIA; obediência; *obedience* **... OBEDIENTE; obediente;** *obedient, compliant, subservient;*
  fú cóng de: 服从的, *obedient;*
  fú cóng: 服从, *obedience;*
  jìng yì: 敬意, *obeisance, respect;*
  shùn cóng (v) (n): 顺从, *to submit/ yield to; obedience, submission;*
  yī shùn: 依顺, *to be obedient;*
SEE (请查看**) DÓCIL**

OBELISCO; obelisco; *obelisk;*
  shí zhù: 石柱, *stela, upright stone, obelisk*

OBESIDAD; obesidade; *obesity, corpulence, plumpness* **... OBESO (A); obeso** (A); *obese, overweight, stout;*
  féi pàng bìng: 肥胖病, *obesity;*
  guò dù féi pàng: 过度肥胖, *obesity;*
  hòu de: 厚的, *fat;*
  pàng zi: 胖子, *fat person, fatty;*
  zhī fáng: 脂肪, *fat, fattiness;*
SEE (请查看**) CORPULENCIA**

OBITUARIO; obituário; *obituary;*
  fù gào: 讣告, *orbituary*

OBJECIÓN; objeção; *objection;*
  yì yì: 异议, *objection, dissent*

OBJETIVAMENTE; objetivamente; *objectively* **... OBJETIVIDAD; objetividade;** *objectivity* **... OBJETIVO** (n); **objetivo,** *aim; objective (MIL);*
  mù biāo: 目标, *target, goal, aim, objective;*
SEE (请查看**) DESINTERÉS, INTENCIÓN**

OBJETO; objeto; *object;*
  shì wù: 事物, *thing, object;*

  wù tǐ: 物体, *body, substance, object;*
SEE (请查看**) ÍTEM**

OBLONGO; oblongo; *oblong;*
  cháng fāng (attr): 长方, *rectangular;*
  cháng fāng tǐ (n): 长方体, *cuboid;*
  cháng fāng xíng (n) (sv): 长方形, *rectangle, oblong; oblong*

OBSCENIDAD; obscenidade; *obscenity;*
  yín huì yǔ yán: 淫秽语言, *obscenity;*
  yín xíng: 淫行, *licentious conduct;*
  zāng huà: 脏话, *swearword, obscene language*

OBSCENO (A); **obsceno** (A); *obscene, vulgar, coarse, dirty;*
  cū sú de: 粗俗的, *vulgar, coarse, earthy;*
  wěi xiè de: 猥亵的, *obscene gesture/ remark/ image;*
  xià liú de: 下流的, *obscene, dirty; low-down, mean;*
  yín huì de: 淫秽的, *obscene, salacious;*
SEE (请查看**) OBSCENIDAD**

OBSEQUIOSO (A); **servil;** *obsequious; servile;*
  bēi gōng qū xī de: 卑躬屈膝的, *servile;*
  dī sān xià sì de (fe): 低三下四的, *lowly, mean, servile;*
  fèng chéng de: 奉承的, *obsequious;*
  nú xìng (sv) (n): 奴性, *servile; servility*

OBSERVACIÓN; observação; *observation;*
  guān chá (v) (n): 观察, *to observe/ inspect; act of observation;*
  guān chá lì (n): 观察力, *discernment,*

observation;
SEE (请查看) ATENCIÓN, CENSURA

OBSERVANCIA; observância;
observance, compliance, regard;
  zūn shǒu (v) (n): 遵守, *to observe/
  abide by; observance*;
SEE (请查看) DEFERENCIA

OBSERVATORIO; observatório;
observatory;
  tiān wén tái: 天文台, *astronomical
  observatory*

OBSESIÓN; obsessão; *obsession,
fixation, mania* ... OBSESIVO (A);
obsessivo (A); *obsessive, dominating*;
  zháo mí (n): 着迷, *obsession*;
  zháo mí de: 着迷的, *obsessive person*;
  zháo mó de: 着魔的, *obsessive
  behaviour/interest*

OBSOLETO (A); obsoleto (A);
obsolete, dated;
  bù zài yòng de: 不再用的, *obsolete*;
  guò shí (sv): 过时, *out-of-date,
  outmoded*;
  táo tài: 淘汰, *to eliminate through
  competition/ selection, to die out;
  obsolete*;
SEE (请查看) ABANDONAR

OBSTÁCULO; obstáculo; *obstacle;
hurdle* (DEP);
  kuà lán sài pǎo: 跨栏赛跑, *hurdle
  race, the hurtles* (DEP);
  tiào lán: 跳栏, *hurdle race*;
  zhàng 'ài (n) (v): 障碍, *barrier,
  obstacle; to hinder/ obstruct*;
SEE (请查看) DIFICULTAR

OBSTETRICIA; obstetrícia; *obstetrics*;
  chǎn kē: 产科, *obstetrics, obstetrical
  department*;
  chǎn kē xué: 产科学, *obstetrics*

OBSTINACIÓN; obstinação;
perseverance, obstinacy ... OBSTINADO
(A); obstinado (A); *persistent, obstinate,
stubborn, mulish*;

bù qū bù náo (fe): 不屈不挠,
unyielding, indomitable;
gù zhí (sv) (v): 固执, *stubborn,
obstinate; to persist in/cling to*;
zhí niù (sv): 执拗, *mulish, stubborn*;
zhí yí (adj) (v): 致意, *stubborn,
obstinate; to persist in/cling to*;
SEE (请查看) ÉNFASIS,
CONTUMACIA, CONSTANTE

OBSTRUCCIÓN; obstrução;
obstruction;
  zhàng 'ài wù: 障碍物, *obstacle,
  barrier*;
SEE (请查看) DIFICULTAR

OBTUSO (A); obtuso (A); *blunt, obtuse,
stupid, insensitive*;
  bù mǐn gǎn (sv): 不敏感, *insensitive*;
  chí dùn (sv): 迟钝, *slow (in thought/
  action); stupid, obtuse*;
  dùn (sv): 钝, *blunt, dull, stupid, dull-
  witted*;
  dùn zhì (sv): 钝滞, *blunt, dull*

OBVIAMENTE; obviamente; *obviously*
... OBVIO (A) (adj); obvio (A); *obvious,
apparent, evident*;
  míng xiǎn (sv): 明显, *clear, obvious,
  evident*;
  míng xiǎn de (adv): 明显地, *obviously,
  clearly, evidently*;
  xiǎn 'ěr yì jiàn (fe): 显而易见,
  obviously, evidently, clearly;
SEE (请查看) EVIDENTE

OCASIONAL; ocasional; *accidental,
occasional*;
  ǒu 'ěr (adv) (sv): 偶尔, *occasionally;
  occasional*;
  ǒu 'ěr (adv): 偶而, *randomly,
  unpredictably*;
SEE (请查看) CIRCUNSTANCIAL

OCCIDENTAL (adj); ocidental;
western;
  xī bù: 西部, *western, the west*

OCÉANO; oceano; *ocean*;
  dà hǎi: 大海, *the open sea*;

hǎi yáng: 海洋, *ocean, seas and oceans*

OCULISTA; oculista; *ophthalmologist;*
  yǎn kē xué: 眼科学, *ophthalmology;*
  yǎn kē yī shēng: 眼科医生,
  ophthalmologist

OCULTO (A); **oculto** (A); *hidden, secret;*
occult, esoteric;
  àn (bf): 暗, *hidden, secret; unclear; (sv)*
  dull, dark, dim;
  àn cáng (v) (sv): 暗藏, *to hide/conceal;*
  hidden, secret;
  chāo zì rán: 超自然, *supernatural;*
  xuán miào: 玄妙, *mysterious, abstruse;*
SEE (请查看**) ARCANO,**
CLANDESTINIDAD, ENIGMÁTICO

OCUPACIÓN; ocupação; *occupation*
... OCUPACIONAL; ocupacional;
occupational;
  háng dang: 行当, *profession, trade,*
  line of business;
  zhí yè (sv) (n): 职业, *occupational;*
  occupation, profession, vocation;
SEE (请查看**) INDUSTRIAL**

OCUPADO (A); **OCUPADO** (A); *busy,*
occupied, engaged;
  fán máng (sv): 繁忙, *busy;*
  máng lù (sv): 忙碌, *be busy/bustle*
  about;
  máng luàn (sv): 忙乱, *slapdash, busy*
  and hurried;
  máng zhe (vp): 忙着, *be busy;*

OCUPANTE; ocupante; *occupant;*
occupying (adj), occupant (n);
  zhàn yòng zhě: 占用者, *long-term*
  occupant;
  jū zhù zhě: 居住者, *occupant, resident;*
  shǐ yòng zhě: 使用者, *short-term*
  occupant, user

ODIO; ódio; *hatred, dislike* **... ODIOSO**
(A); **odioso** (A); *hateful, horrible, nasty;*
  bù xǐ huan: 不喜欢, *dislike;*
  kě wù (sv): 可恶, *detestable,*
  abominable, obnoxious;
SEE (请查看**) AVERSIÓN, ANTIPATÍA,**

ANIMOSIDAD, IGNOMINIA

OFENSA; ofensa; *offense (against),*
slight, insult **... OFENSIVA** (n);
ofensiva; *offensive* **... OFENSIVO** (A)
(adj); **ofensivo** (A); *offensive;*
  líng rén (v): 令人, *to insult/humiliate*
  mào fàn (v) (n): 冒犯, *to offend/affront*
  (a superior person); offense;
  mào fàn xìng de: 冒犯性的, *offensive;*
  wú lǐ de: 无礼的, *impertinent,*
  offensive;
SEE (请查看**) INSULTANTE,**
INSULTO, AGRAVANTE, AGRAVIAR,
DESAGRADO, DISCORDANCIA,
CRIMEN

OFERTA; oferta; *offer;*
  bào jià: 报价, *bid, offer, quoted price;*
  chū jià (v) (n): 出价, *to bid; bid;*
  tè jià: 特价, *special offer, bargain price;*
SEE (请查看**) APROVISIONAR,**
INSINUACIÓN

OFICIAL (adj); **oficial;** *official;*
  guān fāng de: 官方的, *official,*
  approved;
  gōng wù de: 公务的, *official business/*
  matters;
  guān yuán: 官员, *an official*

OFICINA; oficina; *workshop; office;*
  bàn gōng shì: 办公室, *office;*
  chē jiān: 车间, *workshop;*
  gōng chǎng: 工场, *works, atelier;*
  zuō fang: 作坊, *workshop*

OFICIOSO (A); **oficioso** (A); *unofficial,*
informal;
  fēi guān fāng de: 非官方的,
  unofficial;
  fēi zhèng shì de (adv) (sv): 非正式地,
  unofficially; unofficial;
SEE (请查看**) DIARIO**

OFTALMOLOGÍA; oftalmologia;
ophthalmology **... OFTALMÓLOGO** (A);
oftalmologista; *ophthalmologist;*
  yǎn kē xué: 眼科学, *ophthalmology;*
  yǎn kē yī shēng: 眼科医生,

ophthalmologist;
yǎn kē: 眼科, *department of ophthalmology*

ÓLEO; óleo, *oil (GEN); oil, oil paint (ARTE)* ... **OLEOSO** (A) (adj); **oleoso** (A); *greasy; oily*;
hán yóu (v) (sv): 含油, *sthg containing oil; oily*;
jī yóu: 机油, *engine oil, lubricant*;
shí yòng yóu: 食用油, *edible oil*;
shí you: 石油, *petroleum, oil*;
yóu huá (sv): 油滑, *oily, greasy; unctuous; foxy*;
yóu nì (sv) (n): 油腻, *greasy, oily; greasy/oily food*;
yóu rùn (vp) (n): 油润, *oily smooth; lubrication*;
yóu sè: 油色, *oil colors, oils*;
yóu shā: 油砂, *oil sand*;
yóu shuā: 油刷, *oil paint, paint*;
yóu wū: 油污, *greasy/oily dirt*;
yóu zhī: 油脂, *oil, fat*;
yóu (n) (v) (sv) (bf): 油, *oil, fat, grease; to apply paint/oil/varnish; oily, greasy; glib, slick; petroleum*

OLFATO; olfato; *sense of smell, instinct*;
běn xìng: 本性, *nature, instincts*;
chá jué: 察觉, *to have an instinct for/ be aware of*;
qì wèi (n): 气味, *flavor, smell*;
wèi jué: 味觉, *sense of taste*;
xiù jué: 嗅觉, *olfactory; a sense of smell*;
SEE (请查看**) INSTINTO**

OLIGARQUÍA; oligarquia; *oligarchy (government by a few)*;
guǎ tóu zhèng zhì: 寡头政治, *oligarchy*

OMISO (A); **omisso** (A); *negligent, lax, indifferent, derelict*;
lěng dàn (sv) (v): 冷淡, *cold, indifferent; desolate, careless; to treat coldly*;
SEE (请查看**) DESAMOR, APATÍA, DESATENCIÓN**

OMISIÓN; omissão; *omission, deletion*;
pái chú (v) (n): 排除, *to get rid of/ remove/eliminate; deletion*;
shān chú (n) (sv): 删除, *deletion, omission; to delete/leave out*;
shěng lüè (v) (n): 省略, *to leave out/ omit/abridge; abbreviation, deletion, omission*;
yí lòu (v) (n): 遗漏, *to omit/leave out; omission*

ONCOLOGÍA; oncologia; *oncology*;
zhǒng liú xué: 肿瘤学, *oncology*;
zhǒng liú: 肿瘤, *tumor*

ONDULACIÓN; ondulação; *undulation; rippling, ripple, wave* ...
ONDULADO (A); **ondulado** (A); *wavy; curled; wavy* ... **ONDULANTE; ondulante;** *wavy; undulating*;
bō làng shì (n): 波浪式, *wave-like*;
bō làng xìng (sv): 波浪性, *wavy*;
bō làng: 波浪, *wave*;
bō tāo: 波涛, *great waves, billows*;
juǎn qū (vp): 卷曲, *crimp*;
làng tou: 浪头, *tide, wave; trend*;
lián yī (wr): 涟漪, *ripples*;
qǐ fú (v) (n): 起伏, *to rise and fall/ undulate; ups and downs*;
quán qū (v) (vp): 蜷曲, *to curl/coil/ twist; wiggly, twisted*;
yǒu bō wén (sv): 有波纹, *wavy*;
yǒu juǎn máo (sv): 有卷毛, *curly*

ONEROSO (A); **oneroso** (A); *burdensome, onerous*;
bù fāng biàn de: 不方便的, *inconvenient place/situation, etc.*;
bú hé shí yí de: 不合时宜的, *inconvenient, unsuitable, inappropriate time/moment, etc.*;
duō shì (sv) (v): 多事, *troublesome; to be meddlesome*;
fán zhòng (sv): 繁重, *onerous, arduous, heavy, burdensome*;
fèi shì (sv) (v): 费事, *troublesome, difficult; to take a lot of trouble/time doing sthg*;
SEE (请查看**) ARDUO, CONFLICTIVO, IRRITANTE**

OPACIDAD; opacidade; *opacity ...*
OPACO (A); **opaco** (A); *opaque, dull, gloomy; obscure;*
  àn de (bf): 暗的, *obscure, dim, gloomy;*
  bù tòu guāng (sv): 不透光, *not translucent, opaque;*
  bù tòu míng (sv): 不透明, *not transparent/open/ public;*
  huì sè (sv) (n): 晦涩, *grey, ashy; pessimistic, gloomy; obscure, ambiguous;*
  mó hu bù qīng (fe): 模糊不清, *blurred and indistinct; obscure;*
  nán lǐ jiě: 难理解, *difficult to understand;*
  yì yì mó hu: 意义模糊, *blurred, indistinct;*
SEE (请查看) NEBULOSO

ÓPALO; opala; *opal;*
  dàn bái shí: 蛋白石, *opal*

OPCIÓN; opção; *option, choice ...*
OPCIONAL; opcional; *optional ...*
OPTATIVO (A); **opcional;** *optional;*
  kě gōng xuǎn zé de: 可供选择的, *optional;*
  kě xuǎn de: 可选的, *optional;*
  xuǎn zé (n) (v): 选择, *selection, option, choice, alternative; to select/opt for/ choose;*
  zì xuǎn (attr) (v): 自选, *free, optional; to choose;*
SEE (请查看) SELECCIONAR

OPERACIONAL; operacional; *operational;*
  cāo zuò de: 操作的, *operational;*
  kě cāo zuò de: 可操作的, *operable;*
  kě shǐ yòng de: 可使用的, *operational machine/ vehicle/ system; operable;*
  yè wù xì tǒng: 业务系统, *operations, operational system;*
  yùn zhuǎn de: 运转的, *operational, working order*

OPERADOR; operado (A); *operator, (in a general sense);*
  cāo zuò gōng: 操作工, *operator;*
  cāo zuò yuán: 操作员, *operator (generally)*

OPERANTE (adj); **operante;** *operative; operating, effective;*
  yǒu xiào (v) (adj): 有效, *to be effective; effective;*
SEE (请查看) EFECTIVIDAD

OPIO; opio; *opium;*
  yā piàn: 鸦片, *opium*

OPONENTE; oponente; *opponent ...* **OPOSITOR** (A); **adversário** (A); *opponent;*
  duì shǒu: 对手, *adversary, opponent, adversary;*
  fǎn duì zhě: 反对者, *dissenter, opponent;*
  zhèng dí: 政敌, *political opponent*

OPORTUNAMENTE; oportunamente; *opportunely ...*
OPORTUNIDAD; oportunidade; *opportunity, chance ...* **OPORTUNISMO; oportunismo;** *opportunism ...*
OPORTUNISTA; oportunista; *opportunist (n), opportunistic (adj)...*
OPORTUNO (A); **oportuno** (A); *opportune, timely;*
  hé shí: 合时, *timely, opportune;*
  jī huì zhǔ yì (n) (sv): 机会主义, *opportunism; opportunistic;*
  jī huì zhǔ yì zhě: 机会主义者, *opportunist;*
  jī huì: 机会, *opportunity, chance;*
  jí shí de (adv): 及时地, *timely; on time;*
  jī yù: 机遇, *opportunity, favorable circumstances;*
  kòng zi: 空子, *space, room, gap, opening, time, chance, opportunity;*
  qià hǎo (adv): 恰好, *by luck/ coincidence; exactly, just right; opportune;*
  shí jī: 时机, *opportunity, opportune moment;*
  tóu jī (sv) (n): 投机, *opportunistic; to speculate;*
  yìng jǐng (v) (sv): 应景, *to do sthg for the occasion; timely, appropriate*

OPOSICIÓN; oposição; *opposition;*
  fǎn duì (n) (v): 反对, *resistance; to oppose;*

fǎn kàng (v) (n): 反抗, *to revolt/resist/ oppose; opposition*

OPRESIÓN; opressão; *oppression, anxiety ...* **OPRESIVO** (A); **opressivo** (A); *oppressive;*
  yā pò (n) (v): 压迫, *oppression, repression; to oppress/repress;*
  yā yì (sv): 压抑, *oppressive, stifling; depressing*

ÓPTICO (A); **óptico** (A); *optical (adj), optician (n);*
  guāng de: 光的, *optical;*
  guāng xué (sv) (n): 光学, *optical; optics;*
  shì lì (sv) (n): 视力, *optical; vision, sight;*
  yǎn (n) (v) (sv): 眼, *eye; small hole, aperture; to look/glance; optical;*
  yǎn jìng diàn: 眼镜店, *optician (shop/ store);*
  yǎn jìng shāng: 眼镜商, *optician (trade/business)*

OPTIMISMO; otimismo; *optimism ...* **OPTIMISTA; otimista;** *optimistic (adj), optimist (n);*
  lè guān (sv): 乐观, *optimistic, hopeful, sanguine;*
  lè guān de rén: 乐观的人, *optimist;*
  lè guān pài: 乐观派, *optimist;*
  lè guān zhě: 乐观者, *optimist;*
  lè guān zhǔ yì zhě: 乐观主义者, *optimist;*
  lè guān zhǔ yì: 乐观主义, *optimism*

ÓPTIMO (A); **ótimo** (A); *optimum;*
  zuì jiā de: 最佳的, *optimum conditions/ number/ size/etc.*

OPULENCIA; opulência; *opulence, abundance ...* **OPULENTO** (A); **opulento** (A); *opulent, wealthy, luxurious;*
  fù yù (sv): 富裕, *well-to-do, well-off;*
  háo huá (sv): 豪华, *luxurious, extravagant;*
  kuò qi (sv): 阔气, *luxurious, lavish;*
SEE (请查看) ABUNDANCIA, COPIOSO

ORADOR (A); **orador** (A); *orator, speaker;*
  yǎn shuō jiā: 演说家, *orator;*
  yǎn shuō zhě: 演说者, *speaker*

ORBE; orbe; *orb, globe, world;*
  rén jiān: 人间, *the world;*
  shì jiè: 世界, *globe, world;*
  shì shàng: 世上, *in the world, on earth*

ÓRBITA; órbita; *orbit;*
  guǐ dào: 轨道, *orbit*

ORDEN; ordem; *order (GEN); decree;*
  hào lìng: 号令, *order, verbal command;*
  zhǐ lìng (n) (v): 指令, *order, command, direction, directive, instructions; to instruct/order;*
SEE (请查看) MANDATO

ORDENADO (A) (adj); **ordenado** (A); *tidy, neat, organized;*
  gān jìng lì luo (fe): 干净利落, *neat and tidy, efficient;*
  qí zhěng de: 齐整的, *uniform, tidy and orderly;*
  zhěng jié: 整洁, *neat, clean and tidy;*
SEE (请查看) HIGIENE, METÓDICO

ORDINARIO (A); **ordinário** (A); *ordinary, usual;*
  jiǎn dān: 简单, *simple, ordinary, casual, uncomplicated, commonplace;*
  pǔ tōng (sv): 普通, *common, ordinary, average;*
  xún cháng (sv): 寻常, *usual, ordinary, common;*
SEE (请查看) BANAL, MEDIOCRIDAD

ORGÁNICO (A); **orgânico** (A); *organic;*
  qì guān de: 器官的, *organic;*
  yǒu jī (sv): 有机, *organic (QUIM)*

ORGANISMO; organismo; *organism (BIOL); organization (POL);*
  shè tuán: 社团, *mass organization, community;*
  shēng wù (n) (attr): 生物, *living thing, organism; (BIOL);*

zǔ zhī (v) (n): 组织, *to organize/form; organized system; tissue, nerve*;
SEE (请查看) **ASOCIACIÓN**

ORGANIZADOR (A); **organizador** (A); *organizer; organizer (n); organizing (adj)* ... **ORGANIZADO** (A) (adj); **organizado** (A); *organized, structured, arranged*;
  zǔ zhī zhě: 组织者, *organizer of a conference/party, etc.*
SEE (请查看) **ORDENADO, METÓDICO**

ORGASMO; orgasmo; orgasm;
  xìng gāo cháo: 性高潮, *orgasm*

ORGÍA; orgia; *orgy, wildness*;
  fàng dàng (sv): 放荡, *dissolute, unconventional*;
  kuàng huān (n) (v): 狂欢, *revelry, carnival; to revel*;
  zòng jiǔ kuáng huān: 纵酒狂欢, *orgy*

ORIENTE; oriente; *east, (el oriente = The East)*;
  dōng fāng: 东方, *The East, The Orient*;
  dōng: 东, *east*

ORIFICIO; orifício; *hole, opening, orifice*;
  dǎ kāi (v) (n): 打开, *to open/unfold; opening*;
  dòng (n) (adv): 洞, *hole, cavity, cave; penetratingly, thoroughly*;
  kēng (n) (v): 坑, *hole, pit, hollow; tunnel; to bury alive, to cheat, entrap*;
  kǒng (n) (adv): 孔, *hole, aperture; badly, very*;
  kòng quē (n): 空缺, *job opening*;
  kǒu (n): 口, *mouth; opening, entrance; hole, cut*;
  kǒu zi: 口子, *opening, cut, tear*;
  pò dòng: 破洞, *a hole in clothing/pocket/bag, etc.*

ORIGEN; origem; *origin, origin of birth*;
  chū shēn: 出身, *ancestry; family background; class, origin*;
  fā yuán dì: 发源地, *place of origin, birthplace; source*;

  lái lì: 来历, *history, past, origin, background*;
  lài lù: 来路, *origin, background*;
  lài yuán (n) (v): 来源, *origin, source; to originate*;
  qǐ yuán (n) (v): 起源, *origin, genesis; to originate/ stem from*

ORIGINARIO (A); **originário** (A); *indigenous, native; original, initial, first*;
  běn guó de: 本国的, *native*;
  běn guó rén (n): 本国人, *native of a country*;
  běn lái (attr) (adv): 本来, *original; at first*;
  běn tǔ (n): 本土, *one's native country; metropolitan territory/area*;
  chú shēng dì: 出生地, *native, birthplace*;
  chū shǐ: 初始, *initial*;
  dú dào (sv): 独到, *original, unique*;
  gù yǒu de: 固有的, *indigenous*;
  tǔ shēng tǔ zhǎng (fe): 土生土长, *locally born and bred*;
  tǔ zhù rén: 土著人, *native, aborigine*;
  yuán lái (n) (sv): 原来, *originally, formerly; original*;
  yuán lái de: 原来的, *original*;
  yuán shǐ (sv): 原始, *original, first; primitive*;
  yuán zuò de: 原作的, *authentic/ original (work/text, etc.)*;
  zuì chū (n) (attr): 最初, *initially; initial, first, prime*;
  zuì chū de: 最初的, *first, earlier*;
  zuì zǎo de: 最早的, *original, first*;
SEE (请查看) **NATIVO**

ORNAMENTO; ornamento o ornato; *ornament*;
  zhuāng shì huà: 装饰画, *decorative painting*;
  zhuāng shì pǐn: 装饰品, *ornament*;
SEE (请查看) **DECORAR**

ORQUESTA; orquestra; *orchestra*;
  guǎn xián yuè duì: 管弦乐队, *orchestra*

ORTODOXO (A); **ortodoxo** (A); *orthodox*;

bǎo shǒu (v) (sv): 保守, *to keep guard; conservative*;
chuán tǒng de: 传统的, *orthodox*;
zhèng tǒng (n) (attr): 正统, *orthodox ideas/ tradition; orthodox, authorized, classical*;
SEE (请查看) CLÁSICO

ORTOPEDISTA; ortopedia; *orthopedics*;
jiǎo xíng de: 矫形的, *orthopedic*;
jiǎo xíng shù: 矫形术, *orthopedics*

OSCURIDAD ú OBSCURIDAD; obscuridade; *darkness, obscurity*
... OSCURO (A) ú OBSCURO (A); obscuro (A); *dark, overcast, obscure*;
àn (sv): 暗, *dark, dim, dull; obscure; (bf) hidden, secret*;
àn zhōng (adv): 暗中, *in the dark, in secret, surreptitiously*;
bù míng (v) (vp) (n): 不明, *fail to understand; not clear, unknown; obscurity*;
bù qīng chu (sv): 不清楚, *unclear, indistinct, ambiguous*;
bù zhī míng: 不知名, *little known; obscure*;
yīn chén (sv): 阴沉, *overcast, gloomy, somber*;
SEE (请查看) OPACIDAD, OPACO, ARCANO, CRÍPTICO

OSTENTOSO (A); **ostentoso** (A); *ostentatious, showy, pretentious*;
bǎi kuò: 摆阔, *to parade one's wealth*;
fēng tou: 风头, *trend; show off*;
kuò chuò (sv): 阔绰, *ostentatious, extravagant*

OSTEÓPATA; osteopata; *osteopath*;
jiē gǔ yī shēng: 接骨医生, *osteopath*

OSTRA; ostra; *oyster*;
mǔ lì: 牡蛎, *oyster*

OSTRACISMO; ostracismo; *ostracism, blacklist, isolate, shun*;
hēi míng dān (n): 黑名单, *blacklist*;
pái chì (v) (n): 排斥, *to exclude, to black ball; ostracism*

OVACIÓN; ovação; *ovation*;
hè cǎi (v) (n): 喝彩, *to acclaim/cheer; acclamation, ovation*;
rè liè huān yíng (vp): 热烈欢迎, *ovation*

ÓVALO (n); **oval o ovalado** (A); *oval*;
tuǒ yuán (attr): 椭圆, *oval; elliptic, elliptical*;
tuǒ yuán xíng (n) (sv): 椭圆形, *oval*;
SEE (请查看) OVAL

OVARIO; ovário; *ovary*;
luǎn cháo: 卵巢, *ovary*

ÓXIDO; óxido; *oxide*;
yǎng huà wù: 氧化物, *oxide, oxidizing material*

OXÍGENO; oxigênio; *oxygen*;
yǎng qì: 氧气, *oxygen*

OZONO; ozônio; *ozone*;
chòu yǎng: 臭氧, *ozone*

Easily recognizable verbs and their Portuguese and Chinese equivalents
Verbos fácilmente reconocibles en Español-Portugués-Inglés y sus equivalentes en Chino
Verbos facilmente reconhecível em Espanhol-Português-Inglês e seus equivalentes em Chinês
很容易辨认的西班牙语，葡萄牙语，英语动词和他们的中文对等词

OBJETAR; objetar; *to object*;
zuò duì: 作对, *to oppose*;
SEE (请查看) AFRONTAR, PROTESTAR, OPOSICIÓN

OBLIGAR; obrigar; *to oblige, force*;
qiáng xíng: 强行, *to force*;
yāo xié: 要胁, *to force/threaten*;
SEE (请查看) COMPELER,

MANDATO

OBSERVAR; observar; *to observe/ watch*;
  chá kàn: 察看, *to watch/observe/ examine carefully*;
  guān kàn: 观看, *to observe/watch*;
  shì chá: 视察, *to inspect/observe*;
  zhào kàn: 照看, *to look after/watch*;
SEE (请查看) **OBSERVACIÓN, CUSTODIA**

OBSESIONAR; obcecar; *to obsess*;
  mí zhù (sv) (v): 迷住, *confused/lost; to be fascinated/strongly attracted; to infatuate/ enchant/captivate*;
SEE (请查看) **FASCINAR**

OBSTRUIR; obstruir; *to block/ obstruct*;
  yǒu 'ài: 有碍, *to obstruct/be a hindrance*;
  zǔ jī: 阻击, *to block/check*;
  zuò gěng: 作梗, *to obstruct/make things difficult/ create difficulties*;
SEE (请查看) **BLOCAR, DIFICULTAR**

OBTENER; obter; *to get/win/obtain*;
  bó qǔ: 博取, *to win/gain*;
  huò dé: 获得, *to obtain/win/achieve/ gain*;
  huò qǔ: 获取, *to obtain/acquire/gain/ win*;
  lǐng qǔ: 领取, *to get/draw/receive*;
  shèng lì (v) (n) (adv): 胜利, *to win; victory, success; successfully*;
  shōu dào: 收到, *to get/receive/ achieve*;
  yíng dé: 赢得, *to win/gain*;
  zhì shèng: 制胜, *to win/subdue/get the upper hand*;
SEE (请查看) **DERIVAR**

OBTURAR; obturar; *to block/fill/close*;
  bì hé: 闭合, *to close*;
  fēng bì: 封闭, *to close/block; to seal up/off*;
  fēng suǒ: 封锁, *to seal off/block/ blockade; to seal and lock*;
  guān mén (v) (n) (adv): 关门, *to close the doors/ shut down; to shut sb up; gate in a strategic pass; behind closed doors*;
  tián chōng: 填充, *to fill up/stuff up; to fill in the blanks*;
  tián píng: 填平, *to fill and level up*;
  zhē yǎn: 遮掩, *to hide/block; to cover up/cover*;
SEE (请查看) **APREHENDER, BLOCAR, DESACTIVAR**

OCASIONAR; ocasionar; *to cause*;
  chǎn shēng: 产生, *to produce/cause/ engender/ bring about*;
  shǐ de: 使得, *to make/cause; to be usable/feasible*;
  yǐn fā: 引发, *to initiate/trigger/touch off; to evoke*;
  zào chéng (v) (n): 造成, *to create/ bring about; to complete; construction*;
  zhāo rě: 招惹, *to provoke/incur/court/ cause*;
  zhāo zhì: 招致, *to incur/lead to; to recruit/seek*;
  zhì shǐ: 致使, *to cause/result in*;
SEE (请查看) **CAUSAR**

OCULTAR; ocultar; *to hide, conceal*;
  àn cáng: 暗藏, *to hide/conceal*;
  bāo bì: 包庇, *to harbor/cover up/shield*;
  bāo cáng: 保藏, *to contain/harbor/ conceal*;
  mái cáng: 埋藏, *to bury/hide away; to secretly amass*;
  mái mò: 埋没, *to bury/cover up; to ignore/overlook; to stifle*;
  yǐn bì (v) (sv): 隐蔽, *to conceal/take over/hide; concealed*;
  yǐn cáng: 隐藏, *to hide/conceal*;
  yǐn mán: 隐瞒, *to conceal/hide*;
  yǐn nì (wr): 隐匿, *to hide/lie low/ conceal/cover up*;
  zhē bì: 遮蔽, *to hide from view; to obstruct/block*;
  zhē cáng: 遮藏, *to conceal/cover up*;
  zhē gài: 遮盖, *to conceal/cover up; to cover/ overspread*;
  zhē xiū: 遮羞, *to hush up/cover up a scandal/one's embarrassment*;
SEE (请查看) **CLANDESTINIDAD, OBTURAR**

OCUPAR; ocupar; *to occupy/take up/fill;*
  zhàn jù: 占据, *to occupy/hold;*
  zhàn yǒu: 占有, *to own/have; to hold/occupy/take possession of;*
SEE (请查看) APREHENDER, HABITAR

ODIAR; odiar; *to hate; to pester/annoy;*
  shǐ fán nǎo: 使烦恼, *to annoy/drive up the wall;*
SEE (请查看) MOLESTAR, AGRAVAR, DESDÉN, ANIMOSIDAD

OFENDER; ofender; *to insult/offend;*
  mào fàn: 冒犯, *to offend; to affront a superior;*
SEE (请查看) INSULTAR, AGRAVIAR, DESHONRAR

OFERTAR; oferecer; *to offer/tender;*
  chū jià: 出价, *to offer money; to bid;*
  gěi (v) (cov)**:** 给, *to give/give to/offer; for the benefit of; (suf) to;*
  juān zhù: 捐助, *to offer assistance; to donate;*
  kāi jià (v) (n)**:** 开价, *to make an offer; asking/bid;*
SEE (请查看) APROVISIONAR, AVANZAR, INSINUACIÓN

OFUSCAR; ofuscar; *to dazzle/blind;*
  shǎn guāng (v) (n)**:** 闪光, *to flicker/sparkle/dazzle; flash;*
  shǐ mù xuàn: 使目眩, *to be dizzy/dazed;*
  yào yǎn (sv) (v)**:** 耀眼, *dazzling; to be dazzled*

OMITIR; omitir; *to omit;*
  shān qù: 删去, *to omit/cross off/delete;*
SEE (请查看) OMISIÓN

ONDULAR; ondear; *to ripple/undulate;*
  dàng yàng (v) (vp)**:** 荡漾, *to undulate/ripple; excited;*
SEE (请查看) ONDULACIÓN

OPERAR; operar; *to operate/operate on (MED); to perform; to produce/bring about; to operate, use;*
  dòng shǒu shù: 动手术, *to perform an operation;*
  lì yòng: 利用, *to use/exploit;*
  xíng yī: 行医, *to practice medicine;*
  yùn yòng: 运用, *to use/put to use/utilize;*
  yùn zhuàn (v) (n)**:** 运转, *to work/run/operate; to revolve/turn around; sudden change in fortune;*
  zhěng xíng (v) (n)**:** 整形, *to have/perform plastic surgery; plastic surgery;*
SEE (请查看) OPERANTE, ADMINISTRAR, APLICAR

OPTAR; optar; *to choose/opt for;*
  qǔ shě (v) (n)**:** 取舍, *to choose/accept or reject; selection;*
  tiāo jiǎn: 挑拣, *to pick and choose;*
  tiāo xuǎn (v)**:** 挑选, *to choose/select/pick;*
  tuī jǔ: 推举, *to choose/elect;*
  xuǎn qǔ: 选取, *to select/choose;*
SEE (请查看) OPCIÓN

OPTIMIZAR; otimizar; *to optimize;*
  yōu huà (v) (n)**:** 优化, *to optimize, to make superior; optimization*

ORAR; orar; *to pray;*
  dǎo gào: 祷告, *to pray;*
  qí dǎo: 祈祷, *to pray*

ORDENAR; ordenar; *to arrange/put in order/tidy up;*
  ān zhì (v) (n)**:** 安置, *to make arrangements for, to help settle down/find a place for; placement;*
  bǎi bù: 摆布, *to arrange/decorate; to manipulate/ order about;*
  biān pái: 编排, *to arrange/lay out;*
  bù zhì (v) (n)**:** 布置, *to arrange/fix up/decorate; decor;*
  chǔ zhì: 处置, *to deal with/manage/dispose of;*
  shōu shí: 收拾, *to put in order, to tidy/clear up;*
  zhěng lǐ: 整理, *to arrange, to tidy up, to put in order;*

SEE (请查看) **ORDENADO, ACTUAR, DISPOSICIÓN**

ORGANIZAR; organizar; *to organize;*
bù shǔ: 部署, *to deploy/organize;*
chóu huà: 筹划, *to plan and prepare;*
zǔ zhī (v) (n): 组织, *to organize/form; organization, organized system*

ORIENTAR; orientar; *to direct/orient;*
zhǔ bàn: 主办, *to direct/sponsor/host;*
SEE (请查看) **DIRECTOR, LOCALIZAR**

ORIGINAR; originar; *to originate; to cause;*
chuàng shǐ: 创始, *to originate/initiate;*
fā dòng: 发动, *to start/initiate/launch, to arouse;*
fā yuán: 发源, *to originate;*
lái yuán (v) (n): 来源, *to originate; origin, source;*
lài yuán yú: 来源于, *to originate/stem from;*
qǐ yuán (v) (n): 起源, *to originate/stem from; origin, genesis;*
shǒu chuàng: 首创, *to originate/ pioneer/initiate;*
SEE (请查看) **INAUGURAR**

ORNAMENTAR ú ORNAR; ornar; *to decorate/adorn;*
diǎn zhuì (v) (n): 点缀, *to decorate/ embellish; decoration;*
xiū shì: 修饰, *to decorate/modify; to polish (a text);*

SEE (请查看) **DECORAR**

OSCILAR; oscilar; *to swing, fluctuate;*
biàn huàn (v) (attr): 变幻, *to fluctuate/ change irregularly;*
bō dòng (v) (n): 波动, *to undulate/ fluctuate; wave motion (FIS), fluctuation;*
fú dòng: 浮动, *to float/fluctuate;*
SEE (请查看) **ONDULAR, ONDULACIÓN, AGITAR**

OSCURECER; obscurecer; *to darken/ confuse/cloud/ obscure;*
mí huó: 迷惑, *to confuse/puzzle/baffle/ mislead;*
SEE (请查看) **DESCONTROL, DESCONCERTAR**

OSTENTAR; ostentar; *to show, to display; to hold/ have/show off;*
chū fēng tou (fe): 出风头, *to show off/ be in the limelight/seek the forefront;*
kuā yào: 夸耀, *to brag about sthg, to flaunt;*
lòu yī shǒu: 露一手, *to show off;*
mài guāi: 卖乖, *to flaunt one's cleverness;*
SEE (请查看) **OSTENTOSO**

OVACIONAR; ovacionar; *to applaud; to give an ovation;*
pāi shǒu: 拍手, *to applaud/clap;*
SEE (请查看) **ACLAMAR, APLAUDIR**

OXIDAR; oxidar; *to oxidize/rust;*
yǎng huà: 氧化, *to oxidize*

Interchangeable Spanish-Portuguese-English words and their Chinese equivalents
Palabras en Español-Portugués-Inglés y sus equivalentes en Chino
Palavras em Espanhol-Português-Inglês e seus equivalentes em Chinês
西班牙语，葡萄牙语，英语及中文的对等单词

PÁNCREAS; pâncreas;
yí xiàn: 胰腺, *pancreas*

PANDA (ZOOL); **panda;**
dà xióng māo: 大熊猫, *panda*

PANORAMA; panorama;
  quán jǐng: 全景, *panorama*

PAPAL; papal;
  jiào huáng de: 教皇的, *papal*

PARÁBOLA; parábola (MAT);
  pāo wù xiàn: 抛物线, *parabola*

PARANOIA; paranóia;
  wàng xiǎng kuáng: 妄想狂, *paranoia*

PARTICULAR; particular; *special,*
particular;
  jù tǐ (sv): 具体, *concrete, specific,*
  particular, detailed;
  tè bié (sv) (adv): 特别, *special,*
  particular, unusual; especially,
  particularly;
  zhuān mén (sv) (adv): 专门, *special,*
  specialized; technical; especially;
SEE (请查看) **PECULIAR,**
DESIGUAL, DISTINCIÓN

PASTOR (A); **pastor** (A); *shepherd,*
clergyman ... **PASTORAL; pastoral;**
  mù shī (n) (sv): 牧师, *pastor, minister,*
  priest, clergyman; pastoral;
  mù yáng rén: 牧羊人, *shepherd*

PATÉ; patê;
  ròu jiàng: 肉酱, *paté*

PATERNAL; paternal;
  fù qīn de: 父亲的, *paternal*

PATIO; pátio; *courtyard, backyard,*
playground; patio;
  dà yuàn: 大院, *compound, courtyard;*
  píng tái: 平台, *terrace, patio;*
  tíng yuàn: 庭院, *courtyard, patio;*
  yuàn zi: 院子, *courtyard, compound;*
SEE (请查看) **BALCÓN**

PECULIAR; peculiar; *typical,*
particular, distinctive;
  diǎn xíng (sv) (n): 典型, *typical,*
  representative; model, type, typical case;
  dù tè (sv): 独特, *unique, distinctive;*
SEE (请查看) **PARTICULAR,**

CARACTERÍSTICO, INHABITUAL,
EXTRAORDINARIO

PEDESTAL; pedestal;
  jī zuò: 基座, *base, foundation, pedestal*

PEDIGREE ó PEDIGRI; pedigree;
  shì xì: 世系, *pedigree*

PELVIS; pélvis;
  gǔ pén: 骨盆, *pelvis*

PENAL; penal;
  chǔ fá de: 处罚的, *penal*

PENÍNSULA (n); **península;**
  bàn dǎo: 半岛, *peninsula*

PER CÁPITA; per capita;
  měi rén: 每人, *everybody, each person;*
per capita

PERFORMANCE; performance;
  biǎo yǎn (n) (v): 表演, *performance,*
  exhibition; to perform/act/play;
  yǎn chū (n) (v): 演出, *performance,*
  show; to perform

PERFUME; perfume;
  xiāng shuǐ: 香水, *perfume, scent;*
  xiāng wèi: 香味, *fragrance, scent,*
perfume

PERPENDICULAR; perpendicular;
  chuí zhí de: 垂直的, *perpendicular*

PIANO; piano;
  gāng qín: 钢琴, *piano*

PIZZA; pizza;
  bǐ sà bǐng: 比萨饼, *pizza*

PLACEBO; placebo;
  ān wèi jì: 安慰剂, *placebo*

PLACENTA; placenta; *afterbirth;*
  tāi pán: 胎盘, *placenta*

PLASMA; plasma;
  xuè jiāng: 血浆, *plasma*

PLAYBOY ó PLAY-BOY; playboy;
huā huā gōng zǐ: 花花公子, *dandy,*
fop, playboy

PLURAL; plural;
fù shù de (lg): 复述的, *plural*

PLUVIAL; pluvial;
xià yǔ (sv) (n): 下雨, *rainy; summer*
rain;
yǔ jì: 雨季, *rainy season;*
yǔ shuǐ: 雨水, *rainwater, rainfall, rain;*
yǔ: 雨, *rain*

PÓKER ó PÓQUER; pôquer;
pū kè: 扑克, *poker*

POLAR; polar;
běi jí de: 北极的, *polar*

PONCHO; poncho;
yǔ pī: 雨披, *rain cape, poncho*

POPULAR; popular; *traditional;*
dà zhòng (attr): 大众, *popular;*
mín zhòng de: 民众的, *popular*

PÓRTICO; pórtico;
mén láng: 门廊, *porch, portico*

POSE; pose;
zī shì: 姿势, *pose, posture, bearing,*
carriage

POSTAL; postal; *order, money order;*
postal;
yóu zhèng de: 邮政的, *postal service/*
system

PÓSTER; pôster;
guǎng gào: 广告, *poster,*
advertisement;
zhāo tiē huà: 招贴画, *pictorial poster/*
placard;
SEE (请查看**) CARTEL**

PRECURSOR (A); **precursor** (A);
xiān qū: 先驱, *pioneer, forerunner,*
harbinger, predecessor

PRENATAL; pré-natal;
chǎn qián de: 产前的, *antenatal,*
prenatal

PRIMORDIAL; primordial; *primordial;*
chū shēng de: 出生的, *primordial*

PRINCIPAL; principal; *main,*
important;
zhǔ yào (attr): 主要, *main, chief, major,*
principal, fundamental

PRO; pro; *professional;*
yè wù: 业务, *professional (work-*
related);
zhí yè de: 职业的, *professional (not*
amateur);
SEE (请查看**) COMPETENTE,**
EXPERTO, OCUPACIÓN

PROPAGANDA; propaganda;
propaganda/ advertising;
guǎng gào huà (n): 广告画,
advertising poster;
guǎng gào huó dòng (n): 广告活动,
advertising campaign;
xuān chuán (v) (n): 宣传, *to*
propagate/ disseminate/give publicity to;
propaganda;
SEE (请查看**) PÓSTER**

PROVERBIAL; proverbial;
chéng yǔ: 成语, *idiom, proverb;*
yàn yǔ (n) (sv): 谚语, *proverb, saying,*
adage; proverbial

PUBIS; púbis;
chǐ gǔ: 耻骨, *pubic bones, pubis;*
yīn bù: 阴部, *private parts*

PUS; pus;
nóng yè: 脓液, *pus, fester;*
nóng: 脓, *pus*

Easily recognizable Spanish-Portuguese-English nouns, adjectives and adverbs and their Chinese equivalents
Nombres, sustantivos, adjetivos y adverbios en Español-Portugués-Inglés y sus equivalentes en Chino
Nomes, substantivos, adjetivos e advérbios em Espanhol-Português-Inglês e seus equivalentes em Chinês
容易辨认的西班牙语，葡萄牙语，英语的名词，形容词和副词和他们的中文对等词

PACIENCIA; paciência; *patience ...*
PACIENTE (adj); **paciente;** *patient, tolerant;*
  nài xīn (n) (sv): 耐心, *patience, endurance; patient;*
  qì liàng: 气量, *tolerance;*
  rěn nài (n) (v): 忍耐, *patience, forbearance; to be patient/have forbearance;*
SEE (请查看) AUTORIZAR, CLEMENCIA, CONSIDERACIÓN

PACÍFICO (A); **pacifico** (A); *peaceful;*
  ān jìng (sv) (v): 安静, *quiet, peaceful, tranquil; to pacify;*
  ān níng (sv) (n): 安宁, *peaceful, tranquil, undisturbed; calm, composed;*
  níng jìng (sv): 宁静, *peaceful, quiet, calm, tranquil;*
  píng hé (sv): 平和, *gentle, moderate, calm, composed, peaceful;*
  tài píng (sv): 太平, *peaceful;*
SEE (请查看) CALMA, TRANQUILO, TRANQUILIDAD

PACTO; pacto; *pact, agreement, contract;*
  bāo gōng: 包工, *contract;*
  hé tóng: 合同, *contract, agreement;*
  qì yuē: 契约, *contract, deed, agreement;*
  tiáo yuē: 条约, *treaty, pact;*
SEE (请查看) CONTRATO, CONSENSUAL, CONVENCIONAL

PALACIO; palácio; *palace;*
  gōng diàn: 宫殿, *palace*

PALMA; palma; *palm;*
  shǒu xīn: 手心, *palm of the hand, control;*
  shǒu zhǎng: 手掌, *palm;*

  zōng lǘ shù: 棕榈树, *palm tree*

PÁNICO; pânico; *panic;*
  jīng huāng (sv) (n): 惊慌, *become alarmed/panic-stricken; trepidation;*
  kǒng huāng (sv) (n): 恐慌, *panicky, frightened; panic*

PANORÁMICO (A); **panorâmico** (A); *panoramic;*
  quán jǐng (attr) (n): 全景, *panoramic; panorama*

PANTERA; pantera; *panther;*
  bào zi: 豹子, *panther*

PANTOMIMA; pantomima; *pantomime, mime;*
  yǎ jù: 哑剧, *pantomime*

PARADIGMA; paradigma; *paradigm, example;*
  biāo bīng: 标兵, *example, model, pacesetter;*
  shì lì: 事例, *example, instance, precedent;*
SEE (请查看) CLÁSICO, EJEMPLO

PARAFERNALIA; parafernália; *paraphernalia;*
  suí shēn wù pǐn: 随身物品, *paraphernalia;*
SEE (请查看) ARTEFACTO

PARÁFRASIS; paráfrase; *paraphrase;*
  shì yì (v) (n): 释义, *to explain/interpret; paraphrase*

PARAÍSO; paraíso; *paradise, heaven;*
  tiān guó: 天国, *Kingdom of Heaven, paradise;*
  tiān táng: 天堂, *paradise, heaven*

PARALELO (A); **paralelo** (A); *parallel*;
píng xíng (attr) (sv): 平行, *parallel; of equal rank; parallel (walls/lines/streets, etc.); concurrent*

PARÁLISIS; **paralisia**; *paralysis*;
má bì zhèng: 麻痹症, *paralysis*

PARÁMETRO; **parâmetro**; *parameter*;
cān shù: 参数, *parameter (MAT)*

PARAMILITAR; **paramilitar**;
paramilitary;
fǔ zhù jūn shì de: 辅助军事的, *paramilitary*

PARANOICO (A); **paranóico** (A); *paranoid*;
duō yí (sv): 多疑, *distrustful*;
wàng xiǎng kuáng (sv) (n): 妄想狂, *paranoid; paranoia*

PARCIAL; **parcial**; *partial, incomplete*;
bù fen (sv) (n): 部分, *partial; part*;
bù wán quán (sv): 不完全, *incomplete*;
bù wán shàn (sv): 不完善, *incomplete, imperfect*;
cán quē (vp): 残缺, *incomplete, fragmentary*;
jú bù (n) (sv): 局部, *part, portion; local, partial*;
SEE (请查看) INCOMPLETO

PARCIALIDAD; **parcialidade**;
partiality, bias;
chéng jiàn (n): 成见, *preconceived idea, prejudice*;
piān 'ài (v) (n): 偏爱, *to be partial to sb/sthg; partial*;
piān jī (sv): 偏激, *extreme (opinions), radical*;
piān jiàn (n): 偏见, *bias, prejudice*;
piān tǎn (v) (n): 偏袒, *to be partial to and side with; partial*;
piān xīn (sv): 偏心, *partial, biased*;
SEE (请查看) PREJUICIO, CONTRA, PARCIALIDAD, DIGRESIÓN

PARIDAD; **paridade**; *parity, equality*;
děng shì: 等式, *equality*;

duì děng: 对等, *parity, equity*;
jūn děng: 均等, *equality*;
píng děng (sv) (n): 平等, *equal; equality*;
tóng děng (attr): 同等, *of the same class/rank/ status; equivalent*

PARQUE; **parque**; *park*;
gōng yuán: 公园, *park*;
yuán lín: 园林, *park, garden*

PÁRRAFO ó PARÁGRAFO;
parágrafo; *paragraph.. PARTE; parte; part, section*;
duàn luò: 段落, *paragraph*;
piàn duàn: 片断, *section, part; fragment, extract (attr) incomplete, fragmentary*;
zhāng jié: 章节, *chapter(s), section(s)*;
SEE (请查看) PARCIAL, COMPONENTE

PARTICIPANTE; **participante**;
participating;
cān jiā zhě: 参加者, *participant*;
cān yù de: 参与的, *participating*

PARTÍCULA; **partícula**; *particle*;
jí shǎo de: 极少的, *particle; pellet; grain*;
lì zǐ: 粒子, *grain, granule; pellet; particle*;
wēi lì: 微粒, *particle (FIS)*

PASADO (A); **passado** (A); *past; stale, overripe*;
bù xīn xiān (sv): 不新鲜, *stale, drab, tasteless*
fá wèi (sv): 乏味, *stale, drab, tasteless; dull*

PASAPORTE; **passaporte**; *passport*;
hù zhào: 护照, *passport*

PASIVO (A); **passivo** (A); *passive; liabilities (COM)*;
bèi dòng (sv): 被动, *passive; disadvantageous*;
fù zhài (v) (n): 负债, *to be in debt; debt, liabilities*;

SEE (请查看) DESANIMADO

PASTA; pasta; *paste; putty, pastry*;
 hú (v) (n) (sv): 糊, *to paste/plaster;
 paste, plaster; overcooked*

PASTEURIZADO (A); pasteurizado
(A); *pasteurized*;
 miè jūn (n): 灭菌, *sterilization,
 disinfection*;
 xiāo dú (v) (attr): 消毒, *to disinfect,
 sterilize; pasteurized, sterilized,
 disinfected*

PATÉTICO (A); patético (A); *pathetic,
moving*;
 kě lián (sv): 可怜, *pitiable, pitiful;
 pathetic*;
SEE (请查看) LÁSTIMA

PATOLOGÍA; patologia; *pathology
... PATOLÓGICO (A); patológico (A);
pathological*;
 bìng lǐ xuē de: 病理学的,
 pathological;
 bìng lǐ xué: 病理学, *pathology*

PATRIOTA; patriota; *patriot ...
PATRIÓTICO (A); patriótico (A);
patriotic*;
 ài guó (v) (sv): 爱国, *to love one's
 country; patriotic*;
 ài guó de: 爱国的, *patriotic*;
 ài guó zhě: 爱国者, *patriot*;
 ài guó zhǔ yì: 爱国主义, *patriotism*

PATRÓN (A); patrono (A); *boss, master;
owner*;
 gōng tóu: 工头, *foreman, boss*;
 lǎo bǎn: 老板, *boss, manager;
 shopkeeper, proprietor*;
 shàng si: 上司, *superior, boss*;
 tóu zi: 头子, *boss, chieftan; best,
 winner*;
 zhǔ jiàng: 主将, *chief, key person; star
 athletic*;
 zhǔ rén: 主人, *master, host, owner*;
 zhǔ zi: 主子, *master, boss; emperor*

PAUSA; pausa; *pause, break*;

tíng dù (v) (n): 停顿, *to stop/halt/
pause; pause, halt*
SEE (请查看) MORATORIA

PAUSADO (A); pausado (A); *slow,
deliberate*;
 chí chí (adv): 迟迟, *slowly; tardily*;
 màn màn de (adv): 慢慢地, *slowly,
 gradually*;
 tuō lā (sv) (v): 拖拉, *dilatory, stalling,
 slow, sluggish; to put off*;
 tuō tà (sv) (vp): 拖沓, *dilatory, sluggish,
 laggard; to do things in a muddled
 manner*;
SEE (请查看) ENDÉMICO, LENTO

PECULIARIDAD; peculiaridade;
uniqueness, peculiarity;
 gǔ guài (sv): 古怪, *peculiarity,
 eccentric, odd, strange*;
 guāi pì (sv): 乖僻, *eccentric, odd*;
 tè zhì: 特制, *special qualities,
 uniqueness*;
SEE (请查看) CUALIDAD

PEDANTE; pedante; *pedantic,
pretentious; pedant*;
 shū dāi zi: 书呆子, *pedant, bookworm*;
 xué jiū: 学究, *pedant*;
 yū fǔ (sv): 迂腐, *trite, dogmatic,
 pedantic*

PEDESTRE; pedestre; *pedestrian*;
 bù xíng zhě (n): 步行者, *pedestrian*;
 bù xíng (sv) (v): 步行, *pedestrian; to go
 on foot*;
 xíng rén: 行人, *pedestrian*

PENICILINA; penicilina; *penicillin*;
 qīng méi sù: 青霉素, *penicillin*

PENITENTE; penitente; *penitent*;
 huǐ guò de: 悔过的, *penitent*;
 huǐ guò zhě (n): 悔过者, *penitent*

PENSADOR (A); pensador (A);
thinker;
 sī xiǎng jiā: 思想家, *thinker*

PENURIA; penúria; *penury, poverty,
destitution*;

pín kùn (sv) (n): 贫困, *poor, impoverished, poverty*;
SEE (请查看) **DÉFICIT, DIFÍCIL, MISERIA**

PERCEPCIÓN; percepção; *perception*;
  zhī jué: 知觉, *perception, intuition*;
SEE (请查看) **DETECTAR**

PERCUSIÓN; percussão; *percussion*;
  dǎ jī yuè qì: 打击乐器, *percussion*;
  dǎ jī yuè: 打击乐, *percussion (musical instrument)*

PERFECCIÓN; perfeição; *perfection* ... **PERFECCIONISTA; perfeccionista;** *perfectionist* ... **PERFECTAMENTE; perfeitamente;** *perfectly* ... **PERFECTO** (A); **perfeito** (A); *perfect (adj); perfect tense (n)*;
  fēi cháng hǎo de: 非常好地, *perfectly*;
  jué duì (sv): 绝对, *absolute, perfect, definite*;
  wán chéng shí: 完成时, *perfectly*;
  wán měi wú xiá: 完美无暇, *perfection*;
  wán měi zhǔ yì zhě: 完美主义者, *perfectionist*;
  wán shàn: 完善, *perfect, consummate*;
  wú xiá (vp): 无暇, *flawless, without blemish/defect/ fault; perfect*;
SEE (请查看) **CONSUMADO**

PERFIDIA; perfídia; *perfidy, treachery, betrayal* ... **PÉRFIDO** (A); **pérfido** (A); *perfidious, treacherous*;
  bèi pàn (n) (v): 背叛, *treachery, betrayal; to betray*;
  bèi xìn qì yì (fe): 背信弃义, *be perfidious*;
  chū mài (n) (v): 出卖, *betrayal; to sell out/betray*;
  jiān xiǎn (sv): 奸险, *treacherous, malicious*;
SEE (请查看) **CONSPIRACIÓN, INFIDELIDAD, INSIDIOSO**

PERIFERIA; periferia; *periphery, outskirts*;

yuán zhōu: 圆周, *circumference; periphery*;
  zhōu biān: 周边, *periphery*;

PERIÓDICO; periódico (A); *periodic*;
  dìng qī de: 定期的, *periodic*

PERÍODO; período; *period (GEN) (DEP) (MED); time period (GEOL)*;
  shí qī: 时期, *period of time*;
SEE (请查看) **CICLO, FASE**

PERJURIO; perjúrio; *perjury, lying, mendacity, deception*;
  wěi zhèng: 伪证, *perjury, false testimony*;
  wěi zhèng zuì: 伪证罪, *perjury*

PERMANENCIA; permanência; *endurance; staying, continued stay, continuation* ... **PERMANENTE; permanente;** *permanent, fast*;
  cháng jiǔ (sv): 长久, *permanent*;
  cháng rèn (attr): 常任, *permanent, standing*;
  nài lì: 耐力, *endurance, stamina*;
  yǒng héng (attr): 永恒, *eternal, perpetual, permanent*;
  yǒng jiǔ (attr): 永久, *permanent, perpetual, everlasting*;
SEE (请查看) **DURADERO**

PERMISIBLE; permissível; *permissible* ... **PERMISIVO** (A); **tolerante;** *permissive*;
  fàng rèn (sv) (n): 放任, *to let alone, permissive; noninterference*;
  zòng róng (v) (sv): 纵容, *to connive/ wink at; permissive*;
SEE (请查看) **AUTORIDAD**

PERNICIOSO (A); **pernicioso** (A); *damaging, harmful, pernicious*;
  fáng hài (v) (vp): 妨害, *to impair/ jeopardize/be harmful; harmful*;
  yǒu hài (sv): 有害, *harmful, destructive*;
SEE (请查看) **MALICIA**

PERPLEJIDAD; perplexidade;

perplexity, bewilderment, confusion
... PERPLEJO (A)**; perplexo** (A)**;**
perplexed, bewildered, puzzled;
  huáng huò (sv): 惶惑, *perplexed;*
  mí hu (sv): 迷糊, *confused;*
  mí máng (sv): 迷茫, *vast and hazy;*
  perplexed, dazed;
  mí wǎng (sv): 迷惘, *perplexed, to be at*
  a loss;
SEE (请查看) **CAOS, CONFUSO**

PERSEVERANCIA; perseverança;
perseverance, determination ...
PERSISTENCIA; persistência;
persistence;
  bù qū bù náo (fe): 不屈不挠,
  unyielding, indomitable;
  chí xù (sv) (v): 持续, *persistence; to*
  persist/continue;
  yì lì: 毅力, *willpower, will, stamina,*
  perseverance;
SEE (请查看) **DETERMINACIÓN,**
ÉNFASIS, INSISTENCIA

PERSONALIDAD; personalidade;
personality;
  rén gé: 人格, *character, moral quality,*
  personality

PERSONALMENTE; pessoalmente;
personally;
  qīn shǒu (adv): 亲手, *personally, with*
  one's own hands;
  qīn zì (adv): 亲自, *personally, in person*

PERSPECTIVA; perspectiva;
perspective, view, prospect;
  kàn fǎ (n): 看法, *way of seeing sthg,*
  view;
  shì yě: 视野, *perspective;*
  tòu shì (n) (v): 透视, *perspective; to see*
  through/ penetrate;
  yǎn guāng: 眼光, *foresight, insight,*
  perspective

PERSPICACIA; perspicácia;
perceptiveness, insight;
  dòng chá lì: 洞察力, *insight,*
  discernment

PERSPICAZ; perspicaz; *sharp,*
perceptive, shrewd;
  gāo míng (sv) (n): 高明, *brilliant, wise;*
  better qualified; brilliant person;
  jīng míng (sv): 精明, *astute, shrewd;*
  zhī jué (n) (sv): 知觉, *perception;*
  perceptive;
SEE (请查看) **ASTUCIA, DETECTAR**

PERSUASIVO (A)**; persuasivo** (A)**;**
persuasive, convincing, compelling;
  yǒu shuō fú lì de: 有说服力的,
  persuasive;
SEE (请查看) **CONVICCIÓN**

PERTINENCIA; pertinência;
pertinence; appropriateness, relevance
... PERTINENTE; pertinente;
appropriate, pertinent, relevant;
  guān lián (v) (n): 关联, *to be related/*
  connected; connection, correlation;
  qiè tí (v) (sv): 切题, *to keep to the point;*
  relevant, pertinent;
  qiè tí de: 切题的, *relevant, pertinent,*
  appropriate;
  xiāng guān (n) (attr) (vp): 相关,
  correlation; relative; be interrelated;
  xiāng guān xìng: 相关性, *relevance,*
  correlation, pertinence;
  zhòng kěn (sv) (n):中肯, *apropos,*
  pertinent, to the point; critical mass (FIS);
SEE (请查看) **APROPIADO,**
CORRECTAMENTE, CONCERNIR

PERVERSIDAD; perversidade;
wickedness, perversity, depravity...
PERVERSO (A)**; perverso** (A)**;**
depraved, wicked, perverse...
PERVERTIDO (A)**; pervertido** (A)**;**
depraved, perverted, deviant;
  biàn tài de: 变态的, *abnormal,*
  perverse;
  bù hé cháng qíng de: 不合常情的,
  perverse;
  duò luò (sv): 堕落, *degenerate;*
  duò luò zhě: 堕落者, *pervert;*
  fǎn cháng (sv): 反常, *unusual,*
  abnormal; perverse, anomalous;
  gāng bì (vp): 刚愎, *headstrong,*
  perverse;
  jiān chí cuò wù de: 坚持错误的,

perverse;
rèn xìng (sv): 任性, *willful, headstrong; perverse;*
wéi fǎn cháng qìng de: 违反常情的, *perverse;*
SEE (请查看) MAL, VENENOSO

PESIMISMO; pessimismo; *pessimism ... PESIMISTA; pessimista; pessimistic (adj), pessimist (n);*
bēi guān de: 悲观的, *pessimistic;*
bēi guān zhě: 悲观者, *pessimist;*
SEE (请查看) FATALISMO

PÉSIMO (A) (adj); **péssimo** (A); *terrible, awful, dreadful;*
gòu qiàng (sv): 够呛, *unbearable, terrible;*
hài rén (sv): 骇人, *shocking, frightening;*
làn tān zi: 烂摊子, *shambles, awful mess;*
wèi jù (v) (sv): 畏惧, *to fear/dread; dreadful;*
SEE (请查看) DESESPERACIÓN, GRAVE, HORROR

PESTICIDA; pesticida; *pesticide;*
nóng yào: 农药, *pesticide;*
shā chóng jì: 杀虫剂, *insecticide, pesticide*

PESTILENCIA; pestilência; *plague, pestilence;*
wēn yì: 瘟疫, *pestilence; epidemic, plague*

PESTILENTE (adj); **pestilento** (A); *foul-smelling, stink, stench;*
chòu qì: 臭气, *stench;*
è chòu: 恶臭, *stench, stink*

PETRÓLEO; petróleo; *petroleum, crude oil;*
shí yóu: 石油, *petroleum*

PETULANCIA; petulância; *arrogance, conceit, insolence, pride ... PETULANTE; petulante; opinionated, arrogant, brazen;*
ào (sv): 傲, *proud, haughty; (bf) brave,*

refusing to yield
hòu yán (vp): 厚颜, *brazen, shameless;*
jiāo 'ào zì dà: 骄傲自大, *conceited, swollen with pride;*
mán hèng (sv): 蛮横, *overbearing, arbitrary, opinionated;*
zì 'ào (sv): 自傲, *arrogant, conceited;*
zì dà (sv): 自大, *self-important, arrogant, conceited; self-important;*
zì duō (n): 自多, *self-satisfied, conceited;*
zì gāo zì dà (fe): 自高自大, *self-important, conceited, arrogant;*
zì liàn (n) (v): 自恋, *narcissism;*
zì sī (sv): 自私, *selfish, self-centered;*
zì yòng (vp): 自用, *opinionated, self-willed; (attr) personal;*
SEE (请查看) ARROGANCIA, COMPLACIDO, EGOCÉNTRICO

PIANISTA; pianista; *pianist;*
gāng qín jiā: 钢琴家, *pianist*

PICTÓRICO (A); **pictórico** (A); *pictorial;*
yǒu tú huá de: 有图画的, *pictorial;*

PIGMENTO; pigmento; *pigment;*
sè sù: 色素, *pigment (ANAT);*
yán liào: 颜料, *pigment, color (ARTE)*

PIJAMA ó PIYAMA; pajama; *pajama(s);*
shuì kù: 睡裤, *pajama trousers;*
shuì yī: 睡衣, *pajamas*

PILAR; pilar; *pillar, post;*
zhù zi: 柱子, *post, pillar;*
SEE (请查看) COLUMNA

PILOTO; piloto; *pilot (GEN); driver;*
fēi xíng yuán: 飞行员, *pilot, aviator;*
jià shǐ yuán: 驾驶员, *driver, pilot;*
lǐng háng yuán: 领航员, *navigator, pilot*

PIRÁMIDE; pirâmide; *pyramid;*
jīn zì tǎ: 金字塔, *pyramid*

PIRATA; pirate; *pirate;*
hǎi dào xíng wéi: 海盗行为, *piracy;*
hǎi dào: 海盗, *pirate*

PISTOLA; pistol; *pistol, gun ...*
PISTOLERO (A); **pistoleiro** (A);
gunman;
  qiāng shǒu: 抢手, *gunman,*
sharpshooter, gunner;
  shǒu qiāng: 手枪, *pistol*

PLÁSTICO (A); **plástico** (A); *plastic;*
  sù liào bó mó: 塑料薄膜, *plastic film/*
sheeting;
  sù liào dài: 塑料袋, *plastic bags;*
  sù liào: 塑料, *plastics; plastic*

PLATÓNICO (A); **platônico** (A);
platonic, chaste, asexual, detached;
  chún jīng shén de: 纯精神的,
platonic, detached;
  jīng shén liàn 'ài: 精神恋爱, *platonic*
love

PLEBE; plebe; *common people; the*
masses; mob, rabble;
  bào mín: 暴民, *mob;*
  qún zhòng: 群众, *the masses/people*

PLEBISCITO; plebiscito; *plebiscite;*
  gōng mín tóu piào: 公民投票,
referendum, plebiscite

PLEURESÍA; pleurisia; *pleurisy;*
  xiōng mó yán: 胸膜炎, *pleurisy*

PLUMA; pluma; *feather;*
  yǔ máo: 羽毛, *feather; plume*

POEMA; poema; *poem;*
  shī de: 诗的, *poetic;*
  shī rén: 诗人, *pet;*
  shī: 诗, *poem*

POLÉMICA; polêmico (A); *controversy*
(n); polemic (adj);
  lùn zhàn (n) (v): 论战, *polemic; to*
debate
SEE (请查看**) ARGUMENTAR,**
DEBATE, CONFLICTO,
CONTROVERSIA

POLEN; pólen; *pollen;*
  huā fěn zhǐ shù: 花粉指数, *pollen*

count;
  huā fěn: 花粉, *pollen*

POLICÍA; polícia; *police officer, police;*
  jǐng chá: 警察, *police, policeman*

POLIÉSTER; poliéster; *polyester;*
  dí lún: 涤纶, *polyester fiber;*
  jù zhǐ: 聚酯, *polyester*

POLIGAMIA; poligamia; *polygamy;*
  yī fū-duō qī: 一夫多妻, *polygamy;*
  yī qī-duō fū: 一妻多夫, *polyandry*

POLÍTICO (A); **político** (A); *political,*
(POL); tactful;
  yuán tōng de: 圆通的, *smooth, tactful,*
accommodating;
  zhèng zhì (sv) (n): 政治, *political;*
politics, political affairs

POPULARIDAD; popularidade;
popularity;
  chī xiāng (fe): 吃香, *to be very*
popular;
  tōng sú (sv): 通俗, *popular, common;*
  tōng sú xìng: 通俗性, *popularity*

PORCELANA; porcelana; *porcelain;*
  cí qì: 瓷器, *porcelain, chinaware;*
  cí: 瓷, *porcelain*

PORNOGRÁFICO (A); **pornográfico**
(A); *pornographic;*
  huáng sè (n): 黄色, *yellow; (attr)*
decadent, obscene, pornographic;
SEE (请查看**) ERÓTICO**

PORO; poro; *pore;*
  máo kǒng: 毛孔, *pore (ANAT)*

PORTAL; portal; *doorway, entrance,*
main door;
  dà mén: 大门, *main entrance/door/*
gate;
  mén hù: 门户, *door; strategic gateway;*
faction, sect; family;
  mén kǒu: 门口, *doorway, entrance;*
  rù kǒu chù: 入口处, *entrance*

PORTÁTIL; portátil; *portable;*

shǒu tí (attr): 手提, *portable*;
shǒu tí shì (attr): 手提式, *portable*;
SEE (请查看) **CONVENIENTE**

POSESIVO (A); **possessivo** (A);
possessive;
zhàn yǒu yù qiáng de: 占有欲强的,
possessive

POSIBLE; possível; *possible* ...
POSIBILIDAD; possibilidade;
possibility, chance;
kě néng (sv) (aux) (n): 可能, *possible,
probable; probably, maybe; possibility*;
SEE (请查看) **CONTINGENCIA**

POSITIVO (A); **positivo** (A); *positive,
practical*;
xiàn shí (n) (sv): 现实, *reality, actuality;
practical, pragmatic; real, actual*;
SEE (请查看) **AFIRMAR, APLICAR,
EFECTIVIDAD, CONSTRUCTIVO**

POSTERIDAD; posteridade; *posterity*;
zǐ sūn hòu dài: 子孙后代, *posterity*

POSTRERO; último (A); *last*;
zuì zhōng: 最终, *final, last, ultimate*;
SEE (请查看) **DEFINITIVO,
EVENTUAL, ÚLTIMO**

POSTULADO; postulado; *assumption*;
jiǎ dìng (v) (n): 假定, *to suppose/
assume/ grant/presume; hypothesis,
postulate (MAT)*;
jiǎ dìng zhī shì: 假定之事,
assumption;
jiǎ shè (v) (n): 假设, *to suppose/
assume/grant/ presume; hypothesis,
postulate*

PÓSTUMO (A); **póstumo** (A);
posthumous;
sǐ hòu de: 死后的, *posthumous*

POSTURA; postura; *posture, position,
stance*;
tài dù: 态度, *manner, bearing; attitude,
approach*;
zī shì: 姿势, *posture, carriage, bearing*;
zī tài: 姿态, *posture, carriage; attitude,
pose*

POTE; pote; *pot, jar*;
guàn: 罐, *vessel, container; jug, jar; can,
tin; pot*;
guō: 锅, *pot, wok, pan*;
hú: 壶, *kettle, pot*;
SEE (请查看) **RECEPTÁCULO,
BOTELLA, VASO**

POTENCIA; potencia; *potency, power*;
gōng lǜ: 功率, *power (FIS)*;
lì liàng: 力量, *physical strength; power,
force*;
lì qi: 力气, *physical strength, effort*;
néng lì: 能力, *power, capacity;
competence, ability*;
qián lì: 潜力, *latent capacity; potential,
potentiality*;
quán xiàn: 权限, *powers, jurisdiction;
competence*;
shì lì: 势力, *force, power, influence*;
shí lì: 实力, *strength, power, actual
strength*;
shí quán: 实权, *real power*;
tǐ lì: 体力, *physical power/strength*;
zhí quán: 职权, *official powers*;
SEE (请查看) **AUTORIDAD,
EFECTIVIDAD, ÍMPETU, ENERGÍA**

POTENCIAL; potencial; *potential,
conditional*;
qián zài (attr): 潜在, *latent, potential*;
qián zài xìng (n): 潜在性, *potentiality*;
yǒu tiáo jiàn (sv): 有条件, *conditional*;
SEE (请查看) **POSIBLE**

POTENTE; potente; *powerful*;
qiáng dà (sv): 强大, *big and powerful;
formidable*;
qiáng jìn (sv): 强劲, *powerful,
vigorous*;
qiáng shèng (sv): 强盛, *prosperous
and powerful (of a nation)*;
qiáng yǒu lì (attr): 强有力, *strong,
vigorous, forceful, powerful*;
yǒu lì (sv): 有力, *strong, powerful*

PRÁCTICO (A) (adj); **prático**
(A); *practical, dandy; sensible* ...
PRAGMÁTICO (A); **pragmático** (A);
pragmatic (adj), pragmatist (n);
míng lǐ (n) (sv): 明理, *obvious reason/*

fact; sensible, reasonable;

qiè shí (sv) (adv): 切实, *feasible, practical, realistic; practically, honestly, realistically*;

shí yòng (sv): 实用, *practical, functional, pragmatic*;

shí yòng zhǔ yì de: 实用主义的, *pragmatic*;

shí yòng zhǔ yì zhě: 实用主义者, *pragmatist*;

shí yòng zhǔ yì: 实用主义, *pragmatism*;

wù shí (v) (n): 务实, *to try to be sensible/practical/ pragmatic; pragmatism*;

SEE (请查看) POSITIVO, EQUILIBRADO

PRECARIO (A); **precário** (A); *precarious*;

bù què dìng (attr): 不确定, *indeterminate; precarious*;

bù wěn dìng de: 不稳定的, *unstable, precarious*;

fēng yún: 风云, *precarious position; wind and clouds; turmoil*;

kào bu zhù (sv): 靠不住, *unreliable, undependable, precarious*

PRECEPTO; preceito; *precept, order, rule*;

xìn tiáo: 信条, *precept, tenet*

PRECIOSO (A); **precioso** (A); *precious*;

zhēn guì: 珍贵, *valuable, precious*

PRECIPICIO; precipício; *precipice* ...
PRECIPITADO (A); **precipitado** (A); *hasty, headlong*;

cāng cù (adv): 仓促, *hastily; all of a sudden*;

dǒu qiào (sv): 陡峭, *precipitous*;

xiǎn jìng: 险境, *dangerous situation*;

xuán yá: 悬崖, *precipice*

PRECISAMENTE; precisamente; *precisely* ... **PRECISO** (A); **preciso** (A); *precise*;

jīng què (sv) (n): 精确, *accurate, exact, precise; accuracy*;

zhǔn què (sv): 准确, *accurate, exact, precise*;

SEE (请查看) DETERMINADO, EXACTAMENTE

PRECOCIDAD; precocidade; *precociousness, precocity* ... **PRECOZ; precoce**; *premature, early; precocious*

guò zǎo fā yù: 过早发育, *precocity*;

zǎo shú (vp) (n): 早熟, *precocious; precocity*

PREDADOR (A); **predador** (A); *predatory (adj), predator (n)* ...
PREDATORIO (A); **predatório** (A); *predatory instincts, animal instincts*;

lüè duó zhě: 掠夺者, *plunderer, robber, predator*;

pò huài zhě: 破坏者, *destroyer, wrecker*;

ròu shí dòng wù: 肉食动物, *carnivore, predator (ZOOL)*

PREDECESOR (A); **predecessor** (A); *predecessor, ancestor*;

qián rèn (attr) (n): 前任, *ex-; predecessor*

PREDESTINADO (A); **predestinado** (A); *predestined, ordained, fated*;

mìng dìng (attr): 命定, *predestined, fated*;

sù mìng (attr) (n): 宿命, *fated, predestined; fate, predestination*;

SEE (请查看) FATALISMO

PREDISPUESTO; predisposto (A); *predisposed, inclined to, liable to*;

qīng xiàng yú: 倾向于, *predisposed, inclined*;

zàn tóng (v) (sv): 赞同, *to approve of; inclined, predisposed*;

SEE (请查看) INCLINACIÓN

PREDOMINANCIA; predominância; *predominance* ... **PREDOMINANTE; predominante**; *predominant, controlling, ruling* ... **PREDOMINIO; predomínio**; *preponderance, predominance*;

dà liàng: 大量, *preponderance*;
yōu shì: 优势, *predominance*;
zhàn yōu shì de: 占优势的, *predominant*

PREEMINENCIA; preeminência; *preeminence* ... **PREEMINENTE; preeminente;** *preeminent, peerless, unequaled;*
zhuó yuè (vp): 卓越, *unequaled; outstanding, brilliant;*
SEE (请查看**) ATÍPICO, EGREGIO, IMBATIBLE**

PREFABRICADO (A); **pré-fabricado** (A); *prefabricated;*
yù xiān biān zào: 预先编造, *prefabricated*

PREFACIO; prefácio; *preface, foreword;*
xù yán: 序言, *preface, foreword*

PREFERENCIA; preferência; *preference, partiality, inclination, bent* ... **PREFERENCIAL; preferencial;** *preferential* ... **PREFERENTEMENTE; preferivelmente;** *preferably* ... **PREFERIBLE** (A); **preferível;** *preferable(to)* ... **PREFERIDO** (A); **preferido** (A); *preferred, favored;*
chǒng 'ér: 宠儿, *pet, favorite;*
gèng hé yì de: 更合意的, *preferable;*
gèng shì yì de (adv): 更合意地, *preferably;*
piān 'ài (v) (n): 偏爱, *to be partial; preference;*
piān 'ài wù: 偏爱物 , *preference;*
yōu xiān (v) (attr): 优先, *to have priority; preferential, preferred, priority;*
yōu xiān de: 优先的, *preferential;*
yōu xiān quán (n): 优先权, *priority, preference;*
SEE (请查看**) INCLINACIÓN, BENÉFICO**

PRELADO; prelado; *prelate;*
gāo jí jiào shì: 高级教士, *prelate*

PRELIMINAR (adj); **preliminar;** *preliminary; qualifying (DEP);*
chū bù: 初步, *preliminaries, first stages;*
kāi shǐ (n) (v): 开始, *preliminary, beginning; to begin/start*

PRELUDIO; prelúdio; *prelude;*
xù mù: 序幕, *prologue, prelude;*
xù qǔ: 序曲, *overture, prelude (MUS)*

PREMATURO (A); **prematuro** (A); *premature;*
guò zǎo (vp) (adv): 过早, *premature, untimely; prematurely*

PREMEDITADO (A); **premeditado** (A); *premeditated, deliberate;*
yù móu (sv) (n): 预谋, *premeditated; premeditation;*
SEE (请查看**) DELIBERADO**

PREMISA; premissa; *premise;*
jiǎ shè (v) (n) (conj): 假设, *to suppose/ assume; hypothesis; supposing, in case;*
qián tí: 前提, *premise, supposition, prerequisite*

PREOCUPACIÓN; preocupação; *concern, worry* ... **PREOCUPADO** (A); **preocupado** (A); *worried, concerned;*
bù 'ān (sv): 不安, *worried, uneasy, restless, unsettled, troubled;*
dān xīn de: 担心的, *concerned, worried;*
dān yōu (v) (n): 担忧, *to be apprehensive; to worry; to be anxious; concern, worry;*
xīn shì: 心事, *worry, mental stress;*
yōu chóu (vp) (n): 忧愁, *worried, sad, depressed; grief, melancholy;*
zháo jí (sv) (v): 着急, *to worry/feel anxious; anxious, worried;*
SEE (请查看**) APRENSIÓN, BILIOSO, DESCONCERTANTE, CONSTERNACIÓN, CONCERNIR**

PREPARACIÓN; preparação; *preparation* ... **PREPARADO** (A); **preparado** (A); *ready, prepared;*
jiù xù (vp): 就绪, *to be in order, to be ready;*

jiù xù de: 就绪的, *ready*;
qí bèi (v) (sv): 齐备, *to be complete/be all ready; ready*;
tíng dang (sv): 停当, *ready, settled*;
xùn sù de: 迅速的, *ready*;
yǒu zhǔn bèi de: 有准备的, *prepared*;
yuàn yi de: 愿意的, *ready*;
zhǔn bèi hǎo (n) (sv): 准备好, *at the ready; prepared; ready*;
zuò hǎo zhǔn bèi de: 做好准备的, *prepared, available, ready*

PREPARATIVOS; preparativos;
arrangements, preparations;
zhǔn bèi fǎ: 准备法, *preparations*;
SEE (请查看) DISPOSICIÓN

PREPONDERANCIA; preponderância; *preponderance ...*
PREPONDERANTE; preponderante;
prevailing, preponderant;
duō shù de: 多数的, *preponderant*;
SEE (请查看) DOMINANTE

PREPOTENCIA; prepotência;
forcefulness, tyranny, arrogance
... PREPOTENTE; prepotente;
domineering, overbearing, high-handed;
ào man (sv): 傲慢, *arrogant, haughty*;
bà dào (sv) (n): 霸道, *overbearing, high-handed*;
bào zhèng (n): 暴政, *tyranny, despotic rule*;
zhuān hèng (vp): 专横, *imperious, peremptory, domineering*;
zhuān zhì (n) (sv): 专制, *autocracy; autocratic, despotic*

PRERREQUISITO; pré-requisito;
prerequisite;
qián tí: 前题, *prerequisite, premise, presupposition*;
xiān jué (attr): 先决, *prerequisite*;
xiān jué tiáo jiàn: 先决条件, *prerequisite, precondition, premise*

PRERROGATIVA; prerrogativa;
prerogative;
tè quán: 特权, *prerogative*

PRESENCIA; presença; *presence*;
chū xí (v) (n): 出席 , *to be present; presence*;
zài chǎng (n) (v): 在场, *present; to be on the spot/ scene*

PRESENTACIÓN; apresentação
(GEN); *presentation, introduction*;
dǎo yán (n): 导言, *introductory remarks; introduction to a written piece*;
gài lùn (n): 概论, *introduction, outline, general discussion*;
qián yán (n): 前沿, *earlier remarks, preface, foreword, introduction*;
xù yán (n): 序言, *preface, foreword, introduction*;
yǐn yán (n): 引言, *foreword, introduction*

PRESENTADOR (A); **apresentador** (A); *presenter, hostess/host*;
jié mù zhǔ chí rén: 节目主持人, *anchor, master of ceremonies*;
zhǔ chí rén: 主持人, *host, anchor, chair*

PRESENTIMIENTO; premonição;
presentiment, feeling, premonition;
xiáng (bf): 祥, *auspicious*;
yù zhào: 预兆, *omen, sign, harbinger; premonition*;
SEE (请查看) AUGURAR

PRESERVACIÓN; preservação;
preservation;
bǎo hù: 保护, *preservation*;
SEE (请查看) CONSERVACIÓN

PRESIDENCIAL; presidencial;
presidential;
zǒng tǒng de: 总统的, *presidential*

PRESIDIO; presídio; *prison*;
bān fáng (n): 班房, *jail, prison*;
jiān yù (n): 监狱, *prison, jail*;
láo fáng (n): 牢房, *jail, prison cell*;
láo yù (n): 牢狱, *prison*;
SEE (请查看) APREHENDER

PRESTIGIO; prestígio; *prestige ...*
PRESTIGIOSO (A) (adj); **prestigioso**

(A); *prestigious, famous*;
shēng wàng: 声望, *popularity, prestige*;
wēi xìn: 威信, *prestige, popular trust, one's dignity/credit*;
xìn yù: 信誉, *prestige*;
yǒu shēng wàng de: 有声望的, *prestigious*;
SEE (请查看) **FAMOSO, CELEBRIDAD, REPUTACIÓN**

PRESUNCIÓN; presunção; *presumption, conceit, vanity* ...
PRESUNTUOSO (A); **presunçoso** (A); *conceited, presumptuous* ...
PRETENCIOSO (A); **pretencioso** (A); *pretentious, showy, snobbish, vain*;
fàng sì (vp): 放肆, *unbridled, wanton, impudent, presumptuous, licentious*;
jiǎ dìng (v) (n): 假定, *to suppose/ assume/grant/ presume; hypothesis, presumption, postulate (MAT)*;
jiǎ dìng de: 假定的, *presumptive*;
shì lì (sv): 势力, *snobbish*;
tuī cè (v) (n): 推测, *to infer; guess, conjuncture; explanation, presumption*;
xiān yàn (sv): 显眼, *conspicuous, showy*;
xū róng (sv) (n): 虚荣, *vain; vanity*;
xū róng xīn: 虚荣心, *vanity*;
SEE (请查看) **ARROGANCIA, ASUMIR, EGOCÉNTRICO, PETULANCIA**

PRETENDIDO (A); **pretenso** (A); *supposed, alleged*;
shēng chēng (v) (sv): 声称, *to profess/ claim; alleged, claimed*;
suǒ wèi de: 所谓的, *alleged*

PRETENSIÓN; pretensão; *aim, intention, aspiration*;
bào fù: 抱负, *aspiration, ambition*;
běn yì (n): 本意, *original idea, real intention*;
dòng jī (n): 动机, *motive, motivation, intention*;
mù biāo (n): 目标, *objective, goal, target*;
niàn tou (n): 念头, *thought, idea,*

intention;
xīn cháng (n): 心肠, *heart, intention*;
xīn yì (n): 心意, *intention, purpose; kindly feeling*;
yì tú (n): 意图, *intention, intent*;
yòng yì (n): 用意, *intention, purpose*;
zhì qi (n): 志气, *aspiration, ambition*;
zhì qù (n): 志趣, *aspiration and interest, inclination, bent*;
zhǐ yì (n): 旨意, *decree, order; will intention*;
zhì yuàn (n) (v): 志愿, *aspiration, wish, ideal; to volunteer/pledge to do sthg*;
zōng zhǐ (n): 宗旨, *aim, purpose*;
SEE (请查看) **ATENCIÓN, PRETENDER, IDEAL, INTENCIÓN**

PRETEXTO; pretexto; *pretext, excuse* ... **PREVARICACIÓN; prevaricação;** *prevarication*;
huǎng yán (n): 谎言, *lie, falsehood*;
jiǎ huà (n): 假话, *falsehood, lie*;
shuō huǎng (v) (n): 说谎, *to tell a lie; prevarication*;
tuō cí (n) (v): 托辞, *pretext, excuse; to make excuses*;
SEE (请查看) **FALSO, EXCUSA**

PREVENCIÓN; prevenção; *prevention* ... **PREVENTIVO** (A); **preventivo** (A); *preventive (MED)*;
fáng zhì (n): 防治, *prevention and cure*;
kě yù fáng de: 可预防的, *preventable*;
yù fáng xìng: 预防性, *preventive*;
zǔ zhǐ (v) (n): 阻止, *to prevent/stop/ prohibit; prevention*;
SEE (请查看) **PREVENIR**

PREVIO (A); **prévio** (A); *prior, previous*;
guò qù: 过去, *in the past, formerly*;
yǐ qián: 以前, *before, formerly, previously*;
yǐ wǎng: 已往, *before, previously, formerly*;
zài qián: (sv) (adv) (suf): 在前, *previous; formerly; before, prior to*;
zǎo xiān: 早先, *previously, in the past*;
SEE (请查看) **AVANZADO**

PREVISIBLE; previsível; *foreseeable, predictable* ... **PREVISIÓN; previsão,**

previdência; *forecast, foresight, anticipation;*
  yì liào zhī zhōng (n) (sv): 意料之中, *predictable; in accordance with expectation/prediction;*
  yì liào zhōng: 意料中, *predictable; foresight, prevision, prediction; foreseeable;*
  yuǎn jiàn (n): 远见, *foresight, vision;*
SEE (请查看) AUGURAR

PREVISOR (A); **prudente;** *prudent, farsighted;*
  yuǎn shì (n) (attr): 远视, *foresight; forward-looking;*
SEE (请查看) PRUDENCIA, DISCRECIÓN

PREVISTO (A); **previsto** (A); *anticipated, predicted; planned;*
  kě yù liào de: 可预料的, *predictable;*
  qī wáng (v) (n): 期望, *to expect/hope for; expectation, hope;*
  yù liào (v) (n): 预料, *to expect/predict/ anticipate; anticipation, prediction;*
SEE (请查看) ANTICIPAR

PRIMARIO (A); **primário** (A); *primary; elementary, basic;*
  chū děng (attr): 初等, *elementary, primary;*
SEE (请查看) FUNDAMENTAL, DOMINANTE

PRIMERO (A); **primeiro** (A); *first ...*
PRIMITIVO (A); **primitivo** (A); *primitive; first, original;*
  dì-yī (NUM): 第一, *first; primary, foremost;*
  shǒu yào (attr): 首要, *of the first importance, chief, primary, first;*
  yuán shǐ (sv): 原始, *original, firsthand, first; primitive, primeval; (pref) proto-;*
  zuì chū (attr) (n): 最初, *initial, first, prime; initially, at first;*
  zuì zǎo (sv): 最早, *earliest, oldest, original*

PRIMO; primo (A); *prime;*
  jīng huá: 精华, *cream, quintessence;*

shǒu yào (attr): 首要, *of first/prime importance, chief;*
  wán měi zhuàng tài (n): 完美状态, *prime;*
SEE (请查看) PERFECTO, PRIMERO, DOMINANTE, CONSUMADO

PRINCIPIO; princípio; *beginning; onset, start;*
  kāi duān (n): 开端, *beginning, start;*
  kāi shǐ (v) (n): 开始, *to start/begin; initial stage, beginning;*
  kāi tóu (v) (n): 开头, *to begin/start; start, beginning;*
SEE (请查看) ASALTAR

PRIORIDAD; prioridade; *right of way (AUTO), priority;*
  xiān hòu (n) (adv): 先后, *priority; successively;*
  yōu xiān (v) (attr): 优先, *to have priority; preferential, preferred, priority;*
  yōu xiān quán (n): 优先权, *priority, preference*

PRISMA; prisma; *prism;*
  léng jìng: 棱镜, *prism;*
  sān léng jìng (FIS): 三棱镜, *triangular prism;*
  sān lèng xíng (FIS): 三棱形, *prism*

PRIVACIDAD; privacidade; *privacy ... PRIVADO* (A); **privado** (A); *private, confidential ... PRIVATIVO* (A);
privativo (A); *private, exclusive;*
  dú yǒu (v) (sv): 独有, *to possess alone; exclusive;*
  pái chì (v) (sv): 排斥, *to repel/exclude/ reject; exclusive;*
  pái wài (v) (sv): 排外, *to exclude; exclusive, antiforeign, parochial;*
  sī lì (attr): 私立, *privately run, private;*
  sī lì (n): 私利, *private/selfish interest; personal gain;*
  sī rén (n) (attr): 私人, *personal friend; confidant; private, personal; individual;*
  sī shì (n): 私事, *private/personal affair; privacy; secret matter/affair;*
  sī xià (adv): 私下, *in private/secret;*
  sī yíng (attr): 私营, *privately owned/ operated;*

sī yǒu (attr): 私有, *privately owned; private;*
yǐn jū: 隐居, *privacy;*
yǐn sī (n): 隐私, *privacy, personal secrets; privacy;*
SEE (请查看) **ARCANO**

PRIVILEGIO; privilégio; *privilege;*
róng xìng (sv): 荣幸, *honored, privileged;*
tè quán (n): 特权, *privilege, prerogative;*
tè xǔ (v) (sv): 特许, *to give/get special permission; privileged;*
yǒu tè quán de: 有特权的, *privileged;*
SEE (请查看) **BENÉFICO**

PROBABILIDAD; probabilidade; *probability, likelihood ...*
PROBABLEMENTE; provavelmente; *probably, likely, possible;*
duō bàn (adv): 多半, *probably, most likely;*
hěn kě néng de (adv): 很可能地, *likely, probably;*
SEE (请查看) **POSIBLE, CONTINGENCIA**

PROBIDAD; probidade; *probity, integrity, honesty;*
zhèng zhí: 正直, *probity, integrity;*
SEE (请查看) **HONESTO**

PROBLEMA; problema; *problem ...*
PROBLEMÁTICO (A); **problemática;** *problematic;*
chéng wèn tí de: 成问题的, *problematic*
nán tí: 难题, *problem;*
yí wèn (n): 疑问, *question, doubt;*
yǒu yí wèn de: 有疑问的, *problematic, doubtful, questionable*

PROCLAMACIÓN; proclamação; *proclamation;*
shēng míng: 声明, *statement, declaration, proclamation;*
SEE (请查看) **ANUNCIAR**

PROCLIVE (adj); **propensão;**

tendência; *inclined to do sthg ...*
PROCLIVIDAD; propensão o tendência; *proclivity, inclination;*
qù shì: 趋势, *tendency, inclination;*
SEE (请查看) **PROPENSIÓN, INCLINACIÓN, MANÍA**

PRODIGIO; prodígio; *wonder, marvel, prodigy;*
qí cái: 奇才, *rare talent, genius;*
qí jì: 奇迹, *miracle, wonder, marvel;*
tiān cái: 天才, *talent, gift; person of genius*

PRODIGIOSO (A); **prodigioso** (A); *prodigious, marvelous;*
qí miào de: 奇妙的, *marvelous;*
SEE (请查看) **COLOSAL**

PRODUCTIVIDAD; produtividade; *productivity ...* **PRODUCTIVO** (A); **produtivo** (A); *productive;*
shēng chǎn lì: 生产力, *productivity;*
shēng chǎn lǜ: 生产率, *productivity, production rate;*
yǒu shēng chǎn lì: 有生产力, *productivity;*
SEE (请查看) **EFECTIVIDAD, RENTABLE**

PRODUCTO; produto (GEN); *product* (MAT) (AGRIC);
chǎn pǐn: 产品, *product, produce;*
nóng chǎn pǐn: 农产品, *agricultural products, farm produce;*
SEE (请查看) **CAPACIDAD, RESULTA**

PROFANO (A); **profano** (A); *profane, secular;*
xiè dú (v) (sv): 亵渎, *to blaspheme/ profane/pollute; to disturb/trouble/ pester; profane;*
yì jiào (n) (sv): 异教, *paganism, heathenism; secular;*
SEE (请查看) **BANAL**

PROFESOR (A); **professor** (A); *teacher, instructor, lecturer;*
jiǎng shī: 讲师, *lecturer;*
jiào shī: 教师, *teacher, instructor;*

SEE (请查看) EDUCADOR

PROFETA; profeta (ista); *prophet*
... **PROFÉTICO** (A); **profético** (A);
prophetic;
  xiān zhī: 先知, *person of foresight*;
  yù yán de: 预言的, *prophetic*;
  yù yán jiā: 预言家, *prophet*

PROFUNDIDAD; profundidade;
depth ... **PROFUNDAMENTE;**
profundamente; *deeply, profoundly* ...
PROFUNDO (A); **profundo** (A); *deep,*
profound;
  gāo shēn (sv): 高深, *advanced,*
  profound, recondite;
  shēn 'ào (sv) (n): 深奥, *profound,*
  abstruse; profundity;
  shēn cháng (sv): 深长, *profound*;
  shēn chén (sv): 深沉, *deep, profound;*
  grave;
  shēn chù: 深处, *depth, recess,*
  profundity;
  shēn hòu (sv): 深厚, *deep, profound;*
  solid; deep- seated;
  shēn kè (sv) (v): 深刻, *deep, profound;*
  to crave deeply for sthg;
  shēn qiè (sv): 深切, *heartfelt, deep,*
  profound;
  shēn rù (v) (sv) (adv): 深入, *to go deep*
  into/ penetrate; thorough; deep-going;
  shēn shēn: 深深, *very deeply,*
  sincerely, profoundly, keenly;
  shēn yuǎn (sv): 深远, *profound and*
  far-reaching;
SEE (请查看) CLANDESTINIDAD,
ABSTRUSO

PROFUSO (A); **profuso** (A); *profuse,*
extravagant;
  chōng zú (sv): 充足, *sufficient,*
  adequate; abundant;
  dà shǒu dà jiǎo (fe): 大手大脚,
  extravagant;
  duō (sv) (adv) (pref): 多, *many, much,*
  more; to what degree, how; poly-, multi-;
  jí duō (vp): 极多, *very many, abundant,*
  profuse;
  kuò chuò (sv): 阔绰, *ostentatious,*
  liberal with money, extravagant;

pū zhāng (sv) (v) (n): 铺张,
extravagant, exaggerated; to praise
profusely/eulogize; exaggeration

PROGRAMA; programa; *program*
(INFORM); *program, schedule*;
  guī huà (v) (n): 规划, *to program/plan;*
  plan, program;
  jìn dù biǎo: 进度表, *progress chart,*
  schedule;
  rì chéng: 日程, *schedule, itinerary,*
  agenda; program;
  shí jiān biǎo: 时间表, *train/bus/plane*
  schedule;
  shí kè biǎo: 时刻表, *timetable,*
  schedule;
SEE (请查看) DESIGNIO, ITEM,
NORMA

PROGRESIVO (A); **progressivo** (A);
progressive, gradual ... **PROGRESO;**
progresso; *progress, advance*;
  gǎi gé pài rén shì: 改革派人士,
  progressive person;
  jìn bù (v) (n) (sv): 进步, *to progress/*
  advance/ improve; progress,
  improvement, advance; progressive
  (POL);
  shàng jìn (v) (sv): 上进, *to go forward/*
  make progress; progressive;
SEE (请查看) AVANZADO,
EVACUAR, CICLO

PROHIBITIVO (A); **proibitivo** (A);
prohibitive;
  jìn zhǐ (sv) (v): 禁止, *prohibitive; to*
  prohibit/ban

PROLÍFICO (A); **prolifico** (A); *prolific,*
productive, creative;
  chuàng jǔ: 创举, *pioneering work/*
  undertaking;
  chuàng xīn (v) (n): 创新, *to have new*
  ideas, to blaze new trails; creation and
  innovation;
  chuàng zào lì: 创造力, *creativity*;
  chuàng zào xìng: 创造性, *creativity*;
  gé xīn (v) (n): 革新 , *to innovate/*
  reform/improve; innovation;

yǒu chuàng zào lì: 有创造力,
creative;
SEE (请查看) PRODUCTIVIDAD,
PRODUCTIVO

PROLONGADO (A); **prolongado** (A);
prolonged; long, lengthy, extended;
  cháng (sv) (adv) (bf) (v): 长, *long,
  lasting; steadily, regularly; length; strong
  point; to be good/strong in/at sthg*;
  cháng shī jiān (n): 长时间, *long time*;
  cháng shī jiān de: 长时间的,
  prolonged;
SEE (请查看) AMPLIAR,
PERSEVERANCIA

PROMESA; promessa; *promise,
pledge*;
  nuò (bf): 诺, *promise*;
  nuò yán: 诺言, *promise, consent*;
SEE (请查看) COMPROMISO, JURAR

PROMINENCIA; proeminência;
protuberance, bump; prominence;
  qián tū (n): 前突, *protrusion*;
  tǔ chū (sv) (v) (n): 凸出, *convex; to
  protrude/bulge out; bulge*;
SEE (请查看) PROTUBERANCIA

PROMINENTE; destacado (A),
prominent person; **proeminente**,
prominent issues/ideas; **saliente**,
prominent cheekbones; **evidente**;
protruding, prominent;
  tóu miàn rén wù: 头面人物,
  prominent person, bigwig;
  tóu nǎo: 头脑, *brains, mind; head,
  leader*;
SEE (请查看) AFAMADO,
IMPORTANTE

PROMISCUIDAD; promiscuidade;
promiscuity ... **PROMISCUO** (A);
promíscuo (A); *promiscuous*;
  luàn jiāo: 乱交, *promiscuity*;
  nán-nǚ luàn jiāo de: 男女乱交的,
  promiscuous;

PRONÓSTICO; prognóstico; *forecast,
prediction, prognosis*;
  yù cè (v) (n): 预测, *to calculate/*

forecast/predict; prediction, forecast;
SEE (请查看) PREVISIBLE,
PREVISTO, AUGURAR, CÁLCULO

PRONTAMENTE; prontamente;
promptly ... **PRONTITUD;**
pontualidade; *promptness, quickness*;
  jí shí (adv) (n): 即时, *immediately;
  timely, promptly, promptness*;
  lì kè (adv): 立刻, *immediately, at once*;
SEE (请查看) BRUSCO

PRONUNCIADO (A); **pronunciado**
(A); *pronounced, strong, sharp*;
  jiān ruì (sv): 尖锐, *penetrating, incisive,
  intense, acute, sharp*;
  qiáng liè (sv): 强烈, *strong, intense,
  violent; clear-cut, distinct, striking, sharp*;
SEE (请查看) PROMINENTE,
DRÁSTICO, VIGOROSO,
CONSPICUO

PROPAGACIÓN; propagação;
propagation, diffusion;
  chuán bō (v) (n): 传播, *to disseminate/
  propagate; propagation (FIS)*;
SEE (请查看) DIFUSO

PROPENSIÓN; propensão;
propensity, tendency, inclination ...
PROPENSO (A); **propenso** (A); *prone,
susceptible*;
  mǐn gǎn de: 敏感的, *susceptible,
  sensitive; allergic*;
  mǐn gǎn dù: 敏感度, *susceptibility*;
  yì shòu gōng jī xìng: 易受攻击性,
  susceptibility, vulnerability;
  yì yú (vp) (adv): 易于, *be apt to/be easy
  to/prone; easily*;
  yǒu ... qīng xiàng de: 有 ... 倾向的,
  prone;
SEE (请查看) PROCLIVE

PROPICIO (A); **propicio** (A); *propitious,
favorable*;
  jī yù (wr): 机遇, *opportunity, favorable
  circumstances*;
  shùn lì (sv): 顺利, *smooth, successful,
  propitious*;
SEE (请查看) AFORTUNADO,
APROPIADO, AUSPICIOSO,

PROPORCIONADO (A);
proporcionado (A); *shapely, well-proportioned* ... **PROPORCIONAL**;
proporcional; *proportional*;
  chéng bǐ lǜ de (attr): 成比率的, *proportionate*;
  jūn héng (v) (sv): 均衡, *to balance; balanced, even, harmonious, proportionate*;
  yún chèn (sv): 匀称, *well-proportioned, symmetrical*;
SEE (请查看) **COMPARACIÓN**

PROPOSICIÓN; proposição;
proposal, proposition;
  tí 'àn (n) (v): 提案, *motion, proposal, draft, resolution; to call a case (DER)*;
  yì 'àn (n): 议案, *proposal, motion*;
  zhǔ zhāng (v) (n): 主张, *to advocate/ stand for/ hold/maintain; view, position, proposition*;
SEE (请查看) **AVANZAR, INSINUACIÓN**

PROPÓSITO; propósito; *intention, purpose*;
  yì tú (n) (v): 意图, *intention, intent; to intend to do sthg*;
  yì yì (n): 意义, *meaning, purpose, sense, significance*;
  yòng tú (n): 用途, *use, purpose*;
SEE (请查看) **INTENSIÓN, PRETENSIÓN , FUNCIÓN**

PRORRATA; pro rata; *quota, share, pro rata*;
  dìng 'é: 定额, *quota, norm*;
  míng 'é: 名额, *quota of people*;
  rèn wu: 任务, *assignment, job, task, quota*;
  xiàn 'é: 限额, *norm, limit, quota*;
  zhǐ biāo: 指标, *target, quota, norm*

PROSAICO (A); **prosaico** (A); *prosaic, mundane*;
  fá wèi (sv): 乏味, *dull, vapid, drab, tasteless*;
  píng dàn (sv): 平淡, *flat, prosaic, pedestrian, ordinary, insipid; mundane*;
  píng dàn wú qí (fe): 平淡无奇, *prosaic, unremarkable*;
  píng fàn (vp): 平泛, *pedestrian, ordinary, mundane*

PROSPECTO; prospecto; *leaflet, prospectus; directions for use*;
  jì huà shū: 计划书, *prospectus*;
  jiǎn zhāng: 简章, *general regulations; brochure*;
  yòng fǎ: 用法, *use, usage; instructions for use*

PROSPERIDAD; prosperidade;
prosperity ... **PRÓSPERO** (A);
próspero (A); *prosperous, thriving*;
  chāng shèng (sv) (n): 昌盛, *prosperous, glory; prosperity*;
  xīng shèng (sv): 兴盛, *flourishing, prosperous*;
SEE (请查看) **BOOM**

PRÓSTATA; próstata; *prostate*;
  qián liè xiàn: 前列腺, *prostate gland*

PROTAGONISTA; protagonista;
protagonist, main figure;
  chàng dǎo zhě: 倡导者, *imitator, pioneer, advocate, protagonist*;
  zhǔ juér: 主角儿, *leading role, protagonist*;
  zhǔ rén gōng: 主人公, *protagonist, leading role/ part*

PROTECCIÓN; proteção; *protection*;
  bǎo hù (n) (v): 保护, *protection; to protect/ safeguard*;
  jǐng jiè (n) (v): 警戒, *protection; to warn/caution; to guard against*

PROTEÍNA; proteína; *protein*;
  dàn bái zhì: 蛋白质, *protein*

PROTOCOLO; protocolo; *protocol*;
  yì dìng shū: 议定书, *protocol*;
SEE (请查看) **CEREMONIA, AMABILIDAD**

PROTOTIPO; protótipo; *prototype*;
  yuán xíng: 原型, *prototype (machine)*;

SEE (请查看) **EJEMPLO,
SINTOMÁTICO**

PROTUBERANCIA; protuberância;
protuberance, bulge;
   lóng qǐ wù: 隆起物**,** *bulge,
protuberance;*
   tū chū (sv) (v)**:** 突出**,** *projecting;
outstanding, prominent; to break
through; to jut out; to give prominence
to; to stress;*
   tū chū wù: 突出物**,** *protuberance;*
SEE (请查看) **PROMINENCIA,
PROMINENTE, CONVEXO**

PROVERBIO; proverbial; *proverb;*
   gé yán: 格言**,** *maxim, motto, saying;*
   yàn yǔ: 谚语**,** *proverb, saying, adage*

PROVIDENCIAL; providencial;
providential;
   tiān yì de: 天意的**,** *providential; God's
will;*
   xìng yùn (sv) (n)**:** 幸运**,** *providential,
very fortunate; good fortune/luck*

PROVINCIA; província; *province;*
   shěng: 省**,** *province;*
   zhōu: 州**,** *prefecture*

PROVOCATIVO (A)**; provocante;**
provocative;
   tiǎo xìn (v) (sv)**:** 挑衅**,** *to provoke;
provocative;*
SEE (请查看) **AGRAVAR**

PROXIMIDAD; proximidade;
closeness, proximity ... **PRÓXIMO** (A)**;
próximo** (A)**;** *near, close;*
   lín jìn (attr)**:** 邻近**,** *near, close/adjacent
to; (n) neighborhood, vicinity;*
   lín jìn: 临近**,** *closeness, proximity;*
SEE (请查看) **APROXIMACIÓN**

PROYECTO; projeto; *project, plan;*
   fāng 'àn: 方案**,** *scheme, plan, program,
project;*
   fāng lüè: 方略**,** *general plan;*
   gōng chéng: 工程**,** *engineering
project;*
   guī huà (n) (v)**:** 规划**,** *program, plan,*
project; to plan;
   shì yè: 事业**,** *cause, undertaking,
project; enterprise;*
   zhǔ yi: 主意**,** *idea, plan; decision;*
SEE (请查看) **DESIGNIO, INTENCIÓN**

PROYECTOR; projetor; *projector*
(CINE)**;**
   fàng yìng jī: 放映机**,** *projector;*
   huàn dēng jī: 幻灯机**,** *slide projector*

PRUDENCIA; prudência; *caution, care
...* **PRUDENTE; prudente;** *sensible,
prudent;*
   chí zhòng (sv) (v)**:** 持重**,** *prudent,
cautious, discreet; to observe rules of
property/justice;*
   jiǎn diǎn (v) (sv)**:** 检点**,** *to carefully
examine/check/ verify; to be cautious/
restrained in one's conduct; cautious,
careful, restrained, diligent;*
   míng lǐ (sv) (n) (v)**:** 明理**,** *sensible,
reasonable; obvious fact; to understand
the reason/reasoning;*
   qiè nuò (sv) (n)**:** 怯懦**,** *faint-hearted;
cowardice, timidity, cautiousness;*
SEE (请查看) **DILIGENCIA,
DISCRECIÓN, EQUILIBRADO**

PUBLICIDAD; publicidade;
advertising, publicity ... **PÚBLICO** (A)**;
público** (A)**;** *public;*
   dāng zhòng (adv)**:** 当众**,** *in public;*
   gōng yǒu de: 公有的**,** *public;*
   gōng zhòng de zhù yì: 公众的注意**,**
publicity;
   gōng zhòng: 公众**,** *public;*
   guǎng bō (v) (n)**:** 广播**,** *to broadcast/
air; a broadcast, publicity;*
   míng shēng (n)**:** 名声**,** *reputation,
repute, renown, publicity;*
   xuān chuán (v) (n)**:** 宣传**,** *to
propagate/ disseminate/publicize;
propagation, dissemination, publicity*

PUERIL; pueril; *childish, puerile;*
   hái zi bān de: 孩子般的**,** *childish; be
like/act like children;*
   yòu zhì (sv)**:** 幼稚**,** *childish, puerile,
naive*

PULMONÍA; pneumonia; *pneumonia;*
fèi yán: 肺炎, *pneumonia*

PULÓVER; pulóver; *pullover;*
tào tóu máo yī: 套头毛衣, *pullover (sweater);*
tào tóu shān: 套头衫, *pullover (garment)*

PÚLPITO; púlpito; *pulpit;*
bù dào tán: 布道坛, *pulpit*

PULSO; pulso; *pulse (MED);*
mài bó: 脉搏, *pulse (MED), current trend*

PUNITIVO (A); **punitivo** (A); *punitive, retributive;*
chéng fá xìng: 惩罚性, *punitive;*
kē kè (sv): 苛刻, *harsh, punitive;*
SEE (请查看) CASTIGO

PUNKI; punk; *punk music, punk (a person);*
fèi wù (n): 废物, *refuse, trash; a good-for-nothing person;*
péng kè: 朋克, *punk music; a punk, an antisocial person*

PUNTA; ponto; *point (GEN), point, end, tip, side; headland;*
dāo jiān: 刀尖, *point of a knife/sword;*
jiān (n) (sv): 尖, *point, tip; top; sharp;*
jiān duān (n) (attr): 尖端, *pointed end; acme, peak; most advanced, sophisticated;*
zhēn jiān: 针尖, *point of a needle; pinpoint*

PUNTUAL; pontual; *punctual; specific, precise; detailed* ... **PUNTUALIDAD; pontualidade;** *punctuality;*
jí shí (adv): 及时, *timely, in time; promptly;*
jí shí (sv): 及时, *punctual;*
jīng mì (sv) (n): 精密, *precise, exact, accurate; precision;*
jīng què (sv) (n): 精确, *accurate, exact, precise; accuracy;*
jù tǐ (sv): 具体, *concrete, specific,*

detailed;
zhǔn diǎn (adv): 准点, *right on time, on schedule;*
zhǔn què (sv) (n): 准确, *accurate, exact, precise; accuracy;*
zhǔn shí (adv) (sv): 准时, *punctually; on time, on schedule;*
SEE (请查看) DETALLADO, DETERMINADO, DILIGENCIA

PUPILA; pupila; *pupil (ANAT);*
tóng kǒng: 瞳孔, *pupil (of the eye);*
tú dì: 徒弟, *pupil;*
xué sheng: 学生, *pupil/student*

PURÉ; pure; *purée, thick soup; mashed potatoes;*
jiàng (n) (v): 酱, *thick sauce, purée; to cook/pickle in soy sauce;*
ní (n): 泥, *mud, clay; mashed vegetables/fruit*

PURGANTE (adj); **purgative;** *purgative, purifying, cathartic;*
jìng huà (sv) (v): 净化, *purifying; to purge/purify;*
tōng biàn (sv) (v): 通便, *purifying; to take a laxative;*
xiè yào (n): 泻药, *laxative*

PURISTA; purist; *purist* ... **PURO; puro;** *pure, authentic, unalloyed, true, perfect;*
chún cuì zhǔ yì (n): 纯粹主义, *purism;*
chún cuì zhǔ yì zhě: 纯粹主义者, *purist;*
chún jìng (sv): 纯净, *pure, clean;*
chún zhèng (sv): 纯正, *pure, unadulterated; honest, sincere;*
dān chún (sv) (adv): 单纯, *simple, plain, artless, naive, pure; purely, merely;*
dì dao (sv): 地道, *pure, authentic, genuine;*
qīng bái (sv) (n): 清白, *pure, clean, unsullied; innocence;*
SEE (请查看) AUTENTICIDAD, CASTIDAD, COMPLETAMENTE, IDÉNTICO

PÚRPURA (n); **púrpura**; *purple*;
zǐ sè: 紫色, *purple*

PÚSTULA; **pustule**; *pustule, pimple*;
fěn cì: 粉刺, *acne*;
xiǎo nóng pào: 小脓疱, *pustule*

PUTATIVO (A); **putativo** (A); *putative, supposed, reputed*;
bèi gōng rèn de: 被公认的, *putative*

PUTREFACTO (A) ó **PÚTRIDO** (A);
putrefato (A); *rotten, putrid*;
biàn zhì de: 变质的, *rotten*;
fǔ làn de: 腐烂的, *decomposed, putrid, rotten; corrupt*;
yǐ fǔ làn de: 已腐烂的, *rotten, putrid; corrupt*;
SEE (请查看) DECADENTE, CORRUPCIÓN

Easily recognizable Spanish-Portuguese-English verbs and their Chinese equivalents
Verbos fácilmente reconocibles en Español-Portugués-Inglés y sus equivalentes en Chino
Verbos facilmente reconhecível em Espanhol-Português-Inglês e seus equivalentes em Chinês
很容易辨认的西班牙语，葡萄牙语，英语动词和他们的中文对等词

PACIFICAR; **pacificar**; *to pacify/calm/appease*;
fǔ wèi: 抚慰, *to comfort/console/soothe*;
SEE (请查看) AQUIETAR

PALPITAR; **palpitar**; *to beat/throb/palpitate*;
chàn dòng (v) (n): 颤动, *to vibrate/shake/tremble; tremor, vibration*;
xīn zàng jí sù bù tiào dòng: 心脏急速不跳动, *to palpitate*

PARAFRASEAR; **parafrasear**; *to paraphrase*;
shì yì (v) (n): 释义, *to explain/interpret/paraphrase*

PARALIZAR; **paralisar**; *to paralyze/stop*;
má bì (v) (n): 麻痹, *to paralyze/numb; paralysis, palsy, numbness*;
tān huàn (n) (v): 瘫痪, *paralysis, palsy, paralytic; to paralyze*

PARCELAR; **parcelar**; *to parcel out/divide*;
fēn: 分, *to divide/separate*;
guā fēn: 瓜分, *to parcel out/carve up/divide up/partition*

PARLAMENTAR; **parlamentar**; *to negotiate*;
tán pàn (v) (n): 谈判, *to negotiate/talk; negotiations, talks*

PARODIAR; **parodiar**; *to parody/take off on sb*;
cháo nòng: 嘲弄, *to mock/deride*;
mó fǎng (v) (n): 模仿, *to imitate/copy; imitation*;
tōng guò mó fǎng cháo nòng: 通过模仿嘲弄, *to parody*

PARTICIPAR; **participar**; *to participate/take part in*;
cān jiā: 参加, *to join/attend/take part in*

PARTICULARIZAR; **particularizar**; *to specify, to distinguish/characterize*;
jù tǐ guī dìng: 具体规定, *to specify*;
SEE (请查看) NORMA

PARTIR; **partir**; *to break, to leave; to start from, to divide/split/cut*;
bié lí: 别离, *to leave/take leave of*;
chū fā: 出发, *to set out/start off/depart/start a journey*;
chū jìng: 出境, *to leave a country*;
chū qù: 出去, *to exit/go out/get out*;

dǎ duàn: 打断, *to break/interrupt/cut short*;

dòng shēn: 动身, *to leave on a journey*;

fēn céng: 分层, *to stratify/divide into layers*;

fēn jiě: 分解, *to break down/segment*;

fēn kāi (v) (adv): 分开, *to separate/part; separately*;

fēn lí (v) (n): 分离, *to separate/sever; discreteness*;

fēn liè (v) (n): 分裂, *to split/divide/break up; fission, division (BIOL)*;

gào cí: 告辞, *to take leave*;

jué liè: 决裂, *to break with/rupture/burst open*;

lí jìng: 离境, *to leave a country/place*;

lí kāi: 离开, *to leave; to depart/deviate from*;

li zhí: 离职, *to take leave of, to leave office/a job*;

qǐ chéng: 起程, *to leave/set out/start on a trip*;

qǐ shēn: 起身, *to get up/stand up, to get out of bed, to start on a journey*;

SEE (请查看) **EVACUAR, APARTAR, APARTE**

PASTEURIZAR; pasteurizer; *to pasteurize*;

bā shì shā jūn fǎ de: 巴士杀菌法的, *pasteurized*;

xiāo dú: 消毒, *to disinfect/sterilize, (attr) disinfected, sterilized, pasteurized*

PATENTAR; patentear; *to patent*;

qǔ dé ... de zhuān lì quán: 取得...的专利权, *to patent*

PENALIZAR; penalizar; *to distress, to punish, to penalize*;

lùn chǔ: 论处, *to punish, to decide on a punishment*;

pàn chǔ: 判处, *to sentence/condemn/penalize*;

zé fá: 责罚, *to punish*;

SEE (请查看) **PUNITIVO, CASTIGO**

PENETRAR; penetrar; *to enter/get into/penetrate*;

chuān guò: 穿过, *to penetrate/pierce/pass through*;

shí pò: 识破, *to see through, to penetrate*;

SEE (请查看) **ADMITIR**

PENSAR; pensar; *to think/reflect on/think up*;

sī wéi (n) (v): 思维, *thought/thinking; to think/consider*;

xiǎng de dào: 想得到, *to think/imagine/expect*;

xiǎng qǐ: 想起, *to remember/recall/think of*;

xiǎng: 想, *to think/consider*;

zhuó yǎn: 着眼, *to keep in mind/consider*;

SEE (请查看) **CONSIDERACIÓN, CONTEMPLACIÓN, DELIBERAR, CONTEMPLAR, CONCENTRAR, IMAGINAR, REFLEXIÓN**

PERCIBIR; perceber; *to realize, to perceive/notice*;

bù gào (n) (v): 布告, *notice, bulletin; to notice*;

gǎn shòu: 感受, *to be affected by, to experience/feel*;

rèn shi (v) (n): 认识, *to know/recognize; knowledge, understanding*;

rèn shi dào: 认识到, *to realize*;

tǐ huì (v) (n): 体会, *to know or learn from experience; knowledge, understanding*;

tǐ yàn: 体验, *to learn through experience/practice*;

yì huì: 意会, *to sense, to perceive*;

zì jué (sv) (v): 自觉, *on one's own initiate; to be conscious/aware*;

SEE (请查看) **DESILUSIÓN**

PERDONAR; perdoar; *to forgive*;

kuān dài: 宽待, *to treat with leniency*;

kuān shù (v) (n): 宽恕, *to forgive; forgiveness*;

SEE (请查看) **DISCULPAR, DISPENSAR**

PERFORAR; perfurar; *to perforate, pierce*;

cì (v) (n): 刺, *to stab/prick; pierce; to*

assassinate, to irritate/criticize; thorn, splinter;
cì chuān: 刺穿, *to pierce; to prick*

PERJUDICAR; prejudicar; *to disrupt/ impair, to damage/harm/prejudice*;
rǎo luàn: 扰乱, *to throw into disorder*;
sǔn shāng (v) (n): 损伤, *to harm/ damage/injure*;
wēi hài: 危害, *to harm/endanger/ injure/jeopardize*;
xuē ruò: 削弱, *to weaken/cripple*;
SEE (请查看**) ARRUINAR, DESORGANIZAR, DIFICULTAR**

PERJURAR; perjurar-se; *to swear blindly, to commit perjury*;
zuò wěi zhěng: 作伪证, *to give false testimony*

PERMANECER; permanecer; *to stay/ remain*;
zhù sù: 住宿, *to stay, to put up, to get accommodations*;
SEE (请查看**) APREHENDER**

PERMITIR; permitir; *to allow/permit*;
zhǔn yǔ: 准予, *to grant/approve/ permit*;
SEE (请查看**) AUTORIDAD, ADMITIR, AUTORIZAR**

PERMUTAR; permutar; *to permute/ exchange/swap*;
diào huàn: 调换, *to shift/transfer/ exchange*;
hù huàn: 互换, *to exchange*;
jiāo huàn: 交换, *to swap/exchange/ trade*

PERPETRAR; perpetrar; *to perpetrate/commit/ perform*;
biǎo yǎn (v) (n): 表演, *to perform/act/ play; performance, exhibition*;
SEE (请查看**) APLICAR, EJECUTIVO**

PERPETUAR; perpetuar; *to prolong/ to perpetuate/ continue/extend ...*
PROLONGAR; prolonger; *to prolong/ extend*;
shǐ yǒng héng: 使永恒, *to*

perpetuate;
yán xù: 延续, *to flourish and continue*;
SEE (请查看**) AMPLIAR, CONTINUADO, CONSTANTE**

PERSEVERAR; perseverar; *to persevere/persist ...* **PERSISTIR; persistir;** *to persist*;
jiān chí: 坚持, *to persist in, to insist on*;
SEE (请查看**) CONSTANTE, CONTUMACIA**

PERSONIFICAR; personificar; *to personify/embody*;
nǐ rén huà: 拟人化, *to personify*

PERSUADIR; persuader; *to persuade*;
shuō fú: 说服, *to persuade*;
SEE (请查看**) AVISAR**

PERTURBAR; perturbar; *to disrupt/ disturb/perturb*;
shǐ fán nǎo (vp): 使烦恼, *to drive up the wall*;
SEE (请查看**) DESCONCERTAR**

PERVERTIR; perverter; *to corrupt/ pervert/distort*;
qū jiè: 曲解, *to twist/distort/ misconstrue*;
SEE (请查看**) ABUSAR**

PINTAR; pintar; *to paint*;
tú shì: 涂饰, *to cover with paint/white wash*;
yóu qī (n) (v): 油漆, *paint; to paint*;
zuò huà: 作画, *to paint/draw a picture*

PLANIFICAR; planificar; *to plan out; to plan*;
jì huà (v) (n): 计划, *to plan/project; program, project, plan*;
SEE (请查看**) DESIGNIO**

PLANTAR; plantar; *to plant/sow*;
bō zhǒng: 播种, *to sow/plant*;
zāi zhòng: 栽种, *to plant/grow*;
zāi: 栽, *to plant/grow/raise*;
zhòng: 种, *to plant/cultivate*

POLARIZAR; polarizar; *to*

concentrate/polarize;
jí huà (v) (n): 极化, *to polarize; polarization*;
SEE (请查看) **AGRUPAR, CONCENTRAR**

POPULARIZAR; **popularizar**; *to popularize*;
tuī guǎng (v) (n): 推广, *to popularize/ spread/extend; generalization*;
SEE (请查看) **DISEMINAR**

PORTAR; **portar**; *to carry/bear; to behave/conduct*;
chéng shòu: 承受, *to bear/support/ endure; to inherit*;
chǔ shì: 出世, *to conduct/behave os*;
dān fù (v) (n): 担负, *to bear/shoulder/ take on, to be charged with; burden, responsibility*;
fā yáng: 发扬, *to develop/carry on; to make the most of*;
fù dān (v) (n): 负担, *to bear/shoulder/ support; burden, load, encumbrance*;
fù hè (v) (n): 负荷, *to bear/sustain; load (electrical), charge (electrical), weight*;
hòu jì (v) (n): 后继, *to succeed/carry on; successors, posterity*;
rěn nài (v) (n): 忍耐, *to be patient/ forbearing; patience, forbearance*;
rěn ràng: 忍让, *to be conciliatory*;
wéi rén (v) (n) (attr): 为人, *to behave/ conduct os; personal character/make-up; endearing*;
SEE (请查看) **ASUMIR**

PRACTICAR; **practicar**; *to commit; to practice; to exercise/carry out/perform*;
lǚ xíng: 履行, *to perform/carry out*;
SEE (请查看) **APLICAR**

PRECEDER; **precede**; *to go before, to precede*;
xiān yú: 先于, *to precede (in order)*;
zǎo yú: 早于, *to precede (in time)*

PRECIPITAR; **precipitar**; *to throw down/hasten/ precipitate*;
cù chéng: 促成, *to facilitate/effect*;
jiā kuài: 加快, *to speed up/accelerate*;
měng rán xià jiàng: 猛然下降, *to precipitate*

PRECISAR; **precisar**; *to need (GEN); to specify/be necessary; to need/require*;
zhǐ dìng: 指定, *to specify/indicate clearly*;
SEE (请查看) **CÉNTRICO, FALTA, DEMANDAR**

PREDETERMINAR; **predeterminar**; *to predetermine*;
yù dìng: 预定, *to predetermine/ schedule*

PREDOMINAR; **predominar**; *to predominate/prevail over*;
tǒng zhì (v) (n): 统治, *to rule/ dominate; domination*;
yā dǎo: 压倒, *to overwhelm/ overpower/prevail over*

PREFERIR; **preferir**; *to prefer*;
piān 'ài: 偏爱, *to be partial to sb/sthg*;
qíng yuàn (aux): 情愿, *to be willing to; would rather; to prefer*;
SEE (请查看) **INCLINACIÓN**

PREJUZGAR; **prejulgar**; *to prejudge*;
yù xiān jué dìng: 预先决定, *to decide/ resolve beforehand*;
yù xiān pàn duàn: 预先判断, *to prejudge*;
yù xiān qīng xiàng: 预先倾向, *to predetermine/ prejudge*;
SEE (请查看) **PREDETERMINAR**

PREMEDITAR; **premeditar**; *to premeditate on*;
yù móu (v): 预谋, *to premeditate/plan before hand*

PREOCUPAR; **preocupar**; *to be preoccupied*;
guàn zhù: 灌注, *to concentrate on/be absorbed in*
quán shén (vp): 全神, *to be absorbed/ engrossed in*;
shǐ quán shén guàn zhù: 使全神贯注, *to be preoccupied*

PREPARAR; **preparer**; *to prepare; to make/get ready*;

xiě chū: 写出, *to prepare/write out/ draw up*;

yù bèi (v) (n): 预备, *to prepare/get ready; preparation*;

zhì dìng: 制定, *to formulate/prepare/ draft*;

zhǔn bèi: 准备, *to prepare/get ready; to intend to do sthg*

PRESERVAR; preserver; *to protect, preserve, maintain*;

bǎo wèi (v) (n): 保卫, *to defend/ safeguard; guard*;

wéi hù: 维护, *to safeguard/defend/ uphold*;

SEE (请查看) **CONSERVACIÓN, PROTECCIÓN**

PRESIDIAR; presidir; *to lead; to rule/ dominate/ preside/chair*;

zhǔ chí huì yì: 主持会议, *to preside over a meeting/ conference*;

zhǔ chí jié mù: 主持节目, *to preside over a program*;

zhǔ chí: 主持, *to take charge/care of; to manage/ direct, to uphold/preside over*;

SEE (请查看) **CONQUISTA**

PRESTIGIAR; prestigiar; *to honor/ give prestige to*;

biǎo zhāng: 表彰, *to cite/honor/ commend*;

zūn jìng: 尊敬, *to honor/respect/ esteem*

PRESUMIR; presumir; *to presume/ assume*;

jiǎ dìng (v) (n): 假定, *to suppose/ assume/grant/ presume; hypothesis*;

jiǎ shè (v) (n): 假设, *to suppose/ assume/grant/ presume; hypothesis; postulate; (conj) if, in case*;

yì wèi zhe: 意味着, *to mean/imply*

PRETENDER; pretender; *to want to do or intend to do sthg; to aspire to; to expect/mean/try to*;

dǎ suàn (v) (n): 打算, *to plan/intend; plan, intention*;

SEE (请查看) **PREPARAR,**

ANTICIPAR

PREVALECER; prevalecer; *to prevail against*;

huò shèng: 获胜, *to win/triumph*;

SEE (请查看) **DOMINANTE, PREDOMINAR**

PREVARICAR; prevaricar; *to fail in one's duty; to prevent justice*;

táng sè: 搪塞, *to stall, to do sthg perfunctorily*;

zhī wu: 支吾, *to equivocate; to avoid/ evade*

PREVENIR; prevenir; *to warn, to avoid; to prevent*;

bì miǎn: 避免, *to avoid, to dodge a person/obstacle, etc.*;

fáng zhǐ: 防止, *to prevent/guard against/ forestall/avoid*;

jǐng gào (v) (n): 警告, *to warn/caution/ admonish; warning (disciplinary)*;

yù fáng (v) (n): 预防, *to prevent/guard against; prevention*;

SEE (请查看) **BLOCAR, DIFICULTAR, EVADIR, IMPEDIR**

PRIVATIZAR; privatizer; *to privatize*;

shǐ sī yǒu huà: 使私有化, *to privatize*

PROBAR; provar; *to prove*;

xiǎn shì: 显示, *to show/display/ demonstrate/ manifest*;

SEE (请查看) **CERTIFICAR**

PROCLAMAR; proclamar; *to proclaim/declare*;

xuān gào: 宣告, *to declare/proclaim*;

SEE (请查看) **PROMULGAR**

PRODUCIR; produzir; *to produce (CINE) (GEN); to make/generate*;

chǎn shēng: 产生, *to produce/ engender; to emerge/come into being; to generate*;

zhì zào: 制造, *to make/manufacture; to create/ engineer/fabricate*;

zuò: 做, *to make/produce/manufacture; to cook/prepare; to do/act/engage in*;

SEE (请查看) **CAUSAR, REVELAR,**

PROGRAMAR; programar; *to plan, to program (INFORM);*
    ān pái (v) (n): 安排, *to arrange/plan; to fix up; plans, arrangements;*
    zhì dìng: 制订, *to work/map out; to formulate;*
SEE (请查看**) PLANIFICAR, PREPARAR, DESIGNIO**

PROHIBIR; prohibir; *to prohibit/ban;*
    chá jìn: 查禁, *to ban/prohibit/suppress;*
    jìn lìng (n): 禁令, *prohibition, ban;*
    qǔ dì: 取缔, *to ban sthg; to punish sb;*
SEE (请查看**) PREVENIR, BOICOT**

PROLIFERAR; proliferar; *to proliferate;*
    zēng zhí: 增值, *to multiply/proliferate; to breed/propagate;*
SEE (请查看**) MULTIPLICAR**

PROMOCIONAR; promover; *to promote;*
    cù jìn: 促进, *to promote/spur/ accelerate;*
    shēn zhāng: 伸张, *to uphold sthg, to promote/ expand;*
    shēng gé: 升格, *to be promoted/ upgraded;*
    shēng qiān: 升迁, *to be transferred and promoted; to promote sb;*
    tí bá: 提拔, *to promote sb;*
    tí chàng: 提倡, *to advocate/ recommend/promote/ encourage;*
    tí shēng: 提升, *to promote; to hoist/ elevate;*
    tí xié: 提携, *to promote, to lead by the hand, to support/guide sb;*
    tuī xiāo: 推销, *to promote/peddle;*
    zēng jìn: 增进, *to enhance/promote/ further;*
    zhù zhǎng: 助长, *to foment/ encourage/ promote/ foster/abet;*
SEE (请查看**) FOMENTAR**

PROMULGAR; promulgar; *to promulgate; to enact/ announce;*
    xuān bù: 宣布, *to declare/proclaim/ announce;*

SEE (请查看**) ANUNCIAR**

PRONOSTICAR; prever; *to predict/ forecast;*
    yù yán (v) (n): 预言, *to predict/foretell; prophecy, prediction;*
SEE (请查看**) AUGURAR**

PRONUNCIAR; pronunciar; *to pronounce, to deliver/ give an opinion;*
    biǎo tài: 表态, *to declare a stance/ opinion/position;*
    xuān gào: 宣告, *to announce an opinion*

PROPAGAR; propagar; *to spread/ disseminate;*
    sàn bù: 散布, *to disseminate/scatter/ diffuse;*
SEE (请查看**) DISEMINAR**

PROSCRIBIR; proscrever; *to exile; to ban/banish/ prohibit;*
    bù zhǔn (aux) (sv): 不准, *to not allow/ forbid; not accurate;*
SEE (请查看**) PROHIBIR, BOICOT, CONFINAR**

PROSPERAR; prosperar; *to prosper/ thrive;*
    chéng gōng (v) (n): 成功, *to succeed; success;*
SEE (请查看**) BOOM**

PROTESTAR; protestar; *to protest/ complain;*
    fǎn duì: 反对, *to oppose/combat/be against;*
    kàng yì (v) (n): 抗议, *to protest/object; protest, objection*

PROVOCAR; provocar; *to provoke/ incite; upset; stimulus, stimulation;*
    tiǎo dòng: 挑动, *to provoke/incite;*
    tiǎo xìn: 挑衅, *to provoke;*
    zhāo rě: 招惹, *to provoke; to incur/ court;*
SEE (请查看**) AGITAR, AGRAVAR**

PUBLICAR; publicar; *to publish/issue;*
    fā gěi: 发给, *to issue/distribute;*

fā xíng: 发行, *to issue/publish/distribute*;
kān zǎi: 刊载, *to publish in a newspaper/magazine*;
SEE (请查看) PROMULGAR, ANUNCIAR

PURIFICAR; purificar; *to purify/cleanse* ;
jìng huà: 净化, *to purify/purge*;
shǐ chún jìng: 使纯净, *to purify*;
shǐ qīng jié: 使纯洁, *to clean/cleanse*;
SEE (请查看) PURGANTE

Interchangeable Spanish-Portuguese-English words and their Chinese equivalents
Palabras en Español-Portugués-Inglés y sus equivalentes en Chino
Palavras em Espanhol-Português-Inglês e seus equivalentes em Chinês
西班牙语，葡萄牙语，英语及中文的对等单词

QUÓRUM; quórum;
fǎ dìng rén shù: 法定人数, *quorum*

Easily recognizable Spanish-Portuguese-English nouns, adjectives and adverbs and their Chinese equivalents
Nombres, sustantivos, adjetivos y adverbios en Español-Portugués-Inglés y sus equivalentes en Chino
Nomes, substantivos, adjetivos e advérbios em Espanhol-Português-Inglês e seus equivalentes em Chinês
容易辨认的西班牙语，葡萄牙语，英语的名词，形容词和副词和他们的中文对等词

QUIETO (A); **quieto** (A); *calm; still; motionless; Quiet! Be still!*
chén jì (vp) (v): 沉寂, *quiet, still; without news; to lie low*;
chén jìng (sv): 沉静, *quiet, calm, serene*;
lěng jìng (sv): 冷静, *sober, calm*;
wú fēng (attr): 无风, *calm, breezeless, motionless (METEO)*;
zhèn jìng (sv): 镇静, *calm, composed*;
SEE (请查看) CALMA, PACÍFICO

QUIETUD; quitude; *tranquility; stillness*;
píng jìng: 平静, *tranquility; stillness*;
wú fēng: 无风, *stillness*;
SEE (请查看) CALMA

QUININA; quinina; *quinine*;
kuí níng: 奎宁, *quinine*

QUINTAESENCIA; quinta-essência; *quintessence*;
jīng huá: 精华, *quintessence*;
SEE (请查看) EJEMPLO

QUINTETO; quinteto; *quintet*;
wǔ chóng chàng: 五重唱, *vocal quintet*;
wǔ chóng xiàn: 五重线, *quintet (MUS)*;
wǔ chóng zòu: 五重奏, *instrumental quintet (MUS)*

QUÍNTUPLE ó QUÍNTUPLO (A); **quíntuplos;** *quintuple or quintuplet*;
wǔ bāo tāi: 五胞胎, *quintuplets*;
wǔ chóng tài: 五重态, *quintuplet*

Easily recognizable verbs and their Portuguese and Chinese equivalents
Verbos fácilmente reconocibles en Español-Portugués-Inglés y sus equivalentes en Chino
Verbos facilmente reconhecível em Espanhol-Português-Inglês e seus equivalentes em Chinês
很容易辨认的西班牙语，葡萄牙语，英语动词和他们的中文对等词

QUITAR; quitar; *to settle, to cancel, to release; to take down/take off/take out*;
  bá chú (rv): 拔除, *to pull out/take out/ remove*;
  fàng kāi: 放开, *to let go/ set free*;
  gōng kāi (v) (sv): 公开, *to release documents/ information; open, overt*;
  qǔ xià (rv): 取下, *to take down/detach; to unmask*;

  shān chú (rv): 删除, *to cross off/ delete*;
  shì fàng: 释放, *to release/set free*;
  tuō xià (rv): 脱下, *to take off sthg*;
  SEE (请查看) ABSOLVER, ADMINISTRAR, ANULAR, SOLUCIONAR

Interchangeable Spanish-Portuguese-English words and their Chinese equivalents
Palabras en Español-Portugués-Inglés y sus equivalentes en Chino
Palavras em Espanhol-Português-Inglês e seus equivalentes em Chinês
西班牙语，葡萄牙语，英语及中文的对等单词

RACIAL; racial;
  zhǒng zú de: 种族的, *racial*;
  zhǒng zú: 种族, *race (of people)*

RADAR; radar;
  léi dá: 雷达, *radar*

RADIO; radio; *radius (MAT)*;
  bàn jìng: 半径, *radius*

REAL; real (GEN); *authentic, true; royal*;
  zhēn (sv) (adv): 真, *real, true, genuine; really, truly, indeed; clearly*;
  zhēn shí (sv) (n): 真实, *true, real, authentic; truth*;
  SEE (请查看) AUTENTICIDAD, EFECTIVIDAD, PRÁCTICO

RECITAL (MUS); **recital;** *concert*;
  dú zòu huì: 独奏会, *recital*;
  yīn yuè huì: 音乐会, *concert*

REFERÉNDUM; referendum;
  gōng mín fù jué quán: 公民复决权, *referendum*

REGIONAL; regional;
  dì qū (sv) (n): 地区, *regional; area, district, region; prefecture*;
  jú bù de: 局部的, *regional*;
  SEE (请查看) ÁREA, DISTRITO

REGULAR; regular;
  cháng kè: 常客, *regular visitor; a regular customer; a frequenter*;
  dìng qī (v) (attr): 定期, *to fix a date; regular, periodical*;
  dìng qī de: 定期的, *regular*;
  gù dìng (v) (sv): 固定, *to fix/regularize; fixed, regular*;
  gù dìng rén yuàn: 固定人员, *regular staff (member)*;
  gù dìng zhí gōng: 固定职工, *regular/*

permanent workers and staff members;
yǒu guī lǜ (v) (sv) (adv): 有规律, *to be regular; systematic; orderly*

RENAL; renal;
  shèn zàng de: 肾脏的, *renal (MED)*

REPLAY; replay (n); *a recording*;
  chóng sài (v) (n): 重赛, *to replay; replay*;
  lù zhì jié mù: 录制节目, *a recording*

RÉPLICA; replica; *a copy; reply, answer; aftershock; replica (ARTE)*;
  chāo jiàn: 抄件, *duplicate, copy*;
  fān bǎn (v) (n): 翻版, *to reprint; duplicate, copy*;
SEE (请查看**) DUPLICADO**

RESIDUAL; residual;
  cán yú de: 残余的 , *residual*;
  cán yú wù: 残余物, *leftover, remnant*;
  cán yú: 残余, *remains, remnants, vestiges*;
  cán zhā: 残渣, *dregs, residue*;
  zhā zǐ: 渣滓, *dregs, residue; feces*

RETINA; retina;
  shì wǎng mó: 视网膜, *retina*

REVÓLVER; revólver;
  shǒu qiāng: 手枪, *pistol, handgun*;
  zuǒ lún: 左轮, *revolver, six-shooter*

RIFLE; rifle;
  bù qiāng: 步枪, *rifle*;
SEE (请查看**) CARABINA**

RIGOR; rigor; *strictness, accuracy*;
  jīng dù: 精度, *precision*;
  jīng mì (sv) (n):精密 , *accurate, precise, exact; precision*;
  jīng què (sv) (n): 精确, *accurate, precise, exact; accuracy*;
  zhǔn què (sv): 准确, *accurate, exact, precise*;
  zhǔn què: 准确, *accuracy, exactness*

RITUAL; ritual;
  yí shì: 仪式, *ritual, rite*;
SEE (请查看**) CEREMONIA**

RIVAL; rival;
  duì shǒu: 对手, *opponent, adversary*;
  qíng dí: 情敌, *rival in love*;
SEE (请查看**) ENEMIGO**

ROCK ó ROCK AND ROLL; rock (MUS); *rock group*;
  yáo gǔn yuè: 摇滚乐, *rock 'n roll*

ROUND (s); **round;** *as in boxing, golf*;
  huí hé: 回合, *round (in boxing)*;
  yī chǎng: 一场 , *round (in golf)*

RUMOR; rumor; *murmur*;
  dī yǔ: 低语, *murmur; aside*;
  gū nong (n) (v): 咕哝, *murmur, mumble, grumble, mutter; to murmur/ mumble/mutter*

RURAL; rural;
  nóng cūn (pw) (sv): 农村, *rural area, countryside, village; rural, rustic*;
  xiāng cūn (sv): 乡村, *village, countryside, rural area; rural*

Easily recognizable Spanish-Portuguese-English nouns, adjectives and adverbs and their Chinese equivalents
Nombres, sustantivos, adjetivos y adverbios en Español-Portugués-Inglés y sus equivalentes en Chino
Nomes, substantivos, adjetivos e advérbios em Espanhol-Português-Inglês e seus equivalentes em Chinês
容易辨认的西班牙语，葡萄牙语，英语的名词，形容词和副词和他们的中文对等词

RACISMO; racismo; *racism;*
zhǒng zú zhǔ yì: 种族主义, *racism*

RACISTA; racista; *racist;*
zhǒng zú zhǔ yì zhě: 种族主义者, *racist*

RADIACTIVO (A); **radioativo** (A);
radioactive;
fàng shè xìng de: 放射性的, *radioactive;*
fàng shè xìng xiàng: 放射性象, *radioactivity;*
fàng shè xìng: 放射性, *radioactivity*

RADIADOR; radiador; *automobile radiator; radiator;*
nuǎn qì piàn: 暖气片, *radiator, heating radiator;*
sàn rè qì: 散热器, *automobile radiator*

RADIANTE; radiante; *radiant, brilliant, luminous, shining;*
fā guāng (sv): 发光, *luminous;*
fā liàng de: 发亮的, *shiny;*
guāng cǎi duó mù (fe): 光彩夺目, *dazzlingly brilliant;*
guāng máng wàn zhàng (fe): 光芒万丈, *gloriously radiant;*
guāng máng: 光芒, *rays of light, radiance;*
xiān liàng (sv) (wr): 鲜亮, *bright and shining;*
xiǎn liàng (sv): 显亮, *bright;*
xuàn lì (sv): 绚丽, *gorgeous, magnificent, radiant;*
xuàn luàn (vp): 眩乱, *dazzling;*
SEE (请查看) LUCIDEZ, ESPLÉNDIDO, LUSTRE, LUSTROSO

RADIOGRAFÍA; radiografia; *radiography;*
shè xiàn zhào xiàng shù: 射线照相术, *radiography*

RADIOTAXI; radiotáxi; *radio cab, taxi;*
chū zū qì chē: 出租汽车, *taxi*

RAMPA; rampa; *ramp;*
pō dào: 坡道, *sloping road, ramp (for cars, etc.);*

SEE (请查看) BANCO

RANCHERO (A); **rancheiro** (A);
rancher, settler... **RANCHO; rancho;**
mess (MIL); ranch, small farm;
dà mù chǎng zhǔ: 大牧场主, *rancher;*
dà mù chǎng: 大牧场, *ranch; grazing land, pasture;*
dà mù niú chǎng: 大牧牛场, *pasture, ranch;*
mù chǎng: 牧场, *ranch*

RÁPIDAMENTE; rapidamente;
rapidly; quickly... **RAPIDEZ; rapidez;**
speed, rapidity ... **RÁPIDO** (A); **rápido**
(A); *fast, rapid, quick, express; quickly;*
gǎn jǐn (adv): 赶紧, *hurriedly;*
jí cù (adv): 急促, *hastily, rapidly;*
jí jù (adv): 急剧, *rapidly, suddenly;*
kuài xìn: 快信, *express letter;*
kuài yóu: 快邮, *express mail, special delivery;*
mǐn jié (sv): 敏捷, *quick, agile, nimble;*
sù dù (n): 速度, *speed, velocity; tempo; rate, pace (MUS);*
SEE (请查看) ACELERADO, BREVE, BRUSCO

RAPSODIA; rapsódia; *rhapsody;*
kuáng xiǎng qǔ: 狂想曲, *rhapsody*

RARAMENTE (adv); **raramente;** *rarely, seldom, infrequently ...* **RARO** (A); **raro**
(A) (adj), *rare;* **raro** (adv), *rarely; odd, strange, rare;*
bǎo guì (sv) (v): 宝贵, *valuable, rare, precious; to value sthg;*
bù kě duō dé (fe): 不可多得, *rare, hard to get;*
gǔ guài (sv): 古怪, *eccentric; odd, strange;*
hǎn jiàn (sv): 罕见, *rare, seldom/rarely seen;*
hěn shǎo de: 很少地, *rarely;*
lí qí (sv): 离奇, *strange, odd;*
míng guì (sv): 名贵, *precious/rare object; famous and distinguished;*
mò shēng (sv): 陌生, *strange, unfamiliar;*
nán dé (sv): 难得, *rare, hard to come by;*

shǎo jiàn (sv): 少见, *seldom seen, rare, unique*;

shǎo yǒu (sv): 少有, *rare, scarce*;

xī han (sv) (v) (n): 稀罕, *rare, scarce, uncommon; to cherish; rarity*;

xī qí (sv): 稀奇, *rare, strange, curious*;

xī yǒu (sv): 稀有, *rare, unusual*;

SEE (请查看) INHABITUAL, REPELENTE, SINGULAR, ATÍPICO

RATIFICACIÓN; ratificação; *ratification*;

rèn kě (n) (v): 认可, *approval; to approve*;

SEE (请查看) APROBACIÓN, CONFIRMAR

RAYO; raio; *ray, beam, shaft of light*;

guāng bō: 光波, *light-wave*;

guāng xiàn: 光线, *ray, shaft of light; beam*;

guāng zhù: 光柱, *light beam*

RAZONABLE; razoável; *reasonable*;

hé lǐ (sv): 合理, *rational, reasonable, equitable*;

hé qíng hé lǐ (fe): 合情合理, *reasonable; fair*;

hé qíng lǐ (v) (sv): 合情理, *to follow conventional etiquette; reasonable*;

tōng qíng dá lǐ (fe): 通情达理, *reasonable; to show good sense*;

SEE (请查看) DESAPASIONADO

REACCIÓN; reação; *reaction*;

fǎn dòng (sv) (n): 反动, *reactionary; reaction*;

fǎn yìng (v) (n): 反应, *to react/respond; chemical reaction; response; repercussion; feedback*

REALIDAD; realidade; *reality, truth* ... REALISMO; realismo; *realism* ... REALISTA; realista; *realistic (adj), realist (n)*;

bī zhēn (sv) (adv) (sv): 逼真, *lifelike; true to life; distinct; distinctly, clearly; realistic*;

shí jì (n) (sv): 实际, *reality; practice, praxis; practical, realistic, real, actual, concrete*;

shí kuàng: 实况, *actual situation/happening; live broadcast*;

wéi shí lùn: 唯实论, *realism*;

xiàn shí (n) (sv): 现实, *reality, actuality; practical, pragmatic; real, actual*;

xiàn shí (xiě shí) zhǔ yì: 现实 (写实) 主义, *realism*;

xiàn shí zhǔ yì zhě: 现实主义者, *realist*;

xiě shí zhǔ yì zhě: 写实主义者, *realist*;

SEE (请查看) REAL

REALIZABLE; realizável; *achievable; attainable, practical, feasible*;

kě xíng (sv): 可行, *feasible, practical*;

néng gòu dá dào de: 能够达到的, *attainable*;

néng gòu huò dé de: 能够获得的, *attainable*;

qiè shí (sv) (adv): 切实, *feasible, practical, realistic; practically, honestly, realistically*;

shí yòng (sv): 实用, *practical, pragmatic, functionable*;

SEE (请查看) POSITIVO

REALMENTE; realmente; *actually, really, in fact*;

dàng zhēn (vp): 当真, *to take seriously; to be serious; No joking, Really?*

dí què (adv): 的确, *certainly, surely; really*;

guǒ rán (adv) (conj) (n): 果然, *really, as expected, sure enough; if indeed, if really; a long-tailed monkey*;

jiū jìng (adv) (n): 究竟, *actually, exactly; after all, in the end; outcome, what actually happened*;

kě shì (conj) (adv): 可是, *but, yet, however; really, indeed*;

qí shí (adv): 其实, *as a matter of fact, actually, in fact*;

què shí (sv): 确实, *definitely, true, real, certain, reliable; really, certainly, truly indeed*;

què shí de (adv): 确实地, *really, certainly, truly, indeed*;

shí jì shang: 实际上, *as a matter of fact*;

shí shì (n): 实事, *true story, real/ practical/factual things*;
shí shì (vp): 实是, *actually, in fact*
SEE (请查看) **REALIDAD**

REBELIÓN; rebelião; *rebellion, revolt*;
bào luàn: 暴乱, *riot, rebellion, revolt*;
zào fǎn (v) (n): 造反, *to revolt/rebel; revolution, rebellion*;
fǎn pàn (v) n): 反叛, *to revolt/rebel; rebel, traitor, turncoat*;
pàn luàn: 叛乱, *uprising; armed rebellion*

RECALCITRANTE; recalcitrante; *recalcitrant*;
bù fú cóng de: 不服从的, *recalcitrant; obstinate*;
bù shùn cóng de: 不顺从的, *recalcitrant; disobedient, unyielding*;
SEE (请查看) **DESOBEDIENCIA**

RECEPCIÓN; recepção; *reception*;
zhāo dài huì: 招待会, *reception*;
SEE (请查看) **APLAUDIR, BANQUETE**

RECEPCIONISTA; recepcionista; *receptionist*;
jiē dài yuán: 接待员, *receptionist*

RECEPTÁCULO; receptáculo; *receptacle*;
róng qì: 容器, *container, receptacle*

RECEPTIVO (A) (adj); **receptivo** (A); *receptive*;
yǒu jiē shòu néng lì de: 有接受能力的, *receptive*;
jiē shòu (sv) (v): 接受, *receptive; to accept/receive*

RECESIÓN; recessão; *recession (ECON)*;
jīng lì shuāi tuì: 经济衰退, *economic recession*;
SEE (请查看) **DEGENERAR**

RECESO; recesso; *recess, nook*;
jiǎo luò: 角落, *corner, nook; secluded place*;
yǐn bì chù: 隐蔽处, *nook*;
yǐn bì de dì fang: 隐蔽的地方, *nook, recess*

RECIBO; recibo; *receipt, bill*;
dān jù: 单据, *receipts, vouchers, invoices*;
fā piào: 发票, *invoice, receipt*;
huí zhí: 回执, *receipt*;
piào jù: 票据, *bill, note; voucher, receipt*;
shōu jù: 收据, *receipt for purchases*;
shōu tiáo: 收条, *receipt for deposits*

RECIENTE; recente *recent, fresh, new, current* ... **RECIENTEMENTE; recentemente;** *recently, lately*
běn jiè: 本届, *current, this term's/ year's*;
dāng jīn: 当今, *present time, today*;
jìn lái (adv): 近来, *recently; lately, of late*;
xīn (sv): 新, *new, fresh; up-to-date*;
xīn xíng (attr): 新型, *new type/style/ pattern*;
xīn yǐng (sv): 新颖, *new and original; novel*;
yīng jiè: 应届, *current, this year's*;
zhǎn xīn (attr): 崭新, *brand new*;
zuì jìn (vp): 最近, *recently, lately; soon, in the near future*;
SEE (请查看) **CONTEMPORÁNEO, MODERNO**

RECÍPROCO (A); **recíproco** (A); *mutual, reciprocal, common, joint*;
duì děng (n) (attr): 对等, *reciprocity, equity; bilateral*;
gòng tóng (attr) (adv) (pref): 共同, *common, mutual, joint; together, jointly; syn-*;
gòng tóng xìng (n): 共同性, *commonality*;
gòng yòng (attr) (v) (vp): 共用, *shared, common; to share; mutual use*;
gòng yǒu (attr) (v): 共有, *public, common; to jointly possess*;
gōng yǒu (attr) (sv): 共有, *publicity owned, public; common, joint*;
xiāng hù (sv) (adv): 相互, *reciprocal; mutually, reciprocally*

RECLUSO (A); **recluso** (A); *a recluse;*
imprisoned, prisoner;
  qiú fàn: 囚犯: , *prisoner, convict;*
  qiú tú: 囚徒, *convict, prisoner;*
  yǐn shì: 隐士, *recluse, hermit;*
SEE (请查看**) CRIMINAL**

RECOMENDABLE; recomendável;
recommendable, advisable;
  kě qǔ (sv) 可取, *recommendable;*
  xián míng (sv): 贤明, *advisable;*
SEE (请查看**) CORRECTO**

RECOMENDACIÓN; recomendação;
recommendation;
  tuī jiàn (v) (n): 推荐, *to recommend;*
  recommendation;
SEE (请查看**) AVISAR**

RECOMPENSA; recompensa;
reward, recompense;
  bào chou (n): 报酬, *reward,*
  remuneration;
SEE (请查看**) GRATIFICACIÓN**

RECÓNDITO (A); **recôndito** (A);
recondite, hidden, arcane, esoteric;
  àn 'cáng (n) (v): 暗藏, *hidden; to hide/*
  conceal;
  shēn 'ào (sv): 深奥, *esoteric, profound,*
  abstruse;
  yǐn bì (v) (sv): 隐蔽, *to hide/take cover;*
  concealed, hidden;
SEE (请查看**) CLANDESTINIDAD,**
CRÍPTICO, ENIGMÁTICO, ARCANO

RECONOCIBLE; reconhecível;
recognizable;
  biǎo zhāng (n): 表彰, *sign, mark,*
  emblem;
  biǎo zhāng de: 表彰的, *recognizable*

RECREACIÓN; recreação;
divertimento; *recreation, amusement*
... RECREATIVO (A); **recreativo** (A);
recreational, arcade;
  xiāo qiǎn (v) (n): 消遣, *to divert*
  oneself/while away time; pastime;
  yóu lè chǎng: 游乐场 , *amusement*
  park/arcade;

yóu xì (v) (n): 游戏, *to play; recreation,*
  game;
SEE (请查看**) DIVERTIDO,**
JUBILOSO

RECRIMINACIÓN;
recriminação; *reproach,*
recrimination;
  fǎn sù: 反诉, *countercharge;*
  counterclaim (DER);
  hù xiāng gōng jī: 互相攻击,
  recrimination

RECTÁNGULO; retângulo; *rectangle;*
  cháng fāng xíng de: 长方形的,
  rectangular;
  cháng fāng xíng: 长方形, *rectangle;*
  jǔ xíng: 矩形, *rectangle (MAT)*

RECTIFICACIÓN; retificação;
rectification, correction;
  xiū gǎi (n) (v): 修改, *correction,*
  alteration; to revise/amend/alter;
SEE (请查看**) AJUSTAR**

RECTITUD; retidão; *rectitude,*
uprightness;
  zhèng zhí: 正直, *rectitude*

RECTO; reto; *straight (GEN), upright/*
honest person;
  gāng zhí (sv): 刚直, *upright and*
  outspoken;
  lǎo shi (sv): 老实, *honest, frank;*
  tǎn shí (sv): 坦实, *frank and honest;*
  tǎn shuài (sv): 坦率, *frank, sincere,*
  candid, honest;
  zhí lì (sv): 直立, *upright, honest;*
SEE (请查看**) DECENCIA,**
CORRECTAMENTE, HONESTO,
HONESTIDAD

RECURRENTE; recorrente; *recurrent,*
frequent, periodic;
  dìng qī (attr) (v): 定期, *periodical,*
  regular; to fix a date;
  zhōu qī xìng (n) (sv): 周期性,
  periodicity, cyclicity; periodic;
SEE (请查看**) DUPLICADO,**
FRECUENTE

REDACCIÓN; redação; *writing, editing* ... **REDACTOR** (A); **redator** (A); *writer, editor, drafter;*
  biān jì: 编辑, *editor of a book/ newspaper, etc.;*
  jiào dìng zhě: 校订者, *editor of a text/ report, etc.;*
  xiě (n) (v): 写, *writing; to write/ compose/ describe/ depict; (bf) to paint/ draw;*
  zì jì: 字迹, *handwriting, writing;*
  zuò jiā: 作家 , *writer, author;*
  zuò zhě: 作者, *writer of a report/ document, etc.*

REDUCIDO (A); **reduzido** (A); *reduced; small, limited;*
  suō xiǎo (v) (n): 缩小, *to reduce/ shrink; reduction, shrinkage;*
  xiǎo (sv): 小, *small, little, petty, minor;*
SEE (请查看**) DESCENDENTE, LIMITADO**

REDUCTO; reduto; *fort, shelter; stronghold, redoubt;*
  bǎo lěi: 堡垒, *fort;*
  yào sài: 要塞, *stronghold*

REDUNDANCIA; redundância; *redundancy, superfluous* ... **REDUNDANTE; redundante;** *redundant;*
  duō yú (sv): 多余, *unnecessary, superfluous, excessive;*
  guò shèng (vp) (n): 过剩, *to be superfluous/ excessive; surplus;*
SEE (请查看**) DESMEDIDO**

REFECTORIO; refeitório; *dining hall; refectory;*
  cān tīng: 餐厅, *dining room/hall;*
SEE (请查看**) CANTINA**

REFERENCIA; referência; *reference; account, report;*
  bào gào (v) (n): 报告, *to report; report, speech;*
SEE (请查看**) ALUDIR, DESCRIPCIÓN, CERTIFICAR, COMUNICAR, REPORTE**

REFINADO (A); **refinado** (A); *refined;*
  diǎn yǎ (sv): 典雅, *refined, elegant;*
SEE (请查看**) CIVILIZADO, DECORO, DELICADO, EDUCADO, FINURA**

REFINERÍA; refinaria; *refinery;*
  jīng liàn chǎng: 精炼厂, *refinery;*
  liàn yóu chǎng: 炼油厂, *oil refinery*

REFLEXIÓN; reflexão; *reflection, thought* ... **REFLEXIVO** (A); **reflexivo** (A); *reflective, thoughtful;*
  gǎn xiǎng: 感想, *impression(s), reflections, thoughts;*
  niàn tou (n): 念头, *thought, thinking; to think/ consider;*
  sī xiǎng (n): 思想, *thought, thinking, idea, ideology;*
SEE (请查看**) SENSACIÓN, PENSAR**

REFORMA; reforma; *reform; alterations, change;*
  gǎi gé (n) (v): 改革, *reform; to reform;*
  gé xīn (v) (n): 革新, *to innovate/ reform/improve; innovation, reform, improvement*

REFRIGERACIÓN; refrigeração; *refrigeration, cooling* ... **REFRIGERADOR** (A); **geladeira; refrigerador;** *refrigerator, cool, cooler, room, coolant, cooling unit or system;*
  lěng cáng fǎ: 冷藏法, *refrigeration;*
  lěng cáng kù: 冷藏库, *cold storage, freezer;*
  lěng cáng qì: 冷藏器, *freezer;*
  lěng cáng shì: 冷藏室, *cold storage;*
  lěng cáng xiāng: 冷藏箱, *refrigerator;*
  lěng cáng: 冷藏, *refrigeration, cold storage;*
  lěng dòng jì: 冷冻剂, *refrigerant;*
  lěng dòng jī: 冷冻机, *refrigerator, freezer;*
  lěng dòng kù: 冷冻库, *freezer, refrigerated storage room;*
SEE (请查看**) FREEZER ó CONGELADOR**

REFUGIO; refúgio; *refuge, shelter;*
  bì hù (n) (v): 庇护, *shelter, asylum, refuge; to shelter/shield sb*

REFUTACIÓN; refutação;
refutation, rebuttal;
  biàn bó (n) (v): 辩驳, *rebuttal; to dispute/refute;*
  bó chì (v) (n): 驳斥, *to denounce/ refute; rebuttal, refutation*

REGENERACIÓN; regeneração;
regeneration, reform;
  huī fù (v) (sv): 恢复, *to renew; regenerated;*
  xīn shēng (n): 新生, *new life, rebirth, regeneration*

REGRESIÓN; regressão; *regression, fall, decrease* ... **REGRESIVO** (A);
regressivo (A); *regressive, backward;*
  dào tuì de: 倒退的, *regressive;*
SEE (请查看**) DEGENERAR**

REGULARIDAD; regularidade;
regularity; regularly;
  jīng cháng de (adv): 经常地, *frequently, often, regularly*

REITERADO (A); **repetido** (A);
repeated ... **REITERADAMENTE;**
repetidamente; *repeatedly;*
  chóng fù (v) (n) (sv): 重复, *to repeat/ duplicate; repetition; repetitive;*
  fǎn fù de (adv) (n) (sv): 反复地, *repeatedly, again and again; reversal, relapse; not dependable;*
  zài sān de (adv): 再三地, *over and over again*

RELACIÓN; relação; ligação;
relationship, connection;
  guān xi (v) (n): 关系, *to concern/affect/ matter; relation, relationship;*
  lián xì (v) (n): 联系, *to integrate/relate/ link; contact, touch, connection, relation*

RELAJACIÓN; relax; *relaxation* ...
RELAJADO (A); **relaxado** (A); *relaxed, careless;*
  fàng kuān: 放宽, *relaxation (of control, a rule);*
  fàng sōng de: 放松的, *relaxed (person);*

  qīng sōng de: 轻松的, *relaxed (atmosphere);*
SEE (请查看**) CALMA,
RECREACIÓN, NEGLIGENCIA**

RELATIVO (A); **relativo** (A); *relative to, regarding;*
  guān yú (prep): 关于, *with regard to, concerning;*
  yǒu guān: 有关, *relevant to, concerning*

RELATO; relato; *story, tale, account, report;*
  bào dào (v) (n): 报道, *to report the news; a news report;*
  gù shi: 故事, *story, tale; plot;*
  huì bào (v) (n): 汇报, *to report/give an account on; report;*
  liú yán: 留言, *rumor, gossip;*
  yáo yán: 谣言, *rumors;*
SEE (请查看**) COMUNICAR**

RELEVANCIA; relevância;
prominence, relevance, importance ...
RELEVANTE; relevante; *outstanding, important, relevant;*
  guān lián (n) (v): 关联, *relevance, correlation; to be related/connected;*
  qiè tí de (adj) (sv): 切题的 , *relevant, pertinent;*
  xiāng guān (vp) (n) (attr) (sv): 相关, *to be interrelated; correlation; relative; relevant;*
  yào jǐn (sv): 要紧, *important, essential; critical, serious;*
  yǒu guān de: 有关的, *to be interrelated; correlation; relative;*
  zhòng yào xìng: 重要性, *importance, significance;*
SEE (请查看**) APROPIADO,
CONCERNIR, IMPORTANTE**

RELIEVE; relevo; *relief (GEOL) (ARTE);*
  fú diāo: 浮雕, *relief sculpture;*
  dì mào: 地貌, *landforms, configurations of land;*
  dì mào tú: 地貌图, *contour map*

REMEDIO; remédio; *solution, remedy;*

choice, alternative;
   bǔ jiù (n) (v): 补救, remedy; to remedy;
   bǔ jiù bàn fǎ (n): 补救办法, corrective measures, remedy;
   bǔ jiù de fāng fǎ: 补救的方法, remedy for a situation;
   dá 'àn: 答案, solution, answer, key;
   jiě fǎ (n): 解法, solution (MAT);
   zhì liáo (v) (n): 治疗, to treat/cure; treatment, remedy, cure;
   zhì liáo fǎ: 治疗法, remedy for an illness

REMISIBLE; remissível; *forgivable*;
   kě yuán liàng de: 可原谅的, *forgivable*;
SEE (请查看**) CLEMENCIA**

REMISO (A); **relutância**; *reluctant*;
   bù qíng yuàn de: 不情愿的, *reluctant, unwilling*;
SEE (请查看**) RETICENCIA**

REMOTO (A); **remoto** (A); *remote, distant, faraway*;
   liáo yuǎn (sv): 辽远, *distant, faraway*;
   piān pì (sv): 偏僻, *remote, out-of-the-way; rare*;
   yáo yuǎn (sv): 遥远, *remote, isolated; distant*;
   yuǎn chéng (attr): 远程, *long-distance, remote, long-range*;
   yuǎn fāng (n): 远方, *distant place*;
SEE (请查看**) DISTANTE**

RENCOR; rancor; *rancor, bitterness, resentment* ... **RENCOROSO** (A); **ressentido** (A); *resentful, bitter (person)* ... **RESENTIDO** (A); **ressentido** (A); *resentful, bitter* ... **RESENTIMIENTO; ressentimento**; *resentment, bitterness*;
   kǔ (sv) (n) (v) (adv): 苦, *bitter, excessive; hardship, suffering, pain; to cause suffering, to suffer/be troubled by; painstakingly*;
   shēn chóu (n): 深仇, *deep animosity/ hatred; rancor*;
   yuàn fèn (n): 怨愤, *discontent, indignation; grudge*;
SEE (请查看**) DESDÉN,**

DESAGRADO, ANIMOSIDAD, DETESTAR, ENEMISTAD, ACERBO

RENEGADO (A); **renegado** (A); *renegade, rebel; apostate (RELIG)*;
   pàn tú: 叛徒, *traitor, renegade, turncoat*

RENOMBRADO (A); **renomado** (A); *renowned, famous* ... **RENOMBRE; renome**; *renown, fame*;
   zhù míng de: 著名的, *renowned*;
SEE (请查看**) FAMA, FAMOSO, CÉLEBRE, CELEBRIDAD, AFAMADO**

RENOVABLE; renovável; *renewable* ... **RENOVACIÓN; renovação**; *renewal, renovation*;
   gé xīn (v) (n): 革新, *to innovate/ reform/improve; innovation, improvement*;
   gēng xīn (n) (v): 更新, *renewal, renovation; to renew/ replace*;
   kě gēng xīn de: 可更新的, *renewable*

RENTA; lucro, renda; *earnings; profit, income*;
   gōng zī: 工资, *wages, pay, salary; income*;
   lì rùn: 利润, *profit*;
   lì yì: 利益, *interest, benefit, profit*;
   shōu rù (n) (v): 收入, *income; to take in*;
   shōu yì: 收益, *income, profit, earnings, gain*;
   suǒ dé: 所得, *income, gains, earnings*;
   yì chù: 益处, *benefit, profit, good*

RENTABLE; lucrative (A); **lucratividade; rentável**; *profitable, profitability; productive* ... **RENTABILIDAD; rentabilidade**; *profitability*;
   duō chǎn (attr): 多产, *productive, prolific*;
   shēng chǎn (sv) (v): 生产, *productive; to produce/manufacture*;
   yǒu lì kě tú (sv) (v): 有利可图, *profitable; profitability*;

yǒu lì rùn: 有利润, *profitable activity*;
yǒu yì de: 有益的, *profitable; useful, beneficial*;
zhuàn qián de: 赚钱的, *lucrative*

REPARACIÓN; reparação;
reparation, repair, compensation;
bǔ cháng fèi: 补偿费, *compensation, compensatory payment*;
SEE (请查看**) COMPENSACIÓN**

REPARTICIÓN; repartição; *sharing out, distribution*;
fēn fā: 分发, *distribution of items/things, etc.*;
SEE (请查看**) DIFUSO, DISTRIBUCIÓN**

REPELENTE; repelente; *repellent, repulsive; insect repellent*;
kě wù (sv): 可恶, *hateful, abominable, repulsive*;
shā chóng jì: 杀虫剂, *insect repellent, insecticide, pesticide*;
SEE (请查看**) SINGULARIDAD, ESTUPEFACTO**

REPERTORIO; repertório;
repertoire (MUS), selection; index;
bǎo liú jù mù: 保留剧目, *repertoire, repertory*;
quán tào jù mù: 全套剧目, *repertoire*;
SEE (请查看**) DEPÓSITO, INVENTARIO**

REPETICIÓN; repetição; *repetition, reiteration* ... **REPETIDO** (A)**; repetido** (A); *repeated* ... **REPETITIVO** (A)**; repetitivo** (A); *repetitive, redundant; tedious, wordy*;
bèi cái yuán de: 被裁员的, *redundant*;
duō cí (adv): 多次, *repeatedly, on many occasions*;
duō yú (sv): 多余, *unnecessary, superfluous, excessive*;
duō yú dù (n): 多余度, *redundancy*;
fǎn fù (adv) (n) (sv): 反复, *repeatedly, again and again; reversal, relapse; not dependable*;

fǎn fù de: 反复的, *repeated*;
guò duō de: 过多的, *redundant*;
rǒng yú (n) (attr): 冗余, *redundancy; redundant*;
zài sān de (adv): 再三地, *repeatedly*;
SEE (请查看**) DUPLICADO**

REPLETO (A)**; repleto** (A); *full of, crammed with, replete*;
chōng mǎn de: 充满的, *replete*;
chōng shí (v) (sv): 充实, *to substantiate/enrich/ replenish; substantial, rich, replete*

REPORTE; reportage; *report*;
bào gào: 报告, *report*;
SEE (请查看**) REFERENCIA**

REPOSADO (A)**; repousado** (A);
relaxed, calm, quiet;
lìng rén fàng sōng de: 令人放松的, *relaxed person*;
SEE (请查看**) RELAJACIÓN, CALMA, RECREACIÓN, PACÍFICO**

REPOSO; repouso; *rest; repose*;
shuì jiào (v) (n): 睡觉, *to go to bed/sleep; rest*;
xiū xi (n) (v): 休息, *rest; to take a rest*

REPRESENTANTE (n);
representante (n) (adj); *representative*;
dài biǎo (n) (v): 代表, *representative, delegate; to represent*;
dài lǐ (v) (attr) (n): 代理, *to act as an agent/proxy; acting, sub-; representative, agent, substitute, deputy*;
yì yuán: 议员, *representative, member of congress*;
SEE (请查看**) CLÁSICO**

REPRESIÓN; repressão; *repression, suppression*;
zhèn yā: 镇压, *suppression, repression*;
SEE (请查看**) DISCIPLINA**

REPRESIVO (A)**; repressivo** (A);
repressive, restraining, subduing;
cán kù de: 残酷的, *repressive*;
yuē shù de: 约束的, *restraining*

REPRIMENDA; reprimenda;
reprimand, rebuke, reproach, admonish;
  xùn chì (v) (n): 训斥, *to reprimand/
  rebuke; reprimand, rebuke*;
SEE (请查看) DENUNCIA

REPROBABLE; repreensível;
reprehensible;
  yīng shòu zhǐ zé de: 应受指责的,
  reprehensible;
SEE (请查看) CENSURABLE

REPROCHE; censura; *reproach,
censure, disapproval*;
  zhǐ zé (v) (n): 指责, *to censure/criticize;
  censure*;
SEE (请查看) ACUSAR,
DESAPROBACIÓN

REPRODUCCIÓN; reprodução;
reproduction, duplication, replica;
  kǎo bèi jiàn: 拷贝件, *copy,
  reproduction of documents*;
SEE (请查看) DUPLICADO

REPTIL; reptile; *reptile (n), reptilian
(adj)*;
  pá xíng dòng wù: 爬行动物, *reptile*

REPUDIO; repúdio; *rejection,
repudiation*;
  fǒu rèn: 否认, *repudiation*

REPUGNANCIA; repugnância;
disgust, repugnance, loathing
...REPUGNANTE; repugnante;
disgusting, repugnant, revolting ...
REPULSA; repulsa; *repulsion,
rejection, condemnation, rebuff ...*
REPULSIVO (A); **repulsivo** (A);
repulsive, disgusting;
  dé xíng (sv): 德行, *disgusting,
  shameful; vexing, disgraceful*;
  duàn rán jù jué (vp): 断然拒绝,
  rejection; outright, refusal;
  kě wù (sv): 可恶, *repulsive, hateful,
  abominable*;
  lìng rén fǎn gǎn (vp) (sv): 令人反感,
  to be disgusted/ repulsed by; disgusting,

repugnant;
  lìng rén zuò 'ǒu de: 令人作呕的,
  disgusting;
  lìng rén yàn wù de: 令人厌恶的,
  revolting;
SEE (请查看) ABOMINACIÓN,
DESAGRADABLE, ANTIPATÍA,
DESDÉN

REPUTACIÓN; reputação; *reputation*;
  míng shēng: 名声, *reputation, repute,
  renown*;
  shēng wàng (n): 声望, *popularity,
  prestige*;
SEE (请查看) FAMA, CARÁCTER

RESERVADO (A); **reservado** (A);
reserved, discreet, confidential;
  jīn chí (sv): 矜持, *restrained, reserved*;
  jū jǐn (sv): 拘谨, *reserved, overcautious,
  modest*;
SEE (请查看) DISCRETO,
PRUDENCIA

RESIDENCIA; residência;
stay, residence, second home ...
RESIDENCIAL; residencial;
residential ... **RESIDENTE; residente;**
resident;
  cháng zhù (attr): 常驻, *resident,
  permanent*;
  jū mín diǎn: 居民点, *residential area*;
  jū mín: 居民, *resident, inhabitant*;
  jū suǒ: 居所, *residence*;
  zhù chù: 住处, *dwelling place,
  residence, domicile*;
  zhù hù: 住户, *household, resident*;
  zhù zhái lóu: 住宅楼, *residential
  building*;
  zhù zhái qū: 住宅区, *residential
  district*;
  zhù zhái: 住宅, *residence, dwelling*;
  zhù zhǐ: 住址, *address*

RESIDUO; resíduo; *residue, waste;
remainder (MAT)*;
  cán yú: 残余, *residue, remnants,
  remains*;
  fèi liào: 废料 , *waste, scrap, rubbish*;
  fèi (bf): 废, *waste, useless, disused*

RESIGNADO (A); **resignado** (A); *resigned (adj)*;
  qū cóng de: 屈从的, *resigned, submitted*;
  shùn cóng de: 顺从的, *resigned*;

RESINA; resina; *resin*;
  shù zhī: 树脂, *resin*;
  hé chéng shù zhī: 合成树脂, *synthetic resin*

RESISTENTE; resistente; *tough, strong, resistant* ... **RESOLUTO** (A); **resoluto** (A); *resolute, determined, persistent, tenacious, obstinate*;
  gāng yì (sv): 刚毅, *resolute, stalwart*;
  jiān rèn (sv): 坚韧, *firm and tenacious, strong and durable*;
  jiān rěn (sv): 坚忍, *steadfast and preserving*;
  jiē shi (sv): 结实, *strong, solid, durable*;
  láo gù (sv): 牢固, *firm, secure, strong*;
  qiáng yì (sv): 强毅, *resolute and steadfast, staunch*;
  qiáng yìng (sv): 强硬, *strong, tough, unyielding*;
  qiáng zhuàng (sv): 强壮, *strong, sturdy*;
  yǒu lì (sv) (v): 有力, *strong, forceful, powerful; to be strong/forceful*;
SEE (请查看**) INSISTENTE, PERSISTENTE, CONTINUO, DURO, DIFÍCIL, CONSTANTE, OBSTINACIÓN, CRUCIAL, DETERMINACIÓN, CONTUMACIA**

RESONANCIA; ressonância; *resonance, echo*;
  fǎn xiǎng: 反响, *echo, reverberation, repercussion*;
  huí shēng: 回声, *echo*;
  huí yīn: 回音, *echo; reply*

RESPECTIVAMENTE (adv); **respectivamente;** *respectively* ... **RESPECTIVO** (A); **respectivo** (A); *respective*;
  fēn bié (adv) (v) (n): 分别, *separately, respectively, differently; difference; to distinguish/differentiate; to leave/part*

from another; difference;
SEE (请查看**) CORRESPONDIENTE**

RESPETABLE; respeitável; *respectable, considerable*;
  guò de qù de: 过得去的, *adequate, not so bad*;
  zūn guì (attr): 尊贵, *honorable, respected, respectable*;
SEE (请查看**) DECENCIA, CORRESPONDIENTE**

RESPETUOSO (A); **respeitoso** (A); *respectful, courteous, polite, cordial, gracious; civil, accommodating*;
  gōng jìng (sv) (n): 恭敬, *respectful, respect*;
SEE (请查看**) CORDIALIDAD**

RESPIRATORIO (A); **respiratório** (A); *respiratory*;
  hù xī de: 护膝的, *respiratory*

RESPLANDOR; resplendor; *brilliance; brightness, glow, gleam*;
  guāng huī: 光辉, *brilliance, brightness*

RESPONDÓN (A); **respondão;** *insolent, mouthy, cheeky*;
  mán hèng (sv): 蛮横, *overbearing, arbitrary, insolent*;
SEE (请查看**) ARROGANCIA, ABRASIVO**

RESPONSABILIDAD; responsabilidade; *responsibility* ... **RESPONSABLE; responsável;** *responsible for sthg*;
  zhí zé: 职责, *duty, obligation, responsibility*;
SEE (请查看**) COMPROMISO**

RESTAURACIÓN; restauração; *restoration*;
  fù yuán (n) (v): 复原, *restoration; to recover from an illness; to restore/rehabilitate*;
  huī fù (v) (n): 恢复, *to resume/renew; to recover/regain; to restore/to reinstate/rehabilitate; restoration*;
SEE (请查看**) RECONSTRUIR**

RESTAURANTE; restaurante; *restaurant*;
  fàn diàn: 饭店, *restaurant, hotel*;
SEE (请查看**) CANTINA**

RESTRINGIDO; restrito (A); *restricted, limited, prohibited*;
  jìn lìng: 禁令, *prohibition, ban*;
  shòu xiàn zhì de: 受限制的, *restricted*;
SEE (请查看**) BOICOT, DISCIPLINA, CONFINAR, LIMITADO, LIMITACIÓN, INHIBICIÓN**

RESULTA; resultado; *result* ...
RESULTADO; resultado; *result, outcome, score* ... **RESULTANTE; resultante;** *resultant; resulting*;
  bǐ fēn: 比分, *score (DEP)*;
  chǎn wù: 产物, *outcome, result, product*;
  jié guǒ: 结果, *result, outcome*;
  jié jú: 结局, *final results, outcome, ending*;
  jiū jìng (adv) (n): 究竟, *actually, exactly; outcome, what actually happened*;
  zuò wéi jié guǒ: 作为结果 , *resultant*;
SEE (请查看**) CONSECUENCIA, FINAL**

RESUMEN; resumo; *summary, synopsis, abstract, digest*;
  chōu xiàng: 抽象, *abstract*;
  dà gāng: 大纲, *outline, synopsis, summary*;
  gài yào: 概要, *essentials, outline, summary*;
  tí gāng: 提纲, *outline, synopsis*;
  tí yào: 提要, *summary, abstract*;
  wén zhāi: 文摘, *abstract, digest*;
  zhāi yào (v) (n): 摘要, *to summarize; summary, abstract*;
  zǒng jié(v) (n): 总结, *to sum up/ summarize; summary*;
SEE (请查看**) CAPITULAR**

RESURGIMIENTO; ressurgimento; *resurgence, return, revival*;
  fǎn huí (v) (n): 返回, *to return, to come back/go back; return*;
  huī fù huó lì (sv) (n): 恢复活力,

resurgent; resurgence;
  zài cì chū xiàn (sv) (n): 再次出现, *resurgent; resurgence*;
SEE (请查看**) DEVOLVER**

RETALIACIÓN; retaliação; *retaliation, avenge; counter, reciprocate; settle, get even, strike back*;
  bào fu (n) (v): 报复, *retaliation; to retaliate*

RETICENCIA; reticência; *reticence; unwillingness, reluctance, reserved* ...
RETICENTE; reticente; *unwilling, reluctant; shy, timid, reticent*;
  bù qíng yuàn (sv) (n): 不情愿, *reluctant, unwilling; reticence, unwillingness*;
  bù yuàn yì de: 不愿意的, *unwilling*;
  bù yuàn zuò mǒu shì de: 不愿做某事的, *unwilling*;
  dǎn xiǎo (sv): 胆小, *cowardly, timid*
  chén mò (sv): 沉默, *reticent, taciturn; silent*;
  chén mò guǎ yán (fe): 沉默寡言, *reticent*;
  miǎn qiǎng (v) (sv) (adv): 勉强, *to force sb to do sthg; unconvincing, strained; reluctantly, grudgingly*;
SEE (请查看**) TIMIDEZ**

RETÓRICO (A); **retórico** (A); *rhetorical*;
  xiū cí (n) (attr): 修辞, *rhetoric; rhetorical*

RETROACTIVO (A); **retroativo** (A); *retroactive*;
  zhuī sù (sv) (v): 追溯, *retroactive, to trace back/date from* ;
  zhuī bǔ (sv) (v): 追捕, *retroactive; to pursue and capture*

REUMATISMO; reumatismo; *rheumatism*;
  fēng shī bìng: 风湿病, *rheumatism*

REUTILIZABLE; reutilizável; *reusable*;
  kě zài yòng de: 可再用的, *reusable*

REVERSO (A); **inverso** (A); *reverse side, other side, reverse*;
  fǎn miàn (n) (v): 反面, *reverse/wrong side; opposite/negative side; to present a cold look*;
  diān dǎo (v) (vp) (n): 颠倒, *to put upside down/reverse/invert; confused, disordered, topsy-turvy; perversion*;
  bèi miàn (n): 背面, *back, reverse side*;
SEE (请查看) **ANVERSO**

RICAMENTE; **ricamente**; *richly*;
  huá lì de: 华丽的, *richly (decorated); gorgeous, magnificent*;
  nóng hòu de: 浓厚的, *richly (flavored); strong, pronounced*

RICO (A); **rico** (A); *rich*;
  féi měi (sv): 肥美, *fertile, rich; luxuriant; plump, fat*;
  fēng hòu (sv): 丰厚, *thick; rich and generous*;
  fēng shèng (sv): 丰盛, *rich, sumptuous*;
  fù yǒu (v) (sv): 富有, *to be rich/wealthy; to be rich in/full; rich, wealthy*;
  fù yú (vp): 富于, *to be rich in*;
SEE (请查看) **ABUNDANCIA, COPIOSO**

RIDÍCULO (A); **ridículo** (A); *ridiculous, laughable, derisory*;
  huāng miù (sv): 荒谬, *absurd, preposterous; ridiculous*;
  kě xiào (sv): 可笑, *ridiculous, funny*;
SEE (请查看) **ABSURDO**

RIGIDEZ; **rigidez**; *rigidity, stiffness* ... **RÍGIDO** (A); **rígido** (A); *rigid, stiff, inflexible* ... **RIGUROSO** (A); **rigoroso** (A); *strict, rigorous*;
  bù kě wān qū de: 不可弯曲的, *inflexible*;
  bù líng huó: 不灵活, *not nimble/agile; inflexible, inelastic*;
  bù líng huó: 不灵活, *rigidity*;
  kè bǎn (attr): 刻板, *mechanical, stiff, inflexible; dull, stereotyped*;
  kè bǎn: 刻板, *rigidity, stiffness*;
  shēng yìng (sv): 生硬, *stiff, rigid, harsh*;

  yán gé (sv) (n): 严格, *strict, rigorous; stiffness, rigidity*;
  yìng tǐng (v) (sv): 硬挺, *to stick to/hold out; rigid, stiff*
SEE (请查看) **OBSTINADO, RESISTENTE, DIFÍCIL, RÍGIDO, DILIGENCIA, FIRME**

RISA; **riso**; *laugh*;
  dà xiào: 大笑, *loud laugh*;
  cháo xiào (n) (v): 嘲笑, *raillery; to ridicule/laugh at/deride*;
  xiào (v) (n): 笑, *to smile/laugh; to ridicule/laugh at; laugh*;
  xiào shēng: 笑声, *whistling, squeal; laughter*

RÍTMICO (A); **rítmico** (A); *rhythmic, rhythmical*;
  jié zòu de: 节奏的, *rhythmic*

RIVALIDAD; **rivalidade**; *rivalry, competition*;
  jìng zhēng (v) (n): 竞争, *to compete; competition, rivalry*

ROBUSTO (A); **robusto** (A); *robust, tough, strong, sturdy*;
  jiē shi de: 结实的, *strong, robust; solid, durable*;
  qiáng jiàn de: 强健的, *robust, strong and healthy*;
SEE (请查看) **RESISTENTE, RESOLUTO**

ROCA; **rocha**; *rock* ... **ROCOSO** (A); **rochoso** (A); *rocky, stony*;
  duō shí de: 多石的, *stony*;
  yán shí (sv) (n): 岩石, *rocky; rock*

RON; **rum**; *rum*;
  lǎng mǔ jiǔ: 朗姆酒, *rum*

ROTATIVO (A) (adj); **rotatório** (A); *rotary, revolving*;
  xuán zhuàn de: 旋转的, *rotating*;
  zhuàn dòng de: 转动的, *rotating, revolving*

RUDIMENTARIO (A) **rudimentar**;

rudimentary ... RUDIMENTOS;
rudimentos; *rudiments;*
  chū bù (n) (sv): 初步, *the first stages;*
  rudiments; rudimentary;
  jī chǔ (sv) (n) (attr): 基础, *rudimentary;*
  base, foundation, basis; basic,
  fundamental;
SEE (请查看) FUNDAMENTAL

RUFIÁN; rufião (A); *ruffian; villain,*
scoundrel, pimp;
  è gùn: 恶棍, *scoundrel, rogue, bully;*
  pí tiáo kè: 皮条客, *pimp;*
SEE (请查看) GÁNGSTER

RÚSTICO (A); **rústico** (A); *rustic,*
country, rough, coarse;
  nóng cūn (sv) (n): 农村, *rustic;*
  countryside;
  tǔ qì (sv): 土气, *rustic, uncouth;*
SEE (请查看) GROSERO

RUTA; rota; *route, road;*
  dào lù: 道路, *road, way, path;*
  lǚ tú: 旅途, *journey, trip, route;*
  lù xiàn: 路线, *route; itinerary;*
  tōng dào: 通道, *route, passageway;*
  xiàn lù: 线路, *route, line, circuit;*
SEE (请查看) TRAVESÍA

RUTINA; rotina; *normal routine; daily,*
habit ... RUTINARIO (A) (adj); **rotineiro**
(A); *routine, unimaginative;*
  cháng tài (n) (attr): 常态, *normality,*
  normal behavior/conditions; normal;
  cháng wù (n): 常务, *day-to-day*
  business, routine;
  lì xíng gōng shì: 例行公事, *reason,*
  rationality; routine, procedure;
  méi yǒu xiǎng xiàng lì de:
  没有想象力的, *unimaginative;*
SEE (请查看) CONVENCIONAL,
COSTUMBRE

Easily recognizable verbs and their Portuguese and Chinese equivalents
Verbos fácilmente reconocibles en Español-Portugués-Inglés y sus
equivalentes en Chino
Verbos facilmente reconhecível em Espanhol-Português-Inglês e seus
equivalentes em Chinês
很容易辨认的西班牙语，葡萄牙语，英语动词和他们的中文对等词

RACIONALIZAR; racionalizar; *to*
rationalize;
  shǐ hé lǐ huà: 使合理化, *to rationalize*

RACIONAR; racionar; *to ration;*
  dìng liàng (n) (v): 定量, *fixed quantity,*
  ration; to ration;
  dìng liàng gōng yìng: 定量供应, *to*
  ration

RASPAR; raspar; *to smooth down, to*
shave; to scrape, scratch, scratch out;
  cā jìng: 擦净, *to clean/wipe/wipe up; to*
  erase, scratch out; to scour;
  cā shāng (v) (n): 擦伤, *to bruise/graze/*
  scratch/ scrape/abrade/chafe; abrasion,
  scuffing;
  cā: 擦, *to rub/scrub/scrape; to polish/*

wipe; to brush/past/shave; to put/spread
on;
  guā hú zi: 刮胡子, *to shave the beard;*
  guā liǎn: 刮脸, *to shave the face;*
  guā xiāo: 刮削, *to scrape; to exploit/*
  extort;
  guā: 刮, *to scrape/shave;*
  huà diào: 划掉 , *to scratch out; cross*
  off/out;
  tì xū: 剃须, *to shave a beard/mustache;*
  xiāo: 削, *to pare/peel/scrape with a*
  knife;
  xiū miàn: 修面, *to shave;*
SEE (请查看) APLANAR

RATIFICAR; ratificar; *to ratify/confirm;*
to support;
  qiān zì rèn kě: 签字认可, *to ratify;*

què rèn: 确认, *to confirm*;
SEE (请查看**) APROBACIÓN**

REAFIRMAR; reafirmar; *to reaffirm/ confirm/reassert*;
  chóng shēn: 重申, *to reaffirm/restate*

REAJUSTAR; reajustar; *to rearrange/ make changes*;
  gǎi biān: 改编, *to rearrange/ reorganize/ revise/ adapt*;
SEE (请查看**) GRADUAR**

REALIZAR; realizar; *to realize; to make; to carry out/ go on; to do/fulfill*;
  shí xiàn: 实现, *to realize/achieve/bring about*;
  tǐ huì (v) (n): 体会, *to realize, to know/ learn from experience; knowledge, understanding*;
  yì shí (n) (v): 意识, *awareness; to realize*;
SEE (请查看**) DESILUSIÓN, CONCLUIR, COMPLACIDO**

REANIMAR; reanimar; *to revive; to cheer up/ reactivate/liven up/animate*;
  fù xīng: 复兴, *to revive/resurge/ rejuvenate*;
  sū xǐng: 苏醒, *to revive sb*;
  zhèn xīng: 振兴, *to revitalize/promote/ develop*;
  zhèn zuò qǐ lái: 振作起来, *to cheer up sb/brace up sb*;
  zhèn zuò: 振作, *to bestir/exert os*;
SEE (请查看**) AVIVAR, INSPIRAR**

RECAPITULAR; recapitular; *to recapitulate/ summarize*;
  zǒng jié (v) (n): 总结, *to summarize/ sum up*;
SEE (请查看**) RESUMEN, DELINEAR, CONCLUIR, RESUMIR**

RECIBIR; receber; *to receive/get*;
  shòu dào: 受到, *to be given sthg*;
  shōu dào: 收到, *to receive/get/ achieve*;
  shòu jiǎng: 受奖, *to receive an award*;
SEE (请查看**) ACEPTAR**

RECICLAR; reciclar; *to recycle*;
  huí shōu lì yòng: 回收利用, *to recycle*;
  huí shōu: 回收, *to retrieve/recover/ reclaim/recycle*;
  lì yòng: 利用, *to use/utilize; to take advantage of/ exploit*

RECITAR; recitar; *to recite*;
  bèi sòng: 背诵, *to recite, to repeat from memory*;
  lǎng sòng: 朗诵, *to recite; to read aloud*;
SEE (请查看**) ESTUDIAR**

RECLAMAR; reclamar; *to claim/ demand*;
  qiú quán: 求全, *to demand perfection*;
  rèn lǐng: 认领, *to claim sthg; to adopt a child*;
  shēng chēng: 声称, *to profess/claim*;
SEE (请查看**) FALTA, DEMANDAR**

RECOMENDAR; recomendar; *to advise/recommend*;
  guì quàn (v) (n): 规劝, *to admonish/ advise; advice*;
  jiè shào: 介绍, *to introduce/present; to suggest/ recommend; to inform/brief sb*;
  quàn gào (v) (n): 劝告, *to advise/ exhort/counsel; advice, exhortations*;
  tuī jiàn: 推荐, *to recommend*;
SEE (请查看**) AVANZAR, AVISAR**

RECOMPENSAR; recompensar; *to reward/ compensate*;
  chóu bào: 酬报, *to reward*;
  fā jiǎng: 发奖, *to award prizes*;
SEE (请查看**) ADJUDICAR, GRATIFICACIÓN, COMPENSACIÓN, INDEMNIDAD**

RECONCILIAR; reconciliar; *to reconcile*;
  hé jié (v) (n): 和解, *to become reconciled; accomodation*;
  pá jiě: 排解, *to mediate/reconcile; to find a diversion*;
SEE (请查看**) CONCILIAR**

RECONFORTAR; reconfortar; *to*

comfort; to cheer/encourage;
  kuān wèi: 宽慰, *to comfort/console*;
  wèi wèn: 慰问, *to comfort/console; to convey sympathy/greetings*;
  wèi yàn: 慰唁, *to console*;
SEE (请查看) COMFORT, FOMENTAR

RECONQUISTAR; reconquistar; *to reconquer, recapture, recover*;
  duó huí: 夺回, *to recapture/retake*;
  fù yuán: 复原, *to restore/rehabilitate; to recover from an illness*;
  huī fù: 恢复, *to renew/recover/regain/restore*

RECONSIDERAR; reconsiderar; *to reconsider*;
  chóng xīn kǎo lǜ: 重新考虑, *to reconsider*;
  chóng xīn shěn yì (v) (n): 重新审议, *to reconsider; consideration*;
SEE (请查看) CONSIDERACIÓN

RECONSTITUIR; reconstituir; *to reconstitute ...* **RECONSTRUIR; reconstruir;** *to reconstruct ...*
  chóng jiàn: 重建, *to rebuild/reestablish/rehabilitate*;
  chóng xiàn: 重现, *to reappear/reproduce; to reconstruct an event*;
  guī huán: 归还, *to return/revert; to restore*;
  huī fù: 恢复, *to remove/renew; to recover/regain; to restore/reinstate/rehabilitate*;
  xiū fù: 修复, *to repair/restore/reconstruct/renovate*;
SEE (请查看) RESTAURACIÓN

RECUSAR; recusar; *to reject/refuse*;
  bào fèi: 报废, *to discard/reject*;
  bó huí: 驳回, *to reject/overrule*;
  jù jué: 拒绝, *to refuse/reject/decline*;
  pái chì: 排斥, *to repel/exclude/reject*;
  tǔ qì: 吐弃, *to spurn/cast aside/reject*;
SEE (请查看) DECLINAR

REDIMIR; redimir; *to redeem/ransom*;
  wǎn huí: 挽回, *to redeem/retrieve*;

  shú huí: 赎回, *to redeem/ransom*

REFINAR; refinar; *to perfect/refine*;
  gǎi liáng (v) (n): 改良, *to improve/ameliorate; reform*;
  jīng liàn (v) (sv): 精炼, *to refine/purify; smart and capable*;
  jīng zhì: 精致, *to make with extra care/refine*
  shǐ wán shàn: 使完善, *to perfect/consummate*;
  tí chún (sv) (n): 提纯, *to purify/refine; purification, refinement*

REFLEXIONAR; refletir; *to reflect/think*;
  shēn sī: 深思, *to ponder deeply/reflect on*;
SEE (请查看) CONTEMPLACIÓN

REFRIGERAR; refrigerar; *to refrigerate/air-condition/ chill*;
  lěng cáng: 冷藏, *to refrigerate*;
  lěng dòng: 冷冻, *to freeze/refrigerate*

REFUTAR; refuter; *to refute*;
  bó chì: 驳斥, *to refute/renounce/reject*;
  bó dǎo: 驳倒, *to refute*;
  bó huí: 驳回, *to reject/overrule*;
  fǎn bó: 反驳, *to refute/retort/negate*;
  pī bó: 批驳, *to refuse/criticize/rebut/ veto*;
SEE (请查看) IMPUGNAR, DESAUTORIZAR

REGENERAR; regenerar; *to regenerate*;
  fù xīng: 复兴, *to revive/rejuvenate*;
  zài shēng: 再生, *to be reborn/regenerate/reclaim*

REGISTRAR; registrar; *to register; to search/record/ note*;
  bào dào: 报到, *to report for duty; to check in/ register*;
SEE (请查看) ANOTAR, ILUSTRAR, MATRICULAR, ANOTACIÓN

REGLAMENTAR; regrar; *to regulate*;
  jié zhì (v) (n): 节制, *to control/check*;

temperance;
SEE (请查看) ACTUAR, ADAPTAR, ADMINISTRAR

REGULARIZAR; regularizar; *to legalize; to regularize/ standardize;*
   biāo zhǔn huà (n) (v): 标准化, *to standardize; standardization;*
   shǐ hé fǎ huà: 使合法化, *to legalize*

REINSTALAR; reintegrar; *to readmit; to reinstall/ reinstate;*
   shǐ huī fù: 使恢复, *to reinstate/ restore;*
SEE (请查看) RECONSTITUIR

REITERAR; reiterar; *to reiterate/ repeat;*
   chóng shēn: 重申, *to reaffirm/restate/ reiterate;*
   chóng xiū: 重修, *to rebuild; to repeat a course of study;*
   chóng yǎn: 重演, *to recur/reenact/ repeat;*
   chóng zuò: 重做, *to repeat an action;*
SEE (请查看) DUPLICADO

RELATAR; relatar; *to relate/retell;*
   jiǎng shù: 讲述, *to tell about/narrate/ relate;*
   xù shì: 叙事, *to narrate/recount;*
   xù shù (v) (n): 叙述, *to narrate/ recount/relate; narrative*

RELEGAR; relegar; *to relegate;*
   shǐ jiàng jí: 使降级, *to demote; to relegate;*
SEE (请查看) CONFINAR

REMEDIAR; remediar; *to remedy/put right/solve;*
   bǔ jiù (v) (n): 补救, *to remedy; remedy;*
   xiū zhèng: 修正, *to revise/amend/ correct/remedy/ repair*

REMEMORAR; rememorar; *to remember/recall;*
   huí xiǎng qǐ: 回想起, *to remember;*
   jì de: 记得, *to remember;*
   jì zhù: 记住, *to remember/learn by heart;*
   láo jì: 牢记, *to keep firmly in mind;*
   xiǎng qǐ: 想起, *to remember/recall/ think of;*
   zhuī yì: 追忆, *to recollect/recall;*
SEE (请查看) MEMORIA

REMENDAR; remendar; *to rectify; to mend/darn;*
   jiū piān: 纠偏, *to rectify a deviation, to correct an error;*
SEE (请查看) AJUSTAR

REMITIR; remeter; *to remit/send;*
   huì duì (v) (n): 汇兑, *to remit; remittance;*
   huì jí: 汇寄, *to remit;*
   huì kuǎn (v) (n): 汇款, *to remit money; remittance;*
   pài qiǎn: 派遣, *to send/dispatch; to repatriate*

REMOVER; remover; *to remove/dig up/move around, stir;*
   bān kāi: 搬开, *to remove;*
   xiāo chú: 消除, *to eliminate/remove/ clear up;*
   yí dòng: 移动, *to move/shift;*
SEE (请查看) OMISIÓN

RENEGAR; renegar; *to deny strongly/ renounce/ disown ...* **RENUNCIAR; renunciar;** *to renounce/ abandon;*
   fǒu rèn: 否认, *to deny/repudiate/ disown;*
SEE (请查看) ABANDONAR, REPUDIAR, NEGAR, DESAUTORIZAR

RENOVAR; renovar; *to renew/ renovate/upgrade;*
   shǐ shēng jí: 使升级, *to upgrade/ escalate in grade;*
   tí shēng: 提升, *to promote/elevate;*
   gǎi jìn (v) (n): 改进, *to improve/ upgrade; improvement, upgrade;*
SEE (请查看) AUMENTAR

REORGANIZAR; reorganizer; *to reorganize/reshuffle;*

chóng zǔ (n) (v): 重组, *reorganization;
to reorganize;*
gǎi zǔ: 改组, *to reorganize/reshuffle;*
SEE (请查看) ALTERAR

REPARAR; **reparar;** *to repair/mend/
fix;*
  wéi xiū: 维修, *to maintain/keep in
repair;*
  xiū bǔ: 修补, *to mend/repair/revamp;*
  xiū lǐ: 修理, *to repair/mend/fix*

REPARTIR; **repartir;** *to share out/
partition/divide;*
  fēn dān: 分担, *to share responsibility
for;*
  fēn tān: 分摊, *to apportion;*
  fēn xiǎng: 分享, *to share rights/
partake of;*
  gòng yǒu (v) (attr): 共有, *to jointly
possess; common, public*

REPATRIAR; **repatriar;** *to repatriate;*
  huí guó: 回国, *to return to one's
country;*
  qiǎn fǎn: 遣返, *to repatriate;*
  qiǎn sòng: 遣送, *to send back/
repatriate*

REPENSAR; **repensar;** *to rethink/
reconsider;*
  fǎn sī (v) (n): 反思, *to rethink;
rethinking, introspection;*
SEE (请查看) RECONSIDERAR

REPETIR; **repetir;** *to repeat;*
  fù shù: 复述, *to repeat/retell;*
SEE (请查看) REPETICIÓN,
REPETIDO, REPETITIVO,
DUPLICADO

REPRESENTAR; **representar;** *to
represent/look like;*
  xiāng xiàng: 想象, *to resemble/be
similar/alike*

REPROBAR; **reprovar;** *to reprove/
condemn;*
  shēn tǎo: 申讨, *to openly condemn/
denounce;*

SEE (请查看) ACUSAR, ACUSACIÓN,
COMBATIR, CULPAR

REPRODUCIR; **reproduzir;** *to
reproduce/copy/imitate;*
  chāo lù: 抄录, *to make a copy of; to
copy;*
  chāo xiě: 抄写 , *to copy by hand; to
transcribe;*
  fǎng xiào: 仿效, *to imitate/follow an
example;*
  fǎng zhēn: 仿真, *to emulate/simulate;*
  fǎng zhì: 仿制, *to copy/imitate;*
  fǎng zào: 仿造 , *to be modeled on; to
copy;*
  mó fǎng (v) (n): 模仿, *to imitate/copy;
imitation;*
  mó nǐ (v) (n): 模拟, *to imitate/simulate;
simulation;*
  zhào bān: 照搬, *to indiscriminately
imitate/copy;*
  zhào chāo: 照抄, *to copy word-for-
word;*
SEE (请查看) COPIAR, IMITACIÓN,
SIMULACIÓN

REPUDIAR; **repudiar;** *to repudiate/
disown;*
  pī pàn (v) (n): 批判, *to criticize/
repudiate; critique;*
SEE (请查看) NEGAR, RENEGAR,
DESAUTORIZAR

REQUERIR; **requisitar;** *to require/
demand;*
  yào qiú (v) (n): 要求, *to demand/
request; demand, request;*
SEE (请查看) NECESITAR,
REQUERIR, EXIGIR

RESCINDIR; **rescindir;** *to rescind/
cancel;*
  chè xiāo: 撤销, *to cancel/rescind/
revoke;*
SEE (请查看) ANULAR, CANCELAR,
REVOCAR

RESERVAR; **reservar;** *to reserve/
book;*
  bǎo liú chū: 保留出, *to reserve;*

bǎo liú: 保留, *to continue to have/ retain; to hold back/reserve*;
bèi yòng (v) (attr): 备用, *to reserve/ keep in reserve; spare, backup, standby*;
chǔ bèi: 储备, *to lay in/stock up; to reserve*;
yù dìng: 预定, *to subscribe/book/place an order; to reserve a table/seat/book, etc.*

RESIDIR; residir; *to reside*;
jū liú: 居留, *to reside*;
SEE (请查看) **HABITAR**

RESISTIR; resistir; *to resist/withstand/ bear*;
dǐ kàng: 抵抗, *to resist/stand up to*;
dǐng zhù: 顶住, *to withstand/stand up to*;
kàng jī: 抗击, *to resist/beat back*;
SEE (请查看) **AFRONTAR, BOICOT**

RESOLVER; resolver; *to solve; to resolve/settle/ decide*;
jiě mí: 解谜, *to solve a riddle*;
jié zhàng: 结帐, *to settle/square accounts*;
pò 'àn: 破案, *to solve a criminal case*;
pò 'huò: 破获, *to unearth/uncover/ discover/solve*;
shuō dìng: 说定, *to settle/agree on*;
zuò zhǔ: 作主, *to decide; to support, to back*;
zuò zhǔ: 做主, *to make the decision/ decide/back up/support*;
SEE (请查看) **AVISAR, BLOCAR, DETERMINACIÓN, DECIDIR**

RESPIRAR; respirar; *to breathe/ exude*;
chuǎn xī (v) (n): 喘息, *to pant/gasp for breath; breather, respite*;
hū xī (v) (n): 呼吸, *to breathe; breathing*

RESPONDER; responder; *to reply; to answer, respond to*;
dá fù: 答复, *to answer/reply*;
dá huà: 答话, *to answer/reply*;
duì dá: 对答, *to answer/reply*;

huán zuǐ (v) (n): 还嘴, *to answer/talk back; retort*;
huí dá (n) (v): 回答, *answer, reply; to answer*;
xiǎng yìng: 响应, *to respond/answer*;
yìng dá (v) (n): 应答, *to answer/reply; answer, reply*;
yìng shēng: 应声, *to answer/respond*;
SEE (请查看) **REACCIÓN, EXCUSA**

RESTAURAR; restaurar; *to restore ... RESTITUIR; restituir;* *to return/ restore*;
guī huán: 归还, *to return/revert*;
huán yuán: 还原, *to restore/return to the original condition/shape*;
huī fù: 恢复, *to reinstate/restore/ rehabilitate; to resume/renew*;
SEE (请查看) **RESTAURACIÓN**

RESULTAR; resultar; *to become/turn out to be; to be the result of*;
biàn chéng: 变成, *to change into*;
chǎn shēng: 产生, *to produce/ engender/emerge/come into being*;
chéng wéi: 成为, *to become/turn into*;
zhāo zhì: 招致, *to seek recruits/ followers; to incur/lead to*;
zhì shǐ: 致使, *to cause/result in*;
SEE (请查看) **ATRIBUIR, CAUSAR**

RESUMIR; resumir; *to summarize*;
gài shù (v) (n): 概述, *to summarize; summing-up*;
xiǎo jié (v) (n): 小结, *to summarize; brief summary*;
SEE (请查看) **DELINEAR, CONCLUIR, RECAPITULAR, RESUMEN**

RETARDAR; retarder; *to delay/hold up/slow down*;
fàng màn sù dù: 放慢速度, *to slow down (speed)*
fàng màn: 放慢, *to slow down*;
jiǎn huǎn: 减缓, *to retard/slow down*;
màn xià lai: 慢下来, *to slow down*;
SEE (请查看) **DETENCIÓN, DETENER**

RETIRAR; retirar; *to remove (GEN); to retire/ withdraw;*
  chè huí: 撤回, *to recall/withdraw/ revoke/retract;*
  qǔ zǒu: 趋走, *to run away;*
  tuì bīng: 退兵, *to withdraw troops/ force a retreat;*
  tuì què: 退却, *to retreat/withdraw; to shrink back/ flinch;*
SEE (请查看) EVACUAR, REVOCAR

RETORNAR; retornar, *to return from doing sthg;* **revidar,** *to return;*
  chóng fǎn: 重返, *to return;*
  fǎn huí: 返回, *to return; to come back/ go back;*
  huí dào: 回到, *to return to/go back to;*
  huí qù: 回去, *to return/go back;*
  huí xiāng: 回乡, *to return home*

REUTILIZAR; reutilizer; *to reuse;*
  zài shǐ yòng (v) (n): 在使用 , *to reuse; reuse*

REVELAR; reveler; *to reveal, show;*
  bào lù: 暴露, *to reveal/lay bare;*
  biǎo míng: 表明, *to mark/indicate/ reveal;*
  chū shì: 出示, *to show/produce;*
  jiē chuān: 揭穿, *to expose/lay bare;*
  jiē dǐ: 揭底, *to reveal the inside story;*
  jiē lù: 揭露, *to expose/unmask/ferret out/reveal;*
  liú lù: 流露, *to betray/reveal unintentionally;*
  lòu xiànr: 露馅儿, *to be exposed/ expose to public view;*

shuō chuān: 说穿, *to reveal/disclose; to tell what sthg really is;*
  tòu lòu: 透漏, *to divulge/leak;*
  tǔ lù: 吐露, *to reveal/tell;*
  xiàn chū: 显出, *to show/reveal;*
  xie lòu: 泄露, *to disclose/reveal;*
  xiè mì: 泄密, *to divulge a secret;*
SEE (请查看) ANUNCIAR, DIVULGACIÓN, DIVULGAR, COMUNICAR, ILUSTRAR

REVOCAR; revocar; *to recall; to revoke;*
  bà miǎn: 罢免, *to remove/dismiss/ recall;*
  chè fèi: 撤废, *to abolish/rescind/ revoke;*
  chè huàn: 撤换, *to dismiss/recall/ replace;*
  shōu huí: 收回, *to take back/recall/call in; to withdraw/countermand;*
  zhào huí: 召回, *to recall/bring back (diplomats, etc.);*
SEE (请查看) ANULAR, ABOLICIÓN

REVOLVER; revolver; *to rummage through, to search, to turn over; to turn around/stir/mix;*
  fān zhǎo: 翻找, *to rummage through;*
  sōu xún: 搜寻, *to search/look for/seek*

RIDICULIZAR; ridiculizar; *to ridicule/ deride;*
  cháo fěng: 嘲讽, *to sneer at/taunt/ mock;*
  cháo nòng: 嘲弄, *to mock/deride;*
SEE (请查看) IRONÍA

Interchangeable Spanish-Portuguese-English words and their Chinese equivalents
Palabras en Español-Portugués-Inglés y sus equivalentes en Chino
Palavras em Espanhol-Português-Inglês e seus equivalentes em Chinês
西班牙语，葡萄牙语，英语及中文的对等单词

SAFARI; safári;
  yóu liè (n) (v): 游猎, *safari*

SAGA; saga;
  yīng xióng chuán qí: 英雄传奇, *saga*

SALAMI ó SALAME; salami;
  sà lā mǐ xiāng cháng: 萨拉米香肠, *salami*

SALIVA; saliva;
  kǒu shuǐ: 口水, *saliva, spittle, drool*

SAUNA; sauna;
  sāng ná: 桑拿, *sauna*;
  sāng ná yù: 桑拿浴, *sauna, bath*;
  zhēng qì yù: 蒸气浴, *steam/Turkish bath, sauna*

SAVOIR-FAIRE; savoir-faire;
  jiān duān (attr): 尖端, *most advanced, sophisticated*;
  jīng pì (sv): 精辟, *penetrating, incisive*;
  lǎo liàn (sv): 老练, *seasoned, experienced*

SCRIPT (s); script;
  jù běn: 剧本, *drama, play, script*;
  shǒu gǎo: 手稿, *manuscript*;
  shǒu jì: 手迹, *one's handwriting*

SEMEN; sêmen; *seed;*
  jīng yè: 精液, *semen, seminal fluid*

SEMICIRCULAR; semicircular;
  bàn yuán de: 半圆的, *semicircular*

SEMIFINAL; semifinal;
  bàn jué sài: 半决赛, *semifinal*

SEMINAL; seminal;
  chuàng xīn (v) (n): 创新, *to blaze new trails/ produce new ideas; creation, innovation*

SENIOR ó SÉNIOR; sênior;
  nián zhǎng (vp): 年长, *senior, elderly*;
  zī shēn (attr): 资深, *senior*

SENSOR; sensor;
  chuán gǎn qì: 传感器, *sensor*

SENSUAL; sensual; *sensuous;*
  gǎn jué shang de: 感觉上的, *sensuous*;
  gěi rén měi gǎn de: 给人美感的, *sensuous*;
  xìng gǎn de: 性感的, *sensual; sexy*

SENTIMENTAL; sentimental;
  chōng mǎn róu qíng de: 充满柔情的, *sentimental*;
  duō chóu shàn gǎn de (fe): 多愁善感的, *to be sentimental*;
  qíng gǎn (sv) (n): 情感, *sentimental; emotions, feelings*;
  shāng gǎn (vp): 伤感, *sentimental, sensitive*;
  SEE (请查看) **AFECTO, EMOCIÓN**

SET; set; *tennis (DEP);*
  jú: 局, *set in tennis*

SEX-APPEAL; sex appeal ...
SEXUAL; sexual (GEN) **.... SEXY ó SEXI; sexy;**
  xìng de: 性的, *sexual*;
  xìng gǎn (sv) (n): 性感, *sexy; sex appeal*

SIMILAR (to); **similar**;
  xiāng sì (v) (n): 相似, *to resemble, to be similar/alike; resemblance, similarity*

SINGULAR; **singular**; *peculiar, odd, unique, outstanding*;
  dān shù (n): 单数, *odd number, peculiar*;
  gǔ guài (sv): 古怪, *eccentric, odd, strange*;
  hǎn yǒu (v) (vp): 罕有, *to rarely have; rare, unusual, exceptional*;
  qí guài (vp) (sv): 奇怪, *strange, odd; amazing, weird*;
  tè bié (sv) (adv): 特别, *peculiar; unusual; particularly*;
SEE (请查看) **ATÍPICO, CARACTERÍSTICO, EGREGIO, INHABITUAL**

SLOGAN ó ESLOGAN; **slogan**;
  kǒu hào: 口号, *slogan; password*

SOCIAL; **social** (GEN);
  shè huì de: 社会的, *social (society)*;
  shè jiāo de: 社交的, *social (interaction)*

SODA; **soda**; *soda water, club soda*;
  qì shuǐ: 汽水, *soft drink, soda*

SOFÁ (SOFÁ CAMA); **sofa**; *sofa bed, settee, sofa*;
  shā fā chuáng: 沙发床, *studio couch, sofa bed*;
  shā fā: 沙发, *sofa*;
  sū dǎ: 苏打, *sofa, couch*

SOFTWARE (INFORM); **software**;
  ruǎn jiàn: 软件, *software*

SOLAR; **solar**;
  tài yáng (sv): 太阳, *solar*

SONAR; **sonar**; *sonar*;
  shēng nà: 声纳, *sonar*

SONATA; **sonata**;
  zòu míng qǔ: 奏鸣曲, *sonata*

SOPRANO; **soprano**;

gāo yīn: 高音, *high tones (soprano, tenor)*;
  nǚ gāo yīn: 女高音, *soprano (MUS)*

SOUVENIR (s); **souvenir**;
  jì niàn pǐn: 纪念品, *souvenir, keepsake, memento*

SPRAY ó ESPRAY; **spray**; *aerosol*;
  àn niǔ shì pēn wù qì: 按钮式喷雾器, *aerosol*;
  pēn wù qì: 喷雾器, *spray, atomizer*

STÁNDARD ó STANDARD; **standard**;
  shuǐ zhǔn: 水准, *level, standard*;
SEE (请查看) **CRITERIO, NORMA**

STATUS; **status**;
  dì wèi (n): 地位, *position, status*;
SEE (请查看) **CIRCUNSTANCIA**

STATUS QUO; **status quo**;
  xiàn zhuàng: 现状, *status quo*

SUBLIME; **sublime**;
  gāo shàng (sv) (n): 高尚, *sublime, lofty, noble; integrity*;
SEE (请查看) **SOLEMNE**

SUPERFICIAL; **superficial**;
  biǎo miàn (n) (sv): 表面, *surface, face, outside; appearance; superficial*;
  biǎo miàn gōng fū (n): 表面工夫, *superficial work*;
  piāo fú (v) (vp): 漂浮, *to float; superficial, showy (style of work)*;
SEE (请查看) **FRÍVOLO**

SUPERVISOR; **supervisor**;
  dǎo shī: 导师, *tutor, teacher, supervisor*;
  jiān gōng: 监工, *overseer, supervisor*

SUSPENSE; **suspense**;
  xuán niàn (n) (v): 悬念, *suspense (in a story, movie, etc.); to be concerned*;
  xuán yí (n): 悬疑, *suspense*;
SEE (请查看) **DESCONCERTANTE**

Easily recognizable Spanish-Portuguese-English nouns, adjectives and adverbs and their Chinese equivalents

Nombres, sustantivos, adjetivos y adverbios en Español-Portugués-Inglés y sus equivalentes en Chino

Nomes, substantivos, adjetivos e advérbios em Espanhol-Português-Inglês e seus equivalentes em Chinês

容易辨认的西班牙语，葡萄牙语，英语的名词，形容词和副词和他们的中文对等词

SABOTAJE; sabotagem; *sabotage ...*
SABOTEADOR (A); **sabotador** (A); *saboteur;*
  pò huài fèn zǐ: 破坏分子, *saboteur;*
  xù yì pò huài (n): 蓄意破坏, *sabotage*

SACARINA; sacarina; *saccharine or saccharin;*
  táng jīng: 糖精, *saccharin*

SACO (f); **saco;** *sack, bag;*
  bāo: 包, *bag, sack;*
  dài zi: 袋子, *sack, bag*

SÁDICO (A); **sádico** (A); *sadistic (adj), cruel, perverse, monstrous, ruthless, brutal, deviant; sadist (n), pervert, deviate ...* **SADISMO; sadismo;** *sadism, perversity, debauchery, dissipation, brutality, cruelty;*
  duò luò zhě: 堕落者, *degenerate, pervert;*
  fǎn cháng (sv): 反常, *unusual, abnormal, perverse, anomalous;*
  fàng zòng xíng wéi de: 放纵行为的, *perversity;*
  guāi lì (sv): 乖戾, *perverse (behavior), disagreeable (character);*
  jí dù xiōng cán: 极度凶残, *sadism;*
SEE (请查看) CRUELDAD, CRUEL, BRUTAL, BRUTALIDAD, BRUTO, PERVERSO, IMPLACABLE, DECADENTE

SAGACIDAD; sagacidade; *astuteness, shrewdness, cleverness ...* **SAGAZ; sagaz;** *shrewd, astute, clever;*
  cōng míng de: 聪明的, *intelligent, bright, clever;*
  gāo míng de: 高明的, *wise, brilliant;*
  guāi qiǎo de: 乖巧的, *clever; cute, lovely;*

jī ling de: 机灵, *clever, intelligent;*
jiǎo huá (sv) (n): 狡猾, *shrewd, sly, cunning; shrewdness;*
qiǎo miào de: 巧妙的, *ingenious, skillful, clever, shrewd;*
SEE (请查看) PERSPICAZ

SAL; sal; *salt;*
  shí yán: 食盐, *salt*

SALARIO; salário; *wages, wage, salary, pay;*
  gōng zī: 工资, *wages, pay, salary;*
  xīn fèng: 薪俸, *salary;*
  xīn jīn: 薪金, *salary;*
  xīn shuǐ: 薪水, *salary, wages*

SALAZ; lasivo (A); *salacious, prurient, lustful, lecherous;*
  hào sè (sv): 好色, *lustful, lecherous;*
  huáng sè (sv) (attr): 黄色, *decadent, obscene, pornographic;*
  tān qiú (v) (sv): 贪求, *to thirst after/ covet; lustful;*
  wù yù (n): 物欲, *desire for material wealth/worldly things; lust, avarice;*
  xìng yù (n): 性欲, *sexual desire, urge;*
  yín huì (vp): 淫秽, *obscene, salacious;*
  zòng yù (v) (sv): 纵欲, *to indulge in sexual pleasures; be dissolute/ debauched; lecherous;*
SEE (请查看) ÁVIDO

SALIDA; saída; *way out, exit;*
  chū kǒu: 出口, *exit;*
  chū qu (v) (n): 出去, *to exit; exit*

SALIENTE; saliente; *salient, important, conspicuous;*
  tū chū (sv) (v): 突出, *projecting, salient, outstanding, prominent; to break through/jut out;*

zhòng yào (sv): 重要, *important, significant, major*;
SEE (请查看) **EMINENTE, CONSPICUO**

SALINO (A); **salino** (A); *saline*;
 yán de: 盐的, *saline*

SALMONELA; salmonela; *salmonella*;
 shā mén jūn: 沙门菌, *salmonella*

SALUBRE; salubre; *healthy, salubrious, wholesome, pleasant*;
 yǒu yì yú jiàn kāng de: 有益于健康的, *wholesome*;
 jiàn kāng (sv) (n): 健康, *healthy, sound; health*

SANDALIA; sandália; *sandal*;
 liáng xié: 凉鞋, *sandals*;
 tuō xié: 拖鞋, *slippers, sandals, flip-flops*

SARCASMO; sarcasmo; *sarcasm* ...
SARCÁSTICO (A); **sarcástico** (A); *sarcastic, derisive, mocking; scornful, ridiculing, taunting* ... **SARDÓNICO** (A); **sardônico** (A); *sardonic, cynical, ironic*;
 fèn shì jí sú de: 愤世嫉俗的, *cynical*;
 fěng cì wā kǔ de: 讽刺挖苦的, *ironic*;
 jī fěng de: 讥讽的, *sarcastic, derisive*;
 jiān kè de: 尖刻的, *sarcastic, caustic*;
 wā kǔ (sv) (n): 挖苦, *sarcastic, sardonic; sarcasm*;
SEE (请查看) **IRÓNICO, SÁTIRA, IRONÍA**

SARGENTO; sargento; *sergeant*;
 zhōng shì: 中士, *sergeant*

SATÁNICO (A); **satânico** (A); *satanic, diabolical*;
 xié 'è de: 邪恶的, *evil, wicked, vicious, satanic*;
SEE (请查看) **DIABLO**

SATÉLITE; satélite; *satellite*;
 wèi xīng: 卫星, *satellite*

SÁTIRA; sátira; *satire, mockery,*

caricature; lampoon, parody, mimic, pillory* ... **SATÍRICO** (A) (adj); **satírico** (A); *satirical*;
 cháo nòng (v) (n): 嘲弄, *to mock/deride; mockery*;
 fěng cì wén xué: 讽刺文学, *satire*;
 fěng cì zuò pǐn: 讽刺作品, *satire (novel, play)*;
SEE (请查看) **SARCASMO, IRÓNICO**

SATISFACCIÓN; satisfação; *satisfaction, gratification; comfort* ...
SATISFACTORIO (adj); **satisfatório** (A); *satisfactory, acceptable* ...
SATISFECHO (A); **satisfeito** (A); *satisfied, contented*;
 mǎn yì (sv) (n): 满意, *satisfied, pleased; satisfaction*;
 mǎn zú gǎn: 满足感, *satisfaction*;
 shùn xīn (sv): 顺心, *satisfactory*;
 wán mǎn (sv): 完满, *satisfactory, successful*;
 xīn mǎn yì zú de: 心满意足的, *contented*;
 yuán mǎn (sv): 圆满, *satisfactory*;
SEE (请查看) **AGRADABLE, COMPLACIDO, DELEITE , CONSOLACIÓN**

SECRETARIO (A); **secretário** (A); *secretary*;
 mì shū: 秘书, *secretary*

SECRETO (A); **secreto** (A); *secret, confidential*;
 mì mì (sv) (n): 秘密, *secret, confidential; secrecy*;
SEE (请查看) **OCULTAR, CONFIDENCIAL, CLANDESTINIDAD, ARCANO**

SECUENCIA; seqüência; *sequence, progression, chronology, series*;
 cì xù: 次序, *order, sequence*;
 cóng kān: 丛刊, *a series of books; collection*;
 cóng shū: 丛书, *collection of a series*;
 shù cì (adv): 顺次, *in proper order/sequence*;
 shùn xù (n) (adv): 顺序, *sequence,*

order; in turn, in proper order;
xì liè jié mù: 系列节目, *a series of programs/items on a program*;
xì liè: 系列, *series, set*;
xù liè: 序列, *alignment, array; sequence, rank, order*;
yī lián chuàn (fe) (n): 一连串, *series, string, chain of; sequence*;
SEE (请查看) CONTINUADO

SECUNDARIO (A); **secundário** (A); *secondary, minor, supporting role*;
cì jí (n) (attr): 次级, *second class, secondary*;
cóng shǔ (attr): 从属, *subordinate, secondary; dependent*;
dì èr (NUM) (n) (sv): 第二, *second, next; secondary*;
zhōng děng (attr): 中等, *medium, middling; secondary*;
SEE (请查看) CIRCUNSTANCIAL

SEDENTARIO (A); **sedentário** (A); *sedentary*;
zuò zhe de: 坐着的, *sedentary*

SEDICIÓN; sedição; *sedition, disloyalty* ... **SEDICIOSO** (A); **sedicioso** (A); *seditious, dissidence, rabble-rousing*;
shān dòng de: 煽动的, *rabble-rousing*;
SEE (请查看) INFEDILIDAD

SEDIMENTO; sedimento; *sediment, deposit*;
chén jī wù: 沉积物, *sediment, deposit, deposition*;
zhā zi: 渣子, *dregs, scraps*;
SEE (请查看) DEPOSITAR

SEDUCTOR (A); **sedutor** (A); *attractive, charming, seductive*;
yǐn rén rù shèng (fe): 引人入胜, *absorbing, enchanting, fascinating*;
yǐn yòu (v) (sv): 引诱, *to lure/seduce; seductive*;
yòu huò (v) (sv): 诱惑, *to tempt/seduce/lure/ attract/allure; seductive, alluring*;
yòu rén (v) (sv): 诱人, *to attract/allure*;

attractive, alluring, seductive;
SEE (请查看) GLAMOR

SEGMENTO; segmento; *segment (MAT), piece, sector, group*;
bù fen: 部分, *part, section*;
duàn: 段, *section, part; group; paragraph*;
jié: 节, *joint, node, knot; segment*;
jú bù (n) (attr): 局部, *part; partial, local*

SEGUIDO (A); **seguido** (A); *consecutive; continuous*;
lián chuàn (v) (n): 连串, *to string together; string/succession*;
lián mián (vp): 连绵, *to be continuous/ unbroken/uninterrupted*;
SEE (请查看) SECUENCIA, CONTINUADO

SEGURO (A); **seguro** (A); *safe, secure, protected*;
ān quán (sv) (n): 安全, *safe, secure; security, safety*;
ān xīn (v) (sv): 安心, *to feel at ease, to be relieved; secure*;
bǎo xiǎn (n) (sv) (v): 保险, *insurance; safe; to insure/be insured*;
láo gù (sv): 牢固, *firm, secure*;
láo kào (sv): 牢靠, *firm, strong, sturdy, safe, dependable, reliable*;
píng 'ān (sv): 平安, *safe and sound, quiet and stable*;
wěn tuǒ (sv): 稳妥, *safe, reliable*;
yǒu bǎ wò de: 有把握的, *secure*;
SEE (请查看) APRENHENDER

SELECTIVO (A); **seletivo** (A); *selective*;
yǒu xuǎn zé de: 有选择的, *selective*;
SEE (请查看) OPTAR

SEMANAL; semanal; *weekly*;
měi zhōu (n): 每周, *every week*;
měi zhōu yī cì de: 每周一次的, *weekly*;
zhōu bào (n): 周报, *weekly publication (newspaper)*;
zhōu kān (n): 周刊, *weekly publication (magazine/ periodical)*

SEMBLANTE; semblante; *look, countenance, expression, aspect*;
 liǎn miàn: 脸面, *self-respect, feelings, face*;
 liǎn pí: 脸皮, *face, cheek; feelings, sense of shame*;
 liǎn sè: 脸色, *complexion, look, facial expression*;
 miàn mào: 面貌, *face, features, appearance, look, aspect*;
 miàn sè: 面色, *complexion, facial expression*;
 mú yàng (n) (adv): 模样, *appearance, looks; approximately, about, around*;
 qì sè: 气色, *complexion, color, look, expression*;
 shén sè: 神色, *expression, look*;
 zuǐ liǎn: 嘴脸, *looks, features, countenance*;
SEE (请查看) **FACETA, DEFINIR**

SEMESTRE (n); **semestre;** *a period of six months, semester*;
 xué qī: 学期, *semester*

SEMICÍRCULO; semicírculo; *semicircle*;
 bàn yuán: 半圆, *semicircle*

SENIL; senil; *senile, declining, failing* ...
SENILIDAD; senilidade; *senility, old age, dotage*;
 shuāi lǎo: 衰老, *senile*;
 shuāi lǎo zhuàng tài: 衰老状态, *senility*

SENSACIÓN; sensação; *sensation, sense, impression, awareness*;
 chù: 触, *sense of touch*;
 gǎn guān: 感官, *sense, sensory organ*;
 guān niàn: 观念, *sense, idea, conception, concept, notion*;
 qíng miàn: 情面, *feelings*;
 zhí jué: 直觉, *intuition*;
SEE (请查看) **DETECTAR, PERSPICAZ**

SENSACIONAL; sensacional; *sensational, spectacular, great*;
 hōng dòng (sv): 轰动, *cause a*

sensation, make a stir;
 hōng dòng xìng de: 轰动性的, *sensational*;
 hōng dòng xiào yìng: 轰动效应, *sensational effect, wild reaction*;
 jí hǎo (vp): 极好, *extremely good, excellent, sensational*;
 jué miào (sv): 绝妙, *sensational; extremely clever, ingenious*;
SEE (请查看) **ESPECTACULAR, MAGNÍFICO**

SENSATEZ; sensatez; *wisdom, common sense, good sense*;
 dào li: 道理, *reason, rationality*;
 qíng lǐ: 情理, *reason, common sense*;
 zhì huì: 智慧, *wisdom, intelligence*;
 zhī shi: 知识, *knowledge*;
SEE (请查看) **EQUILIBRADO**

SENSATO (A); **sensate** (A), *sensible person*; **prático** (A), *sensible, reasonable, logical, rational*;
 mǐn gǎn xìng: 敏感性, *sensible*;
 míng lǐ (n) (sv): 明理, *truth, fact; sensible, reasonable*

SENSIBILIDAD; sensibilidade; *feeling, sensitivity* ... **SENSIBLE;**
sensível; *sensitive, impressionable*;
 líng mǐn xìng (n): 灵敏性, *sensitivity, sensibility*;
 mǐn gǎn (sv): 敏感, *sensitive, susceptible; allergic*;
 mǐn ruì: 敏锐, *sharp, acute, keen (of the senses)*;
SEE (请查看) **ÁGIL, PROPENSIÓN**

SENSORIAL (adj); **sensorial;** *sensory*;
 gǎn jué de: 感觉的, *sensory*

SENSUALIDAD; sensualidade; *sensuality, eroticism, sexuality*;
 xìng yù: 性欲, *sexuality*

SENTIMENTALISMO; sentimentalismo; *sentimentality* ...
SENTIMIENTO; sentimento; *feeling, to get carried away*;
 duō chóu shàn gǎn (fe): 多愁善感,

to be sentimental;
qíng cāo: 情操, *sentiment*;
qíng diào: 情调, *sentiment, tone and mood, taste*;
shāng gǎn: 伤感, *sentimental, sick at heart, distress*;
SEE (请查看) AFECTO

SEPARACIÓN; separação; *separation, division* ... **SEPARADO** (A); **separado** (A); *separate, separately*;
fēn jū (n) (v): 分居, *separate; to live apart*;
fēn kāi (adv) (v) (n): 分开, *separately; to be separate/apart; division*;
fēn lí (v) (n): 分离, *to separate/server; discreetness, disjunction; separation*;
fēn tóu (adv) (n): 分头, *separately, severally; parted hair*;
SEE (请查看) APARTAR, ADICIONAL

SÉPTICO (A); **séptico** (A); *septic, putrid; putrefying*;
bài xuè bìng de: 败血病的, *septic (MED)*;
bài xuè bìng: 败血病, *septicemia*;
fǔ bài xìng de: 腐败性的, *septic*;
SEE (请查看) CORRUPCIÓN

SEPULCRO; sepulcro; *tomb, grave, sepulcher*;
fén mù: 坟墓, *sepulcher, grave, tomb*

SERENAMENTE; serenamente; *serenely, calmly, quietly*;
píng jìng de: 平静的, *quietly, calmly*

SERENATA; serenata; *serenade*;
xiǎo yè qǔ: 小夜曲, *serenade*

SERENIDAD; serenidade; *tranquility, serenity, calmness* ... **SERENO** (A); **sereno** (A); *calm, serene; settled, fine; clear*;
ān jìng de: 安静的, *peaceful*;
ān mì (sv) (wr): 安谧, *peaceful, tranquil*;
ān xiáng (sv): 安详, *serene, composed*;
qíng lǎng (sv): 晴朗, *sunny, fine and cloudless*;
wú fēng (attr): 无风, *calm, breezeless*;

SEE (请查看) CALMA, TRANQUILIDAD, PACÍFICO

SERIEDAD; seriedade; *seriousness, responsibility, reliability* ... **SERIO** (A); **sério** (A); *serious, grave*;
chén zhòng (sv): 沉重, *heavy, serious; calm, dignified*;
lì hai (sv): 利害, *terrible, devastating; serious; tough, capable; severe, fierce; sharp*;
yán sù (v) (sv): 严肃, *to enforce; serious, solemn*;
zhuāng zhòng (sv): 庄重, *serious, grave, solemn*
SEE (请查看) GRAVE, GRAVEDAD, RELEVANCIA

SERVIL; servile; *servile, menial, obsequious* ... **SERVILISMO; servilismo;** *subservience, servility* ... **SUMISO** (A); **submisso** (A); *submissive, deferential, servile*;
nú cai xiàng: 奴才相, *servility, shameless fawning*;
nú cai: 奴才, *flunky, lackey; slave*;
nú xìng: 奴性, *servility*;
nú yán mèi gǔ (fe): 奴颜媚骨, *sycophancy, obsequiousness*;
qū cóng (v) (sv): 屈从, *to submit/yield to; submissive, compliant*;
yī cóng (v) (sv): 依从, *to comply with/yield to; compliant, deferential; obedient*;
zūn zhòng (v) (attr): 尊重, *to respect/value/esteem; serious, proper*;
SEE (请查看) DEFERENCIA, DESDÉN, DÓCIL, RESPETUOSO, OBEDIENCIA

SESIÓN; sessão; *meeting, session*;
huì qī: 会期, *session*;
SEE (请查看) CONFERENCIA

SEVERIDAD; severidade; *sternness; severity, roughness, strictness* ...
SEVERO (A); **severo** (A); *stern; severe, harsh, rough*;
qīng zhòng: 轻重, *seriousness, severity*;
yán gé (sv): 严格, *strict, rigorous*;

yán kù (attr): 严酷, *harsh, bitter, grim, cruel; ruthless*;
SEE (请查看) SERIEDAD, RIGOR, DRÁSTICO

SHOPPING; shopping; *shopping center or mall*;
  gòu wù zhōng xīn: 购物中心, *shopping center*

SIBILANTE; sibilante; *sibilant*;
  sī sī shēng: 咝咝声, *sibilant*

SIGNIFICACIÓN; significação; *significance, relevance*;
  qiè tí (v) (sv) (n): 切题, *to keep to the point; relevant, pertinent; relevance, pertinence*;
  yì wèi (n): 意味, *meaning, significance, implication*;
  yì yì: 意义, *meaning, sense, significance*;
SEE (请查看) RELEVANCIA

SIGNIFICADO (A); **significado;** *meaning, content, gist, sense, drift ...*
SIGNIFICATIVO (A); **significativo** (A); *significant, meaningful*;
  fù yǒu yì yì de: 富有意义的, *meaningful*;
  hán yì: 含义, *meaning, implication*;
  yì si: 意思, *meaning, idea*;
  yǒu yì yì (v) (sv) (attr): 有意义, *to have meaning/significance; meaningful, significant*;
  zhǔ zhǐ: 主旨, *substance, gist*;
SEE (请查看) SIGNIFICACIÓN, DIVERTIDO

SILENCIO; silêncio; *silence ...*
SILENCIOSO (A); **silencioso** (A); *silent, quiet, mute, still, calm, placid*;
  jì jìng (sv): 寂静, *quiet, still, tranquil, calm*;
  jìng (sv): 静, *calm, quiet, still*;
  jìng qiāo qiāo (vp): 静悄悄, *very quiet*;
SEE (请查看) CALMA, PACÍFICO, RETICENCIA, MUDO

SIMBÓLICO (A); **simbólico** (A);

symbolic, token ... **SIMBOLISMO; simbolismo;** *symbolism, represents, denotes ...* **SÍMBOLO; símbolo;** *symbol*;
  xiàng zhēng (v) (n) (attr): 象征, *to symbolize/signify; symbol, emblem, token; symbolic*;
  xiàng zhēng xìng (sv) (n): 象征性, *symbolic; symbolism, emblem, token*;
  xiàng zhēng zhǔ yì: 象征主义, *symbolism*;
SEE (请查看) DENOTAR, NOTACIÓN

SIMETRÍA; simetria; *symmetry ...* **SIMÉTRICO** (A); **simétrico** (A); *symmetrical*;
  duì chèn de: 对称的, *symmetrical*;
  duì chèn xìng: 对称性, *symmetry*

SÍMIL; simile; *simile (LITER)*;
  míng yù: 明喻, *simile*

SIMILITUD; similitude; *similitude; similarity, resemblance*;
  lèi sì (v) (n): 类似, *be similar to; analogy*;
  tóng diǎn: 同点, *similarity*;
  xiàng (v) (n): 像, *to be like/resemble/take after; likeness, image*;
  xiāng sì (sv) (v) (n): 相似, *to resemble/be similar/ alike; resemblance*;
  xiāng sì xìng: 相似性, *likeness*;
  xiāng tóng yú (vp): 相同于, *to be identical/similar to*;
SEE (请查看) AFÍN, DUPLICADO

SIMPATÍA; simpatia; *warmth; friendliness, affection, sympathy ...* **SIMPÁTICO** (A); **simpático** (A); *pleasant; nice, likeable, friendly*;
  kě 'ài (sv): 可爱, *likeable, loveable, lovely*;
  qíng yì: 情谊, *friendship, friendly feelings*;
  qíng yì: 情意, *tender regards, affection*;
  yǒu 'ài: 友爱, *friendly affection, fraternal love*;
  yǒu qíng: 友情, *friendly sentiments, friendship*;
  yǒu shàn (wr): 友善, *friendly,*

amicable;
yǒu yì: 友谊, *friendship;*
zhì yǒu: 挚友, *intimate/bosom friend;*
SEE (请查看) **DELEITE,**
HOSPITALIDAD, SUAVEMENTE,
AMABILIDAD

SIMPLEMENTE; simplesmente;
simply, just;
  jiǎn zhí (adv) (attr): 简直, *simply, really;*
straightforward;
  wú fēi (adv): 无非, *nothing but, than,*
simply, only;
  zhì bù guò (conj): 只不过, *only, just,*
merely;
  zhǐ gù (vp) (adv): 只顾, *to be absorbed*
in, to be concerned only with; merely,
simply; single-mindedly;
  zhǐ guǎn (vp) (adv): 只管, *by all means;*
merely, simply; only concerned with;
  zhǐ shì (vp) (conj): 只是, *merely, only,*
just, simply; however, but then;
SEE (请查看) **EXACTAMENTE**

SIMPLICIDAD; simplicidade;
simplicity **... SIMPLISTA; simplista;**
simplistic **... SIMPLÓN** (A); **simplório**
(A); *simple, simple minded person;*
  dān chún (sv) (adv): 单纯, *simple,*
plain, artless, naive, pure; purely, merely;
  jiǎn dān (sv) (n): 简单, *simple,*
uncomplicated; simplicity;
  jiǎn dān huà de: 简单化的, *simplistic;*
  jiǎn míng (sv) (n): 简明, *simple and*
clear, concise, simplicity;
  jiǎn pǔ (sv): 俭朴, *thrifty and simple;*
economical;
  jiǎn pǔ (sv): 简朴, *simple and*
unadorned; plain;
  jiǎn yì (n) (sv): 简易, *simplicity; simple*
and easy; unsophisticated;
  pǔ sù (sv): 朴素, *simple, plain, frugal,*
thrifty; naive; undeveloped;
  qiǎn yì (sv): 浅易, *easy and simple;*
  sù yǎ (sv): 素雅, *simple but elegant;*
  tiān zhēn (sv) (n): 天真, *naive, artless,*
innocent; human nature, simplicity;
  zhì pǔ (sv): 质朴, *simple, plain,*
unadorned, unaffected;
SEE (请查看) **BESTIA, CRETINO**

SIMPOSIO; simpósio; *symposium;*
  zuò tán huì: 座谈会, *symposium*

SIMULACIÓN; simulação; *simulation,*
pretense, imitation **... SIMULACRO;**
simulacro; *pretense, mock; simulated*
(as mock trial/fire drill); sham;
  fǎng zhì pǐn (n): 仿制品, *imitation,*
replica, copy;
  guǐ jì (n): 诡计, *ruse, trick;*
  tuō cí (n) (v): 托词, *pretext, excuse; to*
make excuses;
  zì chēng (v) (n): 自称, *to profess*
falsely; pretension;
SEE (请查看) **CAMUFLAJE, FALSO,**
EXCUSA, REPRODUCIR

SIMULTÁNEO (A); **simultâneo** (A);
simultaneous **... SINCRÓNICO** (A);
simultâneo (A); *simultaneous;*
  tóng bù huà (n): 同步化,
synchronization;
  tóng shēng (attr): 同生,
contemporaneous;
SEE (请查看) **CONTEMPORÁNEO,**
SINCRONIZAR

SINCERIDAD; sinceridade; *sincerity,*
frankness, honesty, openness **...**
SINCERO (A); **sincero** (A); *sincere;*
  chéng kěn (sv): 诚恳, *sincere; cordial;*
  chéng zhì (sv) (n): 诚挚, *sincere,*
cordial; sincerity;
  lǎo shi (sv): 老实, *honest, frank; naive,*
simple-minded; well-behaved;
  shuài zhēn (sv): 率真, *forthright and*
sincere;
  shuài zhí (sv): 率直, *straightforward,*
blunt;
  tǎn bái (sv) (v): 坦白, *frank, candid; to*
confess;
  tǎn shuài (sv) (n): 坦率, *candid, frank;*
openness;
  zhēn chéng (sv): 真诚, *sincere,*
genuine, true;
  zhēn qiè (vp) (n): 真切, *vivid, clear,*
distinct; sincerity;
  zhēn xīn: 真心, *sincerity;*
  zhēn zhì (vp): 真挚, *sincere, cordial;*
  zhì chéng (n) (vp): 至诚, *complete*

sincerity; sincere, straightforward;
zhí shuài (sv): 直率, *frank, candid*;
**SEE (请查看) PROFUNDO,
DECENCIA, HONESTO**

SÍNDROME; síndrome; *syndrome;*
zōng hé zhèng: 综合症, *syndrome
(MED)*

SINFÍN; sem fim; *vast number,
countless* ... **SINNÚMERO; inúmero**
(A); *countless, no end of*
lěi lěi (sv) (adv): 累累, *countless; again
and again*;
shǔ bù shèng shǔ (fe): 数不胜数,
innumerable;
wú shù (vp): 无数, *to be innumerable/
countless*

SINGULARIDAD; singularidade;
peculiarity, singularity;
guài dàn (sv): 怪诞, *weird, strange*;
guāi lì (sv): 乖戾, *perverse (behavior),
disagreeable (character)*;
guài li guài qì (fe): 怪里怪气,
eccentric, peculiar;
guài miù (sv): 乖谬, *absurd, abnormal*;
guài pǐ (n): 怪癖, *strange hobby,
eccentricity, peculiarity; oddball, nerd*;
guāi pì (sv): 乖僻, *odd, eccentric*;
SEE (请查看) CUALIDAD

SINIESTRO (A) (adj); **sinistro** (A);
sinister, evil; forbidding, gloomy;
xié 'è de: 邪恶的, *sinister, evil*;
yán jùn de: 严峻的, *forbidding, grim,
severe, stern*;
**SEE (请查看) HORRENDO,
SATÁNICO, NEFASTO, DIABÓLICO,
MALVADO, MALIGNO**

SINIESTRO (n); **sinistro**; *disaster,
accident, crash;*
cháng duǎn (n) (adv) (v): 长短, *length;
accident, mishap; good and bad; anyhow,
anyway; to criticize/scoff at/ridicule*;
sān cháng liǎng duǎn (fe): 三长两短,
unexpected misfortune;
**SEE (请查看) AFLICCIÓN,
APOCALIPSIS, CALAMIDAD,**

DESASTRE, CATASTRÓFICO

SINÓNIMO (A); **sinônimo** (A);
synonymous (adj); synonym (n);
tóng yì (attr): 同义, *synonymous*;
tóng yì cí: 同义词, *synonym*

SINOPSIS; sinopse; *synopsis, diagram*
... **SUMARIAL; sumario** (A); *brief;
summary, synopsis, abstract, digest;*
tí gāng: 提纲, *outline, synopsis*;
**SEE (请查看) ABSTRACTO,
RESUMEN, SUMARIO**

SINTAXIS; sintaxe; *syntax;*
jù fǎ: 句法, *syntax; sentence structure*;
wén fǎ: 文法, *syntax, grammar*

SÍNTESIS; síntese; *synthesis,
summary; integration, mixture;*
zōng hé tǐ: 综合体, *synthesis*
SEE (请查看) RESUMEN, SUMARIO

SINTÉTICO (A); **sintético** (A);
synthetic, artificial; false, fake;
hé chéng (n) (attr): 合成, *to compose/
compound/synthesize; compound,
synthesis; incorporating, synthetic*;
sù jiāo: 塑胶, *synthetic resin; plastic,
plastic cement*;
zōng hé xìng (n) (sv): 综合性,
synthesis, integrity; synthetic;
**SEE (请查看) SIMULACIÓN, FALSO,
EQUIVOCADO**

SÍNTOMA; sintoma; *symptom;*
zhēng hòu: 征候, *sign, indication*;
zhèng hòu: 症候, *disease, symptom
(MED)*;
zhēng zhào (n): 征兆, *sign, omen,
portent, symptom*;
zhèng zhuàng (n): 症状, *symptom
(MED)*

SINTOMÁTICO (A); **sintomático** (A);
symptomatic, characteristic;
diǎn xíng (n) (sv): 典型, *typical case,
model, type; typical, representative*;
**SEE (请查看) SINGULARIDAD,
CARACTERÍSTICO**

SÍSMICO (A); **sísmico** (A); *seismic*
... SISMÓGRAFO; sismógrafo;
seismograph;
  dì zhèn de: 地震的, *seismic*;
  dì zhèn xué: 地震学, *seismograph*

SISTEMA; sistema; *system*
(GEN); group, structure, way, plan ...
SISTEMÁTICO (A); **sistemático** (A);
systematic, organized, planned;
  guī huà (v) (n): 规划, *to program/plan;*
plan, program, project; *internal structure*
of an organization;
  tiáo lì (n): 条例, *regulations , rules,*
ordinances;
  yǒu tiáo yǒu lǐ de: 有条有理的,
organized;
  yǒu xì tǒng de: 有系统的, *systematic*;
SEE (请查看) ASOCIACIÓN,
ORGANISMO, DESIGNIO, GRUPO

SITUACIÓN; situação; *situation,*
position, location, spot, site ... **SITUADO**
(A); **situado** (A); *situated, placed*;
  bù wèi: 部位, *position, place; aspect,*
part;
  dì diǎn: 地点, *place, site, locale*;
  dì fāng (attr) (n): 地方, *local, regional;*
place, site, locality;
  qù chù: 去处, *destinations;*
whereabouts; place, site; occasion,
occurrence;
  suǒ zài: 所在, *place, location*;
  wèi zhi (n): 位置, *seat, place, position,*
location;
  wèi zi: 位子, *seat, place*;
SEE (请查看) CIRCUNSTANCIA,
FACETA

SOBORNO; suborno; *bribery*;
  xíng huì: 行贿, *bribery*

SOBREDOSIS; overdose; *overdose*;
  guò liàng yòng yào: 过量用药,
overdose

SOBREHUMANO (A); **super-homem;**
superhuman;
  chāo rén (sv) (n): 超人, *exceptional;*
superhuman

SOBRENATURAL; sobrenatural;
supernatural;
  chāo jí (sv) (attr): 超级, *super,*
extraordinary;
  chāo zì rán (sv): 超自然, *supernatural*;
  guǐ shén: 鬼神, *supernatural beings*;
  shén qí (sv): 神奇, *magical, mystical,*
miraculous

SOBRENOMBRE; sobrenome;
nickname; epithet;
  chuò hào: 绰号, *nickname*;
  hù míng: 户名, *nickname*

SOBRETASA; sobretaxa; *surcharge*;
  é wài (adv): 额外, *extra, added,*
additional;
  é wài fèi: 额外费, *surcharge*;
  fù jiā fèi: 附加费, *surcharge, extra*
charge

SOBRETODO; sobretudo; *overcoat*;
  dà yī: 大衣, *overcoat, jacket*

SOBRIEDAD; sobriedade; *restraint,*
moderation, sobriety ... **SOBRIO** (A);
sóbrio (A); *sober, serious; restrained,*
moderate, simple;
  kè zhì: 克制, *restraint; moderation*;
  lěng jìng (sv): 冷静, *sober, calm*;
  wēn hé (sv): 温和, *temperate, mild,*
moderate, gentle;
  zhōng yōng (n) (sv): 中庸,
moderation; moderate;
SEE (请查看) SERIO, GRAVE,
DISCRECIÓN, CONVENIENTE,
SINCERO, CORRECTAMENTE,
SERIEDAD

SOCARRÓN (A); **sarcástico**
(A); *sarcastic, snide, sneering ...*
SOCARRONERÍA; sarcasmo;
sarcasm, snide humor;
  chǐ xiào (v) (n): 耻笑, *to laugh/sneer*
at; shame, disgrace, humiliation;
  jī fěng (v) (sv): 讥讽, *to ridicule/satirize;*
sarcastic;
  jī xiào (v) (n): 讥笑, *to ridicule/jeer;*
ridicule, jeer;
  lěng xiào (v) (n): 冷笑, *to sneer/laugh*

grimly; sneer, grim laugh;
SEE (请查看) **SARCASMO,
SARCÁSTICO, SÁTIRA, CÁUSTICO,
IRONÍA, MALICIA**

SOCIEDAD; sociedade; *society;*
 shè huì: 社会, *society*

SODOMÍA; sodomia; *sodomy;*
 jī jiān: 鸡奸, *sodomy*

SOFISMA; sofisma; *sophism;*
 guǐ biàn: 诡辩, *sophism, sophistry*

SOFISTICACIÓN; sofisticação;
sophistication ... **SOFISTICADO** (A);
sofisticado (A); *sophisticated, cultured,
experienced;*
 gāo shēn (sv): 高深, *advanced,
 profound, recondite;*
 jiān duān (attr): 尖端, *most advanced,
 sophisticated;*
 lǎo liàn (sv): 老练, *seasoned,
 experienced;*
 lǎo yú shì gù (fe): 老于世故, *worldly-
 wise, sophisticated;*
 shì gù (sv): 世故, *worldly-wise,
 sophisticated;*
 yǒu jīng yàn de: 有经验的,
 experienced;
 yǒu xiū yǎng de: 有修养的, *cultured;*
SEE (请查看) **AVANZADO**

SOFOCADO; sufocada; *out of
breath, suffocating ...* **SOFOCANTE;
sufocante;** *suffocating, stifling;*
 chén mèn de: 沉闷的, *oppressive,
 stifling, depressing;*
 lìng rén zhì xī de: 令人窒息的,
 stifling;
 zhì xī (v): 窒息, *to stifle/suffocate*

SOLDADO; soldado; *soldier;*
 shì bīng: 士兵, *soldier*

SOLEDAD; solidão; *loneliness,
solitude, desolation, isolation;*
 dú chǔ (v) (n): 独处, *to stay alone;
 solitude;*
 gū jì (sv): 孤寂, *lonely*

gū lì (sv) (v) (n): 孤立, *isolated; to
isolate; isolation;*
jì mò: 寂寞, *loneliness;*
lěng luò (v) (sv) (n): 冷落, *to treat
coldly; unfrequented, desolate;
desolation;*
SEE (请查看) **INTROVERTIDO**

SOLEMNE; solene; *formal, solemn,
serious, dignified ...* **SOLEMNIDAD;
solenidade;** *ceremony; pomp,
solemnity;*
 yī běn zhèng jīng (fe): 一本正经,
 always serious (person, expression, etc.);
 zhuāng yán (vp) (n): 庄严, *solemn,
 dignified, stately; solemnity;*
SEE (请查看) **SERIO, SOBRIEDAD,
DISCRECIÓN**

SOLÍCITO (A); **solícito** (A); *solicitous,
obliging; eager, anxious ...* **SOLICITUD;
solicitude;** *care concern; request,
application;*
 lè yú (vp): 乐于, *to be happy to; to take
 delight in;*
 lè yú zhù rén (fe): 乐于助人, *to
 be happy/willing to help; solicitous,
 obliging;*
SEE (请查看) **APRENSIÓN,
DESCONCERTANTE, ÁVIDO,
CONCERNIR, ATENTO, AMABLE**

SOLIDARIDAD; solidariedade;
solidarity; alone, secluded, single ...
SOLITARIO (A); **solitário** (A); *solitary,
lonely, deserted, unattended;*
 bèi shě qì de: 被舍弃的, *deserted;*
 dān dān (adv): 单单, *only, alone;*
 dān dú (sv): 单独, *solitary, lonely,
 lonesome, single, reclusive;*
 dú zì (adv): 独自, *alone, by oneself;*
 gū dān (attr): 孤单, *all alone,
 friendless;*
 gū pì (sv): 孤僻, *solitary; unsociable;*
 guǎng mò (sv): 广漠, *vast and bare;*
 méi yǒu guān xi de: 没有关系的,
 unattended;
 pì jìng (sv): 僻静, *secluded, lonely;*
 tuán jié yī zhì: 团结一致, *solidarity;*
 wú rén kān guǎn de: 无人看管的,

unattended;
 yǐn jū (sv) (v): 隐居, *secluded; to live in seclusion*;
SEE (请查看) SOLEDAD, SOLO

SOLUCIÓN; solução; *solution, mixture, blend; answer*;
 dá 'àn: 答案, *solution, answer, key*;
 hùn hé wù: 混合物, *mixture, blend*;
 jiě jué fāng 'an: 解决方案, *solution/ answer*

SOLVENCIA; solvência; *solvency, reliability ...* **SOLVENTE; solvente;** *solvent (FIN); reliable, free of debt, sound*;
 cháng fù néng lì: 偿付能力, *solvency*;
 yǒu cháng fù néng lì de: 有偿付能力的, *solvent*;
SEE (请查看) CREÍBLE

SOMBRA; sombra; *shadow, shade; screen, cover; tint*;
 dàn sè: 淡色, *light, color, delicate shade*;
 liáng sǎn: 凉伞, *sunshade, parasol; shade*;
 píng fēng: 屏风, *screen*;
 sè cǎi: 色彩, *color, hue, shade; characteristic quality; flavor*;
 sè diào: 色调, *tone, hue*;
 yǎn hù: 掩护, *screen, shield, cover, camouflage*;
 yīn yǐng: 阴影, *shadow (MED); spot*

SOMBRÍO (A); **sombrio** (A); *gloomy, dark, somber, shaded, murky*;
 àn dàn (sv): 暗淡, *dim, faint, dismal, gloomy; depressing*;
 dī chén (sv): 低沉, *overcast; low and deep (of voice); low-spirited, downcast*;
 hēi 'àn (sv) (n): 黑暗, *dark; dark aspect, seamy side*;
 huì 'àn (sv): 晦暗, *dark, gloomy*;
 huī 'àn (sv): 灰暗, *gray, gloomy; murky*;
 huī mēng mēng (fe): 灰蒙蒙, *dusky, overcast*;
 yīn 'àn (sv) (n): 阴暗, *dark, gloomy; gloominess*;
 yīn lěng (sv): 阴冷, *gloomy and cold; raw (weather); somber, glum*;
 yīn sēn (vp): 阴森, *gloomy, dark;*

gruesome, ghastly;
 yōu 'àn (vp): 幽暗, *dim, gloomy*;
SEE (请查看) DESILUSIÓN, LÍVIDO, OSCURO, NUBLADO, TURBIO, MELANCOLÍA

SOMNOLENCIA; sonolência; *sleepiness, drowsiness ...*
SOMNOLIENTO (A); **sonolento** (A); *sleepy, drowsy*;
 hūn hūn yù shuì (sv) (n): 昏昏欲睡, *drowsy; drowsiness*;
 kē shuì (n) (v): 瞌睡, *nap; to doze off*;
 kě shuì (v) (sv): 渴睡, *to be very sleepy; sleepy*;
 kē shuì chén chén (vp): 瞌睡沉沉, *to be dozing*;
 kē shuì chóng chóng (vp): 瞌睡重重, *to nod drowsily/be heavy with sleep*;
 shuì yì: 睡意, *drowsiness*;
 xiǎo shuì (n) (v): 小睡, *nap; to nap/ doze*

SOPORÍFERO (A) ó **SOPORÍFICO** (A); **soporífero** (A); *soporific (adj), sleeping pill (n)*;
 ān mián yào: 安眠药, *sleeping pill*

SOPORTE; suporte; *support, bracket, base, stand*;
 zhī chéng (attr): 支承, *supporting, bearing*;
 zhī chí (v) (n): 支持, *to sustain/hold out/bear/ support/back/stand by; support*;
SEE (请查看) APROVISIONAR

SÓRDIDO (A); **sórdido** (A); *dirty, sordid, squalid*;
 āng zāng (sv): 肮脏, *dirty, filthy; squalid*;
 è liè (sv): 恶劣, *of very poor quality; vile, nasty*;
 lā ta (sv): 邋遢, *squalid; slovenly*;
 wū gòu: 污垢, *dirt, filth*;
 zāng (sv): 脏, *dirty, filthy*

SOSTÉN; subsistência; *support, prop; sustenance*;
 yōng hù (zhě) (n) (v): 拥护(者),

support (supporter); to support/endorse;
zhī chí zhě: 支持者, *supporter*;
SEE (请查看) SOPORTE, AUXILIO

SUAVEMENTE; suavemente;
gently, softly, smoothly ... **SUAVIDAD;**
suavidade; *mildness; softness,*
smoothness;
  qīng qīng (adv): 轻轻, *lightly, gently,*
softly; quietly;
  róu xìng (n): 柔性, *pliancy, softness,*
gentleness; flexibility;
  wēn róu (adv) (sv): 温柔, *gentle and*
soft; quietly;
  wēn wǎn (sv) (adv): 温婉, *gentle;*
kindly;
  wēn wēn (adv) (sv): 温温, *kindly; mild-*
mannered;
  wēn wén (vp): 温文, *gentle and polite*;
SEE (请查看) FLUÍDO

SUBALTERNO (A); **subalterno** (A);
auxiliary, subordinate, secondary ...
SUBORDINADO (A); **subordinado**
(A); *subordinate, secondary*
  cì yào de: 次要的, *secondary; minor*;
  fǔ zhù de: 辅助的, *auxiliary*;
  xià jí: 下级, *subordinate; lower level*;
  xià shǔ (attr): 下属, *subordinate*;
SEE (请查看) SECUNDARIO

SUBCONSCIENTE; subconsciente;
subconscious;
  qián yì shí: 潜意识, *subconscious*

SUBJETIVIDAD; subjetividade;
subjectivity ... **SUBJETIVISMO;**
subjetivismo; *subjectivism* ...
SUBJETIVO (A); **subjetivo** (A);
subjective;
  zhǔ guān (sv): 主观, *subjective*;
  zhǔ guān zhǔ yì: 主观主义,
subjectivism;
  zhǔ guān: 主观, *subjectivity*

SUBLIMACIÓN; sublimação;
exaltation, sublimation;
  shǐ gāo xìng (n) (v): 使高兴,
exaltation; to delight/amuse

SUBMARINO (A) (adj); **submarino** (A);
underwater; submarine;
  qián shuǐ tǐng: 潜水艇, *submarine*;
  shuǐ xià (attr): 水下, *underwater,*
submerged;
  zài shuǐ xià (sv) (adv): 在水下,
underwater

SUBMUNDO; submundo; *underworld;*
  dì yù: 地域, *Hell, inferno*;
  hēi shè huì: 黑社会, *criminal*
underworld;
  yīn jiān: 阴间, *nether world*

SUBPRODUCTO; subproduto; *by-*
product, derivative, subsidiary;
  fù chǎn pǐn: 副产品, *by-product*;
  pài shēng cí: 派生词, *derivative (lg)*;
  yǎn shēng (sv) (n): 衍生, *derivative;*
derivation
SEE (请查看) DERIVADO

SUBSIDIARIO (A); **subsidário** (A);
subsidiary, ancillary, accessory;
  fēn gōng sī: 分公司, *branch/subsidiary*
office;
  zǐ gōng sī: 子公司, *subsidiary*
company/corporation;
SEE (请查看) ACCESORIO, ANEXAR,
DEPARTAMENTO, SERVIR,
COMPLEMENTARIO, SECUNDARIO

SUBSIDIO; subsídio; *allowance,*
benefit, subsidy;
  bǔ tiē (n) (v): 补贴, *subsidy, to*
subsidize;
  bǔ zhù (v) (n): 补助, *to subsidize;*
subsidy, allowance;
  bǔ zhù jīn: 补助金, *subsidy, grant-in-*
aid;
  jīn tiē (n) (v): 津贴, *subsidy, allowance;*
to subsidize

SUBSIGUIENTE; subseqüente;
subsequent;
  hòu lái de: 后来地, *afterward, later*;
  suí hòu de: 随后地, *soon afterward,*
subsequent;
SEE (请查看) POSTERIOR

SUBSISTENCIA; subsistência; *subsistence;*
  kǒu liáng: 口粮, *grain, ration; subsistence;*
  shēng cún (v) (n): 生存, *to subsist/ exist/live; subsistence;*
SEE (请查看**) SUSTENTO**

SUBSTANCIA ó SUSTANCIA; substância; *substance;*
  běn zhì: 本质, *essence, nature, substance;*
  shí zhì: 实质, *substance, essence, being;*
SEE (请查看**) MATERIAL**

SUBSTANCIOSO ó SUSTANCIOSO; substancial; *substantial;*
  jiān shí (sv): 坚实, *solid, robust, substantial;*
  shí jù: 实据, *substantial evidence;*
  zhòng shǎng (n) (v): 重赏, *handsome/ substantial reward; to reward generously;*
SEE (请查看**) DESMEDIDO, IMPORTANTE, SUBSTANCIAL, SÓLIDO**

SUBSTITUCIÓN ó SUSTITUCIÓN; substituição; *replacement, substitution, alternate ...* **SUBSTITUTIVO (A) ó SUSTITUTIVO (A)** (adj)**; substituto** (A)**; sucedâneo** (A) (adj)**;** *substitute;*
  dài tì rén: 代替人, *replacement, substitute (person); agent, deputy;*
  dài tì pǐn: 代替品, *substitute (product, goods);*
  dài tì wù: 代替物, *replacement/ substitute object;*
  dài tì zhě: 代替者, *substitute;*
  dài tì: 代替, *substitution;*
  tì huàn (v) (n): 替换, *to replace/ displace; alteration, substitution; replacement;*
  tì huàn zhě: 替换者, *alternate;*
SEE (请查看**) SUSTITUIR, ALTERNAR, SUPLEMENTO**

SUBTERFUGIO; subterfúgio; *subterfuge, artifice, trick, scheme;*

  guǐ jì: 诡计, *ruse, trick;*
  huā zhāo: 花招, *trick, game;*
SEE (请查看**) FRAUDE, ARTIFICIO, ESTRATAGEMA**

SUBTERRÁNEO (A); subterrâneo (A); *subterranean, underground; concealed;*
  dì miàn xià de: 地面下的, *subterranean;*
  dì xià: 低下, *underground; secret activity;*
  yǐn bì (sv) (v): 隐蔽, *concealed; to conceal;*
SEE (请查看**) SUBMUNDO**

SUBTÍTULO; subtítulo; *subtitle, caption, secondary title;*
  biāo tí: 标题, *caption;*
  fù biāo tí: 副标题, *subheading, subtitle;*
  zǐ mù: 子目, *subtitle, caption*

SUBURBANO (A); suburbano (A); *suburban;*
  chéng jiāo: 城郊, *outskirts, suburbs;*
  jiāo qū : 郊区, *suburbs, outskirts;*
  jìn jiāo: 近郊, *city suburbs/environs;*
  shì jiāo (sv) (n): 市郊, *suburban; suburb, outskirts*

SUBVERSIVO (A); subversivo (A); *subversive, seditious, treasonous;*
  diān fù de: 颠覆的, *subversive;*
  gǎo pò huài de: 搞破坏的, *subversive;*
  pàn guó (sv) (v): 叛国, *treasonous; to betray one's country/commit treason;*
  pàn nì (n) (v) (sv): 叛逆, *rebel; to rebel/ revolt against; treasonous;*
  shān dòng xìng de: 煽动性的, *seditious;*
SEE (请查看**) SEDICIOSO, SUBVERSIVO, INCONFORMISTA**

SUCESIVO (A); sucessivo (A); *successive, consecutive, following;*
  jiē lián de: 接连的, *successive, repeatedly;*
  lián xù de: 连续的, *successive, continuous, running;*
SEE (请查看**) REPETIDO, REPETIDAMENTE**

SUCESOR (A); **sucessor** (A); *successor*;
  jì chéng rén: 继承人, *heir, successor; inheritor*;
  jì rèn zhě: 继任者, *successor in a job*;
  jiē bān rén: 接班人, *successor*

SUCESORIO (A) (adj); **sucessão**; *succession*;
  jì chéng (v) (n): 继承, *to inherit/ succeed; succession*;
  jiē tì (v) (n): 接替, *to take over/replace; succession*;
SEE (请查看) **CONTINUADO, SECUENCIA, SUCESIVO**

SUCINTO (A); **sucinto** (A); *succinct, concise, pithy, short, brief* ... **SUMARIO** (A); **sumario** (A); *summary, brief, concise*;
  jiǎn duǎn de: 简短的, *brief, succinct, terse*;
  jiǎn jié de: 简洁的, *succinct, terse, to-the-point*;
  jiǎn liàn de: 简练的, *terse, succinct*;
  jiǎn míng de: 简明的, *succinct, concise*;
  jiǎn yào de: 简要的, *concise, brief, to-the-point*;
  jiǎn yuē de: 简约的, *brief, concise, sketchy*;
SEE (请查看) **CONCISO, BREVE**

SUÉTER; **suéter**; *sweater*;
  máo yī: 毛衣, *sweater*

SUFICIENCIA; **suficiência**; *sufficiency; competence*;
  ná shǒu (sv) (n): 拿手, *adept, expert, good at; special ability/skill*;
SEE (请查看) **APTITUD, CRACK**

SUFICIENTE; **suficiente**; *sufficient; enough, adequate*;
  chōng zú (sv): 充足, *adequate, sufficient, abundant, ample*;
  zú gòu (adv) (vp) (sv): 足够, *sufficiently; enough, fully, amply; adequate, sufficient*;
SEE (请查看) **COPIOSO**

SUFLÉ; **suflê**; *soufflé*;
  dàn nǎi sū: 蛋奶酥, *soufflé*

SUGESTIÓN; **sugestão**; *suggestion*;
  tí yì (v) (n): 提议, *to propose/suggest/ move; proposal, motion, suggestion*;
SEE (请查看) **ALUDIR, AVANZAR, INSINUACIÓN**

SUGESTIONABLE; **sugestionável**; *suggestible, impressionable*;
  yì shòu yǐng xiǎng de: 易受影响的, *impressionable*;
  yì shòu 'àn shì (fe): 易受暗示, *suggestibility*

SUGESTIVO (A); **SUGESTIVO** (A); *evocative, stimulating, exciting, arousing, stirring*;
  huàn qǐ de: 唤起的, *evocative*;
  shǐ xīng fèn de: 使兴奋的, *stimulating*;
SEE (请查看) **INSINUACIÓN**

SUICIDA; **suicida**; *suicidal* ...
SUICIDIO; **suicídio**; *suicide*;
  zì shā (n) (sv): 自杀, *suicide; suicidal*

SUMA; **soma**; *sum; addition, total*;
  jiā fǎ: 加法, *addition (MAT)*;
  jīn 'é: 金额, *amount, sum (of money)*;
  quán shù: 全数, *total number, whole amount*;
  zǒng jià: 总价, *grand total, total price*;
  zǒng shù (v) (n): 总数, *to summarize/ sum up; sum, total*

SUMAMENTE; **sumamente**; *extremely, highly*;
  shí fēn (adv): 十分, *very extremely, utterly, fully*;
  wàn fēn (adv): 万分, *extremely*;
SEE (请查看) **ATÍPICO**

SUPERESTRUCTURA; **superestrutura**; *superstructure*;
  shàng céng jiàn zhù: 上层建筑, *superstructure of a building*;
  shàng céng jié gòu: 上层结构, *superstructure; structure, composition, texture*;

shàng céng lǐng yù: 上层领域, *superstructure; composition, structure of a territory/domain, realm*

SUPERFICIALIDAD; superficialidade; *superficially, externally, cursory;*
  qiǎn bó (sv) (adv): 浅薄, *shallow, superficial, meager; superficially;*
SEE (请查看) BRUSCO, FRÍVOLO, VACUO, SUPERFICIAL

SUPERFLUO (A); **supérfluo** (A); *superfluous, unnecessary, excessive;*
  duō yú (sv): 多余, *excessive, superfluous; unnecessary, uncalled-for;*
  guò shèng (vp): 过剩, *excess, to be superfluous, surplus*

SUPERIORIDAD; superioridade; *superiority, supremacy, dominance;*
  yōu yuè xìng: 优越性, *superiority; advantage;*
SEE (请查看) DOMINANTE

SUPERLATIVO (A) (adj); **superlativo** (A); *exceptional, superlative;*
  zuì gāo (vp): 最高, *superlative (highest, supreme, tallest, maximum);*
SEE (请查看) ATÍPICO, EXAGERACIÓN, SENSACIONAL, EXCEPCIONAL, EXTRAORDINARIO

SUPERMERCADO; supermercado; *supermarket;*
  chāo jí shì chǎng: 超级市场, *supermarket*

SUPERPOTENCIA; superpotência; *superpower;*
  chāo jí dà guó: 超级大国, *superpower*

SUPERSÓNICO (A); **supersônico** (A); *supersonic;*
  chāo yīn sù: 超音速, *supersonic speed*

SUPERSTICIÓN; superstição; *superstition ...* **SUPERSTICIOSO** (A); **supersticioso** (A); *superstitious;*
  mí xìn (v) (sv) (n): 迷信, *to have blind faith in/make a fetish of; superstitious;*

superstition

SUPINO (A); **supino** (A); *supine;*
  yǎng wò (sv) (v): 仰卧, *supine; to lie supine;*
SEE (请查看) DESATENCIÓN

SUPLEMENTO; suplemento; *supply; supplement;*
  bǔ chōng (attr) (v): 补充, *additional, supplementary; supplement; to replenish/supplement;*
  gōng yìng pǐn: 供应品, *supplies;*
SEE (请查看) APROVISIONAR, AUMENTAR

SUPLENTE; suplente; *substitute, deputy;*
  bāng bàn (v) (n): 帮办, *to help manage sthg; deputy, assistant;*
  tì shēn: 替身, *substitute, replacement; stand-in; scapegoat;*
  tì sǐ guǐ: 替死鬼, *scapegoat (coll);*
  tì zuì yáng: 替罪羊, *scapegoat (loan);*
SEE (请查看) SUBSTITUTIVO, AGENTE, SUBSTITUCIÓN, SUBSTITUIR

SÚPLICA; súplica; *plea; request, supplication;*
  kàng biàn: 抗辩, *plea, demurrer;*
  kěn qiú (v) (n): 恳求, *to implore/ entreat; plea;*
SEE (请查看) APELAR

SUPOSICIÓN; suposição; *supposition, belief, assumption ...* **SUPUESTO** (A) (n); **suposto** (A); *assumption, supposition, hypothesis;*
  jiǎ dìng (v) (n): 假定, *to suppose/ assume/grant/ presume; hypothesis, supposition;*
  jiǎ shè (v) (n): 假设, *to suppose/ assume/grant/ presume; hypothesis; postulation;*
  tuī cè (v) (n): 推测, *to conjecture/ guess/infer; assumption; explanation;*
SEE (请查看) CONVICCIÓN, IMAGINAR

SUPREMACÍA; supremacia;

supremacy ... **SUPREMO** (A); **supremo** (A); *supreme, highest*;
 zhì gāo wú shàng (fe): 至高无上, *paramount, supreme*;
 zhì shàng (attr) (v): 至上, *supreme, highest; most revered; to come first*;
SEE (请查看) **SUPERLATIVO**

SUSPENSO (n); **suspenso**; *suspense; anxiety, agitation, tension*;
 bù 'ān: 不安, *agitation*;
 bù què dìng (attr) (n): 不确定, *indeterminate, uncertain; suspense*;
 xīn jiāo (sv): 心焦, *anxious, worried*;
 xuán yí (n): 悬疑, *suspense*;
SEE (请查看) **AGITACIÓN, APRENSIÓN, BILIOSO, DESCONCERTANTE, INQUIETO, INTRIGA**

SUSPENSO (A) (adj); **suspenso** (A); *suspended (GEN), postponed, cancelled (GEN)*;
 shān chú (v) (n): 删除, *to delete/leave out; cancellation*;
SEE (请查看) **ANULAR, MORATORIA**

SUSPICACIA; **suspeita**; *suspicion, mistrust* ... **SUSPICAZ**; **suspeito** (A); *suspicious, doubtful, skeptical, distrustful*;
 cāi rěn (vp): 猜忍, *suspicious and ruthless*;
 duō xīn (sv): 多心, *suspicious, wary; oversensitive*;
 kě yí (sv): 可疑, *suspicious, dubious; questionable, doubtful*;
 ná bù zhǔn (v) (sv): 拿不准, *to be unsure/uncertain; doubtful*;
 xián yí (v) (n): 嫌疑, *to raise a doubt; suspicion*;
 yí diǎn (n): 疑点, *doubtful/suspicious point/ argument*;
SEE (请查看) **DESCONFIADO, DESCONFIANZA, DUDA, PARANOICO**

SUSTANCIA; **sustância**; *substance*;

běn zhì (n): 本质, *essence, nature, intrinsic quality, substance*;
 cái liào (n): 材料, *material, data, stuff, ingredients*;
 shí zhì (n): 实质, *substance, essence, being*;
 wù zhì (n) (attr): 物质, *matter; substance, material; materialistic*;
SEE (请查看) **ESENCIA, FORTUNA, CORPOREIDAD**

SUSTANCIAL; **substancial**; *essential, vital, significant*;
 hěn zhòng yào de: 很重要的, *vital*;
 zhì guān zhòng yào de: 至关重要的, *essential, vital*;
SEE (请查看) **IMPORTANTE, FUNDAMENTAL, DIVERTIDO, IMPORTANCIA**

SUSTENTO; **sustento**; *sustenance, support, provision*;
 yíng yǎng: 营养, *nutrition, nourishment*;
 shēng jì: 生计, *livelihood, means of livelihood*;
 wéi chí (v) (n): 维持, *to keep/preserve; preservation, sustenance*;
SEE (请查看) **SOPORTE, SUBSISTIR**

SUTIL; **sutil**; *subtle; delicate, fine* ... **SUTILEZA**; **sutileza**; *subtlety, guile, cunning*;
 dàn yǎ (sv): 淡雅, *quietly elegant, quiet and refined*;
 nán yǐ zhuō mō (fe): 难以捉摸, *to be elusive/ unintelligible, subtle*;
 qiǎo miào (sv) (n): 巧妙, *ingenious, skillful; clever, shrewd; subtlety*;
 xì wēi (n) (sv): 细微, *fine distinction, subtle difference; subtle*;
 xì wēi chā bié: 细微差别, *subtlety, nuance; fine distinction*;
SEE (请查看) **SIMULACIÓN, ARTIFICIO, DELICADO, SAGAZ, VAGAMENTE, VAGO**

Easily recognizable verbs and their Portuguese and Chinese equivalents
Verbos fácilmente reconocibles en Español-Portugués-Inglés y sus equivalentes en Chino
Verbos facilmente reconhecível em Espanhol-Português-Inglês e seus equivalentes em Chinês
很容易辨认的西班牙语，葡萄牙语，英语动词和他们的中文对等词

SABOTEAR; sabotar; *to sabotage*;
  zǔ náo: 阻挠, *to obstruct/thwart/ prevent*;
SEE (请查看**) ARRUINAR, DIFICULTAR**

SACRIFICAR; sacrificar; *to sacrifice*;
  xī shēng: 牺牲, *to sacrifice*

SALUDAR; saudar; *to greet*;
  huān yíng: 欢迎, *to welcome/ greet*;
SEE (请查看**) APLAUDIR**

SALVAGUARDAR; salvaguardar; *to safeguard*;
  bǎo hù: 保护, *to protect/safeguard*
SEE (请查看**) PROTECCIÓN**

SALVAR; salvar; *to save*;
  dā jiù: 搭救, *to rescue/go to the rescue of*;
  jiù (v): 救, *to rescue/save/salvage; (bf) help, relieve*

SANCIONAR; sancionar; *to sanction/ penalize*;
  pī zhǔn (v) (n): 批准, *to ratify/approve/ sanction; approval, sanction*;
SEE (请查看**) APROBACIÓN**

SATIRIZAR; satirizar; *to satirize*;
  chǐ xiào: 耻笑, *to mock/sneer at/ ridicule*;
SEE (请查看**) SARCASMO, IRONÍA**

SATISFACER; satisfazer; *to satisfy/ please/fulfill*;
  lè yì (v) (sv): 乐意, *to be willing/ready to; pleased, happy*;
SEE (请查看**) COMPLACIDO**

SATURAR; saturar; *to saturate/flood/ soak/drench*;

  jìn tòu: 浸透, *to soak through/saturate*;
SEE (请查看**) INFESTAR**

SECUESTRAR; seqüestrar; *to kidnap/confiscate/seize*;
  bǎng jià (v) (n): 绑架, *to kidnap; staking (AGRIC)*;
  bǎng piào: 绑票, *to kidnap for ransom*;
  duó dé: 夺得, *to carry off/seize; to win/ obtain through competition*;
  duó quán: 夺权, *to seize power*;
  duó zǒu: 夺走, *to snatch away*;
  mò shōu: 没收, *to confiscate/ expropriate*;
  qiáng duó: 强夺, *to grasp/snatch/rob/ seize*;
  qiǎng zhàn: 强占, *to forcibly occupy/ seize*;
  yòu guǎi: 诱拐, *to abduct/kidnap*;
SEE (请查看**) ACTUAR, APREHENDER, RECONQUISTAR**

SECUNDAR; secundar; *to help, to reinforce; to second/join/support*;
  jiā gù: 加固, *to reinforce/consolidate*;
  jiā qiáng: 加强, *to consolidate/ reinforce*;
  jiù (bf): 救, *to help/relieve; to rescue/ save/salvage*;
  xié lì: 协力, *to assist/help with sthg*;
  zēng dà: 增大, *to extend/magnify/ amplify*;
  zēng yì: 增益, *to add/increase/ augment*;
  zēng yuán: 增援, *to reinforce (MIL)*;
  zuò zhǔ: 作主, *to make the decision; to back up/ support sb/sthg*;
SEE (请查看**) SOPORTE, SERVIR, AUXILIO, APROVISIONAR, ASISTIR, AUMENTAR, COORDINACIÓN, COLABORAR**

SEDUCIR; seduzir; *to attract/charm/ seduce;*

  gōu yǐn: 勾引, *to seduce/tempt/entice;*
  lì yòu: 利诱, *to lure/entice;*
  xī yǐn: 吸引, *to attract/draw/fascinate;*
  yǐn yòu: 引诱, *to lure/seduce;*
  yòu chū: 诱出, *to lure out;*
  yòu dǎo: 诱导, *to guide/lead/induce;*
  yòu jiān (v) (n): 诱奸, *to induce sexually; statutory rape;*
  yòu rù: 诱入, *to lure into;*
  yòu shǐ: 诱使, *to inveigle into/lure/ seduce;*

SEE (请查看**) OBSESIONAR, INCITAR, SEDUCTOR**

SEGMENTAR; segmentar; *to cut or divide into pieces/segment ...* **SEGREGAR; segregar;** *to segregate ...* **SEPARAR; separar;** *to separate, split up, detach, sever ...* **SECCIONAR; seccionar;** *to cut into sections, to divide; to section, cut off;*

  duàn jué: 断绝, *to break off/sever;*
  duàn kāi: 断开, *to break/sever;*
  duàn lù: 断路, *to cut off a road, to break relations, to break an electric current; to way lay/hold up sb;*
  fēn bān: 分班, *to divide into classes (in school), to divide into squads (MIL);*
  fēn céng (v) (n): 分层, *to stratify, to divide into layers; stratification, tier;*
  fēn duàn (v): 分段, *to fragment, to divide into sections;*
  fēn féi: 分肥, *to share/divide stolen property;*
  fēn gōng (v) (n): 分工, *to divide the work, to be assigned a job; division of labor;*
  fēn kāi (v) (adv): 分开, *to detach/ separate; separately;*
  fēn lí (v) (n): 分离, *to separate/sever; discreteness, disjunction;*
  gē chú: 割除, *to cut off/cut out, to excise;*
  gé duàn: 隔断, *to cut off/separate; to obstruct;*
  gē duàn: 割断, *to cut off/sever;*
  gé kāi: 隔开, *to separate/set apart; to segregate;*

  gē lí: 割离, *to sever/cut off; to segregate;*
  gé lí: 隔离, *to keep apart; to segregate/ isolate;*
  gē liè: 割裂, *to cut apart/separate;*
  jiǎn diào: 剪掉, *to cut off;*
  jié duàn: 截断, *to cut off/block, to cut short/to interrupt, to divide/separate;*
  jié huò: 截获, *to intercept/cut off and capture;*
  jūn fēn: 均分, *to divide equally;*
  píng fēn: 平分, *to divide equally/go halves;*
  qiē chéng: 切成, *to cut into pieces/ sections, etc.;*
  qiē diào: 切掉, *to cut off;*

SEE (请查看**) RUPTURA, AMPUTAR, DIVIDIR, PARCELAR, DESMEMBRAR, APARTAR, CONFINAR**

SEGUIR; seguir; *to follow/follow up; to chase/pursue;*

  bàn suí: 伴随, *to accompany, to follow;*
  gēn dìng: 跟定, *to follow determinedly;*
  gēn jìn: 跟进, *to follow sb into; to follow up (MIL);*
  gēn pái: 跟牌, *to follow suit (card game);*
  gēn rén (n) (v): 跟人, *attendant, follower, retainer; to follow sb;*
  gēn suí (v) (n): 跟随, *to follow; follower, retinue;*
  gēn zōng: 跟踪, *to track/trail after; to follow sb;*
  jǐn gēn: 紧跟, *to follow closely, to keep in step with/ comply with;*
  máng cóng: 盲从, *to follow blindly;*
  wěi suí: 尾随, *to follow, to tail behind;*
  zhuī bī: 追逼, *to pursue closely; to press (for payment), to extort (a confession);*
  zhuī bǔ: 追捕, *to pursue and capture;*
  zhuī gǎn: 追赶, *to chase after/pursue;*
  zhuī jī: 追击, *to pursue and attack;*
  zhuī jī: 追缉, *to pursue and capture;*
  zhuī jiān: 追歼, *to pursue and wipe out (an enemy);*
  zhuī jiǎo: 追剿, *to pursue and wipe out/eliminate;*
  zhuī ná: 追拿, *to pursue and apprehend;*

zhuī qiú dào: 追求到, *to pursue*;
zhuī qiú: 追求, *to seek/pursue; to woo/ court*;
zhuī suí: 追随, *to follow (a leader/ doctrine, etc.); to adhere to sthg; to accompany sb*;
zhuī suǒ: 追索, *to pursue/explore/ trace/seek; to dun/demand payment*;
zhuī xún: 追寻, *to pursue/search/track down*;
zhuī zhú: 追逐, *to pursue/chase/seek*

SELECCIONAR; selecionar; *to select/ pick/choose*;
dìng míng (v) (n): 定名, *to denominate/choose a name for; denomination*;
jiǎn xuǎn: 拣选, *to select/choose*;
tiāo chū: 挑出, *to select/choose*;
tiāo lái tiāo qù (vp): 挑来挑去, *to be choosy*;
xuǎn bá: 选拔, *to select sb for some task/job*;
xuǎn cái: 选材, *to select material, to select a suitable person*;
xuǎn chū: 选出, *to pick out/select; to elect*;
xuǎn cuì: 选萃, *to select the best*;
xuǎn diào: 选调, *to select and transfer, to recruit*;
xuǎn dìng: 选定, *to select/designate*;
xuǎn gòu: 选购, *to choose and buy*;
xuǎn jí (v) (n): 选集, *to select and compile; selections*;
xuǎn jiǎn: 选拣, *to select*;
xuǎn jǔ: 选举, *to elect by vote, to select by examination*;
xuǎn sòng: 选送, *to select and send (the best persons/things, etc.)*;
xuǎn yòng: 选用, *to select and use/ apply*;
xuǎn yuè: 选阅, *to review and select*;
xuǎn zhòng: 选中, *to pick/decide/ settle on*;
xuǎn zhǔn: 选准, *to make the right choice*;
zé jiāo: 择交, *to choose friends*;
SEE (请查看**) OPTAR**

SENTENCIAR; sentenciar; *to decide;*

to sentence/ condemn; to give an opinion;
xuān pàn: 宣判, *to pronounce judgment*;
SEE (请查看**) ADJUDICAR, DECIDIR**

SEPULTAR; sepultar; *to bury*;
mái zàng: 埋葬, *to bury (a dead person)*;
yǎn mái: 掩埋, *to bury*

SERPENTEAR; serpentear; *to meander; to wind/ meander; to creep*;
màn bù (v): 漫步, *to stroll/ramble*;
wān yán (v) (vp): 蜿蜒, *to meander; zigzag, long and winding*

SERVIR; servir; *to serve/help/assist*;
fǔ zhù (v) (attr): 辅助, *to assist from the sidelines; supplementary, auxiliary*;
gǎi shàn (v): 改善, *to improve/perfect*;
yǒu yòng (sv): 有用, *useful*;
SEE (请查看**) AUXILIO, ASISTIR**

SIGNIFICAR; significar; *to mean/ express/signify*;
shì yì: 释义, *to explain/interpret*;
SEE (请查看**) COMUNICAR, EXPRESAR, INDICAR**

SILENCIAR; silenciar; *to hush up/keep quiet/silence*;
shǐ ān jìng: 使安静, *to keep quiet/ silence*;
zhē chǒu: 遮丑, *to conceal (a shame/ crime, etc.)*;
SEE (请查看**) SUPRIMIR, OCULTAR**

SIMBOLIZAR; simbolizar; *to symbolize*;
xiàng zhēng (v) (n): 象征, *to symbolize/signify/ stand for; symbol, emblem, token*;
SEE (请查看**) DENOTAR, REPRESENTANTE, REPRESENTAR**

SIMPLIFICAR; simplificar; *to simplify/ clarify/ untangle*;
biǎo míng: 表明, *to make clear/show/ indicate*;
jiǎn huà (v) (n): 简化, *to simplify; simplification*;

nòng qīng: 弄清, *to clarify/make clear*

SIMULAR; simular; *to simulate; to feign/sham;*
  guǐ chēng: 诡称, *to pretend/falsely allege;*
  jiǎ chōng: 假充, *to pretend to be/pose as;*
  mào chōng: 冒充, *to pass os/sthg off as/pretend to be;*
  yǎn xì: 演戏, *to playact/pretend; to put on or act in a play;*
  zhuāng bàn: 装扮, *to dress up/deck out; to disguise/masquerade; to pretend/feign;*
  zhuāng suàn: 装蒜, *to act stupid/play dumb;*
  SEE (请查看**) CAMUFLAJE, FALIBLE, REPRODUCIR**

SINCRONIZAR; sincronizar; *to synchronize;*
  shǐ tóng bù: 使同步, *to synchronize;*
  tóng bù (attr) (v): 同步, *coordinated, synchronized; to be in step with;*
  tóng shí fā shēng: 同时发生, *to synchronize*

SINGULARIZAR; singularizar; *to distinguish/single out/stand out;*
  biàn bié (v) (n): 辨别, *to differentiate/discriminate; discrimination;*
  qū fēn: 区分, *to differentiate/set apart;*
  SEE (请查看**) DIFERENCIA, CATEGORIZAR, DIFERENCIAR**

SINTETIZAR; sintetizar; *to synthesize (QUIM); to summarize;*
  zǒng jié: 总结, *to summarize/sum up/add up;*
  hé chéng: 合成, *to synthesize (QUIM)*

SISTEMATIZAR; sistematizar; *to systematize;*
  shǐ xì tǒng huà: 使系统化, *to systematize*

SITUAR; situar; *to place/put; to post (MIL);*
  fàng: 放, *to place/put;*

fàng jìn: 放进, *to put sthg into;*
fàng qǐ: 放起, *to put sthg up;*
fàng shang: 放上, *to put/add sthg into;*
fàng xià lai: 放下来, *to put sthg down;*
fàng xia: 放下, *to lay/put down, to put aside*

SOBREESTIMAR; superestimar; *to overestimate;*
  guò gāo gū jì: 过高估计, *to overestimate*

SOBREVIVIR; sobreviver; *to survive/outlive;*
  cán cún: 残存, *to be left over, to survive;*
  huó mìng (v) (n): 活命, *to survive, to earn a living; life;*
  shēng cún: 生存, *to survive;*
  xìng cún: 幸存, *to survive by good luck;*
  xìng miǎn: 幸免, *to survive/escape by luck;*
  yuè dōng: 越冬, *to survive the winter*

SOCIALIZAR; sociabilizar o socializar; *to socialize;*
  jiāo jì (v) (n): 交际, *to socialize; social communications;*
  jiāo yǒu (v) (n): 交友, *to make friends/have friendly contact with; friends;*
  shè jiāo (v) (n): 社交, *to have social contacts; social contact/interaction;*
  SEE (请查看**) ALTERNAR**

SOFOCAR; sufocar; *to suffocate/stifle/put out/crush/ stop;*
  mēn sǐ: 闷死, *to choke to death, to suffocate;*
  xūn zhēng (v) (vp): 熏蒸, *to stifle/suffocate; suffocating, sultry, sweltering, stifling;*
  zhǐ bù: 止步, *to halt/stop; to go no further;*
  zhì zhù: 制住, *to check/subdue;*
  SEE (请查看**) SILENCIAR, SUPRIMIR, APREHENDER, BLOCAR, DIFICULTAR**

SOLDAR; soldar; *to solder/weld/join;*
  hàn jiē (v): 焊接, *welding, soldering;*
SEE (请查看**) SOLIDIFICAR**

SOLICITAR; solicitar; *to solicit/ask for/seek/canvass;*
  gào dài: 告贷, *to ask for a loan;*
  gào jí: 告急, *to ask for/need emergency help; to report an emergency;*
  zhēng qiú: 征求, *to solicit/seek;*
SEE (请查看**) APELAR, SUPLICAR, IMPLORAR, INFORMAR**

SOLIDIFICAR; solidificar; *to solidify/ harden;*
  gǔ huà: 骨化, *to ossify;*
  gù huà: 固化, *to weld/solder; to solidify/consolidate;*
  yìng huà: 硬化, *to harden; to become inflexible/ rigid in opinions/ideas; to ossify;*
  yìng jié (v) (n): 硬结, *to harden; scleroma (MED);*

SOLUCIONAR; solucionar; *to solve/ resolve/settle ...* **SOLVENTAR; solver;** *to dissolve; to settle/resolve/ pay;*
  jiě jué: 解决, *to solve/resolve/settle/ dispose of;*
  jié zhàng: 结帐, *to settle/square accounts;*
  liào lǐ: 料理, *to settle/pay;*
  liǎo shì: 了事, *to dispose of a matter/ get sthg over with;*
SEE (请查看**) ASENTIR, DETERMINACIÓN, DECIDIR, DISOLVER**

SONDAR; sondar; *to probe; to sound/ take soundings;*
  shì tàn: 试探, *to sound out/probe;*
  tàn cè (v) (n): 探测, *to probe/survey/ search/sound; probe, survey, search;*
  tàn chá: 探察, *to observe/explore;*
  tàn chá: 探查, *to scout/examine/ investigate;*
  tàn jiū (v) (attr): 探究, *to investigate/ explore; exploratory;*
  tàn suǒ (v) (n): 探索, *to explore/probe; explorations;*

  tàn tīng: 探听, *to find out/make inquiries;*
  tàn wàng: 探望, *to look about, to visit;*
  tàn xiǎn (v) (n): 探险, *to explore; adventure, exploration;*
  tàng míng: 探明, *to ascertain/verify; to find out;*
SEE (请查看**) SEGUIR, INVESTIGAR, DOCUMENTAR**

SUBDIVIDIR; subdividir; *to subdivide;*
  zài fēn: 再分, *to subdivide;*

SUBESTIMAR; subestimar; *to underestimate/ underrate;*
  dī gū: 低估, *to underestimate/ underrate;*
  kàn qīng: 看轻, *to underestimate/look down upon*

SUBLIMAR; sublimar; *to out; to sublimate/divert, alter;*
  shǐ gāo shàng: 使高尚, *to sublimate;*
  shǐ lǐ xiǎng huà: 使理想化, *to sublimate; to idealize;*
  shǐ zhuǎn xiàng: 使 转向, *to change direction/divert;*
SEE (请查看**) SOFOCAR**

SUBORDINAR; subordinar; *to subordinate;*
  cóng shǔ (v) (attr): 从属, *to subordinate; subordinate, dependent;*
  shǐ shùn cóng: 使顺从, *to subordinate;*
  zhēng fú: 征服, *to conquer/subjugate*

SUBSIDIAR; subsidiar; *to subsidize ...* **SUBVENCIONAR; subvencionar;** *to subsidize;*
  gěi yǔ bǔ zhù: 给予补助, *to subsidize*

SUBSISTIR; subsistir; *to live/exist/ survive/subsist;*
  wéi chí shēng huó: 维持生活, *to make a living;*
  wéi chí shēng jì: 维持生计, *to support os or one's family;*
SEE (请查看**) SOBREVIVIR, SUBSISTENCIA, SUSTENTO**

SUBVERTIR; subverter; *to subvert;*
  bài huài: 败坏, *to ruin/corrupt/ undermine;*
  diān fù: 颠覆, *to overturn/subvert;*
SEE (请查看) AFECTAR, ARRUINAR

SUCCIONAR; sugar; *to suck up/soak up/absorb;*
  xī shōu: 吸收, *to absorb/suck up/ assimilate*

SUCEDER; suceder; *to follow; to happen; to succeed/ replace sb;*
  fā shēng: 发生, *to occur/happen/take place;*
  pèng qiǎo: 碰巧, *to happen by chance;*
SEE (请查看) SEGUIR

SUCUMBIR; sucumbir; *to succumb (to)/die/fall;*
  dǐ dǎng bù zhù: 抵挡不住, *to succumb to sthg;*
  qū fú: 屈服, *to surrender/yield*
SEE (请查看) SERVIL

SUFRIR; sofrer; *to suffer/bear/put up with;*
  chī kǔ: 吃苦, *to suffer/bear hardship;*
  huó shòu zuì (vp): 活受罪, *to have a hellish life;*
  kǔ yú (sv): 苦于, *to suffer from;*
  méng shòu: 蒙受, *to suffer/sustain/ incur sthg bad;*
  rěn qì tūn shēng (fe): 忍气吞声, *to swallow anger, to keep quiet and suffer insults;*
  rěn tòng: 忍痛, *to suffer pain with dignity, to bear pain, to do sthg reluctantly;*
  shòu cuò: 受挫, *to be baffled/ thwarted;*
  shòu hài: 受害, *to suffer injury/loss, to be victimized;*
  shòu jìn: 受尽, *to suffer excessively, to have one's fill of, to suffer enough from;*
  shòu kǔ: 受苦, *to suffer hardship;*
  shòu nàn: 受难, *to suffer hardship/ calamity; to die a martyr;*
  shòu zuì: 受罪, *to endure torture/ hardship;*

  zāo dào: 遭到, *to meet with sthg bad;*
  zāo jié: 遭劫, *to meet with catastrophe;*
  zāo shòu: 遭受, *to suffer/sustain;*
  zāo yāng (v) (n): 遭殃, *to meet with disaster; misfortune;*
  zhī chí zhù: 支持住, *to be able to hold out/bear/ sustain;*
SEE (请查看) SOPORTE, VIVIR

SUGERIR; sugerir; *to suggest;*
  tí chū: 提出, *to put forward/pose/raise;*
SEE (请查看) AVANZAR

SUMERGIR; submergir; *to submerge/ immerse/dip/ sink;*
  chén jìn: 沉浸, *to immerse/steep; to soak;*
  tā xiàn: 塌陷, *to sink/cave in;*
  xiàn luò: 陷落, *to subside/sink/cave in;*
  xiàn rù: 陷入, *to sink/fall into/get bogged down in;*
  yān mò: 淹没, *to flood/inundate/ drown; to submerge*

SUPERVISAR; supervisionar; *to supervise;*
  jiān cè: 监测, *to examine/monitor/ supervise;*
  jiān gōng (v) (n): 监工, *to supervise/ overseer; supervisor;*
SEE (请查看) ACTUAR, ADMINISTRAR, DIRECTOR, MONITORIZAR

SUPLANTAR; suplantar; *to supplant, take the place of ...* **SUSTITUIR;**
substituir; *to replace/substitute;*
  dài xiè: 代谢, *to supersede/replace;*
  dài yòng: 代用, *to substitute/replace;*
  jiē tì: 接替, *to take over/replace;*
  qǔ dài: 取代, *to replace/supersede/ substitute;*
  tì bǔ: 替补, *to replace/substitute; to fill vacancies;*
  tì dài: 替代, *to substitute for; to replace/supersede;*
  zhì huàn: 置换, *to displace/replace (QUIM);*
SEE (请查看) SUBSTITUCIÓN, ALTERNAR

SUPLICAR; suplicar; *to plead for sthg, implore, beg*;
  kěn qiú (vp): 恳求, *to earnestly demand/plead for/ require; to be eager; to be eager for*;
SEE (请查看**) SOLICITAR**

SUPRIMIR; suprimir; *to abolish/ suppress/remove*;
  yā zhì: 压制, *to suppress/stifle/inhibit*;
  zhèn yā: 镇压, *to suppress/repress/put down*;
SEE (请查看**) SOFOCAR**

SUPURAR; supurar; *to suppurate/ fester (MED)*;
  huà nóng: 化脓, *to fester/suppurate*;

SEE (请查看**) AGRAVANTE**

SUSPENDER; suspender; *to hang up/ hang from sthg/suspend*;
  guà duàn diàn huà: 挂断电话, *to hang up*;
  guà: 挂, *to hang/put up*;
  xuán guà: 悬挂, *to hang/fly (a flag); to be suspended*

SUSTENTAR; sustentar; *to hold up/ support/sustain*;
  shù qǐ: 竖起, *to hold up; to erect*;
  zhī de qǐ: 支得起, *to be able to prop up*;
SEE (请查看**) APROVISIONAR**

Interchangeable Spanish-Portuguese-English words and their Chinese equivalents
Palabras en Español-Portugués-Inglés y sus equivalentes en Chino
Palavras em Espanhol-Português-Inglês e seus equivalentes em Chinês
西班牙语，葡萄牙语，英语及中文的对等单词

TANGO; tango;
  tàn gē wǔ (v) (n): 探戈舞, *to tango; tango*

TAXI; táxi;
  chū zū chē: 出租车, *taxi*

TÉLEX; telex;
  diàn chuán: 电传, *telex*

TEMPERAMENTAL; temperamental;
  qíng xù bō dòng de: 情绪波动的, *temperamental*;
  shén jīng zhì de: 神经质的, *nervous, temperamental*;
  shí hǎo shí huài de: 时好时坏的, *temperamental car, machine, etc.*;
  xǐ nù wú cháng de: 喜怒无常的, *temperamental person*

TEMPORAL (adj); **temporal** (adj);
temporal; relative to time; temporary,

provisional;
  duǎn zàn de: 短暂的, *temporal, temporary*;
  lín shí (adv) (attr): 临时, *at a time when sthg happens; temporary, provisional*;
  lín shí bàn fǎ: 临时办法, *temporary arrangement, makeshift*;
  lín shí cuò shī: 临时措施, *stopgap measure*;
  lín shí de: 临时的, *temporary, provisional*;
  lín shí xìng: 临时性, *temporary*;
SEE (请查看**) BREVE**

TENOR (MUS); **tenor;**
  nán gāo yīn gē shǒu: 男高音歌手, *tenor*

TERMINAL; terminal (adj) (GEN); *ending (MED); a station*;
  jué zhèng: 绝症, *incurable/fatal illness*;

mò qī (n) (sv): 末期, *last/final phase/ stage; terminal/final*;
zhōng dǐ (attr): 终底, *terminal*;
zhōng duān (n) (attr): 终端, *terminal*;
zhōng mò (attr): 终末, *terminal*;
zhōng (bf) (adv): 终, *end, finish; whole, entire time; eventually, after all, in the end*;
zhōng diǎn: 终点, *end of a journey, destination, terminal point; finish line (DEP)*;
SEE **(**请查看**) FINAL, ÚLTIMO, ESTACIÓN**

TERRITORIAL; territorial;
lǐng tǔ (sv) (n): 领土, *territorial; territory*

TERROR; terror;
kǒng jù (n) (v) (sv): 恐惧, *terror; to fear/dread/be afraid of; horrifying, fearsome*;
SEE **(**请查看**) HORROR**

TEXTUAL; textual (adj); *precise; exact; textual*;
jīng què de: 精确的, *precise*;
yuán wén de: 原文的, *textual (original text)*;
SEE **(**请查看**) EXACTAMENTE, DEFINIDO**

TOPLESS ó TOP-LESS; topless;
tǎn xiōng de: 坦胸的, *topless*

TORNADO; tornado;
jù fēng: 飓风, *hurricane, typhoon*;
lóng juǎn fēng: 龙卷风, *tornado, cyclone*

TORPEDO; torpedo;
shuǐ léi: 水雷, *submarine mine*;
yú léi: 鱼雷, *torpedo*

TORSO; torso;
qū gàn: 躯干, *trunk, torso*

TOTAL; total;
jué duì (sv): 绝对, *absolute, perfect, definite, total*;
zǒng (bf) (adv) (v): 总, *total, comprehensive, general, overall; always, invariably; anyway, after all; sooner or later; surely, certainly; to assemble/ put together/sum up*;
zǒng chǎn: 总产, *total output*;
zǒng de: 总的, *total (number, cost, etc.)*;
zǒng gòng jǐ: 总供给, *aggregate/ total/gross supply*;
zǒng hé: 总合, *sum, total*;
zǒng zhí: 总值, *gross/total value*;
SEE **(**请查看**) COMPLETO, GENERAL, TODO, SUMA**

TRAUMA; trauma;
chuāng shāng: 创伤, *wound, trauma*

TRIANGULAR (adj); **triangular** (adj);
sān jiǎo xíng de: 三角形的, *triangular*

TRÍO; trio;
sān chóng chàng: 三重唱, *vocal trio*;
sān chóng zòu: 三重奏, *instrumental trio*

TRIVIAL; trivial; *ordinary, trivial;*
ér xì: 儿戏, *children's play; trifling matter*;
píng fán (sv): 平凡, *ordinary, common, mediocre*;
píng fàn (vp): 平泛, *pedestrian, ordinary*;
suǒ shì: 琐事, *trifle, trivial matter*;
suǒ suì (sv) (n): 琐碎, *trifling, trivial; slight indisposition, trivia*;
SEE **(**请查看**) BANAL, DIMINUTO, FRÍVOLO, INSIGNIFICANTE**

TROPICAL; tropical;
rè dài de: 热带的, *tropical*

TUMOR (MED); **tumor;**
zhǒng liú: 肿瘤, *tumor*

TWEED; tweed;
cū huā ní (sv) (n): 粗花呢, *tweed (coat, etc.); tweed*

Easily recognizable Spanish-Portuguese-English nouns, adjectives and adverbs and their Chinese equivalents
Nombres, sustantivos, adjetivos y adverbios en Español-Portugués-Inglés y sus equivalentes en Chino
Nomes, substantivos, adjetivos e advérbios em Espanhol-Português-Inglês e seus equivalentes em Chinês
容易辨认的西班牙语，葡萄牙语，英语的名词，形容词和副词和他们的中文对等词

TABACO; tabaco; *tobacco products and plant*;
  yān cǎo: 烟草, *tobacco; tobacco plant*

TABERNA; taberna; *tavern, bar*;
  jiǔ diàn: 酒店, *wine shop, hotel, public house*;
  xiǎo lǚ guǎn: 小旅馆, *inn*

TABÚ; tabu; *taboo*;
  jìn jì (n) (v): 禁忌, *taboo; to avoid*;
  jì huì (v) (n): 忌讳, *to avoid as a taboo; taboo*

TÁCITO (A); **tácito** (A); *tacit, unwritten, unspoken*;
  àn shì de: 暗示的, *suggestive, implied*;
  xīn zhào bù xuān de: 心照不宣的, *tacit understanding*

TACITURNO (A); **taciturno** (A); *taciturn, silent, reticent; sullen, moody*;
  guǎ yán (sv): 寡言, *taciturn*;
  qì nǎo (sv): 气恼, *to be sullen/sulky/ruffled*;
  xǐ nù wú cháng (fe): 喜怒无常, *subject to changing moods, moody*;
SEE (请查看) DESILUSIÓN, MALHUMORADO, RETICENCIA

TÁCTICA; tática; *tactics, tactic, gambit, strategy, approach* ... **TÁCTICO** (A); **tático** (A); *tactical (adj); tactician (n)*;
  cè lüè de: 策略的, *tactical (strategies)*;
  cè lüè: 策略, *tactics*;
  zhàn lüè (sv) (n): 战略, *tactical (policies); strategy, tactics*;
  zhàn shù (sv) (n): 战术, *tactical (weapons); military tactics, tactics*;
  zhàn shù jiā: 战术家, *tactician*;
SEE (请查看) MÉTODO

TÁCTIL; tátil; *tactile; tangible*;
  què shí de: 确实的, *definite, real, true, tangible*;
  yǒu xíng de: 有形的, *tangible, visible*;
SEE (请查看) GENUINO

TALENTO; talento; *ability, talent* ... **TALENTOSO** (A); **talentoso** (A); *talented, gifted*;
  cái huá: 才华, *literary/artistic talent*;
  cái qì: 才气, *literary talent*;
  cái qíng: 才情, *literary and artistic talent, imaginative power*;
  cái shì: 才士, *a man of ability or talent, a brilliant man*;
  cái tóng: 才童, *talented child, whiz kid, child prodigy*;
  cái wàng: 才望, *reputation for talent*;
  rén cái: 人才, *a person of ability/talent*;
  tiān cái: 天才, *a man of genius; talent, gift*;
  tiān fèn gāo (vp): 天分高, *gifted, talented*;
  tiān fèn: 天分, *natural gift, talent*;
  tiān fù (vp) (n): 天赋, *inborn, innate; natural gift/talent*;
  yīng cái: 英才, *person of outstanding ability, a talented person*;
  yǒu cái néng de: 有才能的, *talented*;
SEE (请查看) APTITUD, CAPACIDAD, TALENTO, COMPETENCIA, CAPAZ

TANGENTE; tangent; *tangent*;
  tū rán lí tí: 突然离题, *tangent*

TARDÍO (A) (adj); **tardio** (A); *late, belated; slow*;
  chí (sv) (bf): 迟, *tardy, late, belated; slow*;
  chí dào (v) (sv): 迟到, *to be/come/arrive late; late*;
  chí huǎn zhě (n): 迟缓者, *laggard*;

màn chē: 慢车, *slow/local train/bus*;

shāo wǎn de: 稍晚的, *late (after the usual time)*;

wǎn shú (sv)**:** 晚熟, *late maturing (of a person), late ripening (of a plant)*;

SEE (请查看) DILATADO, ENDÉMICO, LENTO

TARIFA; tarifa; *charge, fare, flat rate, tariff;*

chē fèi: 车费, *fare, carfare;*

guān shuì: 关税, *tariff, customs duty;*

shuì lǜ: 税率, *tax, tariff rate;*

SEE (请查看) COSTO

TAXATIVO (A)**; taxativo** (A)**;** *categorical; limited, restricted, sharp, emphatic;*

duàn rán (adv) (vp)**:** 断然, *absolutely, flatly, categorically; resolute, drastic;*

jué duì (sv)**:** 绝对, *absolute, perfect, definite, categorically;*

wú tiáo jiàn (attr) (sv)**:** 无条件, *unconditional, unconditioned; categorical;*

SEE (请查看) CONFINAR, LIMITADO

TAXISTA; taxista; *taxi driver;*

chū zū chē sī jī: 出租车司机, *taxi driver;*

chū zū chē: 出租车, *taxi;*

TÉCNICA; técnica; *technique, craftsmanship ...* **TÉCNICO** (A)**;**
técnico (A)**;** *technical (adj); technician (n) ...* **TECNOLOGÍA; tecnologia;** *technology;*

gōng yì jì qiǎo: 工艺技巧, *craftsmanship;*

gōng yì xué: 工艺学, *technology;*

jì néng: 技能, *technical ability, mastery of a technique/skill;*

jì qiǎo: 技巧, *technique, skill, craftsmanship; dexterity;*

jì shù de: 技术的, *technical;*

jì shù: 技术, *technology, skill, technique;*

shǒu fǎ: 手法, *skill, technique;*

shǒu yì: 手艺, *craftsmanship, workmanship;*

zhuān yè xìng: 专业性, *specialization,*

technicality;

jì shī: 技师, *technician;*

zhuān yè: 专业, *specialty, discipline, special field of study/research;*

SEE (请查看) CALIFICADO

TEDIO; tédio; *boredom, tedium, monotony, ennui ...* **TEDIOSO** (A)**;**
tedioso (A)**;** *tedious;*

chén mèn (sv) (n)**:** 沉闷, *oppressive, depressing, tedious, depressed, in low spirits; withdrawn; tedium;*

dān diào (sv) (n)**:** 单调, *monotonous, dull, drab, boring; tedium;*

fá wèi (sv)**:** 乏味, *dull, vapid, drab, tasteless;*

kū zào (sv)**:** 枯燥, *dull and dry, uninteresting, tedious;*

rǒng cháng (sv) (n)**:** 冗长, *long and tedious; redundant, superfluous, verbose; supernumerary;*

yàn juàn (v) (sv)**:** 厌倦, *to be weary of; tedious;*

SEE (请查看) ENERVANTE, ESTUPIDEZ

TELÉFONO; telephone; *telephone, phone ...* **TELÉGRAFO; telegrafar;**
telegraph ... **TELEGRAMA; telegram;**
telegram;

diàn huà: 电话, *telephone, phone;*

SEE (请查看) CALEGRAMA

TELEPATÍA; telepatia; *telepathy ...*
TELEPÁTICO (A)**; telepático** (A)**;**
telepathic, clairvoyant, psychic;

dòng chá lì (n)**:** 洞察力, *clairvoyance;*

xīn lǐ de: 心理的, *psychic;*

xīn líng gǎn yìng: 心灵感应, *telepathy;*

yǒu dòng chá lì de rén (n)**:** 有洞察力的人, *clairvoyant*

TELEVISOR; televisor; *television set;*

diàn shì jī: 电视机, *television set*

TEMERIDAD; temeridade; *temerity; recklessness, folly, boldness;*

bù gù hòu guǒ (sv) (n)**:** 不顾后果, *reckless; recklessness;*

dà dǎn (sv)**:** 大胆, *audacious, bold,*

daring;

dǎn dà bāo tiān (fe): 胆大包天, *extremely audacious*;

lèng tóu lèng nǎo (fe): 愣头愣脑, *rash, impetuous, reckless*;

máo cao (sv): 毛草, *careless*;

máo jìn (n) (sv): 冒进, *rash, recklessness, adventurous*;

mào mào shī shī (sv) (adv): 冒冒失失, *thoughtless, careless; recklessly and abruptly*;

SEE (请查看) ESTUPIDEZ, IMPACIENCIA

TEMEROSO (A); temeroso (A); *afraid, dreadful; frightened* ... TEMIBLE; temível; *fearsome, frightful* ... TEMOR; temor; *fear, dread, terror, fright*;

bèi xià dǎo: 被吓倒, *frightened*;

hài pà (v) (n) (sv): 害怕, *to be afraid/scared; fear, dread; frightful; frightened*;

jīng huáng (sv) (n): 惊惶, *to become alarmed/panic stricken; trepidation*;

kǒng jù (v) (sv): 恐惧, *to fear/dread, to be afraid of; scared, afraid*;

kǒng jù gǎn: 恐惧感, *feeling/sense of fear*;

kǒng jù zhèng: 恐惧症, *phobia*;

shòu jīng: 受惊, *to be frightened/startled*;

xià yī tiào (v) (sv): 吓一跳, *to startle/frighten; frightened, startled*;

xià zhù (vp): 吓住, *to startle/stop by intimidation*;

SEE (请查看) TERROR, ALARMA, APRENSIÓN, HORROR, DESCONCERTANTE

TEMPERAMENTO; temperament; *temperament, nature, disposition*;

pí qi: 脾气, *temperament, disposition; bad temper; behavior*;

yì qì: 意气, *temperament, spirit; impulse*;

SEE (请查看) TEMPERAMENTAL, HUMOR

TEMPERATURA; temperature; *temperature*;

qì wēn: 气温, *air temperature*;

rè dù: 热度, *temperature of a fever/furnace, etc.; heat, enthusiasm*;

tǐ wēn: 体温, *body temperature*;

wēn dù: 温度, *temperature*

TEMPESTAD; tempestade; *tempest, storm* ... TEMPESTUOSO (A); tempestuoso (A); *stormy*;

bào fēng xuě: 暴风雪, *snowstorm, blizzard*;

bào fēng yǔ: 暴风雨, *rainstorm, tempest*;

bào fēng zhòu yǔ: 暴风骤雨, *violent storm*;

bāo fēng: 暴风, *storm, wind, gale; storminess*;

fēng bào: 风暴, *windstorm, tempest*;

fēng bō: 风波, *storm, disturbance; crisis*;

jì fēng: 季风, *monsoon; storm, strong mind*;

yǒu bào fēng yǔ de: 有暴风雨的, *stormy weather*;

SEE (请查看) VEHEMENTE

TENACIDAD; tenacidade; *tenacity; persistence, resolute*;

jiān rěn (sv): 坚忍, *steadfast and persevering*;

jiān rèn (sv): 坚韧, *firm and tenacious; strong and durable*;

SEE (请查看) DETERMINACIÓN, ÉNFASIS, CONTUMACIA

TENDENCIA; tendência; *tendency, trend*;

qū shì (n) (v): 趋势, *trend, tendency; to follow the trend*;

SEE (请查看) INCLINACIÓN, ONDULACIÓN

TENIS; tênis; *tennis* ... TENISTA; tenista; *tennis player*;

wǎng qiú chǎng: 网球场, *tennis court*;

wǎng qiú pāi: 网球拍, *tennis racket*;

wǎng qiú sài: 网球赛, *tennis match*;

wǎng qiú shǒu: 网球手, *tennis player*;

wǎng qiú yùn dòng: 网球运动, *tennis*;

wǎng qiú: 网球, *tennis, tennis ball*

TENSO; tenso; *taut, stiff, rigid; tense, nervous;*

jǐn bēng bēng (sv): 紧绷绷, *tight, taut; tense;*

jǐn zhāng (sv): 紧张, *nervous, keyed up; tense, intense, strained;*

shēng yìng (sv): 生硬, *stiff, rigid, harsh;*

SEE (请查看) DESCONCERTANTE, DOGMÁTICO

TENTACIÓN; tentação; *temptation, draw, lure, inducement ...* **TENTADOR** (A); **tentador** (A); *tempting (adj);*

gōu yǐn (v) (n): 勾引, *to tempt/entice/ seduce; temptation;*

yǐn yòu (v) (n): 引诱, *to lure/seduce; temptation;*

yòu huò wù: 诱惑物, *lure, attraction;*

SEE (请查看) SEDUCIR, SEDUCCIÓN, SEDUCTOR, CARISMA

TENTATIVA; tentative; *attempt;*

cháng shì (n) (v): 尝试, *attempt; to attempt/try;*

shì tú (v) (n): 试图, *to attempt/try; attempt*

TENUE; tênue; *slight, tenuous;*

kōng dòng wú lì: 空洞无力, *tenuous, weak*

wú zú qīng zhòng: 无足轻重, *slight, insubstantial;*

xiān xì (sv): 纤细, *very thin, slender, fine, tenuous; insignificant;*

SEE (请查看) DIMINUTO

TEORÍA; teoria; *theory;*

lǐ lùn: 理论, *theory, principle; -ism;*

xué shuō: 学说, *theory, doctrine;*

yì jiàn: 意见, *idea, view, opinion; theory; suggestion;*

yuán lǐ: 原理, *principle, tenant, theory;*

zhǔ yì: 主义, *doctrine, theory; -ism*

TERAPEUTA; terapeuta; *therapist* ... **TERAPÉUTICO** (A); **terapêutico** (A); *therapeutic ...* **TERAPIA; terapia;** *therapy;*

liáo fǎ: 疗法, *therapy, treatment;*

yǒu lì yú jiàn kāng (sv): 有利于健康, *therapeutic;*

yǒu liáo xiào (sv): 有疗效, *therapeutic;*

zhì liáo xué: 治疗学, *therapeutics;*

zhì liáo zhuān jiā: 治疗专家, *therapist;*

zhì liáo (n) (v): 治疗, *therapy, treatment; to treat/ cure*

TÉRMICO (A); **térmico** (A); *thermal, heat;*

bǎo nuǎn (sv) (v): 保暖, *thermal; to keep warm;*

rè liàng de: 热量的, *thermal;*

rè liàng: 热量, *heat; quantity of heat (FIS);*

rè néng: 热能, *thermal energy*

TERMINADO; concluído; *finished, accomplished, closed, stopped ...* **TERMINANTE; terminante;** *categorical, conclusive, final, outright ...* **TERMINANTEMENTE; terminantemente;** *categorically, conclusively ...* **TÉRMINO; término;** *end, conclusion;*

jié jú: 结局, *final result, outcome, ending;*

mò duàn: 末段, *finale;*

mò hòu (adv) (n): 末后, *finally; the end, final part;*

mò wěi: 末尾, *end, ending;*

mò zhàn: 末站, *terminal (concluding, final);*

wán bì (v) (sv): 完毕, *to finish/ complete; finished, done, completed;*

wán chéng (v) (sv): 完成, *to accomplish/fulfill/ complete; accomplished, completed;*

SEE (请查看) CATEGÓRICO, TERMINAL, TAXATIVO, AFIRMAR, APREHENDER, COMPLETO, DEDUCCIÓN, DESINTEGRACIÓN, CONCRETO, FINAL

TERMINOLOGÍA; terminologia; *terminology, nomenclature, wording;*

shù yǔ: 术语, *terminology*

TERMÓMETRO; termômetro;
thermometer;
  wēn dù jì: 温度计, *thermometer*

TERMOSTATO; termostato;
thermostat;
  héng wēn qì: 恒温器, *thermostat*

TERREMOTO; terremoto; *earthquake*;
  dì zhèn (n) (v): 地震, *earthquake; to shake the earth*

TERRENO; terreno; *land, terrain (GEOL); earthly* **... TERRITORIO;**
território; *territory; region, district* (POL);
  dà dì: 大地, *earth, mother earth; world*;
  dì qiú (sv) (n): 地球, *earthly; The Earth/ globe*;
  dì shì: 地势, *terrain; topography relief*;
  lǐng tǔ: 领土, *territory*;
  lù dì: 陆地, *dry land; land surface*;
  ní tǔ: 泥土, *earth, soil; muddy soil; clay*;
SEE (请查看**) DISTRITO**

TERRORÍFICO (A) (adj); **terrível;**
terrible, terrifying, frightening;
  gòu qiàng (vp): 够呛, *unbearable, terrible*;
  lìng ré hài pà de: 令人害怕的, *terrifying*;
  wēi xié (v) (sv): 威胁, *to menace/ imperil/ threaten/ intimidate; terrified, terrifying*;
  xià huài (v) (sv): 吓坏, *to be terribly frightened; terrified*;
SEE (请查看**) TEMEROSO, HORROR, SERIEDAD**

TERRORISMO; terrorismo; *terrorism*
... TERRORISTA; terrorista; *terrorist*;
  kǒng bù fèn zǐ de (adj): 恐怖分子的, *terrorist*;
  kǒng bù fèn zǐ: 恐怖分子, *terrorist*;
  kǒng bù zhǔ yì: 恐怖主义, *terrorism*;
SEE (请查看**) TERROR**

TESÓN; tenacidade; *tenacity, perseverance, persistence*;
  bù qū bù náo (fe): 不屈不挠, *unyielding*;

  jiān rèn (sv): 坚韧, *firm and tenacious, strong and durable*;
SEE (请查看**) TENACIDAD, DETERMINACIÓN, PERSEVERANCIA, INSISTIR, ÉNFASIS, CONSTANTE, CONTUMACIA**

TESTAMENTO; testament; *legacy, will, testament*;
  yí chǎn: 遗产, *legacy*;
  yí zhǔ: 遗嘱, *testament, will; deathbed behest*

TESTARUDO (A); **teimoso** (A);
stubborn person; stubborn, pigheaded;
  jué jiàng de: 倔强的, *stubborn*;
SEE (请查看**) TESÓN, INDOMABLE , CONTUMACIA**

TEXTIL; têxtil *textile*;
  fǎng zhī pǐn: 纺织品, *textile*;
SEE (请查看**) COTÓN**

TEXTO; texto; *text*;
  kè běn: 课本, *text book*;
  zhèng wén: 正文, *written material*

TEXTURA; textura; *texture*;
  zhì dì: 质地, *texture, quality of material; character*;
  zhī dì: 织地, *texture*

TIFUS; tifo; *typhus*;
  shāng hán: 伤寒, *typhoid (fever), typhus (MED)*

TIMIDEZ; timidez; *shyness, timidity ...*
TÍMIDO (A); **tímido** (A); *shy, timid*;
  dǎn qiè: 胆怯, *timid, shy, cowardly*;
  dǎn xiǎo (sv): 胆小, *timid, cowardly*;
  dǎn xiǎo bēi qiè (fe): 胆小卑怯, *chicken-hearted*;
  dǎn xiǎo guǐ: 胆小鬼, *coward*;
  dǎn xiǎo pà shì (vp): 胆小怕事, *timid and overcautious*;
  dǎn xiǎo rú shǔ (vp): 胆小如鼠, *lily-livered, chicken-hearted*;
  hài xiū (sv): 害羞, *be bashful/shy*;
  hán xiū (adv): 含羞, *shyly, timidly*;

liǎn nèn (vp): 脸嫩, *to be bashful/shy*;
liǎn pí báo (vp): 脸皮薄, *to be shy, sensitive*;
liǎn pí nèn (fe): 脸皮嫩, *bashful, shy*;
liǎn xiǎo (vp): 脸小, *to be bashful/shy with women; to have little or no prestige; to be a nobody*;
pà shēng (v) (sv): 怕生, *to be shy with strangers (of a child)*;
pà xiū (sv): 怕羞, *shy, bashful*;
qiè (bf) (sv): 怯, *timid, cowardly; uncouth*;
qiè fū: 怯夫, *coward*;
qiè qiè (sv): 怯怯, *timid*;
qiè shēng (sv): 怯生, *shy with strangers*;
qiè shēng shēng (sv): 怯生生, *timid, shy*;
qiè yí (vp): 怯疑, *timid and vacillating*;
qiè yì: 怯意, *timidity, shyness*;
xiū sè (sv): 羞涩, *shy, bashful, embarrassed*;
SEE (请查看**) INTROVERTIDO, PRUDENCIA**

TÍPICO (A); **típico** (A); *typical*;
diǎn xíng de: 典型的, *typical*;
yǒu dài biǎo xìng de: 有代表性的, *representative*

TIPO; tipo; *type, kind, sort*;
pǐn pái: 品牌, *type, brand*;
xìng: 性, *sort, type, nature, character*;
SEE (请查看**) CLASIFICACIÓN, GÉNERO**

TIRANÍA; tirania; *tyranny* ...
TIRÁNICO (A); **tirânico** (A); *a tyrannical, possessive government*;
bào zhèng: 暴政, *tyranny*;
yā pò (v) (n): 压迫, *to oppress/repress/ constrict; oppression, repression, constriction*;
SEE (请查看**) ABUSIVO**

TODO (A); **todo** (A); *all* ...
TOTALIDAD; totalidade; *whole, totality* ... **TOTALMENTE; totalmente;** *totally, completely*;
quán bù (n) (adj): 全部, *whole, complete, total, all*;

SEE (请查看**) TOTAL, CASTO, GENERAL**

TOLERANCIA; tolerancia; *tolerance, patience, leniency* ... **TOLERANTE; tolerante;** *tolerant, fair, considerate*;
kǎo lǜ zhōu dào: 考虑周到的 *considerate*;
nài xīn (sv) (n): 耐心, *patient; patience, endurance*;
nài xīn xì zhì (fe): 耐心细致, *patient, painstaking*;
nài xìng (n): 耐性, *patience, endurance*;
SEE (请查看**) ATENCIÓN, AUTORIZAR, CLEMENCIA, DESAPASIONADO**

TOMATE; tomate; *tomato*;
fān qié: 番茄, *tomato*;
xī hóng shì: 西红柿, *tomato*

TOMO; tomo; *tome, book, volume*;
cè zi: 册子, *book, volume*;
shǒu gǎo: 手稿, *manuscript*;
shū jí: 书籍, *books, works of literature*;
shū: 书, *book*

TÓNICO (A); **tônico** (A); *revitalizing, tonic, stimulating* ... **TONIFICACIÓN; tonificação;** *invigoration* ...
TONIFICADOR (A) (adj); **tonificante;** *invigorating*;
lìng rén gǔ wǔ de: 令人鼓舞的, *invigorating*;
shǐ xīng fèn de: 使兴奋的, *stimulating*;
shǐ xīng fèn: 使兴奋, *stimulation*;
zī bǔ (attr) (v): 滋补, *nourishing, nutritious*;
SEE (请查看**) DESCONCERTANTE, VITALIDAD**

TOPOGRAFÍA; topografia; *topography* ... **TOPOGRÁFICO** (A); **topográfico** (A); *topographical*;
dì xíng xué: 地形学, *topography*;
dì xíng xué de: 地形学的, *topographical*;
SEE (请查看**) TERRENO**

TORMENTA; tormenta; *storm (METEO); turmoil* ... **TORMENTOSO** (A); **tormentoso** (A); *stormy; troubled;*
  páo xiào (v) (sv): 咆哮, *to roar/ thunder; to rage (of a person); stormy;*
  são dòng (v) (n): 骚动, *to become restless; to disturb/ upset; disturbance, turmoil;*
SEE (请查看) **TEMPESTAD, CAOS, FUROR**

TORMENTO; tormento; *torment, torture, anguish, agony* ... **TORTURA; tortura;** *torture;*
  hūn luàn (sv): 昏乱, *decrepit and muddle-headed;*
  jí dù tòng kǔ: 极度痛苦, *mental anguish;*
  jù tòng: 剧痛, *physical anguish, severe pain;*
  kù xíng: 酷刑, *cruel torture;*
  zhé mo (v) (n): 折磨, *to persecute/ torment; torment, torture;*
SEE (请查看) **AFLICCIÓN, ACOSAR**

TORRE; torre; *tower (GEN); high-rise;*
  gāo céng (attr):高层 , *high-level; high-rise;*
  gāo céng jiàn zhù (n): 高层建筑, *high-rise*

TORRENCIAL; torrencial; *torrential* ... **TORRENTE; torrente;** *torrent, flood;*
  bēn liú (n) (v): 奔流, *torrent, racing current; to flow a great speed;*
  hóng liú: 洪流, *mighty torrent;*
  hóng shuǐ: 洪水, *flood;*
  jī liú: 激流, *torrent, rapids;*
  pāng tuó (vp): 滂沱, *torrential;*
  shuǐ zāi: 水灾, *flood, inundation*

TÓRRIDO (A); **tórrido;** *torrid;*
  dú rè (vp): 毒热, *scorching hot, torrid;*
  yán rè (sv): 炎热, *torrid, scorching, blazing hot;*
  zhuó rè (vp): 灼热, *scorching hot;*
SEE (请查看) **EFUSIVO**

TORTUOSO (A); **tortuoso** (A); *tortuous, winding;*

yū huí (attr) (v): 迂回, *circuitous, roundabout; to outflank;*
SEE (请查看) **DIFICULTAR, CONTORSIÓN, CURVATURA**

TÓXICO (A) (adj); **tóxico** (A); *toxic, poisonous* ... **TÓXICO** (n); **toxina;** *toxin; poison, toxic substance;*
  dú (n) (v) (sv): 毒, *poison, toxin; to poison; poisonous, malicious, cruel*
  dú hài (n) (v): 毒害, *poison; to poison sb's mind, to poison;*
  dú qì: 毒气, *poison(ous) gas;*
  dú shé: 毒蛇, *poisonous snake;*
  dú wù: 毒物, *poisonous substance, poison;*
  dú xìng: 毒性, *toxicity;*
  dú yào: 毒药, *poison, toxicant;*
  dú yè: 毒液, *venom, poisonous fluid;*
  dú zhèng: 毒症, *poisoning;*
  dú zhì: 毒质, *poisonous matter;*
  dú zhī: 毒汁, *venom; poisonous fluid;*
  yǒu dú (attr) (v): 有毒, *poisonous, venomous, deleterious;*
SEE (请查看) **VENENO**

TRADICIÓN; tradição; *tradition* ... **TRADICIONAL; tradicional;** *traditional;*
  chuán tǒng (n) (sv): 传统, *tradition, convention; traditional, conventional;*
  chuán tǒng xí guàn: 串通习惯, *traditional habit/ custom;*
SEE (请查看) **CONVENCIONAL**

TRÁFICO; tráfico; *traffic; trade;*
  mào yì: 贸易, *trade;*
  shāng yè: 商业, *commerce, trade, business;*
SEE (请查看) **NEGOCIO**

TRAGEDIA; tragédia; *tragedy* ... **TRÁGICO** (A); **trágico** (A); *tragic;*
  āi yuàn (sv) (n): 哀怨, *sad, plaintive, tragic;*
  bēi cǎn (sv): 悲惨, *miserable, tragic;*
  bēi jù xìng: 悲剧性, *tragedy, tragic nature;*
  bēi jù: 悲剧, *tragedy;*
  jí dà de bù xìng: 极大的不幸, *tragedy,*

misfortune, adversity

TRAICIONERO (A); **traiçoeiro** (A);
perfidious, unreliable; treacherous;
  wēi xiǎn (sv) (n): 危险, *treacherous
  (conditions); dangerous, perilous; danger,
  peril*;
SEE (请查看**) CONSPIRACIÓN,
INFIDELIDAD**

TRAIDOR (A) (adj); **traidor** (A);
traitorous, deceitful; traitor;
  mài guó zéi: 卖国贼, *traitor to one's
  country*;
  pàn tú: 叛徒, *traitor*;
SEE (请查看**) DUPLICIDAD**

TRAMPOLÍN; trampolim; *trampoline,
springboard*;
  bèng chuáng: 蹦床, *trampoline*

**TRANQUILAMENTE;
tranqüilamente;** *calmly; peacefully,
leisurely* ... **TRANQUILIDAD;
tranqüilidade;** *peaceful, calm,
tranquility* ... **TRANQUILO** (A) (adj);
tranqüilo (A); *peaceful, calm; quiet
(MUS)*;
  ān mì (sv) (wr): 安谧, *peaceful,
  tranquil*;
  ān wěn (sv) (adv): 安稳, *smooth and
  steady, peaceful*;
  jì jìng (sv): 寂静, *quiet, calm, still,
  tranquil*;
  píng 'ān (sv): 平安, *safe and sound,
  quiet and stable*;
SEE (请查看**) CALMO, PACÍFICO,
CALMA, APLOMO, QUIETO**

**TRANSCRIPCIÓN; trascrição o
transcrição;** *transcription, transcript*;
  chāo běn: 抄本, *transcript, manuscript,
  hand-copied*;
  jiǎng gǎo: 讲稿, *transcript; draft;
  notes*;
SEE (请查看**) DUPLICAR**

**TRANSFORMACIÓN;
transformação;** *transformation,
change*;

gǎi biàn: 改变, *transformation*

TRANSGRESIÓN; transgressão;
transgression, offense, misdeed ...
TRANSGRESOR (A); **transgressor**
(A); **offender;** *transgressor*;
  zuì xíng wéi bèi: 罪行违背, *violation,
  criminal acts*;
  wéi fǎn: 违反, *transgression*;
  zuì xíng: 罪行, *criminal acts*;
SEE (请查看**) INFRACTOR, CRIMEN**

TRANSICIÓN; transição; *transition,
changeover; alteration*;
  guò dù (v) (n) (attr): 过渡, *to ferry over;
  intermediate stage/state; transition,
  interim; transitional*;
SEE (请查看**) ALTERAR**

TRANSIGENCIA; transigência;
willingness to compromise, tolerance ...
TRANSIGENTE; transigente*(adj)*;
*compliant, yielding; compromising,
tolerant, forgiving*;
  tuǒ xié: 妥协, *appeasement, amity*;
SEE (请查看**) TOLERANCIA,
OBEDIENCIA**

TRANSITORIO (A); **transitório** (A);
transitory, temporary, provisional;
  piàn kè (n) (sv): 片刻, *a short while, a
  moment; transitory*;
SEE (请查看**) BREVE, TEMPORAL**

TRANSLÚCIDO (A); **translúcido** (A);
translucent;
  bàn tòu míng de: 半透明的,
  translucent;
SEE (请查看**) DEFINIDO**

TRANSPARENCIA; transparência;
transparency, openness ...
TRANSPARENTE (adj); **transparente;**
transparent, diaphanous, filmy;
  tòu chè (sv) (n): 透澈, *clear,
  transparent, lucid; transparency*;
  tòu guāng (sv): 透光, *translucent*;
  tòu liang (sv): 透亮, *bright,
  transparent; perfectly clear*;
  tòu míng dù: 透明度, *transparency*

(literally and figuratively); degree of
political openness;
  yì dǒng: 易懂, *transparent*;
SEE (请查看**) DIÁFANO**

TRANSPLANTE ó TRASPLANTE;
transplante; *transplant (MED)*;
  yí zhí (n) (v): 移植, *transplant (MED); to*
transplant/ graft (MED);
  yí zhí qì guān: 移植器官, *transplant*

TRATABLE; tratável; *easy going,*
friendly, sociable;
  hào jiāo jì de: 好交际的, *sociable*;
SEE (请查看**) GREGARIO**

TRAUMÁTICO (A)**; traumático** (A)**;**
traumatic, shocking, upsetting;
  chuāng shāng de: 创伤的, *traumatic*;
  tòng kǔ nán wàng de: 痛苦难忘的,
traumatic;
  zāo tòu: 糟透, *very bad, shocking*;
SEE (请查看**) ALARMA, INDIGNANTE**

TRAVESÍA; travessia; *journey;*
crossing, voyage;
  háng chéng: 航程, *voyage, passage*;
  háng xíng (v) (n): 航行, *to sail/fly;*
voyage, trip;
  lù tú: 路途, *road, path; way, journey*;
SEE (请查看**) RUTA**

TREMENDO (A)**; tremendo** (A)**;**
terrible; tremendous, overpowering;
  bù kě dǐ kàng de: 不可抵抗的,
irresistible, overpowering;
  bù néng yā zhì de: 不能压制的,
irresistible, oppressive;
  jí bàng de: 极棒的, *tremendous*;
  nán yǐ yì zhì de: 难以抑制的,
overpowering (urge, desire, etc.);
SEE (请查看**) ENORME,**
ESTUPENDO, IRRESISTIBLE,
FORMIDABLE, TREMENDO,
DESORBITANTE

TRÉMULO; trêmulo (A)**;** *trembling,*
faltering; tremulous, shaky; quavering;
  bù jiān dìng (sv): 不坚定, *shaky*;
  bù kě kào (sv): 不可靠, *unreliable,*

shaky; untrustworthy;
  bù wěn (sv): 不稳, *unstable, unsteady;*
unsure, uncertain;
  bù wěn dìng (adj) (v): 不稳定,
unstable, unsteady; to stabilize;
  chàn dǒu (v) (sv): 颤抖, *to shake/*
quiver/shiver; tremulous, trembling;
  chéng wèn tí (v) (sv): 成问题, *to be a*
problem/open to question; questionable,
shaky;
  dǎn qiè (sv): 胆怯, *timid, cowardly;*
quavering, faltering;
  fā dǒu (v) (sv): 发抖, *to shiver/shake/*
quiver/ tremble; shaky;
  yáo huàng (sv) (v): 摇晃, *rocky, shaky;*
to rock/ sway/shake;
SEE (请查看**) INESTABLE,**
PRECARIO, FRÁGIL

TREPIDANTE; trepidante; *restive;*
frantic; intolerable, anxious;
  bù 'ān níng de: 不安宁的, *restive,*
anxious;
  wú fǎ rěn shòu de: 无法忍受的,
intolerable;
SEE (请查看**) APRENSIÓN,**
FRENÉTICO

TRIBULACIÓN; tribulação;
tribulation, hardship;
  kùn nan: 困难, *difficulty, problem;*
straitened circumstances; dire straits;
SEE (请查看**) DIFÍCIL**

TRIMESTRAL; trimestral; *trimester,*
quarterly;
  jì dù (n): 季度, *quarter of a year*;
  jì dù de: 季度的, *quarterly*;
  jì kān: 季刊, *quarterly (publication)*

TRIVIALIDAD; trivialidade; *triviality,*
triteness;
  suǒ (bf): 锁, *trivial, petty*;
  suǒ shì (n): 琐事, *trifle, trivial matter;*
triviality;
  suǒ suì (sv) (n): 琐碎, *trifling, trivial;*
slight indisposition, triviality;
  suǒ xì (sv): 琐细, *trifling, trivial*

TRÓPICO; trópico; *tropic*;
  huí guī xiàn: 回归线, *tropic*

TRUNCADO (A); **truncado** (A); *truncated, shortened; incomplete*;
  bù chè dǐ de: 不彻底的, *incomplete*;
  bù wán quán de: 不完全的, *incomplete*;
  bù wán shàn de: 不完善的, *imperfect*;
  cán quē (vp): 残缺, *incomplete, fragmentary*;
  wèi wán chéng de: 未完成的, *incomplete, unfinished*

TUBO; tubo; *tube*;
  guǎn dào: 管道, *pipeline, conduit; piping*;
  guǎn zi: 管子, *tube, pipe*

TUMULTO; tumulto; *commotion; riot, disturbance, uproar, turmoil*;
  sāo luàn (v) (n): 骚乱, *to create a disturbance; riot, chaos*;
SEE (请查看) **CAOS, CAÓTICO, DISTURBIO, CONFUSIÓN**

TÚNEL; túnel; *tunnel*;
  dì dào: 地道, *causeway*;
  kēng (n) (v): 坑, *hole, pit; tunnel, hollow; to bury alive*;
  kēng dào: 坑道, *gallery; tunnel*;
  suì dào: 隧道, *tunnel; tunnel in a mine; subterranean passage*

TÚNICA; túnica; *tunic, robe*;
  cháng páo: 长袍, *robe*;
  wú xiù shàng yī: 无袖上衣, *tunic*

TURBACIÓN; distúrbio; *upset, disturbance, alarm, worry* ... **TURBADO; perturbado** (A); *disturbed, alarmed, worried* ... **TURBADOR** (adj); **perturbador** (A); *disturbing, alarming, embarrassing*;
  bù 'ān de: 不安的, *disturbed, worried, anxious*;
  gān gà (sv): 尴尬, *embarrassed; awkward*;
  gān rǎo: 干扰, *disturbance*;

  jiào lǜ (sv): 焦虑, *anxious, apprehensive*;
  lìng rén bù 'ān de: 令人不安的, *disturbing*;
  lìng rén gān ga de: 令人尴尬的, *embarrassing*;
  lìng rén jīng kǒng de: 令人惊恐的, *alarming*;
  mèn mèn bù lè de: 闷闷不乐的, *worried*;
SEE (请查看) **TREPIDANTE, TORMENTA, TUMULTO, PREOCUPADO, ALARMA, ALARMANTE, APRENSIÓN**

TURBINA; turbina; *turbine*;
  wō lún ji: 涡轮机, *turbine*;
  wō lún: 涡轮, *turbine*

TURBIO; túrbido (A); *turbid, cloudy, muddy*;
  hún zhuó (sv): 混浊, *muddy, turbid*;
  ní nìng (sv) (n): 泥泞, *muddy, turbid; mire*;
SEE (请查看) **DESORDEN, CONFUNDIDO, CONFUSO, CAOS**

TURBULENCIA; turbulência; *turbulence, tumultuous, commotion ...*
TURBULENTO (A); **turbulento** (A); *turbulent, rebellious, stormy, troubled*;
  bào fēng yǔ (n) (sv): 暴风雨, *rainstorm, tempest; stormy*;
  bào fēng: 暴风, *storm, wind gale; storminess*;
  bào jǔ: 暴举, *savage/violent act*;
  duō shi (vp): 多事, *troubled, eventful*
  sāo luàn (sv): 骚乱, *turbulent, chaotic*;
SEE (请查看) **TUMULTO, TEMPESTAD, TURBULENTO, DISTURBIO, PREOCUPADO, INQUIETO, AGITADO, BRAVÍO, CAOS, DESCONCERTANTE**

TURGENTE; túrgido (A); *turgid, swollen, inflated; pompous*;
  zhàng gǎn: 胀感, *puffiness, bloatedness*;

zhǒng zhàng (vp) (sv) (v): 肿胀,
swelling; swollen; to swell/be swollen;
SEE (请查看) PRETENCIOSO,
OSTENTOSO

TURISMO; turismo; *tourism* ...
TURISTA; turista; *tourist*;
 lǚ yóu yè: 旅游业, *tourism*;
 yóu kè: 游客, *tourist*

Easily recognizable verbs and their Portuguese and Chinese equivalents
Verbos fácilmente reconocibles en Español-Portugués-Inglés y sus
equivalentes en Chino
Verbos facilmente reconhecível em Espanhol-Português-Inglês e seus
equivalentes em Chinês
很容易辨认的西班牙语，葡萄牙语，英语动词和他们的中文对等词

TABULAR; tabular; *to tabulate*;
 liè biǎo: 列表, *to tabulate*

TELEFONEAR; telefonar; *to
telephone*;
 dǎ diàn huà: 打电话, *to be on the
 telephone*

TELEVISAR; televisionar; *to televise*;
 diàn shì bō sòng: 电视播送, *to
 televise*

TEMER; temer; *to fear*;
 jù pà: 惧怕, *to fear/dread*;
 kǒng pà (v) (aux): 恐怕, *to fear; I'm
 afraid, I fear; perhaps, maybe*;
 wèi jù: 畏惧, *to fear/dread/be
 apprehensive*;
SEE (请查看) TEMOR

TERMINAR; terminar; *to finish*;
 (shǐ) wán dàn: (使) 完蛋, *to be done
 for; to be finished/destroyed*;
 (shǐ) wán měi: (使) 完美, *to perfect/
 consummate/finish*;
 (shǐ) wán shàn: (使) 完善, *to perfect/
 consummate/finish*;
 hào jìn (rv): 耗尽, *to exhaust/use up/
 finish*;
 yòng wán: 用完, *to finish/use up/
 exhaust*;
 zuò wán: 作完, *to finish doing sthg*;
SEE (请查看) APREHENDER,
DEDUCCIÓN, CONCLUIR

TIPIFICAR; tipificar; *to classify/
standardize/ typify*;

 fēn lèi (v) (n): 分类, *to classify/sort;
 classification, type*;
SEE (请查看) CLASIFICAR,
CATEGORIZAR, REGULARIZAR

TIRANIZAR; tiranizar; *to tyrannize/
domineer*;
 shī xíng bào zhèng: 施行暴政, *to
 tyrannize*;
 yā pò (v) (n): 压迫, *to oppress/repress;
 oppression, repression*

TOLERAR; tolerar; *to tolerate*;
 rěn shòu: 忍受, *to endure/bear*;
 róng xū (v) (adv): 容许, *to permit/
 tolerate; perhaps, possibly*;
SEE (请查看) RESISTIR, DURAR,
ACOMODAR, AUTORIZAR,
CONSENTIR

TORTURAR; torturar; *to torment/
torture*;
 shǐ tòng kǔ: 使痛苦, *to torment/
 torture*;
 zhé mó: 折磨, *to persecute/torment*

TRAFICAR; traficar; *to traffic in; to
deal in*;
 fàn mài: 贩卖, *to peddle/sell*;
SEE (请查看) NEGOCIO

TRANQUILIZAR; tranqüilizar; *to calm
(down)/ reassure*;
 shǐ ān xīn: 使安心, *to calm/reassure*;
 shǐ fàng xīn: 使放心, *to reassure*;
SEE (请查看) CONSOLACIÓN

TRANSCENDER (DE); **transcender;** *to transcend/ go beyond;*
  chāo yuè: 超越, *to exceed/surmount/ transcend/surpass*

TRANSFERIR; transferir; *to transfer/ convey/ hand over;*
  bān qiān: 搬迁, *to move/transfer/ relocate;*
  zhuǎn yí (v) (n): 转移, *to shift/transfer/ divert; to change/transform; transition, removal*

TRANSFORMAR; transformar; *to transform/ convert/modify;*
  biàn huà (v) (n): 变化, *to change/vary; change, transformation;*
SEE (请查看) **AJUSTAR, ALTERAR, REMEDIAR**

TRANSGREDIR; transgredir; *to transgress;*
  wéi fǎn: 违反, *to violate/transgress/ infringe*

TRANSMITIR; transmitir; *to transmit/ send/transfer;*
  chuán sòng: 传送, *to transmit/deliver;*
SEE (请查看) **AMPLIAR**

TRANSPORTAR; transportar; *to transport/ move/ transfer/send;*
  yùn shū (n) (v): 运输, *transport; to transport;*
SEE (请查看) **CONSIGNAR**

TRASPASAR; traspassar o transpassar; *to pierce/ penetrate;*
  chuān guò (rv): 穿过, *to pierce/pass through;*

cì (v) (n): 刺, *to stab/prick; to penetrate; to irritate; to criticize; thorn, splinter;*
dǎ rù: 打入, *to throw into/infiltrate; to pierce;*
kàn chuān (v): 看穿, *to see through (sb, sthg); to penetrate;*
shí pò: 识破, *to see through/penetrate;*
tòu guò: 透过, *to go through; via;*
SEE (请查看) **ADMITIR**

TRASPLANTAR; transplantar; *to transplant/ shift/uproot;*
  yí zhí (v) (n): 移植, *to transplant/graft; transplant, graft*

TRAUMATIZAR; traumatizar; *to injure/ traumatize/shock;*
  shāng (v) (n): 伤, *to injure/wound; injury, wound;*
SEE (请查看) **ARRUINAR**

TRUNCAR; truncar; *to truncate/ shorten/cut short;*
  jié duàn: 截断, *to cut off, block; to cut short/ interrupt; to divide/separate;*
  shān jié: 删节, *to delete and revise; to abbreviate/condense/shorten;*
SEE (请查看) **INTERCEPTAR, SEPARAR**

TUTELAR; tutelar; *to act as a guardian (DER); to protect/guard/supervise;*
  kān shǒu (v) (n): 看守, *to watch/ guard; turnkey;*
  shǒu wèi: 守卫, *to guard/defend;*
SEE (请查看) **ACTUAR, PROTECCIÓN, PREVENIR**

Interchangeable Spanish-Portuguese-English words and their Chinese equivalents
Palabras en Español-Portugués-Inglés y sus equivalentes en Chino
Palavras em Espanhol-Português-Inglês e seus equivalentes em Chinês
西班牙语，葡萄牙语，英语及中文的对等单词

ULTERIOR; ulterior;
 yǐn mì (sv) (n): 隐秘, *hidden, secret; secret;*
SEE (请查看) SECRETO, CLANDESTINIDAD

UMBILICAL; umbilical;
 qí dài: 脐带, *umbilical cord*

UNILATERAL; unilateral;
 dān fāng (attr) (n): 单方, *unilateral; one side; folk prescription, home remedy;*
 dān fāng miàn (attr) (n): 单方面, *one side; unilateral;*
 piàn miàn (sv): 片面, *unilateral, one-sided;*
SEE (请查看) UNÁNIME

UNIVERSAL; universal;
 quán shì jiè (n) (sv): 全世界, *the whole world; universal;*
SEE (请查看) DISEMINAR, UNIVERSALIDAD

UTOPÍA; utopia;
 wū tuō bāng: 乌托邦, *Utopia*

Easily recognizable Spanish-Portuguese-English nouns, adjectives and adverbs and their Chinese equivalents
Nombres, sustantivos, adjetivos y adverbios en Español-Portugués-Inglés y sus equivalentes en Chino
Nomes, substantivos, adjetivos e advérbios em Espanhol-Português-Inglês e seus equivalentes em Chinês
容易辨认的西班牙语，葡萄牙语，英语的名词，形容词和副词和他们的中文对等词

ÚLCERA; úlcera; *ulcer, sore (MED);*
 chuāng (n): 疮, *sore, skin ulcer; (bf) wound;*
 kuì yáng (n) (v): 溃疡, *ulcer; to ulcerate;*
 téng tòng (n): 疼痛, *ache, pain, soreness;*
 tòng (sv): 痛, *sore, painful*

ULTERIORMENTE; ulteriormente;
subsequently;
 hòu lái: 后来, *afterward, later, subsequent;*
 suí hòu (adv): 随后, *soon afterward; subsequently*

ULTIMACIÓN; conclusão; *conclusion, completion;*
 jié jú: 结局, *final result, outcome, ending, conclusion;*
SEE (请查看) CONCLUSIÓN, TÉRMINO, DEDUCCIÓN

ÚLTIMAMENTE; ultimamente;
recently, of late, lately;
 jìn lái (adv): 进来, *recently, lately;*
 zuì jìn (vp): 最近, *recently, lately; soon, in the near future*

ÚLTIMO (A); **último** (A); *last, ultimate;*
 zhōng jí (n) (attr): 终极, *end, final outcome; ultimate;*
SEE (请查看) DEFINITIVO, FINAL, TERMINAL, POSTRERO

ULTRAMAR; ultramar; *overseas, abroad;*
 hǎi wài: 海外, *overseas, abroad;*
 xiàng hǎi wài: 向海外, *overseas;*
 zài guó wài: 在国外, *abroad*

ULTRASÓNICO (A); **ultra-sônico** (A); *ultrasonic ...* **ULTRASONIDO; ultra-som;** *ultrasound;*
 chāo shēng bō (n): 超声波, *ultrasonic;*
 chāo yīn bō: 超音波, *ultrasonic wave, supersonic*

ULTRAVIOLETA; ultravioleta;
ultraviolet;
 zǐ wài (attr): 紫外, *ultraviolet;*
 zǐ wài guāng: 紫外光, *ultraviolet light;*
 zǐ wài xiàn: 紫外线, *ultraviolet*

UMBRAL; umbral; *doorway; threshold, verge;*
  mén kǎn (n): 门坎, *threshold;*
  mén kǒu: 门口, *entrance, doorway;*
  xiàn (bf) (n): 线, *brink, verge; demarcation line, boundary;*
SEE (请查看) MARGEN

UNÁNIME; unânime; *unanimous* **... UNANIMIDAD; unanimidade;** *unanimity*
  quán tǐ yī zhì (attr) (vp): 全体一致, *unanimous; to a man;*
  wú yì yì (vp): 无异议, *unanimous;*
SEE (请查看) UNILATERAL, UNIFICACIÓN

UNICIDAD; unicidade; *uniqueness* **... ÚNICO** (A); **único** (A); *only, unique, single;*
  kōng qián (vp): 空前, *unprecedented;*
  wéi yī (attr): 惟一, *only, sole; unparalleled, unequaled;*
  wú shuāng (vp): 无双, *unparalleled, unrivaled;*
SEE (请查看) DIFERENCIA, SOLAMENTE, SOLO, EXÓTICO

UNIDO (A); **unido** (A); *joined; united, close; close-knit;*
  jié gòu jǐn mì (sv): 结构紧密, *close-knit;*
  jǐn mì (sv): 紧密, *close, together, inseparable;*
  qì yǒu: 契友, *close friend;*
  tiē xīn rén: 贴心人, *close friend;*
SEE (请查看) APROXIMAR, ÍNTIMO, CORDIALIDAD, CONEXIÓN, CONJUNTO, CONECTAR, RECÍPROCO

UNIDIRECCIONAL; unidirecional; *unidirectional, one way;*
  dān biān (attr): 单边, *unilateral (FIN);*
  dān cè (attr): 单侧, *unilateral;*
  dān chéng (attr): 单程, *one-way;*
  dān chéng piào: 单程票, *one-way ticket;*
  dān fāng miàn: 单方面, *one side; unilateral;*
  dān xiàng (attr): 单向, *one-way, unidirectional;*
  dān xiàng lù: 单项路, *one-way street;*
  dān xíng dào: 单行道, *one-way street/ traffic;*
  dān xíng xiàn: 单行线, *one-way road*

UNIFICACIÓN; unificação; *unification, standardization* **... UNIFICADOR** (A); **unificador** (A); *unifying;*
  tǒng yī (attr) (sv): 统一, *unified, centralized; unifying;*
  xiāng pèi (sv): 相配, *match, fit;*
SEE (请查看) COHESIONAR, CORRESPONDIENTE, EQUIVALENTE, NORMATIVO, SIMILITUD, REGULARIZAR

UNIFORME; uniforme; *uniform, even, smooth, level* **... UNIFORMIDAD; uniformidade;** *uniformity, regularity; evenness, smoothness;*
  guāng huá (sv): 光滑, *smooth; glossy, sleek;*
  píng (sv) (bf) (v): 平, *flat, level, even; ordinary, common, uniform; to level/ pacify/make peace;*
  píng tǎn (sv): 平坦, *level, even, smooth, flat;*
  yī zhì (sv) (n): 一致, *identical, unanimous, consistent; agreement; uniformity, consistency;*
SEE (请查看) DUPLICADO

UNIPERSONAL (adj); **unipessoal;** *single, individual;*
  dān gè (attr) (adv) (n): 单个, *single, alone, individually; an odd one;*
  dān rén: 单人, *single person (for one person) ;*
  dān shēn (n) (attr): 单身, *unmarried/ single person; alone, unaccompanied;*
  dān yī (attr): 单一, *single, unitary;*
  wèi hūn (attr): 未婚, *unmarried, single;*
SEE (请查看) ATÍPICO

UNIVERSIDAD; universidade; *university, institute;*
  dà xué: 大学, *university, college*

UNIVERSO; universo; *universe (ASTROM);*
  yǔ zhòu: 宇宙, *universe, cosmos*

URBANO (A); **urbano** (A); *urban, urbane;*
  bīn bīn yǒu lǐ de: 彬彬有礼的, *urbane;*
  chéng shì: 城市, *town, city;*
  chéng shì de: 城市的, *urban*

URBE; urbe; *large city, metropolis;*
  (dà) dū shì: (大) 都市, *(big, great) city, metropolis;*
  dū huì: 都会, *city, metropolis*

URGENCIA; urgência; *urgency, emergency (MED), urgent need ...*
URGENTE; urgente; *urgent, express, pressing, rush ...* **URGENTEMENTE** (adv); **urgentemente;** *urgently;*
  jí pò (sv) (n): 急迫, *urgent, pressing, imperative; urgency;*
  jí qiè (sv): 急切, *eager, impatient; in a hurry;*
  jǐn pò (sv): 紧迫, *pressing, imminent;*
  pò qiè (sv) (n): 迫切, *urgent, pressing, imperative; urgency;*
  tè kuài (n): 特快, *express;*
SEE (请查看**) EMERGENCIA, EXPRÉS**

USADO (A); **usado** (A); *secondhand, used;*
  èr shǒu (attr): 二手, *secondhand;*
  yòng guò de: 用过的, *used;*

SEE (请查看**) APLICAR**

USURA; usura; *avarice; usury*
... USURARIO (A); **usurário** (A); *avaricious; usurious ...* **USURERO** (A); **usurário** (A); *usurer;*
  gāo lì dài (sv) (n): 高利贷, *usurious; usury;*
  gāo lì dài zhě: 高利贷者, *usurer;*
SEE (请查看**) AVARICIA**

UTENSILIO; utensílio; *tool, implement, utensil;*
  jiā huo: 家伙, *implement, tool;*
  qì mǐn: 器皿, *household utensils;*
SEE (请查看**) ARTEFACTO**

UTILIDAD; utilidade; *usefulness, utility ...* **UTILIZABLE; utilizável;** *utilizable, practical; useable, available, ready for use;*
  gōng lì: 功力, *skill, craftsmanship; utility; efficiency;*
  jiù xù (vp): 就绪, *to be in order, be ready;*
  kě yǐ shǐ yòng de: 可以使用的, *available;*
  kě yǒng (vp): 可用, *available, usable;*
  yì yú shǐ yòng de: 易于使用的, *user-friendly;*
  yǒu yòng (sv): 有用, *useful;*
SEE (请查看**) AUXILIO, EFECTIVIDAD, CONSTRUCTIVO, REALIZABLE**

Easily recognizable verbs and their Portuguese and Chinese equivalents
Verbos fácilmente reconocibles en Español-Portugués-Inglés y sus equivalentes en Chino
Verbos facilmente reconhecível em Espanhol-Português-Inglês e seus equivalentes em Chinês
很容易辨认的西班牙语，葡萄牙语，英语动词和他们的中文对等词

ULTIMAR; ultimar; *to conclude/finalize/ finish, complete;*
  wán chéng: 完成, *to complete/ accomplish/fulfill;*
SEE (请查看**) DEDUCCIÓN, CONCLUIR**

ULULAR; ulular; *to scream/howl/ ululate;*
  jiān jiào: 尖叫, *to scream;*
  jiào hǎn: 叫喊, *to shout/howl/scream*

UNIFICAR; unificar; *to unite/join/ unify;*

(shǐ) lián hé: (使) 联合, *to unite/ally*;
(shǐ) tuán jié (n) (v): (使) 团结, *to unite/rally*;
lián jié: 联合, *to join/link*

UNIFORMIZAR; uniformizar, *to standardize/blend*;
  shǐ biāo zhǔn huà: 使标准化, *to standardize*

URBANIZAR; urbanizar; *to urbanize/ become civilized/develop*;
  jiào huà (v) (n): 教化, *to educate; culture*;
SEE (请查看) CIVILIZAR

USAR; usar; *to use (GEN), to wear out*;
  bù néng zài yòng: 不能再用, *to wear out*;

chuān pò: 穿破, *to wear out/perforate sthg*;
yòng huài: 用坏, *to wear out*

USURPAR; usurpar; *to usurp/ encroach/seize*;
  cuàn duó: 篡夺, *to usurp/seize*;
  qīn zhàn: 侵占, *to invade and occupy/ seize*

UTILIZAR; utilizar; *to use/make use of/ utilize*;
  shǐ chū: 使出, *to use/exert*;
  xiāo hào: 消耗, *to consume/use up/ deplete*;
  yùn yòng: 运用, *to use/wield/apply*;
SEE (请查看) APLICAR, CAPITALIZAR, HABITAR

Interchangeable Spanish-Portuguese-English words and their Chinese equivalents
Palabras en Español-Portugués-Inglés y sus equivalentes en Chino
Palavras em Espanhol-Português-Inglês e seus equivalentes em Chinês
西班牙语，葡萄牙语，英语及中文的对等单词

VAPOR; vapor; *steam*;
  rè qì: 热气, *steam, hot vapor; hot gas/ air; ardor, fervor*;
  shuǐ qì: 水气, *vapor, steam, moisture*;
  zhēng qì: 蒸气, *vapor, steam (FIS)*

VERBAL; verbal;
  dòng cí de: 动词的, *verbal*;
  kǒu tóu de: 口头的, *verbal, oral*;
  yǔ yán de: 语言的, *verbal*

VERSUS; versus;
  duì: 对, *versus*;
  duì (bf): 对, *opposite*

VÉRTEBRA; vértebra;
  jǐ zhù: 脊柱, *spinal column*;
  jǐ zhuī gǔ: 脊椎骨, *vertebra, spine, backbone*

VERTICAL; vertical;
  chuí zhí (attr): 垂直, *vertical; perpendicular*;
  lì shì (attr): 立式, *vertical, upright*;
  zhí lì (v) (sv): 直立, *to stand erect/ straight; vertical*

VETO; veto;
  fǒu jué (v) (n): 否决, *to veto/vote down/overrule; veto*;
SEE (请查看) BOICOT

VICEVERSA ó VICE VERSA; vice-versa;
  fǎn zhī yì rán: 反之亦然, *vice-versa*

VIDEO; vídeo (GEN); *system, recorder …*
VIDEOCASSETTE ó VIDEOCASETE;

videocassete; *video cassette*;
lù xiàng dài: 录像带, *video cassette,
videotape*;
lù xiàng jī: 录像机, *video recorder*;
lù xiàng: 录像, *video system, videotape*

VIOLA; viola;
zhōng tí qín: 中提琴, *viola*

VIRTUAL; virtual (TECNOL);
xū nǐ xiàn shí: 虚拟现实, *virtual*;
SEE (请查看) DUPLICIDAD,
POSITIVO

VIRUS; vírus;
bìng dú: 病毒, *virus*;
xì jūn: 细菌, *germ, bacterium, virus*;
SEE (请查看) BUG

VISCERAL; visceral (GEN);
nèi zàng de: 内脏的, *visceral*;
nèi zàng: 内脏, *internal organs, viscera*

VISOR; visor; *viewfinder* (FOTO);
qǔ jǐng qì: 取景器, *viewfinder*

VISUAL; visual;
shì jué (n) (sv): 视觉, *visual sense,
vision; visual*;
shì lì (n) (sv): 视力, *vision, sight; visual*

VITAL; vital;
bì yào de: 必要的, *necessary, essential,
indispensable*;
SEE (请查看) NECESARIO,
ESENCIAL, INDISPENSABLE,
CÉNTRICO, SUSTANCIAL

VOCAL; vocal;
fā shēng (v) (sv): 发声, *to produce
sound; vocal*;
shēng yīn (n) (sv): 声音, *sound, voice;
vocal*

VOYEUR; voyeur;
tōu kuī zhě: 偷窥者, *voyeur*

VULGAR; vulgar; *common, coarse,
vulgar*;
cū sú (sv): 粗俗, *vulgar, coarse, earthy*;
yōng sú (sv): 庸俗, *vulgar, philistine*;
SEE (请查看) ABRASIVO, BANAL,
GROSERO

**Easily recognizable Spanish-Portuguese-English nouns, adjectives and
adverbs and their Chinese equivalents
Nombres, sustantivos, adjetivos y adverbios en Español-Portugués-Inglés y
sus equivalentes en Chino
Nomes, substantivos, adjetivos e advérbios em Espanhol-Português-Inglês
e seus equivalentes em Chinês**
容易辨认的西班牙语，葡萄牙语，英语的名词，形容词和副词和他们的中文对等词

VACANTE (adj); vacante; *vacant,
empty; vacancy (n)*;
kòng bái (n): 空白, *blank space*;
kòng bái diǎn (n): 空白点, *blank,
blank spot*;
kōng dàng (n): 空荡, *deserted, empty*;
kōng dào (n): 空道, *deserted way/
road*;
kòng 'é (n): 空额, *vacancy*;
kòng fáng: 空房, *vacant room; vacant/
deserted house*;
kōng pì (sv): 空僻, *empty and quiet (of
a place)*;

kōng píng (n): 空瓶, *empty bottle*;
kòng yú (attr): 空余, *spare, extra; free;
vacant, unoccupied*;
quē (v) (n): 缺, *to be short of/lack;
vacancy, opening*;
quē biān (attr) (n): 缺编, *understaffed;
vacancy*;
quē 'é: 缺额, *vacancy; opening (job
position)*;
SEE (请查看) ABANDONADO,
ABANDONAR, DESHABITADO

VACILACIÓN; vacilação; *hesitation,*

indecision, vacillation ... **VACILANTE;**
vacilante; *hesitant, indecisive, faltering*;
 chí yí (v) (n): 迟疑, *to hesitate/falter; hesitation*;
 chí yí bù jué de: 迟疑不决的, *hesitant; (fe) to be uncertain/irresolute/ undecided*;
 chóu chú: 踌躇, *hesitation, vacillation*;
 yōu róu (vp): 优柔, *indecisive, hesitating*;
 yōu róu guǎ duàn de: 优柔寡断的, *indecisive*;
 yóu yù (v) (sv): 犹豫, *to hesitate/be irresolute; hesitant, wavering*;
 yóu yù bù jué (bf): 犹豫不决, *shilly-shally*;
 yóu yù bù jué de: 犹豫不决的, *indecisive*;

VACIO (A); **vácuo;** *vacuum (FIS); low (METEO); vacant, empty*;
 dī shuǐ píng: 低水平, *low*;
 kòng bái: 空白, *vacuum, blank, space*;
 zhēn kōng: 真空, *vacuum (FIS)*;
SEE (请查看**) VACANTE**

VACUIDAD; vacuidade; *shallowness, vacuity* ... **VACUO** (A); **vácuo;** *vacuum, void; shallow, vacuous*;
 kōng (sv): 空, *empty, hollow, void; fictitious, unreal, impractical; vain and useless; (bf) sky, space; (n) emptiness, void; (v) to empty/exhaust; to leave empty*;
 méi yǒu (v) (adv) (sv): 没有, *to not have, there is not, to be void; to be without; less than, not more than; void*;
 piāo fú (v) (vp): 漂浮, *to float; superficial, showy*;
 qiǎn (sv) (sv) (n): 浅, *shallow, superficial; easy, simple; not close/ intimate; shallowness*;
 wú yì yì (vp): 无意义, *to lack meaning, be meaningless*;
 zhēn kōng (n) (sv): 真空, *vacuum (FIS); vacuum*;
SEE (请查看**) VACÍO, VACANTE, FRÍVOLO, ESTUPIDEZ**

VAGABUNDO (A); **vagabundo** (A);
vagabond, tramp; wandering, roving; stray;
 liú làng zhě: 流浪者, *tramp, vagrant*;
 piāo bó (n) (v): 漂泊, *vagrant; to drift aimlessly*;
 piāo bó bù dìng (fe): 漂泊不定, *to drift about/lead a vagrant life*;
 yóu mín: 游民, *vagrant, vagabond*;
SEE (请查看**) BRONCO**

VAGAMENTE; vagamente; *vaguely, indistinctly*;
 bù qīng chǔ de: 不清楚的, *unclear, indistinct*;
 bù qīng xī de: 不清晰的, *indistinct, unclear*;
 bù què qiè de: 不确切的, *unclear and ambiguous*;
 hán hú bù qīng (fe): 含糊不清, *vague, woolly*;
 hán hú qí cí (fe): 含糊其辞, *equivocal*;
 hán hùn (vp): 含混, *indistinct, ambiguous*;
 hán hú bù míng (fe): 含糊不明, *vague and ambiguous*;
 máng rán (sv) (sv): 茫然, *boundless and indistinct, vast; ignorant, in the dark; at a loss; distracted, vague; vaguely*;
 yǐn yuē (vp): 隐约, *indistinct, faint, vague*;
SEE (请查看**) VACÍO, VACUIDAD, DESOCUPADO, NEBULOSO**

VÁLIDO (A); **válido** (A); *valid*;
 lìng rén xìn fú de: 令人信服的, *valid (argument, reason, etc.)*;
SEE (请查看**) EFECTIVIDAD**

VALIOSO (A) (adj); **valioso** (A);
valuable, precious, costly; cherished ...
VALOR; valor; *value, worth; desirability, utility* ... **VALORACIÓN; valorização;**
valuation, assessment;
 bǎo guì (sv) (v): 宝贵, *valuable, precious; to value/set store by*;
 gū jià (v) (n): 估价, *to appraise/ evaluate; appraisal, valuation*;
 guì zhòng (sv): 贵重, *valuable, precious*;
 kě guì (sv): 可贵, *valuable,*

praiseworthy;
píng jià (v) (n): 评价, *to appraise/ evaluate; evaluation*;
wú jià (attr): 无价, *priceless, invaluable*;
wú jià zhī bǎo (n): 无价之宝, *priceless treasure, invaluable asset*;
zhēn (bf): 珍, *precious, rare*;
zhēn guì (sv): 珍贵, *valuable, precious*;
zhēn qí (attr): 珍奇, *rare*;
zhēn yì (attr): 珍异, *rare*;
zhí qián (sv): 值钱, *costly, valuable*;
SEE (请查看) **COSTOSO, MÉRITO**

VÁLVULA; válvula; *valve (MECAN)*;
huó mén: 活门, *valve*

VAMPIRO; vampiro; *vampire*;
xī xuè guǐ: 吸血鬼, *vampire, bloodsucker*

VANAGLORIA; vanglória; *vainglory, extreme vanity* ... **VANIDAD; vaidade;** *vanity, conceit; arrogance, pride* ...
VANIDOSO (A); **vaidoso** (A); *vain, conceited*;
ài xū róng de: 爱虚荣的, *vainglorious*;
ài xū róng: 爱虚荣, *vainglory*;
jiāo 'ào gǎn (n): 骄傲感, *self-satisfaction, pride*;
jiāo 'ào zì mǎn (fe): 骄傲自满, *be conceited and arrogant*;
xū róng xīn: 虚荣心, *vanity*;
xū róng: 虚荣, *vanity*;
zì fù: 自负, *vanity, conceit*;
zì gāo zì dà (fe): 自高自大, *conceited, arrogant, self-important*;
zì gāo zì dà de: 自高自大的, *conceited, self-important, arrogant*;
SEE (请查看) **ARROGANCIA**

VANDALISMO; vandalismo; *vandalism, damage, injury, loss* ...
VÁNDALO (A); **vândalo** (A); *loutish; vandal, hooligan*;
cū rén: 粗人, *rough fellow, boor*;
è gùn: 恶棍, *scoundrel, rogue, bully*;
liú máng: 流氓, *hooligan, hoodlum, gangster*;
xù yì pò huài gōng wù de xíng wéi: 蓄意破坏公物的行为, *vandalism*;
xù yì pò huài gōng wù zhě: 蓄意破

坏公物者, *vandal*;
SEE (请查看) **GÁNGSTER**

VANGUARDIA; vanguarda; *vanguard, forefront, spearhead*;
jiān bīng: 尖兵, *pioneer, trailblazer; vanguard*;
xiān fēng: 先锋, *vanguard*;
xiān qū zhě: 先驱者, *pioneer*;
xiān qū: 先驱, *pioneer, forerunner, harbinger, predecessor*;
zuì qián xiàn: 最前线, *forefront*;
SEE (请查看) **AVANZADO**

VANO (A); **vão** (A); *worthless, futile; vain, empty, groundless*;
háo wú jià zhí de: 毫无价值的, *worthless*;
méi yòng (sv) (v): 没用, *useless; to be useless*;
nóng bāo: 脓包, *pustule (MED); worthless person*;
tú láo: 徒劳, *futile/fruitless labor/effort*;
wú gēn jù de: 无根据的, *groundless, worthless*;
wú xiào yì de: 无效益的, *vain, unprofitable*;
SEE (请查看) **INVÁLIDO**

VAPORIZADOR; vaporizador; *vaporizer*;
pēn wù qì: 喷雾器, *vaporizer*

VARIADO (A); **variado** (A); *varied, assorted, mixed* ... **VARIANTE; variante;** *version, variety, variant* ...
VARIEDAD; variedade; *variety* ...
VARIO (A) ó **VARIOS; vário** (A); *diverse; several, various; motley*;
bǎn běn (n): 版本, *edition (of a book), version*;
biàn tǐ (n): 变体, *variety; deviant style (lg)* ;
duō bèi (attr): 多倍, *multiple*;
duō chóng (attr): 多重, *multiple, diverse*;
duō duān (n): 多端, *many kinds, many ways; a great variety*;
duō fāng miàn (attr): 多方面, *many-faceted, in many ways, many-sided*;
duō zhǒng duō yàng (fe): 多种多样,

diverse; varied;

fēng fù duō cǎi (fe): 丰富多彩, *rich and varied*;

gè zhǒng gè yàng (fe): 各种各样, *all sorts/ varieties*;

gè zhǒng gè yàng de: 各种各样的, *assorted; various*;

hào fán (sv): 浩繁, *vast; many and numerous; varied*;

huā yàng: 花样, *pattern, variety*;

huā yàng bǎi chū (fe): 花样百出, *a great variety*;

ruò gān: 若干, *varied*;

shí (bf): 什, *assorted, various, miscellaneous*;

shí jǐn (attr): 什锦, *assorted, mixed*;

shuō fǎ: 说法, *version*;

xíng xíng sè sè (): 形形色色, *mixed, of every shade and description*;

xǔ duō (attr): 许多, *many, much, a lot of, various*;

xǔ duō zhǒng: 许多种, *variety*;

zhǒng lèi (n): 种类, *kind, type, variety; category*;

SEE (请查看) DESIGUAL, DIFERENCIA, DIVERSIDAD, DIVERSO, DIVERSIFICAR

VARONIL; varonil; *virile, manly, mannish*;

qiáng jiàn (sv): 强健, *strong and healthy*;

yǒu nán zǐ qì: 有男子气, *manly*;

SEE (请查看) MASCULINO

VASO; vaso; *pot, flower vase, glass*;

chá hú (n): 茶壶, *teapot*;

guàn (m): 罐, *vessel, container; jug, jar; can, tin*;

guō (n): 锅, *pot, pan, wok, boiler; bowl (of a pipe, etc.)*;

guō zi: 锅子, *bowl, chafing dish; pot, pan*;

hú (n): 壶, *kettle, pot; bottle, flask; jar*;

huā pén (n): 花盆, *flowerpot*;

huā píng (n): 花瓶, *flower vase; a secretary kept only because of her looks; a pretty and coquettish woman*;

kā fēi hú (n): 咖啡壶, *coffee pot*;

niào hú (n): 尿壶, *chamber pot*;

yī hú chá: 一壶茶, *a pot of tea*;

yī hú kā fēi: 一壶咖啡, *a pot of coffee*;

SEE (请查看) POTE

VASTO (A); **vasto** (A); *vast, wide, huge*;

hào dàng (vp): 浩荡, *vast and mighty; irresolute*;

SEE (请查看) DESMEDIDO, DILATADO, ABISMAL, GIGANTESCO, INMENSO, GRANDIOSO

VEGETACIÓN; vegetação; *vegetation* ... **VEGETAL** (adj); **vegetal;** *vegetable; plant*;

cǎo mù: 草木, *vegetation*;

shū cài: 蔬菜, *vegetables and greens*;

zhí wù: 植物, *vegetation, plant*

VEGETARIANO (A); **vegetariano** (A); *vegetarian*;

sù shí zhě: 素食者, *vegetarian*

VEHEMENTE; veemente; *vehement, forceful, ardent*;

jī liè (sv): 激烈, *intense, sharp, fierce, acute; vehement*;

pō là (sv): 泼辣, *bad-tempered, aggressive; forceful*;

rè xīn (sv) (n): 热心, *enthusiastic, ardent; enthusiasm*;

SEE (请查看) DRÁSTICO, EFUSIVO

VEHÍCULO; veículo; *vehicle; carrier* (MED);

chē liàng: 车辆, *vehicles, cars*

VELOCIDAD; velocidade; *speed* (GEN), *velocity*;

sù dù: 速度, *speed, velocity*;

sù lǜ: 速率, *speed, rate of speed*

VELOCÍMETRO; velocímetro; *speedometer*;

jì sù qì: 计速器, *speedometer*

VELOCISTA; velocista; *sprinter*;

duǎn pǎo jiàn jiàng: 短跑健将, *sprinter; short distance runner*

VENDIBLE (adj); **vendável;** *salable,*

marketable;
   yǒu xiāo lù de: 有销路的, *marketable*

VENENO; veneno; *poison, venom,
toxin; malice, spite* **... VENENOSO** (A);
VENENOSO (A); *poisonous, venomous;
malicious;*
   dú (n) (v) (sv): 毒, *poison, toxin;
   narcotics; to kill with poison; poisonous,
   malicious, cruel;*
   dú zhī (n): 毒汁, *venom, poisonous
   fluid;*
   huái yǒu è yì de: 怀有恶意的,
   spiteful;
   jiān xiǎn (sv): 艰险, *treacherous/
   malicious person, wicked, wily;*
   xià dú (n): 下毒, *poisoning;*
SEE (请查看**) TÓXICO, INTOXICAR,
MALICIA, MALICIOSO, CRUEL**

VENÉREO (A); **venéreo** (A); *venereal
(MED);*
   xìng bìng: 性病, *venereal disease*

VENTILACIÓN; ventilação; *ventilation*
... VENTILADOR; ventilador;
ventilator, fan, air vent;
   hū xī qì: 呼吸器, *ventilator (MED);*
   tōng fēng jī: 通风机, *ventilator, fan,
   air pump;*
   tōng fēng jǐng: 通风井, *ventilation/
   air shaft;*
   tōng fēng shè bèi: 通风设备,
   ventilating system/ facilities

VENTOSO (A); **ventoso** (A); *windy,
blustery, gusty, blowing;*
   duō fēng de: 多风的, *windy;*
   fēng dà de: 风大的, *windy;*
   fēng kuáng chuī de: 风狂吹的,
   blustery;
   kuáng chuī (v): 狂吹, *to blow
   violently/wildly;*
   kuáng fēng: 狂风, *gale-force wind;*
   yī zhèn (n): 一阵, *a burst of temper/
   rain/wind, etc. ;*
   zhèn fēng (n): 阵风, *gust of wind;*
   zhèn fēng de: 阵风的, *gusty*

VERACIDAD; veracidade;
truthfulness, veracity **... VERAZ; veraz;**
truthful;
   chéng shí de: 诚实的, *truthful;*
   rú shí de: 如实地, *truthful, according
   to the facts;*
   zhēn shí xìng: 真实性, *truthfulness,
   authenticity, validity;*
   zhèng què dù: 正确度, *accuracy,
   truthfulness;*
SEE (请查看**) CONFIANZA,
HONESTIDAD**

VERBO; verbo; *verb;*
   dòng cí: 动词, *verb*

VERBOSO (A) (adj); **verborrágico** (A);
verbose, wordy;
   duō yán (attr): 多言, *talkative;*
   duō yán de: 多言的, *verbose;*
   luō suo (sv): 罗嗦, *long and tedious,
   redundant, superfluous; verbose (writing)*

VERDAD; verdade; *the truth;
real* **... VERDADERAMENTE;
verdadeiramente;** *truly; really;*
   shì shí: 事实, *fact, point of fact, real;*
   zhēn (sv) (adv): 真, *true, real, genuine;
   really, truly, indeed; clearly;*
   zhēn lǐ: 真理, *truth;*
SEE (请查看**) CORRESPONDIENTE,
REALMENTE**

VEREDICTO; veredicto; *verdict (DER);*
   dìng lùn: 定论, *final conclusion;
   accepted argument;*
   SEE (请查看**) ADJUDICAR**

VERIFICACIÓN (n); **verificação;**
verification, confirmation;
   hé shí (v) (n): 核实, *to verify/check; on-
   the-spot investigation;*
   què rèn (n) (v): 确认, *verification; to
   affirm/confirm;*
SEE (请查看**) APROBACIÓN**

VERNÁCULO (A) (adj); **vernáculo** (A);
vernacular, jargon, dialect;
   bái huà: 白话, *vernacular;*
   tǔ huà: 土话, *local/colloquial
   expressions/dialect; slang*

VERSÁTIL; versátil; *versatile; fickle*
... VERSATILIDAD; versatilidade;
versatility; fickleness;
  duō biān (attr): 多边, *multilateral;*
  fickle, changeable;
  duō cái duō yì (fe): 多才多艺,
  versatile; gifted in many ways;
  tōng yòng (vp) (attr): 通用, *in common*
  use, current, general; interchangeable;
  versatility;
  yì biàn: 易变, *fickle*

VERSO; verso; *verse, poem;*
  shī: 诗, *poetry, verse, poem, hymn;*
  yùn wén: 韵文, *prose, poetry*

VERTEBRADO (A); **vertebrado** (A);
vertebrate;
  jǐ zhuī dòng wù: 脊椎动物,
  vertebrate;
SEE (请查看) **VÉRTEBRA**

VESTÍBULO; vestíbulo; *entrance hall,*
lobby, foyer, vestibule;
  dà tīng: 大厅, *main hall; lobby, hall;*
  jìn kǒu (v) (n): 进口, *to import;*
  entrance;
  mén kǒu: 门口, *entrance, doorway;*
  mén tīng: 门厅, *entrance hall,*
  vestibule;
  tōng dào: 通道, *passageway*

VESTIGIO; vestígio; *vestige, sign,*
trace; suggestion, hint;
  hén jì: 痕迹, *mark, trace, vestige;*
  jì xiàng: 迹象, *sign, indication;*
  wēi liàng: 微量, *trace;*
  yí jì (n): 遗迹, *historical remains,*
  vestiges, traces;
  zōng jì: 踪迹, *trace, track;*
SEE (请查看) **MARCA**

VETERANO (A); **veterano** (A); *veteran*
(MIL); *experienced, old hand;*
  lǎo bīng: 老兵, *old soldier, veteran;*
  tuì yì jūn rén: 退役军人, *military*
  veteran

VETERINARIO (A); **veterinário** (A);
veterinary (adj), veterinary doctor (n);
  shòu yī: 兽医, *veterinarian, vet;*

shòu yī xué: 兽医学, *veterinary*
medicine/science

VIABILIDAD; viabilidade; *viability,*
feasibility, possibility;
  kě shí shī de: 可实施的, *feasible;*
  viable;
  kě xíng xìng: 可行性, *feasibility;*
  viability;
SEE (请查看) **POSIBLE, FACTIBLE,**
CONTINGENCIA

VIADUCTO; viaduto; *viaduct;*
  gāo jià qiáo: 高架桥, *viaduct*

VÍBORA; víbora; *viper;*
  dú shé: 毒蛇, *viper*

VIBRACIÓN; vibração; *vibration ...*
VIBRADOR (A); **vibrador** (A); *vibrating*
(adj), vibrator (n) **... VIBRANTE;**
vibrante; *vibrating, vibrant, resonant;*
  huí shēng de: 回声的, *resonant;*
  yòu huò lì (sv) (n): 诱惑力, *vibrant;*
  attractiveness;
  zhèn dòng qì: 震动器, *vibrator,*
  oscillator

VICIO; vício; *vice, bad habit; fault,*
shortcoming;
  quē hàn: 缺憾, *flaw, shortcoming,*
  defect;
SEE (请查看) **DEBILIDAD**

VICIOSO (A); **vicioso** (A); *corrupt,*
vicious; dissolute, depraved;
  fǔ huà duò luò (fe): 腐化堕落,
  depraved; to be corrupt and degenerate;
  fǔ huà fèn zǐ: 腐化分子, *a corrupt/*
  depraved/ degenerate person;
  tān wū (attr) (n): 贪污, *corrupt, venal;*
  corruption, graft;
SEE (请查看) **PERVERTIDO,**
DEPRAVADO, BRUTAL, ATROZ,
MALICIOSO, MAL, CRUEL,
DECADENTE, CORRUPCIÓN,
ORGÍA

VICISITUD; vicissitude; *vicissitude;*
uncertainty, shift, change;
  biàn qiān (n) (v): 变迁, *vicissitudes/*

changes; to change;
xīng shuāi (n): 兴衰, *rise and decline; ups and downs; vicissitudes*

VÍCTIMA; vítima; *victim, casualty;*
  shòu hài rén: 受害人, *victim, victimized party;*
  shòu hài zhě: 受害者, *victim;*
  xī shēng pǐn: 牺牲品, *victim, prey; loss leader;*
  yù nàn zhě: 遇难者, *victim*

VIGENCIA; vigência; *validity, applicability; authenticity* ... **VIGENTE; vigente;** *in force, in use, current;*
  kě kào xìng (n): 可靠性, *reliability, authenticity;*
  liú xíng de: 流行的, *prevalent, popular, fashionable;*
  què shí xìng: 确实性, *authenticity, validity*
  shí yòng xìng: 实用性, *suitability, applicability;*
  zhēn shí xìng (n): 真实性, *truthfulness, authenticity, validity;*
  zhèng què xìng: 正确性, *validity;*
SEE (请查看) **ACTUALIDAD, TENDENCIA**

VIGÍA; vigia; *surveillance, watch tower, lookout;*
  dīng shāo (n) (v): 盯梢, *surveillance, observation; to shadow/tail sb;*
SEE (请查看) **MONITORIZAR**

VIGILANCIA; vigilância; *vigilance, care* ... **VIGILANTE; vigilante;** *vigilant (adj), guard, watchman (n);*
  jǐng jué xìng: 警觉性, *vigilance, alertness;*
  jǐng tì (n) (v): 警惕, *vigilance; to be on guard against*

VIGOROSO (A); **vigoroso** (A); *vigorous, energetic; strenuous;*
  jīng lì chōng pèi de: 精力充沛的, *energetic;*
  jīng shen (n) (sv): 精神, *vigor; animated;*
  qiáng jìng (sv): 强劲, *powerful,*

forceful, vigorous;
  yǒu lì (sv) (v): 有力, *strong, forceful, powerful, energetic, vigorous;*
SEE (请查看) **EFUSIVO, ENÉRGICO**

VINO; vinho; *wine;*
  pú tao jiǔ: 葡萄酒, *grape wine*

VIOLENCIA; violência; *violence, vehemence, ferocity* ... **VIOLENTO** (A); **violento** (A); *violent, intense, forceful, powerful;*
  bào lì (n): 暴力, *violence, force;*
  bào liè (sv): 暴烈, *violent, fierce;*
  kuáng (sv) (n): 狂, *mad, crazy; violent, wild, unrestrained; arrogant, overbearing; mania, insanity;*
  měng hàn (vp): 猛焊, *bold and vigorous; violent, ferocious;*
  měng lì (sv): 猛力, *fierce, vigorous, violent;*
  měng měng rán (adv): 猛猛然, *suddenly, abruptly;*
  měng ruì (vp): 猛锐, *bold, forceful, dashing;*
  qiáng dà (sv): 强大, *big and powerful, formidable;*
  qiáng liè (sv): 强烈, *strong, intense, violent; distinct, clear cut, striking, sharp;*
  yǒu shuō fú lì (v) (sv): 有说服力, *convincing, persuasive, forceful;*
SEE (请查看) **BRAVÍO, FANÁTICO, DRÁSTICO, POTENTE, FRENÉTICO**

VIOLETA; violeta; *violet□;*
  zǐ luó lán: 紫罗兰, *violet (the flower);*
  zǐ luó lán sè de: 紫罗兰色的, *violet (the color)*

VIOLINISTA; violinista; *violinist;*
  xiǎo tí qín shǒu: 小提琴手, *violinist*

VIRIL; viril; *virile, manly, macho* ... **VIRILIDAD; virilidade;** *virility, manliness, machismo;*
  dà nán zǐ qì gài de: 大男子气概的, *macho;*
  nán xìng (n) (sv): 男性, *male sex, man; manly;*
  nán zǐ qì (n) (sv): 男子气, *manliness;*

manly;
SEE (请查看) MASCULINO

VIRTUD; virtude; *virtue;*
  měi dé: 美德, *virtue, moral excellence*

VIRTUOSISMO; virtuosidade;
virtuosity;
  háng jiā: 行家, *expert, connoisseur*

VIRULENCIA; virulência; *virulence
(MED)* **... VIRULENTO** (A); **virulento**
(A); *virulent (MED); bitter, hostile;*
  bìng dú de: 病毒的, *virulent (MED);*
  jù dú de: 剧毒的, *deadly;*
  kǔ de (adj) (n): 苦的, *bitter; hardship;*
  yǒu dí yì de: 有敌意的, *hostile;*
SEE (请查看) MALICIA

VISCOSIDAD; viscosidade; *viscosity,
slime, thickness* **... VISCOSO** (A);
viscoso (A); *viscous, slimy, thick;*
  ní jiāng de: 泥浆的, *slimy;*
  nián xìng de: 粘性的, *viscous;*
  nián xìng: 粘性, *viscosity, stickiness;*
SEE (请查看) DENSO

VISIBILIDAD; visibilidade; *visibility;*
  néng jiàn dù: 能见度, *visibility*

VISIONARIO (A); **visionário** (A);
visionary;
  yǒu yuǎn jiàn de rén: 有远见的人,
visionary;
  yǒu yuǎn jiàn (sv): 有远见, *farsighted*

VISITA; visita; *visit, call* **... VISITANTE;**
visitante; *visitor (n); visiting (adj);*
  bài fǎng (v) (n): 拜访, *to pay a visit/call
on; visit;*
  bīn kè: 宾客, *guests, visitors;*
  cān guān (v) (sv): 参观, *to visit/tour;
visiting;*
  fǎng wèn (v) (sv): 访问, *to visit/call on;
to interview; visiting;*
  fǎng wèn zhě: 访问者, *visitor;*
  kè ren: 客人, *visitor, guest; traveling
trader;*
  lái bīn: 来宾, *guest, visitor;*
  lái kè: 来客, *visitor; guest;*
  yóu kè: 游客, *visitor; tourist, traveler;*

yóu lǎn (v) (n) (sv): 游览, *to go sight-
seeing; tour, visit; visiting;*
SEE (请查看) TURISMO

VITALIDAD; vitalidade; *vitality;*
  huó lì: 活力, *vigor, vitality, energy;*
  shēng mìng lì: 生命力, *vitality, life-
force;*
  yuán qì: 元气, *vitality, vigor*

VITAMINA; vitamina; *vitamin;*
  wéi shēng sù: 维生素, *vitamin*

VIVACIDAD; vivacidade; *liveliness,
vigor, vivacity* **... VIVARACHO** (A);
vivaldino (A); *lively, vivacious, bright*
*... **VIVAZ** (adj); **vivaz;** *vivid, lively ...*
VIVENCIA; vivência; *experience ...*
VIVEZA; viveza; *liveliness, vividness ...*
VÍVIDO (A) (n); **vívido** (A); *vivid (GEN);
vivacious, graphic;*
  huǒ bào (sv): 火暴, *fiery, flourishing;
exuberant, lively;*
  huǒ chì: 火炽, *white-hot (fig), lively,
bustling with noise and excitement;*
  jīng yàn (n) (v): 经验, *experience; to
experience;*
  qīng kuài (sv): 轻快, *brisk, lively, agile;
light hearted;*
  qīng sōng yú kuài (fe) (n): 轻松愉快,
happy and relaxed; vivacity;
  rè nao (sv) (v) (n): 热闹, *lively, buzzing
with excitement; to have a lively time;
excitement, lively scene, merry-making,
mirth, fun, hilarity;*
  shēng dòng de: 生动的, *vivid, lively;*
  xíng xiàng (n) (sv): 形象, *image, form,
figure; imagery, visualization; vivid;*
  yǒu shēng qì (sv) (n): 有生气,
vivacious; vivacity;
SEE (请查看) ARDOROSO,
ANIMOSO, CALMA, CÓLERA,
DELEITE, DETALLADO, DINÁMICO,
APARENTE, EXPERIENCIA,
SINCERIDAD

VIVAMENTE; vivamente; *vividly,
deeply, intensely;*
  fēi cháng de: 非常的, *deeply,
intensely;*
  shēn (adv): 深, *deeply (felt);*

shēn rù (v) (sv) (adv): 深入, *to go deep into/penetrate into; thorough; deeply, deep going*;
SEE (请查看) **PROFUNDO**

VOCABLO; **vocábulo**; *word, term*;
  cí jù (lg): 词句, *expression, phrases, words and phrases*;
  cí: 词, *word, term*;
  dān cí (lg): 单词, *word*;
  kǒu tóu (n) (sv): 口头, *word; oral, verbal; flavor, taste*;
  yán cí (n): 言辞, *words, expression*;
  yán yǔ (n) (v): 言语, *spoken language, speech, words; to speak/talk*;
  yòng yǔ (lg): 用语, *wording, phraseology, term*;
  yǔ cí (n): 语词, *words and phrases*

VOCABULARIO; **vocabulário**; *vocabulary*;
  cí huì: 词汇, *vocabulary*;
  yǔ huì: 语汇, *vocabulary, lexicon*

VOCACIONAL; **vocacional**; *vocational*;
  zhí yè de: 职业的, *vocational*

VOCALISTA; **vocalista**; *vocalist, singer*;
  gē shǒu: 歌手, *singer, vocalist*

VOLÁTIL; **volátil**; *volatile, unpredictable* ... **VOLATILIDAD**; **volatilidade**; *volatility*;
  bù wěn dìng de: 不稳定的, *volatile (situation)*;
  duō biàn de: 多变的, *volatile (person)*;
  duō biàn: 多变, *volatility*;
  yì huī fā de: 易挥发的, *volatile (substance)*

VOLCÁN; **vulcão**; *volcano* ...
VOLCÁNICO (A); **vulcânico** (A); *volcanic*;
  bào liè de: 暴烈的, *violent, fierce, volcanic*;
  huǒ zào (sv): 火燥, *irascible, irritable, volcanic*;
  huǒ shān (sv) (n): 火山, *volcanic; volcano*;

SEE (请查看) **VOLÁTIL**

VOLUMINOSO (A); **volumoso** (A); **vultoso** (A); *weighty, considerable, bulky, voluminous*;
  bèn zhòng (sv): 笨重, *heavy, cumbersome, unwieldy, voluminous, bulky*;
  bèn (sv): 笨, *stupid, dull; clumsy, awkward, cumbersome*;
  bèn dà de: 笨大的, *bulky, cumbersome*;
  dà de: 大的, *bulky (big, large, great)*;
SEE (请查看) **CUANTÍA**

VOLUNTAD; **vontade**; *willpower, will, volition*;
  yì zhì lì (n): 意志力, *willpower*;
  yì zhì (n): 意志, *will, determination, volition, willpower*

VOLUNTARIO (A); **voluntário** (A); *voluntary, arbitrary; volunteer*;
  zì yuàn de (adv): 自愿地, *voluntarily*;
  zhǔ dòng (attr) (adv) (sv): 主动, *active, initiative; voluntarily; active, voluntary*

VOLUNTARIOSO (A); **voluntarioso** (A); *headstrong, willing, persistent, dedicated*;
  rèn xìng (sv): 任性, *willful, headstrong*;
SEE (请查看) **CONTUMACIA, PERVERSO, OBSTINADO**

VOLUPTUOSO (A); **voluptuoso** (A); *voluptuous*;
  xìng gǎn (n) (sv): 性感, *sex appeal, sexuality; eroticism; sexy, voluptuous*;
  xìng gǎn de: 性感的, *sexy*;
  yāo ráo de (vp) (wr): 妖娆的, *enchanting, bewitching, voluptuous*

VORAZ; **voraz**; *voracious, raging, ravenous; fierce*;
  tān lán (sv): 贪婪, *greedy, ravenous, rapacious*;
  tān chī de (v) (sv): 贪吃的, *be gluttonous*

VOTANTE; **votante**; *voter (n), voting (adj)* ... **VOTO**; **voto**; *vote*;

xuǎn jǔ rén: 选举人, *voter*;
xuǎn jǔ: 选举, *voting*;
SEE (请查看) BALOTA

VULGARIDAD; vulgaridade; *vulgarity, coarseness* ... VULGARMENTE; vulgarmente; *commonly, popularly*;
cū sú (sv) (n): 粗俗, *common, vulgar; vulgarity, coarseness*;
tōng sú: 通俗, *commonness*;
yōng sú: 庸俗, *vulgarity*;

SEE (请查看) VULGAR, NORMALMENTE

VULNERABILIDAD; vulnerabilidade; *vulnerability*;
cuì ruò (n) (sv): 脆弱, *vulnerability; fragile, weak*;
mǐn gǎn (n) (sv): 敏感, *vulnerability; sensitive, susceptible, allergic*;
yì sǔn huài xìng: 易损坏性, *vulnerability*;
SEE (请查看) PROPENSO

Easily recognizable verbs and their Portuguese and Chinese equivalents
Verbos fácilmente reconocibles en Español-Portugués-Inglés y sus equivalentes en Chino
Verbos facilmente reconhecível em Espanhol-Português-Inglês e seus equivalentes em Chinês
很容易辨认的西班牙语，葡萄牙语，英语动词和他们的中文对等词

VACILAR; vacilar; *to hesitate/be indecisive/sway; stagger*;
chóu chú: 踌躇, *to hesitate/dilly-dally*;
yóu yù: 犹豫, *to hesitate/be irresolute*

VAGAR; vagar; *to vacant/leave*;
cí qù: 辞去, *to resign (a job)/vacate (a position)*;
SEE (请查看) DESOCUPAR

VALIDAR; validar; *to validate/ratify/sanction*;
yàn zhèng (v) (n): 验证, *to verify/validate; verification*;
SEE (请查看) APROBACIÓN

VAPORIZAR; vaporizar; *to vaporize/spray*;
(shǐ) qì huà (v) (n): (使) 气化, *to vaporize; vaporization*;
(shǐ) zhēng fā: (使) 蒸发, *to evaporate/vaporize*

VARIAR; variar; *to alter/change/vary*;
yǒu chā yì: 有差异, *to make a difference*;
SEE (请查看) AJUSTAR, ADAPTAR, MODIFICACIÓN

VENTILAR; ventilar; *to air/clear/ventilate*;
(shǐ) huàn qì: (使) 换气, *to change the air, to ventilate*;
pái qì: 排气, *to exhaust/ventilate/vent*;
tōng qì: 通气, *to ventilate/aerate*

VERBALIZAR; verbalizar; *to verbalize/express*;
chū diǎn zi: 出点子, *to express an opinion, to give an opinion, to think of a way*;
dá xiè: 答谢, *to express appreciation, to acknowledge*;
dá yì: 达意, *to convey one's thoughts, to express an opinion/one's ideas*;
míng shì: 明示, *to express sthg clearly/explicitly, to instruct*;
shēn shù: 申述, *to explain/express/state in detail*;
shēn xiè: 申谢, *to express thanks*;
yòng yán yǔ biǎo dá: 用言语表达, *to verbalize*;
zhì xiè: 致谢, *to extend/express one's thanks*;
zhù sòng: 祝颂, *to express good wishes, to congratulate and command*;
SEE (请查看) ADMIRAR, ANUNCIAR, COMUNICAR, VINDICAR

VERIFICAR; verificar; *to verify/check/ authenticate;*
  jiǎn dìng (v) (n): 检定, *to examine/ certify; examination;*
  jiàn dìng (v) (n): 鉴定, *to appraise/ identify/ authenticate; appraisal;*
  zhèng shí: 证实, *to authenticate;*
SEE (请查看) **VERIFICACIÓN**

VIBRAR; vibrar; *to vibrate/shake;*
  shǐ zhèn dòng: 使震动, *to shake/rock/ vibrate;*
  zhèn chàn: 震颤, *to tremble/quiver/ vibrate*

VILIPENDIAR; vilipendiar; *to belittle/ vilify/revile; despise;*
  biǎn dī: 贬低, *to belittle/play down;*
  fěi bàng míng yù: 诽谤名誉, *to defame someone's reputation, to libel sb;*
  màn mà: 谩骂, *to curse/rail against;*
  wǔ miè: 诬蔑, *to insult/look down upon;*
SEE (请查看) **ABUSAR, CALUMNIA, DIFAMAR**

VINDICAR; vindicar; *to avenge/ vindicate;*
  bào chóu: 报仇, *to avenge/commit an act of revenge;*
  biàn hù: 辩护, *to vindicate;*
  biǎo bái: 表白, *to vindicate/explain os;*
  zì bái (v) (n): 自白, *to explain/vindicate os, to confess; explanation*

VIOLAR; violar; *to violate/rape; to break/infringe;*
  jiān wū: 奸污, *to rape/seduce;*
  jiān yín (v) (n): 奸淫, *to rape/seduce; adultery, sexual relations;*
  qiáng jiān: 强奸, *to rape/assault sexually;*
  qīn fàn: 侵犯, *to violate, to infringe on sb's rights;*
  qīn hài: 侵害, *to encroach on/violate sb's rights;*
  qīn rù: 侵入, *to invade/violate/intrude into;*
  wéi bèi: 违背, *to violate/go against;*
  wéi biāo: 违标, *to go against the stipulated criteria;*

  wéi fǎn: 违反, *to violate/transgress/ infringe;*
  wéi jì: 违纪, *to breach principle/break precedent;*
  wéi jìn: 违禁, *to violate a ban;*
  wéi xiàn: 违宪, *to violate the constitution;*
  wéi yuē: 违约, *to violate a treaty, to break a promise/contract/engagement;*
  wéi zhāng: 违章, *to break regulations;*
  wéi: 违, *to disobey/violate, to be separated;*
SEE (请查看) **ARRUINAR, DESHONRAR, ILEGAL, INSUBORDINADO**

VISITAR; visitar; *to visit/call on (MED);*
  bài huì: 拜会, *to pay an official visit/ call on;*
  bài jiàn: 拜见, *to pay a formal visit/call on/pay respects;*
  dēng mén: 登门, *to call at sb's house/ call on/visit;*
  fǎng yǒu: 访友, *to call on/visit friends;*
  kàn wàng: 看望, *to call on/visit/see;*
  lái fǎng: 来访, *to come to visit/call on;*
  tàn fǎng: 探访, *to search out/visit;*
  tàn qīn: 探亲, *to visit relatives;*
  tàn shì: 探视, *to visit;*
  yóu lǎn (v) (n): 游览, *to visit/tour/go sight-seeing; sight-seeing tour, visit;*
  zǒu dòng: 走动, *to walk about/stretch one's legs, to visit each other, to go to the toilet;*
SEE (请查看) **VISITA, SONDAR**

VISUALIZAR; visualizar; *to visualize/ make out; to display;*
  xiǎng xiàng (v) (n): 想象, *to visualize/ image/fancy; imagination, picture;*
SEE (请查看) **ASUMIR, IMAGINAR**

VITALIZAR; vitalizar; *to vitalize/ revitalize, strengthen ... **VIVIFICAR; vivificar;** *to revive/ revitalize;*
  (shǐ) fù huó: (使) 复活, *to be revived; to come back to life;*
  chóng yǎn: 重演, *to revive a play, etc.; to recur/ reenact/repeat;*
  chóng zhèn: 重振, *to restore/*

regenerate;
fù sū: 复苏, to resuscitate/recover;
fù xīng: 复兴, to revive/rejuvenate; to resurge;
huàn qǐ: 唤起, to arouse; to call/recall;
jiā gù: 加固, to reinforce/consolidate/strengthen;
qiáng huà (v) (n): 强化, to strengthen/intensify/ consolidate; reinforcement;
shǐ sū xǐng: 使苏醒, to revive a person, to regain consciousness, to come to;
zēng qiáng: 增强, to strengthen/enhance;
zhèn xīng: 振兴, to vitalize/promote, to develop vigorously;
SEE (请查看) COMPLETO, INSPIRAR, INTENSO

VITRIFICAR; vitrificar; to vitrify;
biàn chéng bō li wù tǐ: 变成玻璃物体, to vitrify

VIVIR; viver; to experience/live/be alive;
jīng shòu: 经受, to undergo/experience/withstand;
lǐng jiào: 领教, to experience/ask for advice;
shēng cún (v) (n): 生存, to live/exist/subsist; life, existence;
shēng huó (v) (n): 生活, to live,

existence; livelihood, profession;
zāo yù (v) (n): 遭遇, to meet with/encounter/ experience sthg bad; calamity;
SEE (请查看) NEÓFITO

VOCIFERAR; vociferar; to shout/proclaim/yell;
gāo hū: 高呼, to shout loudly, to cheer;
hǎn yuān: 喊冤, to cry out a grievance;
hǒu jiào: 吼叫, to call/shout/howl;
hū hǎn: 呼喊, to shout/call out; to yell;
hū huàn: 呼唤, to call/shout; to summon, to give orders;
hū jiào: 呼叫, to call out/yell;
jiào rǎng: 叫嚷, to shout/howl/clamor;
rāng rāng: 嚷嚷, to holler/shout; to argue noisily;
SEE (请查看) CLAMAR

VOMITAR; vomitar; to vomit/bring up;
ǒu tù: 呕吐, to vomit

VOTAR; votar; to vote for/vote on;
biǎo jué: 表决, to decide by vote;
xuǎn chū: 选出, to pick out/select/elect;
xuǎn: 选, to select/choose/elect;
SEE (请查看) SELECCIONAR, INDICAR

Interchangeable Spanish-Portuguese-English words and their Chinese equivalents
Palabras en Español-Portugués-Inglés y sus equivalentes en Chino
Palavras em Espanhol-Português-Inglês e seus equivalentes em Chinês
西班牙语，葡萄牙语，英语及中文的对等单词

WALKIE-TALKIE; walkie-talkie;
bù huà jī: 步话机, walkie-talkie

WALKMAN; Walkman ®;
suí shēn tīng: 随身听, Walkman ®

WATT ó WAT; watt; electric wattage, watt;

wǎ tè shù: 瓦特数, wattage;
wǎ tè: 瓦特, watt;
wǎ: 瓦, watt

WEB ó WWW; web; (world wide web);
wǎng yè: 网页, webpage;
wǎng zhǐ: 网址, website;
SEE (请查看) INTERNET

Y

Interchangeable Spanish-Portuguese-English words and their Chinese equivalents
Palabras en Español-Portugués-Inglés y sus equivalentes en Chino
Palavras em Espanhol-Português-Inglês e seus equivalentes em Chinês
西班牙语，葡萄牙语，英语及中文的对等单词

YEN (FIN); **yen;**
  yuán: 元, *yen*

YUPPIE ó YUPPY; yuppie;
  yǎ pí shì: 雅皮士, *yuppie (loan)*

Z

Interchangeable Spanish-Portuguese-English words and their Chinese equivalents
Palabras en Español-Portugués-Inglés y sus equivalentes en Chino
Palavras em Espanhol-Português-Inglês e seus equivalentes em Chinês
西班牙语，葡萄牙语，英语及中文的对等单词

ZOO; zôo;
  dòng wù yuán: 动物园, *zoo*

ZOOM (FOTO); **zoom;** *zoom lens;*
  lā jìn (v) (n): 拉近, *to draw close; zoom lens*

Easily recognizable Spanish-Portuguese-English nouns, adjectives and adverbs and their Chinese equivalents
Nombres, sustantivos, adjetivos y adverbios en Español-Portugués-Inglés y sus equivalentes en Chino
Nomes, substantivos, adjetivos e advérbios em Espanhol-Português-Inglês e seus equivalentes em Chinês
容易辨认的西班牙语，葡萄牙语，英语的名词，形容词和副词和他们的中文对等词

ZÍPER ó SÍPER; zíper;
  lā liàn: 拉链, *zipper*

ZONA; zona; *zone;*

dì dài: 地带, *zone, belt, region, district*

ZOOLOGÍA; zoologia; *zoology;*
  dòng wù xué: 动物学, *zoology*

Easily recognizable Spanish-Portuguese-English nouns, adjectives and adverbs and their Chinese equivalents
Nombres, sustantivos, adjetivos y adverbios en Español-Portugués-Inglés y sus equivalentes en Chino
Nomes, substantivos, adjetivos e advérbios em Espanhol-Português-Inglês e seus equivalentes em Chinês
容易辨认的西班牙语，葡萄牙语，英语的名词，形容词和副词和他们的中文对等词

ZIGZAGUEAR; ziguezaguear; *to zigzag;*

qū zhé qián jì: 曲折前进, *to zigzag*

Now available in eBook at Amazon.com and other eBook outlets

Need additional copies?

To order more copies of
A Comparative Vocabulary Study Guide
Spanish to Portuguese to English to Chinese
contact NewBookPublishing.com

❐ Order online at:
NewBookPublishing.com/Bookstore

❐ Call 877-311-5100 or

❐ Email Info@NewBookPublishing.com

Reliance
Media

Now available in eBook at Amazon.com and other eBook outlets

Need additional copies?

To order more copies of
A Comparative Vocabulary Study Guide
Spanish to English to Portuguese
contact NewBookPublishing.com

❐ Order online at:
   NewBookPublishing.com/Bookstore

❐ Call 877-311-5100 or

❐ Email Info@NewBookPublishing.com

Reliance
Media